Eating Disorders and Addictions: Clinical Perspectives and Treatment

Eating Disorders and Addictions: Clinical Perspectives and Treatment

Editor: Ellie Morrison

AMERICAN
MEDICAL PUBLISHERS
www.americanmedicalpublishers.com

AMERICAN
MEDICAL PUBLISHERS
www.americanmedicalpublishers.com

Cataloging-in-Publication Data

Eating disorders and addictions : clinical perspectives and treatment / edited by Ellie Morrison.
p. cm.
Includes bibliographical references and index.
ISBN 979-8-88740-082-2
1. Eating disorders. 2. Eating disorders--Diagnosis. 3. Eating disorders--Treatment. 4. Addicts--Rehabilitation.
5. Appetite disorders. 6. Psychology, Pathological. 7. Psychiatry. I. Morrison, Ellie.
RC552.E18 E28 2023
616.852 6--dc23

American Medical Publishers,
41 Flatbush Avenue,
1st Floor, New York,
NY 11217, USA

ISBN 979-8-88740-082-2 (Hardback)

Contents

Preface .... **VII**

Chapter 1 **Eating Disorders, Heredity and Environmental Activation: Getting Epigenetic Concepts into Practice** **1**
Howard Steiger and Linda Booij

Chapter 2 **Increasing Chocolate's Sugar Content Enhances its Psychoactive Effects and Intake** **14**
Shanon L. Casperson, Lisa Lanza, Eram Albajri and Jennifer A. Nasser

Chapter 3 **Somatotype Components as Useful Predictors of Disordered Eating Attitudes in Young Female Ballet Dance Students** **26**
José Ramón Alvero-Cruz, Verónica Parent Mathias and Jerónimo C. García-Romero

Chapter 4 **Health Professionals' and Health Professional Trainees' Views on Addictive Eating Behaviours** **37**
Tracy Burrows, Antonio Verdejo-Garcia, Adrian Carter, Robyn M. Brown, Zane B. Andrews, Chris V. Dayas, Charlotte A. Hardman, Natalie Loxton, Priya Sumithran and Megan Whatnall

Chapter 5 **Separating the Signal from the Noise: How Psychiatric Diagnoses Can Help Discern Food Addiction from Dietary Restraint** **52**
David Wiss and Timothy Brewerton

Chapter 6 **Polygenic Score for Body Mass Index is Associated with Disordered Eating in a General Population Cohort** **81**
Mohamed Abdulkadir, Moritz Herle, Bianca L. De Stavola, Christopher Hübel, Diana L. Santos Ferreira, Ruth J. F. Loos, Rachel Bryant-Waugh, Cynthia M. Bulik and Nadia Micali

Chapter 7 **The Clinical Utility of Food Addiction: Characteristics and Psychosocial Impairments in a Treatment-Seeking Sample** **97**
Edgar Oliveira, Hyoun S. Kim, Emilie Lacroix, Mária de Fátima Vasques, Cristiane Ruiz Durante, Daniela Pereira, Janice Rico Cabral, Paula Sanches Bernstein, Ximena Garcia, Emma V. Ritchie and Hermano Tavares

Chapter 8 **Validation of the Japanese Version of the Yale Food Addiction Scale 2.0 (J-YFAS 2.0)** **107**
May Thet Khine, Atsuhiko Ota, Ashley N. Gearhardt, Akiko Fujisawa, Mamiko Morita, Atsuko Minagawa, Yuanying Li, Hisao Naito and Hiroshi Yatsuya

Chapter 9 **Food Addiction is Associated with Binge Eating and Psychiatric Distress among Post-Operative Bariatric Surgery Patients and May Improve in Response to Cognitive Behavioural Therapy** **119**
Stephanie Cassin, Samantha Leung, Raed Hawa, Susan Wnuk, Timothy Jackson and Sanjeev Sockalingam

Chapter 10 **Fat Addiction: Psychological and Physiological Trajectory....130**
Siddharth Sarkar, Kanwal Preet Kochhar and Naim Akhtar Khan

Chapter 11 **Food Addiction: Implications for the Diagnosis and Treatment of Overeating....145**
Rachel C. Adams, Jemma Sedgmond, Leah Maizey, Christopher D. Chambers and Natalia S. Lawrence

Chapter 12 **Unexpected Association of Desacyl-Ghrelin with Physical Activity and Chronic Food Restriction: A Translational Study on Anorexia Nervosa....181**
Philibert Duriez, Lauralee Robichon, Roland Dardennes, Guillaume Lavoisy, Dominique Grouselle, Jacques Epelbaum, Nicolas Ramoz, Philip Gorwood, Virginie Tolle and Odile Viltart

Chapter 13 **Food Addiction Symptoms and Amygdala Response in Fasted and Fed States....200**
Kirrilly M. Pursey, Oren Contreras-Rodriguez, Clare E. Collins, Peter Stanwell and Tracy L. Burrows

Chapter 14 **Assessment of Physical Activity Patterns in Adolescent Patients with Anorexia Nervosa and their Effect on Weight Gain....210**
Miriam Kemmer, Christoph U. Correll, Tobias Hofmann, Andreas Stengel, Julia Grosser and Verena Haas

Permissions

List of Contributors

Index

Preface

The main aim of this book is to educate learners and enhance their research focus by presenting diverse topics covering this vast field. This is an advanced book which compiles significant studies by distinguished experts in the area of analysis. This book addresses successive solutions to the challenges arising in the area of application, along with it; the book provides scope for future developments.

Eating disorders are a range of psychological conditions characterized by severe and persistent abnormal eating behaviors. Addiction to food is a compulsive or uncontrollable urge to eat food that does not relate to the feelings of hunger. These conditions are associated with distressing thoughts and emotions that may affect physical, psychological and social function. Some common symptoms of eating disorders include food binges, restriction of food, and purging behaviors like vomiting or over exercising. Heritability and genes play a significant role in the development of eating disorders, but people having no family history can also develop these disorders. There are several types of eating disorders including anorexia nervosa, bulimia nervosa, binge eating disorder, etc. A variety of physical and psychological evaluations, as well as lab tests are used to diagnose eating disorders. The treatment of an eating disorder is based on the type and severity the condition. Cognitive behavioral therapy (CBT), nutrition counseling and medical nutrition therapy are some methods of treating eating disorders. This book unravels the recent studies on eating disorders and addictions. It will provide comprehensive knowledge to the readers.

It was a great honour to edit this book, though there were challenges, as it involved a lot of communication and networking between me and the editorial team. However, the end result was this all-inclusive book covering diverse themes in the field.

Finally, it is important to acknowledge the efforts of the contributors for their excellent chapters, through which a wide variety of issues have been addressed. I would also like to thank my colleagues for their valuable feedback during the making of this book.

Editor

1

Eating Disorders, Heredity and Environmental Activation: Getting Epigenetic Concepts into Practice

Howard Steiger [1,2,3,*,†] and Linda Booij [3,4,5,*,†]

1 Eating Disorders Continuum, Douglas University Institute, Montreal, Quebec H4H 1R3, Canada
2 Douglas Institute Research Centre, McGill University, Montreal, Quebec H4H 1R3, Canada
3 Department of Psychiatry, McGill University, Montreal, Quebec H3A 1A1, Canada
4 Department of Psychology, Concordia University, Montreal, Quebec H4B 1R6, Canada
5 Sainte-Justine Hospital Research Centre, University of Montreal, Montreal, Quebec H3T 1C5, Canada
* Correspondence: stehow@douglas.mcgill.ca (H.S.); linda.booij@concordia.ca (L.B.)
† Authorship for this paper is shared equally.

Abstract: Epigenetic mechanisms are believed to link environmental exposures to alterations in gene expression, and in so doing, to provide a physical substrate for the activation of hereditary potentials by life experiences. In keeping with this idea, accumulating data suggest that epigenetic processes are implicated in eating-disorder (ED) etiology. This paper reviews literature on putative links between epigenetic factors and EDs, and examines ways in which epigenetic programming of gene expression could account for gene-environment interactions acting in the EDs. The paper also presents evidence suggesting that epigenetic processes link malnutrition and life stresses (gestational, perinatal, childhood, and adult) to risk of ED development. Drawing from empirical evidence and clinical experience, we propose that an epigenetically informed understanding of ED etiology can benefit patients, caregivers, and clinicians alike, in the sense that the perspective can reduce judgmental or blameful attitudes on the part of clinicians and caregivers, and increase self-acceptance and optimism about recovery on the part of those affected.

Keywords: epigenetics; anorexia nervosa; bulimia nervosa; eating disorders; DNA methylation; gene-environment interactions

---

1. Introduction

Anorexia nervosa (AN), bulimia nervosa (BN), and related eating disorders (EDs) have traditionally been viewed as "sociocultural creations," or as products of disturbed family environments [1,2]. Not to downplay social and family influences in certain instances of ED, empirical evidence suggests that environmental "impacts" influence ED development by acting upon an environmentally malleable, heritable biology. In this paper, we review evidence for the concept that EDs involve the environmental regulation (through epigenetic processes) of hereditary susceptibilities, and discuss various potential benefits of providing patients, caregivers, and clinicians with a good understanding of a putative causal interplay, in the EDs, between genetic and environmental processes. Our intention with this paper is not to conduct a systematic review on epigenetics in the eating disorders (as such reviews exist elsewhere (e.g., [3,4]), but rather to provide an informed update on the latest findings, along with a discussion of clinical implications. Nonetheless, our review covers important recent articles related to the topic, as identified using PubMED and Google Scholar.

2. What are Eating Disorders (EDs)?

Eating disorders (EDs) are characterized by intense preoccupations with eating, weight, and body image, and such maladaptive eating practices as excessive caloric restraint, binge eating, self-induced vomiting, and compulsive exercise [5]. These disorders are often associated with marked morbidity and mortality [6,7], and high personal and social costs, including lower educational and vocational achievement, decreased quality of life, and social isolation [7–9]. The current version of the Diagnostic and Statistical Manual of Mental Disorders (DSM-5) refers to EDs as "Feeding and Eating Disorders" (FEDs), and recognizes six subtypes: anorexia nervosa (AN), bulimia nervosa (BN), binge eating disorder (BED), avoidant/restrictive food intake disorder (ARFID), rumination disorder (RD), and pica. Two residual diagnoses (other specified feeding or eating disorder and unspecified feeding or eating disorder) capture ED variants that have clinical significance without fulfilling criteria for full-threshold syndromes [5].

AN is defined by restriction of energy intake and persistent avoidance of weight gain, resulting in subnormal body weight. The disorder has two sub-types: AN-restricting type, characterized by restriction of food intake without binging or purging; and AN-binge-eating/purging type, in which individuals regularly engage in binge-eating followed by compensatory behaviors (like self-induced vomiting or misuse of laxatives). People with BN also display recurrent binge-eating and compensatory behaviors, but in the absence of marked weight loss [5]. Individuals with BED, roughly 40% of whom are obese [10], show recurrent binge-eating without compensatory behaviors [5]. Newly introduced in DSM-5, ARFID is characterized by restriction of food intake for reasons unrelated to weight and body image—for instance, compulsive avoidance of foods judged to be impure or unhealthy, or that elicit disgust or aversion [5]. People affected by RD bring already swallowed foods back up and re-chew, whereas pica is a disorder in which people eat non-food items [5]. To date, there are no genetic or epigenetic studies involving ARFID, RD, or pica and, thus, our review does not address these entities.

3. Etiology

EDs are understood to be multiply determined by genetic factors (that shape emotion regulation, reward sensitivity, energy metabolism, appetite, and other variations), environmental triggers (including perinatal insults, developmental stressors, later-life stressors), state-related effects (owing to the nutritional and mental status) and ultimately, social inducements toward intensive caloric restraint [11,12].

3.1. Heredity

Multiple sources of evidence point to the importance of heredity in the EDs. Family aggregation studies have shown that AN and BN are substantially more common in female first-degree relatives of people who themselves have AN or BN (e.g., Strober, et al. [13]), and one study shows that levels of eating and body-image concerns correspond in biological sister pairs, but not in adoptive pairs [14]. Even more convincingly, studies comparing concordance rates for EDs between mono- and dizygotic twin pairs reveal heritability coefficients for AN, BN, and BED ranging from 32% to 76% [15], 28% to 83% [15], and 39% to 45% [15], respectively. Aside from emphasizing unique genetic effects, these studies generally indicate non-shared environmental factors (e.g., a particular stressor experienced by one twin) to be more influential in ED development than are shared environmental factors (e.g., living in the same family environment) [15]. The preceding tends to refute ED formulations that are couched strongly in terms of family dynamics.

3.2. Genetics

There have been various efforts to identify gene variants that may be associated with risk of an ED. Candidate-gene approaches (which examine single gene variants) are generally driven by a theory-based "guess" about which of the tens of thousands of genes may be an important contributor to risk for a disorder—something akin to guessing around which star in the night sky might there be a life-harboring planet. Nonetheless, some findings point to associations between EDs and polymorphisms of genes regulating key neurotransmitters (e.g., serotonin [16]), neuromodulators (e.g., brain-derived neurotropic factor (BDNF) [17]), hormones (e.g., estrogen [18]), or eating behavior (e.g., ghrelin [19]). Despite some leads, the candidate approach has not yielded many replicable findings. Detailed reviews of findings from candidate-gene studies in EDs can be found in several previous reviews (e.g., [3,20]).

Recent technologies support genome-wide association studies (GWASs), which allow for hypothesis-free investigations aimed at uncovering novel genetic markers that reach what is called "genome-wide statistical significance" for association with a phenotype of interest. Given that genome-wide methods test thousands of common human gene variant markers at a time, a strict threshold for significance ($p < 5 \times 10^{-8}$) has been established to correct for chance associations that could occur when conducting large numbers of simultaneous comparisons. The cost of maintaining such stringency, however, is that genome-wide studies require enormous sample sizes.

To date, GWASs in the field have been completed only for AN—although studies examining BN and BED are underway. The earliest published GWASs in AN were underpowered, and hence failed to yield findings of genome-wide significance [21–24]. However, two recently published GWASs, both conducted by the Eating Disorders Work Group of the Psychiatric Genomics Consortium (PGC-ED), have yielded intriguing findings reaching genome-wide significance. The first of these, involving DNA from 3,495 people with AN and 10,982 normal-eater controls, associated a locus on chromosome 12 with AN, at a site linked to type-1 diabetes and autoimmune diseases [25]. In addition, genetic correlations (computed using linkage disequilibrium scores) associated AN with mental-illness phenotypes (e.g., neuroticism) and physical-health phenotypes (rapid glucose and lipid metabolism, low body mass index (BMI)). In other words, in addition to expected psychiatric components, findings characterized AN as having important metabolic and autoimmune components. The autoimmune aspect of these findings, incidentally, corroborates a report from a study in more than 930,000 Swedish hospital records showing that children having a parent with an auto-immune disorder are unusually likely to develop an ED [26].

The second GWAS, involving data from 16,992 people with AN and 55,525 controls [27], identified eight significant genetic loci, and again implicated psychiatric traits (e.g., obsessive-compulsive and major depressive disorders), metabolic traits (e.g., insulin resistance, lipid metabolism) and anthropometric traits (e.g., low BMI, low fat mass). According to these studies, the genetic architecture of AN not only implicates psychiatric traits, but also metabolic factors and particular physical (anthropometric) characteristics.

4. Genes and Environmental Activation

It is an intuitive point that the genetic contribution to many mental-health problems acts only when triggered by the environment—and the preceding is very likely to be true of EDs. As we have already noted, twin data have shown that EDs involve a strong genetic diathesis, but also a contribution from the non-shared environment [15]. In other words, ED development is likely to implicate gene-environment interaction effects. Supporting this point, animal data suggest that genetic susceptibility, in combination with adolescent social stress and caloric restraint can produce a mouse "analog" to AN—mice that let themselves starve [28]. Similarly, clinical data show risk of AN to be increased in genetically disposed individuals when subjected to familial distress [29]. Diverse environmental influences have been postulated to act in AN, including obstetric insults, gestational stress, childhood trauma, familial conflict, adult victimization experiences, social inducement towards caloric restraint, and one's actual nutritional state [30].

Epigenetic Processes

Epigenetic processes influence gene expression (and corresponding phenotypic variations) in the absence of actual DNA sequence changes, and are believed to act in an environmentally responsive fashion [31,32]. Mechanisms involved include DNA methylation/demethylation and hydroxylmethylation, histone acetylation/deacetylation, histone phosphorylation/ dephosphorylation, noncoding RNA and microRNAs, as well as transcriptome actions [32]. The most widely studied of these, DNA methylation, involves the addition of methyl groups to regions of the gene referred to as CpG sites—at which cytocine is followed by guanine [32]. Methylation in certain CpGs can silence or suppress gene expression—in theory, allowing for environmental programming of gene expression [31,32]. Available findings provide compelling evidence of a role of DNA methylation in rendering gene expression responsive to environmental exposures. However, these findings are not without limitations—from both methodological and conceptual standpoints. As a full discussion of such limitations is beyond the scope of this paper, the interested reader is referred to full treatments of such questions presented elsewhere [4,33].

Environments of Concern

The Prenatal Environment

A famous study, capitalizing on a "natural experiment" in malnutrition, showed that Dutch children born to starving mothers (due to a World War II induced food blockade) showed altered physical stature and emotional adjustment and, after six decades, altered DNA methylation in genes regulating growth and metabolism compared to those of their siblings [34]. In a similar vein, studies have linked maternal depression during gestation to altered methylation of the glucocorticoid receptor (*NR3C1*) gene and altered stress reactivity in the offspring [35]. Likewise, Suarez et al. [36] observed that maternal antenatal depression was associated with an epigenetic marker (lower epigenetic gestational age) associated with mental-health problems in pre-school age boys. Fathers matter, too. Germ cells in the sperm line convey epigenetic information, meaning that fathers can also influence fetal programming in their offspring [37]. There is a now-sizable literature demonstrating that stress in parents of both sexes can impact neurodevelopment in their offspring via epigenetic processes (see [38] for a thorough review). Also of relevance are findings of a recent study associating fathers' periconception BMI with DNA methylation patterns in their children at age 3 and 7 years, independently of mothers' BMI [39].

One of our group's recent studies showed that children of mothers who were exposed to intense, third-trimester gestational distress during very-severe weather conditions—the 1998 Quebec Ice Storm (regarded as Canada's worst natural disaster)—showed more ED symptoms at age 13 $\frac{1}{2}$ than did children of mothers who had less environmental-stress exposure [40]. Indicating the effect to have likely epigenetic origins, in a separate study, degree of *in utero* stress exposure in the same children was associated with extent of alteration of methylation in genes involved in Type-1 and -2 diabetes mellitus [41]. Interestingly, children who had higher methylation levels at age 13 concurrently had a lower BMI and lower central adiposity [41]. Investigating possible epigenetic effects of maternal EDs upon their offspring, Kazmi and colleagues [42] measured genome-wide methylation of cord blood DNA in 21 babies of women with active AN, 43 with a past AN, and 126 normal-eater controls. Infants of women with AN had lower global methylation levels than did controls. In addition, babies of women who were actively eating-disordered during pregnancy had altered methylation in genes implicated in biosynthesis of cholesterol and neuronal survival, whereas those whose mothers once had AN showed altered methylation in a gene linked to inflammation and immune response.

The Childhood Environment

Although it is uncertain to what extent findings obtained in animal studies inform processes in humans, animal studies have one advantage when studying possible epigenetic effects of early-life stress—as environmental stress exposures can be randomized across animals and experimentally manipulated and controlled in a way that could never be done in studies on developing humans. The preceding allows for differentiation of gene-environment correlations (in which the actor, because of a particular trait, induces an environmental effect) from gene-environment interactions (in which the environment has an action that is fully independent of the actor). There are many demonstrations that animals raised in stressful conditions show altered DNA methylation in systems associated with stress accommodation (e.g., [43–45]. Studies by Roth and colleagues indicate that infant rats exposed to adverse rearing experiences evinced lasting changes in the methylation status of the *BDNF* gene, and corresponding behavioral alterations [45]. Likewise, studies by Meaney and colleagues showed that rat pups receiving low maternal care compared to pups, that received high maternal care had greater hippocampal DNA methylation of the glucocorticoid receptor gene (*NR3C1*) and decreased hippocampal glucocorticoid receptor messenger RNA (mRNA) expression (e.g., [43,46]). In parallel, in a postmortem study, human suicide victims who had experienced childhood abuse have been shown to display higher methylation of the *NR3C1* gene promoter and decreased levels of glucocorticoid receptor mRNA in the hippocampus relative to non-abused suicide victims and controls [44]. Numerous other observations in humans associate early-life stress exposures (such as physical or sexual abuse, deprivation from parental care, or natural disasters), with epigenetic alterations and later behavioral and mental-health outcomes [33,47–51].

Suggesting that comparable effects apply in EDs, we previously found that women with BN who report a history of suicidality have greater methylation of specific CpG sites in the *NR3C1* gene promoter region [52]. We also observed hypermethylation of specific CpG sites in the promoter region of the *BDNF* gene in bulimic women who report a history of childhood sexual or physical abuse [53]. BDNF is thought to play a role in neural plasticity, learning of traumatic memory and binge eating [54]. Furthermore, we reported that women with BN and comorbid borderline personality disorder, who tend to report high levels of childhood adversity, show hypermethylation of the dopamine *DRD2* receptor gene promoter region [55].

The Nutritional Environment

Since EDs profoundly affect nutritional status, an important question is "How do ED-induced nutritional deficits affect the epigenome?" An even more important question may be: "Does nutritional rehabilitation during ED recovery reverse disorder-linked epigenetic alterations?". Central to the preceding questions is that nutrients, such as folate, B12, and choline, influence the functioning of one carbon metabolism—a physiological process crucial for generating methyl-transfer reactions upon which DNA methylation depends [56]. While most of the evidence for the influence of nutrients on DNA methylation comes from animal studies, there is now increasing evidence in humans that dietary intake of folate, choline, and B-vitamins also affect DNA methylation and brain function across the life-cycle [56,57]. Furthermore, numerous studies suggest that peoples' nutritional state can make epigenetically mediated contributions to psychiatric disorders [58]. Our group is presently studying pathways, in people with AN, linking self-reported eating behaviors, plasma levels of nutrients involved in one-carbon metabolism, and DNA methylation levels. At the time of this writing, results are in a preliminary state. However, initial indices suggest that nutritional factors do impinge directly upon DNA methylation levels [59].

5. Findings on DNA Methylation in People with EDs

5.1. Methylation Studies in Candidate Genes

We emphasize from the start that candidate-gene methylation studies are subject to all of the limitations inherent in any candidate study—including problems of power and stability of results. Nonetheless, interpreted judiciously, available studies offer some intriguing indications: Available studies in AN have reported altered methylation of genes regulating expression of alpha-synuclein (involved in neurotransmitter release) [60], dopamine [61] (implicated in mood, impulse-control, reward sensitivity and binge-like eating), oxytocin [62,63] (linked to social attachment), histone deacetylase [64] (broadly influencing gene expression), and leptin [65] (which inhibits hunger). Combining measures of serotonin transporter (*SLC6A4*) gene methylation with resting-state functional connectivity data, Boehm, et al. [66] associated epigenetic variation in the *SLC6A4* gene with neural connectivity in the salience network—an important brain circuit for emotion regulation. Another research group reported that individuals with BN had greater methylation of the atrial natriuretic peptide (ANP) gene promoter (involved in cardiovascular homeostasis) than controls [67]. Similarly, studies noted earlier have documented alterations in the methylation of candidate genes that might, in theory, be relevant to bulimic ED variants—including glucocorticoid receptor [52] and dopamine *DRD2* receptor genes [55]. However, we note that available findings seem to indicate that the epigenetic variations noted may be more pertinent to comorbidity (e.g., suicidality or personality disorders) than to BN itself.

We identified no studies investigating methylation differences between patients with a primary diagnosis of BED and normal-eater controls. However, one study reported that patients who showed concurrent bipolar disorders and binge-eating had hypomethylation of the *SLC1A2* gene (involved in removing glutamate from the synaptic cleft) relative to patients with bipolar disorder who displayed no binge eating [68].

5.2. *Global Methylation Level Studies*

A handful of recent studies has attempted to quantify global methylation across the whole genome. Such studies allow for the evaluation of hypotheses about global variations in methylation levels, but are "blind" to possibly more meaningful variations in methylation acting at specific genomic loci. Studies of this type have tended to produce inconsistent results, largely (we suspect) because of small samples and a diversity of methods involved. Across available studies comparing participants with AN to those with no ED, we find one reporting no global differences [69], two reporting global hypomethylation in AN [60,70], and one reporting hypermethylation [71].

5.3. *Epigenome-Wide Methylation Studies*

Superior to either candidate-gene or global methylation measures, genome-wide methylation measures allow for the analysis of site-specific alterations at multiple genomic loci. A first study of this kind, performed by our group, used a high-throughput (Illumina 450K) technology to perform a genome-wide comparison of methylation levels in DNA obtained from leukocytes in 30 women with active AN and 15 normal-weight, normal eaters [71]. False discovery rate corrected comparisons identified differentially methylated CpG probes corresponding to genes associated with histone acetylation, cholesterol storage, lipid transport, and dopamine and glutamate signaling. Findings also linked chronicity of illness to DNA methylation levels at probes that mapped onto genes associated with anxiety, immunity, and central nervous system functioning. An independent study (using the same technology) reported on methylation in 47 females with AN and 100 population-based control females [72]. Intriguingly, two of the differentially methylated genes identified in case-control comparisons—*NR1H3* (involved in lipid metabolism and inflammation) and *TNXB* (associated with connective-tissue disorders)—corresponded to those identified by our group. TNXB encodes an extracellular matrix glycoprotein, absence of which has been associated with Ehlers–Danlos syndrome, a connective tissue disorder characterized by joint hypermobility that is noted to co-occur with AN [73].

Our group subsequently reported on an expanded methylome-wide study, involving enlarged samples of participants with active AN or no ED, and a new sample of individuals in whom AN had remitted for at least one year [74]. Methylation levels in members of the remitted group differed from those in the active group on probes that, among others, isolated genes associated with serotonin and insulin activity, glucose metabolism, and immunity. Intriguingly, the direction of methylation effects in remitted participants tended to be opposite to that seen in individuals with active AN, suggesting that epigenetic alterations in actively ill individuals may be reversible. If so, DNA methylation could serve as a marker of disease staging or therapeutic response. Furthermore, we find it intriguing that altered methylation findings seem to parallel results of the GWASs described earlier [25]—i.e., they also implicate psychiatric, metabolic, and immune functions.

6. Clinical Applications

Traditional etiological models are replete with blameful and pathologizing innuendos concerning roles in ED development of "maladaptive personality traits" in affected individuals and "problematic interaction patterns" in their families. As our review has shown, contemporary conceptualizations refute such notions—promoting instead the point that people do not develop EDs because of "character weaknesses," "stubbornness," "superficial concern with appearance," or "bad parenting" but because they carry real genetic susceptibilities that get "switched on" by a lifetime of environmental exposures. In other words, EDs are understood to result from factors that are far beyond the willful control of those affected. It is our belief that perspectives on ED development that properly accommodate genetic and epigenetic influences improve clinicians' sensitivity to their patients' realities, and help make treatment more palatable and humane.

We take inspiration from several recent efforts to apply gene x environment interaction concepts clinically in the ED area. One recent study showed that an approach to ED psychoeducation that was couched in epigenetic terms (referred to as "malleable biology"), when compared to approaches framed in purely biological or cognitive terms, led to greater recovery optimism and felt self-efficacy on ED patients' part [75]. A recent paper makes a similar point, that when counseling for people affected by EDs places causal responsibility upon interacting genetic and environmental influences, it has potential to relieve blame and to legitimize patients' experiences [76]. One of the co-authors of the paper in question, Jehannine Austin, has been a strong proponent of the application, across a variety of mental-health contexts, of a new "breed" of genetic counseling. She and her colleagues have shown that counseling that informs patients and those close to them about gene-environment interactions helps empower and increase self-efficacy in individuals with mental illness [77]. In one of their studies, patients reported that this style of counseling made them better able to manage their illnesses, and more open to talking about them with family and friends [77]. We have similarly argued that epigenetically informed models improve clinicians' empathy surrounding the ways in which EDs can become entrenched and difficult to overcome [30]. Encouragingly (and a bit paradoxically), formulations of ED development that accommodate neuroscience concepts actually seem to "humanize" the understanding of ED illness and recovery. Arguably, genetically and epigenetically informed models of ED development contribute positively to efforts of clinicians and carers in various ways:

1. They blame affected individuals less. Since the causes of EDs are increasingly understood to involve the activation of real physical susceptibilities by real environmental exposures, it becomes possible to trace with patients the sequence of life events (that may include perinatal insults, childhood adversities, school-related stresses and, invariably, the effects of prolonged caloric restraint) that served to activate inherited susceptibilities toward ED development. Likewise, because they take into account multiple causal factors (and complex interactions among them), informed models do less "finger pointing" at parents and other caregivers. It is never a single event or action (e.g., parents' divorce, or a care-taker's depressive episode) that caused someone's ED.
2. They help promote greater self-acceptance. Clinical experience dictates that a common "symptom" of an ED is shame. People invariably feel stupid to have developed their disorder, weak to not yet have overcome it, and guilty for the distress their disorder causes relatives and friends. When with someone experiencing shame around his/her ED, and speaking from an epigenetically informed understanding, we might often say something like: "You didn't ask to have an ED. At the end of the day, when you fully understand why you developed this disorder, you won't have to feel ashamed. You'll just say, 'I see why I got an ED'". This stance on therapists' part, when sincere, helps promote self-acceptance in people who are prone instead to self-disparagement. Likewise, especially when afflicted by an ED after several rounds of therapy, or decades of suffering, it is natural for affected people to feel inadequate, and perhaps deserving of messages they may have received from uninformed carers or therapists that "you aren't trying hard enough" or "You're choosing to keep your ED". Findings from the epigenetic literature suggest that chronic exposure

to malnutrition and dietary distress amplify psychological tendencies (e.g., compulsivity, anxiety) and metabolic adaptations (e.g., altered lipid metabolism) that help "lock" the ED into place. The difficulty one may experience in recovering from an ED becomes understood, not as an index of character weakness or obstinacy, but of the extent to which biological processes anchor symptoms and behaviors into place.

3. They help patients (and therapists) accept "incremental response." Epigenetic data in AN suggest that there are many disorder-induced alterations in the expression of genes that affect mental status, metabolism, and immune/inflammatory processes—and that such alterations become more pronounced with increasing chronicity of illness (see [71,74]). It is likely that these same factors need to be "reset" before someone affected can take back control. Encouragingly, some findings show that nutritional rehabilitation does help undo problematic changes—but it remains unclear over what span of time such alterations take place.
4. They assign proper importance to nutritional factors. It is clear that malnutrition and dietary distress amplify physical and psychological problems in ED patients, and help lock the disorder into place. Various recent findings suggest that epigenetic processes may contribute to ED entrenchment through nutritionally-induced alterations in gene expression [71,72,74]. An implicit message is that: "Your ED was triggered by too much caloric restraint and, logically, recovery will depend upon re-establishing a healthy nutritional state". Although further research is required to establish parameters, a related concern may help moderate messages aimed at preventing obesity that encourage dietary restraint.
5. They help separate the person affected from his/her illness. "Externalizing the illness" is an explicit operation in family-based treatment approaches [78], and an implicit one in Cognitive Behavioral Therapy [79] and other established ED treatments. Recognizing that one is separate from one's disorder (and the behaviors that it drives) helps affected people overcome shame, and increases empathy on the part of family members, partners, and friends. A genetically/epigenetically informed model implicitly separates individuals from the factors that caused and perpetuate their illnesses—in the sense that the model makes explicit the point that EDs represent the activation of heritable physical susceptibilities by real-life experiences. We often say: "You did not ask to have this disorder. You are responsible for repairing the damage and recovering, but not for what caused the illness in the first place". In a related vein, because of its ego-syntonic nature, people with AN sometimes identify positively with their disorder, or assume it as an identity. We believe that an epigenetically informed perspective helps counteract such tendencies. It helps people affected by the disorder recognize that "you are not 'an anorexic'. Rather, you are someone in whom a vulnerability has been switched on by too much dieting. And the effect is that restricting food intake feels good in a bit the same way that abusing drugs feels good to a person with an addiction."

The following clinical vignette illustrates the potential value of an epigenetically informed stance: Some time ago, we admitted a woman with severe anorexia nervosa onto our inpatient unit. She was bewildered and frightened in the early days of her stay on our unit. A voluntary patient, after only a few days she took essentially the stance: "Thank you, I'm feeling much better and would like to go home." This was not a plan that could be safe for her. As a program invested in practices governed by notions of autonomy support (See [80,81]), we made efforts to avoid involuntary admission. But rational arguments aimed at helping this woman opt to stay voluntarily failed to be convincing, and she became increasingly adamant about returning home. Thankfully, serendipity made involuntary admission unnecessary. This woman spontaneously asked why she felt so bloated after eating, and we explained that this was a symptom of delayed stomach emptying time typical in AN. She replied: "You mean it's not in my head". We replied: "No. It's not in your head; it's in your stomach. There's a real physical cause". We explained further. "And speaking of real physical causes, you know that study on epigenetics in which we asked you to take part? Can we talk about that a bit?" We elaborated on what epigenetics is, how it is a science that promises to explain how genetic tendencies get activated by the environment. How life stresses and too much dieting seem to be among the factors that cause epigenetic changes in AN. After a brief discussion, and after addressing the patient's various questions and confusions, she stated: "That's so interesting". Signs of indignity fell away. She not only consented to take part in the study, but agreed to stay longer on the unit.

Author Contributions: H.S. conceptualized the review. H.S. and L.B. drafted the article. Both authors have read and agreed to the published version of the manuscript. All authors have read and agreed to the published version of the manuscript.

References

1. Gordon, R. *Eating Disorders: Anatomy of a Social Epidemic*, 2nd ed.; Wiley-Blackwell: Hoboken, NJ, USA, 2000.
2. Minuchin, S.; Baker, L.; Rosman, B.L.; Liebman, R.; Milman, L.; Todd, T.C. A conceptual model of psychosomatic illness in children. Family organization and family therapy. *Arch. Gen. Psychiatry* **1975**, *32*, 1031–1038. [CrossRef]
3. Himmerich, H.; Bentley, J.; Kan, C.; Treasure, J. Genetic risk factors for eating disorders: An update and insights into pathophysiology. *Ther. Adv. Psychopharmacol.* **2019**, *9*. [CrossRef]
4. Hubel, C.; Marzi, S.J.; Breen, G.; Bulik, C.M. Epigenetics in eating disorders: A systematic review. *Mol. Psychiatry* **2019**, *24*, 901–915. [CrossRef] [PubMed]
5. American Psychiatric Association. *Diagnostic and Statistical Manual of Mental Disorders*, 5th ed.; American Psychiatric Publishing: Washington, DC, USA, 2013.
6. Arcelus, J.; Mitchell, A.J.; Wales, J.; Nielsen, S. Mortality rates in patients with anorexia nervosa and other eating disorders. A meta-analysis of 36 studies. *Arch. Gen. Psychiatry* **2011**, *68*, 724–731. [CrossRef] [PubMed]
7. Weigel, A.; Konig, H.H.; Gumz, A.; Lowe, B.; Brettschneider, C. Correlates of health related quality of life in anorexia nervosa. *Int. J. Eat. Disord.* **2016**, *49*, 630–634. [CrossRef] [PubMed]
8. Maxwell, M.; Thornton, L.M.; Root, T.L.; Pinheiro, A.P.; Strober, M.; Brandt, H.; Crawford, S.; Crow, S.; Fichter, M.M.; Halmi, K.A.; et al. Life beyond the eating disorder: Education, relationships, and reproduction. *Int. J. Eat. Disord.* **2011**, *44*, 225–232. [CrossRef]
9. Wentz, E.; Gillberg, I.C.; Anckarsater, H.; Gillberg, C.; Rastam, M. Adolescent-onset anorexia nervosa: 18-year outcome. *Br. J. Psychiatry* **2009**, *194*, 168–174. [CrossRef]
10. Kessler, R.C.; Berglund, P.A.; Chiu, W.T.; Deitz, A.C.; Hudson, J.I.; Shahly, V.; Aguilar-Gaxiola, S.; Alonso, J.; Angermeyer, M.C.; Benjet, C.; et al. The prevalence and correlates of binge eating disorder in the World Health Organization World Mental Health Surveys. *Biol. Psychiatry* **2013**, *73*, 904–914. [CrossRef]
11. Steiger, H.; Coelho, J.; Thaler, L.; Van den Eynde, F. Eating disorders. In *Oxford Textbook of Psychopathology*; Blaney, P., Krueger, R., Millon, T., Eds.; Oxford University Press: New York, NY, USA, 2015.
12. Striegel-Moore, R.H.; Bulik, C.M. Risk factors for eating disorders. *Am. Psychol.* **2007**, *62*, 181–198. [CrossRef]
13. Strober, M.; Freeman, R.; Lampert, C.; Diamond, J.; Kaye, W. Controlled family study of anorexia nervosa and bulimia nervosa: Evidence of shared liability and transmission of partial syndromes. *Am. J. Psychiatry* **2000**, *157*, 393–401. [CrossRef]
14. Klump, K.L.; Suisman, J.L.; Burt, S.A.; McGue, M.; Iacono, W.G. Genetic and environmental influences on disordered eating: An adoption study. *J. Abnorm. Psychol.* **2009**, *118*, 797–805. [CrossRef] [PubMed]
15. Wade, T.C.; Bulik, C.M. Genetic Influences on Eating Disorders. In *The Oxford Handbook of Eating Disorders*; Agras, W.S., Robinson, A., Eds.; Oxford University Press: New York, NY, USA, 2018.
16. Calati, R.; De Ronchi, D.; Bellini, M.; Serretti, A. The 5-HTTLPR polymorphism and eating disorders: A meta-analysis. *Int. J. Eat. Disord.* **2011**, *44*, 191–199. [CrossRef] [PubMed]
17. Ceccarini, M.R.; Tasegian, A.; Franzago, M.; Patria, F.F.; Albi, E.; Codini, M.; Conte, C.; Bertelli, M.; Dalla Ragione, L.; Stuppia, L.; et al. 5-HT2AR and BDNF gene variants in eating disorders susceptibility. *Am. J. Med. Genet. B NeuroPsychiatr. Genet.* **2019**, *183*, 155–163. [CrossRef] [PubMed]
18. Nilsson, M.; Naessen, S.; Dahlman, I.; Linden Hirschberg, A.; Gustafsson, J.A.; Dahlman-Wright, K. Association of estrogen receptor beta gene polymorphisms with bulimic disease in women. *Mol. Psychiatry* **2004**, *9*, 28–34. [CrossRef] [PubMed]
19. Muller, T.D.; Tschop, M.H.; Jarick, I.; Ehrlich, S.; Scherag, S.; Herpertz-Dahlmann, B.; Zipfel, S.; Herzog, W.; de Zwaan, M.; Burghardt, R.; et al. Genetic variation of the ghrelin activator gene ghrelin O-acyltransferase (GOAT) is associated with anorexia nervosa. *J. Psychiatr. Res.* **2011**, *45*, 706–711. [CrossRef]

20. Baker, J.H.; Schaumberg, K.; Munn-Chernoff, M.A. Genetics of anorexia nervosa. *Curr. Psychiatry Rep.* **2017**, *19*, 84. [CrossRef]
21. Boraska, V.; Franklin, C.S.; Floyd, J.A.; Thornton, L.M.; Huckins, L.M.; Southam, L.; Rayner, N.W.; Tachmazidou, I.; Klump, K.L.; Treasure, J.; et al. A genome-wide association study of anorexia nervosa. *Mol. Psychiatry* **2014**, *19*, 1085–1094. [CrossRef]
22. Huckins, L.M.; Hatzikotoulas, K.; Southam, L.; Thornton, L.M.; Steinberg, J.; Aguilera-McKay, F.; Treasure, J.; Schmidt, U.; Gunasinghe, C.; Romero, A.; et al. Investigation of common, low-frequency and rare genome-wide variation in anorexia nervosa. *Mol. Psychiatry* **2018**, *23*, 1169–1180. [CrossRef]
23. Wang, K.; Zhang, H.; Bloss, C.S.; Duvvuri, V.; Kaye, W.; Schork, N.J.; Berrettini, W.; Hakonarson, H.; Price Foundation Collaborative, G. A genome-wide association study on common SNPs and rare CNVs in anorexia nervosa. *Mol. Psychiatry* **2011**, *16*, 949–959. [CrossRef]
24. Li, D.; Chang, X.; Connolly, J.J.; Tian, L.; Liu, Y.; Bhoj, E.J.; Robinson, N.; Abrams, D.; Li, Y.R.; Bradfield, J.P.; et al. A genome-wide association study of anorexia nervosa suggests a risk locus implicated in dysregulated leptin signaling. *Sci. Rep.* **2017**, *7*, 3847. [CrossRef]
25. Duncan, L.; Yilmaz, Z.; Gaspar, H.; Walters, R.; Goldstein, J.; Anttila, V.; Bulik-Sullivan, B.; Ripke, S.; Eating Disorders Working Group of the Psychiatric Genomics; Thornton, L.; et al. Significant locus and metabolic genetic correlations revealed in genome-wide association study of anorexia nervosa. *Am. J. Psychiatry* **2017**, *174*, 850–858. [CrossRef] [PubMed]
26. Zerwas, S.; Larsen, J.T.; Petersen, L.; Thornton, L.M.; Quaranta, M.; Koch, S.V.; Pisetsky, D.; Mortensen, P.B.; Bulik, C.M. Eating disorders, autoimmune, and autoinflammatory disease. *Pediatrics* **2017**, *140*. [CrossRef] [PubMed]
27. Watson, H.J.; Yilmaz, Z.; Thornton, L.M.; Hubel, C.; Coleman, J.R.I.; Gaspar, H.A.; Bryois, J.; Hinney, A.; Leppa, V.M.; Mattheisen, M.; et al. Genome-wide association study identifies eight risk loci and implicates metabo-psychiatric origins for anorexia nervosa. *Nat. Genet.* **2019**, *51*, 1207–1214. [CrossRef] [PubMed]
28. Madra, M.; Zeltser, L.M. BDNF-Val66Met variant and adolescent stress interact to promote susceptibility to anorexic behavior in mice. *Transl. Psychiatry* **2016**, *6*, e776. [CrossRef]
29. Karwautz, A.F.; Wagner, G.; Waldherr, K.; Nader, I.W.; Fernandez-Aranda, F.; Estivill, X.; Holliday, J.; Collier, D.A.; Treasure, J.L. Gene-environment interaction in anorexia nervosa: Relevance of non-shared environment and the serotonin transporter gene. *Mol. Psychiatry* **2011**, *16*, 590–592. [CrossRef]
30. Steiger, H.; Thaler, L. Eating disorders, gene-environment interactions and the epigenome: Roles of stress exposures and nutritional status. *Physiol. Behav.* **2016**, *162*, 181–185. [CrossRef]
31. Szyf, M. DNA methylation, behavior and early life adversity. *J. Genet. Genom.* **2013**, *40*, 331–338. [CrossRef]
32. Szyf, M. Epigenetics, a key for unlocking complex CNS disorders? Therapeutic implications. *Eur. Neuropsychopharmacol.* **2015**, *25*, 682–702. [CrossRef]
33. Cecil, C.A.M.; Zhang, Y.; Nolte, T. Childhood maltreatment and DNA methylation: A systematic review. *NeuroSci. BioBehav. Rev.* **2020**, *112*, 392–409. [CrossRef]
34. Tobi, E.W.; Goeman, J.J.; Monajemi, R.; Gu, H.; Putter, H.; Zhang, Y.; Slieker, R.C.; Stok, A.P.; Thijssen, P.E.; Muller, F.; et al. DNA methylation signatures link prenatal famine exposure to growth and metabolism. *Nat. Commun.* **2014**, *5*, 5592. [CrossRef]
35. Nemoda, Z.; Szyf, M. Epigenetic alterations and prenatal maternal depression. *Birth Defects Res.* **2017**, *109*, 888–897. [CrossRef] [PubMed]
36. Suarez, A.; Lahti, J.; Czamara, D.; Lahti-Pulkkinen, M.; Knight, A.K.; Girchenko, P.; Hamalainen, E.; Kajantie, E.; Lipsanen, J.; Laivuori, H.; et al. The epigenetic clock at birth: Associations with maternal antenatal depression and child psychiatric problems. *J. Am. Acad Child. Adolesc. Psychiatry* **2018**, *57*, 321–328. [CrossRef] [PubMed]
37. Marcho, C.; Oluwayiose, O.A.; Pilsner, J.R. The preconception environment and sperm epigenetics. *Andrology* **2020**. [CrossRef] [PubMed]
38. Chan, J.C.; Nugent, B.M.; Bale, T.L. Parental advisory: Maternal and paternal stress can impact offspring neurodevelopment. *Biol. Psychiatry* **2018**, *83*, 886–894. [CrossRef]
39. Noor, N.; Cardenas, A.; Rifas-Shiman, S.L.; Pan, H.; Dreyfuss, J.M.; Oken, E.; Hivert, M.F.; James-Todd, T.; Patti, M.E.; Isganaitis, E. Association of periconception paternal body mass index with persistent changes in DNA methylation of offspring in childhood. *JAMA Netw. Open* **2019**, *2*. [CrossRef]

40. St-Hilaire, A.; Steiger, H.; Liu, A.; Laplante, D.P.; Thaler, L.; Magill, T.; King, S. A prospective study of effects of prenatal maternal stress on later eating-disorder manifestations in affected offspring: Preliminary indications based on the Project Ice Storm cohort. *Int. J. Eat. Disord.* **2015**, *48*, 512–516. [CrossRef]
41. Cao-Lei, L.; Dancause, K.N.; Elgbeili, G.; Massart, R.; Szyf, M.; Liu, A.; Laplante, D.P.; King, S. DNA methylation mediates the impact of exposure to prenatal maternal stress on BMI and central adiposity in children at age 13(1/2) years: Project Ice Storm. *Epigenetics* **2015**, *10*, 749–761. [CrossRef]
42. Kazmi, N.; Gaunt, T.R.; Relton, C.; Micali, N. Maternal eating disorders affect offspring cord blood DNA methylation: A prospective study. *Clin. Epigenet.* **2017**, *9*, 120. [CrossRef]
43. Weaver, I.C.; Cervoni, N.; Champagne, F.A.; D'Alessio, A.C.; Sharma, S.; Seckl, J.R.; Dymov, S.; Szyf, M.; Meaney, M.J. Epigenetic programming by maternal behavior. *Nat. NeuroSci.* **2004**, *7*, 847–854. [CrossRef]
44. McGowan, P.O.; Sasaki, A.; D'Alessio, A.C.; Dymov, S.; Labonte, B.; Szyf, M.; Turecki, G.; Meaney, M.J. Epigenetic regulation of the glucocorticoid receptor in human brain associates with childhood abuse. *Nat. NeuroSci.* **2009**, *12*, 342–348. [CrossRef]
45. Roth, T.L.; Sweatt, J.D. Epigenetic marking of the BDNF gene by early-life adverse experiences. *Horm. Behav.* **2011**, *59*, 315–320. [CrossRef] [PubMed]
46. Suderman, M.; McGowan, P.O.; Sasaki, A.; Huang, T.C.; Hallett, M.T.; Meaney, M.J.; Turecki, G.; Szyf, M. Conserved epigenetic sensitivity to early life experience in the rat and human hippocampus. *Proc. Natl. Acad. Sci. USA* **2012**, *109*, 17266–17272. [CrossRef] [PubMed]
47. Holmes, L., Jr.; Shutman, E.; Chinaka, C.; Deepika, K.; Pelaez, L.; Dabney, K.W. Aberrant epigenomic modulation of glucocorticoid receptor gene (NR3C1) in early life stress and major depressive disorder correlation: Systematic review and quantitative evidence synthesis. *Int. J. Environ. Res. Public Health* **2019**, *16*, 4280. [CrossRef] [PubMed]
48. Jawahar, M.C.; Murgatroyd, C.; Harrison, E.L.; Baune, B.T. Epigenetic alterations following early postnatal stress: A review on novel aetiological mechanisms of common psychiatric disorders. *Clin. Epigenet.* **2015**, *7*, 122. [CrossRef] [PubMed]
49. Park, C.; Rosenblat, J.D.; Brietzke, E.; Pan, Z.; Lee, Y.; Cao, B.; Zuckerman, H.; Kalantarova, A.; McIntyre, R.S. Stress, epigenetics and depression: A systematic review. *NeuroSci. BioBehav. Rev.* **2019**, *102*, 139–152. [CrossRef] [PubMed]
50. Jawaid, A.; Roszkowski, M.; Mansuy, I.M. Transgenerational epigenetics of traumatic stress. *Prog. Mol. Biol. Transl. Sci.* **2018**, *158*, 273–298. [CrossRef]
51. Watkeys, O.J.; Kremerskothen, K.; Quide, Y.; Fullerton, J.M.; Green, M.J. Glucocorticoid receptor gene (NR3C1) DNA methylation in association with trauma, psychopathology, transcript expression, or genotypic variation: A systematic review. *NeuroSci. BioBehav. Rev.* **2018**, *95*, 85–122. [CrossRef]
52. Steiger, H.; Labonte, B.; Groleau, P.; Turecki, G.; Israel, M. Methylation of the glucocorticoid receptor gene promoter in bulimic women: Associations with borderline personality disorder, suicidality, and exposure to childhood abuse. *Int. J. Eat. Disord.* **2013**, *46*, 246–255. [CrossRef]
53. Thaler, L.; Gauvin, L.; Joober, R.; Groleau, P.; de Guzman, R.; Ambalavanan, A.; Israel, M.; Wilson, S.; Steiger, H. Methylation of BDNF in women with bulimic eating syndromes: Associations with childhood abuse and borderline personality disorder. *Prog. Neuropsychopharmacol. Biol. Psychiatry* **2014**, *54*, 43–49. [CrossRef]
54. Notaras, M.; van den Buuse, M. Neurobiology of BDNF in fear memory, sensitivity to stress, and stress-related disorders. *Mol. Psychiatry* **2020**. [CrossRef]
55. Groleau, P.; Joober, R.; Israel, M.; Zeramdini, N.; DeGuzman, R.; Steiger, H. Methylation of the dopamine D2 receptor (DRD2) gene promoter in women with a bulimia-spectrum disorder: Associations with borderline personality disorder and exposure to childhood abuse. *J. Psychiatr. Res.* **2014**, *48*, 121–127. [CrossRef] [PubMed]
56. Amenyah, S.D.; Hughes, C.F.; Ward, M.; Rosborough, S.; Deane, J.; Thursby, S.-J.; Walsh, C.P.; Kok, D.E.; Strain, J.J.; McNulty, H.; et al. Influence of nutrients involved in one-carbon metabolism on DNA methylation in adults—a systematic review and meta-analysis. *Nutr. Rev.* **2020**. [CrossRef] [PubMed]
57. McGarel, C.; Pentieva, K.; Strain, J.J.; McNulty, H. Emerging roles for folate and related B-vitamins in brain health across the lifecycle. *Proc. Nutr. Soc.* **2015**, *74*, 46–55. [CrossRef] [PubMed]
58. Stevens, A.J.; Rucklidge, J.J.; Kennedy, M.A. Epigenetics, nutrition and mental health. Is there a relationship? *Nutr. NeuroSci.* **2018**, *21*, 602–613. [CrossRef]

59. Burdo, J.; Booij, L.; Kahan, E.; McGregor, K.; Greenlaw, K.; Agellon, L.B.; Thaler, L.; Labbe, A.; Israël, M.; Wykes, L.; et al. Association between plasma nutrient levels and methylation of selected genomic probes in women with anorexia nervosa. In Proceedings of the International Conference on Eating Disorders, New York, NY, USA, 15 March 2019.
60. Frieling, H.; Gozner, A.; Romer, K.D.; Lenz, B.; Bonsch, D.; Wilhelm, J.; Hillemacher, T.; de Zwaan, M.; Kornhuber, J.; Bleich, S. Global DNA hypomethylation and DNA hypermethylation of the alpha synuclein promoter in females with anorexia nervosa. *Mol. Psychiatry* **2007**, *12*, 229–230. [CrossRef]
61. Frieling, H.; Römer, K.D.; Scholz, S.; Mittelbach, F.; Wilhelm, J.; De Zwaan, M.; Jacoby, G.E.; Kornhuber, J.; Hillemacher, T.; Bleich, S. Epigenetic dysregulation of dopaminergic genes in eating disorders. *Int. J. Eat. Disord.* **2010**, *43*, 577–583. [CrossRef]
62. Kim, Y.-R.; Kim, J.-H.; Kim, M.J.; Treasure, J. Differential methylation of the oxytocin receptor gene in patients with anorexia nervosa: A pilot study. *PLoS ONE* **2014**, *9*, e88673. [CrossRef]
63. Thaler, L.; Brassard, S.; Booij, L.; Kahan, E.; McGregor, K.; Labbe, A.; Israel, M.; Steiger, H. Methylation of the OXTR gene in women with anorexia nervosa: Relationship to social behavior. *Eur. Eat. Disord. Rev.* **2020**, *28*, 79–86. [CrossRef]
64. Subramanian, S.; Braun, P.R.; Han, S.; Potash, J.B. Investigation of differential HDAC4 methylation patterns in eating disorders. *Psychiatr. Genet.* **2018**, *28*, 12–15. [CrossRef]
65. Neyazi, A.; Buchholz, V.; Burkert, A.; Hillemacher, T.; de Zwaan, M.; Herzog, W.; Jahn, K.; Giel, K.; Herpertz, S.; Buchholz, C.A.; et al. Association of leptin gene DNA methylation with diagnosis and treatment outcome of anorexia nervosa. *Front. Psychiatry* **2019**, *10*, 197. [CrossRef]
66. Boehm, I.; Walton, E.; Alexander, N.; Batury, V.L.; Seidel, M.; Geisler, D.; King, J.A.; Weidner, K.; Roessner, V.; Ehrlich, S. Peripheral serotonin transporter DNA methylation is linked to increased salience network connectivity in females with anorexia nervosa. *J. Psychiatry NeuroSci.* **2019**, *45*, 190016. [CrossRef]
67. Frieling, H.; Bleich, S.; Otten, J.; Romer, K.D.; Kornhuber, J.; de Zwaan, M.; Jacoby, G.E.; Wilhelm, J.; Hillemacher, T. Epigenetic downregulation of atrial natriuretic peptide but not vasopressin mRNA expression in females with eating disorders is related to impulsivity. *Neuropsychopharmacology* **2008**, *33*, 2605–2609. [CrossRef] [PubMed]
68. Jia, Y.F.; Choi, Y.; Ayers-Ringler, J.R.; Biernacka, J.M.; Geske, J.R.; Lindberg, D.R.; McElroy, S.L.; Frye, M.A.; Choi, D.S.; Veldic, M. Differential SLC1A2 promoter methylation in bipolar disorder with or without addiction. *Front. Cell NeuroSci.* **2017**, *11*, 217. [CrossRef] [PubMed]
69. Saffrey, R.; Novakovic, B.; Wade, T.D. Assessing global and gene specific DNA methylation in anorexia nervosa: A pilot study. *Int. J. Eat. Disord.* **2014**, *47*, 206–210. [CrossRef]
70. Tremolizzo, L.; Conti, E.; Bomba, M.; Uccellini, O.; Rossi, M.S.; Marfone, M.; Corbetta, F.; Santarone, M.E.; Raggi, M.E.; Neri, F.; et al. Decreased whole-blood global DNA methylation is related to serum hormones in anorexia nervosa adolescents. *World J. Biol. Psychiatry* **2014**, *15*, 327–333. [CrossRef]
71. Booij, L.; Casey, K.F.; Antunes, J.M.; Szyf, M.; Joober, R.; Israel, M.; Steiger, H. DNA methylation in individuals with anorexia nervosa and in matched normal-eater controls: A genome-wide study. *Int. J. Eat. Disord.* **2015**, *48*, 874–882. [CrossRef]
72. Kesselmeier, M.; Putter, C.; Volckmar, A.L.; Baurecht, H.; Grallert, H.; Illig, T.; Ismail, K.; Ollikainen, M.; Silen, Y.; Keski-Rahkonen, A.; et al. High-throughput DNA methylation analysis in anorexia nervosa confirms TNXB hypermethylation. *World J. Biol. Psychiatry* **2018**, *19*, 187–199. [CrossRef]
73. Lee, M.; Strand, M. Ehlers-Danlos syndrome in a young woman with anorexia nervosa and complex somatic symptoms. *Int. J. Eat. Disord.* **2018**, *51*, 281–284. [CrossRef]
74. Steiger, H.; Booij, L.; Kahan, E.; McGregor, K.; Thaler, L.; Fletcher, E.; Labbe, A.; Joober, R.; Israel, M.; Szyf, M.; et al. A longitudinal, epigenome-wide study of DNA methylation in anorexia nervosa: Results in actively ill, partially weight-restored, long-term remitted and non-eating-disordered women. *J. Psychiatry NeuroSci.* **2019**, *44*, 205–213. [CrossRef]
75. Farrell, N.R.; Lee, A.A.; Deacon, B.J. Biological or psychological? Effects of eating disorder psychoeducation on self-blame and recovery expectations among symptomatic individuals. *Behav. Res. Ther.* **2015**, *74*, 32–37. [CrossRef]
76. Bulik, C.M.; Blake, L.; Austin, J. Genetics of eating disorders: What the clinician needs to know. *Psychiatr. Clin. North. Am.* **2019**, *42*, 59–73. [CrossRef] [PubMed]

77. Semaka, A.; Austin, J. Patient perspectives on the process and outcomes of psychiatric genetic counseling: An "empowering encounter". *J. Genet. Couns* **2019**, *28*, 856–868. [CrossRef] [PubMed]
78. Lock, J.; Le Grange, D. *Treatment Manual for Anorexia Nervosa*, 2nd ed.; Guilford Press: New York, NY, USA, 2012.
79. Fairburn, C.G. *Cognitive Behavior Therapy and Eating Disorders*; Guilford Press: New York, NY, USA, 2008.
80. Steiger, H. Evidence-informed practices in the real-world treatment of people with eating disorders. *Eat. Disord.* **2017**, *25*, 173–181. [CrossRef] [PubMed]
81. Steiger, H.; Sansfacon, J.; Thaler, L.; Leonard, N.; Cottier, D.; Kahan, E.; Fletcher, E.; Rossi, E.; Israel, M.; Gauvin, L. Autonomy support and autonomous motivation in the outpatient treatment of adults with an eating disorder. *Int. J. Eat. Disord.* **2017**, *50*, 1058–1066. [CrossRef]

2

Increasing Chocolate's Sugar Content Enhances its Psychoactive Effects and Intake

Shanon L. Casperson [1,*], Lisa Lanza [2], Eram Albajri [2] and Jennifer A. Nasser [2,*]

1 USDA, Agricultural Research Service, Grand Forks Human Nutrition Research Center, 2420 2nd Ave. North, Grand Forks, ND 58203-9034, USA

2 College of Nursing and Health Professions, Drexel University, 1601 Cherry St MS31030 RM 389, Philadelphia, PA 19102-1320, USA; lisa.marcelalanza.lanza@drexel.edu (L.L.); eram.abdullah.albajri@drexel.edu (E.A.)

* Correspondence: shanon.casperson@ars.usda.gov (S.L.C.); jan57@drexel.edu (J.A.N.)

Abstract: Chocolate elicits unique brain activity compared to other foods, activating similar brain regions and neurobiological substrates with potentially similar psychoactive effects as substances of abuse. We sought to determine the relationship between chocolate with varying combinations of its main constituents (sugar, cocoa, and fat) and its psychoactive effects. Participants consumed 5 g of a commercially available chocolate with increasing amounts of sugar (90% cocoa, 85% cocoa, 70% cocoa, and milk chocolates). After each chocolate sample, participants completed the Psychoactive Effects Questionnaire (PEQ). The PEQ consists of questions taken from the Morphine-Benzedrine Group (MBG), Morphine (M,) and Excitement (E) subscales of the Addiction Research Center Inventory. After all testing procedures, participants completed the Binge Eating Scale (BES) while left alone and allowed to eat as much as they wanted of each of the different chocolates. We found a measurable psychoactive dose–effect relationship with each incremental increase in the chocolate's sugar content. The total number of positive responses and the number of positive responses on the E subscale began increasing after tasting the 90% cocoa chocolate, whereas the number of positive responses on the MBG and M subscales began increasing after tasting the 85% cocoa chocolate sample. We did not find a correlation between BES scores and the total amount of chocolate consumed or self-reported scores on the PEQ. These results suggest that each incremental increase in chocolate's sugar content enhances its psychoactive effects. These results extend our understanding of chocolate's appeal and unique ability to prompt an addictive-like eating response.

Keywords: chocolate; Addiction Research Center Inventory; sugar; craving; addictive-like eating; eating behavior

1. Introduction

Chocolate holds a special status in our society. Indeed, it is one of the most loved and craved, but problematic, foods [1]. Consuming chocolate evokes pleasant feelings, reduces tension, and improves mood [2,3]. Furthermore, chocolate elicits unique brain activity compared to other high-sugar and high-fat foods, recruiting brain structures that respond to craving-inducing stimuli, and is therefore more likely to provoke an addictive-like eating response [4]. The particular combination of cocoa, sugar, and fat in chocolate may play important, yet distinct, roles in chocolate's unique ability to elicit an addictive-like eating response. Smit et al. [5] demonstrated a role of the main psychopharmacological active constituents of cocoa in producing psychostimulant effects but determined that other attributes, such as sweetness and texture, may be more important. In a prior study, we observed effects of the percent cocoa and sugar contents on "desire to consume more chocolate", while fat content trended towards significance for this effect [6]. Defeliceantonio et al. [7] demonstrated a supra-additive effect of combining sugar and fat on food reward in humans, while others have demonstrated that the sugar component (in a sugar/fat combination) in particular is more effective at activating reward [8,9] and gustatory brain circuits [9]. Additionally, we have demonstrated that the highly reinforcing properties of sugar are difficult to overcome [10,11]. Taken together, chocolate's desirability appears to arise from the synergistic relationship among its components.

Fat and sugar are known to stimulate both the dopamine and the opioid neurotransmitter systems to regulate a food's rewarding potential [12–14]. The dopamine neurotransmitter system stimulates 'wanting', or the motivation to consume the food [12,14], whereas the opioid neurotransmitter system modulates the consumption of a desired food by amplifying 'liking', or the hedonic value, of the desired food [12,13]. Thus, the sight, smell, and taste of a highly palatable food such as chocolate work together to trigger motivational and hedonic reward mechanisms that result in the pursuit and consumption of the desired food. Subjective dopaminergic and opioidergic effects of food consumption can be differentiated using the Addiction Research Center Inventory (ACRI) [15]. We previously utilized the ARCI, specifically the Morphine-Benzedrine Group (MBG), Morphine (M), and Excitement (E) subscales, in a between-group design (groups identified by percent cocoa of the sample tasted), to provide indices of the psychoactive effects of chocolate that are associated with addictive-like eating [6]. We showed that simply tasting chocolate increases the number of positive responses on the MBG subscale of the ARCI, consistent with responses obtained on the MBG subscale after dopaminergic–opioidergic drug administration [16]. These results help explain chocolate's high reinforcing value, as foods that elevate feelings of euphoria have a greater reinforcing potential [17]. However, different individuals may specifically crave a particular combination of chocolate's main components (dark vs milk chocolate).

To continue our study of the psychoactive effects of chocolates varying in percent cocoa and sugar and fat content, we repeated our 2011 study using a within-subject design. Because some have postulated that "food addiction" is more of an "eating behavior addiction" similar to binge eating [18,19], we added the Binge Eating Scale (BES) [20] to our data collection. We hypothesized that self-reported scores on the MBG and E subscales of the ARCI would correlate with the particular combination of the main components (cocoa, sugar, and fat) of the chocolate and the amount of each of the different chocolates consumed after the tasting session. Consistent with our 2011 study, we expected no correlation between self-reported scores on the M subscale of the ARCI and the particular combination of chocolate's main components. In addition, we hypothesized that the amount of chocolate consumed after the tasting session would positively correlate with the increasing sugar content and decreasing cocoa and fat content of the chocolate. Furthermore, we hypothesized that BES scores would positively correlate with self-reported scores on the ARCI questionnaire and chocolate consumption.

2. Materials and Methods

2.1. Participants

Healthy adults (Table 1) were recruited from the greater Grand Forks, ND, and Philadelphia, PA, areas. Our participant population consisted of 57% non-overweight, 30% overweight, and 13% class 1 obese participants. Screening for study eligibility included height, weight, and a medical health history questionnaire. Exclusion criteria included: presence of food and non-food allergies; current status as a dieter; current or past metabolic illnesses (diabetes, renal failure, thyroid illness, hypertension); psychiatric, neurological, or eating disorders (schizophrenia, depression, Parkinson's Disease, Huntington's Disease, cerebral palsy, stroke, epilepsy, anorexia nervosa, or bulimia nervosa); taking prescription medications except for oral contraceptives or antihyperlipidemia agents. The study was approved by both the University of North Dakota and the Drexel University Institutional Review Boards and registered on clinicaltrials.gov as NCT03364413. Informed written consent was obtained from all participants prior to any study-related procedures.

Table 1. Participant characteristics. BMI, body mass index.

	Grand Forks	Philadelphia	Total
N (F/M)	20 (14/6)	10 (6/4)	30 (20/10)
Age, years	24.1 ± 6.8	26.1 ± 6.0	24.8 ± 6.5
Height, cm	168.7 ± 9.3	172.3 ± 11.1	169.9 ± 9.9
Weight, kg	72.1 ± 10.9	70.3 ± 11.1	70.7 ± 9.4
BMI, kg/m^2	25.3 ± 3.5	23.8 ± 4.3	24.8 ± 3.8

Values are means ± SD.

2.2. Experimental Procedures

Participants reported to the Center at which they were recruited 3–4 h postprandial to determine the psychoactive effect of consuming chocolate with varying amounts of fat, sugar, and cocoa (Table 2). Participants were instructed to have a light meal (e.g., sandwich with side salad or cup of soup) and to then refrain from eating or drinking (except water) before reporting for their study visit. Upon arrival, participants rated their appetite using 10 cm visual analog scales and completed a baseline Psychophysical Effects Questionnaire (PEQ; based on the ARCI) [6]. Participants were then presented with 5 g of commercially available chocolate varying in cocoa, sugar, and fat concentrations (Table 2). Chocolates were tested in order from least to most amount of sugar, and the PEQ was completed immediately after each chocolate tasting. Participants completed the Binge Eating Scale (BES) after the tasting session. Participants at the Grand Forks site were then left alone and allowed to eat as much as they wanted of each of the different chocolates.

Table 2. Characteristics of each 5 g chocolate sample.

Chocolate Type	kcal	Cocoa (%)	Sugar (g)	Fat (g)
Lindt® milk	29	38	2.4	1.9
Lindt® dark	30	70	1.5	2.4
Lindt® extra dark	29	85	0.6	2.3
Lindt® supreme dark	30	90	0.4	2.8

2.3. Questionnaires

Subjective homeostatic and hedonic hunger ratings were assessed using 100 mm visual analogue scales. Questions asked included: 1. How hungry do you feel; 2. How strong is your desire to eat; 3. How full do you feel; 4. How satisfied do you feel; 5. How much do you think you could eat right now; 6. Would you like to eat something sweet; and 7. Would you like to eat something fatty.

The PEQ is composed of 30 questions taken from the ARCI Morphine-Benzedrine Group (MBG), Morphine (M), and Excitement (E) subscales that assess subjective dopaminergic and opioidergic effects of psychoactive drugs [15]. The MBG subscale contains questions that center on feelings of well-being and euphoria, which correlate with the activation of both the dopaminergic and the opioidergic neurotransmitter systems. The M subscale focuses on attitude and physical sensations, and the E subscale relates to physical and psychological feelings of excitement, both of which correlate with activation of the dopaminergic neurotransmitter system [16]. Participants completed the PEQ before and after tasting each of the different chocolates.

The BES is composed of 16 questions used to assess the presence of binge eating behavior [20]. The BES contains questions that assess both behavioral manifestations of binge eating and of the feelings that either cue or follow a binge episode. Participants completed the BES after completing all testing procedures.

2.4. Anthropometric Measurements

Height, measured to the nearest 0.1 cm using a stadiometer (SECA Model 214, Hamburg, Germany), and body weight, measured using a calibrated digital scale to the nearest 0.1 kg (Fairbanks model 50735; Kansas City, MO, USA), were obtained at the end of the testing session.

2.5. Statistical Analysis

General linear models were used to compare general participant characteristics (i.e., sex, age, body mass index (BMI), hunger, testing site) and ARCI subscale scores of each chocolate type (defined by the percent cocoa in the chocolate sample tasted) and the amount of chocolate consumed. Tukey's post hoc analysis was used to determine differences. The threshold of significance was set at alpha = 0.05. JMP V14 (SAS Institute, Inc., Cary, NC, USA) was used for all analyses.

3. Results

3.1. Subjective Appetite Responses

On a scale from 0 (not at all) to 100 (very much), participants' rating of hunger was 58 $\pm$ 21 and of the desire to eat was 66 $\pm$ 28, while fullness was 25 $\pm$ 24 and feeling of being satisfied was 31 $\pm$ 21. There was no main effect of hunger or fullness on the total number of positive responses and on the number of positive responses on the MBG and M subscales; however, there was a main effect of hunger ($F(1,15) = 4.73$, $p = 0.046$) and fullness ($F(1,15) = 8.06$, $p = 0.012$) on self-reported scores on the E subscale of the PEQ.

Participants also rated their desire to eat foods with a specific taste profile on a scale from 0 (not at all) to 100 (very much). Participants' rating of the desire to eat something sweet was 79 $\pm$ 14 and that of the desire to eat something fatty was 48 $\pm$ 27. There was no main effect of the desire to eat something sweet or fatty on the total number of positive responses or on the number of positive responses on the MBG, M, and E subscales.

3.2. Psychophysical Effects Questionnaire

There was no main effect of testing site, sex, age, BMI, or BES on the total number of positive responses or on the number of positive responses on the MBG, M, and E subscales. Because of the direct correlation between the percent cocoa and sugar contents and the simultaneous changes of the fat and cocoa contents, we were not able to assess the direct effects of the individual chocolate components in this within-subject study design.

There was a significant main effect of chocolate type on the total number of positive responses ($F(4,106) = 30.10$, $p < 0.0001$) and on the number of positive responses on the MBG ($F(4,106) = 15.83$, $p < 0.0001$), M ($F(4,106) = 10.34$, $p < 0.0001$) and E ($F(4,106) = 16.57$, $p < 0.0001$) subscales. Tukey's post hoc analysis revealed slight differences in the effect of chocolate type on the total number of positive responses and on the number of positive responses on MBG, M, and E subscales.

The total number of positive responses (Figure 1) significantly increased after the consumption of all the different types of chocolate, with milk chocolate eliciting the greatest increase.

The number of positive responses on the MBG subscale (Figure 2) significantly increased after the consumption of the 85% cocoa chocolate and continued to increase in a dose-dependent manner in response to tasting each of the other chocolates. The number of positive responses on the MBG subscale after the consumption of the milk chocolate was significantly greater than after consumption of any of the other chocolates.

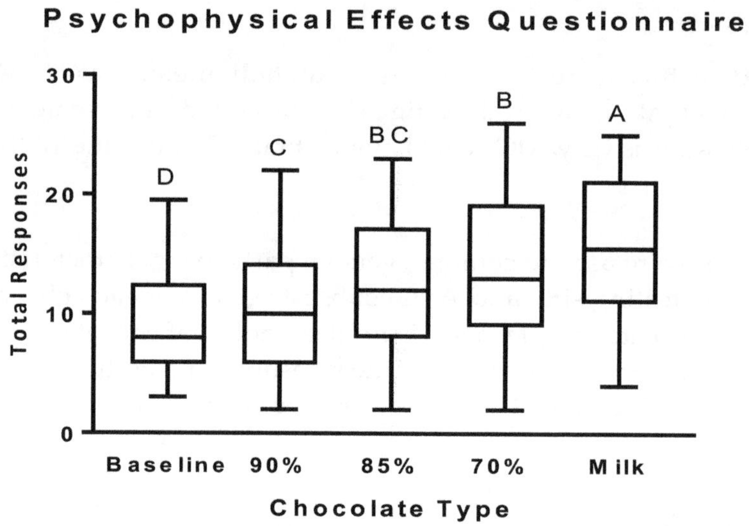

Figure 1. Total Psychophysical Effects Questionnaire (PEQ) scores after the consumption of chocolates differing in cocoa, sugar, and fat content. Self-reported scores on the PEQ questionnaire are presented as box and whiskers plots with the line representing the median, the box representing the 25th to 75th percentiles, and the whiskers representing the minimum to maximum values. Least-squares means are Baseline: 8.26 ± 1.16 (SE), 95% CI [5.93, 10.58]; 90% cocoa: 10.87 ± 1.10 (SE), 95% CI [8.65, 13.08]; 85% cocoa: 12.37 ± 1.10 (SE), 95% CI [10.15, 14.58]; 70% cocoa: 13.70 ± 1.10 (SE), 95% CI [11.49, 15.91]; Milk: 15.87 ± 1.10 (SE), 95% CI [13.65, 18.08]. Levels not connected by the same letter are significantly different.

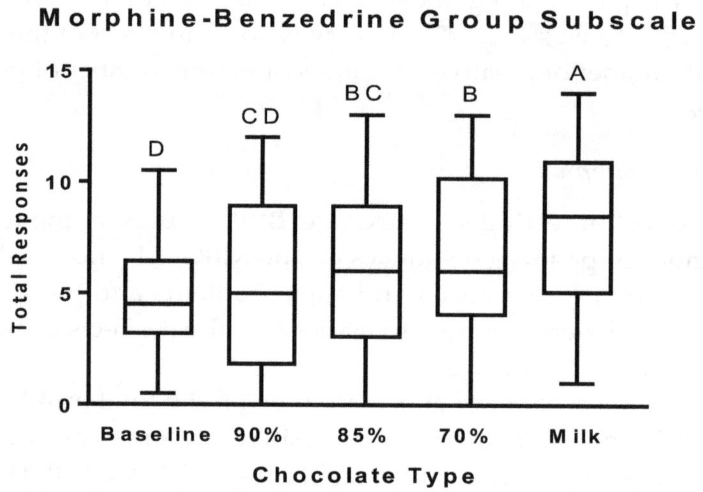

Figure 2. Morphine-Benzedrine Group (MBG) subscale scores after the consumption of chocolates differing in cocoa, sugar, and fat content. Self-reported scores on the MBG subscale are presented as box and whiskers plots with the line representing the median, the box representing the 25th to 75th percentiles, and the whiskers representing the minimum to maximum values. Least-squares means are Baseline: 4.28 ± 0.71 (SE), 95% CI [2.86, 5.69]; 90% cocoa: 5.37 ± 0.66 (SE), 95% CI [4.03, 6.70]; 85% cocoa: 6.10 ± 0.66 (SE), 95% CI [4.77, 7.43]; 70% cocoa: 6.63 ± 0.66 (SE), 95% CI [5.30, 7.97]; Milk: 7.97 ± 0.66 (SE), 95% CI [6.63, 9.30]. Levels not connected by the same letter are significantly different.

The number of positive responses on the M subscale (Figure 3) did not increase after the consumption of the 90% cocoa chocolate. A significant increase above baseline was not observed until participants consumed the 85% cocoa chocolate, with no further increases for each sequential chocolate consumption.

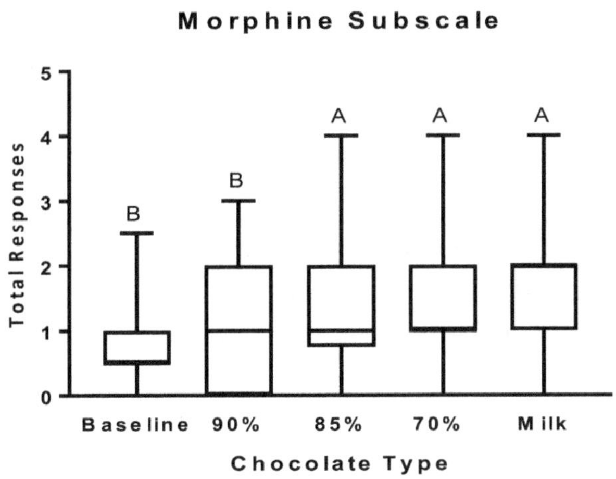

Figure 3. Morphine (M) subscale scores after the consumption of chocolates differing in cocoa, sugar, and fat content. Self-reported scores on the M subscale are presented as box and whiskers plots with the line representing the median, the box representing the 25th to 75th percentiles, and the whiskers representing the minimum to maximum values. Least-squares means are Baseline: 0.78 ± 0.20 (SE), 95% CI [0.37, 1.19]; 90% cocoa: 1.00 ± 0.19 (SE), 95% CI [0.62, 1.38]; 85% cocoa: 1.47 ± 0.19 (SE), 95% CI [1.09, 1.84]; 70% cocoa: 1.57 ± 0.19 (SE), 95% CI [1.19, 1.94]; Milk: 1.57 ± 0.19 (SE), 95% CI [1.19, 1.94]. Levels not connected by the same letter are significantly different.

The number of positive responses on the E subscale (Figure 4) significantly increased after the consumption of the 90% cocoa chocolate. As with the MBG subscale, the number of positive responses on the E subscale continued to increase in a dose-dependent manner in response to each incremental increase in the chocolate's sugar content and decrease in the percent cocoa and fat content.

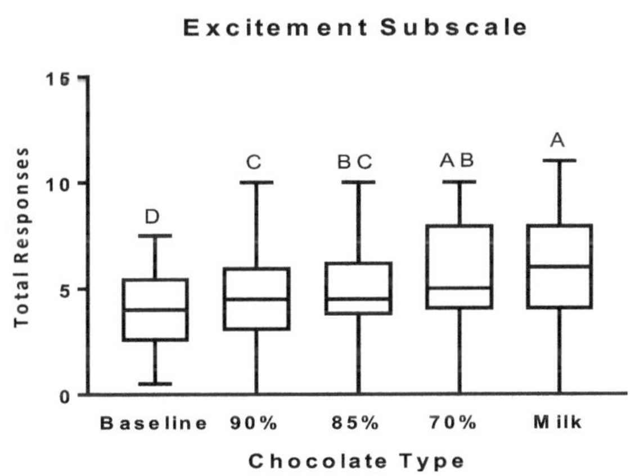

Figure 4. Excitement (E) subscale scores after the consumption of chocolates differing in cocoa, sugar, and fat content. Self-reported scores on the E subscale are presented as box and whiskers plots with the line representing the median, the box representing the 25th to 75th percentiles, and the whiskers representing the minimum to maximum values. Least-squares means are Baseline: 3.51 ± 0.47 (SE), 95% CI [2.56, 4.46]; 90% cocoa: 4.57 ± 0.44 (SE), 95% CI [3.68, 5.45]; 85% cocoa: 4.80 ± 0.44 (SE), 95% CI [3.92, 5.68]; 70% cocoa: 5.53 ± 0.44 (SE), 95% CI [4.65, 6.42]; Milk: 6.27 ± 0.44 (SE), 95% CI [5.38, 7.15]. Levels not connected by the same letter are significantly different.

3.3. Chocolate Consumption

There was a main effect of chocolate type on the amount of chocolate consumed ($p < 0.0001$). Overall, participants consumed significantly more milk chocolate (21 g ± 25 (SD)) than any other chocolate type (90% cocoa: 3 g ± 9; 85% cocoa: 2 g ± 4; 70% cocoa: 6 g ± 10 (SD)). There was no correlation between the amount of chocolate consumed and the total number of positive responses or the number of positive responses on the MBG, M, or E subscales. There was a main effect of hunger

($F(1,18) = 11.74$, $p = 0.003$) on the total amount of chocolate consumed. Post hoc analysis revealed a main effect of hunger ($F(1,17) = 8.64$, $p = 0.009$) on the amount of milk chocolate consumed only. There was no main effect of BES score on the total amount of chocolate consumed.

4. Discussion

The current study aimed to extend our previous findings on the psychoactive effects of consuming chocolate varying in cocoa, sugar, and fat concentrations using a validated ARCI "drug effects" questionnaire in a within-subject design. The questions used simultaneously reflect alterations in motivation, mood, sensation, and perception, and, therefore, provide insight into the interrelation of these variables and chocolate consumption [16]. Our data indicate a measurable psychoactive dose–effect relationship with each incremental increase in the chocolate's sugar content and decrease in the percent cocoa and fat contents. Overall, there were an inverse dose–effect relationship with cocoa concentration and fat content and a positive dose–effect relationship with the sugar content of a chocolate. In addition, our data indicate that the dose–effect relationship of the different chocolates was slightly different for each ARCI subscale. Thus, the present study is the first to demonstrate a dose-dependent relationship between self-reported scores on the PEQ and chocolate consumption.

Increased feelings of well-being, euphoria, and physical and psychological feelings of excitement after chocolate consumption are consistent with chocolate's ability to modulate both the opioid and the dopamine neurotransmitter systems. Both human and animal research has demonstrated the reinforcing potential and comforting and mood-ameliorating effects of chocolate [2,3,21–23]. Contrary to our hypothesis, we did not find an association between self-reported scores on the MBG subscale and chocolate consumption. These results are also inconsistent with our previous study in which self-reported scores on the MBG subscale were associated with an increased desire to eat more chocolate [6]. A possible explanation for these findings is that subjective appetite measurements were obtained prior to the tasting session rather than after; however, participants were allowed to consume as much of the different chocolates as they wanted after the tasting session. On average, participants consumed 8 ± 15 g more chocolate than what was provided to them for the tasting session. Another possible explanation for this difference is that the smell and tasting of four different chocolates in the same session as opposed to only one type of chocolate could have satiated the desire to eat more chocolate. Massolt et al. [24] demonstrated that not only eating but simply smelling chocolate (85% cocoa) suppresses appetite. Additionally, Sørensen and Astrup [25] demonstrated that dark chocolate (70% cocoa) increases satiety and decreases the desire to eat something sweet more than milk chocolate. In the current study, participants consumed 15 g of dark chocolate before tasting the milk chocolate, and this could have decreased their appetite for more chocolate.

The sugar content, which plays a key role in chocolate's pleasurable taste and texture, is important in determining chocolate's reinforcing potential [26]. Research has shown that the added sugar component of a food is greatly associated with its reinforcing value [8,9,27]. We have also shown that the highly reinforcing properties of sugar are difficult to overcome [10,11]. The activation of sweet taste receptors, the speed at which the information about a food is delivered from the chemosensory and somatosensory neurons in the mouth to the brain, and the magnitude of the activation of the food reward system govern the reinforcing and rewarding effect of sugar [28,29]. Low et al. [30] recently reported that the average concentration at which sugar can be differentiated from water is 9 mass percent (m%); however, interindividual variability is large (reported range from 2 m% to 32 m%). The sugar content of the chocolates provided in this study were 8 m%, 13 m%, 30 m%, and 48 m% for the 90% cocoa, 85% cocoa, 70% cocoa, and milk chocolates, respectively. Therefore, our finding that consuming the 85% cocoa, 70% cocoa, and milk chocolates resulted in significant increases in self-reported scores on the PEQ, and each subscale, above baseline is supported by the fact that all of these chocolates were above the 9 m% detection threshold.

In agreement with our prior study [6], consuming milk chocolate elicited a greater increase, compared to all the other chocolates, in the total number of positive responses as well as a greater increase in positive responses on the MBG subscale. The sugar content of the milk chocolate, which was equivalent to the upper sucrose detection threshold reported by Low et al. [30], may explain these results, as well as the mass appeal of milk chocolate. Indeed, participants in the current study consumed an average of 21 $\pm$ 25 g of milk chocolate compared to 6 $\pm$ 10 g of the 70% cocoa and 2 $\pm$ 4 g of the 85% cocoa chocolates. Taken together, these results agree substantively with other indicators of reinforcement essential for motivational behavior [15,31] and support the "addictive-like" behavior response individuals can experience with chocolate, in particular milk chocolate, consumption.

The finding that consuming chocolate containing 90% cocoa increased the total number of positive responses and the number of positive responses on the E subscale is of interest, given its reported "bitter" taste. The bioactive compounds found in dark chocolate may explain these positive results. In two double-blind, placebo control studies, Smit et al. [5] demonstrated that the amount of methylxanthines (theobromine and caffeine) found in dark chocolate can produce psychostimulant effects. They found that the consumption of both encapsulated cocoa powder and a "typical portion" of dark chocolate increases energetic arousal ("energetic", "alert", etc. versus "tired", "sluggish"). This is consistent with our results demonstrating chocolate's ability to increase physical and psychological feelings of excitement. Interestingly, when examined separately, the amount of theobromine found in a "typical portion" of chocolate (200–300 mg) does not appear to play a psychopharmacological role [32], whereas the amount of caffeine (25–35 mg) is well above the previously reported stimulatory threshold (12.5 mg [33]). The amount of caffeine consumed from the 90% cocoa chocolate sample in the current study was 9 mg, well below the stimulatory threshold. It may be that the theobromine found in chocolate enhances the stimulatory effect of caffeine. Thus, it is plausible that the combination of theobromine and caffeine found in chocolate provides an additive psychostimulant effect. While the methylxanthines in chocolate provide psychostimulant effects, Smit et al. [5], as well as Michener and Rozin [26], reported no difference in chocolate cravings between the ingestion of cocoa powder versus placebo, whereas consuming chocolate, including white chocolate (albeit to a lesser extent), immediately reduced chocolate cravings. As mentioned above, another explanation for this finding is that the sugar content of the 90% cocoa chocolate (8 m%) is well above the lowest and close to the average sucrose detection threshold previously reported [30]. Taken together, these results confirm that the combination of the main chocolate constituents is necessary to produce its psychoactive effects.

As expected, more milk chocolate was consumed than any of the other chocolates, indicating its reinforcing potential. This is consistent with the greater number of positive responses on the PEQ. However, contrary to our hypothesis, we did not find an association between the total amount of chocolate consumed or the total number of positive responses on the PEQ and BES scores. A potential explanation for this finding is all of our study participants had a score less than or equal to 17 and thus would be classified as non-binge eaters [20]. The narrow range in BES scores (2–17) of our participants may not have provided the heterogeneity needed to reliably determine a correlation between BES scores and chocolate consumption or self-reported PEQ scores. Further studies are needed to determine the potential correlation between BES scores and chocolate consumption or self-reported PEQ scores. Additionally, the low BES scores may also explain why we did not find an association between self-reported scores on the MBG subscale and chocolate consumption.

This study is not without limitations. The direct correlation between the percent cocoa and sugar content and the simultaneous changes of the fat content in the chocolate samples did not allow us to assess the independent psychoactive effects of each component. However, using commercially available chocolate provides a "real-world" value to our observations. Furthermore, tasting the chocolate samples sequentially in a relatively short amount of time may have produced an additive effect on our outcomes, such as habituation or sensory-specific satiety [34]. For this study, each participant consumed a total of 20 g of chocolate (5 g/sample) compared to the 12.5 g provided in our previous study [6] with similar PEQ results. Therefore, it does not appear that our within-subject study design had a significant impact on our results. Lastly, the participants in this study tended to be healthy-weight individuals (57% of the participants), thus, the results may not reflect the response of overweight and obese individuals. Although we did not find a significant effect of BMI on self-reported scores on the PEQ or any of the subscales, research has shown that food reinforcement can vary significantly between lean, overweight, and obese individual [35–37] and individuals with an eating disorder [38,39]. Further research is needed to determine if there exist differential psychoactive effects of chocolate consumption between lean, overweight, and obese populations and individuals with an eating disorder.

Our prior work suggests that obese individuals who engage in binge eating may do so because of an inherent reward deficiency, resulting in overeating high-sugar foods. We previously found an increase in food reinforcement after the consumption of a liquid chocolate-based preload, indicating a "sensitization" response to foods that increase the dopaminergic response [39]. Davis et al. [38] found that obese individuals diagnosed with binge eating disorder have a "hyper-reactivity to the hedonic properties of food, coupled with the motivation to engage in appetitive behaviors." In women diagnosed with bulimia nervosa (BN), Bulik et al. [40] reported that food reinforcement decreases following deprivation. On the basis of these results, we posit that obese individuals with an eating disorder would demonstrate an overall increase in their self-reported scores on the PEQ due to reward sensitization. However, we would not anticipate a significant increase per se in obese individuals who do not exhibit a binge eating-related eating disorder.

Although questionnaires provide validated subjective measurements about food reward and eating behavior, the use of objective methodologies provide insight into the effect of highly palatable food on central dopamine activity and brain regions known to have a high density of dopamine neurons (positron emission tomography and functional magnetic resonance imaging, respectively). However, the cost of instrumentation, the expertise needed to operate the equipment and interpret the data, as well as the engineering and mechanical constraints of the scanners make objective measurements of the dopaminergic response to food challenging. A promising methodology, electroretinography (ERG), may provide a more efficient way to objectively assess central dopamine activity. ERG is a clinical ophthalmological procedure that overcomes the impediments of other neuroimaging methods. ERG records the electrical potential from the retina, which is dependent upon dopamine signaling [41,42], in response to light simulation. ERG has been used to show a negative correlation between self-reported cocaine craving and dopamine-mediated retinal signal [43,44] and a positive correlation between dopamine metabolite levels in the cerebrospinal fluid [45] and dopamine-mediated retinal signal. We have also used ERG to demonstrate a positive correlation between increased dopamine-mediated retinal signal with food stimulation and BES scores [46], consistent with positron emission tomography [47]. We are currently conducting research to extend those findings to chocolates varying in cocoa, sugar, and fat content. Results from this ongoing study should provide further evidence that ERG should be considered as a low-cost, non-invasive method for objective evaluation of the stimulating properties of food in conjunction with ARCI questionnaires.

5. Conclusions

Chocolate's ability to modulate both the opioidergic and the dopaminergic systems, evident by the significant increase in self-reported scores on the PEQ, is consistent with research demonstrating chocolate's reinforcing potential and comforting and mood-ameliorating effects [2,3,21–23]. These results help explain chocolate's high reinforcing value, as foods that elevate feelings of euphoria, as indicated by an increase in the number of positive responses on the MBG subscales, have a greater reinforcing potential [17]. Given the measurable psychoactive dose–effect relationship observed in this study, we posit that chocolate's ability to provoke "addictive-like" eating behavior is initiated by its bioactive compounds, and each incremental increase in added sugar further enhances these effects.

Author Contributions: The authors' responsibilities were as follows—S.L.C. and J.A.N.: conceived the project, developed the overall research plan, oversaw the study, wrote and edited the manuscript, and had primary responsibility for final content; S.L.C., L.L., and E.A.: collected the data, analyzed the data, and edited the manuscript; and all authors read and approved the final manuscript.

Acknowledgments: The authors would like to thank Clint Hall and Joshua Severud for their assistance with the implementation of the protocol, data collection, and data entry, and Wei DU, MD, MS (Chair, Department of Psychiatry, Drexel University College of Medicine (DUCOM), for his insights on the physiological/pharmacological effects of addictive substances.

References

1. Schulte, E.M.; Avena, N.M.; Gearhardt, A.N. Which foods may be addictive? The roles of processing, fat content, and glycemic load. *PLoS ONE* **2015**, *10*, e0117959. [CrossRef]
2. Macht, M.; Dettmer, D. Everyday mood and emotions after eating a chocolate bar or an apple. *Appetite* **2006**, *46*, 332–336. [CrossRef] [PubMed]
3. Meier, B.P.; Noll, S.W.; Molokwu, O.J. The sweet life: The effect of mindful chocolate consumption on mood. *Appetite* **2017**, *108*, 21–27. [CrossRef]
4. Asmaro, D.; Liotti, M. High-caloric and chocolate stimuli processing in healthy humans: An integration of functional imaging and electrophysiological findings. *Nutrients* **2014**, *6*, 319–341. [CrossRef] [PubMed]
5. Smit, H.J.; Gaffan, E.A.; Rogers, P.J. Methylxanthines are the psycho-pharmacologically active constituents of chocolate. *Psychopharmacology* **2004**, *176*, 412–419. [CrossRef]
6. Nasser, J.A.; Bradley, L.E.; Leitzsch, J.B.; Chohan, O.; Fasulo, K.; Haller, J.; Jaeger, K.; Szulanczyk, B.; Del Parigi, A. Psychoactive effects of tasting chocolate and desire for more chocolate. *Physiol. Behav.* **2011**, *104*, 117–121. [CrossRef] [PubMed]
7. DiFeliceantonio, A.G.; Coppin, G.; Rigoux, L.; Edwin Thanarajah, S.; Dagher, A.; Tittgemeyer, M.; Small, D.M. Supra-additive effects of combining fat and carbohydrate on food reward. *Cell Metab.* **2018**, *28*, 33–44.e3. [CrossRef] [PubMed]
8. Epstein, L.H.; Carr, K.A.; Lin, H.; Fletcher, K.D. Food reinforcement, energy intake, and macronutrient choice. *Am. J. Clin. Nutr.* **2011**, *94*, 12–18. [CrossRef]
9. Stice, E.; Burger, K.S.; Yokum, S. Relative ability of fat and sugar tastes to activate reward, gustatory, and somatosensory regions. *Am. J. Clin. Nutr.* **2013**, *98*, 1377–1384. [CrossRef]
10. Casperson, S.L.; Johnson, L.; Roemmich, J.N. The relative reinforcing value of sweet versus savory snack foods after consumption of sugar- or non-nutritive sweetened beverages. *Appetite* **2017**, *112*, 143–149. [CrossRef]
11. Casperson, S.L.; Roemmich, J.N. Impact of dietary protein and gender on food reinforcement. *Nutrients* **2017**, *9*, 957. [CrossRef] [PubMed]
12. Berridge, K.C. 'Liking' and 'wanting' food rewards: Brain substrates and roles in eating disorders. *Physiol. Behav.* **2009**, *97*, 537–550. [CrossRef]
13. Pecina, S. Opioid reward 'liking' and 'wanting' in the nucleus accumbens. *Physiol. Behav.* **2008**, *94*, 675–680. [CrossRef] [PubMed]
14. Wise, R.A. Role of brain dopamine in food reward and reinforcement. *Philos. Trans. R. Soc. B Biol. Sci.* **2006**, *361*, 1149–1158. [CrossRef]
15. Balster, R.L.; Walsh, S.L. Addiction research center inventory. In *Encyclopedia of Psychopharmacology*; Stolerman, I.P., Ed.; Springer: Berlin/Heidelberg, Germany, 2010; p. 20.
16. Haertzen, C.A. Development of scales based on patterns of drug effects, using the addiction research center inventory (arci). *Psychol. Rep.* **1966**, *18*, 163–194. [CrossRef] [PubMed]
17. Schulte, E.M.; Smeal, J.K.; Gearhardt, A.N. Foods are differentially associated with subjective effect report questions of abuse liability. *PLoS ONE* **2017**, *12*, e0184220. [CrossRef]
18. Leigh, S.J.; Morris, M.J. The role of reward circuitry and food addiction in the obesity epidemic: An update. *Biol. Psychol.* **2018**, *131*, 31–42. [CrossRef]
19. Novelle, M.G.; Dieguez, C. Food addiction and binge eating: Lessons learned from animal models. *Nutrients* **2018**, *10*, 71. [CrossRef] [PubMed]
20. Gormally, J.; Black, S.; Daston, S.; Rardin, D. The assessment of binge eating severity among obese persons. *Addict. Behav.* **1982**, *7*, 47–55. [CrossRef]
21. Scholey, A.; Owen, L. Effects of chocolate on cognitive function and mood: A systematic review. *Nutr. Rev.* **2013**, *71*, 665–681. [CrossRef]
22. Bruinsma, K.; Taren, D.L. Chocolate: Food or drug? *J. Am. Diet. Assoc.* **1999**, *99*, 1249–1256. [CrossRef]

23. Parker, G.; Parker, I.; Brotchie, H. Mood state effects of chocolate. *J. Affect. Disord.* **2006**, *92*, 149–159. [CrossRef] [PubMed]
24. Massolt, E.T.; van Haard, P.M.; Rehfeld, J.F.; Posthuma, E.F.; van der Veer, E.; Schweitzer, D.H. Appetite suppression through smelling of dark chocolate correlates with changes in ghrelin in young women. *Regul. Pept.* **2010**, *161*, 81–86. [CrossRef]
25. Sorensen, L.B.; Astrup, A. Eating dark and milk chocolate: A randomized crossover study of effects on appetite and energy intake. *Nutr. Diabetes* **2011**, *1*, e21. [CrossRef]
26. Michener, W.; Rozin, P. Pharmacological versus sensory factors in the satiation of chocolate craving. *Physiol. Behav.* **1994**, *56*, 419–422. [CrossRef]
27. Avena, N.M.; Rada, P.; Hoebel, B.G. Evidence for sugar addiction: Behavioral and neurochemical effects of intermittent, excessive sugar intake. *Neurosci. Biobehav. Rev.* **2008**, *32*, 20–39. [CrossRef] [PubMed]
28. *Treatment for Stimulant Use Disorders*; Treatment Improvement Protocol (TIP) Series, No. 33; Center for Substance Abuse Treatment: Rockville, MD, USA, 1999.
29. Lee, A.A.; Owyang, C. Sugars, sweet taste receptors, and brain responses. *Nutrients* **2017**, *9*, 653. [CrossRef]
30. Low, J.Y.; McBride, R.L.; Lacy, K.E.; Keast, R.S. Psychophysical evaluation of sweetness functions across multiple sweeteners. *Chem. Senses* **2017**, *42*, 111–120. [CrossRef]
31. Noori, H.R.; Cosa Linan, A.; Spanagel, R. Largely overlapping neuronal substrates of reactivity to drug, gambling, food and sexual cues: A comprehensive meta-analysis. *Eur. Neuropsychopharmacol.* **2016**, *26*, 1419–1430. [CrossRef] [PubMed]
32. Baggott, M.J.; Childs, E.; Hart, A.B.; de Bruin, E.; Palmer, A.A.; Wilkinson, J.E.; de Wit, H. Psychopharmacology of theobromine in healthy volunteers. *Psychopharmacology* **2013**, *228*, 109–118. [CrossRef] [PubMed]
33. Smit, H.J.; Rogers, P.J. Effects of low doses of caffeine on cognitive performance, mood and thirst in low and higher caffeine consumers. *Psychopharmacology* **2000**, *152*, 167–173. [CrossRef] [PubMed]
34. Hetherington, M.; Rolls, B.J.; Burley, V.J. The time course of sensory-specific satiety. *Appetite* **1989**, *12*, 57–68. [CrossRef]
35. Temple, J.L.; Bulkley, A.M.; Badawy, R.L.; Krause, N.; McCann, S.; Epstein, L.H. Differential effects of daily snack food intake on the reinforcing value of food in obese and nonobese women. *Am. J. Clin. Nutr.* **2009**, *90*, 304–313. [CrossRef] [PubMed]
36. Volkow, N.D.; Wang, G.J.; Tomasi, D.; Baler, R.D. Obesity and addiction: Neurobiological overlaps. *Obes. Rev.* **2013**, *14*, 2–18. [CrossRef]
37. Epstein, L.H.; Carr, K.A.; Lin, H.; Fletcher, K.D.; Roemmich, J.N. Usual energy intake mediates the relationship between food reinforcement and bmi. *Obesity* **2012**, *20*, 1815–1819. [CrossRef]
38. Davis, C.A.; Levitan, R.D.; Reid, C.; Carter, J.C.; Kaplan, A.S.; Patte, K.A.; King, N.; Curtis, C.; Kennedy, J.L. Dopamine for "wanting" and opioids for "liking": A comparison of obese adults with and without binge eating. *Obesity* **2009**, *17*, 1220–1225. [CrossRef]
39. Nasser, J.A.; Evans, S.M.; Geliebter, A.; Pi-Sunyer, F.X.; Foltin, R.W. Use of an operant task to estimate food reinforcement in adult humans with and without bed. *Obesity* **2008**, *16*, 1816–1820. [CrossRef]
40. Bulik, C.M.; Brinded, E.C. The effect of food deprivation on the reinforcing value of food and smoking in bulimic and control women. *Physiol. Behav.* **1994**, *55*, 665–672. [CrossRef]
41. Witkovsky, P.; Veisenberger, E.; Haycock, J.W.; Akopian, A.; Garcia-Espana, A.; Meller, E. Activity-dependent phosphorylation of tyrosine hydroxylase in dopaminergic neurons of the rat retina. *J. Neurosci.* **2004**, *24*, 4242–4249. [CrossRef]
42. Lavoie, J.; Illiano, P.; Sotnikova, T.D.; Gainetdinov, R.R.; Beaulieu, J.M.; Hebert, M. The electroretinogram as a biomarker of central dopamine and serotonin: Potential relevance to psychiatric disorders. *Biol. Psychiatry* **2014**, *75*, 479–486. [CrossRef]
43. Roy, M.; Smelson, D.A.; Roy, A. Abnormal electroretinogram in cocaine-dependent patients. Relationship to craving. *Br. J. Psychiatry* **1996**, *168*, 507–511. [CrossRef]
44. Smelson, D.A.; Roy, A.; Roy, M.; Tershakovec, D.; Engelhart, C.; Losonczy, M.F. Electroretinogram and cue-elicited craving in withdrawn cocaine-dependent patients: A replication. *Am. J. Drug Alcohol Abuse* **2001**, *27*, 391–397. [CrossRef]
45. Roy, A.; Roy, M.; Berman, J.; Gonzalez, B. Blue cone electroretinogram amplitudes are related to dopamine function in cocaine-dependent patients. *Psychiatry Res.* **2003**, *117*, 191–195. [CrossRef]

46. Nasser, J.A.; Del Parigi, A.; Merhige, K.; Wolper, C.; Geliebter, A.; Hashim, S.A. Electroretinographic detection of human brain dopamine response to oral food stimulation. *Obesity* **2013**, *21*, 976–980. [CrossRef]
47. Wang, G.J.; Geliebter, A.; Volkow, N.D.; Telang, F.W.; Logan, J.; Jayne, M.C.; Galanti, K.; Selig, P.A.; Han, H.; Zhu, W.; et al. Enhanced striatal dopamine release during food stimulation in binge eating disorder. *Obesity* **2011**, *19*, 1601–1608. [CrossRef]

Somatotype Components as Useful Predictors of Disordered Eating Attitudes in Young Female Ballet Dance Students

José Ramón Alvero-Cruz [1,2,3,*], Verónica Parent Mathias [1] and Jerónimo C. García-Romero [1,2]

1 Department of Human Physiology, Histology, Pathological Anatomy and Physical Education and Sport, University of Málaga-Andalucía Tech, 29071 Málaga, Spain; veronicaparent@hotmail.com (V.P.M.); jeronimo@uma.es (J.C.G.-R.)
2 The Biomedical Research Institute of Málaga (IBIMA), 29010 Málaga, Spain
3 Edificio López de Peñalver, Campus de Teatinos, Universidad de Málaga, 29071 Málaga, Spain
* Correspondence: alvero@uma.es

Abstract: The current study used receiver operating characteristic (ROC) curve analysis to examine the accuracy of somatotype components in correctly classifying disordered eating attitudes (DEA) in female dance students. Participants were a sample of 81 female dancers distributed in two groups: beginner training (BT; age (mean ± SD) = 10.09 ± 1.2 years, n = 32) and advanced training (AT; age = 15.37 ± 2.1 years, n = 49). For evaluation of DEA, the Eating Attitudes Test- 26 (EAT-26) questionnaire was used. We defined an EAT-26 score ≥20 as positive for DEA. Somatotype components were calculated using the Heath-Carter anthropometric method. The risk of presenting DEA was 28.1% (n = 9) in the BT group and 6.1% (n = 3) in the AT group. In the BT group, mesomorphy demonstrated moderate–high accuracy in predicting DEA (area under the curve (AUC) = 0.82, 95% confidence interval (CI): 0.64–0.93). The optimal cut-off of 6.34 yielded a sensitivity of 0.77 and a specificity of 0.95. Ectomorphy showed moderate accuracy in predicting DEA (AUC = 0.768, 95% CI: 0.58–0.89). The optimal cut-off of 2.41 yielded a sensitivity of 0.78 and a specificity of 0.78. In the AT group, none of the components demonstrated accuracy in predicting DEA. Somatotype components were good predictors of disordered eating attitudes in the younger dance student group (beginner training). Further research is needed to identify the determinants of these differences between the two groups.

Keywords: dance students; disordered eating attitudes; Eating Attitudes Test-26 (EAT-26); mesomorphy; ectomorphy; Receiver Operating Characteristics (ROC) curve analysis

1. Introduction

Eating disorders (EDs) are mental disorders defined by abnormal eating habits that negatively affect a person's physical or mental health. Anorexia nervosa, one of the main EDs, has two distinct symptoms: low body weight (body mass index (BMI) less than 17.5 kg/m^2 or less than 85% of the expected weight for height, age and sex) and body image disturbance. Bulimia nervosa is defined by three criteria: recurrent binge eating, recurrent compensatory behavior, and preoccupation with one's body weight or shape. Others EDs include avoidant/restrictive food intake disorder, pica, regurgitation disorders, and other specified feeding and eating disorder [1]. In most EDs, the association with depression and anxiety states and substance abuse is common [1,2].

The influence of cultural and social factors on the development of EDs and their manifestations have been investigated from multiple perspectives [3]. The reasons for these rates of EDs have been centered on elements including personality factors and traits such as perfectionism and low self-esteem.

Epigenetic reasons are currently found in the etiology of EDs, with evidence suggesting that epigenetic processes link malnutrition and life stresses (gestational, perinatal, childhood, and adult) to the risk of developing EDs [4]. In dancers, it is well known that they spend countless hours practicing in front of mirrors where their bodies are closely examined by themselves and others. In addition, high levels of perfectionism concerning dance and a specific body shape, combined with the socio-cultural pressures for thinness inherent in the dance profession and expectations of high performance, produce the ideal social climate for the development of EDs [5,6].

Similarly, the Tripartite Influence Model, which is an etiological model of body image disturbance and eating disorders, proposes that social agents, such as family, friends, and the media, promote ideals of appearance that emphasize a slim ideal for women and a lean, muscular ideal for men [7]. EDs today are a health problem in Western countries [8], and their incidence and prevalence are increasing. The prevalence of EDs in female athletes appears to be high when competitive weight is important [9]. This prevalence is higher in athletes (18%) compared to non-athletes (5%) [10], and is also higher in female athletes (20%) than in non-athletes (5%) [11]. The highest prevalence of EDs is found in aesthetic sports, as well as in sports where athletes are classified by body weight (45%) compared to other sports (12%) [11]. Similar to the trend in the prevalence of Eds, athletes in lean sports exhibit more disordered eating behaviors than those in non-lean sports [12]. Female dancers, in particular, show high levels of perfectionism and when in highly competitive environments, such as dance companies or professional conservatories, may present a higher risk for developing an ED [13,14]. EDs are characterized by chronicity and relapses of disordered eating behavior in which the attitudes of adolescent girls towards body weight, as well as their perception of body shape, are frequently altered.

Numerous efforts have been made to develop instruments to improve the predictive value in the diagnostic screening of these diseases and various tests have been developed (EAT, Children's Eating Attitudes Test (ChEAT), Eating Disorders Examination-Questionnaire (EDE-Q), Sick, Control, One, Fat, Food (SCOFF), Eating Disorder Inventory (EDI), etc.). Of all these questionnaires, the Eating Attitudes Test (EAT) has been the most extensively used because of its reliability and reproducibility in the detection of EDs in the general population [15]; it has also been widely used in sports and dance [16–19]. EDs are complex and have an impact on both the physical and social–emotional health of adolescents as well as young adults [20]. EDs such as anorexia nervosa and bulimia, have well-established effects on body composition, such as decreased fat mass, fat-free mass, and total body water [21], as well as decreased bone mineral density [22].

The somatotype is defined as the quantification of the present shape and composition of the human body. It is expressed as a three-number rating representing the endomorphy, mesomorphy, and ectomorphy components, respectively, always in the same order. Endomorphy is the relative fatness; mesomorphy is the relative musculoskeletal robustness; and ectomorphy is the relative linearity or slenderness of a physique. The Heath-Carter method uses various anthropometric measurements including weight, height, upper arm circumference, maximal calf circumference, femur and humerus breadths, and triceps, subscapular, supraspinal, and medial calf skinfolds [23]. Somatotype determination is useful in the characterization of body shape in contemporary dance and sports dance [24], but the relationship between anthropometric somatotype components and EDs has been rarely studied [25]. Mesomorphy, the second component of the anthropometric somatotype [23], reflects the development of skeleton and muscle tissues. Studies have found associations between body shape and muscularity and an increase in eating problems [26]. The rationale for studying the somatotype components and their association with DEA is that this measurement is a reflection of body shape based on the three components: endomorphy (fatness), mesomorphy (robustness), and ectomorphy (slenderness). In addition, body dissatisfaction seems to be a determining factor for risk behavior for EDs [2,26].

The present study therefore aimed to establish the accuracy of somatotype components using receiver operating characteristic (ROC) curve analysis to assess disordered eating attitudes (DEA) in a group of dance students engaged in beginner and advanced dance training.

2. Methods

This cross-sectional and correlational study conducted in 2017 was approved by the Research Ethics Committee of the University of Málaga, Spain (EMEFYDE 2016–011 report) and carried out according to the principles of the Declaration of Helsinki.

2.1. *Participants*

A total of 81 female students between the ages of 8 and 21 years participated in this study. All were enrolled in the Professional Conservatory of Granada, Spain, in courses from beginner training (BT) through advanced training (AT). The students in the AT group were distributed into four dance specialties: Flamenco, Spanish, Classical, and Contemporary. Participation in the study was voluntary, and prior to its initiation, written informed consent was obtained from the participants or the legal guardians of those under 18 years of age. The exclusion criteria were the inability to perform some of the anthropometric measurements, incorrectly completing the EAT-26, and male gender.

2.2. *Eating Behavior*

Eating behavior was assessed with the EAT-26, which is a self-administered questionnaire used worldwide. It has been validated for assessing symptoms, concerns, and attitudes associated with abnormal eating behavior. The EAT-26 consists of 26 items forming three scales: dieting (related to the avoidance of fattening foods and the preoccupation with being thinner), bulimia and food preoccupation (involving items reflecting thoughts about food and those indicating bulimia), and oral control (associated with the self-control of eating and the perceived pressure from others to gain weight). A total score equal to or greater than 20 on the questionnaire is indicative of disordered eating behavior [15]. The EAT-26 has been validated for the Spanish population [16,27,28].

2.3. *Anthropometric Assessment*

All anthropometric measurements were conducted after a 12-h fast. Weight was measured on a SECA 813 electronic scale (SECA, Hamburg, Germany) accurate to 0.1 kg., and stretch stature was measured using a wall-mounted SECA 216 stadiometer (SECA, Hamburg, Germany) accurate to 0.1 cm. Skinfolds were measured at the following sites: triceps, subscapular, supraspinal, and medial calf with a Holtain skinfold caliper (Holtain, Crymych, UK) accurate to 0.2 mm, computing the means for subsequent calculations. Girths were measured at the following sites: flexed and tensed arm and calf with a Lufkin W606PM anthropometric tape (Apex Tool Group, Lufkin, México) accurate to 0.1 cm. Biepicondylar humerus and Bicondylar femur breadths were measured with a Holtain sliding caliper (Holtain, Crymych, UK) accurate to 0.1 cm. BMI was calculated as weight in kilograms divided by height in meters squared. Anthropometric measurements were performed following standardized techniques adopted by the International Society for the Advancement of Kinanthropometry [29]. The technical error of measurement of the Level 3 anthropometrist was less than 3% for skinfolds and less than 1% for the rest of the anthropometric measurements.

2.4. *Anthropometric Somatotype*

Anthropometric somatotypes were determined according to the Heath-Carter method [23] by the following equations:

$$\text{Endomorphy} = -0.7182 + 0.1451\,(X) - 0.00068\,(X^2) + 0.0000014\,(X^3) \text{ where } X = \text{sum of triceps, subscapular and supraspinal skinfolds) multiplied by (170.18/height in cm).} \tag{1}$$

This is called height-corrected endomorphy and is the preferred method for calculating endomorphy.

$$\text{Mesomorphy} = 0.858 \times \text{humerus breadth} + 0.601 \times \text{femur breadth} + 0.188 \times \text{corrected arm girth} + 0.161 \times \text{corrected calf girth} - 0.131 \times \text{height} + 4.5 \tag{2}$$

Three different equations are used to calculate ectomorphy according to the height–weight ratio (HWR). If the HWR is greater than or equal to 40.75, then ectomorphy = 0.732 HWR – 28.58. If HWR is less than 40.75 but greater than 38.25, then ectomorphy = 0.463 HWR – 17.63. If HWR is equal to or less than 38.25, then ectomorphy = 0.1.

2.5. Statistical Analysis

Normality was analyzed using the Shapiro-Wilk test. The descriptive characteristics of the group variables were expressed as mean ± standard deviation. Comparisons between groups were performed using a Mann-Whitney U or one-way ANOVA test when appropriate. Associations between EAT-26 subscale scores and somatotype components were assessed by Spearman's rank correlation coefficient (rho) for the two groups separately. The following criteria were adopted to interpret the magnitude of the correlations: $r \leq 0.1$ = trivial; $0.1 < r \leq 0.3$ = small; $0.3 < r \leq 0.5$ = moderate; $0. < r \leq 0.7$ = large; $0.7 < r \leq 0.9$ = very large; and $r > 0.9$ = almost perfect [30]. Cronbach's alpha was performed for investigating the internal consistency of the subscales and the total score of the EAT-26 questionnaire. Test–retest reliability was assessed by intraclass correlation coefficient (ICC). The effect size was calculated using Rosenthal's R-test and the power (1-β) to analyze the type II error by G*Power [31].

ROC curve analysis was used to test the performance of the somatotype components in predicting disordered eating status and to identify a cut-off score. The ROC curve is a graphical representation of a measure's sensitivity plotted against its false positive rate (i.e., 1-specificity). The area under the curve (AUC) summarizes a test's overall accuracy, or ability to distinguish cases from non-cases, based on the average value of sensitivity for all possible values of specificity. AUC values are defined as non-informative (≤0.50), less accurate (0.51 to 0.70), moderately accurate (0.71 to 0.90), highly accurate (0.91 to 0.99), or perfect (1.0) [32]. The likelihood ratios were calculated for each somatotype component. Binary logistic regression was used to evaluate the association between independent variables (somatotype components) and risk behaviors for DEA. The level of significance was set at $p < 0.05$. The statistical analysis was performed on MedCalc Statistical Software version 19.3.1 (MedCalc Software bvba, Ostend, Belgium).

3. Results

The risk of presenting DEA was 28.1% ($n = 9$) in the BT group and 6.1% ($n = 3$) in the AT group. Table 1 shows the comparative data of the study groups. Regarding the anthropometric variables; significant differences were found in age, weight, height, and BMI (all $p = 0.000001$). Similarly, differences were seen in both endomorphy ($p = 0.003$) and mesomorphy ($p = 0.04$). The psychometric assessment of the EAT-26 subscales showed differences between the groups only in bulimia ($p = 0.004$), although the values of the diet subscale and the total score were higher in the BT group (Table 1).

The internal consistency of the EAT-26 was assessed with Cronbach's alpha. The results revealed satisfactory levels for the subsample ($n = 25$). Cronbach's alpha for the total EAT-26 score, bulimia, oral control, and dieting were 0.87, 0.915, 0.89, and 0.906, respectively. The subsample of 25 participants completed the retest after 3-week intervals. Test–retest reliability was good (ICC = 0.864, $p < 0.001$). A Mann–Whitney U test showed no significant differences between the test and re-test scores for the total EAT-26 score ($p = 0.467$).

Bivariate correlations in the beginner training group: bulimia correlated inversely with age (rho = −0.37, $p = 0.035$) and height (rho = −0.465, $p = 0.007$); oral control correlated with mesomorphy (rho = 0.46. $p = 0.007$); bulimia correlated inversely with height (rho = −0.39. $p = 0.027$) and directly with mesomorphy (rho = 0.40, $p = 0.021$); and the total score correlated inversely with height (rho = −0.45, $p = 0.0089$) and directly with mesomorphy (rho = 0.40, $p = 0.02$) (Table 2).

Table 1. Descriptive data for anthropometrics and the Eating Attitudes Test-26 (EAT-26) subscales of the study groups.

Variables	Beginner Training (n = 32)		Advanced Training (n = 49)		p-Value	Effect Size	Statistical Power
	Mean	SD	Mean	SD		r	1-β
Age (years)	10.09	1.23	15.37	2.11	<0.0001	0.84	0.99
Weight (kg)	34.93	3.63	52.28	5.79	<0.0001	0.87	0.99
Height (m)	1.40	0.07	1.59	0.08	<0.0001	0.79	0.99
BMI (kg/m^2)	18.00	1.89	20.69	1.96	<0.0001	0.57	0.99
Endomorphy	3.85	1.23	3.19	0.64	0.003	0.32	0.81
Mesomorphy	5.64	0.95	5.17	1.04	0.041	0.23	0.51
Ectomorphy	2.77	1.27	2.62	1.29	0.60	0.09	0.08
Bulimia	0.94	1.50	0.16	0.55	0.004	0.33	0.83
Oral control	3.44	4.06	3.10	3.05	0.66	0.05	0.07
Dieting	6.72	7.35	4.22	5.21	0.21	0.19	0.38
Total score	11.09	11.58	7.49	8.01	0.46	0.18	0.33

Table 2. Spearman's rank correlation coefficient between body composition variables, somatotype components and the EAT-26 subscales in the Beginner Training group.

	Bulimia	Oral Control	Dieting	Total Score	Age	Weight	Height	BMI	Endo	Meso
Oral control	0.786 **									
Dieting	0.667 **	0.60 **								
Total Score	0.772 **	0.821 **	0.936 **							
Age	−0.37 *	−0.243	−0.158	−0.218						
Weight	−0.132	−0.212	−0.093	−0.17	0.54 **					
Height	−0.46 **	−0.48 **	−0.39 *	−0.45 **	0.81 **	0.528 **				
BMI	0.193	0.197	0.204	0.184	−0.169	0.537 **	−0.37 *			
Endo	0.254	0.206	0.116	0.121	−0.56 **	0.058	−0.65 **	0.63 **		
Meso	0.422 *	0.466 **	0.405 *	0.438 *	−0.166	0.32	−0.43 **	0.82 **	0.49 **	
Ecto	−0.319	−0.338	−0.27	−0.294	0.415 *	-0.291	0.62 **	−0.94 **	−0.73 **	−0.8 **

BMI: body mass index. Endo: endomorphy. Meso: mesomorphy. Ecto: ectomorphy. * $p < 0.05$. ** $p < 0.001$.

Bivariate correlations in the advanced training group: bulimia did not correlate with body composition variables or somatotype components ($p > 0.05$); oral control correlated directly with age (rho = 0.28, $p = 0.047$) and BMI (rho = 0.29, $p = 0.04$); the mesomorphic component correlated inversely with height (rho = −0.75, $p < 0.0001$) and directly with BMI (rho = 0.62, $p < 0.0001$); ectomorphy also correlated directly with diet (rho = 0.34, $p = 0.016$) and height (rho = 0.69, $p < 0.001$); and the total EAT-26 score did not correlate with any of the body composition variables or somatotype components ($p > 0.05$) (Table 3).

Analysis of ROC Curves

Ectomorphy showed moderate accuracy for the diagnosis of DEA (AUC: 0.768, $p = 0.0158$), and mesomorphy showed moderately high accuracy (AUC: 0.82, $p = 0.0003$) in the BT group. Endomorphy in the BT group and all three components for the AT group indicated low accuracy ($p > 0.05$), (Figure 1 and Table 4).

Table 3. Spearman's rank correlation coefficients between body composition variables, somatotype components, and the EAT-26 subscales in the Advanced Training group.

	Bulimia	Oral Control	Dieting	Total Score	Age	Weight	Height	BMI	Endo	Meso
Oral control	0.469 **									
Dieting	0.489 **	0.141								
Total Score	0.482 *	0.828 **	0.616 **							
Age	0.23	0.284 *	−0.093	0.127						
Weight	0.237	0.35 *	−0.035	0.214	0.803 **					
Height	0.187	0.066	0.258	0.219	0.414 **	0.594 **				
BMI	0.103	0.294 *	−0.277	−0.011	0.474 **	0.51 **	−0.322 *			
Endo	−0.016	0.066	−0.107	−0.021	−0.165	−0.213	−0.57 **	0.431 **		
Meso	−0.09	0.102	−0.281	−0.112	−0.022	−0.146	−0.76 **	0.629 **	0.544 **	
Ecto	0.026	−0.177	0.342 *	0.119	−0.127	−0.118	0.692 **	−0.88 **	−0.59 **	−0.80 **

BMI, body mass index; Endo, endomorphy; Meso, mesomorphy; Ecto, ectomorphy. * $p < 0.05$. ** $p < 0.001$.

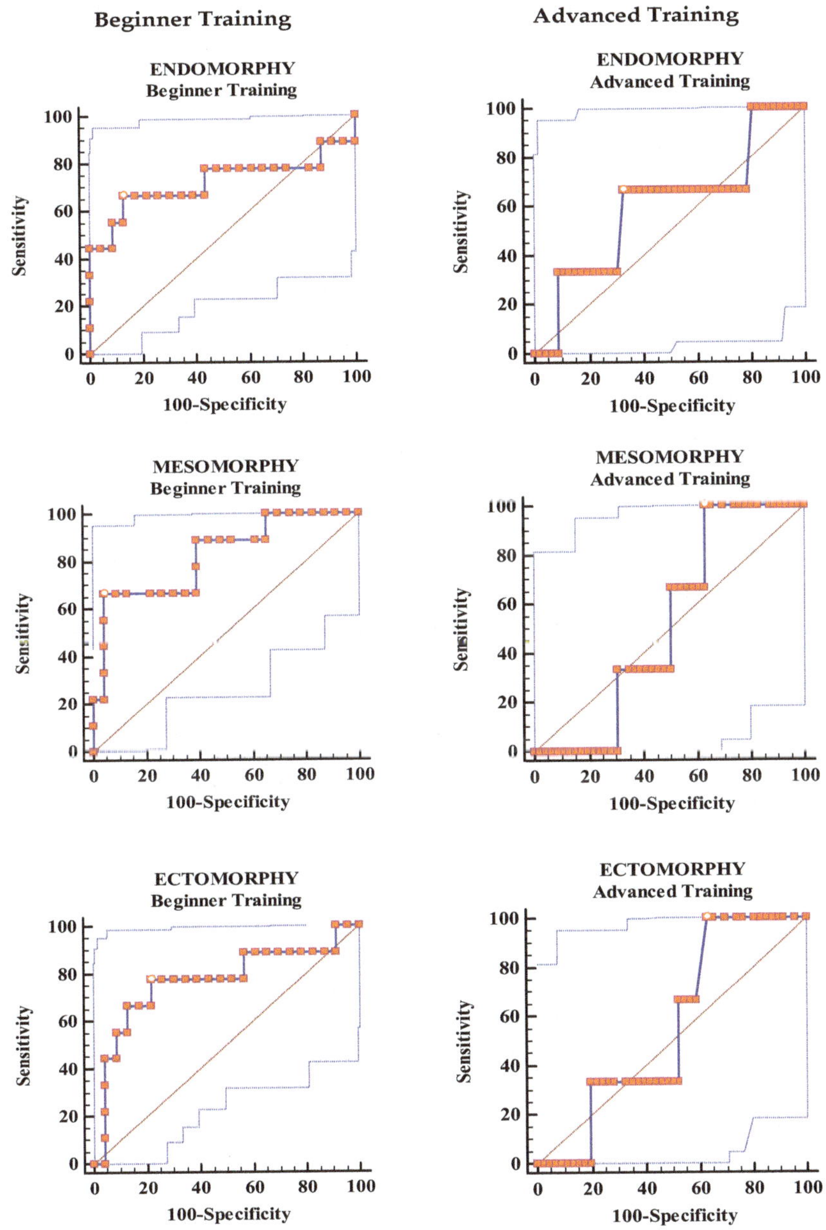

Figure 1. Receiver Operating Characteristics (ROC) curve analysis showing the area under the curve for the prediction of disordered eating attitudes using the Eating Attitudes Test-26 (EAT-26) total score.

Table 4. Characteristics of the ROC curves for somatotype components in the beginner training and advanced training groups.

	Beginner Training			Advanced Training		
	Endo	Meso	Ecto	Endo	Meso	Ecto
Area under the curve	0.72	0.82	0.768	0.601	0.522	0.558
Standard error	0.135	0.089	0.111	0.212	0.114	0.139
95% CI	0.53 to 0.86	0.64 to 0.93	0.58 to 0.89	0.45 to 0.74	0.37 to 0.66	0.41 to 0.70
z statistic	1.631	3.61	2.41	0.477	0.191	0.418
***p*-value**	0.1030	0.003	0.0158	0.633	0.8483	0.6758
Youden's J index	0.5362	0.6232	0.564	0.3406	0.3696	0.3696

ROC, receiver operating characteristic; Endo, endomorphy; Meso, mesomorphy; Ecto, ectomorphy; CI, confidence interval.

The BT group had moderate specificity values for ectomorphy (78.6%) and high values for mesomorphy (95.6%) and endomorphy (87%). Sensitivity values were low and moderate, respectively. In this group, of note is the cut-off point of 6.34 for mesomorphy with a very high positive likelihood ratio value of (15.33). In the AT group, sensitivity values were moderate for endomorphy (67%) and highest for mesomorphy and ectomorphy (both 100%) (Table 5).

Table 5. Sensitivity. specificity and likelihood ratios of somatotype components in the beginner and advanced training groups.

Somatotype Component	Training	Cut-Off	Sens	95% CI	Spec	95% CI	+LR	95% CI	−LR	95% CI
Endomorphy	BT	>4.36	66.67	29.9–92.5	86.96	66.4–97.2	5.11	1.6–16.2	0.38	0.2–1.0
	AT	≤2.88	66.67	9.4–99.2	67.39	52.0–80.5	2.04	0.8–5.0	0.49	0.10–2.5
Mesomorphy	BT	>6.34	66.67	29.9–92.5	95.65	78.1–99.9	15.33	2.1–110	0.35	0.1–0.9
	AT	≤5.72	100	29.2–100.0	36.96	23.2–52.5	1.59	1.3–2.0	0	
Ectomorphy	BT	≤2.41	77.78	40.0–97.2	78.6	56.3–92.5	3.58	1.5–8.4	0.28	0.08–1.0
	AT	>1.76	100	29.2–100.0	36.96	23.2–52.5	1.59	1.3–2.0	0	

BT, beginner training; AT, advanced training; Sens, sensitivity; CI, confidence interval; Spec, specificity; +LR, positive likelihood ratio; −LR, negative likelihood ratio.

A logistic regression analysis was performed to examine independent associations between somatotype components and the probability of DEA (Table 6). The model provided a good fit for all three components in the BT group, particularly the mesomorphic component. However, in the AT group, none of the components achieved a significant fit.

Table 6. Associations between somatotype components and eating disorders.

				Overall Model Fit		Hosmer & Lemeshow	
Group	Variable	OR	95% CI	X^2	*p*-Value	X^2	*p*-Value
BT	Endo	2.44	1.1608 to 5.1493	6.878	0.0087	7.3902	0.5966
	Meso	7.14	1.7214 to 29.672	12.47	0.0004	11.0945	0.2693
	Ecto	0.42	0.2041 to 0.8972	6.22	0.0126	9.5698	0.3864
AT	Endo		Not retained in the model				
	Meso		Not retained in the model				
	Ecto		Not retained in the model				

BT, beginner training; AT, advanced training; Endo, endomorphy; Meso, mesomorphy; Ecto, ectomorphy; OR, odds ratio; CI, confidence interval; X^2, chi-squared.

4. Discussion

This study addresses the diagnostic accuracy of somatotype components (endomorphy, mesomorphy, and ectomorphy) to discriminate DEA in two groups of female dance students. The results show important significant differences and indicate that the ectomorphic and mesomorphic components in the BT group (younger students) can discriminate DEA with moderate and high accuracy, respectively; however, none of the somatotype components can do this in the AT group.

The emerging importance of somatotype components in predicting DEA in young female dance students is poorly reflected in the literature. Only one recent study showed that women who support attitudes and/or behaviors aimed at achieving the female muscle ideal may be susceptible to experiencing symptoms of DEA and negative emotional states, such as depression, stress, and anxiety [33].

The differences in the somatotype component associations between the study groups can be explained by the following reasons: the shorter height in the BT group increased mesomorphy scores, and although no significant differences in mesomorphy scores were found between groups, the levels were slightly higher in the BT group. In other words, the musculoskeletal structure was proportionally larger, and therefore a negative body image could have been internalized [34]. This also occurred with ectomorphy, since higher weight in relation to shorter height resulted in a lower ectomorphy value.

Similar results were found by Bartsch et al. who associate bulimia episodes with heavier somatotypes, such as pycnomorphic and metromorphic (similar to Heath and Carter's endomorphic and mesomorphic components) [25]. In the present study, we also observed a relationship between the bulimia subscale and mesomorphy, but this was only in the BT group. It should be noted that all the subscales of the EAT-26 as well as the total score had a significant direct association with the mesomorphic component. The substantial increase in DEA in Western societies may be associated with sociocultural pressures to maintain a slim body shape as well as with the combined influence of perfectionism and learning [5]. This condition becomes more pronounced in aesthetic activities such as dance [35].

Investigating the nature and distribution of DEA in dance students is important for several reasons. First, these studies can provide information about the extent of DEA and weight control in female dancers. Second, on a broader level, many dancers face specific pressures to control their weight and body shape, and this enables us to explore the association between this type of pressure and the development of disordered eating attitudes and behaviors [36].

Although no reference was made to the prevalence of bulimia, anorexia nervosa, or non-specific disorders, due both to this not being an aim of the study and to the limited sample size, the prevalence of these disorders was higher in the BT group, comprising younger students, similar to results published by other authors. In the BT group, this prevalence was around 26% and in the AT group it was 6% [37].

In a study by Fortes et al. that sought to establish the extent to which anthropometric variables can explain body dissatisfaction and eating behavior disturbances in teenage boys and girls, the findings showed that body dissatisfaction was modulated by body fat percentage ($R^2 = 0.18$), but this modulation was low. This was also low for its interaction with BMI ($R^2 = 0.18$). The interaction between eating behavior disturbances and body fat percentage and between body fat percentage and BMI were both ($R^2 = 0.03$) [38]. In contrast, Jáuregui et al. found that although there were correlations between BMI and EAT-40 scores, this did not result in an increased risk of developing an DEA [6]. These associations between BMI and the EAT-26 subscales were not confirmed in either of our study groups. The study by Toro et al. also found no significant inverse correlations between BMI and EAT-26 in dance students aged 14.4 years [39].

Another study in women found associations between BMI and DEA, and when these were mediated by a degree of body dissatisfaction, the associations disappeared [40]. This could explain the different associations between BMI and EAT-26 scores in our study, noting an association between BMI and oral control in the AT group, which implies greater self-control over food intake. In young people, being female, overweight, depressed, and having a high BMI are associated with DEA [41]. The results of a study of athletes competing in weight categories (taekwondo and judo) demonstrated that eating patterns and good dietary management decrease the likelihood of developing an DEA, which appears to be a good strategy [42].

Rouzitalab et al. analyzed a group of physical education students between the ages of 18 and 25 years. They found that EAT-26 had low but significant correlations with body weight and waist circumference in women, indicating these variables as good markers associated with an increase in

DEA [43]. In our study, no correlations were found between weight or BMI and the total score in the AT group, and none of these correlations were found in the BT group.

Several studies are available showing values for the subscales and total score on the EAT-26 in dance students of various ages, with no major differences found between these scores. These studies were performed in ballet dancers between the ages of 11 and 19, the same as those of our study. All the subscale scores in all the studies are higher in dieting than in oral control and bulimia [3,16,44,45].

Female gender, excess weight, living in urban areas, a distorted perception of weight, and body dissatisfaction were factors associated with DEA, suggesting that multiple factors contributed to the development of DEA [46,47]. The highest odds ratios were attributed to factors such as distorted perception of weight and body shape dissatisfaction [42,43]. In a study of 15- to 18-year-olds, the analysis showed significant negative associations between the total EAT-26 score and perceived physical appearance (rho = −0.290, $p < 0.001$) [37]. These data do not agree with those obtained in our study regarding correlations, although the EAT-26 score is very similar. However, for their assessment these differences should be compared with other determinants such as anxiety, stress, dissatisfaction, or body image and with other psychometric instruments that could explain those differences.

The results of this study can be used for prevention and early detection of DEA among young female dance students. Educational programs addressing adolescent eating behaviors should be developed. Future training programs on the significance of somatotype variations with growth, physical activity, and nutrition may be useful in preventing DEA.

5. Limitations

Several limitations of this study should be mentioned including the cross-sectional design, which limits the interpretation of causality. In addition, there was only one study stage, with no clinical interview performed to diagnose DEA. The EAT-26 was used as a screening tool only as the use of a questionnaire alone is not sufficient to diagnose DEA. Another limitation was that our study had a relatively small sample and only female students were included, although the statistical power was acceptable.

6. Conclusions

The ROC curve analysis showed that the mesomorphy and ectomorphy components for the BT group had a high and moderate discriminatory power for classifying DEA. This study allows the identification of a population at risk of DEA, such as young female dance students. We believe that the results found in the group comprising the youngest dancers should serve as an alert for greater control in the onset of DEA.

Author Contributions: Conceptualization, J.R.A.-C.; Data curation, J.R.A.-C. and V.P.M.; Formal analysis, J.R.A.-C., V.P.M., and J.C.G.-R.; Funding acquisition, J.R.A.-C.; Investigation, J.R.A.-C.; Methodology, J.R.A.-C., V.P.M., and J.C.G.-R.; Resources, J.R.A.-C.; Supervision, J.R.A.-C. and J.C.G.-R.; Writing–review and editing, J.R.A.-C., V.P.M., and J.C.G.-R. All authors have read and agreed to the published version of the manuscript.

Acknowledgments: This study was supported by IBIMA (The Biomedical Research Institute of Málaga). We would like to thank to dance students and their parents for their voluntary participation in this study. We also thank Maria Repice for her help with the English version of the text and Manuel Jiménez for his statistical advice.

References

1. American Psychiatric Association American Psychiatric Association. *Diagnostic and Statistical Manual of Mental Disorders*, 5th ed.; American Psychiatric Publishing: Gloucester, UK, 2013; ISBN 9780890425541.
2. Treasure, J.; Duarte, T.A.; Schmidt, U. Eating disorders. *Lancet* **2020**, *395*, 899–911. [CrossRef]
3. Toro, J.; Gomez-Peresmitré, G.; Sentis, J.; Vallés, A.; Casulà, V.; Castro, J.; Pineda, G.; Leon, R.; Platas, S.; Rodriguez, R. Eating disorders and body image in Spanish and Mexican female adolescents. *Soc. Psychiatry Psychiatr. Epidemiol.* **2006**, *41*, 556–565. [CrossRef]
4. Steiger, H.; Booij, L. Eating disorders, heredity and environmental activation: Getting epigenetic concepts into practice. *J. Clin. Med.* **2020**, *9*, e1332. [CrossRef] [PubMed]

5. Penniment, K.J.; Egan, S.J. Perfectionism and learning experiences in dance class as risk factors for eating disorders in dancers. *Eur. Eat. Disord. Rev.* **2012**, *20*, 13–22. [CrossRef] [PubMed]
6. Jáuregui-Lobera, I.; Bolaños-Rios, P.; Valero-Blanco, E.; Ortega-de-la-Torre, A. Eating attitudes, body image and risk for eating disorders in a group of Spanish dancers. *Nutr. Hosp.* **2016**, *33*, 1213–1221.
7. Tylka, T.L. Refinement of the tripartite influence model for men: Dual body image pathways to body change behaviors. *Body Image* **2011**, *8*, 199–207. [CrossRef]
8. Uher, R.; Rutter, M. Classification of feeding and eating disorders: Review of evidence and proposals for ICD-11. *World Psychiatry* **2012**, *11*, 80–92. [CrossRef]
9. Joy, E.; Kussman, A.; Nattiv, A. 2016 update on eating disorders in athletes: A comprehensive narrative review with a focus on clinical assessment and management. *Br. J. Sports Med.* **2016**, *50*, 154–162. [CrossRef]
10. Martinsen, M.; Sundgot-Borgen, J. Higher prevalence of eating disorders among adolescent elite athletes than controls. *Med. Sci. Sports Exerc.* **2013**, *45*, 1188–1197. [CrossRef] [PubMed]
11. Sundgot-Borgen, J.; Torstveit, M.K. Prevalence of eating disorders in elite athletes is higher than in the general population. *Clin. J. Sport Med.* **2004**, *14*, 25–32. [CrossRef]
12. Glazer, J.L. Eating disorders among male athletes. *Curr. Sports Med. Rep.* **2008**, *7*, 332–337. [CrossRef]
13. Goodwin, H.; Arcelus, J.; Geach, N.; Meyer, C. Perfectionism and eating psychopathology among dancers: The role of high standards and self-criticism. *Eur. Eat. Disord. Rev.* **2014**, *22*, 346–351. [CrossRef] [PubMed]
14. Abraham, S. Characteristics of eating disorders among young ballet dancers. *Psychopathology* **1996**, *29*, 223–229. [CrossRef] [PubMed]
15. Garner, D.M.; Bohr, Y.; Garfinkel, P.E. The eating attitudes test: Psychometric features and clinical correlates. *Psychol. Med.* **1982**, *12*, 871–878. [CrossRef] [PubMed]
16. Arcelus, J.; Witcomb, G.L.; Mitchell, A. Prevalence of eating disorders amongst dancers: A systemic review and meta-analysis. *Eur. Eat. Disord. Rev.* **2014**, *22*, 92–101. [CrossRef]
17. Sepúlveda, A.R.; Compte, E.J.; Faya, M.; Villaseñor, A.; Gutierrez, S.; Andrés, P.; Graell, M. Spanish validation of the Eating Disorder Examination Questionnaire for Adolescents (EDE-Q-A): Confirmatory factor analyses among a clinical sample. *Eat. Disord.* **2019**, *27*, 565–576. [CrossRef]
18. Rivas, T.; Bersabé, R.; Jimenez, M.; Berrocal, C. The eating attitudes test (EAT-26): Reliability and validity in Spanish female samples. *Span. J. Psychol.* **2010**, *13*, 1044–1056. [CrossRef]
19. Peláez-Fernández, M.A.; Ruiz-Lázaro, P.M.; Labrador, F.J.; Raich, R.M. Validation of the Eating Attitudes Test as a screening instrument for eating disorders in general population. *Med. Clin.* **2014**, *20*, 153–155. [CrossRef]
20. Neumark-Sztainer, D.; Wall, M.; Larson, N.I.; Eisenberg, M.E.; Loth, K. Dieting and disordered eating behaviors from adolescence to young adulthood: Findings from a 10-year longitudinal study. *J. Am. Diet. Assoc.* **2011**, *111*, 1004–1011. [CrossRef]
21. Hübel, C.; Yilmaz, Z.; Schaumberg, K.E.; Breithaupt, L.; Hunjan, A.; Horne, E.; García-González, J.; O'Reilly, P.F.; Bulik, C.M.; Breen, G. Body composition in anorexia nervosa: Meta-analysis and meta-regression of cross-sectional and longitudinal studies. *Int. J. Eat. Disord.* **2019**, *52*, 1205–1223. [CrossRef]
22. Robinson, L.; Micali, N.; Misra, M. Eating disorders and bone metabolism in women. *Curr. Opin. Pediatr.* **2017**, *29*, 488–492. [CrossRef]
23. Heath, B.H.; Carter, J.E.L. A modified somatotype method. *Am. J. Phys. Anthropol.* **1967**, *27*, 57–74. [CrossRef] [PubMed]
24. Liiv, H.; Wyon, M.A.; Jürimäe, T.; Saar, M.; Mäestu, J.; Jürimäe, J. Anthropometry, somatotypes, and aerobic power in ballet, contemporary dance, and DanceSport. *Med. Probl. Perform. Art.* **2013**, *28*, 207–211. [CrossRef] [PubMed]
25. Bartsch, A.J.; Brümmerhoff, A.; Greil, H.; Neumärker, K.J. Shall the anthropometry of physique cast new light on the diagnoses and treatment of eating disorders? *Eur. Child Adolesc. Psychiatry* **2003**, *12*, i54. [CrossRef] [PubMed]
26. Hoffmann, S.; Warschburger, P. Weight, shape, and muscularity concerns in male and female adolescents: Predictors of change and influences on eating concern. *Int. J. Eat. Disord.* **2017**, *50*, 139–147. [CrossRef]
27. De Irala, J.; Cano-Prous, A.; Lahortiga-Ramos, F.; Gual-García, P.; Martínez-González, M.A.; Cervera-Enguix, S. Validation of the Eating Attitudes Test (EAT) as a screening tool in the general population. *Med. Clin.* **2008**, *12*, 487–491. [CrossRef]
28. Castro, J.; Toro, J.; Salamero, M.; Guimerá, E. The eating attitudes test: Validation of the Spanish version. *Evaluación Psicológica* **1991**, *7*, 175–190.

29. Marfell-Jones, M.; Olds, L. *International Standards for Anthropometric Assessment*; International Society for the Advancement of Kinanthropometry: Potchefstroom, South Africa, 2006.
30. Hinkle, D.; Wiersma, W.; Jurs, S. *Applied Statistics for the Behavioural Sciences*, 5th ed.; Houghton Mifflin: Boston, MA, USA, 2003; ISBN 978-0618124053.
31. Faul, F.; Erdfelder, E.; Lang, A.G.; Buchner, A. G*Power 3: A flexible statistical power analysis program for the social, behavioral, and biomedical sciences. *Behav. Res. Methods* **2007**, *39*, 175–191. [CrossRef]
32. Zweig, M.H.; Campbell, G. Receiver-operating characteristic (ROC) plots: A fundamental evaluation tool in clinical medicine. *Clin. Chem.* **1993**, *39*, 561–577. [CrossRef]
33. Cunningham, M.L.; Szabo, M.; Kambanis, P.E.; Murray, S.B.; Thomas, J.J.; Eddy, K.T.; Franko, D.L.; Griffiths, S. Negative psychological correlates of the pursuit of muscularity among women. *Int. J. Eat. Disord.* **2019**, *52*, 1326–1331. [CrossRef]
34. Douglas, V.J.; Kwan, M.Y.; Minnich, A.M.; Gordon, K.H. The interaction of sociocultural attitudes and gender on disordered eating. *J. Clin. Psychol.* **2019**, *75*, 2140–2146. [CrossRef]
35. Ringham, R.; Klump, K.; Kaye, W.; Stone, D.; Libman, S.; Stowe, S.; Marcus, M. Eating disorder symptomatology among ballet dancers. *Int. J. Eat. Disord.* **2006**, *39*, 503–508. [CrossRef] [PubMed]
36. Byrne, S.; McLean, N. Eating disorders in athletes: A review of the literature. *J. Sci. Med. Sport* **2001**, *4*, 145–159. [CrossRef]
37. Costarelli, V.; Antonopoulou, K.; Mavrovounioti, C. Psychosocial characteristics in relation to disordered eating attitudes in Greek adolescents. *Eur. Eat. Disord. Rev.* **2011**, *19*, 322–330. [CrossRef] [PubMed]
38. Fortes, L.D.S.; Almeida, S.D.S.; Ferreira, M.E.C. Impacto de variáveis antropométricas sobre a insatisfação corporal e o comportamento alimentar em jovens atletas. *J. Bras. Psiquiatr.* **2012**, *61*, 235–241. [CrossRef]
39. Toro, J.; Guerrero, M.; Sentis, J.; Castro, J.; Puértolas, C. Eating disorders in Ballet dancing students: Problems and risk factors. *Eur. Eat. Disord. Rev.* **2009**, *17*, 40–49. [CrossRef] [PubMed]
40. Jones, C.L.; Fowle, J.L.; Ilyumzhinova, R.; Berona, J.; Mbayiwa, K.; Goldschmidt, A.B.; Bodell, L.P.; Stepp, S.D.; Hipwell, A.E.; Keenan, K.E. The relationship between body mass index, body dissatisfaction, and eating pathology in sexual minority women. *Int. J. Eat. Disord.* **2019**, *53*, 730–734. [CrossRef]
41. Dooley-Hash, S.; Banker, J.D.; Walton, M.A.; Ginsburg, Y.; Cunningham, R.M. The prevalence and correlates of eating disorders among emergency department patients aged 14–20 years. *Int. J. Eat. Disord.* **2012**, *45*, 883–890. [CrossRef]
42. Rodriguez, A.M.; Salar, N.V.; Carretero, C.M.; Gimeno, E.C.; Collado, E.R. Eating disorders and diet management in contact sports; EAT-26 questionnaire does not seem appropriate to evaluate eating disorders in sports. *Nutr. Hosp.* **2015**, *32*, 1708–1714.
43. Rouzitalab, T.; Gargari, B.P.; Amirsasan, R.; Jafarabadi, M.A.; Naeimi, A.F.; Sanoobar, M. The relationship of disordered eating attitudes with body composition and anthropometric indices in physical education students. *Iran. Red Crescent Med. J.* **2015**, *17*, e20727. [CrossRef] [PubMed]
44. Dotti, A.; Fioravanti, M.; Balotta, M.; Tozzi, F.; Cannella, C.; Lazzari, R. Eating behavior of ballet dancers. *Eat. Weight Disord.* **2002**, *71*, 60–67. [CrossRef]
45. Hayakawa, N.; Tanaka, S.; Hirata, N.; Ogino, S.; Ozaki, N. A battery of self-screening instruments and self-reported body frame could not detect eating disorders among college students. *BMC Res. Notes* **2019**, *12*, 613. [CrossRef] [PubMed]
46. Al-Kloub, M.I.; Al-Khawaldeh, O.A.; ALBashtawy, M.; Batiha, A.M.; Al-Haliq, M. Disordered eating in Jordanian adolescents. *Int. J. Nurs. Pract.* **2019**, *25*, e12694. [CrossRef] [PubMed]
47. Fortes, L.D.S.; Cipriani, F.M.; Ferreira, M.E.C. Risk behaviors for eating disorder: Factors associated in adolescent students. *Trends Psychiatry Psychother.* **2013**, *35*, 279–286. [CrossRef] [PubMed]

4

Health Professionals' and Health Professional Trainees' Views on Addictive Eating Behaviours

Tracy Burrows [1,2,*], Antonio Verdejo-Garcia [3], Adrian Carter [3], Robyn M. Brown [4], Zane B. Andrews [4,5], Chris V. Dayas [6,7], Charlotte A. Hardman [8], Natalie Loxton [9,10], Priya Sumithran [11,12] and Megan Whatnall [1,2]

1 Priority Research Centre for Physical Activity and Nutrition, University of Newcastle, Callaghan, NSW 2308, Australia; megan.whatnall@newcastle.edu.au
2 School of Health Sciences, Faculty of Health and Medicine, University of Newcastle, Callaghan, NSW 2308, Australia
3 Turner Institute for Brain and Mental Health, Monash University, Clayton, VIC 3800, Australia; antonio.verdejo@monash.edu (A.V.-G.); adrian.carter@monash.edu (A.C.)
4 Florey Institute of Neuroscience and Mental Health, University of Melbourne, Parkville, VIC 3052, Australia; robyn.brown@florey.edu.au (R.M.B.); zane.andrews@monash.edu (Z.B.A.)
5 Monash Biomedicine Discovery Institute and Department of Physiology, Monash University, Clayton, VIC 3800, Australia
6 School of Biomedical Sciences & Pharmacy, Faculty of Health and Medicine, University of Newcastle, Callaghan, NSW 2308, Australia; christopher.dayas@newcastle.edu.au
7 Hunter Medical Research Institute (HMRI), New Lambton Heights, NSW 2305, Australia
8 Department of Psychology, Institute of Population Health, University of Liverpool, Liverpool L69 7ZA, UK; cah@liverpool.ac.uk
9 School of Applied Psychology, Griffith University, Brisbane, QLD 4122, Australia; n.loxton@griffith.edu.au
10 Centre for Youth Substance Abuse Research, University of Queensland, Brisbane, QLD 4072, Australia
11 Department of Medicine (Austin), University of Melbourne, Heidelberg, VIC 3084, Australia; priyas@unimelb.edu.au
12 Department of Endocrinology, Austin Health, Heidelberg Heights, VIC 3081, Australia
* Correspondence: tracy.burrows@newcastle.edu.au

Abstract: Despite increasing research on the concept of addictive eating, there is currently no published evidence on the views of health professionals who potentially consult with patients presenting with addictive eating behaviours, or of students training to become health professionals. This study aimed to explore the views and understanding of addictive eating behaviours among health professionals and health professionals in training and to identify potential gaps in professional development training. An international online cross-sectional survey was conducted in February–April 2020. The survey (70 questions, 6 key areas) assessed participants' opinions and clinical experience of addictive eating; opinions on control, responsibility, and stigma relating to addictive eating; and knowledge of addictive eating and opinions on professional development training. In total, 142 health professionals and 33 health professionals in training completed the survey (mean age 38.1 ± 12.5 years, 65% from Australia/16% from the U.K.) Of the health professionals, 47% were dietitians and 16% were psychologists. Most participants (n = 126, 72%) reported that they have been asked by individuals about addictive eating. Half of the participants reported that they consider the term food addiction to be stigmatising for individuals (n = 88). Sixty percent (n = 105) reported that they were interested/very interested in receiving addictive eating training, with the top two preferred formats being online and self-paced, and face-to-face. These results demonstrate that addictive eating is supported by health professionals as they consult with patients presenting with this behaviour, which supports the views of the general community and demonstrates a need for health professional training.

Keywords: addictive eating; food addiction; health professional; clinician

1. Introduction

Addictive eating (i.e., an abnormal, recurrent pattern of excessive food consumption despite negative consequences) [1], often referred to as food addiction, is not currently recognised in the Diagnostic and Statistical Manual of Mental Disorders as a distinct diagnosis from other eating and substance use disorders. There exists an ongoing scientific debate in this regard, which centres around whether the symptoms of addictive eating are covered appropriately under other recognised disorders, such as binge eating disorder [2,3]. If addictive eating is a distinct disorder, the debate is also around whether it should be considered a substance (i.e., food) addiction or a behavioural (i.e., eating) addiction, or on a spectrum of overeating [2,3]. Further, there is the question of what the addictive substance/s are or whether it relates to the level of food processing [2,3]. Regardless of whether addictive eating should be recognised, 15–20% of the population report experiencing symptoms that align with addictive eating as determined by self-reported tools [4]. This is higher among certain groups, including females, those with binge eating disorder and other mental health conditions, and those with overweight and obesity [4]. Further, rates of self-perceived addictive eating among community samples range from 27% to 50% [5]. There is also widespread support from community samples that the concept of addictive eating exists [5,6]. For example, a survey of over 600 American and Australian adults reported that 86% believed certain foods may be addictive, and 72% believed addictive eating is linked with an increased risk of obesity [6].

Unhealthy lifestyle behaviours such as poorer dietary intake, physical inactivity, greater time spent sitting, and poor sleep quality are associated with addictive eating [7,8]. This association extends to conditions such as depression, anxiety, and overweight and obesity [9,10]. In terms of clinical management of addictive eating, the published evidence is scarce [11,12]. A recent systematic review conducted by Cassin et al. to assess psychosocial interventions for addictive eating identified only eight studies [12]. Of these, only two studies included individuals with addictive eating and interventions that specifically targeted addictive eating symptoms. The two interventions were abstinence-based (i.e., abstaining from overeating, snacking, and/or from identified problem foods), while the remaining studies included an outcome measure of addictive eating in intervention studies targeting either bulimia nervosa or overweight and obesity. Additionally, all of the included studies were deemed to exhibit poor or fair methodological quality, and most were pilot or feasibility studies. Importantly, the review was limited to psychosocial interventions and did not consider alternate options such as dietary advice alone. Overall, the review's authors concluded that no effective psychosocial interventions currently exist for the treatment of addictive eating. There is however a high volume of self-help support groups for individuals with addictive eating [13]. A recent review of websites identified 13 online support groups for addictive eating; however only three of these involved credentialed health professionals [13]. Evidently, research exploring the clinical utility of recognising addictive eating as a diagnostic entity and evidence-based best practices for treatment are limited.

There is currently no published evidence on the views of health professionals who likely consult with patients who report addictive eating behaviours, or of those training to become health professionals. Research should examine clinicians' and future clinicians' understanding of addictive eating, their support for it as a diagnostic category, and whether professional development training is needed regarding understanding and treating addictive eating. This work is critical to advancing the field of addictive eating in terms of treatment and informing best practice. The aims of this study were to explore the opinions and understanding of addictive eating behaviours among health professionals with experience in weight management and students undertaking relevant health professional training. The study also aimed to explore the needs and preferences for professional development training in addictive eating.

2. Materials and Methods

2.1. Study Design

An international online cross-sectional survey was conducted. An online survey was used as a convenient method of completion for participants and to maximise the survey reach and response rate. The survey was hosted via Qualtrics (https://www.qualtrics.com/au/) and was open from 21 February to 27 April 2020. The survey took approximately 25 min to complete and was initially pilot tested among a sample of five health professionals and university students to assess for readability and comprehension. The survey consisted of 70 questions including demographic questions and questions across six key areas (opinions and clinical experience of addictive eating; opinions on control, responsibility, and stigma relating to addictive eating; knowledge of addictive eating and opinions on professional development training; opinions on weight gain; treatment of disordered eating and overweight/obesity; and agreement with statements regarding addictive eating symptoms). This paper reports on the questions relating to opinions and clinical experience of addictive eating; opinions on control, responsibility, and stigma relating to addictive eating; and knowledge of addictive eating and opinions on professional development training. Questions relating to the other key areas were outside the scope of the current paper (see File S1 and Table S1). The survey questions used were developed by the research team for the purpose of this study. The survey was set up to require a response to each question before participants could progress to the next question, with the exception of the qualitative questions, which were optional to complete. Survey logic was used so that only relevant questions were displayed to each participant, based on their previous responses. The use of survey logic also limits participants from being able to go back and change previous responses. The study conduct and reporting comply with the Strengthening the Reporting of Observational Studies in Epidemiology (STROBE) guidelines for cross-sectional studies [14]. All participants gave informed consent prior to completing the survey. Participation was voluntary, and no incentives were offered for participation. Ethical approval for the study was obtained from the University of Newcastle Human Research Ethics Committee (H-2019-0349).

2.2. Participants and Recruitment

Individuals were eligible to participate if they were a health professional with experience in the management or research of overweight or obesity or disordered eating, or were a student currently enrolled in health professional training at a university. Relevant disciplines included allied health professionals; medical professionals; psychologists; other health professionals; public health, nutrition, or other health researchers; or university students training in one of these professions. University students of relevant disciplines were also included as they represent the next generation of health professionals. Individuals from any country were eligible to participate; however, the survey was written in English. Health professionals and university students completed the same survey; however, some of the survey questions were worded differently by asking health professionals about their practical experience and university students about their opinions. Additionally, the questions regarding experience in treating clients were only asked of health professionals. Recruitment was via convenience sampling and used a range of strategies. Email invitations were sent from the members of the research team to their networks of health professionals and students and contained a link to the online survey. The survey was also advertised via posts from the research team on Twitter, a brief advertisement in the member e-newsletter of Dietitians Australia (professional body for Dietitians in Australia), and an advertisement to students was posted via the online learning management system at the University of Newcastle, Australia. All advertisements used the same recruitment materials and information, which described the survey as a "cross-sectional survey to identify the current understanding of addictive eating behaviours and whether a need exists for professional development training."

2.3. Measures

2.3.1. Demographic Characteristics

Demographic data collected included age, gender, country of residence, and highest qualification completed. Health professionals were also asked their occupation, primary work setting (e.g., hospital, private practice, research), the population group/life stage they primarily work with (e.g., adolescents, adults), and whether they provide advice to individuals with disordered eating or overweight/obesity. University students were also asked the degree for which they were currently studying.

2.3.2. Opinions and Clinical Experience of Addictive Eating

The survey included 14 questions about opinions and clinical experiences regarding addictive eating. Participants were asked whether they had encountered patients/individuals asking or speaking about addictive eating, their thoughts around whether people can develop compulsive eating patterns that resemble an addictive disorder, and whether addictive eating exists (yes, no, or maybe). Of those who indicated that addictive eating does or may exist, participants were asked whether they think different populations may be more vulnerable. Of those who indicated that they provide advice to individuals with disordered eating or overweight/obesity, participants were asked what proportion of their clients may benefit from a specific treatment of addictive eating, if available. Participants were also asked to rate their level of interest in addictive eating becoming a diagnostic term and a referral pathway being introduced for the treatment/management of addictive eating (1/very interested to 5/not at all interested). In terms of treatment for addictive eating, participants were asked their opinion on which health professionals would be best placed to identify and treat people with addictive eating, and which services they would be more/less likely to refer individuals to, as well as whether any particular sub-groups of overweight and obese people would benefit more from a diagnosis of addictive eating. Two open-ended questions were also asked of those who indicated that addictive eating does or may exist, including what they thought were the strengths and weaknesses of using the addictive eating concept to explain eating and weight to individuals.

2.3.3. Opinions on Control, Responsibility, and Stigma Relating to Addictive Eating

Three questions were included relating to opinions on control and responsibility for eating and weight. Participants were asked to rate how much they think it is the responsibility of the individual with addictive eating to gain control over their eating and weight status (1/not responsible to 5/100% responsible) and how much control they think individuals have over their eating and weight (1/a great deal to 5/none at all). Three questions were included relating to their opinions around the different terminology used for addictive eating and stigma. Participants were asked how well they think the term food addiction relates to the experiences of people with weight issues, whether they think the term food addiction is stigmatising, and to indicate which term (if any) they think is most appropriate to describe food addiction/addictive eating.

2.3.4. Knowledge of Addictive Eating and Opinions on Professional Development Training

Three questions asked about participants' knowledge of addictive eating. Participants were asked what sources of information informed their understanding of addictive eating and to rate their current knowledge of addictive eating and their level of confidence in their knowledge. Six questions asked about participants' professional development training needs and preferences. Participants were asked about what kinds of professional development training on addictive eating assessment and treatment would be needed, who should receive this training, and their preferred method of training delivery. They were also asked to rate their level of interest in receiving addictive eating training delivered online, whether this would be of interest to colleagues/peers, and whether individuals/clients would be interested in training/management/treatment delivered online.

2.4. Analysis

Data were analysed using Stata statistical software version 14.2. In total, 274 individuals accessed the online survey, of these, 175 consented and completed all survey questions (i.e., 64% of those who accessed the survey). Of those that did not complete the survey (n = 99), 14 opened the link/viewed the first page but did not start the survey, one did not provide consent and exited the survey, 15 filled in some of the demographics questions only, and the remaining 69 completed the demographics questions and some but not all of the rest of the survey. Quantitative data are reported as number and percentage for categorical variables and mean and standard deviation for continuous variables. Open-response questions are described qualitatively. Qualitative data were analysed using a theoretical thematic analysis approach [15], including (1) identifying codes from the responses based on keywords/phrases, (2) grouping codes into themes, (3) reviewing themes in relation to the contributing codes, and (4) defining and naming themes. One researcher initially conducted the thematic analysis, and this was checked by a second researcher, with any discrepancies discussed and results amended. Themes are presented in the order of most to least frequent/recurrent. Results for health professional and health professional trainee participants were compared using chi-square tests for questions with mutually exclusive response options, to determine whether these were significantly different. There were differences between responses for nine of the questions; however, with further investigation these differences were driven by the large number of response options. As the pattern of the most common responses were similar between the two groups, and due to the small sample size of the health professionals in training, it was deemed appropriate to combine the responses for reporting (see Table S2 for responses by group).

3. Results

3.1. Sample Characteristics

Of the 175 participants, 81% (n = 142) were health professionals, and 19% (n = 33) were university students (Table 1). The mean ± SD age of participants was 38.1 + 12.5 years, the majority were female (n = 150, 86%), and participants were from six different countries with most residing in Australia (n = 113, 65%) or the U.K. (n = 28, 16%). Among the health professional participants, the most common occupations were dietitian (n = 66, 47%) and psychologist (n = 23, 16%), with the highest proportion working in hospitals (n = 39, 28%) and private practice (n = 39, 28%), and working with population groups of adults 25–65 years (n = 109, 77%) and young adults 18–24 years (n = 52, 37%). Sixty-three percent of health professional participants (n = 90) reported that they provide advice to clients for disordered eating, while 70% (n = 100) provide advice to clients for overweight/obesity.

Table 1. Demographic characteristics of health professionals participating in a survey on addictive eating (n = 175).

Demographic Characteristic	n	%
Age (years) Mean ± SD	38.1 ± 12.5	
Gender		
Female	150	85.7
Male	22	12.6
Other	3	1.7
Country of residence		
Australia	113	64.6
U.K.	28	16.0
USA	23	13.1
Other	11	6.3

Table 1. *Cont.*

Demographic Characteristic	*n*	%
Highest qualification completed		
School certificate/Higher school certificate	21	12.0
Trade or diploma	2	1.1
Undergraduate university degree	50	28.6
Postgraduate university degree	71	40.6
Higher research degree	31	17.7
Occupation		
Dietitian	66	37.7
Tertiary health or medical student [a]	33	18.9
Psychologist	23	13.1
Other health practitioner	18	10.3
Health researcher	12	6.9
Tertiary academic/teacher	6	3.4
Medical specialist/registrar	4	1.7
General practitioner	3	1.7
Counsellor	3	1.7
Pharmacist	3	1.7
Psychotherapist	2	1.1
Social worker	2	1.1
Primary work situation [b]		
Hospital	39	27.5
Private practice	39	27.5
Research and teaching	29	20.4
Community/population/public health program	19	13.4
Primary care	7	4.9
Food service	1	0.7
Other	8	5.6
Population group worked with [b,c]		
Infants < 2 years	13	9.2
Children 2–12 years	20	14.1
Adolescents 13–17 years	39	23.2
Young adults 18–24 years	52	36.6
Adults 25–65 years	109	76.8
Adults > 65 years	41	28.9
Not applicable	4	2.8

[a] Of the tertiary health and medical students, $n = 29$ (88%) were studying a degree in Nutrition and Dietetics. [b] Responses are for health professionals only ($n = 142$). [c] Multiple response question i.e., percentages add to >100.

3.2. Description of Quantitative Results

3.2.1. Opinions and Clinical Experience of Addictive Eating

The majority of participants ($n = 126$, 72%) reported that they have been asked by individuals about addictive eating (Table 2). Sixty percent of participants ($n = 105$) indicated that they think addictive eating exists. The proportion of the sample who reported being interested/very interested in addictive eating being a diagnostic term was 48% ($n = 83$).

Table 2. Opinions and clinical experience of addictive eating among health professionals participating in a survey on addictive eating (n = 175).

Survey Item	n	%
Have you experienced individuals asking or speaking about addictive eating?		
Yes	126	72.0
Maybe	14	8.0
No	35	20.0
In your opinion, do you feel that people can develop compulsive patterns of eating that resemble an addictive disorder?		
Yes	120	68.6
Maybe	33	18.9
No	22	12.6
In your opinion, does addictive eating exist?		
Yes	105	60.0
Maybe	33	18.9
No	37	21.1
In your opinion, do you feel that there are population groups who may be more vulnerable to addictive eating? [a]		
Yes	75	54.3
Unsure	18	13.0
No	45	32.6
Estimated percentage of clients to benefit from a specific treatment of addictive eating (Mean SD) [b]	40.9 ± 27.9	
How interested would you be in addictive eating being a diagnostic term?		
Very interested	43	24.6
Interested	40	22.9
Somewhat interested	29	16.6
Not very interested	23	13.1
Not at all interested	40	22.9
How interested would you be if there was a referral pathway for the treatment/management of addictive eating?		
Very interested	72	41.1
Interested	41	23.4
Somewhat interested	20	11.4
Not very interested	6	3.4
Not at all interested	36	20.6
Who do you think would be best placed to identify people with behaviours suggestive of addictive eating? [c]		
Dietitians/nutritionists	99	56.6
Psychologists	93	53.1
Psychiatrists	51	29.1
Counsellor	49	28.0
General practitioner	48	27.4
Medical specialists	30	17.1
All of the above	75	42.9
Other	30	17.1
Who do you think is best placed to provide treatment for people with addictive eating? [c]		
Psychologists	114	65.1
Dietitians/nutritionists	107	61.1
Psychiatrists	52	29.7
Counsellor	49	28.0
General practitioner	16	9.1
Medical specialists	17	9.7
All of the above	34	19.4
Other	29	16.6
Are there any services you would be more likely to refer to or suggest to clients/individuals with addictive eating? [c]		
Psychologist	124	70.9
Counselling	77	44.0
Addiction specialist	75	42.9
General practitioner	19	10.9
Pharmacological	8	4.6
All of the above	96	54.9
Other	14	8.0
None	34	19.4

Table 2. *Cont.*

Survey Item	n	%
Are there any services you would be less likely to refer to or suggest to clients/individuals with addictive eating? [c]		
Pharmacological	86	49.1
General practitioner	76	43.4
Addiction specialist	33	18.9
Counselling	6	3.4
Psychologist	2	1.1
All of the above	7	4.0
Other	3	1.7
None	46	26.3
Are there any particular sub-groups of overweight and obese people you feel would benefit more from a diagnosis of addictive eating? [c]		
Individuals with binge eating disorder	80	45.7
Overeaters	79	45.1
Individuals with a mental health condition	60	34.3
Individuals with other mental illnesses	44	25.1
Individuals with substance disorders	36	20.6
Individuals with low motivation to engage with treatment	30	17.1
Children	14	8.0
Other	17	9.7
No	58	33.1

[a] n = 138 responses (i.e., those that believe addictive eating exists). [b] n = 80 responses from health professionals (i.e., those that believe addictive eating exists and provide treatment for overweight/obesity and/or disordered eating). [c] Multiple response questions, i.e., percentages add to >100.

3.2.2. Opinions on Control, Responsibility, and Stigma Relating to Addictive Eating

The largest proportion of participants reported that they think individuals with addictive eating have "a little" control over their eating habits (n = 89, 51%) and weight (n = 77, 44%) (Table 3). However, the majority reported that individuals with addictive eating are very/moderately responsible for gaining control over their eating and weight (n = 118, 67%). Half of the participants reported that they think food addiction is a stigmatising term for individuals (n = 88). Participants' preferences regarding the terminology used to describe addictive eating/food addiction were varied. From the proposed list of terms, the largest proportion of participants selected compulsive overeating (n = 41, 23%), followed by addictive eating (n = 34, 19%), and other (n = 29, 17%). Of those that selected other, some indicated that eating disorder terminology should be used, some indicated that more than one term is needed as the most appropriate term may differ for different clients/individuals, while other suggested terms included disordered eating, eating addiction, highly processed food addiction, refined food addiction, and restriction–rebound overeating.

Table 3. Opinions on control, responsibility, and stigma relating to addictive eating among health professionals participating in a survey on addictive eating (n = 175).

Survey Item	n	%
In your opinion, how much control does someone with addictive eating have over their eating habits?		
A great deal	5	2.9
A lot	9	5.1
A moderate amount	60	34.3
A little	89	50.9
None at all	12	6.9
In your opinion, how much control does someone with addictive eating have over their weight?		
A great deal	2	1.1
A lot	2	1.1
A moderate amount	44	25.1
A little	77	44.0
None at all	50	28.6

Table 3. *Cont.*

Survey Item	*n*	%
In your opinion, how much responsibility does someone with addictive eating have to gain control over their eating and weight?		
100% responsible	12	6.9
Very responsible	51	29.1
Moderately responsible	67	38.3
Not very responsible	20	11.4
Not responsible	25	14.3
Do you think that the term "food addiction" is stigmatising for individuals?		
Yes	88	50.3
Unsure	52	29.7
No	35	20.0
How well do you think the term food addiction relates to the experiences of people with weight issues?		
Extremely/very well	59	33.7
Neutral	35	20.0
Not well	81	46.3
Select which term you feel is most appropriate to describe food addiction/addictive eating?		
Compulsive overeating	41	23.4
Addictive eating	34	19.4
Compulsive overeating disorder	27	15.4
Food addiction	23	13.1
None, no term needed	21	12.0
Other	29	16.6

3.2.3. Knowledge of Addictive Eating and Opinions on Professional Development Training

The majority of participants rated their knowledge of addictive eating as average or poor (n = 106, 61%) (Table 4). The most common source of information that participants used to inform their understanding of addictive eating was colleagues (n = 123, 70%), followed by the scientific literature (n = 116, 66%). Sixty percent of participants (n = 105) reported that they were interested/very interested in receiving training on addictive eating delivered via technologies such as the internet and/or smartphones. When participants were asked who should be trained in addictive eating, the most common responses were dietitians (n = 87, 50%) and psychologists (n = 82, 47%). In terms of the types of professional development training that is needed, most commonly, participants indicated training in evidence-based treatment (n = 142, 81%), followed by understanding medical and non-medical treatments (n = 134, 77%) and assessment and diagnosis (n = 134, 77%).

Table 4. Knowledge of addictive eating and opinions on professional development training among health professionals participating in a survey on addictive eating (n = 175).

Survey Item	*n*	%
How confident do you feel in your knowledge on the latest evidence relating to addictive eating (i.e., assessment methodologies/treatment)?		
Extremely confident	26	14.9
Very confident	26	14.9
Neutral	41	23.4
Somewhat confident	34	19.4
Not at all confident	48	27.4
How would you rate your current knowledge about addictive eating?		
Excellent	30	17.1
Good	36	20.6
Average	57	32.6
Poor	49	28.0
Terrible	3	1.7

Table 4. *Cont.*

Survey Item	*n*	%
What sources of information have informed your understanding of addictive eating? [a]		
Colleagues	123	70.3
Scientific literature	116	66.3
Education	102	58.3
Conferences	68	38.9
Social media	36	20.6
Other reading	27	15.4
Traditional media	21	12.0
Have not heard of addictive eating	7	4.0
If training for addictive eating were available, how interested would you be in participating in training delivered using technologies such as the internet and/or smartphones?		
Very interested	75	42.9
Interested	30	17.1
Somewhat interested	24	13.7
Not very interested	10	5.7
Not at all interested	36	20.6
In your opinion, who should be trained in addictive eating assessment and treatment? [a]		
Dietitians	87	49.7
Psychologists	82	46.9
Psychiatrists	55	31.4
General practitioners	52	29.7
Undergraduate students	38	21.7
Medical specialists	33	18.9
Practice nurses	25	14.3
All of the above	73	41.7
Other	38	21.7
If food addiction/addictive eating became a diagnostic term, what kinds of professional development training do you think would be needed (for yourself/other professions)? [a]		
Evidence-based treatment	142	81.1
Understanding treatment (medical and non-medical)	134	76.6
Assessment/diagnosis	134	76.6
Treatment approaches focusing on other behaviours as well as food, e.g., sleep, physical activity	129	73.7
Understanding addiction terminology	123	70.3
Neuroscience behind addictive eating	119	68.0
How to minimise stigma	114	65.1
Foods to avoid	59	33.7
Other	36	20.6
What would be your preferred method of delivery for professional development training? [b]		
Face to face	81	46.3
Online, self-paced	77	44.0
Professional development	65	37.1
Structured short course	63	36.0
Delivered by a credential source	51	29.1
Other	13	7.4
Do you think online training/management/treatment delivered by health professionals would be of interest to clients/individuals?		
Yes/Maybe	157	89.7
No	18	10.3
Do you think online training would be of interest to your co-workers/colleagues/peers?		
Yes/Maybe	154	88.0
No	21	12.0

[a] Multiple response questions i.e., percentages add to >100. [b] Reported as the *n*(%) who ranked responses as 1 or 2.

3.2.4. Description of Qualitative Results

Thematic analysis results are presented in Table 5. Sixty-three percent ($n = 111$) of the participants responded to the question "What are some strengths/benefits to using the addictive eating approach to explain eating and weight to clients/individuals?" Five themes were identified, including from most to least frequent: (1) provides an explanation/assists understanding; (2) relieves guilt/stigma; (3) provides acknowledgement/validation; (4) provides a framework/pathway for future treatment;

and (5) encourages hope for overcoming addictive eating. Fifty-nine percent (n = 103) of participants responded to the question "What are some of the downsides/weaknesses to using the addictive eating approach to explain eating and weight to clients/individuals?" Six themes were identified, including from most to least frequent: (1) reason/barrier not to change; (2) negative response from clients/individuals; (3) stigma; (4) lack of evidence/recognition; (5) implications for treatment; and (6) clinician training/time.

Table 5. Qualitative findings among health professionals participating in a survey on addictive eating (n = 175).

Question: What are some strengths/benefits to using the addictive eating approach to explain eating and weight to clients/individuals?	
Themes and quotes	(1) Provides an explanation/assists understanding "Help clients realise the link between behaviours, thoughts, and food ... " "Help people understand the role of psychology in food choice"
	(2) Relieves guilt/stigma "May help to reduce stigma and some of the extreme negative thoughts people have in relation to their eating." "Clients may feel less guilty about weight/weight gain."
	(3) Provides acknowledgement/validation "Legitimises their problem" "'Giving it a name' may help people externalise and tackle the issue better."
	(4) Provides a framework/pathway for future treatment "Current knowledge about addiction medicine would provide potential avenues for treatment."
	(5) Encourages hope for overcoming addictive eating "When they [clients] feel understanding and empowered it is easier to facilitate health promoting changes and more effective strategies."
Question: What are some of the downsides/weaknesses to using the addictive eating approach to explain eating and weight to clients/individuals?	
Themes and quotes	(1) Reason/barrier not to change "Some people may like another label as a reason not to try to change." "Dissolves some responsibility for lifestyle decisions that are outside of addictive behaviours."
	(2) Negative response from clients/individuals "[It] may induce a sense of helplessness." "Some people may get offended when using the word addictive, may bring up deep rooted emotional issues associated with why they overeat."
	(3) Stigma "It can become a stigmatised label of being an 'addict', which may impact on their recovery journey."
	(4) Lack of evidence/recognition "I do not see this [food addiction] at the moment as true addiction." "The fact that scientific literature and other health care professionals don't support this."
	(5) Implications for treatment "The abstinence model may have the potential to increase binge eating if it is too restrictive regarding food rules." "Limited psychological support to help manage the condition"
	(6) Clinician training/time "Clinicians need to be trained to identify and safely address addictive eating ... Identifying the eating behaviour without appropriate treatment may be detrimental."

Questions were only asked of those participants who responded yes or maybe to the question, "do you believe addictive eating exists?"

4. Discussion

This study aimed to explore the opinions and understanding of addictive eating in an international sample of practising health professionals and health professionals in training. The needs and preferences for professional development training in addictive eating were also explored. The majority of the survey sample reported that they support that addictive eating exists, have experienced individuals/patients asking about addictive eating, and expressed interest in receiving training about addictive eating. Overall, the study findings provide important insight into the perspective of currently practicing health professionals and health professionals in training (i.e., future health professionals) on addictive eating.

This adds to and provides a point of comparison for the larger evidence base of opinions among the general population.

Sixty percent of the health professionals and health professionals in training surveyed supported that addictive eating exists, while a higher proportion (69%) expressed the view that people can develop compulsive patterns of eating resembling an addictive disorder. These results are substantially lower than in community samples such as the survey by Lee et al. where 86% of adults believed that certain foods may be addictive [6]. Results show that over 70% of health professionals reported that individuals had enquired about addictive eating. Moreover, participants expressed interest in addictive eating being officially recognised as a formal diagnosis and in the use of a specific referral pathway. However, self-rating of knowledge of addictive eating was rated below average in the majority of participants and confidence in knowledge of the evidence base was low. Thus, it is potentially not surprising that our data revealed a definite interest for training and education in this specific topic. Two-thirds of health professionals were interested or very interested in receiving addictive eating training, with almost half reporting that they would prefer training to be online and self-paced and almost half preferring face-to-face training. The most common types of professional development training that were reportedly needed included training in evidence-based treatment, understanding medical and non-medical treatments, and training in assessment and diagnosis. Participants identified dietitians and psychologists as the two major professions who should receive training, followed by psychiatrists and general practitioners, while the majority reported that training in addictive eating would also be useful for individuals or clients. This is not surprising given the pertinent roles that these health professionals have in other recognised forms of disordered eating. These findings indicate that this is a significant issue faced by clients and health professionals.

Overall, there was a mixed response in terms of the preferred terminology to be used to describe this compulsive form of eating. Compulsive overeating was the most preferred term, indicated by 23% of participants, followed by addictive eating (19%). However, a large proportion of participants indicated other responses including that more than one term may be needed as the most appropriate term may differ between clients/individuals. This difference may suggest that a multidimensional or domain-based approach is needed rather than a categorical diagnosis. This also shows that reaching a consensus on a common term may not be achievable. Despite there being a lack of consensus in existing research over the preferred terminology [16,17], the term "food addiction" was the least preferred. This illustrates the recognition amongst those surveyed of the highly stigmatising nature of this descriptor. Indeed, the majority of participants expressed a belief that the term food addiction is stigmatising, which supports consumer research [18]. Many existing research reports discuss the terminology, and it may be time to move beyond the terminology to focus on greater understanding and possible management options, given that many health professionals in the current study have patients seeking help for this behaviour. The qualitative findings from the current study also provide further insight into the discussion of stigma, as this was a recurrent theme when health professionals were asked to explain the benefits and downsides of using the addictive eating approach to explain eating and weight to individuals. Views were divided, in that, some health professionals commented that it may reduce stigma, while others explained that it may introduce the stigma that is associated with addictions and other mental health conditions in general. This may be linked with the number of views expressed about the terminology. Further exploration of the views of health professionals regarding addictive eating and stigma is warranted [19].

The survey identified mixed opinions regarding the relationship between addictive eating behaviours and weight. Over two-thirds of the participants reported that individuals with addictive eating have little to no control over their eating habits and weight. This highlights acceptance of the lack of control experienced by those with addictive eating; yet, approximately half of the participants reported that addictive eating does not relate well to the experiences of people with weight issues. These findings could relate to the fact that individuals may not have been directed to the appropriate services for the management of their addictive eating, i.e., the lack of control relates to numerous unsuccessful attempts at treatment/management by the individual with addictive eating. Comparatively, the study by Lee et al. found that among the community sample of >600 adults, almost three-quarters supported that addictive eating causes obesity, while views were divided close to 50:50 in terms of individuals having control over their weight and eating [6]. These are important findings, as the way that health professionals view these factors would have implications for the treatment that they may provide or refer individuals on to. Further, if these views differ from those of the general population and/or their patients, this may also influence the efficacy of treatment. There has been increasing research of the overlap of disordered eating and obesity [20]. Given that addictive eating often overlaps with binge eating and presents with obesity, this offers an interesting opportunity for further exploration.

The major strength of this study is that it is the first to explore opinions on addictive eating in a sample of health professionals and health professionals in training. Further, a moderate sample size was obtained, which is a strength given the challenges of engaging health professionals in research (e.g., due to busy workloads). The sample was an international sample with health professionals from a range of backgrounds, which is a strength for this exploratory study as it provides a broad range of perspectives; however, the fact that different countries have different professional standards and structures is also a potential limitation. In terms of limitations, health professionals who have an interest in or have been asked about addictive eating may have been motivated to participate in the current study, while a large proportion were dietitians or psychologists. Therefore, the representativeness of the sample is a limitation, and the views presented may not represent the generalised community of health professionals and students. Further, females were over-represented in the study population. However, this can be explained by the higher percentage of women among the health professions surveyed [21] and by the fact that females are more likely to participate in online survey studies than males [22]. The use of convenience sampling is also a limitation in terms of the representativeness of the sample, for example, this likely contributed to the high percentage of dietitians and participants residing in Australia. The survey included a large number and scope of questions as it is the first to explore this topic among health professionals and the intention was to obtain a broad overview of opinions. However, this may have contributed to some participants not completing the survey. Additionally, the survey is based on self-report and, while some qualitative data were collected, the survey included primarily quantitative questions, which may limit the scope of opinions. Many of the participants surveyed also rated their knowledge of addictive eating as below average and their confidence in their knowledge of the latest evidence as low, which could be a limitation to their views on the topic.

The implications of the study findings for research and practice include that practitioners are being asked about addictive eating and there is a need for practitioners to understand addictive eating and the related comorbidities with weight and other mental health conditions such as depression. This would ensure that individuals are provided or directed to the most appropriate service rather than just standard dietary, weight management or psychology advice. One avenue for this could be achieved through professional development training. The focus of professional development training will need to consider the needs of different health professions based on their role in the referral or treatment pathway, for example, focusing on awareness of addictive eating and appropriate services to refer individuals to, compared with evidence-based treatment approaches for those delivering/managing treatment. Despite the lack of consistent terminology, addictive eating may be a means of people seeking help for a mental illness evidenced through having an unhealthy relationship with food. Therefore, there is a need for greater understanding of addictive eating behaviour and possible management options regardless of the terminology that is used to describe it. Future studies should aim to include a varied representation of health professions who may have a role in the care of individuals presenting with addictive eating. For example, GPs who may be the first point of contact for individuals and psychologists, dietitians, or other health professionals who may provide ongoing treatment. As addictive eating is an emerging field of research, health professionals' views on the topic may change over time, and research into this should be updated accordingly.

5. Conclusions

Overall, this survey of an international sample of practising health professionals and health professionals in training identified support for the concept of addictive eating and interest in professional development training. Additional exploration of health professionals' views on addictive eating is warranted, as this information is critical to advancing the field of addictive eating and informing best practice for assessment and treatment.

Author Contributions: Conceptualisation, T.B., A.V.-G., A.C., R.M.B., Z.B.A., C.V.D., C.A.H., N.L., and P.S.; methodology, T.B., A.V.-G., A.C., R.M.B., Z.B.A., C.V.D., C.A.H., N.L., P.S., and M.W.; data curation, M.W. and T.B.; formal analysis, M.W. and T.B.; writing—original draft preparation, M.W. and T.B.; writing—review and editing, T.B., A.V.-G., A.C., R.M.B., Z.B.A., C.V.D., C.A.H., N.L., P.S., and M.W. All authors have read and agreed to the published version of the manuscript.

References

1. Gearhardt, A.N.; Corbin, W.R.; Brownell, K.D. Food Addiction: An Examination of the Diagnostic Criteria for Dependence. *J. Addict. Med.* **2009**, *3*, 1–7. [CrossRef]
2. Davis, C. From passive overeating to "food addiction": A spectrum of compulsion and severity. *ISRN Obes.* **2013**, *2013*, 435027. [CrossRef]
3. Fletcher, P.C.; Kenny, P.J. Food addiction: A valid concept? *Neuropsychopharmacology* **2018**, *43*, 2506–2513. [CrossRef] [PubMed]
4. Pursey, K.M.; Stanwell, P.; Gearhardt, A.N.; Collins, C.E.; Burrows, T.L. The prevalence of food addiction as assessed by the Yale Food Addiction Scale: A systematic review. *Nutrients* **2014**, *6*, 4552–4590. [CrossRef] [PubMed]
5. Ruddock, H.K.; Hardman, C.A. Food Addiction Beliefs Amongst the Lay Public: What Are the Consequences for Eating Behaviour? *Curr. Addict. Rep.* **2017**, *4*, 110–115. [CrossRef] [PubMed]
6. Lee, N.M.; Lucke, J.; Hall, W.D.; Meurk, C.; Boyle, F.M.; Carter, A. Public Views on Food Addiction and Obesity: Implications for Policy and Treatment. *PLoS ONE* **2013**, *8*, e74836. [CrossRef]
7. Li, J.T.E.; Pursey, K.M.; Duncan, M.J.; Burrows, T. Addictive Eating and Its Relation to Physical Activity and Sleep Behavior. *Nutrients* **2018**, *10*, 1428. [CrossRef]
8. Pursey, K.M.; Collins, C.E.; Stanwell, P.; Burrows, T.L. Foods and dietary profiles associated with 'food addiction' in young adults. *Addict. Behav. Rep.* **2015**, *2*, 41–48. [CrossRef]
9. Pedram, P.; Wadden, D.; Amini, P.; Gulliver, W.; Randell, E.; Cahill, F.; Vasdev, S.; Goodridge, A.; Carter, J.C.; Zhai, G.; et al. Food Addiction: Its Prevalence and Significant Association with Obesity in the General Population. *PLoS ONE* **2013**, *8*, e74832. [CrossRef]
10. Burrows, T.; Skinner, J.; McKenna, R.; Rollo, M. Food Addiction, Binge Eating Disorder, and Obesity: Is There a Relationship? *Behav. Sci.* **2017**, *7*, 54. [CrossRef]
11. Wiss, D.A.; Brewerton, T.D. Incorporating food addiction into disordered eating: The disordered eating food addiction nutrition guide (DEFANG). *Eat. Weight Disord. EWD* **2017**, *22*, 49–59. [CrossRef] [PubMed]
12. Cassin, S.E.; Sijercic, I.; Montemarano, V. Psychosocial Interventions for Food Addiction: A Systematic Review. *Curr. Addict. Rep.* **2020**. [CrossRef]
13. McKenna, R.A.; Rollo, M.E.; Skinner, J.A.; Burrows, T.L. Food Addiction Support: Website Content Analysis. *JMIR Cardio* **2018**, *2*, e10. [CrossRef] [PubMed]
14. Vandenbroucke, J.P.; von Elm, E.; Altman, D.G.; Gotzsche, P.C.; Mulrow, C.D.; Pocock, S.J.; Poole, C.; Schlesselman, J.J.; Egger, M. Strengthening the Reporting of Observational Studies in Epidemiology (STROBE): Explanation and elaboration. *Epidemiology* **2007**, *18*, 805–835. [CrossRef]
15. Braun, V.; Clarke, V. Using thematic analysis in psychology. *Qual. Res. Psychol.* **2006**, *3*, 77–101. [CrossRef]
16. Hebebrand, J.; Albayrak, Ö.; Adan, R.; Antel, J.; Diéguez, C.; De Jong, J.; Leng, G.; Menzies, J.; Mercer, J.G.; Murphy, M.; et al. "Eating addiction", rather than "food addiction", better captures addictive-like eating behavior. *Neurosci. Biobehav. Rev.* **2014**, *47*, 295–306. [CrossRef]
17. Ruddock, H.K.; Christiansen, P.; Halford, J.C.G.; Hardman, C.A. The development and validation of the Addiction-like Eating Behaviour Scale. *Int. J. Obes.* **2017**, *41*, 1710–1717. [CrossRef]
18. DePierre, J.A.; Puhl, R.M.; Luedicke, J. Public perceptions of food addiction: A comparison with alcohol and tobacco. *J. Subst. Use* **2014**, *19*, 1–6. [CrossRef]

19. Cassin, S.E.; Buchman, D.Z.; Leung, S.E.; Kantarovich, K.; Hawa, A.; Carter, A.; Sockalingam, S. Ethical, Stigma, and Policy Implications of Food Addiction: A Scoping Review. *Nutrients* **2019**, *11*, 710. [CrossRef]
20. da Luz, F.Q.; Hay, P.; Touyz, S.; Sainsbury, A. Obesity with Comorbid Eating Disorders: Associated Health Risks and Treatment Approaches. *Nutrients* **2018**, *10*, 829. [CrossRef]
21. Australian Institute of Health & Welfare. Health Workforce Snapshot. Available online: https://www.aihw.gov.au/reports/australias-health/health-workforce (accessed on 25 August 2020).
22. Cull, W.L.; O'Connor, K.G.; Sharp, S.; Tang, S.-F.S. Response rates and response bias for 50 surveys of pediatricians. *Health Serv. Res.* **2005**, *40*, 213–226. [CrossRef] [PubMed]

5

Separating the Signal from the Noise: How Psychiatric Diagnoses Can Help Discern Food Addiction from Dietary Restraint

David Wiss [1,*] and Timothy Brewerton [2]

[1] Department of Community Health Sciences, Fielding School of Public Health, University of California Los Angeles, Los Angeles, CA 90025, USA

[2] Department of Psychiatry and Behavioral Sciences, Medical University of South Carolina, Charleston, SC 29425, USA; drtimothybrewerton@gmail.com

* Correspondence: dwiss@ucla.edu

Abstract: Converging evidence from both animal and human studies have implicated hedonic eating as a driver of both binge eating and obesity. The construct of food addiction has been used to capture pathological eating across clinical and non-clinical populations. There is an ongoing debate regarding the value of a food addiction "diagnosis" among those with eating disorders such as anorexia nervosa binge/purge-type, bulimia nervosa, and binge eating disorder. Much of the food addiction research in eating disorder populations has failed to account for dietary restraint, which can increase addiction-like eating behaviors and may even lead to false positives. Some have argued that the concept of food addiction does more harm than good by encouraging restrictive approaches to eating. Others have shown that a better understanding of the food addiction model can reduce stigma associated with obesity. What is lacking in the literature is a description of a more comprehensive approach to the assessment of food addiction. This should include consideration of dietary restraint, and the presence of symptoms of other psychiatric disorders (substance use, posttraumatic stress, depressive, anxiety, attention deficit hyperactivity) to guide treatments including nutrition interventions. The purpose of this review is to help clinicians identify the symptoms of food addiction (true positives, or "the signal") from the more classic eating pathology (true negatives, or "restraint") that can potentially elevate food addiction scores (false positives, or "the noise"). Three clinical vignettes are presented, designed to aid with the assessment process, case conceptualization, and treatment strategies. The review summarizes logical steps that clinicians can take to contextualize elevated food addiction scores, even when the use of validated research instruments is not practical.

Keywords: food addiction; eating disorder; dietary restraint; substance use disorder; posttraumatic stress disorder; trauma; adverse childhood experience; early life adversity; psychiatric comorbidity; clinical vignette

1. Background

The Yale Food Addiction Scale (YFAS) was created in 2009 to match criteria for Substance Abuse in the Diagnostic and Statistical Manual of Mental Disorders (DSM-IV) and has been validated as a tool for identifying eating patterns which resemble alcohol and drug addictions [1]. The YFAS 2.0 (released 2016) reflects updated criteria in the DSM-5 [2]. Prevalence estimates of food addiction (FA) in a nationally representative US sample are approximately 15%, with higher rates in those who are obese [3]. A meta-analysis of 51 studies suggests the mean prevalence of FA worldwide is 16.2% [4]. Unlike obesity, rates of FA in the US are elevated among individuals with higher incomes [3]. In other studies of patients with obesity seeking weight loss, prevalence estimates range from 6.7–16.5% [5,6]

which closely mirror national prevalence rates for alcohol and substance use disorders (SUDs) [7]. Estimates are lower in adolescents [8], suggesting that FA develops over time. There has been a growing interest in early life psychosocial risk factors (e.g., trauma—defined as a deeply distressing or disturbing experience) in the development of both FA and obesity [9–12]. The current review employs a biopsychosocial perspective on FA, considering predisposing factors such as early life adversity which occurs in the first 18 years of life and can become biologically embedded, impacting reward function and eating behavior over the life course.

There has been considerable debate regarding the utility of an FA "diagnosis" without considering the contribution of dietary restraint in increasing FA symptoms [13–17]. While FA is not recognized by the DSM, the term diagnosis is used loosely throughout this manuscript. A common criticism of the YFAS in clinical applications is that the measure itself does not detect restrained eating (tendency to restrict food intake for weight control). The Disordered Eating and Food Addiction Nutrition Guide (DEFANG) attempted to conceptualize a role for FA into the common eating disorder (ED) paradigm which rejects the concept of food having addictive qualities by favoring an "all foods fit" ("no bad foods") approach [18]. However, the DEFANG did not incorporate restrained eating into the framework, nor did it consider the impact of trauma. The current review aims to help clinicians consider divergent nutritional strategies in patients with elevated YFAS scores, and to avoid misconceptions regarding treatment. Importantly, FA does not always necessitate rigid nutrition interventions. Arguments for and against the FA construct in the context of binge eating have recently been published [15]. Here, the position that FA can be relevant as a clinical entity is presented, and it is suggested that the presence of other psychiatric conditions such as ED, SUD, and posttraumatic stress disorder (PTSD) can be useful in determining if an individual requires targeted nutritional treatment (e.g., abstinence from specific foods). Alternatively, related psychopathology (e.g., chronic dieting based on body dissatisfaction) might indicate an opposite approach (e.g., inclusion of the foods persistently avoided). An understanding of different FA phenotypes may help guide intervention strategies.

1.1. Food Addiction Stigma

Alcohol use disorder (AUD) and SUDs were once viewed as individual choices but scientific progress and changing social norms have reduced this stigma. A survey study found that FA is more vulnerable to stigmatization than alcohol and may be perceived as a behavioral rather than substance addiction [19]. This position has favored the term "eating addiction" which has gained some traction and stimulated scholarly debate [20,21]. Meanwhile, FA is becoming increasingly accepted by the lay public, as evidenced by growing numbers of self-perceived food addicts [22,23]. Study participants express a desire to have their perceived condition formally recognized in order to receive more appropriate treatment [24]. While some research suggests that the FA label may increase stigmatizing attitudes [25], other studies show that the FA explanation reduces weight stigma [26,27]. It has also been suggested that while FA reduces externalized stigma, it may increase internalized stigma [28]. Furthermore, believing that certain food products can be addictive has been associated with support for policies intended to curb their use [29]. However, it remains unclear how a better understanding of FA neurobiology can reduce stigma in the context of ED treatment and recovery.

1.2. Food Addiction Controversy

Efforts to clear confusion around the FA construct have focused on semantics. For example, some authors have proposed the terms "refined food addiction" or "processed food addiction" to better capture FA as a substance-related disorder [30,31]. This approach targets specific foods which have been identified as addictive, such as chocolate, ice cream, French fries, pizza, cookies, chips, and cake [32]. More importantly, individuals would identify foods to avoid ("trigger foods") as part of their personal recovery program, which has been endorsed by some 12-Step groups (whereas other 12-Step groups have fixed food plans for all members). These approaches have come under scrutiny because success rates have not been well documented. Meanwhile, some authors posit that saying abstinence is ineffective because people binge when they finally eat sweets is like saying that abstinence from alcohol is ineffective because those with AUD binge after taking the first drink [31]. Another reason "abstinence-based" approaches are criticized is because they often place emphasis on weight loss, which current data suggests is not sustainable over the long term. A study based on a large prospective cohort from the UK suggests that over a 9-year period, the probability of going from obese to normal was 1 in 210 for men, and 1 in 124 for women [33]. Understandably, with such small chances of sustaining weight loss, classic ED treatment has favored targeting dietary restraint rather than weight loss, or the removal of specific foods.

1.3. Dietary Restraint

In 2003, Fairburn introduced a transdiagnostic theory of EDs proposing that diagnosis is not relevant to the treatment [34], when binge eating disorder (BED) was in the DSM-IV appendix and not yet an official diagnosis. A core assumption is that dieting precipitates bingeing; therefore, the pursuit of weight loss will be counterproductive with most ED presentations. However, among women with body image concerns ($n = 1165$), weight suppression correlated with future onset of EDs characterized by dietary restriction or compensatory weight control behaviors, but not with BED [35]. In one study of BED outpatients ($n = 98$), 65% reported an onset of dieting prior to their first binge and 35% reported that binge eating preceded their first diet [36]. Thus, dieting may not necessarily be a precursor to all forms of binge eating [37,38]. There is less consensus regarding the pursuit of weight loss in the presence of FA without an ED. Some advocates for reconceptualizing weight as a social justice issue believe that no person at all should engage in weight-loss behaviors. Rather, treatment professionals should target the problem of fat shame in society [39]. Others support the idea that new treatments are needed to address ED pathology and weight loss concurrently [40]. A recent systematic review and meta-analysis found that structured and professionally run obesity treatments are associated with reduced ED prevalence, risk, and symptoms in children [41]. However, because clinicians who work with patients with EDs often discover that the onset of disordered eating follows the first attempt to diet, many prefer a "do no harm" approach. Additionally, many professionals who work with these populations have abandoned weight loss [42] in some cases to avoid being targeted (shamed) by colleagues.

The current standard ED treatment is associated with high rates of relapse and poor long-term outcomes [43–45]. It has been suggested that contemporary ED models devote relatively little attention to biological factors driving binge eating, and that changes in the food environment interacting with individual vulnerability are key predisposing risk factors [46]. Newly proposed models suggest that clinicians go beyond a "no dieting" approach for all ED presentations and should incorporate addiction neuroscience [46,47]. Some authors recommend that researchers and clinicians distinguish between flexible and rigid restraint [14]. In some cases, restraint is related to a lower body weight, better weight regulation, and a better diet quality while in others, restraint predicts poor diet, overeating, and obesity [48]. While short-term deprivation increases cravings for avoided foods, long-term restriction results in reduction of food cravings that can facilitate extinction of conditioned responses [16]. Meule states that "the wide-held notion that dieting inevitably leads to food cravings is strongly oversimplified as the relationship between food restriction and food craving is more complex" [16]. This paper explores the nuances of different FA phenotypes, which have not been adequately described.

2. Eating Disorders

2.1. Bulimia Nervosa and Anorexia Nervosa

The highest prevalence rates of YFAS 2.0 diagnoses have been found in individuals with bulimia nervosa (BN) [49]. The relationship between FA and BMI has been described as non-linear: FA symptomatology can be higher in some underweight groups, in some cases related to compensatory behaviors that maintain lower BMIs [50]. In fact, some studies suggest that when separating anorexia nervosa restrictive type (AN-R) with the binge–purge type (AN-BP), FA prevalence is the highest in AN-BP [51]. Compensatory weight control behaviors in individuals with BN and AN-BP likely dampen the association between FA and BMI [52]. Several key reviews have summarized neurobiological overlaps with BN and SUDs, including dopamine (DA) D2 receptor-related vulnerabilities, structural and functional alterations in the frontal cortex, glutamatergic signaling, and the opioid system [53–55]. A recent systematic review of neuroimaging studies on BN and BED found diminished activity in frontostriatal circuits (associated with self-regulation) [56]. Treatment studies suggest that FA most likely improves when BN symptoms remit [57]. In an intervention study among women with BN (n = 66), those with higher FA severity at baseline were less likely to obtain abstinence from binge–purge episodes following treatment [58]. Taken together, there is preliminary support for the role of FA in the maintenance of BN via neuroadaptive changes in reward circuits. The challenge is discerning which came first (or would be considered "primary") in order to conceptualize an effective nutrition strategy. Here, it is suggested that consideration of the temporal sequence of disorder onset can be useful in discerning the truly positive FA "signal" from the falsely positive "noise," but that no rule can be applied to all cases.

2.2. Binge Eating Disorder

It has been suggested that subtyping BED based on psychiatric comorbidity may have important implications for treatment [59]. Researchers question whether the presence of BED vs. FA vs. BED + FA requires tailored treatment approaches [60]. One study suggested that when diagnostic subtypes are considered separately, FA is associated with a poor prognosis in the BED group [61]. It is possible that poor BED outcomes stem from the transdiagnostic assumption that BED patients do not need to emphasize the quality of their food ("it's not about the food"). Patient interest in weight loss may increase their risk of dropout from nonspecific ED treatment (not tailored to BED) [62]. Different phenotypes in BED are likely related to their dopaminergic response to highly palatable foods. For example, some individuals may develop particular eating expectancies in the face of poor emotion regulation and high anticipatory rewards [63]. The presence of FA may represent a more disturbed group of BED characterized by greater psychopathology [64]. To illustrate, in one study of 788 adults enrolled in BED treatment, shape/weight overvaluation differentiated BED severity more strongly than binge eating frequency [65]. Relatedly, those with heightened body image disturbance are more likely to engage in dietary restraint [66] which may contribute to bingeing as well as FA symptoms. Importantly, fear of being stigmatized predicts worsening FA status over time [67]. Stigma leads to maladaptive eating behaviors, stress, and weight gain [68]. Meanwhile, other findings do not support prevailing models that posit dietary or cognitive restraint as the predominant risk factor in BED [69]. Taken together, there appears a timely need to identify phenotypes of BED that require different treatment strategies, specifically those that would aim to reduce addiction-like eating versus those that would aim to reduce dietary restraint.

3. Substance Use Disorders

Given the neurobiological overlap between SUDs, EDs, and FA, considering an individual's relationship to alcohol, drugs, and other substances such as nicotine and caffeine may be helpful in separating the FA signal from the noise. For example, in a sample of Dutch adolescents (n = 2653), symptoms of FA were positively associated with alcohol use, cannabis use, smoking, and sugar intake [8]. Men with heroin use disorder (n = 100) had triple the odds of meeting criteria for BED or FA compared to controls [70]. Not surprisingly, FA diagnosis was associated with more severe craving. In a community-based sample of women (n = 3756), those with lifetime AUD or nicotine dependence were at higher risk for ED symptoms and diagnoses [71]. Based on the concept of reward dysfunction (reviewed below), it is likely that such ED symptoms represent those that overlap with FA. A recent systematic review and meta-analysis confirmed a higher prevalence of comorbid SUD in binge–purge ED presentations [72]. Among individuals with EDs, the pooled lifetime prevalence of comorbid SUD was 21.9% [72]. In an Italian sample of SUD patients (n = 575), the prevalence of FA was 20.2% [73], which is very close to the prevalence of ED estimated in meta-analysis. In a large longitudinal study from Australia, illicit substance users had significant risk of developing recurrent binge eating in addition to, or in place of, their substance use; however, the reverse was not found [74]. This suggests that individuals who engage in dysfunctional food-related behaviors prior to using drugs and alcohol may represent a different phenotype than those who develop addiction-like eating as a result of their drug use. In a study of women in SUD treatment (n = 297), a third reported starting drug use (in part) to lose weight and nearly half were concerned that gaining weight could trigger relapse [75]. In a non-treatment sample of drug-using women (college setting), 15.3% reported drug use for weight control purposes [76]. Patients with co-occurring SUD and ED are more sensitive to reward, have more difficulty engaging in goal-directed activity, are more impulsive, and have less access to emotion regulation skills [77]. The assessment of other addictions may prove helpful in determining the underpinnings of a high FA score, specifically as they relate to reward dysfunction and impulsivity. Meanwhile, genome wide association studies have found limited support for shared underpinnings for FA and SUD [78] whereas other lines of research have implicated DA-D2 receptors [79–83].

3.1. *Reward Dysfunction*

Convergence from neuroscience findings with case reports from the field have made clear that dysregulation of DA function is important for reward-related processes driving substance-seeking behavior [84]. Many authors have speculated that the bidirectional association between food and alcohol/drug dysfunction represents an "addiction transfer" [85] which has been supported by many studies of bariatric patients [86]. In a large twin study from the Netherlands, genetic factors explained 48% of the variation in high sugar consumption (52% explained by unique environmental factors), suggesting that neuronal circuits underlying the development of addiction and obesity are related, possibly due to DA receptor dysfunction that lead to difficulties resisting rewarding stimuli [87]. DA contributes to addiction and obesity through its differentiated role in reinforcement, motivation, and self-regulation [88]. In addition to deficiencies identified at striatal DA-D2 receptors [89,90], individuals with obesity and BED have widespread reduction in binding at mu-opioid receptors (MOR) [91]. The mesolimbic dopaminergic circuit is clearly affected by both highly palatable foods and diet-induced obesity similar to exposure to drugs of abuse [92]. Recent review articles have discussed highly processed foods (often high in glycemic index) as impacting neurohormonal and inflammatory signaling pathways in ways that create a vicious cycle of impulsivity, compulsivity, FA, and EDs [93–95]. The Regulatory Model of Addictive Vulnerability (RMAV) proposes that susceptibility to addictive disorders is linked to how well an individual's regulatory system responds to challenges, also referred to as allostasis [96]. According to these authors, both obesity and drug addiction are examples of major disorders characterized by dysregulated control systems. To date, this information has not been integrated into mainstream ED treatment programs, possibly because the translation of these findings contradicts the popular assumption that "it's not about the food." No trials have been conducted using strategies designed to reduce reward-based eating in patients with EDs; however, there are data suggesting that medications commonly used in SUD treatment (naltrexone/bupropion) in conjunction with lifestyle changes can reduce FA severity among those with BED [97]. Prospective research is needed to determine if reduction of highly palatable foods can improve reward dysfunction in people with FA.

3.2. *Impulsivity*

Impulsivity can be separated into attentional (inability to focus attention or concentrate) and motor (acting without thinking). In a sample of individuals with obesity presenting for bariatric surgery (n = 193), FA emerged when both attentional and motor impulsivity levels were elevated [98]. Impulsivity has been identified as a key shared mechanism between BED and addictive disorders [99].

For example, patients with EDs who have problems pursuing tasks to the end and focusing on long-term goals are more likely to develop addiction-like eating patterns [100]. A recent systematic review reported that across 45 studies, impulsivity was consistently associated with FA [101]. Given that FA has been reported as a mediator between impulsivity and obesity [102], it is possible that in certain susceptible individuals, ED behaviors develop along this trajectory to suppress unwanted weight. In a recent study of 145 patients with EDs, those with alcohol and drug abuse symptoms represented a specific phenotype characterized by greater impulsive personality, emotion dysregulation, and problems with executive functioning [103]. Among male military veterans (n = 106), impulsivity moderated the relationship between PTSD symptoms and alcohol consumption [104], with relevance discussed in more detail below. In addition to higher levels of impulsivity, individuals with FA are more likely to report a family history of addiction [105] which may be consistent with genetic underpinnings. While addiction research has primarily focused on the mesolimbic dopaminergic projection, impulsivity has also been linked to the serotonin system. Several genetic studies have linked polymorphisms at 5HTTLPR (codes for serotonin transporters) to higher levels of impulsivity among individuals with BN [106,107], with associated aberrations of serotonergic functioning being exacerbated by early life adversity (ELA) [108–110]. However, meta-analysis has linked the 5HTTLPR allele strongest to AN [111] and to date no study has linked this polymorphism to FA. Taken together, assessment of impulsivity in conjunction with assessment of SUD may prove beneficial in separating the FA signal (true positives) from the noise (false positives), but more research is needed before the impulsivity construct can be used in predicting the clinical utility of FA.

4. Trauma and PTSD

The Adverse Childhood Experiences (ACE) study from 1998 highlighted 5- to 10-fold increase in the risk of AUD and SUD following exposure to four or more ACEs in the first 18 years of life [112]. As traumatic stress affects a variety of brain structures and functions, ACEs impact a variety of functions and behaviors therefore have been determined nonspecific [113]. ACEs captured by the various forms of the questionnaire are referred to as a form of ELA; however, it is important to acknowledge there are many other measures used, such as the childhood trauma questionnaire (CTQ) [114,115]. Why is it that some individuals exposed to childhood trauma have a heightened risk for psychiatric disorder while others demonstrate resilience over the lifespan? The Theory of Latent Vulnerability suggests that one's genotype interacts with an adverse environment to create a neurocognitive phenotype, characterized by changes in reward processing (DA), threat processing (amygdala), and memory processing (hippocampus) [116]. One pathway which might in part explain the enduring biological impact of adversity is inflammation. A longitudinal study of adolescent girls (n = 147) showed that ELA was associated with greater odds of displaying a proinflammatory phenotype, generating low-level non-resolving inflammation (higher levels of IL-6 and decreased sensitivity to cortisol) [117]. Meta-analysis has linked childhood trauma to cognitive deficits, with the greatest deficits among those with a PTSD diagnosis [118]. If any abuse is identified in children or adolescents, it is likely they have also previously experienced, are currently experiencing, or are at risk for experiencing additional forms of abuse [119], which highlights the importance of social and environmental factors in a biopsychosocial model. While it is outside the scope of this review to clearly distinguish between trauma, adversity, chronic stress, and PTSD, the importance of these events early in life are emphasized as increasing risk for various addictions. Important for the understanding of trauma is that events be differentiated from their effects, which varies based on the experience of the individual [120]. Exposures by themselves do not define PTSD.

4.1. Addictions

Functional magnetic resonance imaging (fMRI) studies have linked ELA to blunted subjective responses to reward-predicting cues and dysfunction in the left basal ganglia regions implicated in reward-related learning and motivation [121]. Other neuroimaging studies have indicated an increase in dopamine transporter (DAT) density in PTSD, which may reflect a higher DA turnover among trauma survivors [122]. Both an increase in the number of traumatic events early in life and an increase in levels of perceived stress were associated with a higher ventral striatal DA response to amphetamine [123]. This evidence supports the biological embedding hypothesis [124] which links ELA to addictive behaviors [125]. ELA can be viewed as nonspecific because it predisposes individuals to a wide range of addictive behaviors. For example, in a sample of healthy young adults (n = 200), greater lifetime stress exposure was related to increased impulsivity and FA [126], suggesting that food is a predictable go-to for self-medication [127]. A nationally representative sample of young adults' (n = 10,813) exposure to multiple forms of maltreatment predicted excessive sugar sweetened beverage consumption [128]. Not surprisingly, childhood physical abuse and childhood sexual abuse both increase risk for FA by approximately 90% [10]. Higher numbers of PTSD symptoms predict increased prevalence of FA and the strength of this association increased when symptom onset occurred at an earlier age [11]. In this study (n = 49,408), the PTSD-FA association did not differ substantially by trauma type, suggesting that all forms of ELA impact reward-related behaviors. Among overweight/obese women (n = 301), the association between FA and childhood trauma was significant after controlling for potential confounders such as socioeconomic status [129]. Compared to women with no addictions, women with FA and with SUD endorsed more depression and PTSD symptoms and had more difficulties with goal-directed behaviors, acceptance of emotions, and impulse control [130]. Taken together, exposure to trauma significantly increases risk for FA and therefore should be considered during comprehensive psychiatric/psychological and nutrition assessments.

4.2. Eating Disorders

All forms of childhood maltreatment are associated with all forms of EDs, although some more than others [131]. The odds of BED following maltreatment is consistently higher than AN [132], yet meta-analysis confirms that, when pooled, the risk for BN is the highest [133]. Given the link between early life trauma and addictive disorders, it is likely that FA is an important pathway on the trajectory toward binge-type EDs. Meanwhile, there are also associations from ELA to EDs which may not include FA as a mediator, capturing a different phenotype with different treatment implications (discussed further below). In one sample of adult patients with EDs from Sweden (n = 853), a quarter had a lifetime diagnosis of PTSD [134]. Other estimates suggest traumatic events occur in over a third of adolescents in ED outpatients (n = 182), and the prevalence is highest among those with BN [135]. A recent review article suggests that the prevalence of comorbid PTSD and EDs ranges from 9% to 24% [136], although estimates are consistently higher when looking specifically at binge-type EDs [137–141]. Several studies have suggested that adverse events experienced early in life predict binge eating symptoms in both men and women [142–144]. Evidence consistently shows that ED symptoms such as anxiety and depression are more severe among those with a PTSD diagnosis [145], and those with the dissociative subtype are even worse off [146]. Some authors believe that it may be helpful to modify current ED treatments to better address the overlapping risk among EDs and obesity among those who have been exposed to trauma [147]. Others posit that any effort to lose weight or restrict food will only make eating problems worse [66,148,149]. In this paper, our aim is to resolve this debate by presenting three clinical vignettes that are fictional yet rooted in extensive clinical experience.

5. Other Psychiatric Diagnoses

5.1. Depression

Multiple lines of evidence suggest that individuals with FA have more depressive symptoms than controls [60,105,130,150–152]. A recent review of studies using YFAS identified depressive symptoms as a clinically relevant correlate [49]. Meta-analysis suggests that FA is significantly correlated to depression (r = 0.459) [4]. The directionality of this relationship remains less clear. While it is likely that depressed individuals may turn to highly palatable foods to alleviate negative affect, several recent studies have suggested that a low-quality diet increases depressive symptoms. A cross-sectional study from the US (n = 16,807) suggests that intakes of total fiber, specifically from fruits and vegetables, was inversely associated with depressive symptoms [153]. In a French cohort of adults (n = 3523) with mean follow-up 12.6 years, diets high in anti-inflammatory properties prevented depressive symptoms, particularly among men, smokers, or physically inactive individuals [154]. In a Spanish cohort of graduate students initially free of depression (n = 14,907), followed for a median 10.3 years, participants with the highest consumption of ultra-processed foods had the highest risk of developing depression, particularly among those with low levels of physical activity [155]. Another large French cohort of adults followed for a mean of 5.4 years demonstrated a positive association between ultra-processed food and the risk of incident depression [156].

While there appears to be preliminary support that low-quality diets can lead to depression, there is also evidence that high-quality diets can mitigate or reverse depressive symptoms. A randomized controlled trial (RCT) showed that dietary support (nutrition counseling by a dietitian) for 12 weeks can improve symptoms [157]. Systematic review and meta-analysis suggest that the most compelling evidence for reducing incident depression exists for the Mediterranean diet, known for its anti-inflammatory properties [158]. Since depressive disorders correlate and cross-associate with EDs, SUDs, and PTSD [138,159,160] the diagnosis may prove important for informing nutrition treatment. While the presence of depressive symptoms might not be informative of whether or not an individual has an actual addiction to food (the signal), it is worth considering the potential role of dietary intake in contributing to symptoms. For example, for a person engaging excess consumption of highly palatable foods, it may be worth experimenting with dietary manipulation before psychiatric medication. Further, if a patient receiving ED treatment with the "all foods fit" philosophy is consistently eating low-fiber foods ("intuitively") and has non-resolving depressive symptoms, it may indicate that a more targeted nutrition strategy is warranted.

5.2. *Anxiety*

In addition to reducing depressive symptoms, the Mediterranean diet may also be helpful in reducing the odds of anxiety [161]. However, a recent meta-analysis of RCTs concluded that no effect of dietary interventions is observed for anxiety [162]. Meanwhile, anxiety disorders show a dose–response association with worsening diet quality [163]; however, directionality remains unclear. Omega-3 fatty acids have been investigated for their role in anxiety disorders, but results are inconsistent, and data are too sparse to draw conclusions [164,165]. The role of gastrointestinal microbiota has also received attention as a potential mediator linking diet quality to anxiety symptoms [166–169]. Meanwhile, anxiety has been significantly correlated with FA (r = 0.483) [4] which is not surprising given the strong associations between anxiety and SUDs [170]. Anxiety is a well-established risk factor for EDs, SUDs, and PTSD. A recent systematic review suggested that anxiety may mediate the association between PTSD and SUD [171]; therefore, it is biologically plausible that anxiety is on the pathway from ELA to FA, though this has not yet been shown. Among treatment-seeking youth (n = 490), social anxiety predicts binge eating [172]. A rodent model suggests that consumption of a Western diet may lead to long-lasting damage to fear neurocircuitry, particularly during adolescence [173]. In an Australian sample of adults (n = 1344), anxiety sensitivity predicted severe FA [174]. The association between FA and current anxiety disorders has also been reported in bariatric surgery candidates (n = 128) [175]. One study suggested that irrational beliefs may be the source of the anxiety associated with FA [176]. Among adult females with anxiety (n = 51), impulsivity predicted higher intakes of sugar and saturated fat [177], which is consistent with reports of "comfort food" consumption when under stress [178]. Taken together, the presence of an anxiety diagnosis by itself is not likely to be informative of an FA phenotype; however, it may prove beneficial to discern between anxiety that is symptomatic of PTSD/ELA and generalized [145,179] versus other forms of anxiety such as body image disturbance or dysmorphia (likely indicative of dietary restraint). Either way, FA treatment should include positive anxiety management and coping skills [46].

5.3. *Attention Deficit Hyperactivity Disorder (ADHD)*

ADHD is defined by inattention and/or hyperactivity and is often characterized by impulsivity. Both ADHD and SUDs are characterized by choice impulsivity [180]. There are recent data to support the possibility that choice impulsivity in ADHD results from substance misuse [181]. A popular explanation for the association between ADHD and EDs is that impulsive behavior generates the disordered eating [182,183]. Both conditions rely on a dopaminergic signaling which makes their cooccurrence a logical comorbidity [182]. However, the evidence reviewed above suggests that among those with EDs, impulsivity is also linked to serotonergic genes (i.e., 5HTTLPR). In both sexes, binge eaters have significantly higher prevalence of ADHD [184]. In a nationally representative sample of adults in the US ($n = 4719$), only the association between ADHD and BN remained significant after confounders were adjusted for [185]. In a sample of patients with obesity ($n = 105$), adult and childhood ADHD were significantly associated with self-reported FA and binge eating severity [186]. In a recent study of 136 patients with EDs, a positive screen for ADHD related to worse eating symptoms and the presence of high ED levels contributed to treatment dropout [187]. Meanwhile, a large genome-wide association study suggests that higher BMI increases risk of developing ADHD but not the other way around [188]; therefore, directionality remains unclear. It is worth noting that stimulant medications (i.e., amphetamines) often used in the treatment of ADHD can have an impact on appetite, with suppressing effects while using and rebound appetite when not. In one study of undergraduate students ($n = 705$), nearly 12% reported using prescription stimulants to lose weight [189] however these students were not diagnosed with ADHD. Lisdexamfetamine, which is FDA approved for ADHD as well as BED, works by enhancing dorsofrontal cortex function [190,191]. Meanwhile, it remains unclear whether ADHD symptomatology (e.g., impulsivity) or the effect of ADHD medications (including their discontinuation) drive the potential association with FA. Research is needed to test long-term outcomes of lisdexamfetamine on BED + FA. It may prove important to consider ADHD when conceptualizing FA phenotypes in the context of nutrition strategies.

6. Clinical Vignettes

6.1. *Phenotype A*

Alma is a 23-year-old, single Columbian female who grew up in a troubled household. Her parents were not married but lived together off and on until she was 10, when her father left. Alma had two older brothers from a different father. Her mother divorced her first husband when the two boys were two and four, right before she met Alma's father, who attempted to parent all three children. However, Alma's father struggled with a severe alcohol use disorder and would be absent for days at a time. Alma's brothers never accepted him as a parent figure. When Alma's father was gone completely, she began to seek attention from boys by playing sports with her brothers. She became athletic and thrived in volleyball. As a freshman in high school, she joined the volleyball team and made many friends among the athletic crowd. Alma loved to play sports and cook food, often referring to herself as a "foodie", known for baking Columbian desserts for her teammates. She grew close to the assistant coach of the girls' volleyball team who had a reputation for drinking with the students after games. Alma never drank alcohol or did drugs because of what she had seen them do to her father. She swore she would never smoke a cigarette. One night the male assistant coach offered to take Alma home and kissed her in the car. Alma felt confused but kept the secret to herself. During the summer after her freshman year, she agreed to visit his home where she was coerced into sex (statutory rape). Alma kept it a secret due to shame, but people close to her knew something had changed.

Alma did not return to the volleyball team for her sophomore year. She became promiscuous with several seniors at her school and some of her brother's friends. She lost interest in sports completely and began binge eating on highly processed foods at night to help her sleep. She often skipped breakfast but never engaged in any compensatory behaviors. Her academic performance began to decline, and she started drinking coffee, soda, and energy drinks throughout the day. Between her sophomore and senior year, Alma gained forty pounds, meanwhile experimenting with a few popular diets that never stuck for more than two days. When she graduated from high school, she moved in with her boyfriend who was 30 years old, owning a small shop that sold electronic cigarettes. Alma began vaping daily. However, she stuck by her commitment to never smoke a cigarette, drink alcohol, or use drugs. They mostly ate fast food and ordered take-out together, but Alma would frequently bake and cook. Alma got a job as an office administrator and slowly stopped responding to texts from her mother and brothers. She never posted any pictures on social media because she did not want people to see how much weight she had gained. Eventually, she learned that her boyfriend was cheating on her and moved back in with her mother after he told her that she had to leave. At this point the mother brought Alma to a psychiatrist for an evaluation, but Alma did not tell the doctor about the rape, in part because she was amnestic for the memories. The doctor identified complex PTSD and a dissociative disorder, prescribing sertraline and trazadone. She was referred to an outpatient psychotherapist who began working with her twice per week, at which point Alma opened up about the sexual abuse. When the trauma therapy started, the bingeing escalated significantly. At this point, Alma was referred to a registered dietitian nutritionist (RDN) specializing in mental and behavioral health. Several assessment tools were administered, including the eating disorder examination questionnaire (EDE-Q) which indicated an absence of dietary restraint and the YFAS 2.0 where she met criteria for severe food addiction (BMI = 36.8).

6.2. Phenotype B

Jeffrey is a 27-year-old, single, half-Taiwanese, half-white male who grew up in a wealthy household as an only child. His father was a cardiologist with mild undiagnosed obsessive compulsive personality disorder (OCPD) and, before getting married, his mother was a swimsuit model with a long history of dieting. Both parents ran marathons together and revered the thin ideal, frequently making negative comments about fat people. Jeffrey's parents were very adamant about their son playing sports and at one point hired a running coach for him. Jeffrey spent a lot of time with nannies and babysitters, including extended periods when his parents vacationed without him. When Jeffrey was nine, he was sent to a psychiatrist for behavioral problems where he was diagnosed with ADHD and prescribed dextroamphetamine/amphetamine. Jeffrey was a straight-A student with the help of the medication and several tutors. Jeffrey also began running with his parents by age 13. His mother told Jeffrey to only eat carbohydrates before, during, and after a run, and to avoid them at all other times. Jeffrey completed his first marathon at age 15 and wore the medal at his private high school the next day, where he was photographed for the cover of the school magazine and website. One of his mother's friends provided an opportunity for Jeffrey to model for a large international fashion company and, at age 17, he was on a billboard in his 6′2″ frame with his shirt off. His agent helped him build a following on Instagram, and Jeffrey began to spend more time exercising to prepare for photo shoots. The agreement was that Jeffrey could continue to model as long as he went to college and earned decent grades. He went to a private university as a communications major.

As a freshman in college, Jeffrey was switched from mixed amphetamine salts to a high-dose lisdexamfetamine and was also prescribed clonazepam for anxiety. Jeffrey never told anyone that he spent up to an hour each day looking in the mirror, obsessed with the fat on his abdominal area. During his junior year Jeffrey did a "Freeze the Fat" procedure with the physician who had done several cosmetic surgeries on his mother. He was very disappointed with the results. As Jeffrey continued to get modeling jobs, his performance in school began to decline. Jeffrey continued to run 10 miles per day on a treadmill in the gym at his apartment complex. He also did 30 minutes of abdominal workouts daily and rarely missed a workout. Jeffrey cut out all grains and dairy from his diet and only got small amounts of carbohydrates from fruits, starchy vegetables, and occasionally beans. Jeffrey frequently made negative comments about processed food and did not like to eat at restaurants. Jeffrey had several short-lived relationships with women, but as he became increasingly concerned about his appearance, he lost interest in dating. Jeffrey sought out an RDN to help him lose his stubborn abdominal fat; the dietitian determined that his BMI was 17.2 and contacted the psychiatrist to discuss potential body dysmorphic disorder. The psychiatrist told Jeffrey that being on a stimulant was contraindicated at such a low BMI, discontinuing the lisdexamfetamine and starting him on fluoxetine. At this point Jeffrey starting bingeing on carbohydrates and would "run it off" in his apartment gym, even if it was late at night. One evening, Jeffrey rolled his ankle and due to the sprain was told not to run for several weeks. Jeffrey purged for the first time after ordering Chinese food and eating a whole container of fried rice. He hated the experience of purging but continued to engage that behavior whenever he ate carbohydrates. He began to order food delivery and would often flush the food down the toilet because once he retrieved it from the trash. At the request of the psychiatrist, Jeffrey made another appointment with the RDN and obliged because he was feeling very depressed. Several assessment tools were administered, including the EDE-Q, which indicated high levels of dietary restraint, and the YFAS 2.0, where he met criteria for moderate food addiction (BMI = 17.0).

6.3. *Phenotype C*

Whitney is a 30-year-old, single, white female, and the oldest of three daughters to happily married parents who had no formal psychiatric diagnoses. Her mother was a professor at a small university and her father a certified public accountant who became obese in his late 40s. Her two sisters looked up to Whitney who was quite popular in middle school. Whitney got a lot of attention from boys but found herself attracted to women. In high school, she had a girlfriend for two years and the relationship made a lot of people in school uncomfortable. Despite becoming somewhat of an outcast, Whitney got good grades and was accepted into a local college as a sociology major. She was passionate about gender studies and started her own blog about sexuality. For a class assignment, Whitney filled out the ACE measure and scored a zero. Some of her friends began frequenting rave parties and taking ecstasy; Whitney fell in love with this culture. Whitney attended the Burning Man festival each year during college and graduated with honors. Whitney's family was proud of her and she maintained successful relationships with her parents and siblings. Everyone in the family loved Whitney's girlfriend. After college, they opened a business selling handmade jewelry, which was a big success in the Burning Man crowd. They eventually moved into a condo together and had two dogs who they took with them on long hikes at nearby trails.

At age 26, Whitney was hit by a drunk driver which killed her partner, witnessing her take her last breath at the scene. Whitney shattered her femur along with several other minor fractures and was in the hospital for two weeks, completely devastated by the loss of her lover. Despite having family by her side constantly and a doctor who gave a positive prognosis of her recovery, Whitney began to express suicidal ideation. She was on heavy doses of opioid medications and everyone assumed her mental health would improve after discharging from the hospital. However, upon returning back to her parents' house, it was obvious that Whitney had PTSD. She was prescribed oxycodone for pain management which she quickly became dependent on. The family found a therapist to do Eye Movement Desensitization and Reprocessing (EMDR), but Whitney would often show up sedated from the medication and the work was not productive. After several months of both physical and emotional therapy, the doctor took her off opioids and prescribed gabapentin. However, Whitney was able to purchase oxycodone on the street and within a matter of months she was buying heroin (which she smoked rather than injected) because it was much more affordable.

Whitney went into her first treatment center for heroin use disorder at age 29. She was prescribed gabapentin, buspirone, methocarbamol, venlafaxine, and quetiapine. During this time, she developed a strong preference for sweets and would eat several bags of candy daily. It was normal for people in her rehab to smoke cigarettes and drink sugary energy drinks, so she did the same. For the first time in her life, Whitney began gaining weight and by six months sober had gained 30 pounds. At this time, she was in a sober living house, which provided restaurant-style catered food. One of her roommates with severe bulimia nervosa taught Whitney how to induce vomiting to lose unwanted pounds. Whitney had never struggled with body image issues until she was sober and on several medications.

She quickly learned that purging was quite soothing and began vomiting daily, yet never tried any specific diets. Sometimes she would purge "healthy foods" simply because it felt relieving to do so. When these behaviors were discovered, her sober living required her to attend an ED outpatient clinic where she was instructed to eat three meals, two snacks, plus dessert every single day. After reaching her highest weight, Whitney relapsed on heroin and, within two weeks, was back in detox, where she began bingeing on ice cream, candy, and grilled cheese sandwiches. Whitney was referred to an RDN specializing in mental and behavioral health. Several assessment tools were administered including the EDE-Q which indicated moderate dietary restraint and the YFAS 2.0 where she met criteria for severe food addiction (BMI = 26.4).

7. Discussion

Phenotype A is a clear example of an FA signal (true positive) not blocked by the noise of dietary restraint (false positive). With an absence of restrictive eating there is little convincing evidence that the addiction is driven by dieting, a relic of internalized weight bias, or other forms of compensation often generated by socially constructed forces such as weight stigma. This case illustrates the link between ELA and FA which is likely mediated by biological mechanisms including altered DA signaling [121,122,192–194]. FA has been independently associated with exposure to early life sexual abuse [195]. Alma's father has AUD, which can be useful in evaluating biological susceptibility to addictive disorders. Furthermore, Alma was a "foodie" prior to the rape incident, suggesting that her tendency to seek highly palatable food may have a genetic basis as well as linked to her early psychosocial environment (and cultural background). The traumatic event did not create the FA but rather exacerbated her symptoms and severity by creating dependence on food for self-medication. Her weight gain may have reinforced incentive salience assigned to food stimuli [196]. Alma did not develop alcohol or drug problems due to important social factors during her upbringing where she witnessed the devastating impact they had on her father. While many people with high susceptibility to addictions struggle with multiple substances, Alma did not cross-addict into intoxicating substances; however, her clinical history indicates evidence of both caffeine and nicotine use disorders. Based on our clinical experience, we have observed that some (not all) of the most severe FA cases develop addictions to food with limited cross-addictions. We recommend considering cross-addiction in discerning the signal from the noise (true versus false positives); however, the absence of cross-addiction does not always indicate a weaker signal. In fact, in some cases it may be more severe because other addictive substances fail to compete with the experience of food. As this phenotype exemplifies FA, it suggests that FA-informed nutritional strategies may be warranted as well as safe (low risk of developing an ED). We suggest that strategies be assessed individually rather than a "one size fits all" approach.

Phenotype B is an example of how "noise" can muddle the FA signal and produce a false positive. In this case, dietary restraint is clearly driving the FA symptoms. Jeffrey is a classic example of how thin ideals can be perpetuated by the family system, become internalized, and eventually become pathological. Jeffrey's modeling career appears influenced by his mother's history of modeling and related social network. There is no AUD/SUD in the immediate family, which can be helpful information when assessing potential FA (reward dysfunction). The fact that Jeffrey never struggled with AUD/SUD is also informative. However, the ADHD diagnosis indicates the potential for higher levels of impulsivity and the stimulant medications may have appetite dysregulating effects [182,189,197]. When Jeffrey was taken off lisdexamfetamine after clinical concerns about under eating and body dysmorphic disorder, the loss-of-control eating began. Binge eating was accompanied by compensatory exercise behaviors, indicating classic ED pathology. The period of time when Jeffrey was depressed and experiencing heightened conflict around food is likely the source of the increased FA scores. He was previously successful in restraining himself with food but eventually lost his ability to do so, which is not uncommon over longer periods of time [34]. This case study exemplifies how an underweight individual can have elevated YFAS scores; however, the diagnosis of moderate FA is not informative for treatment. Rather, FA is a product of restrained eating stemming from body dissatisfaction. Therefore, intervention strategies should focus on dietary inclusion rather than exclusion, targeting the underlying psychological and family system issues rather than focus on avoiding specific foods (e.g., carbohydrates).

Phenotype C is an example of a case that could be interpreted as an FA signal (true positive), or as a more classic ED presentation (false positive), depending on the training (and bias) of the practitioner. Whitney had no evidence of ELA, although did experience adversity in high school. However, she was resilient to this exposure. She did not develop SUD early on despite regularly using "party drugs" (methylenedioxyamphetamine or MDMA). However, following her serious injury and PTSD warranting opioid medications, she developed an opioid use disorder, implicating trauma as an important risk factor. Once becoming sober and being prescribed several medications, her PTSD symptoms and reward-seeking behavior led to FA and associated distress. Evidence of cross-addiction can be found with caffeine and nicotine. The ED developed after the FA and weight gain, eventually contributing to her relapse with heroin. While body dissatisfaction initially drove the ED behaviors, there was no history of dietary restraint before the SUD. In this case, FA preceded the dietary restraint, meaning that the signal existed before the noise. It is likely that practitioners who do not endorse the clinical utility of FA will observe the PTSD–ED connection and ignore the contribution of addiction-like eating into Whitney's assessment and treatment plan. The best direction for nutrition treatment is not clear and could be effective in multiple ways as long as Whitney had "buy-in" with adequate clinical and social support. Regular inclusion of highly palatable foods appears to be the safest course in order to prevent further progression of restriction and/or purging. However, it is possible that this approach can increase risk for SUD relapse if Whitney continues to gain weight and is unable to accept her body at a higher BMI [75]. Meanwhile, some might argue that FA-informed nutrition strategies that reduce reward-based eating may increase risk for SUD relapse by depriving the brain of DA that it has been conditioned to get from comforting foods. This has been widely endorsed by a "first things first" message from *Alcoholics Anonymous*, suggesting that sweets and chocolate are helpful in early recovery [198], but data to support this are lacking. This is another example of how a nutrition strategy is best assessed on an individual basis. Importantly, the treatment team should be on the same page since consistent messaging from providers appears critical [47].

The three clinical vignettes bring attention to heterogeneity that is possible given an FA diagnosis using the YFAS 2.0. All three cases meet criteria for FA (A and C are severe while B is moderate). However, a comprehensive biopsychosocial assessment identified divergent phenotypes that may warrant different nutrition interventions. While no trials have been reported using targeted nutrition interventions for FA, several studies have shown that non-diet approaches such as intuitive eating can be effective in reducing dietary restraint [199–201]. The present review suggests that it would be effective to identify FA phenotypes based on the presence of other psychiatric disorders such as ED, AUD/SUD, PTSD, depression, anxiety, and ADHD as part of a comprehensive biopsychosocial assessment, and to assign nutrition treatment based on the relative strength of the FA signal amidst the noise (true versus false positive). Recent studies have identified different phenotypic characterizations of the FA construct [60,61,202,203]. However, Table 1 suggests a guide for clinicians to consider in settings where the use of extensive validated instruments is not always practical.

Table 1. Eight Step Process for Clinicians to Discern Food Addiction from Dietary Restraint in Order to Inform Inclusive vs. Exclusive Nutrition Strategies.

Step	Assessment	If Negative	If Positive
1	Food Addiction (FA) • YFAS 2.0 [2] or mYFAS [204]	FA is unlikely to be a relevant construct	⇒ Step 2
2	Dietary Restraint • Examine history of dieting behavior and role of body image as well as internalized weight bias • Can use EDE-Q (long or short) [205] or EAT-26 [206] or similar validated tools	FA is likely to be a relevant construct • Consider ruling out food insecurity since it is also a form of deprivation that may increase FA symptoms [207,208]	Consider if the FA preceded the restraint, or if the restraint created the FA • If FA came first, it is likely to be informative that FA is a relevant construct ⇒ Step 3, and → Step 7
3	Substance Use Disorder (SUD) • Can use clinical diagnosis or self-report or validated measure • Can assess reward dysfunction by also considering addictions to caffeine and nicotine • Can also assess impulsivity using BIS-11 [209,210] which may help to better understand loss-of-control behavior	Absence of other addictions does not rule out FA. However, concurrent low levels of impulsivity may suggest that the individual is unlikely to have an actual FA. Will want to also consider ADHD when assessing impulsivity ⇒ Step 4, and ⇒ Step 8	FA is likely to be a relevant construct. It is worth considering if the FA or SUD came first • If SUD came first, it may indicate that inclusive nutrition strategies are the most practical ⇒ Step 4
4	PTSD including complex PTSD • Can use clinical diagnosis or validated measure such as PCL-5 [211] • Qualified professionals are required to assess the presence of CPTSD because it can be difficult for some patients to "connect the dots" across multiple life events	If there is an absence of SUD and PTSD, the presence of dietary restraint suggests that FA symptoms are driven by restriction rather than an actual FA. An exception would be if it was clear that FA preceded the restraint; however, in the absence of SUD and PTSD, inclusive nutritional strategies are likely to be the most practical ⇒ Step 6	FA is likely to be a relevant construct regardless of whether there is SUD history. However, history of SUD likely strengthens the confidence in the FA signal ⇒ Step 5
5	Early Life Adversity (ELA) • Can use validated measures such as ACE [112], CTQ [114,115], ETI-SR [212]	Suggests an absence of biological embedding. While later life traumatic experiences can alter physiology, an absence of ELA indicates that inclusive nutritional strategies may be more plausible. There may be some cases of ELA in the absence of PTSD which can indicate high levels of biological resilience, also warranting inclusive nutritional strategies ⇒ Step 6	FA is very likely to be a relevant construct, and in the presence of ELA, PTSD, and SUD and no evidence of dietary restraint as a predisposing risk factor, exclusive/restricted nutritional strategies may be warranted, assuming there are adequate resources including social support and access to nutritious unprocessed foods
6	Depression • Can use clinical diagnosis or self-report or validated measures such as PHQ-9 [213], BDI [214], or CESD [215]	With low levels of depressive symptoms, an inclusive nutritional strategy is likely to be the most practical strategy ⇒ Step 7	If depressive symptoms persist, it may be worth making drastic dietary changes such as the exclusion of highly processed foods in order to improve mood

Table 1. *Cont.*

Step	Assessment	If Negative	If Positive
7	Anxiety • Can use clinical diagnosis or self-report or validated measures such as the BAI [216], STAI [217], GAD-7 [218] or similar validated tools	Low levels of anxiety indicate that an inclusive nutritional strategy is likely to be most practical ⇒ Step 8	Consider if anxiety is related to body image disturbance. If body image drives anxiety (or vice versa), it may indicate dietary restraint, suggesting an inclusive nutritional strategy. If anxiety is not associated with body image, improving nutritional status by excluding certain foods may be warranted (and safe)
8	ADHD • Can use clinical diagnosis or validated measures such as ASRS [219]	If ADHD is negative but there are high levels of impulsivity, it may indicate higher likelihood of FA	Consider if eating behavior has been altered by the impact of stimulant medications

Legend: YFAS: Yale Food Addiction Scale; FA: Food Addiction; EDE-Q: Eating Disorder Examination Questionnaire; EAT-26: Eating Attitudes Test-26; SUD: Substance Use Disorder; BIS-11: Barratt Impulsiveness Scale-11; ADHD: Attention Deficit Hyperactivity Disorder; PTSD: Post Traumatic Stress Disorder; PCL-5: PTSD Checklist for DSM-5; CPTSD: Complex Post Traumatic Stress Disorder; ELA: Early Life Adversity; ACE: Adverse Childhood Experience; CTQ: Childhood Trauma Questionnaire; ETI-SR: Early Trauma Inventory Self-Report; PHQ-9: Patient Health Questionnaire-9; BDI: Beck Depression Inventory; CESD: Center for Epidemiological Studies Depression; BAI: Beck Anxiety Inventory; STAI: State Trait Anxiety Inventory; GAD-7: General Anxiety Disorder-7; ASRS: Adult ADHD Self-Report Scale.

8. Interventions for Food Addiction

There are few successful interventions for reducing FA in the literature. Likewise, there are no articles describing effective interventions for the treatment of obesity in individuals with a history of ACEs [220] which is likely mediated by FA [9,192]. In a study of 60 women, 12-Step self-help groups for compulsive eating have been shown to reduce anxiety and depression, but not FA [221]. A 14-week group lifestyle modification program including caloric reduction (n = 178) significantly reduced addictive eating behaviors [222]. A 6-week integrative group for weight management (n = 51) reduced FA from pre to post, with strategies such as mindful eating, keeping a food diary, carrying out an exercise plan, regular weigh-ins, and planning for social eating [223]. In a study of 47 different internet sources, self-perceived sugar addicts shared actional strategies that worked for them, including avoidance, consumption planning, environmental restructuring, professional and social support, addressing underlying issues, and urge management, among others [23]. Qualitative interviews have found that the YFAS does not adequately assess social and situational cues for overeating [224]. Importantly, interventions aimed to reduce weight and FA scores generally do not have strategies in place to mitigate progression into disordered eating. This highlights the difference between dietary restraint that can be helpful for some versus pathological for others. Some authors recommend that if an ED is present in addition to FA, clinicians should first provide evidence-based treatments for those conditions [225]. Notwithstanding, it is worth repeating that among women with BN, patients with higher FA severity at baseline were less likely to obtain abstinence from bingeing/purging episodes after treatment [58]. Thus, it is being suggested to view EDs with co-occurring FA on a continuum rather than as discrete conditions, using the eight-step process as a guide, rather than simply to dichotomize inclusive vs. exclusive nutrition strategies.

It is well established that earlier intervention is beneficial for addressing ED pathology [226]. With respect to reducing FA symptoms and severity, it appears that earlier intervention matters, given that ELA does not lead to obesity immediately but develops over time [227,228]. Recently, there have been recommendations for interventions among adolescents that promote executive functioning in the context of salience and reward processing [196]. Among adolescents with obesity (n = 18), an FA-informed mobile health (app) intervention reduced zBMI in a more cost-effective manner than the in-clinic intervention, and there is currently an RCT underway in a larger sample using this approach [229,230]. It has been suggested that the more interactive, engaging and person centered a mobile health treatment is, the more appealing it will be to those suffering from compulsive overeating [231]. Meanwhile, many people with more classic ED training may view these apps as a causal factor to ED pathology, either in the short term or over the life course. It seems that until researchers and clinicians determine who is a good candidate for an FA-based nutrition intervention, FA science will continue to stimulate disagreement. In the meantime, recommended treatments might include abstinence from trigger foods, deliberate inclusion of health-promoting foods, interventions that target impulsivity and habitual patterns of responding, anxiety management, coping mechanisms, positive social connections, spirituality, and deterrence of maladaptive compensatory behaviors [46].

9. Summary

The DEFANG (2017) was the first effort to disentangle FA from more classic ED pathology by incorporating the presence or history of SUD into the nutrition intake process [47]. The current review using three clinical vignettes extends that work by adding trauma and PTSD history, particularly early in life, as well as histories of depression, anxiety, and ADHD to guide treatment. The aim in including psychiatric diagnoses, self-report, scores on validated measures, or even informal assessment (clinical intuition) is to reduce the potential for false FA positives (enhance specificity and sensitivity). We have recognized dietary restraint as a primary contributor of "noise" in the FA signal. Failure to consider restrictive eating patterns is an important criticism of FA that has led many ED professionals to reject the construct altogether [15]. The eight-step process outlined in Table 1 might improve the FA assessment process and help clinicians further integrate FA into ED treatment protocols. Currently, most EDs are treated with an inclusive nutrition strategy aimed to reduce fears around food and desensitize individuals to highly palatable foods through regular consumption. Meanwhile, standard ED treatment is associated with suboptimal results, possibly because existing treatments sometimes fail to recognize impulsivity as part of the eating pathology [232,233]. Our clinical experience suggests that failure to recognize/treat trauma/PTSD is a major contributor to poor outcomes. We have suggested that the proper interpretation of an FA diagnosis may improve treatment for those who would benefit from a different nutritional approach, such as excluding problematic foods like added refined sugars [234]. Evidence supports the validity of FA as a diagnostic construct, particularly as it relates to foods high in added sweeteners and refined ingredients [235]. Similar to how SUD patients exhibit different patterns of abuse, patients with FA may have very different behavioral characteristics such as those that binge versus those that do not. Tailor-made hybrid models between inclusive and exclusive approaches have been useful in our clinical experience but have yet to be formally described or tested. These nutrition interventions usually require some trial-and-error and are best done under the supervision of an RDN and a psychiatrist/psychotherapist who understands EDs, FA, SUDs, trauma, and the associations with other psychiatric diagnoses described herein. A multidisciplinary team approach can be helpful, but it is essential that all team members understand the science of FA.

Emerging data on FA may contribute to reduced stigma around body weight, by clearing up confusion and controversy around why humans consume food beyond physiological need. Better terminology will be important to progressing FA science, with several authors proposing new descriptors such as "food use disorder" [236] among others described earlier. The area of greatest controversy surrounding FA appears to be in those with clinically significant EDs, particularly those with purging behaviors where FA symptoms can become elevated [51]. An understanding of the SUD recovery culture including harm reduction may be useful in helping clinicians integrate FA into ED treatment. However, it will be very challenging to implement divergent nutritional strategies in residential treatment settings where there is comparison on the unit and heightened interest in each other's food plans. Currently, exclusive nutritional strategies might be best conducted in an outpatient setting. These strategies may run the risk of exacerbating restrict–binge patterns, therefore should be supervised by clinicians experienced in EDs as well as in detecting reward dysfunction (through examination of cross-addictions) and impulsivity (with respect to food and other behaviors). Treatment professionals should be aware of the various pathways in which ELA and PTSD can become biologically embedded and alter human physiology. ELA increases vulnerability for FA and obesity later in life [192] and highly palatable foods can become a way to distract from disturbing and intrusive trauma-related thoughts [237]. When food alters DA circuitry, efforts to moderate become more difficult and "intuitive eating" can feel impossible. Trauma-informed care should be applied to recovery systems and providers servicing EDs [238,239].

Future Directions

A large prospective study of individuals meeting criteria for FA separated into a restricted diet group (excluding identified trigger foods) and a non-diet group (including challenging foods) would be informative, timely, and warranted. However, given the heterogeneity associated with FA described herein, it could be more effective to categorize FA phenotypes before implementing nutrition-related treatment. Future research using exclusive nutrition strategies might exclude participants revealing moderate or high levels of dietary restraint in order to assess risk for progression from exclusion into disordered eating, as well as into "orthorexia" [240]. The inclusion of orthorexia into future versions of the DSM might prove useful when conceptualizing treatment strategies and research related to FA. It would be valuable to analyze the benefits vs. risks in reducing reward-based eating in those who meet criteria for FA. Research on medications commonly used on patients with SUD for patients with FA is also needed. There is a growing interest in genetic risk for EDs and it would be valuable to know if genetic counseling would be of benefit [241]. More data on food insecurity and other forms of deprivation as predictors of FA may also elucidate the link between undereating and overeating. The temporal sequence of disorder onset may prove beneficial in terms of case conceptualization with respect to nutrition. Consideration of other psychiatric diagnoses such as obsessive compulsive, bipolar, and borderline personality disorders may prove beneficial for FA treatment as new data becomes available. We have proposed that identifying different phenotypes for FA as well as for EDs might improve nutrition interventions and even modify treatment models. An important question at this time remains unanswered: where does all the dieting stem from in the first place? How have sociocultural influences engrained highly palatable foods into the brain's reward expectancy? Furthermore, can public health interventions aimed at reducing exposure to highly processed foods eventually reduce FA and subsequently reduce chronic dieting?

10. Conclusions

While there is disagreement regarding FA, it appears that much of the controversy pertains to the treatment (lacking data) rather than the existence of the problem (robust data). More specifically, nutrition interventions for individuals with FA and co-occurring ED characterized by high levels of dietary restraint are less clear than for individuals with FA and no history of restrictive ED. Individualized treatment might be helpful based on the existence of FA, but only after it has been determined that the FA signal represents an addiction to food (true positive), rather than a consequence of dietary restraint, food insecurity or insufficiency, or other forms of deprivation or food-related neglect (false positive). Dismissing FA as a clinical entity is ill informed and not helpful. FA may warrant consideration as a distinct category in the DSM, which might lead to additional research at the individual and group level, as well as public health efforts to improve the national food environment. The impact of contemporary Westernized foods may be contributing to poor ED treatment outcomes. Patients may become increasingly distrustful of the message that "there are no bad foods." EDs are far more heterogenous than the transdiagnostic theory originally proposed, and recent data on FA supports this conclusion. Treatment models must be trauma informed. Food philosophies must be dynamic, continually incorporating new findings. In summary, one size will not fit all in FA treatment, and collaboration with the patient is crucial to develop a mutually agreeable/achievable plan. Steps and assessment tools offered herein may improve the clinical utility of FA and, in doing so, improve quality of life in individuals seeking care.

Author Contributions: Conceptualization and first draft preparation (D.W.). Conceptual contribution and draft revisions (T.B.). All authors have read and agreed to the published version of the manuscript.

References

1. Gearhardt, A.; Corbin, W.; Brownell, K. Preliminary validation of the yale food addiction scale. *Appetite* **2009**, *52*, 430–436. [CrossRef]
2. Gearhardt, A.; Corbin, W.; Brownell, K. Development of the yale food addiction scale version 2.0. *Psychol. Addict. Behav.* **2016**, *30*, 113–121. [CrossRef] [PubMed]
3. Schulte, E.M.; Gearhardt, A.N. Associations of food addiction in a sample recruited to be nationally representative of the united states. *Eur. Eat. Disord. Rev.* **2018**, *26*, 112–119. [CrossRef] [PubMed]
4. Burrows, T.; Kay-Lambkin, F.; Pursey, K.; Skinner, J.; Dayas, C. Food addiction and associations with mental health symptoms: A systematic review with meta-analysis. *J. Hum. Nutr. Diet.* **2018**, *4*, 544–572. [CrossRef] [PubMed]
5. Brunault, P.; Ducluzeau, P.-H.; Bourbao-Tournois, C.; Delbachian, I.; Couet, C.; Réveillère, C.; Ballon, N. Food addiction in bariatric surgery candidates: Prevalence and risk factors. *Obes. Surg.* **2016**, *26*, 1650–1653. [CrossRef]
6. Chao, A.M.; Shaw, J.A.; Pearl, R.L.; Alamuddin, N.; Hopkins, C.M.; Bakizada, Z.M.; Berkowitz, R.; Wadden, T.A. Prevalence and psychosocial correlates of food addiction in persons with obesity seeking weight reduction. *Compr. Psychiatry.* **2017**, *73*, 97–104. [CrossRef]
7. SAMHSA. *Key Substance use and Mental Health Indicators in the United States: Results from the 2018 National Survey on Drug Use and Health [Internet]*; Center for Behavioral Health Statistics and Quality, Substance Abuse and Mental Health Services Administration: Rockville, MD, USA, 2019; (HHS Publication No. PEP19-5068, NSDUH Series H-54). Available online: https://www.samhsa.gov/data (accessed on 1 September 2020).
8. Mies, G.W.; Treur, J.L.; Larsen, J.K.; Halberstadt, J.; Pasman, J.A.; Vink, J.M. The prevalence of food addiction in a large sample of adolescents and its association with addictive substances. *Appetite* **2017**, *118*, 97–105. [CrossRef]
9. Wiss, D.A.; Brewerton, T.D. Adverse childhood experiences and adult obesity: A systematic review of plausible mechanisms and meta-analysis of cross-sectional studies. *Physiol Behav.* **2020**, *223*, 112964. [CrossRef]
10. Mason, S.M.; Flint, A.J.; Field, A.E.; Austin, B.S.; Rich-Edwards, J.W. Abuse victimization in childhood or adolescence and risk of food addiction in adult women. *Obesity* **2013**, *21*, E775–E781. [CrossRef]
11. Mason, S.M.; Flint, A.J.; Roberts, A.L.; Agnew-Blais, J.; Koenen, K.C.; Rich-Edwards, J.W. Posttraumatic stress disorder symptoms and food addiction in women by timing and type of trauma exposure. *JAMA Psychiatry* **2014**, *71*, 1271–1278. [CrossRef]
12. Mason, S.; Santaularia, N.; Berge, J.; Larson, N.; Neumark-Sztainer, D. Is the childhood home food environment a confounder of the association between child maltreatment exposure and adult body mass index? *Prev. Med.* **2018**, *110*, 86–92. [CrossRef] [PubMed]
13. Polk, S.E.; Schulte, E.M.; Furman, C.R.; Gearhardt, A.N. Wanting and liking: Separable components in problematic eating behavior? *Appetite* **2017**, *115*, 45–53. [CrossRef]
14. Linardon, J. The relationship between dietary restraint and binge eating: Examining eating-related self-efficacy as a moderator. *Appetite* **2018**, *127*, 126–129. [CrossRef] [PubMed]
15. Wiss, D.A.; Avena, N.M. *Food Addiction, Binge Eating, and the Role of Dietary Restraint: Converging Evidence From Animal and Human Studies*; Frank, K.W., Berner, L.A., Eds.; Springer Nature: Cham, Switzerland, 2020; pp. 193–209.
16. Meule, A. The psychology of food cravings: The role of food deprivation. *Curr. Nutr. Rep.* **2020**, *9*, 251–257. [CrossRef] [PubMed]
17. Racine, S.E.; Burt, A.S.; Iacono, W.G.; McGue, M.; Klump, K.L. Dietary restraint moderates genetic risk for binge eating. *J. Abnorm. Psychol.* **2011**, *120*, 119. [CrossRef]
18. Freeland-Graves, J.H.; Nitzke, S. Dietetics a of and. position of the academy of nutrition and dietetics: Total diet approach to healthy eating. *J. Acad. Nutr. Diet.* **2013**, *113*, 307–317. [CrossRef]

19. DePierre, J.A.; Puhl, R.M.; Luedicke, J. Public perceptions of food addiction: A comparison with alcohol and tobacco. *J. Subst. Use* **2013**, *19*, 1–6. [CrossRef]
20. Hebebrand, J.; Albayrak, Ö.; Adan, R.; Antel, J.; Diéguez, C.; De Jong, J.; Leng, G.; Menzies, J.; Mercer, J.G.; Murphy, M.; et al. "Eating addiction", rather than "food addiction", better captures addictive-like eating behavior. *Neurosci. Biobehav. Rev.* **2014**, *47*, 295–306. [CrossRef]
21. Schulte, E.M.; Potenza, M.N.; Gearhardt, A.N. A commentary on the "eating addiction" versus "food addiction" perspectives on addictive-like food consumption. *Appetite* **2017**, *115*, 9–15. [CrossRef]
22. Ruddock, H.K.; Hardman, C.A. food addiction beliefs amongst the lay public: What are the onsequences for eating behaviour? *Curr. Addict. Rep.* **2017**, *4*, 110–115. [CrossRef]
23. Rodda, S.N.; Booth, N.; Brittain, M.; McKean, J.; Thornley, S. I was truly addicted to sugar: A consumer-focused classification system of behaviour change strategies for sugar reduction. *Appetite* **2019**, *144*, 104456. [CrossRef]
24. Edwards, S.; Lusher, J.; Murray, E. The lived experience of obese people who feel that they are addicted to food. *Int. J. Psychol. Cogn. Sci.* **2019**, *5*, 79–87.
25. Ruddock, H.K.; Orwin, M.; Boyland, E.J.; Evans, E.H.; Hardman, C.A. Obesity stigma: Is the 'food addiction' label feeding the problem? *Nutrients* **2019**, *11*, 2100. [CrossRef]
26. O'Brien, K.; Puhl, R.M.; Latner, J.D.; Lynott, D.; Reid, J.D.; Vakhitova, Z.I.; Hunter, J.A.; Scarf, D.; Jeanes, R.; Bouguettaya, A.; et al. The Effect of a Food Addiction Explanation Model for Weight Control and Obesity on Weight Stigma. *Nutrients* **2020**, *12*, 294.
27. Latner, J.D.; Puhl, R.M.; Murakami, J.M.; O'Brien, K.S. Food addiction as a causal model of obesity. Effects on stigma, blame, and perceived psychopathology. *Appetite* **2014**, *77*, 79–84. [CrossRef]
28. Cassin, S.E.; Buchman, D.Z.; Leung, S.E.; Kantarovich, K.; Hawa, A.; Carter, A.; Sockalingam, S. Ethical, Stigma, and Policy Implications of Food Addiction: A Scoping Review. *Nutrition* **2019**, *11*, 710. [CrossRef]
29. Moran, A.; Musicus, A.; Soo, J.; Gearhardt, A.N.; Gollust, S.E.; Roberto, C.A. Believing that certain foods are addictive is associated with support for obesity-related public policies. *Prev. Med.* **2016**, *90*, 39–46. [CrossRef] [PubMed]
30. Ifland, J.R.; Preuss, H.; Marcus, M.; Rourke, K.; Taylor, W.; Burau, K.; Jacobs, W.; Kadish, W.; Manso, G. Refined food addiction: A classic substance use disorder. *Med Hypotheses* **2009**, *72*, 518–526. [CrossRef]
31. Ifland, J.; Preuss, H.G.; Marcus, M.T.; Rourke, K.M.; Taylor, W.; Wright, T.H. Clearing the confusion around processed food addiction. *J. Am. Coll. Nutr.* **2015**, *34*, 240–243. [CrossRef]
32. Schulte, E.M.; Avena, N.M.; Gearhardt, A.N. Which foods may be addictive? The roles of processing, fat content, and glycemic load. *PloS ONE* **2015**, *10*, e0117959. [CrossRef]
33. Fildes, A.; Charlton, J.; Rudisill, C.; Littlejohns, P.; Prevost, A.T.; Gulliford, M. Probability of an obese person attaining normal body weight: Cohort study using electronic health records. *Am. J. Public Health* **2015**, *105*, e54–e59. [CrossRef] [PubMed]
34. Fairburn, C.G.; Cooper, Z.; Shafran, R. Cognitive behaviour therapy for eating disorders: A "transdiagnostic" theory and treatment? *Behav. Res. Ther.* **2003**, *41*, 509–528. [CrossRef]
35. Stice, E.; Rohde, P.; Shaw, H.; Desjardins, C. Weight suppression increases odds for future onset of anorexia nervosa, bulimia nervosa, and purging disorder, but not binge eating disorder. *Am. J. Clin. Nutr.* **2020**, nqaa146. [CrossRef]
36. Grilo, C.M.; Masheb, R.M. Onset of dieting vs binge eating in outpatients with binge eating disorder. *Int. J. Obes.* **2000**, *24*, 404–409. [CrossRef]
37. Mussell, M.P.; Mitchell, J.E.; Fenna, C.J.; Crosby, R.D.; Miller, J.P.; Hoberman, H.M. A comparison of onset of binge eating versus dieting in the development of bulimia nervosa. *Int. J. Eat. Disord.* **1997**, *21*, 353–360. [CrossRef]
38. Brewerton, T.D.; Dansky, B.S.; Kilpatrick, D.G.; O'Neil, P.M. Which comes first in the pathogenesis of bulimia nervosa: Dieting or bingeing? *Int. J. Eat. Disord.* **2000**, *28*, 259–264. [CrossRef]
39. Brown-Bowers, A.; Ward, A.; Cormier, N. Treating the binge or the (fat) body? Representations of fatness in a gold standard psychological treatment manual for binge eating disorder. *Health Interdiscip. J. Soc. Study Health Illn. Med.* **2016**, *21*, 21–37. [CrossRef] [PubMed]
40. Dakanalis, A.; Clerici, M. Tackling excess body weight in people with binge eating disorder. *Aust. N. Z. J. Psychiatry* **2019**, *53*, 1027. [CrossRef]

41. Jebeile, H.; Gow, M.L.; Baur, L.A.; Garnett, S.P.; Paxton, S.J.; Lister, N.B. Treatment of obesity, with a dietary component, and eating disorder risk in children and adolescents: A systematic review with meta-analysis. *Obes. Rev.* **2019**, *20*, 1287–1298. [CrossRef]
42. Hunger, J.M.; Smith, J.P.; Tomiyama, A.J. An Evidence-based rationale for adopting weight-inclusive health policy. *Soc. Issues Policy Rev.* **2020**, *14*, 73–107. [CrossRef]
43. Kordy, H.; Krämer, B.; Palmer, R.L.; Papezova, H.; Pellet, J.; Richard, M.; Treasure, J. Remission, recovery, relapse, and recurrence in eating disorders: Conceptualization and illustration of a validation strategy. *J. Clin. Psychol.* **2002**, *58*, 833–846. [CrossRef] [PubMed]
44. Clausen, L. Time to remission for eating disorder patients: A $2\frac{1}{2}$-year follow-up study of outcome and predictors. *Nord. J. Psychiatry* **2009**, *62*, 151–159. [CrossRef] [PubMed]
45. Grilo, C.M.; Pagano, M.; Stout, R.L.; Markowitz, J.C.; Ansell, E.B.; Pinto, A.; Zanarini, M.C.; Yen, S.; Skodol, A.E. Stressful life events predict eating disorder relapse following remission: Six-year prospective outcomes. *Int. J. Eat. Disord.* **2011**, *45*, 185–192. [CrossRef]
46. Treasure, J.; Leslie, M.; Chami, R.; Fernández-Aranda, F. Are trans diagnostic models of eating disorders fit for purpose? A consideration of the evidence for food addiction. *Eur. Eat. Disord. Rev.* **2018**, *26*, 83–91. [CrossRef]
47. Wiss, D.; Brewerton, T.D. Incorporating food addiction into disordered eating: The disordered eating food addiction nutrition guide (DEFANG). *Eat. Weight. Disord. Stud. Anorexia, Bulim. Obes.* **2016**, *22*, 49–59. [CrossRef]
48. Bryant, E.; Rehman, J.; Pepper, L.B.; Walters, E.R. Obesity and Eating Disturbance: The Role of TFEQ Restraint and Disinhibition. *Curr. Obes. Rep.* **2019**, *8*, 363–372. [CrossRef]
49. Meule, A.; Gearhardt, A.N. Ten Years of the Yale Food Addiction Scale: A Review of Version 2.0. *Curr. Addict. Rep.* **2019**, *6*, 218–228. [CrossRef]
50. Meule, A. Food addiction and body-mass-index: A non-linear relationship. *Med. Hypotheses* **2012**, *79*, 508–511. [CrossRef]
51. Granero, R.; Hilker, I.; Agüera, Z.; Jiménez-Murcia, S.; Sauchelli, S.; Islam, M.A.; Fagundo, A.B.; Sanchez, I.; Riesco, N.; Diéguez, C.; et al. Food addiction in a spanish sample of eating disorders: Dsm-5 diagnostic subtype differentiation and validation data. *Eur. Eat. Disord. Rev.* **2014**, *22*, 389–396. [CrossRef]
52. De Vries, S.-K.; Meule, A. Food addiction and bulimia nervosa: New data based on the yale food addiction scale 2.0. *Eur. Eat. Disord. Rev.* **2016**, *24*, 518–522. [CrossRef]
53. Kaye, W.H.; Wierenga, C.E.; Bailer, U.F.; Simmons, A.N.; Wagner, A.; Bischoff-Grethe, A. Does a shared neurobiology for foods and drugs of abuse contribute to extremes of food ingestion in anorexia and bulimia nervosa? *Biol. Psychiatry* **2013**, *73*, 836–842. [CrossRef] [PubMed]
54. Frank, G.K. Altered brain reward circuits in eating disorders: Chicken or egg? *Curr. Psychiatry Rep.* **2013**, *15*, 396. [CrossRef] [PubMed]
55. Hadad, N.A.; Knackstedt, L.A. Addicted to palatable foods: Comparing the neurobiology of bulimia nervosa to that of drug addiction. *Psychopharmacology* **2014**, *231*, 1897–1912. [CrossRef]
56. Donnelly, B.; Touyz, S.W.; Hay, P.; Burton, A.; Russell, J.; Caterson, I. Neuroimaging in bulimia nervosa and binge eating disorder: A systematic review. *J. Eat. Disord.* **2018**, *6*, 3. [CrossRef] [PubMed]
57. Meule, A.; Von Rezori, V.; Blechert, J. Food addiction and bulimia nervosa. *Eur. Eat. Disord. Rev.* **2014**, *22*, 331–337. [CrossRef]
58. Hilker, I.; Sánchez, I.; Steward, T.; Jiménez-Murcia, S.; Granero, R.; Gearhardt, A.N.; Rodríguez-Muñoz, R.C.; Diéguez, C.; Crujeiras, A.B.; Tolosa-Sola, I.; et al. Food Addiction in bulimia nervosa: Clinical correlates and association with response to a brief psychoeducational intervention. *Eur. Eat. Disord. Rev.* **2016**, *24*, 482–488. [CrossRef]
59. Becker, D.F.; Grilo, C.M. Comorbidity of mood and substance use disorders in patients with binge-eating disorder: Associations with personality disorder and eating disorder pathology. *J. Psychosom. Res.* **2015**, *79*, 159–164. [CrossRef]
60. Ivezaj, V.; White, M.A.; Grilo, C.M. Examining binge-eating disorder and food addiction in adults with overweight and obesity. *Obesity* **2016**, *24*, 2064–2069. [CrossRef]
61. Romero, X.; Agüera, Z.; Granero, R.; Sánchez, I.; Riesco, N.; Jiménez-Murcia, S.; Gisbert-Rodriguez, M.; Sánchez-González, J.; Casalé, G.; Baenas, I.; et al. Is food addiction a predictor of treatment outcome among patients with eating disorder? *Eur. Eat. Disord. Rev.* **2019**, *27*, 700–711. [CrossRef]

62. Agüera, Z.; Lozano-Madrid, M.; Mallorquí-Bagué, N.; Jiménez-Murcia, S.; Menchón, J.M.; Fernández-Aranda, F. A review of binge eating disorder and obesity. *Neuropsychiatry* **2020**, 1–11. [CrossRef]
63. Smith, K.E.; Mason, T.B.; Peterson, C.B.; Pearson, C.M. Relationships between eating disorder-specific and transdiagnostic risk factors for binge eating: An integrative moderated mediation model of emotion regulation, anticipatory reward, and expectancy. *Eat. Behav.* **2018**, *31*, 131–136. [CrossRef] [PubMed]
64. Linardon, J.; Messer, M. Assessment of food addiction using the Yale Food Addiction Scale 2.0 in individuals with binge-eating disorder symptomatology: Factor structure, psychometric properties, and clinical significance. *Psychiatry Res. Neuroimaging* **2019**, *279*, 216–221. [CrossRef] [PubMed]
65. Forest, L.N.; Jacobucci, R.C.; Grilo, C.M. Empirically determined severity levels for binge-eating disorder outperform existing severity classification schemes. *Psychol. Med.* **2020**, 1–11. [CrossRef]
66. Andrés, A.; Saldaña, C. Body dissatisfaction and dietary restraint influence binge eating behavior. *Nutr. Res.* **2014**, *34*, 944–950. [CrossRef] [PubMed]
67. Meadows, A.; Higgs, S. Internalized weight stigma and the progression of food addiction over time. *Body Image* **2020**, *34*, 67–71. [CrossRef]
68. Puhl, R.M.; Himmelstein, M.; Pearl, R.L. Weight stigma as a psychosocial contributor to obesity. *Am. Psychol.* **2020**, *75*, 274–289. [CrossRef]
69. Masheb, R.M.; Grilo, C.M. On the relation of attempting to lose weight, restraint, and binge eating in outpatients with binge eating disorder. *Obes. Res.* **2000**, *8*, 638–645. [CrossRef]
70. Canan, F.; Karaca, S.; Sogucak, S.; Gecici, O.; Kuloglu, M. Eating disorders and food addiction in men with heroin use disorder: A controlled study. *Eat. Weight. Disord. Stud. Anorexia Bulim. Obes.* **2017**, *22*, 249–257. [CrossRef]
71. Munn-Chernoff, M.A.; Few, L.R.; Matherne, C.E.; Baker, J.H.; Men, V.Y.; McCutcheon, V.V.; Agrawal, A.; Bucholz, K.K.; Madden, P.A.; Heath, A.C.; et al. Eating disorders in a community-based sample of women with alcohol use disorder and nicotine dependence. *Drug Alcohol Depend.* **2020**, *212*, 107981. [CrossRef]
72. Bahji, A.; Mazhar, M.N.; Hawken, E.; Hudson, C.C.; Nadkarni, P.; MacNeil, B.A. Prevalence of substance use disorder comorbidity among individuals with eating disorders: A systematic review and meta-analysis. *Psychiatry Res.* **2019**, *273*, 58–66. [CrossRef]
73. Tinghino, B.; Lugoboni, F.; Amatulli, A.; Biasin, C.; Araldi, M.B.; Cantiero, D.; Cremaschini, M.; Galimberti, G.L.; Giusti, S.; Grosina, C.; et al. The fodrat study (FOod addiction, DRugs, Alcohol and Tobacco): First data on food addiction prevalence among patients with addiction to drugs, tobacco and alcohol. *Eat Weight Disord.* **2020**, 1–7. [CrossRef] [PubMed]
74. Lu, H.K.; Mannan, H.; Hay, P. Exploring relationships between recurrent binge eating and illicit substance use in a non-clinical sample of women over two years. *Behav. Sci.* **2017**, *7*, 46. [CrossRef] [PubMed]
75. Warren, C.S.; Lindsay, A.R.; White, E.; Claudat, K.; Velasquez, S.C. Weight-related concerns related to drug use for women in substance abuse treatment: Prevalence and relationships with eating pathology. *J. Subst. Abus. Treat.* **2013**, *44*, 494–501. [CrossRef] [PubMed]
76. Bruening, A.B.; Perez, M.; Ohrt, T.K. Exploring weight control as motivation for illicit stimulant use. *Eat. Behav.* **2018**, *30*, 72–75. [CrossRef] [PubMed]
77. Claudat, K.; Brown, T.A.; Anderson, L.; Bongiorno, G.; Berner, L.A.; Reilly, E.E.; Luo, T.; Orloff, N.; Kaye, W.H. Correlates of co-occurring eating disorders and substance use disorders: A case for dialectical behavior therapy. *Eat. Disord.* **2020**, *28*, 1–15. [CrossRef]
78. Cornelis, M.C.; Flint, A.; Field, A.E.; Kraft, P.; Han, J.; Rimm, E.B.; Van Dam, R.M. A genome-wide investigation of food addiction. *Obesity* **2016**, *24*, 1336–1341. [CrossRef] [PubMed]
79. Blum, K.; Sheridan, P.J.; Wood, R.C.; Braverman, E.R.; Chen, T.J.H.; Cull, J.G.; E Comings, D. The D2 dopamine receptor gene as a determinant of reward deficiency syndrome. *J. R. Soc. Med.* **1996**, *89*, 396–400. [CrossRef] [PubMed]
80. Blum, K.; Braverman, E.R.; Holder, J.M.; Lubar, J.F.; Monastra, V.J.; Miller, D.; Lubar, J.O.; Chen, T.J.; Comings, D.E. The reward deficiency syndrome: A biogenetic model for the diagnosis and treatment of impulsive, addictive and compulsive behaviors. *J. Psychoact. Drugs* **2000**, *32*, 1–112. [CrossRef]
81. Blum, K.; Chen, A.L.; Giordano, J.; Borsten, J.; Chen, T.J.; Hauser, M.; Simpatico, T.; Femino, J.; Braverman, E.R.; Barh, D. The addictive brain: All roads lead to dopamine. *J. Psychoact. Drugs* **2012**, *44*, 134–143. [CrossRef]
82. Blum, K. Dopamine genetics and function in food and substance abuse. *J. Genet. Syndr. Gene Ther.* **2013**, *4*, 1–13.

83. Blum, K.; Thanos, P.K.; Wang, G.-J.; Febo, M.; Demetrovics, Z.; Modestino, E.J.; Braverman, E.R.; Baron, D.; Badgaiyan, R.D.; Gold, M.S.; et al. The food and drug addiction epidemic: Targeting dopamine homeostasis. *Curr. Pharm. Des.* **2018**, *23*, 6050–6061. [CrossRef] [PubMed]
84. Hb, C. Common phenotype in patients with both food and substance dependence: Case reports. *J. Genet. Syndr. Gene Ther.* **2013**, *4*, 1–4. [CrossRef] [PubMed]
85. Brunault, P.; Salamé, E.; Jaafari, N.; Courtois, R.; Réveillère, C.; Silvain, C.; Benyamina, A.; Blecha, L.; Belin, D.; Ballon, N. Why do liver transplant patients so often become obese? The addiction transfer hypothesis. *Med. Hypotheses* **2015**, *85*, 68–75. [CrossRef] [PubMed]
86. Kanji, S.; Wong, E.; Aikioyamen, L.; Melamed, O.; Taylor, V. Exploring pre-surgery and post-surgery substance use disorder and alcohol use disorder in bariatric surgery: A qualitative scoping review. *Int. J. Obes.* **2019**, *43*, 1659–1674. [CrossRef] [PubMed]
87. Treur, J.L.; Boomsma, R.I.; Ligthart, L.; Willemsen, G.; Vink, J.M. Heritability of high sugar consumption through drinks and the genetic correlation with substance use. *Am. J. Clin. Nutr.* **2016**, *104*, 1144–1150. [CrossRef]
88. Volkow, N.D.; Wise, R.A.; Baler, R. The dopamine motive system: Implications for drug and food addiction. *Nat. Rev. Neurosci.* **2017**, *18*, 741–752. [CrossRef]
89. Wang, G.-J.; Volkow, N.D.; Logan, J.; Pappas, N.R.; Wong, C.T.; Zhu, W.; Netusll, N.; Fowler, J.S. Brain dopamine and obesity. *Lancet* **2001**, *357*, 354–357. [CrossRef]
90. Wang, G.-J.; Volkow, N.D.; Thanos, P.K.; Fowler, J.S. Similarity between obesity and drug addiction as assessed by neurofunctional imaging. *J. Addict. Dis.* **2004**, *23*, 39–53. [CrossRef]
91. Joutsa, J.; Karlsson, H.K.; Majuri, J.; Nuutila, P.; Helin, S.; Kaasinen, V.; Nummenmaa, L. Binge eating disorder and morbid obesity are associated with lowered mu-opioid receptor availability in the brain. *Psychiatry Res. Neuroimaging* **2018**, *276*, 41–45. [CrossRef]
92. Leigh, S.-J.; Morris, M.J. The role of reward circuitry and food addiction in the obesity epidemic: An update. *Biol. Psychol.* **2016**, *131*, 31–42. [CrossRef]
93. Small, D.M.; DiFeliceantonio, A.G. Processed foods and food reward. *Sciences* **2019**, *363*, 346–347. [CrossRef] [PubMed]
94. Leslie, M.; Lambert, E.R.; Treasure, J. Towards a translational approach to food addiction: Implications for bulimia nervosa. *Curr. Addict. Rep.* **2019**, *6*, 258–265. [CrossRef]
95. Tobore, T.O. Towards a comprehensive theory of obesity and a healthy diet: The causal role of oxidative stress in food addiction and obesity. *Behav. Brain Res.* **2020**, *384*, 112560. [CrossRef] [PubMed]
96. Ramsay, D.S.; Kaiyala, K.J.; Woods, S.C. Individual differences in biological regulation: Predicting vulnerability to drug addiction, obesity, and other dysregulatory disorders. *Exp. Clin. Psychopharmacol.* **2020**, *28*, 388–403. [CrossRef]
97. Carbone, E.A.; Caroleo, M.; Rania, M.; Calabrò, G.; Staltari, F.A.; De Filippis, R.; Aloi, M.; Condoleo, F.; Arturi, F.; Segura-García, C. An open-label trial on the efficacy and tolerability of naltrexone/bupropion SR for treating altered eating behaviours and weight loss in binge eating disorder. *Eat. Weight. Disord. Stud. Anorex. Bulim. Obes.* **2020**, 1–10. [CrossRef]
98. Meule, A.; de Zwaan, M.; Müller, A. Attentional and motor impulsivity interactively predict 'food addiction' in obese individuals. *Compr. Psychiatry* **2017**, *72*, 83–87. [CrossRef]
99. Schulte, E.M.; Grilo, C.M.; Gearhardt, A.N. Shared and unique mechanisms underlying binge eating disorder and addictive disorders. *Clin. Psychol. Rev.* **2016**, *44*, 125–139. [CrossRef]
100. Wolz, I.; Hilker, I.; Granero, R.; Jiménez-Murcia, S.; Gearhardt, A.N.; Diéguez, C.; Casanueva, F.F.; Crujeiras, A.B.; Menchon, J.M.; Fernández-Aranda, F. "Food Addiction" in patients with eating disorders is associated with negative urgency and difficulties to focus on long-term goals. *Front. Psychol.* **2016**, *7*, 61. [CrossRef]
101. Maxwell, A.L.; Gardiner, E.; Loxton, N.J. Investigating the relationship between reward sensitivity, impulsivity, and food addiction: A systematic review. *Eur. Eat. Disord. Rev.* **2020**, *28*, 368–384. [CrossRef]
102. VanderBroek-Stice, L.; Stojek, M.; Beach, S.R.H.; Vandellen, M.R.; MacKillop, J. Multidimensional assessment of impulsivity in relation to obesity and food addiction. *Appetite* **2017**, *112*, 59–68. [CrossRef]
103. Lozano-Madrid, M.; Bryan, D.C.; Granero, R.; Sánchez, I.; Riesco, N.; Mallorquí-Bagué, N.; Jiménez-Murcia, S.; Treasure, J.; Fernández-Aranda, F. Impulsivity, emotional dysregulation and executive function deficits could be associated with alcohol and drug abuse in eating disorders. *J. Clin. Med.* **2020**, *9*, 1936. [CrossRef] [PubMed]

104. Mahoney, C.T.; Cole, H.E.; Gilbar, O.; Taft, C.T. The Role of impulsivity in the association between posttraumatic stress disorder symptom severity and substance use in male military veterans. *J. Trauma. Stress* **2020**, *33*, 296–306. [CrossRef] [PubMed]
105. Wenzel, K.R.; Weinstock, J.; McGrath, A.B. The clinical significance of food addiction. *J. Addict. Med.* **2020**, *1*. [CrossRef]
106. Steiger, H.; Joober, R.; Israël, M.; Young, S.N.; Kin, N.M.K.N.Y.; Gauvin, L.; Bruce, K.R.; Joncas, J.; Torkaman-Zehi, A. The 5HTTLPR polymorphism, psychopathologic symptoms, and platelet [3H-] paroxetine binding in bulimic syndromes. *Int. J. Eat. Disord.* **2004**, *37*, 57–60. [CrossRef] [PubMed]
107. Bruce, K.R.; Steiger, H.; Joober, R.; Kin, N.; Israel, M.; Young, S.N. Association of the promoter polymorphism −1438G/A of the 5-HT2A receptor gene with behavioral impulsiveness and serotonin function in women with bulimia nervosa. *Am. J. Med. Genet. Part B Neuropsychiatr. Genet.* **2005**, *137*, 40–44. [CrossRef] [PubMed]
108. Steiger, H.; Gauvin, L.; Israël, M.; Koerner, N.; Kin, N.M.K.N.Y.; Paris, J.; Young, S.N. Association of serotonin and cortisol indices with childhood abuse in bulimia nervosa. *Arch. Gen. Psychiatry* **2001**, *58*, 837–843. [CrossRef]
109. Steiger, H.; Richardson, J.; Joober, R.; Gauvin, L.; Israel, M.; Bruce, K.R.; Kin, N.M.K.N.Y.; Howard, H.; Young, S.N. The 5HTTLPR polymorphism, prior maltreatment and dramatic–erratic personality manifestations in women with bulimic syndromes. *J. Psychiatry Neurosci.* **2007**, *32*, 354–362.
110. Akkermann, K.; Kaasik, K.; Kiive, E.; Nordquist, N.; Oreland, L.; Harro, J. The impact of adverse life events and the serotonin transporter gene promoter polymorphism on the development of eating disorder symptoms. *J. Psychiatr. Res.* **2012**, *46*, 38–43. [CrossRef]
111. Calati, R.; De Ronchi, D.; Bellini, M.; Serretti, A. The 5-HTTLPR polymorphism and eating disorders: A meta-analysis. *Int. J. Eat. Disord.* **2011**, *44*, 191–199. [CrossRef]
112. Felitti, V.J.; Anda, R.F.; Nordenberg, D.; Williamson, D.F.; Spitz, A.M.; Edwards, V.; Koss, M.P.; Marks, J.S. Relationship of childhood abuse and household dysfunction to many of the leading causes of death in adults. The Adverse Childhood Experiences (ACE) Study. *Am. J. Prev. Med.* **1998**, *14*, 245–258. [CrossRef]
113. Anda, R.F.; Felitti, V.J.; Bremner, J.D.; Walker, J.D.; Whitfield, C.; Perry, B.D.; Dube, S.R.; Giles, W.H. The enduring effects of abuse and related adverse experiences in childhood. *Eur. Arch. Psychiatry Clin. Neurosci.* **2005**, *256*, 174–186. [CrossRef] [PubMed]
114. Bernstein, D.P.; Ahluvalia, T.; Pogge, D.; Handelsman, L. Validity of the Childhood Trauma Questionnaire in an Adolescent Psychiatric Population. *J. Am. Acad. Child Adolesc. Psychiatry* **1997**, *36*, 340–348. [CrossRef] [PubMed]
115. Bernstein, D.P.; Stein, J.A.; Newcomb, M.D.; Walker, E.; Pogge, D.; Ahluvalia, T.; Stokes, J.; Handelsman, L.; Medrano, M.; Desmond, D.; et al. Development and validation of a brief screening version of the Childhood Trauma Questionnaire. *Child Abus. Negl.* **2003**, *27*, 169–190. [CrossRef]
116. McCrory, E.J.; Viding, E. The theory of latent vulnerability: Reconceptualizing the link between childhood maltreatment and psychiatric disorder. *Dev. Psychopathol.* **2015**, *27*, 493–505. [CrossRef]
117. Ehrlich, K.B.; Ross, K.M.; Chen, E.; Miller, G.E. Testing the biological embedding hypothesis: Is early life adversity associated with a later proinflammatory phenotype? *Dev. Psychopathol.* **2016**, *28*, 1273–1283. [CrossRef]
118. Malarbi, S.; Abu-Rayya, H.M.; Muscara, F.; Stargatt, R. Neuropsychological functioning of childhood trauma and post-traumatic stress disorder: A meta-analysis. *Neurosci. Biobehav. Rev.* **2017**, *72*, 68–86. [CrossRef]
119. Ziobrowski, H.N.; Buka, S.L.; Austin, S.B.; Sullivan, A.J.; Horton, N.J.; Simone, M.; Field, A.E. Using latent class analysis to empirically classify maltreatment according to the developmental timing, duration, and co-occurrence of abuse types. *Child Abus. Negl.* **2020**, *107*, 104574. [CrossRef]
120. SAMHSA. *SAMHSA Concept of Trauma and Guidance for a Trauma-Informed Approach*; Substance Abuse and Mental Health Services Administration: Rockville, MD, USA, 2014; (HHS Publication No. (SMA) 14-4884).
121. Dillon, D.G.; Holmes, A.J.; Birk, J.L.; Brooks, N.; Lyons-Ruth, K.; Pizzagalli, D.A. Childhood adversity is associated with left basal ganglia dysfunction during reward anticipation in adulthood. *Biol. Psychiatry* **2009**, *66*, 206–213. [CrossRef]
122. Hoexter, M.Q.; Fadel, G.; Felício, A.C.; Calzavara, M.B.; Batista, I.R.; Reis, M.A.; Shih, M.C.; Pitman, R.K.; Andreoli, S.B.; De Mello, M.F.; et al. Higher striatal dopamine transporter density in PTSD: An in vivo SPECT study with [99mTc]TRODAT-1. *Psychopharmacology* **2012**, *224*, 337–345. [CrossRef]

123. Oswald, L.M.; Wand, G.S.; Kuwabara, H.; Wong, D.F.; Zhu, S.; Brašić, J.R. History of childhood adversity is positively associated with ventral striatal dopamine responses to amphetamine. *Psychopharmacology* **2014**, *231*, 2417–2433. [CrossRef]
124. Hertzman, C. The biological embedding of early experience and its effects on health in adulthood. *Ann. N. Y. Acad. Sci.* **1999**, *896*, 85–95. [CrossRef]
125. Duffy, K.A.; McLaughlin, K.A.; Green, P.A. Early life adversity and health-risk behaviors: Proposed psychological and neural mechanisms. *Ann. N. Y. Acad. Sci.* **2018**, *1428*, 151–169. [CrossRef] [PubMed]
126. McMullin, S.D.; Shields, G.S.; Slavich, G.M.; Buchanan, T.W. Cumulative lifetime stress exposure predicts greater impulsivity and addictive behaviors. *J. Health Psychol.* **2020**. [CrossRef]
127. Brewerton, T.D. Posttraumatic stress disorder and disordered eating: Food addiction as self-medication. *J. Women's Health* **2011**, *20*, 1133–1134. [CrossRef] [PubMed]
128. Cammack, A.L.; Gazmararian, J.A.; Suglia, S.F. History of child maltreatment and excessive dietary and screen time behaviors in young adults: Results from a nationally representative study. *Prev. Med.* **2020**, *139*, 106176. [CrossRef]
129. Imperatori, C.; Innamorati, M.; Lamis, D.A.; Farina, B.; Pompili, M.; Contardi, A.; Fabbricatore, M. Childhood trauma in obese and overweight women with food addiction and clinical-level of binge eating. *Child Abus. Negl.* **2016**, *58*, 180–190. [CrossRef] [PubMed]
130. Hardy, R.; Fani, N.; Jovanovic, T.; Michopoulos, V. Food addiction and substance addiction in women: Common clinical characteristics. *Appetite* **2017**, *120*, 367–373. [CrossRef]
131. Molendijk, M.L.; Hoek, H.W.; Brewerton, T.D.; Elzinga, B.M. Childhood maltreatment and eating disorder pathology: A systematic review and dose-response meta-analysis. *Psychol. Med.* **2017**, *47*, 1402–1416. [CrossRef]
132. Afifi, T.O.; Sareen, J.; Fortier, J.; Taillieu, T.; Turner, S.; Cheung, K.; Henriksen, C.A. Child maltreatment and eating disorders among men and women in adulthood: Results from a nationally representative United States sample. *Int. J. Eat. Disord.* **2017**, *50*, 1281–1296. [CrossRef]
133. Caslini, M.; Bartoli, F.; Crocamo, C.; Dakanalis, A.; Clerici, M.; Carrà, G. Disentangling the association between child abuse and eating disorders. *Psychosom. Med.* **2016**, *78*, 79–90. [CrossRef]
134. Isomaa, R.; Backholm, K.; Birgegård, A. Posttraumatic stress disorder in eating disorder patients: The roles of psychological distress and timing of trauma. *Psychiatry Res.* **2015**, *230*, 506–510. [PubMed]
135. White, A.A.H.; Pratt, K.J.; Cottrill, C.B. The relationship between trauma and weight status among adolescents in eating disorder treatment. *Appetite* **2018**, *129*, 62–69.
136. Rijkers, C.; Schoorl, M.; Van Hoeken, D.; Hoek, H.W. Eating disorders and posttraumatic stress disorder. *Curr. Opin. Psychiatry* **2019**, *32*, 510–517. [PubMed]
137. Dansky, B.S.; Brewerton, T.D.; Kilpatrick, D.G.; O'Neil, P.M. The national women's study: Relationship of victimization and posttraumatic stress disorder to bulimia nervosa. *Int. J. Eat. Disord.* **1997**, *21*, 213–228.
138. Hudson, J.I.; Hiripi, E.; Pope, H.G.; Kessler, R.C. The prevalence and correlates of eating disorders in the national comorbidity survey replication. *Biol. Psychiatry* **2007**, *61*, 348–358.
139. Romans, S.E.; Gendall, K.A.; Martin, J.L.; Mullen, P.E. Child sexual abuse and later disordered eating: A New Zealand epidemiological study. *Int. J. Eat. Disord.* **2001**, *29*, 380–392.
140. Sanci, L.; Coffey, C.; Olsson, C.; Reid, S.; Carlin, J.B.; Patton, G. Childhood sexual abuse and eating disorders in females. *Arch. Pediatr. Adolesc. Med.* **2008**, *162*, 261–267.
141. Johnson, J.G.; Cohen, P.; Kotler, L.; Kasen, S.; Brook, J.S. Psychiatric disorders associated with risk for the development of eating disorders during adolescence and early adulthood. *J. Consult. Clin. Psych.* **2002**, *70*, 1119.
142. Quilliot, D.; Brunaud, L.; Mathieu, J.; Quenot, C.; Sirveaux, M.-A.; Kahn, J.-P.; Ziegler, O.; Witkowski, P. Links between traumatic experiences in childhood or early adulthood and lifetime binge eating disorder. *Psychiatry Res. Neuroimaging* **2019**, *276*, 134–141.
143. Braun, J.; El-Gabalawy, R.; Sommer, J.L.; Pietrzak, R.H.; Mitchell, K.; Mota, N. Trauma Exposure, DSM-5 Posttraumatic Stress, and Binge Eating Symptoms: Results From a Nationally Representative Sample. *J. Clin. Psychiatry* **2019**, *80*, 19m12813.
144. Hazzard, V.M.; Bauer, K.W.; Mukherjee, B.; Miller, A.L.; Sonneville, K.R. Associations between childhood maltreatment latent classes and eating disorder symptoms in a nationally representative sample of young adults in the United States. *Child Abus. Negl.* **2019**, *98*, 104171. [CrossRef] [PubMed]

145. Scharff, A.; Ortiz, S.N.; Ma, L.N.F.; Smith, A.R. Comparing the clinical presentation of eating disorder patients with and without trauma history and/or comorbid PTSD. *Eat. Disord.* **2019**, 1–15. [CrossRef] [PubMed]
146. Gidzgier, P.; Grundmann, J.; Lotzin, A.; Hiller, P.; Schneider, B.; Driessen, M.; Schaefer, M.; Scherbaum, N.; Hillemacher, T.; Schäfer, I. The dissociative subtype of PTSD in women with substance use disorders: Exploring symptom and exposure profiles. *J. Subst. Abus. Treat.* **2019**, *99*, 73–79. [CrossRef] [PubMed]
147. Cuthbert, K.; Hardin, S.; Zelkowitz, R.; Mitchell, K.S. Eating disorders and overweight/obesity in veterans: Prevalence, risk factors, and treatment considerations. *Curr. Obes. Rep.* **2020**, *9*, 98–108.
148. Polivy, J.; Coleman, J.; Herman, C.P. The effect of deprivation on food cravings and eating behavior in restrained and unrestrained eaters. *Int. J. Eat. Disord.* **2005**, *38*, 301–309. [CrossRef]
149. Herman, C.P.; Mack, D. Restrained and unrestrained eating1. *J. Pers.* **1975**, *43*, 647–660. [CrossRef]
150. Racine, S.E.; Hagan, K.E.; Schell, S.E. Is all nonhomeostatic eating the same? Examining the latent structure of nonhomeostatic eating processes in women and men. *Psychol. Assess.* **2019**, *31*, 1220–1233. [CrossRef]
151. Mills, J.G.; Thomas, S.J.; Larkin, T.A.; Deng, C. Overeating and food addiction in Major Depressive Disorder: Links to peripheral dopamine. *Appetite* **2020**, *148*, 104586. [CrossRef]
152. Kiyici, S.; Koca, N.; Sigirli, D.; Aslan, B.B.; Guclu, M.; Kisakol, G. Food addiction correlates with psychosocial functioning more than metabolic parameters in patients with obesity. *Metab. Syndr. Relat. Disord.* **2020**, *18*, 161–167.
153. Xu, H.; Li, S.; Song, X.; Li, Z.; Zhang, D. Exploration of the association between dietary fiber intake and depressive symptoms in adults. *Nutrition* **2018**, *54*, 48–53. [CrossRef]
154. Adjibade, M.; Andreeva, V.A.; Lemogne, C.; Touvier, M.; Shivappa, N.; Hébert, J.R.; Wirth, M.D.; Hercberg, S.; Galan, P.; Julia, C.; et al. The inflammatory potential of the diet is associated with depressive symptoms in different subgroups of the general population. *J. Nutr.* **2017**, *147*, 879–887. [CrossRef] [PubMed]
155. Gómez-Donoso, C.; Sánchez-Villegas, A.; Martínez-González, M.A.; Gea, A.; Mendonça, R.D.D.; Lahortiga-Ramos, F.; Bes-Rastrollo, M. Ultra-processed food consumption and the incidence of depression in a Mediterranean cohort: The SUN Project. *Eur. J. Nutr.* **2019**, *59*, 1093–1103. [CrossRef] [PubMed]
156. Adjibade, M.; Julia, C.; Allès, B.; Touvier, M.; Lemogne, C.; Srour, B.; Hercberg, S.; Galan, P.; Assmann, K.E.; Kesse-Guyot, E. Prospective association between ultra-processed food consumption and incident depressive symptoms in the French NutriNet-Santé cohort. *BMC Med.* **2019**, *17*, 78. [CrossRef]
157. Jacka, F.N.; O'Neil, A.; Opie, R.; Itsiopoulos, C.; Cotton, S.; Mohebbi, M.; Castle, D.; Dash, S.; Mihalopoulos, C.; Chatterton, M.L.; et al. A randomised controlled trial of dietary improvement for adults with major depression (the 'SMILES' trial). *BMC Med.* **2017**, *15*, 23.
158. Lassale, C.; Batty, G.D.; Akbaraly, T. Reply to Veronese and Smith: Healthy dietary indices and risk of depressive outcomes: A systematic review and meta-analysis of observational studies. *Mol. Psychiatry* **2019**, *24*, 1–2. [CrossRef] [PubMed]
159. Davis, L.L.; Uezato, A.; Newell, J.M.; Frazier, E. Major depression and comorbid substance use disorders. *Curr. Opin. Psychiatry* **2008**, *21*, 14–18. [CrossRef] [PubMed]
160. Flory, J.D.; Yehuda, R. Comorbidity between post-traumatic stress disorder and major depressive disorder: Alternative explanations and treatment considerations. *Dialog- Clin. Neurosci.* **2015**, *17*, 141–150.
161. Sadeghi, O.; Keshteli, A.H.; Afshar, H.; Esmaillzadeh, A.; Adibi, P. Adherence to mediterranean dietary pattern is inversely associated with depression, anxiety and psychological distress. *Nutr. Neurosci.* **2019**, 1–12. [CrossRef]
162. Firth, J.; Marx, W.; Dash, S.; Carney, R.; Teasdale, S.B.; Solmi, M.; Stubbs, B.; Schuch, F.B.; Carvalho, A.F.; Jacka, F.; et al. The effects of dietary improvement on symptoms of depression and anxiety. *Psychosom. Med.* **2019**, *81*, 265–280.
163. Gibson-Smith, D.; Bot, M.; Brouwer, I.A.; Visser, M.; Penninx, B.W. Diet quality in persons with and without depressive and anxiety disorders. *J. Psychiatr. Res.* **2018**, *106*, 1–7. [CrossRef]
164. Bozzatello, P.; Rocca, P.; Mantelli, E.; Bellino, S. Polyunsaturated fatty acids: What is their role in treatment of psychiatric disorders? *Int. J. Mol. Sci.* **2019**, *20*, 5257. [CrossRef]
165. Bozzatello, P.; Brignolo, E.; De Grandi, E.; Bellino, S. Supplementation with omega-3 fatty acids in psychiatric disorders: A review of literature data. *J. Clin. Med.* **2016**, *5*, 67. [CrossRef] [PubMed]
166. Cryan, J.F.; O'Riordan, K.J.; Cowan, C.S.M.; Sandhu, K.V.; Bastiaanssen, T.F.S.; Boehme, M.; Codagnone, M.G.; Cussotto, S.; Fulling, C.; Golubeva, A.V.; et al. The microbiota-gut-brain axis. *Physiol. Rev.* **2019**, *99*, 1877–2013. [CrossRef] [PubMed]

167. Cryan, J.F.; Dinan, T.G. Mind-altering microorganisms: The impact of the gut microbiota on brain and behaviour. *Nat. Rev. Neurosci.* **2012**, *13*, 701–712. [CrossRef]
168. Noonan, S.; Zaveri, M.; MacAninch, E.; Martyn, K. Food & mood: A review of supplementary prebiotic and probiotic interventions in the treatment of anxiety and depression in adults. *BMJ Nutr. Prev. Health* **2020**. [CrossRef]
169. Foster, J.A.; Neufeld, K.-A.M. Gut–brain axis: How the microbiome influences anxiety and depression. *Trends Neurosci.* **2013**, *36*, 305–312. [CrossRef]
170. Smith, J.P.; Book, S.W. Anxiety and substance use disorders: A review. *Psychiatric Times.* **2008**, *10*, 19–23.
171. Vujanovic, A.A.; Farris, S.G.; Bartlett, B.A.; Lyons, R.C.; Haller, M.; Colvonen, P.J.; Norman, S.B. Anxiety sensitivity in the association between posttraumatic stress and substance use disorders: A systematic review. *Clin. Psychol. Rev.* **2018**, *62*, 37–55. [CrossRef] [PubMed]
172. Spettigue, W.; Obeid, N.; Santos, A.; Norris, M.; Hamati, R.; Hadjiyannakis, S.; Buchholz, A. Binge eating and social anxiety in treatment-seeking adolescents with eating disorders or severe obesity. *Eat. Weight. Disord. Stud. Anorexia, Bulim. Obes.* **2019**, *25*, 787–793. [CrossRef] [PubMed]
173. Vega-Torres, J.D.; Haddad, E.; Bin Lee, J.; Kalyan-Masih, P.; George, W.I.M.; Pérez, L.L.; Vázquez, D.M.P.; Torres, Y.A.; Santana, J.M.S.; Obenaus, A.; et al. Exposure to an obesogenic diet during adolescence leads to abnormal maturation of neural and behavioral substrates underpinning fear and anxiety. *Brain Behav. Immun.* **2018**, *70*, 96–117. [CrossRef] [PubMed]
174. Burrows, T.L.; Hides, L.; Brown, R.; Dayas, C.V.; Kay-Lambkin, F. Differences in Dietary Preferences, Personality and Mental Health in Australian Adults with and without Food Addiction. *Nutrition* **2017**, *9*, 285. [CrossRef] [PubMed]
175. Benzerouk, F.; Gierski, F.; Ducluzeau, P.-H.; Bourbao-Tournois, C.; Gaubil-Kaladjian, I.; Bertin, E.; Kaladjian, A.; Ballon, N.; Brunault, P. Food addiction, in obese patients seeking bariatric surgery, is associated with higher prevalence of current mood and anxiety disorders and past mood disorders. *Psychiatry Res.* **2018**, *267*, 473–479. [CrossRef] [PubMed]
176. Nolan, L.J.; Jenkins, S.M. Food Addiction Is Associated with Irrational Beliefs via Trait Anxiety and Emotional Eating. *Nutrition* **2019**, *11*, 1711. [CrossRef] [PubMed]
177. Fonseca, N.K.d.O.d.; Molle, R.D.; Costa, M.d.A.; Gonçalves, F.G.; Silva, A.C.; Rodrigues, Y.; Price, M.; Silveira, P.P.; Manfro, G.G. Impulsivity influences food intake in women with generalized anxiety disorder. *Rev. Bras. Psiquiatr.* **2020**, *42*, 382–388. [CrossRef]
178. Tomiyama, A.J.; Dallman, M.F.; Epel, E. Comfort food is comforting to those most stressed: Evidence of the chronic stress response network in high stress women. *Psychoneuroendocrinology* **2011**, *36*, 1513–1519. [CrossRef]
179. Kaplow, J.B.; Widom, C.S. Age of onset of child maltreatment predicts long-term mental health outcomes. *J. Abnorm. Psychol.* **2007**, *116*, 176–187. [CrossRef]
180. Hamilton, K.R.; Mitchell, M.R.; Wing, V.C.; Balodis, I.M.; Bickel, W.K.; Fillmore, M.; Lane, S.D.; Lejuez, C.; Littlefield, A.K.; Luijten, M.; et al. Choice impulsivity: Definitions, measurement issues, and clinical implications. *Pers. Disord. Theory Res. Treat.* **2015**, *6*, 182–198. [CrossRef]
181. Paraskevopoulou, M.; Van Rooij, D.; Schene, A.H.; Scheres, A.P.; Buitelaar, J.K.; Schellekens, A.F.A. Effects of substance misuse and family history of substance use disorder on delay discounting in adolescents and young adults with attention-deficit/hyperactivity disorder. *Eur. Addict. Res.* **2020**, *26*, 295–305. [CrossRef]
182. Ptacek, R.; Stefano, G.B.; Weissenberger, S.; Akotia, D.; Raboch, J.; Papezova, H.; Domkarova, L.; Stepankova, T.; Goetz, M. Attention deficit hyperactivity disorder and disordered eating behaviors: Links, risks, and challenges faced. *Neuropsychiatr. Dis. Treat.* **2016**, *12*, 571–579. [CrossRef]
183. Van Blyderveen, S.; Lafrance, A.; Emond, M.; Kosmerly, S.; O'Connor, M.; Chang, F. Personality differences in the susceptibility to stress-eating: The influence of emotional control and impulsivity. *Eat. Behav.* **2016**, *23*, 76–81. [CrossRef]
184. Brewerton, T.D.; Duncan, A.E. Associations between attention deficit hyperactivity disorder and eating disorders by gender: Results from the national comorbidity survey replication. *Eur. Eat. Disord. Rev.* **2016**, *24*, 536–540. [CrossRef] [PubMed]
185. Ziobrowski, H.; Brewerton, T.D.; Duncan, A.E. Associations between ADHD and eating disorders in relation to comorbid psychiatric disorders in a nationally representative sample. *Psychiatry Res. Neuroimaging* **2018**, *260*, 53–59. [CrossRef]

186. Brunault, P.; Frammery, J.; Montaudon, P.; De Luca, A.; Hankard, R.; Ducluzeau, P.-H.; Cortese, S.; Ballon, N.; Pierre-Henri, P.-H.D.; Nicolas, N.B. Adulthood and childhood ADHD in patients consulting for obesity is associated with food addiction and binge eating, but not sleep apnea syndrome. *Appetite* **2019**, *136*, 25–32. [CrossRef] [PubMed]
187. Testa, G.; Baenas, I.; Vintró-Alcaraz, C.; Granero, R.; Agüera, Z.; Sánchez, I.; Riesco, N.; Jiménez-Murcia, S.; Fernández-Aranda, F. Does ADHD symptomatology influence treatment outcome and dropout risk in eating disorders? A longitudinal study. *J. Clin. Med.* **2020**, *9*, 2305. [CrossRef] [PubMed]
188. Martins-Silva, T.; Vaz, J.S.; Hutz, M.H.; Salatino-Oliveira, A.; Genro, J.P.; Hartwig, F.P.; Moreira-Maia, C.R.; Rohde, L.A.; Borges, M.C.; Tovo-Rodrigues, L. Assessing causality in the association between attention-deficit/hyperactivity disorder and obesity: A Mendelian randomization study. *Int. J. Obes.* **2019**, *43*, 2500–2508. [CrossRef] [PubMed]
189. Jeffers, A.J.; Benotsch, E.G.; Koester, S. Misuse of prescription stimulants for weight loss, psychosocial variables, and eating disordered behaviors. *Appetite* **2013**, *65*, 8–13. [CrossRef]
190. Hudson, J.I.; McElroy, S.L.; Ferreira-Cornwell, M.C.; Radewonuk, J.; Gasior, M. Efficacy of lisdexamfetamine in adults with moderate to severe binge-eating disorder: A randomized clinical trial. *JAMA Psychiatry* **2017**, *74*, 903–910. [CrossRef]
191. McElroy, S.L.; Hudson, J.I.; Mitchell, J.E.; Wilfley, D.; Ferreira-Cornwell, M.C.; Gao, J.; Wang, J.; Whitaker, T.; Jonas, J.; Gasior, M. Efficacy and safety of lisdexamfetamine for treatment of adults with moderate to severe binge-eating disorder. *JAMA Psychiatry* **2015**, *72*, 235–246. [CrossRef]
192. Osadchiy, V.; Mayer, E.A.; Bhatt, R.; Labus, J.S.; Gao, L.; Kilpatrick, L.A.; Liu, C.; Tillisch, K.; Naliboff, B.; Chang, L.; et al. History of early life adversity is associated with increased food addiction and sex-specific alterations in reward network connectivity in obesity. *Obes. Sci. Pr.* **2019**, *5*, 416–436. [CrossRef]
193. McCutcheon, A.R.; Bloomfield, M.A.; Dahoun, T.; Mehta, M.; Howes, O.D. Chronic psychosocial stressors are associated with alterations in salience processing and corticostriatal connectivity. *Schizophr. Res.* **2019**, *213*, 56–64. [CrossRef]
194. Bloomfield, M.A.P.; McCutcheon, R.A.; Kempton, M.; Freeman, T.P.; Howes, O.D. The effects of psychosocial stress on dopaminergic function and the acute stress response. *eLife* **2019**, *8*, e46797. [CrossRef]
195. Nunes-Neto, P.R.; Köhler, C.A.; Schuch, F.B.; Solmi, M.; Quevedo, J.; Maes, M.; Murru, A.; Vieta, E.; McIntyre, R.S.; McElroy, S.L.; et al. Food addiction: Prevalence, psychopathological correlates and associations with quality of life in a large sample. *J. Psychiatr. Res.* **2018**, *96*, 145–152. [CrossRef] [PubMed]
196. Borowitz, M.A.; Yokum, S.; Duval, E.R.; Gearhardt, A.N. Weight-Related differences in salience, default mode, and executive function network connectivity in adolescents. *Obesity* **2020**, *28*, 1438–1446. [CrossRef] [PubMed]
197. Grant, E.J.; Redden, S.A.; Lust, K.; Chamberlain, S.R. Nonmedical use of stimulants is associated with riskier sexual practices and other forms of impulsivity. *J. Addict. Med.* **2018**, *12*, 474–480. [CrossRef] [PubMed]
198. Wilson, B. *Alcoholics Anonymous*; Alcoholics Anonymous World Services, Inc.: New York, NY, USA, 1939.
199. Tylka, T.L.; Wilcox, J.A. Are intuitive eating and eating disorder symptomatology opposite poles of the same construct? *J. Couns. Psychol.* **2006**, *53*, 474–485. [CrossRef]
200. Linardon, J.; Mitchell, S.A. Rigid dietary control, flexible dietary control, and intuitive eating: Evidence for their differential relationship to disordered eating and body image concerns. *Eat. Behav.* **2017**, *26*, 16–22. [CrossRef]
201. Katzer, L.; Bradshaw, A.J.; Horwath, C.C.; Gray, A.; O'Brien, S.; Joyce, J. Evaluation of a "Nondieting" stress reduction program for overweight women: A randomized trial. *Am. J. Health Promot.* **2008**, *22*, 264–274. [CrossRef]
202. Jiménez-Murcia, S.; Agüera, Z.; Paslakis, G.; Munguía, L.; Granero, R.; Sánchez-González, J.; Sánchez, I.; Riesco, N.; Gearhardt, A.N.; Diéguez, C.; et al. Food addiction in eating disorders and obesity: Analysis of clusters and implications for treatment. *Nutrition* **2019**, *11*, 2633. [CrossRef]
203. Fauconnier, M.; Rousselet, M.; Brunault, P.; Thiabaud, E.; Lambert, S.; Rocher, B.; Challet-Bouju, G.; Grall-Bronnec, M. Food addiction among female patients seeking treatment for an eating disorder: Prevalence and associated factors. *Nutrition* **2020**, *12*, 1897.
204. Schulte, E.M.; Gearhardt, A.N. Development of the modified yale food addiction scale version 2.0. *Eur. Eat. Disord. Rev.* **2017**, *25*, 302–308. [CrossRef]

205. Gideon, N.; Hawkes, N.; Mond, J.; Saunders, R.; Tchanturia, K.; Serpell, L. Development and psychometric validation of the ede-qs, a 12 item short form of the eating disorder examination questionnaire (EDE-Q). *PLoS ONE* **2016**, *11*, e0152744. [CrossRef] [PubMed]
206. Garner, D.M.; Olmsted, M.P.; Bohr, Y.; Garfinkel, P.E. The eating attitudes test: Psychometric features and clinical correlates. *Psychol. Med.* **1982**, *12*, 871–878. [CrossRef] [PubMed]
207. Stinson, E.J.; Votruba, S.B.; Venti, C.; Perez, M.; Krakoff, J.; Gluck, M.E. Food Insecurity is associated with maladaptive eating behaviors and objectively measured overeating. *Obesity* **2018**, *26*, 1841–1848. [CrossRef] [PubMed]
208. Rasmusson, G.; Lydecker, J.A.; Coffino, J.A.; White, M.A.; Grilo, C.M. Household food insecurity is associated with binge-eating disorder and obesity. *Int. J. Eat. Disord.* **2018**, *52*, 28–35. [CrossRef] [PubMed]
209. Stanford, M.S.; Mathias, C.W.; Dougherty, D.M.; Lake, S.L.; Anderson, N.E.; Patton, J.H. Fifty years of the Barratt Impulsiveness Scale: An update and review. *Pers. Individ. Differ.* **2009**, *47*, 385–395. [CrossRef]
210. Patton, J.H.; Stanford, M.S.; Barratt, E.S. Factor structure of the barratt impulsiveness scale. *J. Clin. Psychol.* **1995**, *51*, 768–774. [CrossRef]
211. Blevins, C.A.; Weathers, F.W.; Davis, M.T.; Witte, T.; Domino, J.L. The posttraumatic stress disorder checklist for DSM-5 (PCL-5): Development and initial psychometric evaluation. *J. Trauma. Stress* **2015**, *28*, 489–498. [CrossRef]
212. Bremner, J.D.; Bolus, R.; Mayer, E.A. Psychometric properties of the early trauma inventory? Self report. *J. Nerv. Ment. Dis.* **2007**, *195*, 211–218. [CrossRef]
213. Kroenke, K.; Spitzer, R.L.; Williams, J.B.W. The PHQ-9: Validity of a brief depression severity measure. *J. Gen. Intern. Med.* **2001**, *16*, 606–613. [CrossRef]
214. Beck, A.T.; Steer, R.A.; Carbin, M.G. Psychometric properties of the beck depression inventory: Twenty-five years of evaluation. *Clin. Psychol. Rev.* **1988**, *8*, 77–100. [CrossRef]
215. Radloff, L.S. The CES-D Scale. *Appl. Psychol. Meas.* **1977**, *1*, 385–401. [CrossRef]
216. Fydrich, T.; Dowdall, D.; Chambless, D.L. Reliability and validity of the beck anxiety inventory. *J. Anxiety Disord.* **1992**, *6*, 55–61. [CrossRef]
217. Spielberger, C.D. *The Corsini Encyclopedia of Psychology*; John Wiley & Sons: Hoboken, NJ, USA, 2010.
218. Spitzer, R.L.; Kroenke, K.; Williams, J.B.W.; Löwe, B. A brief measure for assessing generalized anxiety disorder. *Arch. Intern. Med.* **2006**, *166*, 1092–1097. [CrossRef] [PubMed]
219. Kessler, R.C.; Adler, L.; Ames, M.; Demler, O.V.; Faraone, S.; Hiripi, E.; Howes, M.J.; Jin, R.; Secnik, K.; Spencer, T.; et al. The world health organization adult ADHD self-report scale (ASRS): A short screening scale for use in the general population. *Psychol. Med.* **2005**, *35*, 245–256. [CrossRef] [PubMed]
220. McDonnell, C.J.; Garbers, S.V. Adverse childhood experiences and obesity: Systematic review of behavioral interventions for women. *Psychol. Trauma: Theory, Res. Pr. Policy* **2018**, *10*, 387–395. [CrossRef]
221. Weinstein, A.M.; Zlatkes, M.; Gingis, A.; Lejoyeux, M. The effects of a 12-step self-help group for compulsive eating on measures of food addiction, anxiety, depression, and self-efficacy. *J. Groups Addict. Recover.* **2015**, *10*, 190–200. [CrossRef]
222. Chao, A.M.; Wadden, T.A.; Tronieri, J.S.; Pearl, R.L.; Alamuddin, N.; Bakizada, Z.M.; Pinkasavage, E.; Leonard, S.M.; Alfaris, N.; Berkowitz, R.I. Effects of addictive-like eating behaviors on weight loss with behavioral obesity treatment. *J. Behav. Med.* **2018**, *42*, 246–255. [CrossRef]
223. Miller-Matero, L.R.; Brescacin, C.; Clark, S.M.; Troncone, C.L.; Tobin, E.T. Why WAIT? Preliminary evaluation of the weight assistance and intervention techniques (WAIT) group. *Psychol. Health Med.* **2019**, *24*, 1029–1037. [CrossRef]
224. Paterson, C.; Lacroix, E.; Von Ranson, K.M. Conceptualizing addictive-like eating: A qualitative analysis. *Appetite* **2019**, *141*, 104326. [CrossRef]
225. Cassin, S.E.; Sijercic, I.; Montemarano, V. Psychosocial interventions for food addiction: A systematic review. *Curr. Addict. Rep.* **2020**, *7*, 9–19. [CrossRef]
226. Romano, K.A.; Heron, K.E.; Amerson, R.; Howard, L.M.; MacIntyre, R.I.; Mason, T.B. Changes in disordered eating behaviors over 10 or more years: A meta-analysis. *Int. J. Eat. Disord.* **2020**, *53*, 1034–1055. [CrossRef]
227. Elsenburg, L.K.; Van Wijk, K.J.E.; Liefbroer, A.C.; Smidt, N. Accumulation of adverse childhood events and overweight in children: A systematic review and meta-analysis. *Obesity* **2017**, *25*, 820–832. [CrossRef] [PubMed]

228. Elsenburg, L.K.; Smidt, N.; Liefbroer, A.C. The longitudinal relation between accumulation of adverse life events and body mass index from early adolescence to young adulthood. *Psychosom. Med.* **2017**, *79*, 365–373. [CrossRef]
229. Vidmar, A.P.; Salvy, S.J.; Pretlow, R.; Mittelman, S.D.; Wee, C.P.; Fink, C.; Fox, D.S.; Raymond, J.K. An addiction-based mobile health weight loss intervention: Protocol of a randomized controlled trial. *Contemp. Clin. Trials* **2019**, *78*, 11–19. [CrossRef]
230. Vidmar, A.P.; Pretlow, R.; Borzutzky, C.; Wee, C.P.; Fox, D.S.; Fink, C.; Mittelman, S.D. An addiction model-based mobile health weight loss intervention in adolescents with obesity. *Pediatr. Obes.* **2018**, *14*, e12464. [CrossRef] [PubMed]
231. Moghimi, E.; Davis, C.; Rotondi, M.A. eHealth treatments for compulsive overeating: A narrative review. *Curr. Addict. Rep.* **2020**, *7*, 395–404. [CrossRef]
232. Bergh, C.; Callmar, M.; Danemar, S.; Hölcke, M.; Isberg, S.; Leon, M.; Lindgren, J.; Lundqvist, A.; Niinimaa, M.; Olofsson, B.; et al. Effective treatment of eating disorders: Results at multiple sites. *Behav. Neurosci.* **2013**, *127*, 878–889. [CrossRef]
233. Manasse, S.M.; Espel, H.M.; Schumacher, L.M.; Kerrigan, S.G.; Zhang, F.; Forman, E.M.; Juarascio, A.S. Does impulsivity predict outcome in treatment for binge eating disorder? A multimodal investigation. *Appetite* **2016**, *105*, 172–179. [CrossRef]
234. Wiss, D.A.; Avena, N.; Rada, P. Sugar addiction: From evolution to revolution. *Front. Psychiatry* **2018**, *9*, 545. [CrossRef] [PubMed]
235. Gordon, E.L.; Ariel-Donges, A.H.; Bauman, V.; Merlo, L.J. What is the evidence for "Food Addiction?" A systematic review. *Nutrition* **2018**, *10*, 477. [CrossRef] [PubMed]
236. Nolan, L.J. Is it time to consider the food use disorder? *Appetite* **2017**, *115*, 16–18. [CrossRef] [PubMed]
237. Brewerton, T.D. Chapter 15 Food addiction and its associations to trauma, severity of illness, and comorbidity. *Compuls. Eat. Behav. Food Addict.* **2019**, 449–468.
238. Brewerton, T.D. An overview of trauma-informed care and practice for eating disorders. *J. Aggress. Maltreatment Trauma* **2018**, *28*, 1–18. [CrossRef]
239. Brewerton, T.D.; Alexander, J.; Schaefer, J. Trauma-informed care and practice for eating disorders: Personal and professional perspectives of lived experiences. *Eat. Weight. Disord. Stud. Anorexia, Bulim. Obes.* **2018**, *24*, 329–338. [CrossRef]
240. Dunn, T.M.; Bratman, S.V. On orthorexia nervosa: A review of the literature and proposed diagnostic criteria. *Eat. Behav.* **2016**, *21*, 11–17. [CrossRef] [PubMed]
241. Michael, J.E.; Bulik, C.M.; Hart, S.J.; Doyle, L.; Austin, J.; Msc, J.E.M. Perceptions of genetic risk, testing, and counseling among individuals with eating disorders. *Int. J. Eat. Disord.* **2020**, *53*, 1496–1505. [CrossRef]

6

Polygenic Score for Body Mass Index is Associated with Disordered Eating in a General Population Cohort

Mohamed Abdulkadir [1], Moritz Herle [2,3], Bianca L. De Stavola [2], Christopher Hübel [4,5,6], Diana L. Santos Ferreira [7,8], Ruth J. F. Loos [9], Rachel Bryant-Waugh [10], Cynthia M. Bulik [6,11,12] and Nadia Micali [1,2,13,*]

1 Department of Psychiatry, Faculty of Medicine, University of Geneva, CH–1205 Geneva, Switzerland; mohamed.abdulkadir@unige.ch
2 Great Ormond Street Institute of Child Health, University College London, London WC1N 1EH, UK; moritz.herle.12@ucl.ac.uk (M.H.); b.destavola@ucl.ac.uk (B.L.D.S.)
3 Department of Biostatistics & Health Informatics, Institute of Psychiatry, Psychology & Neuroscience, King's College London, London SE5 8AB, UK
4 Social, Genetic & Developmental Psychiatry Centre, Institute of Psychiatry, Psychology & Neuroscience, King's College London, London SE5 8AF, UK; christopher.1.huebel@kcl.ac.uk
5 UK National Institute for Health Research (NIHR) Biomedical Research Centre, South London and Maudsley Hospital, London SE5 8AF, UK
6 Department of Medical Epidemiology and Biostatistics, Karolinska Institutet, SE-171 77 Stockholm, Sweden; cynthia_bulik@med.unc.edu
7 Medical Research Council Integrative Epidemiology, University of Bristol, Bristol BS8 2BN, UK; diana.santosferreira@bristol.ac.uk
8 Population Health Sciences, Bristol Medical School, University of Bristol, Bristol BS8 2PS, UK
9 The Charles Bronfman Institute for Personalized Medicine, The Mindich Child Health and Development Institute, Icahn School of Medicine at Mount Sinai, New York, NY 10029, USA; ruth.loos@mssm.edu
10 Maudsley Centre for Child and Adolescent Eating Disorders, Michael Rutter Centre for Children and Young People, Maudsley Hospital, London SE5 8AZ, UK; rachel.bryant-waugh@slam.nhs.uk
11 Department of Psychiatry, University of North Carolina at Chapel Hill, Chapel Hill, NC 27599, USA
12 Department of Nutrition, University of North Carolina at Chapel Hill, Chapel Hill, NC 27599, USA
13 Department of Pediatrics, Gynecology and Obstetrics, University of Geneva, CH–1205 Geneva, Switzerland
* Correspondence: n.micali@ucl.ac.uk or nadia.micali@unige.ch

Abstract: Background: Disordered eating (DE) is common and is associated with body mass index (BMI). We investigated whether genetic variants for BMI were associated with DE. *Methods*: BMI polygenic scores (PGS) were calculated for participants of the Avon Longitudinal Study of Parents and Children (ALSPAC; $N = 8654$) and their association with DE tested. Data on DE behaviors (e.g., binge eating and compensatory behaviors) were collected at ages 14, 16, 18 years, and DE cognitions (e.g., body dissatisfaction) at 14 years. Mediation analyses determined whether BMI mediated the association between the BMI-PGS and DE. *Results*: The BMI-PGS was positively associated with fasting (OR = 1.42, 95% CI = 1.25, 1.61), binge eating (OR = 1.28, 95% CI = 1.12, 1.46), purging (OR = 1.20, 95% CI = 1.02, 1.42), body dissatisfaction (Beta = 0.99, 95% CI = 0.77, 1.22), restrained eating (Beta = 0.14, 95% CI = 0.10, 1.17), emotional eating (Beta = 0.21, 95% CI = 0.052, 0.38), and negatively associated with thin ideal internalization (Beta = −0.15, 95% CI = −0.23, −0.07) and external eating (Beta = −0.19, 95% CI = −0.30, −0.09). These associations were mainly mediated by BMI. *Conclusions*: Genetic variants associated with BMI are also associated with DE. This association was mediated through BMI suggesting that weight potentially sits on the pathway from genetic liability to DE.

Keywords: Avon Longitudinal Study of Parents and Children (ALSPAC); body mass index; disordered eating behaviors; disordered eating cognitions; polygenic scores

1. Introduction

Disordered eating (DE) behaviors [1–3], including fasting, binge eating, and related cognitions (such as body dissatisfaction) are widely prevalent in the general population (14–22%) and are considered behavioral and psychological features of a clinical diagnosis of anorexia nervosa (AN), bulimia nervosa (BN), and binge-eating disorder (BED) [1,4–7]. DE typically arises during pre-adolescence and adolescence [1,7,8] and individuals with DE are at greater risk for mood disorders, psychosocial impairment, and suicidal behavior, as well as at elevated risk for developing a full eating disorder [9,10]. Identification of risk factors that may contribute to DE is an active area of inquiry and may offer new prevention and therapeutic interventions as the current treatment strategies for eating disorders (ED) are limited in their efficacy [11,12].

DE and related cognitions are moderate to highly heritable, with estimates from twin studies ranging between 20–85% making it suitable for genetic analyses [13,14]. Polygenic score (PGS) analyses are an effective method that allow for direct testing of whether common genetic variants associated with one trait are also associated with another [15,16]. PGS approaches to understand DE are of interest as they allow interrogation of the shared genetic etiology of two traits that are associated at the phenotypic level, such as DE and body mass index (BMI) [17,18]. Previous research has highlighted that DE and related cognitions are present across the entire weight spectrum, including AN (at one extreme of the weight spectrum) and BED (often at the other extreme of the weight spectrum) [19]. In addition, children who develop an ED have been shown to follow different BMI trajectories prior to diagnosis [20–22]. More specifically, children who go on to develop AN show consistently lower childhood BMI, whereas children who later develop BED show higher premorbid childhood BMIs [20].

It is well established that BMI has a substantial genetic component [23] with the SNP-based heritability ranging between 17–27% [24]. Recent studies have shown a negative genetic correlation between AN and BMI ($r_g \sim -0.24$) suggesting shared genetic etiology between AN and BMI, whereby genetic variants associated with higher BMI were associated with lower risk for AN [25,26]. However, less is known about the extent to which DE shares genetic etiology with BMI.

The first study to investigate the association between DE and a BMI-PGS found that a BMI-PGS is associated with weight loss behaviors [27]. Nagata et al. reported that the BMI-PGS was associated with a higher odds of weight loss behaviors (e.g., dieting, vomiting) and a lower odds of weight gain behaviors (e.g., eating more or different foods than normal). In addition, Nagata et al. found that the association between the BMI-PGS and weight loss behaviors was mediated by measured BMI; a higher BMI-PGS was associated with a higher measured BMI, which in turn was associated with higher odds of engaging in weight loss behaviors. However, this study [27] investigated the association only in a sample of young adults and evidence is currently lacking in adolescence—a critical period for the development of EDs and DE. Furthermore, this study failed to include pre-morbid BMI (measurement of BMI prior to DE) in the mediation analyses, which complicates establishing potential causal pathways that lead from measured BMI to DE.

In the current study, we investigated whether a BMI-PGS is longitudinally associated with a broad range of DE behaviors and cognitions in a large UK-based population study across adolescence. We hypothesized that the BMI-PGS will be positively correlated with binge eating, emotional eating, and inappropriate compensatory behaviors, such as purging and fasting for weight loss. Based on a previous positive correlation of higher body weight with higher adolescent body dissatisfaction [1] and restrained eating [27,28], we hypothesized that the BMI-PGS will positively correlate with later body dissatisfaction and restrained eating. We also expected a negative association between BMI-PGS and both thin ideal internalization and high external eating—both of which have been found to be negatively correlated with weight or BMI in population-based studies [28,29]. One possible pathway that genetic risk could lead to DE could be through changes in measured BMI which then could lead to increased risk for DE; therefore, we aimed to determine the role of measured BMI as a mediator of these associations. Considering the prospective nature of the data, we also examined developmental differences, determining whether the strength of the association between the BMI-PGS and DE differs across the three time-points during adolescence.

2. Methods and Materials

2.1. Participants

The Avon Longitudinal Study of Parents and Children (ALSPAC) study is an ongoing population-based birth cohort study of 15,454 mothers and their children (that were born between 1 April 1991 and 31 December 1992) residing in the south west of England (UK) [30–33]. From the 15,454 pregnancies, 13,988 were alive at 1 year. At age 7 years this sample was bolstered with an additional 913 children. Participants are assessed at regular intervals using clinical interviews, self-report questionnaires, medical records, and physical examinations. We included children based on three waves of data collection which were at age 14 (wave 14, N = 10,581), 16 (wave 16, N = 9702), and 18 years (wave 18, N = 9505). Further details on ALSPAC are available in previous publications [30,32] and the study website contains details of available data through a fully searchable data dictionary: http://www.bristol.ac.uk/alspac/researchers/our-data/. To avoid potential confounding due to relatedness, one sibling per set of multiple births was randomly selected to guarantee independence of participants (N = 75). Furthermore, individuals who were closely related to each other, defined as a phi hat > 0.2 (calculated using PLINK v1.90b), were removed; this meant removal of any duplicates or monozygotic twins, first-degree relatives (i.e., parent-offspring and full siblings), and second-degree relatives (i.e., half-siblings, uncles, aunts, grandparents, and double cousins). The authors assert that all procedures contributing to this work comply with the ethical standards of the relevant national and institutional committees on human experimentation and with the Helsinki Declaration of 1975, as revised in 2008.Ethical approval for the study was obtained from the ALSPAC Ethics and Law Committee and the Local Research Ethics Committees (Bristol and Weston Health Authority: E1808 Children of the Nineties: ALSPAC. 28th November 1989. for details see: http://www.bristol.ac.uk/alspac/researchers/research-ethics/). Informed consent for the use of data collected via questionnaires and clinics was obtained from participants following the recommendations of the ALSPAC Ethics and Law Committee at the time. The main caregiver initially provided consent for child participation and from the age 16 years the offspring themselves have provided informed written consent.

2.2. Measures

2.2.1. Binary Outcomes

Information on fasting, binge eating, and purging, were assessed at ages 14, 16, and 18 years using questions modified from the Youth Risk Behavior Surveillance System questionnaire [34]. For fasting (N age 14 = 4584, N age 16 = 3844, N age 18 = 2586), participants were asked, "During the past year, how often did you fast (not eat for at least a day) to lose weight or avoid gaining weight?" with the response options "Never", "Less than once a month", "1–3 times a month", "Once a week", and "2 or more times a week". This variable was dichotomized as fasting at least once a month in the previous year versus no fasting [8]. For binge eating (N age 14 = 4144, N age 16 = 3336, N age 18 = 1910), participants were asked how often they engaged in overeating (eating a very large amount of food) in the previous year. Participants who answered this question positively were subsequently asked whether they felt out of control during these episodes. We dichotomized the binge eating variable as eating a very large of amount of food at least once a month (with the feeling of loss of control) versus no binge eating. Regarding purging (N age 14 = 4588, N age 16 = 3871, N age 18 = 2582), participants were asked how often they self-induced vomiting or had taken laxatives (or other weight loss medications) to lose weight or avoid weight gain in the previous year; this variable was then dichotomized as purging at least once a month versus no purging.

2.2.2. Continuous Outcomes

All continuous DE outcomes were assessed at age 14 years and included thin ideal internalization, body dissatisfaction, emotional eating, external eating, and restrained eating. Thin ideal internalization (N = 4496) was assessed using the Ideal-Body Stereotype Scale-Revised with gender-specific items used to assess different aspects of appearance-ideal internalization for boys (six items) and girls (five items) [8,35,36]. The responses were rated on a five-point Likert scale from "strongly agree" to "strongly disagree" and the items from this scale were summed to obtain a total score; a higher score corresponded with increased internalization of the thin ideal Body dissatisfaction (N = 4625) was assessed using the Body Dissatisfaction Scale [36,37]. Participants were asked gender-specific questions rating their satisfaction with nine body parts with responses on a six-point Likert scale ranging from 'extremely satisfied' to 'extremely dissatisfied'. We constructed a continuous score from this scale with a higher score corresponding to higher body dissatisfaction [8,36]. Restrained eating (N = 4530), emotional eating (N = 4345), and external eating (N = 3995) were assessed using a modified version of the Dutch Eating Behavior Questionnaire (DEBQ; [38]). The restrained eating subscale was assessed with two questions, the emotional eating subscale with 14, and the external eating subscale with seven [36,39].

2.2.3. Body Mass Index.

BMI (weight/height^2) was calculated using objectively measured weight and height obtained during a face-to-face assessment at age 11 years (N = 5902) [30–32]. Height was measured to the nearest millimeter using a Harpenden Stadiometer (Holtain Ltd., Crymych, UK) and weight was measured using the Tanita Body Fat analyzer (Tanita TBF UK Ltd., Middlesex, UK) to the nearest 50 g. Age- and sex-standardized BMI z-scores (zBMI) were calculated according to UK reference data, indicating the degree to which a child is heavier (>0) or lighter than expected according to his/her age and sex [40].

2.3. *Genotyping*

Genotype data were available for 9915 children out of the total of 15,247 ALSPAC participants. Participants were genome-wide genotyped on the Illumina HumanHap550 quad chip. Details of the quality control checks are described in the Supplementary Information.

2.4. *PGS Calculations*

PGS were derived from summary statistics of the Genetic Investigation of Anthropometric Traits (GIANT) consortium, referred to as the discovery cohort [41]. The calculation, application, and evaluation of the PGS was carried out with PRSice (2.1.3 beta; github.com/choishingwan/PRSice/) [42,43]. PRSice relies on PLINK to carry out necessary cleaning steps prior to PGS calculation [42,44]. Strand-ambiguous SNPs were removed prior to the scoring. A total of 1,488,001 SNPs were present in both the discovery and in the target cohort. Clumping was applied to extract independent SNPs according to linkage disequilibrium and p-value: the SNP with the smallest p-value in each 250 kilobase window was retained and all those in linkage disequilibrium ($r^2 > 0.1$) with this SNP were removed. To calculate the PGS, for each participant the sum of the risk alleles was taken and was then weighted by the effect size estimated from the discovery cohort. The PGS were calculated using the high-resolution scoring (PGS calculated across a large number of p-value thresholds) option in PRSice, to identify an optimal p-value threshold at which the PGS is optimally associated with the outcome.

2.5. *Statistical Analyses*

2.5.1. Sensitivity Analyses (Linkage Disequilibrium Score Regression)

The discovery genome-wide association study (GWAS) from which the BMI-PGS was derived included participants from the UK Biobank [41]. Considering a potential overlap in participants between ALSPAC and the UK Biobank we performed a BMI GWAS with biological sex as a covariate using PLINK in the ALSPAC sample [44]. Subsequently we determined the genetic covariance with the BMI GWAS [41] using linkage disequilibrium score regression (LDSC) v1.0.0. [45].

2.5.2. Regression Analyses

Logistic regressions models were applied for binary outcomes (e.g., fasting at age 14, 16, and 18 years) and linear regression models were used for continuous variables (e.g., thin ideal internalization) with biological sex and the first four ancestry-informative principal components as covariate in all models. We also tested for an interaction between the BMI-PGS and sex and conducted gender stratified analyses.

As confirmatory analyses, we investigated the association between the BMI-PGS and BMI at age 11 and 18 years and the association between the BMI-PGS and the age and sex standardized BMI (i.e., BMI z-scores) measured at age 11 years. We then investigated the association of DE symptoms at age 14 years, except for purging due to its low endorsement and hence exclusion from our analyses (*N* purging at age 14 years = 74). We repeated the same analyses at age 16 and 18 years for fasting, binge eating, and purging. We report the regression models that explain the largest R^2 or Nagelkerke's pseudo-R^2 at the optimal BMI-PGS *p*-value threshold. For the binary outcome measures we report the Nagelkerke's pseudo-R^2 on the liability scale [46]. Empirical *p*-values were calculated through permutation ($N = 11{,}000$) that account for multiple testing (i.e., number of *p*-value thresholds tested) and overfitting [42]. We additionally calculated False Discovery Rate-corrected *Q*-values adjusting for the number of phenotypes tested [47]. The significance threshold was met if the False Discovery Rate-adjusted Q was <0.05.

2.5.3. Generalized Linear Mixed Models (GLMM)

To understand whether the association of the BMI-PGS with DE differs across the ages (i.e., developmental differences), we used generalized linear mixed models, including BMI-PGS, biological sex, the first four ancestry-informative principal components as fixed effects, and age at self-report as an interaction term. We included random intercepts for each individual in the model, to take into account variance in DE that is due to inter-individual differences. To generate comparable results across the ages, we calculated the PGS at a *p*-value threshold (P_t) of 1 for each behavioral trait at each age.

2.5.4. Exploratory Causal Mediation Analysis

The association between BMI-PGS and adolescent DE could be explained through childhood BMI prior to assessment of DE. We used sex- and age-adjusted BMI z-scores (zBMI) measured around the age of 11 years (prior to assessment of DE and related cognitions) to capture a possible pathway linking genetic liability measured by the standardized BMI-PGS to DE (Figure S1). We estimated the BMI-PGS effects that are mediated and not mediated by childhood zBMI scores using concepts proposed in modern causal inference; the natural direct and indirect effects [48]. The natural direct effect (also known as the "average direct effect", ADE) measures the expected risk difference of the binary outcome measures (e.g., fasting) had the BMI-PGS been hypothetically set to change by 1 SD from 0 to 1, while at the same time childhood zBMI scores had been set to take their natural value (i.e., the zBMI value that would be experienced had the BMI-PGS been set at the reference value of 0, i.e., under no exposure). For the continuous outcome measures (e.g., thin ideal internalization), the ADE measured as the mean difference of the outcome had the BMI-PGS been set to change by 1 SD while childhood zBMI scores were set to take their natural value under no exposure. The natural indirect effect ("average causal mediated effect", ACME) measures the expected risk difference in binary outcome measures had the BMI-PGS been hypothetically set to take the value 1, while at the same time childhood zBMI scores had been set to take their potential values had BMI-PGS been set to 0 or 1. The ADE was defined in a similar fashion for the continuous outcome measures except that the ACME measured the expected mean difference of the outcome. When summed together, these direct and indirect effects give the total causal effects and therefore are useful measures of the contribution made by a particular pathway to a causal relationship.

We estimated these effects, expressed as risk differences/mean differences, using the R package 'mediation' (version 4.4.6; [49]). Our analyses were controlled for biological sex, and the first four ancestry-informative principal components. Furthermore, we assumed that there were no additional unaccounted confounders nor any intermediate confounders [48].

2.5.5. Missing Data

Considering the longitudinal nature of ALSPAC, study participants tend to drop out as time goes on leading to missing data. In our analyses we carried out complete cases analyses (CCA) and to counter potential bias introduced by carrying out CCA we included relevant confounders (sex), as well as BMI-PGS, both of which are related to missingness in our data [50]. Hence estimates are unbiased under the missing at random (MAR) assumption.

3. Results

3.1. Sample Description

Following quality control of the genetic data, a total of 8654 children with genotyping data and at least one outcome measure were included in the analyses (Table 1). Information regarding age, sex, and ancestry for each timepoint can be found in Table S1. Our sensitivity analyses did not find evidence of sample overlap between our discovery (i.e., BMI GWAS; 25) and target cohort (i.e., ALSPAC) using LDSC, as the intercept from the genetic covariance (0.0068) was less than one standard error (0.0103) from zero, suggesting no sample overlap.

Table 1. Descriptive statistics of disordered eating behaviors and cognitions and BMI of the participants in the Avon Longitudinal Study of Parents and Children [a].

			Cases		Controls	
Binary Outcomes	**Age Outcome Measured (Years)**	**Total N**	**N (%)**	**% Female**	**N**	**% Female**
Fasting [b]	14	4584	300 (3.4%)	83.7%	4284	53.3%
Fasting [b]	16	3844	516 (5.9%)	90.7%	3328	53.8%
Fasting [b]	18	2586	143 (1.6%)	93%	2443	62.1%
Binge eating [b]	14	4144	257 (2.9%)	71.6%	3887	53.4%
Binge eating [b]	16	3336	434 (5.0%)	83.2%	2902	55.3%
Binge eating [b]	18	1910	365 (4.2%)	85.2%	1545	62.2%
Purging [b]	16	3871	237 (2.7%)	92.4%	3634	56.7%
Purging [b]	18	2582	166 (1.9%)	90.9%	2416	62.0%
Continuous Outcomes	**Age Outcome Measured (Years)**	**Total N**	**Mean**	**SD**	**Observed Range (min)**	**Observed Range (max)**
Thin ideal internalization [c]	14	4496	15.33	2.69	5	25
Body dissatisfaction [d]	14	4625	21.85	7.75	9	46.3
Restrained eating [e]	14	4530	0.68	1.13	0	5
Emotional eating [e]	14	4345	5.22	5.53	0	28
External eating [e]	14	3995	8.45	3.34	0	21
Age- and sex-adjusted body mass index (zBMI) [f]	11	4037	0.59	1.13	−3.22	3.78
Total sample size [g]		8654				

SD = standard deviation. [a] Full description of the Avon Longitudinal Study of Parents and Children is described elsewhere; [30–33]. [b] Assessed using questions modified from the Youth Risk Behavior Surveillance System questionnaire [34]. [c] Assessed the Ideal-Body Stereotype Scale-Revised with gender-specific items used to assess different aspects for boys and girls [8,35,36]. [d] Assessed using the Body Dissatisfaction scale [36,37]. [e] As measured by a modified version of the Dutch Eating Behavior Questionnaire [38]. [f] Calculated as weight in kilograms divided by height in meters squared. Height was measured to the nearest millimeter using a Harpenden Stadiometer (Holtain Ltd., Crymych, UK) and weight was measured using the Tanita Body Fat analyzer (Tanita TBF UK Ltd., Middlesex, UK) to the nearest 50 g. zBMI was calculated by standardizing BMI by age and sex. [g] Individuals with at least one outcome measurement (e.g., fasting, binge eating, body dissatisfaction) and available genotyping data.

3.2. *PGS Analyses*

3.2.1. BMI

In our confirmatory analyses we found that the BMI-PGS was significantly associated with BMI at age 11 years and 18 years and to zBMI measured at age 11 years (Table S2).

3.2.2. DE Behaviors

The BMI-PGS was positively associated with fasting and binge eating at the ages 14, 16, and 18 years and with purging at age 16 years but not at age 18 years (Table 2, Figure 1). There was no significant interaction between the BMI-PGS and sex. When female participants were investigated separately we found similar effect sizes (Table S3). The effect of the best-fit BMI-PGS on fasting was fairly consistent; for one SD increase in the BMI-PGS children were 1.42 (95% CI 1.25, 1.61), 1.29 (95% CI 1.17, 1.42), and 1.26 (95% CI 1.06, 1.51) times more likely to engage in fasting behavior at age 14, 16, and 18 years, respectively. We did not find evidence for a significant interaction between the PGS-BMI and fasting across the three ages indicating that the effect of the BMI-PGS is not age-dependent.

Table 2. Associations of body mass index polygenic score (BMI-PGS) with disordered eating behaviors and cognitions correcting for biological sex in the Avon Longitudinal Study of Parents and Children.

Binary Outcomes	Age Outcome Measured (Years)	Threshold [a]	N SNPs	R^2	OR (95% CI) [b]	Q [c]
Fasting	14	0.085	33,379	0.021	1.42 (1.25, 1.61)	<0.001
Fasting	16	0.17	43,956	0.012	1.29 (1.17, 1.42)	<0.001
Fasting	18	0.1	36,088	0.008	1.26 (1.06, 1.51)	0.045
Binge eating	14	0.014	17,929	0.010	1.28 (1.12, 1.46)	0.003
Binge eating	16	0.0016	9523	0.006	1.20 (1.08, 1.34)	0.006
Binge eating	18	0.0047	12,708	0.008	1.23 (1.09, 1.39)	0.008
Purging	16	0.00025	6115	0.007	1.22 (1.07, 1.41)	0.02
Purging	18	0.033	23,731	0.005	1.20 (1.02, 1.42)	0.10
Continuous Outcomes	**Age Outcome Measured (Years)**	**Threshold [a]**	**N SNPs**	**R^2**	**β (95% CI) [d]**	**Q [c]**
Thin ideal internalization	14	0.5	66,077	0.003	−0.15 (−0.23, −0.07)	0.003
Body dissatisfaction	14	0.0013	9075	0.015	0.99 (0.77, 1.22)	<0.001
Restrained eating	14	0.1	36,088	0.015	0.14 (0.10, 0.17)	<0.001
Emotional eating	14	0.0091	15,467	0.001	0.21 (0.052, 0.38)	0.046
External eating	14	0.0026	10,780	0.003	−0.19 (−0.30, −0.09)	0.003

SNP = single nucleotide polymorphism; R^2, Nagelkerke's Pseudo squared multiple correlation on the liability scale for the binary outcome measures and the squared multiple correlation for the continuous outcomes; OR, odds ratio; CI, confidence interval. [a] The optimal *p*-value threshold for the inclusion of SNPs in the calculation of the body mass index (BMI) polygenic score (PGS) as determined by PRSice's high-resolution scoring [42]. [b] Odds ratios reflect one standard deviation change in the standardized (to mean zero and standard deviation of one) BMI-PGS. [c] Benjamini & Hochberg False Discovery Rate adjustment for the number of phenotypes tested [47]. [d] Standardized betas reflect one standard deviation increase in the standardized (to mean zero and standard deviation of one) BMI-PGS.

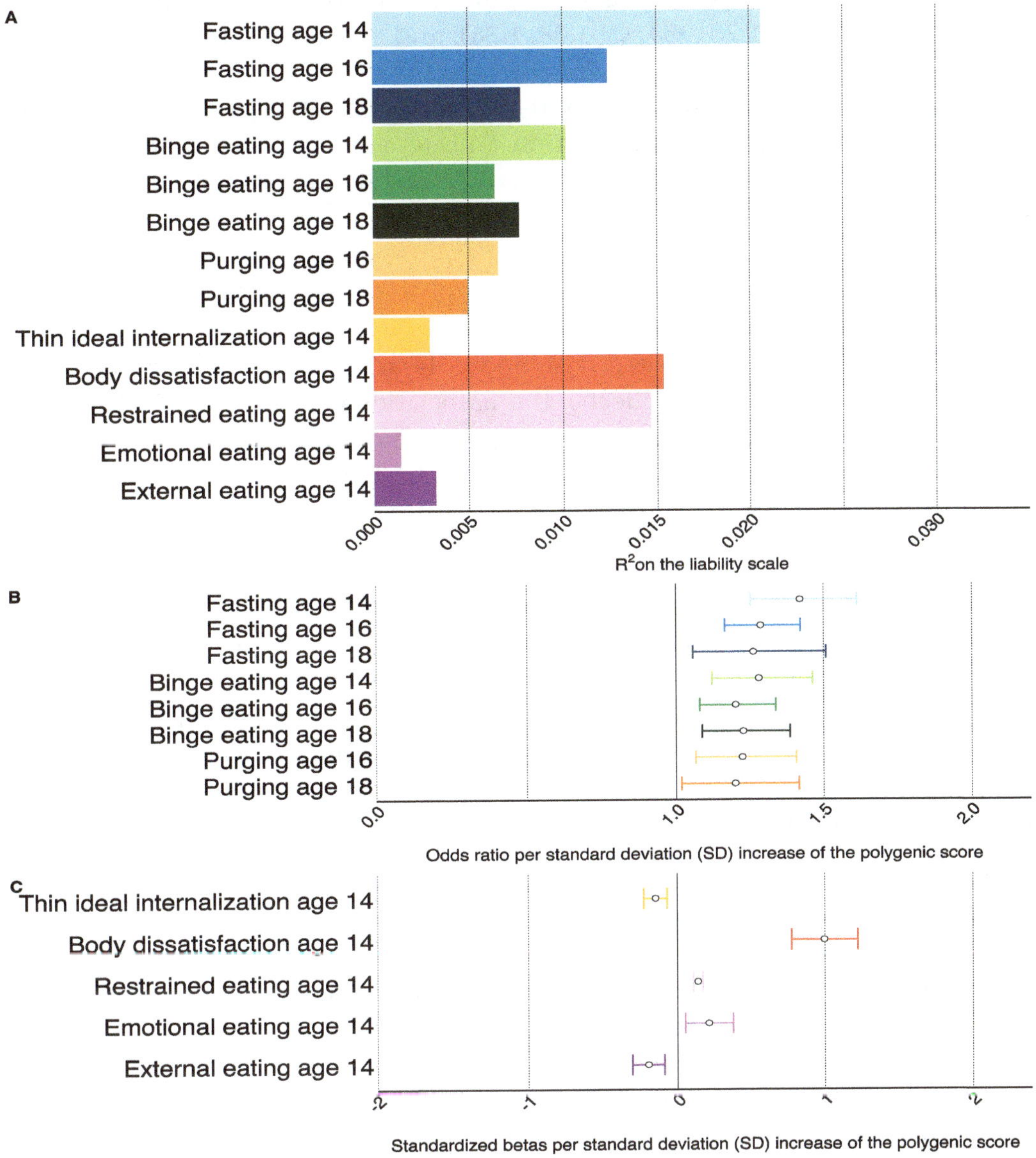

Figure 1. Association between the body mass index polygenic score (BMI-PGS) and disordered eating (DE) behaviors and cognitions in the Avon Longitudinal Study of Parents and Children using generalized linear models [30–33]. Analyses were corrected for biological sex. Age is measured in years. Sample sizes per outcome were fasting (age 14, n cases = 300, n controls = 4284; age 16, n cases = 516, n controls = 3328; age 18, n cases =143, n controls = 2443;), binge eating (age 14, n cases = 257, n controls = 3887; age 16, n cases = 434, n controls = 2902; age 18, n cases =365, n controls = 1545;), and purging (age 16, n cases = 237, n controls = 3634; age 18, n cases= 166, n controls = 2416), thin ideal internalization (n = 4496), body dissatisfaction (n = 4625), restrained eating (n = 4530), emotional eating (n = 4345), external eating (n = 3995). (**A**) Explained variance as measured by Nagelkerke's Pseudo squared multiple correlation (R^2) for the DE phenotypes. All associations were statistically significant (False Discovery Rate-corrected Q-values < 0.05) except for purging at age 18 years. (**B**) Effect size of the association between the standardized BMI-PGS (to mean zero and standard deviation of one) as measured by odds ratios (ORs) and the DE behaviors. The dots represent the point estimates of the ORs for an increase of one standard deviation in the BMI-PGS and the lines represent the 95% confidence interval of the point estimate. (**C**) Effect size of the association between the standardized BMI-PGS (to mean zero and standard deviation of one) as measured by standardized betas and the DE cognitions. The dots represent the point estimates of the standardized betas for an increase of one standard deviation in the BM-PGS and the lines represent the 95% confidence interval of the point estimate.

Children with higher BMI-PGS were also more likely to report binge eating at all three ages with ORs of 1.28 (95% CI 1.12, 1.46), 1.20 (95% CI 1.08, 1.34), and 1.23 (95% CI: 1.09, 1.39), for the ages 14, 16, and 18 years, respectively. Furthermore, the effect of the BMI-PGS on binge eating did not differ across the three ages. Individuals with higher BMI-PGS were 1.22 (95% CI 1.07, 1.41) times more likely to report purging at age 16 years. We did not find an interaction between the BMI-PGS and age at reporting suggesting that the effect of the BMI-PGS did not differ across the reported ages (Table S4).

3.2.3. DE Cognitions

The BMI-PGS was positively correlated with body dissatisfaction and with the DEBQ restrained and emotional eating scale (Table 2). The effect of this association was strongest for body dissatisfaction; children with a higher BMI-PGS (an increase of 1 SD) were more likely to have higher scores on body dissatisfaction at age 14 years ($\beta = 0.99$, 95% CI 0.77, 1.22). This effect was less pronounced for the restrained ($\beta = 0.14$, 95% CI: 0.10, 1.17) and emotional eating ($\beta = 0.21$, 95% CI: 0.05, 0.38) scale of the DEBQ in which a higher BMI-PGS corresponded with lower scores for both behaviors.

In contrast to all other DE outcomes, we found that the BMI-PGS was negatively correlated with thin ideal internalization and with external eating; i.e., individuals with a higher BMI-PGS reported lower scores for thin ideal internalization ($\beta = -0.15$, 95% CI: −0.23, −0.07) and external eating ($\beta = -0.19$, 95% CI: −0.30, −0.09). There was no significant interaction between the BMI-PGS and sex in relation to the DE cognitions. Furthermore, the effect sizes of the association between the BMI-PGS and DE cognitions did not differ (95% confidence intervals overlapped) when female participants were analyzed separately (Table S3).

3.3. *Exploratory Causal Mediation Analyses*

Causal mediation analyses indicated that the zBMI scores mediated the association between the BMI-PGS and DE except for thin ideal internalization (Table 3). Estimate (β_{ACME}) of the average causal mediation effect ranged between −0.11 (external eating) and 0.93 (body dissatisfaction). For almost all mediation models, one standard deviation (SD) increase in the BMI-PGS corresponded to an increase in zBMI scores at age 11 years, which in turn led to an increased probability of endorsing DE. The exception to this direction of effect was external eating; one standard deviation increase in the BMI-PGS led to an increase in zBMI scores at age 11 years, which corresponded to lower external eating scores at 14 years.

Table 3. Exploratory causal mediation analysis of the association between the disordered eating outcomes and the standardized body mass index polygenic score (BMI-PGS) with the age- and sex-adjusted body mass index z-scores at age 11 years as mediator [a]. *p*-values for mediation were generated with bootstrapping methods.

Phenotype	Age [b]	Total Effect Estimate $\beta_{total\ effect}$ (95% CI)	Total Effect *p*-Value	Average Direct Effect β_{ADE} (95% CI)	Average Direct Effect *p*-Value	Average Causal Mediation Effect β_{ACME} (95% CI)	Average Causal Mediation Effect *p*-Value
Fasting	14	0.022 (0.01, 0.032)	<0.0001	0.011 (0.001, 0.022)	0.038	0.011 (0.007, 0.014)	<0.0001
Fasting	16	0.035 (0.019, 0.051)	<0.0001	0.021 (0.005, 0.037)	0.004	0.014 (0.008, 0.019)	<0.0001
Fasting	18	0.014 (0.002, 0.028)	0.02	0.009 (−0.002, 0.024)	0.146	0.005 (0.001, 0.01)	0.03
Binge eating	14	0.01 (−0.001, 0.02)	0.07	0.004 (−0.007, 0.014)	0.464	0.006 (0.002, 0.01)	<0.0001
Binge eating	16	0.015 (0.001, 0.031)	0.04	−0.001 (−0.015, 0.014)	0.95	0.016 (0.01, 0.022)	<0.0001
Binge eating	18	0.028 (0.006, 0.053)	0.01	0.01 (−0.013, 0.034)	0.348	0.017 (0.009, 0.026)	<0.0001
Purging	16	0.011 (0.002, 0.022)	0.02	0.007 (−0.003, 0.018)	0.168	0.004 (0.001, 0.008)	0.006
Purging	18	0.014 (0.001, 0.03)	0.04	0.004 (−0.008, 0.019)	0.494	0.009 (0.005, 0.014)	<0.0001
Thin ideal internalization	14	−0.133 (−0.245, −0.017)	0.03	−0.118 (−0.228, −0.001)	0.042	−0.015 (−0.055, 0.027)	0.47
Body dissatisfaction	14	1.097 (0.819, 1.378)	<0.0001	0.171 (−0.097, 0.439)	0.218	0.926 (0.798, 1.061)	<0.0001
Restrained eating	14	0.161 (0.819, 0.208)	<0.0001	0.03 (−0.014, 0.072)	0.162	0.13 (0.113, 0.149)	<0.0001
Emotional eating	14	0.129 (−0.071, 0.356)	0.26	0.03 (−0.181, 0.269)	0.804	0.098 (0.023, 0.176)	0.01
External eating	14	−0.195 (−0.335, −0.053)	0.006	−0.087 (−0.228, 0.06)	0.212	−0.108 (−0.162, −0.057)	<0.0001

[a] The BMI-PGS was derived from summary statistics of the genome-wide association study (GWAS) carried out by the Genetic Investigation of Anthropometric Traits (GIANT) consortium [41] and were calculated for participants in the Avon Longitudinal Study of Parents and Children [30–33]. The age- and sex-adjusted BMI (zBMI) at age 11 years was included as a mediator in the causal mediation analyses that was carried out using the R package 'mediation' (version 4.4.6; 32) which is based on concepts proposed in modern causal inference [48]. Prior to the mediation analyses the BMI-PGS was standardized and the analysis was controlled for biological sex. [b] Age was measured in years. [c] Measured using the Dutch Eating Behavior Questionnaire (DEBQ; [38]).

4. Discussion

To our knowledge this is the largest study to date that has investigated whether a BMI-PGS is longitudinally associated with DE in a general population cohort (N = 8654). We demonstrate that genetic factors that underlie BMI are also associated with DE suggesting possible shared genetic etiology between BMI and DE. This association was mainly mediated through measured age- and sex-adjusted BMI (i.e., zBMI at age 11 years). Our results mirror findings from epidemiological studies that report higher BMI to be positively correlated with binge eating, emotional eating, restrained eating, purging, fasting, and body dissatisfaction, and negatively correlated with external eating [28,51–55]. The negative genetic correlation between the BMI-PGS and thin ideal internalization is also consistent with findings for AN, reported to be negatively genetically correlated ($r_g = -0.32$) with BMI [25,26]. The non-significant association between the BMI-PGS and purging at age 18 years was likely due to the relatively rare endorsement of purging behavior ($N = 166$) emphasizing the need for larger samples. Furthermore, we did not find evidence for developmental differences; i.e., the strength of the association between the BMI-PGS and DE did not differ across ages.

It is important to emphasize that our study focused on DE as present in a general population cohort, which has important implications in interpreting our findings. Given the high incidence of overweight and obesity [56] in the general population, more individuals than ever could be at risk of developing DE and particularly those with elevated BMI-PGS could be at greater risk. Consistent with our findings, Nagata et al. reported that higher BMI-PGS is positively correlated with weight loss behaviors (e.g., fasting, use of laxatives) in a population cohort [27]. Findings from our group have also previously implicated BMI-related genes in adolescent binge eating in this sample [51]. Taken together, our data and those of others support the notion of a shared genetic etiology between DE and propensity for higher BMI [27,51,57].

Results from our mediation analyses extend previous findings from Reed et al. that reported a causal effect of higher BMI in childhood on increased risk of DE at age 13 years using Mendelian randomization [52]. The importance of BMI in predicting ED has also been highlighted in prospective studies in which BMI trajectories of children who develop an ED during adolescence were found to significantly deviate from children without an eating disorder [20]. We found differences in the estimates of the mediated effect by age- and sex-corrected BMI (zBMI) in the association between the BMI-PGS and DE; suggesting that the effect of actual BMI in late childhood is important for body dissatisfaction, but less for DE behaviors (e.g., purging and fasting for weight loss). As previously shown [1], cognitions such as body dissatisfaction are likely to be influenced by body image distortion and might be more influenced by environmental factors (e.g., comments and teasing about shape and weight). Furthermore, it is important to note that the zBMI scores did not mediate the association between the BMI-PGS and thin ideal internalization. The non-significant mediation for thin ideal internalization might suggest that other pathways apart from prior BMI might account for this association (e.g., environmental factors such as exposure to family or peer factors; [58]). Overall, our findings add to the considerable wealth of literature suggesting an important role for BMI in DE [1,20,25–27,52].

This study benefitted from a large discovery sample ($N \sim 789{,}224$) that included participants from the GIANT consortium and the UK Biobank [41,59] and a relatively large target sample ($N = 8654$). In addition, the availability of a wide range of DE outcomes collected at different time points enriched our analyses. The availability of objectively measured BMI at age 11 years allowed us to investigate the possible role that BMI plays in the association between the BMI-PGS and DE.

Findings from this study should be interpreted in the context of some limitations. Participants were all recruited from the same geographical region in the southwest of England and therefore the results of this study might not be broadly generalizable to other populations. However, the homogeneity of the sample lends itself to genetic analyses as bias from population stratification is expected to be less pronounced [60]. It is important to note that ED symptoms included in this study were derived from self-reports and the questions asked pertained to the previous year, which may have resulted in misclassification and recall bias. However, we emphasize that observational measures on eating behaviors are not feasible in large cohort studies such as ALSPAC. We did not have information on DE behaviors and related cognitions in late childhood; occurrence of these behaviors prior to the measurement of BMI at age 11 years could have biased estimates of our mediation analysis. However, it is likely that prevalence of these behaviors and cognitions would have been very low in late childhood. We also highlight that the focus of our study was on DE as present in the general population and while this information could improve our understanding of threshold ED, caution should be taken when interpreting these results in the context of threshold ED; a proportion of the individuals endorsing DE do not go on to develop an ED. The dichotomizing of categorical behaviors (fasting, binge eating, and purging) might have resulted in grouping less severe cases with more severe cases and in a loss of variance in the outcome which could have weakened our findings. Furthermore, considering the longitudinal nature of the study, participants tend to drop out as time goes on leading to missing data. Attrition (i.e., loss to follow up) in longitudinal studies such as ALSPAC was reported to be associated with higher BMI-PGS [61]. Given what is known about this cohort, we have assumed that the missingness observed in our data was at random, given certain individual characteristics, including the BMI-PGS; for this reason we do not expect substantial bias affecting our complete cases analyses because they included covariates that were related to missingness in our dataset. We acknowledge that some remaining bias might result from selective attrition (i.e., more severe cases dropping out from the study) [50].

The results of our mediation analyses are promising and suggest that joint approaches to the prevention of both obesity and DE might yield better clinical outcomes than those targeting the former or the latter independently [7]. Furthermore, increased awareness amongst pediatricians or general practitioners that children who have overweight or obesity are at increased risk of DE might aid in early screening, detection, and prevention of DE potentially mitigating the development of threshold ED [3]. BMI-PGS can also be used in conjunction with other PGS (e.g., eating disorder PGS) and environmental risk factors in constructing clinical risk prediction models for ED. A robust clinical risk prediction model could for example aid in prediction and guide personalization of treatment, an approach that has shown to be fruitful in many somatic illnesses including coronary artery diseases [62]. However, given the effect sizes observed in this study, the utility of PGS for clinical application for DE is premature.

In conclusion, our results suggest that genetic propensity for higher BMI is associated with DE, and that this association is mediated by actual measured BMI. Our findings add to the consistent epidemiological literature that implicates BMI in DE. The current study has demonstrated that DE and related cognitions need to be understood in a broad context that includes anthropometry as well as behavioral and developmental components. Future research should focus on multifactorial risk and consider the role of environment as well as genetic predisposition to other DE-related traits.

Author Contributions: Conceptualization, B.L.D.S., C.M.B. and N.M.; Data curation, M.H. and N.M.; Formal analysis, M.A., M.H., B.L.D.S. and N.M.; Funding acquisition, N.M. Investigation, M.A., M.H., B.L.D.S. and N.M.; Project administration, N.M.; Supervision, B.L.D.S., R.J.F.L., R.B.-W., C.M.B. and N.M.; Visualization, M.A.; Writing—original draft, M.A., M.H., B.L.D.S. and N.M.; Writing—review & editing, M.A., M.H., B.L.D.S., C.H., D.L.S.F., R.J.F.L., R.B.-W., C.M.B. and N.M. All authors have read and agreed to the published version of the manuscript.

Acknowledgments: We wish to thank the Genetic Investigation of Anthropometric Traits (GIANT) consortium for providing the summary statistics of the GWAS on BMI. We are also extremely grateful to all the families who took part in the ALSPAC study, the midwives for their help in recruiting them, and the whole ALSPAC team, which includes interviewers, computer and laboratory technicians, clerical workers, research scientists, volunteers, managers, receptionists, and nurses.

References

1. Micali, N.; De Stavola, B.; Ploubidis, G.; Simonoff, E.; Treasure, J.; Field, A.E. Adolescent eating disorder behaviours and cognitions: Gender-specific effects of child, maternal and family risk factors. *Br. J. Psychiatry* **2015**, *207*, 320–327. [CrossRef] [PubMed]
2. Micali, N.; Horton, N.J.; Crosby, R.D.; Swanson, S.A.; Sonneville, K.R.; Solmi, F.; Calzo, J.P.; Eddy, K.T.; Field, A.E. Eating disorder behaviours amongst adolescents: Investigating classification, persistence and prospective associations with adverse outcomes using latent class models. *Eur. Child Adolesc. Psychiatry* **2017**, *26*, 231–240. [CrossRef] [PubMed]

3. Hayes, J.F.; Fitzsimmons-Craft, E.E.; Karam, A.M.; Jakubiak, J.; Brown, M.L.; Wilfley, D.E. Disordered Eating Attitudes and Behaviors in Youth with Overweight and Obesity: Implications for Treatment. *Curr. Obes. Rep.* **2018**, *7*, 235–246. [CrossRef] [PubMed]
4. Swanson, S.A.; Crow, S.J.; Le Grange, D.; Swendsen, J.; Merikangas, K.R. Prevalence and Correlates of Eating Disorders in Adolescents. *Arch. Gen. Psychiatry* **2011**, *68*, 714–723. [CrossRef]
5. Field, A.E.; Sonneville, K.R.; Micali, N.; Crosby, R.D.; Swanson, S.A.; Laird, N.M.; Treasure, J.; Solmi, F.; Horton, N.J. Prospective Association of Common Eating Disorders and Adverse Outcomes. *Pediatrics* **2012**, *130*, e289–e295. [CrossRef]
6. Solmi, F.; Sonneville, K.R.; Easter, A.; Horton, N.J.; Crosby, R.D.; Treasure, J.; Rodriguez, A.; Jarvelin, M.R.; Field, A.E.; Micali, N. Prevalence of purging at age 16 and associations with negative outcomes among girls in three community-based cohorts. *J. Child Psychol. Psychiatry Allied Discip.* **2015**, *56*, 87–96. [CrossRef]
7. Neumark-Sztainer, D.; Wall, M.; Guo, J.; Story, M.; Haines, J.; Eisenberg, M. Obesity, disordered eating, and eating disorders in a longitudinal study of adolescents: How do dieters fare 5 years later? *J. Am. Diet. Assoc.* **2006**, *106*, 559–568. [CrossRef] [PubMed]
8. Micali, N.; Solmi, F.; Horton, N.J.; Crosby, R.D.; Eddy, K.T.; Calzo, J.P.; Sonneville, K.R.; Swanson, S.A.; Field, A.E. Adolescent Eating Disorders Predict Psychiatric, High-Risk Behaviors and Weight Outcomes in Young Adulthood. *J. Am. Acad. Child Adolesc. Psychiatry* **2015**, *54*, 652–659.e1. [CrossRef]
9. Crow, S.; Eisenberg, M.E.; Story, M.; Neumark-Sztainer, D. Are body dissatisfaction, eating disturbance, and body mass index predictors of suicidal behavior in adolescents? A longitudinal study. *J. Consult. Clin. Psychol.* **2008**, *76*, 887–892. [CrossRef]
10. Chamay-Weber, C.; Narring, F.; Michaud, P.-A. Partial eating disorders among adolescents: A review. *J. Adolesc. Heal.* **2005**, *37*, 416–426. [CrossRef]
11. Berkman, N.; Bulik, C.; Brownley, K.; Lohr, K.; Sedway, J.; Rooks, A.; Gartlehner, G. *Management of Eating Disorders. Evidence Report/Technology Assessment No. 135*; (Prepared by the RTI International-University of North Carolina Evidence-Based Practice Center under Contract No. 290-02-0016.) AHRQ Publication No. 06-E010; Agency for Healthcare Research and Quality: Rockville, MD, USA, 2006.
12. Keel, P.K.; Haedt, A. Evidence-Based Psychosocial Treatments for Eating Problems and Eating Disorders. *J. Clin. Child Adolesc. Psychol.* **2008**, *37*, 39–61. [CrossRef] [PubMed]
13. Culbert, K.M.; Racine, S.E.; Klump, K.L. Research Review: What we have learned about the causes of eating disorders—A synthesis of sociocultural, psychological, and biological research. *J. Child Psychol. Psychiatry* **2015**, *56*, 1141–1164. [CrossRef] [PubMed]
14. Culbert, K.M.; Racine, S.E.; Klump, K.L. The influence of gender and puberty on the heritability of disordered eating symptoms. In *Behavioral neurobiology of eating disorders*; Springer: Berlin/Heidelberg, Germany, 2010; pp. 177–185.
15. Martin, A.R.; Daly, M.J.; Robinson, E.B.; Hyman, S.E.; Neale, B.M. Predicting Polygenic Risk of Psychiatric Disorders. *Biol. Psychiatry* **2019**, *86*, 97–109. [CrossRef] [PubMed]
16. Choi, S.W.; Shin, T.; Mak, H.; Reilly, P.F.O. A guide to performing Polygenic Risk Score analyses. *bioRxiv* **2018**, *5*, 11–13.
17. Tanofsky-Kraff, M.; Yanovski, S.Z.; Wilfley, D.E.; Marmarosh, C.; Morgan, C.M.; Yanovski, J.A. Eating-Disordered Behaviors, Body Fat, and Psychopathology in Overweight and Normal-Weight Children. *J. Consult. Clin. Psychol.* **2004**, *72*, 53–61. [CrossRef] [PubMed]
18. Torstveit, M.K.; Aagedal-Mortensen, K.; Stea, T.H. More than half of high school students report disordered eating: A cross sectional study among Norwegian boys and girls. *PLoS ONE* **2015**, *10*, 1–15. [CrossRef]
19. Flament, M.F.; Henderson, K.; Buchholz, A.; Obeid, N.; Nguyen, H.N.T.; Birmingham, M.; Goldfield, G. Weight Status and DSM-5 Diagnoses of Eating Disorders in Adolescents from the Community. *J. Am. Acad. Child Adolesc. Psychiatry* **2015**, *54*, 403–411.e2. [CrossRef]
20. Yilmaz, Z.; Gottfredson, N.C.; Zerwas, S.C.; Bulik, C.M.; Micali, N. Developmental Premorbid Body Mass Index Trajectories of Adolescents with Eating Disorders in a Longitudinal Population Cohort. *J. Am. Acad. Child Adolesc. Psychiatry* **2019**, *58*, 191–199. [CrossRef]
21. Herle, M.; De Stavola, B.; Hübel, C.; Abdulkadir, M.; Ferreira, D.S.; Loos, R.J.F.; Bryant-Waugh, R.; Bulik, C.M.; Micali, N. A longitudinal study of eating behaviours in childhood and later eating disorder behaviours and diagnoses. *Br. J. Psychiatry* **2019**, 1–7. [CrossRef]

22. Föcker, M.; Bühren, K.; Timmesfeld, N.; Dempfle, A.; Knoll, S.; Schwarte, R.; Egberts, K.M.; Pfeiffer, E.; Fleischhaker, C.; Wewetzer, C.; et al. The relationship between premorbid body weight and weight at referral, at discharge and at 1-year follow-up in anorexia nervosa. *Eur. Child Adolesc. Psychiatry* **2015**, *24*, 537–544. [CrossRef]
23. Albuquerque, D.; Stice, E.; Rodríguez, R.; Licíno, L.-R.; Manco, L.; Nóbrega, C. Current review of genetics of human obesity: From molecular mechanisms to an evolutionary perspective. *Mol. Genet. Genomics* **2015**, *290*, 1191–1221. [CrossRef] [PubMed]
24. Khera, A.V.; Chaffin, M.; Wade, K.H.; Zahid, S.; Brancale, J.; Xia, R.; Distefano, M.; Senol-Cosar, O.; Haas, M.E.; Bick, A.; et al. Polygenic Prediction of Weight and Obesity Trajectories from Birth to Adulthood. *Cell* **2019**, *177*, 587–596.e9. [CrossRef] [PubMed]
25. Watson, H.J.; Yilmaz, Z.; Thornton, L.M.; Hübel, C.; Coleman, J.R.I.I.; Gaspar, H.A.; Bryois, J.; Hinney, A.; Leppä, V.M.; Mattheisen, M.; et al. Genome-wide association study identifies eight risk loci and implicates metabo-psychiatric origins for anorexia nervosa. *Nat. Genet.* **2019**, *51*, 1207–1214. [CrossRef] [PubMed]
26. Duncan, L.; Yilmaz, Z.; Gaspar, H.; Walters, R.; Goldstein, J.; Anttila, V.; Bulik-Sullivan, B.; Ripke, S.; Thornton, L.; Hinney, A.; et al. Significant locus and metabolic genetic correlations revealed in genome-wide association study of anorexia nervosa. *Am. J. Psychiatry* **2017**, *174*, 850–858. [CrossRef]
27. Nagata, J.M.; Braudt, D.B.; Domingue, B.W.; Bibbins-Domingo, K.; Garber, A.K.; Griffiths, S.; Murray, S.B. Genetic risk, body mass index, and weight control behaviors: Unlocking the triad. *Int. J. Eat. Disord.* **2019**, *52*, 825–833. [CrossRef]
28. Snoek, H.M.; Engels, R.C.M.E.; van Strien, T.; Otten, R. Emotional, external and restrained eating behaviour and BMI trajectories in adolescence. *Appetite* **2013**, *67*, 81–87. [CrossRef]
29. Juarascio, A.S.; Forman, E.M.; Timko, C.A.; Herbert, J.D.; Butryn, M.; Lowe, M. Implicit internalization of the thin ideal as a predictor of increases in weight, body dissatisfaction, and disordered eating. *Eat. Behav.* **2011**, *12*, 207–213. [CrossRef]
30. Fraser, A.; Macdonald-wallis, C.; Tilling, K.; Boyd, A.; Golding, J.; Davey smith, G.; Henderson, J.; Macleod, J.; Molloy, L.; Ness, A.; et al. Cohort profile: The avon longitudinal study of parents and children: ALSPAC mothers cohort. *Int. J. Epidemiol.* **2013**, *42*, 97–110. [CrossRef]
31. Golding; Pembrey; Jones; The Alspac Study Team ALSPAC-The Avon Longitudinal Study of Parents and Children. *Paediatr. Perinat. Epidemiol.* **2001**, *15*, 74–87. [CrossRef]
32. Golding, J.; Team, S. The Avon Longitudinal Study of Parents and Children (ALSPAC) – Study design and collaborative opportunities. *Eur. J. Endocrinol.* **2004**, *151* (Suppl. 3), U119–U123. [CrossRef] [PubMed]
33. Boyd, A.; Golding, J.; Macleod, J.; Lawlor, D.A.; Fraser, A.; Henderson, J.; Molloy, L.; Ness, A.; Ring, S.; Smith, G.D. Cohort profile: The 'Children of the 90s'-The index offspring of the avon longitudinal study of parents and children. *Int. J. Epidemiol.* **2013**, *42*, 111–127. [CrossRef] [PubMed]
34. Kann, L.; Warren, C.W.; Harris, W.A.; Collins, J.L.; Williams, B.I.; Ross, J.G.; Kolbe, L.J. Youth Risk Behavior Surveillance-United States, 1995. *J. Sch. Health* **1996**, *66*, 365–377. [CrossRef] [PubMed]
35. Stice, E. Modeling of eating pathology and social reinforcement of the thin-ideal predict onset of bulimic symptoms. *Behav. Res. Ther.* **1998**, *36*, 931–944. [CrossRef]
36. Calzo, J.P.; Austin, S.B.; Micali, N. Sexual orientation disparities in eating disorder symptoms among adolescent boys and girls in the UK. *Eur. Child Adolesc. Psychiatry* **2018**, *27*, 1–8. [CrossRef]
37. Stice, E. A prospective test of the dual-pathway model of bulimic pathology: Mediating effects of dieting and negative affect. *J. Abnorm. Psychol.* **2001**, *110*, 124–135. [CrossRef]
38. van Strien, T.; Frijters, J.E.R.; Bergers, G.P.A.; Defares, P.B. The Dutch Eating Behavior Questionnaire (DEBQ) for assessment of restrained, emotional, and external eating behavior. *Int. J. Eat. Disord.* **1986**, *5*, 295–315. [CrossRef]
39. Schaumberg, K.; Zerwas, S.; Goodman, E.; Yilmaz, Z.; Bulik, C.M.; Micali, N. Anxiety disorder symptoms at age 10 predict eating disorder symptoms and diagnoses in adolescence. *J. Child Psychol. Psychiatry Allied Discip.* **2018**. [CrossRef]
40. Cole, T.J.; Bellizzi, M.; Flegal, K.; Dietz, W. Establishing a standard definition for child overweight and obesity worldwide: International survey. *BMJ* **2000**, *320*, 1240. [CrossRef]
41. Yengo, L.; Sidorenko, J.; Kemper, K.E.; Zheng, Z.; Wood, A.R.; Weedon, M.N.; Frayling, T.M.; Hirschhorn, J.; Yang, J.; Visscher, P.M. Meta-analysis of genome-wide association studies for height and body mass index in ~700000 individuals of European ancestry. *Hum. Mol. Genet.* **2018**, *27*, 3641–3649. [CrossRef]

42. Euesden, J.; Lewis, C.M.; O'Reilly, P.F. PRSice: Polygenic Risk Score software. *Bioinformatics* **2015**, *31*, 1466–1468. [CrossRef]
43. Choi, S.W.; O'Reilly, P.F. PRSice-2: Polygenic Risk Score software for biobank-scale data. *Gigascience* **2019**, *8*, 1–6. [CrossRef] [PubMed]
44. Purcell, S.; Neale, B.; Todd-Brown, K.; Thomas, L.; Ferreira, M.A.R.; Bender, D.; Maller, J.; Sklar, P.; de Bakker, P.I.W.; Daly, M.J.; et al. PLINK: A tool set for whole-genome association and population-based linkage analyses. *Am. J. Hum. Genet.* **2007**, *81*, 559–575. [CrossRef] [PubMed]
45. Bulik-Sullivan, B.; Loh, P.R.; Finucane, H.K.; Ripke, S.; Yang, J.; Patterson, N.; Daly, M.J.; Price, A.L.; Neale, B.M.; Corvin, A.; et al. LD score regression distinguishes confounding from polygenicity in genome-wide association studies. *Nat. Genet.* **2015**, *47*, 291–295. [CrossRef] [PubMed]
46. Lee, S.H.; Goddard, M.E.; Wray, N.R.; Visscher, P.M. A better coefficient of determination for genetic profile analysis. *Genet. Epidemiol.* **2012**, *36*, 214–224. [CrossRef]
47. Benjamini, Y.; Hochberg, Y. Controlling the False Discovery Rate: A Practical and Powerful Approach to Multiple Testing. *J. R. Stat. Soc. Ser. B* **1995**, *57*, 289–300. [CrossRef]
48. VanderWeele, T. *Explanation in Causal Inference: Methods for Mediation and Interaction*; Oxford University Press: Oxford, UK, 2015.
49. Tingley, D.; Yamamoto, T.; Hirose, K.; Keele, L.; Imai, K. mediation: R Package for Causal Mediation Analysis. *J. Stat. Softw.* **2014**, *59*, 1–38. [CrossRef]
50. White, I.R.; Carlin, J.B. Bias and efficiency of multiple imputation compared with complete-case analysis for missing covariate values. *Stat. Med.* **2010**, *29*, 2920–2931. [CrossRef]
51. Micali, N.; Field, A.E.; Treasure, J.L.; Evans, D.M. Are obesity risk genes associated with binge eating in adolescence? *Obesity* **2015**, *23*, 1729–1736. [CrossRef]
52. Reed, Z.E.; Micali, N.; Bulik, C.M.; Davey Smith, G.; Wade, K.H. Assessing the causal role of adiposity on disordered eating in childhood, adolescence, and adulthood: A Mendelian randomization analysis. *Am. J. Clin. Nutr.* **2017**, ajcn154104. [CrossRef]
53. Bucchianeri, M.M.; Arikian, A.J.; Hannan, P.J.; Eisenberg, M.E.; Neumark-Sztainer, D. Body dissatisfaction from adolescence to young adulthood: Findings from a 10-year longitudinal study. *Body Image* **2013**, *10*, 1–7. [CrossRef]
54. Keel, P.K.; Baxter, M.G.; Heatherton, T.F.; Joiner, T.E. A 20-year longitudinal study of body weight, dieting, and eating disorder symptoms. *J. Abnorm. Psychol.* **2007**, *116*, 422–432. [CrossRef] [PubMed]
55. Stice, E.; Gau, J.M.; Rohde, P.; Shaw, H. Risk factors that predict future onset of each DSM–5 eating disorder: Predictive specificity in high-risk adolescent females. *J. Abnorm. Psychol.* **2017**, *126*, 38–51. [CrossRef] [PubMed]
56. Bentham, J.; Di Cesare, M.; Bilano, V.; Bixby, H.; Zhou, B.; Stevens, G.A.; Riley, L.M.; Taddei, C.; Hajifathalian, K.; Lu, Y.; et al. Worldwide trends in body-mass index, underweight, overweight, and obesity from 1975 to 2016: A pooled analysis of 2416 population-based measurement studies in 128·9 million children, adolescents, and adults. *Lancet* **2017**, *390*, 2627–2642.
57. Hinney, A.; Kesselmeier, M.; Jall, S.; Volckmar, A.-L.; Föcker, M.; Antel, J.; Heid, I.M.; Winkler, T.W.; Grant, S.F.A.; Guo, Y.; et al. Evidence for three genetic loci involved in both anorexia nervosa risk and variation of body mass index. *Mol. Psychiatry* **2017**, *22*, 192–201. [CrossRef]
58. Field, A.E.; Javaras, K.M.; Aneja, P.; Kitos, N.; Camargo, C.A.; Taylor, C.B.; Laird, N.M. Family, Peer, and Media Predictors of Becoming Eating Disordered. *Arch. Pediatr. Adolesc. Med.* **2008**, *162*, 574. [CrossRef]
59. Bycroft, C.; Freeman, C.; Petkova, D.; Band, G.; Elliott, L.T.; Sharp, K.; Motyer, A.; Vukcevic, D.; Delaneau, O.; O'Connell, J.; et al. The UK Biobank resource with deep phenotyping and genomic data. *Nature* **2018**, *562*, 203–209. [CrossRef]
60. Hellwege, J.N.; Keaton, J.M.; Giri, A.; Gao, X.; Velez Edwards, D.R.; Edwards, T.L. Population Stratification in Genetic Association Studies. *Curr. Protoc. Hum. Genet.* **2017**, *95*, 1.22.1–1.22.23. [CrossRef]
61. Taylor, A.E.; Jones, H.J.; Sallis, H.; Euesden, J.; Stergiakouli, E.; Davies, N.M.; Zammit, S.; Lawlor, D.A.; Munafò, M.R.; Smith, G.D.; et al. Exploring the association of genetic factors with participation in the Avon Longitudinal Study of Parents and Children. *Int. J. Epidemiol.* **2018**, *47*, 1207–1216. [CrossRef]
62. Lambert, S.A.; Abraham, G.; Inouye, M. Towards clinical utility of polygenic risk scores. *Hum. Mol. Genet.* **2019**, *00*, 1–10. [CrossRef]

The Clinical Utility of Food Addiction: Characteristics and Psychosocial Impairments in a Treatment-Seeking Sample

Edgar Oliveira [1,*], Hyoun S. Kim [2,*], Emilie Lacroix [3], Mária de Fátima Vasques [1], Cristiane Ruiz Durante [1], Daniela Pereira [1], Janice Rico Cabral [1], Paula Sanches Bernstein [1], Ximena Garcia [3], Emma V. Ritchie [4] and Hermano Tavares [1]

1 Department of Psychiatry, University of São Paulo, Rua Artur de Azevedo, 145, Cerqueira Cesar, São Paulo CEP 05404-010, SP, Brasil; vasquesfatima10@gmail.com (M.d.F.V.); crisnutrition@hotmail.com (C.R.D.); dani.psico8@gmail.com (D.P.); janice.rcabral@gmail.com (J.R.C.); paulabernstein@ciencias.com.br (P.S.B.); hermanot@usp.br (H.T.)

2 Department of Psychology, Ryerson University, 350 Victoria Street, Toronto, ON M5B 2K3, Canada

3 Department of Psychology, University of Calgary, 2500 University Drive, NW, Calgary, AB T2N 1N4, Canada; emilie.lacroix@ucalgary.ca (E.L.); xgarcia@ucalgary.ca (X.G.)

4 Department of Psychology, York University, 4700 Keele St, Toronto, ON M3J 1P3, Canada; evritchi@yorku.ca

* Correspondence: dredgaroliveirapq@gmail.com (E.O.); andrewhs.kim@ryerson.ca (H.S.K.)

Abstract: Little is known about the characteristics of individuals seeking treatment for food addiction (FA), and the clinical utility of FA has yet to be established. To address these gaps, we examined (i) the demographic, eating pathology, and psychiatric conditions associated with FA and (ii) whether FA is associated with psychosocial impairments when accounting for eating-related and other psychopathology. Forty-six patients seeking treatment for FA completed self-report questionnaires and semi-structured clinical interviews. The majority of the sample were women and self-identified as White, with a mean age of 43 years. Most participants (83.3%) presented with a comorbid psychiatric condition, most commonly anxiety and mood disorders, with a mean of 2.31 comorbid conditions. FA was associated with binge eating severity and anxiety symptoms, as well as psychological, physical, and social impairment. In regression analyses controlling for binge eating severity, food cravings, depression, and anxiety, FA remained a significant predictor only of social impairment. Taken together, the results suggest that individuals seeking treatment for FA are likely to present with significant comorbid conditions, in particular anxiety disorders. The results of the present research provide evidence for the clinical utility of FA, particularly in explaining social impairment.

Keywords: food addiction; clinical utility; psychosocial impairment; comorbidity; quality of life

1. Introduction

The food addiction (FA) hypothesis posits that foods that are highly processed and rich in salt, sugar, and fat have "addictive potential". In other words, certain foods may have the ability to provoke symptoms of substance use disorders [1]. Empirical research on the concept of food addiction is rapidly growing, and animal and human studies have demonstrated similarities between food and drugs that are abused, particularly with respect to their effects on reward pathways in the brain [2,3]. FA, assessed using the self-report Yale Food Addiction Scale [4], which applies substance use disorder criteria to food and eating has been found to be relatively common, ranging from 3% to 20% in non-clinical samples [4]. Rates of FA are higher in eating disorder samples, with some studies finding rates as high as 95% among women with bulimia nervosa [4]. FA is also relatively common in Brazil, with Nunes-Neto and colleagues (2018) reporting a prevalence rate of 4.3% in a large web-based sample [5].

The concept of FA is heavily debated, with some arguing that it pathologizes everyday eating behaviors [6] or does not hold incremental clinical utility beyond existing eating disorder diagnoses [7]. According to the 5th edition of the Diagnostic and Statistical Manual of Mental Disorders, "The diagnosis of a mental disorder should have clinical utility: it should help clinicians to determine prognosis, treatment plans, and potential outcomes for their patients" (p. 20) [8]. However, the clinical utility of FA constitutes an important gap in the field. A systematic review examining the correlates of FA reported a relationship with body mass index, binge eating, and mixed results with other psychopathology including depression [9]. Since the review, studies have also revealed an association between FA and demographic characteristics [10], lower quality of life [11], psychological distress [12,13], problematic eating behaviors [13–15], and impulsivity [5,14]. Regarding psychosocial impairments, FA has been shown to have moderate to strong associations that remain significant when other forms of eating pathology are controlled for [16]. Within a Brazilian context, Nunes-Neto and colleagues also found associations between FA and psychopathology and lower quality of life in psychological, physical, social, and environment domains [5]. Thus, there is evidence to suggest that FA may be associated with unique characteristics and psychosocial impairments, providing preliminary support for its clinical utility.

Although these studies are informative, a major limitation is that they have all consisted of non-clinical samples or people experiencing difficulties with weight and eating disorders. Additionally, previous studies have not controlled for the impact of comorbid psychopathology on psychosocial impairments. As such, it is unclear whether the documented clinical characteristics and psychosocial impairments stem from FA or from other conditions, which provides a limited understanding of the clinical utility of FA. Furthermore, the incremental clinical utility of FA is not known, that is, whether it contributes useful information above and beyond what may be explained by the comorbid psychopathology. It is critical to examine the incremental utility of FA among individuals seeking treatment for this concern, given that there is already emerging literature recommending various treatment strategies for FA [17,18]. In this light, the aim of the present study was to address gaps in the understanding of the clinical utility of FA by examining clinical characteristics (demographics, eating disorders, cravings, psychiatric conditions) and psychosocial impairments (controlling for common psychopathology) in a clinical sample with the primary concern of FA.

2. Materials and Methods

2.1. Participants and Procedures

Participants were 46 patients seeking treatment for food addiction at a specialized university outpatient clinic associated with the University of São Paulo, Faculty of Medicine in São Paulo, Brazil. Patients were self-referred through the community or referred by other treatment programs affiliated with the University. At intake, patients were assessed by a registered psychiatrist to determine their suitability for treatment. The eligibility criteria for treatment were as follows: (i) meet criteria for moderate-to-severe FA as assessed by the Yale Food Addiction Scale 2.0 (YFAS 2.0) [19] and (ii) 18 years of age or over. Exclusion criteria included (i) an organic condition that may explain eating pathology (e.g., endocrine disturbances); (ii) acute psychosis, mania, or borderline personality disorder; (iii) cognitive impairments that may interfere with treatment; and (iv) being currently pregnant or breastfeeding. Current psychiatric conditions were assessed by psychiatrists using the Brazilian Portuguese version of the Mini International Neuropsychiatric Interview (MINI) [20] using the Diagnostic and Statistical Manual of Mental Disorders - IV criteria. The MINI is a brief, semi-structured clinical interview with strong psychometric properties and high inter-rater reliability compared to the Structured Clinical Interview for the DSM [20]. The treatment consisted of 15 weekly sessions of group schema therapy and six sessions of behavioral nutrition delivered by two psychologists and two nutritionists [21].

Ethics approval was obtained from the Faculty of Medicine, University of São Paulo (12820813.5.0000.0068). The research was conducted in accordance with the Declaration of Helsinki. All patients were informed that research participation was voluntary and would not impact their treatment. All participants provided their consent to participate in the study.

2.2. *Measures*

2.2.1. Demographic Information

Participants reported their age, gender, ethnicity, and marital and employment status.

2.2.2. Food Addiction Severity

The Yale Food Addiction Scale 2.0 (YFAS 2.0) [19] was used to assess FA severity. The YFAS 2.0 contains 35 items ($\alpha = 0.90$) assessing the 11 DSM-5 substance use disorder criteria applied to FA, including two items to assess distress and impairment. The items are anchored from 0 (never) to 7 (every day) with total scores ranging from 0 to 235. In addition to providing a total score, the YFAS 2.0 provides a total symptom count, as well as a categorical "diagnosis" of food addiction (None = $\leq$1 symptom and/or lack of distress or impairment; Mild = 2 to 3 symptoms plus distress and/or impairment; Moderate = 4 to 5 symptoms plus distress and/or impairment; Severe = $\geq$6 symptoms plus distress and/or impairment). The YFAS 2.0 was translated and back-translated to Brazilian Portuguese by the senior author (H.T.), a content expert who is fluent in both languages.

2.2.3. Binge Eating Severity

Binge eating severity was assessed using the Brazilian-Portuguese version of the Binge Eating Scale (BES) [22]. The BES consists of 16 items ($\alpha = 0.80$) assessing the behavioral, affective, and cognitive components associated with binge eating. The response options for BES range from 0 to 3, with two questions containing three response options. As such, the total scores on the BES range from 0 to 46, with higher scores indicating greater binge eating severity.

2.2.4. Food Craving (Trait)

The Brazilian-Portuguese validated version of the Food Cravings Questionnaire—Trait version (FCQ-T) [23] was used to assess the frequency and intensity of participants' food-related cravings. The FCQ-T contains 39 items ($\alpha = 0.94$) assessing a variety of dimensions related to food cravings. The items are anchored from 1 (never or not applicable) to 6 (always). Total scores (39–234) are calculated by summing the items with higher scores indicating greater food-related cravings.

2.2.5. Psychiatric Comorbidities

Symptoms of depression and anxiety were assessed using the Brazilian-Portuguese validated versions of the 21-item Beck Depression Inventory (BDI-II) [24] ($\alpha = 0.90$) and the 21-item Beck Anxiety Inventory (BAI) [25] ($\alpha = 0.87$), respectively. Both the BDI and BAI are anchored from 0 to 3 with total scores ranging from 0 to 63. The MINI provided diagnostic coverage of current psychiatric conditions, including mood, anxiety, substance use, and eating disorders.

2.2.6. Quality of Life

A Brazilian-Portuguese validated version of the WHOQOL-bref [26] was used to assess quality of life in four domains: psychological, physical, social, and environment. The WHOQOL-bref contains 26 items ($\alpha = 0.91$) with items ranging from 1 to 5. Mean scores were computed for each domain, with lower scores indicating worse quality of life in the domains.

2.3. Data Analytic Plan

First, descriptive statistics were used to examine demographic characteristics and current psychiatric conditions. Next, two-tailed bivariate correlation analyses were conducted to examine associations among YFAS 2.0 total scores, food cravings, binge eating severity, symptoms of depression/anxiety, and quality of life. Lastly, a multiple regression analysis was conducted with the psychological, physical, social, and environmental domains of the WHOQOL-bref as the criterion variable and binge eating severity, food craving, symptoms of depression, and anxiety as the predictor variables to examine whether FA predicted psychosocial impairments above and beyond common comorbidities associated with FA.

3. Results

3.1. Clinical Characteristics

The sample consisted of more women (n = 37; 80.4%) than men (n = 9; 19.6%). The mean age was 43.28 (*Standard Deviation [SD]* = 10.82) years. Regarding ethnicity, the majority of the sample self-identified as White (n = 36; 78.3%), five as mixed (10.9%), three as Black (6.5%), and one as Asian (2.2%). One participant did not disclose their ethnicity. Roughly half (n = 24; 52.2%) of the participants reported being in a relationship, and the majority (n = 43; 93.48%) reported being employed. The mean score on the YFAS 2.0 was 9.12 (*SD* = 1.81), which corresponds to severe symptoms of food addiction.

Of the 42 patients who completed the MINI, 35 (83.3%) met criteria for at least one current psychiatric condition, with a mean of 2.31 (*SD* = 1.87) comorbid conditions (Table 1). The most common current psychiatric condition was generalized anxiety disorder (n = 26; 61.9%), followed by major depressive episode (n = 20; 47.6%), suicidality (n = 11; 26.8%), agoraphobia (n = 9; 21.4%), and social anxiety (n = 8; 19.0%). Regarding eating disorders, seven (16.7%) participants met criteria for bulimia nervosa, and none met criteria for anorexia nervosa. Relatively few, if any, participants met current diagnostic criteria for post-traumatic stress disorder (n = 1; 2.4%) or alcohol or substance use/dependence (n = 1; 2.4%).

Table 1. Frequencies of current psychiatric conditions met by participants using the Mini International Neuropsychiatric Interview (MINI).

Psychiatric Diagnoses	Yes	No
Major Depressive Episode	20 (47.6%)	22 (52.4%)
Dysthymia	4 (9.5%)	38 (90.5%)
Suicidality	11 (26.8%)	30 (73.2%)
Panic Disorder	4 (9.5%)	38 (90.5%)
Agoraphobia	9 (21.4%)	33 (78.6%)
Social Anxiety	8 (19.0%)	34 (81.0%)
Generalized Anxiety	26 (61.9%)	15 (38.1%)
Obsessive Compulsive Disorder	6 (14.3%)	36 (85.7%)
Post-Traumatic Stress Disorder	1 (2.4%)	41 (97.6%)
Alcohol Abuse/Dependence	1 (2.4%)	41 (97.6%)
Substance Abuse/Dependence	0 (0.0%)	42 (100.0%)
Anorexia Nervosa	0 (0.0%)	42 (100.0%)
Anorexia Nervosa Binge/Purge Type	0 (0.0%)	42 (100.0%)
Bulimia Nervosa	7 (16.7%)	35 (83.3%)
Any Current Condition	35 (83.3%)	7 (16.7%)

3.2. Correlation Analyses

Means, standard deviations, and correlations among the variables of interest are presented in Table 2. Food addiction severity was positively correlated with binge eating severity and anxiety symptoms, and negatively correlated with the psychological, physical, and social domains of the WHOQOL-bref. Food addiction severity was not significantly correlated with food craving, depression symptoms, or the environment domain of the WHOQOL-bref, $p > 0.055$.

Table 2. Means, standard deviation, and correlations between our variables of interest.

	M	SD	1	2	3	4	5	6	7	8	9
1. YFAS2.0	142.45	34.89	-	0.42 **	0.26	0.28	0.50 ***	−0.37 *	−0.32 *	−0.44 **	−0.29
2. BES	30.46	7.60		-	0.63 ***	0.43 **	0.36 *	−0.54 **	−0.63 ***	−0.12	−0.22
3. FCQ-T	166.39	30.27			-	0.22	0.30 *	−0.35 *	−0.39 **	−0.09	−0.14
4. BDI	20.31	10.37				-	0.53 **	−0.86 ***	−0.73 ***	−0.43 **	−0.53 ***
5. BAI	16.66	10.42					-	−0.57 ***	−0.55 ***	−0.25	−0.42 **
6. WHO_Psyc	10.77	2.94						-	0.81 ***	0.52 ***	0.64 ***
7. WHO_Phys	12.07	2.74							-	0.42 **	0.51 ***
8. WHO_Soc	11.68	3.63								-	0.56 ***
9. WHO_Env	12.65	2.36									-

Note. YFAS 2.0 = Yale Food Addiction Scale 2.0; BES = Binge Eating Scale; FCQ-T = Food Craving Questionnaire—Trait; BDI = Beck Depression Inventory; BAI = Beck Anxiety Inventory; WHO = WHOQOL-bref; Psyc = psychological; Phys = physical; Soc = social; Env = environmental. * $p < 0.05$; ** $p < 0.01$; *** $p < 0.001$. M = Mean, SD = Standard deviation.

3.3. Multiple Regression

3.3.1. Psychological Impairment

The multiple regression model predicting psychological impairment was statistically significant $F(5,35) = 29.84$, $p < 0.001$, adj. $R^2 = 0.78$. In this model, only symptoms of depression significantly predicted psychological impairment. FA, binge eating, symptoms of anxiety, and food craving were not significant predictors (Table 3). A post hoc power analysis indicated a power of 1.0 based on our results.

Table 3. Multiple regression results predicting psychological impairments measured using the WHOQOL-bref.

Psychological Impairment	b	LL	UL	SE b	B	adj. R^2	R^2C
Model						0.78	0.81 ***
Constant	17.62 ***	14.92	20.33				
Food Addiction	−0.01	−0.02	0.01	0.01	−0.08		
Anxiety Symptoms	−0.01	−0.06	0.05	0.03	−0.03		
Depression Symptoms	−0.22 ***	−0.27	−0.17	0.03	−0.78 ***		
Binge Eating Symptoms	−0.07	−0.13	−0.01	0.04	−0.19		
Food Craving	0.003	−0.02	0.02	0.01	0.04		

Note. b = unstandardized beta, LL = Lower limit, UL = Upper limit, SE b = Standard error of unstandardized beta, B = standardized beta, adj.R^2 = adjusted R^2, R^2C = R^2 Change. *** $p < 0.001$.

3.3.2. Physical Impairment

The multiple regression model was statistically significant, $F(5,35) = 13.36$, $p < 0.001$, adj. $R^2 = 0.61$. Symptoms of depression and binge eating significantly predicted physical impairments. On the other hand, FA, symptoms of anxiety, and food craving were not significant predictors of physical impairments (Table 4). A post hoc power analysis indicated a power of 0.99 based on our results.

Table 4. Multiple regression results predicting physical impairments measured using WHOQOL-bref.

Physical Impairment	b	LL	UL	SE b	B	adj. R^2	R^2C
Model						0.61	0.66 ***
Constant	19.24 ***	15.68	22.79				
Food Addiction	0.01	−0.01	0.03	0.01	0.09		
Anxiety Symptoms	−0.05	−0.12	0.02	0.03	−0.17		
Depression Symptoms	−0.13 ***	−0.20	−0.06	0.03	−0.48 ***		

Table 4. *Cont.*

Physical Impairment	b	LL	UL	SE b	B	adj. R^2	R^2C
Binge Eating Symptoms	−0.14 **	−0.23	−0.04	0.05	−0.38 **		
Food Craving	−0.003	−0.03	0.02	0.01	−0.04		

Note. b = unstandardized beta, LL = Lower limit, UL = Upper limit, SE b = Standard error of unstandardized beta, B = standardized beta, adj.R^2 = adjusted R^2, R^2C = R^2 Change. ** $p < 0.01$, *** $p < 0.001$.

3.3.3. Social Impairment

The multiple regression model was statistically significant, F(5,35) = 4.10, $p = 0.005$, adj. $R^2 = 0.28$. FA and symptoms of depression were significant predictors of social impairments. Symptoms of anxiety, binge eating severity, and food craving were not significant predictors (Table 5). A post hoc power analysis indicated a power of 0.95 with the parameters of our observed results. FA symptoms remained a significant predictor of social impairment $b = -0.049$, $t = -3.20$, $p = 0.004$ when controlling for age, gender, marital status, ethnicity, and body mass index.

Table 5. Multiple regression results predicting social impairments measured using WHOQOL-bref.

Social Impairment	b	LL	UL	SE b	B	adj. R^2	R^2C
Model						0.28	0.37 **
Constant	16.57 ***	10.38	22.77				
Food Addiction	−0.05 **	−0.08	−0.02	0.02	−0.49 **		
Anxiety Symptoms	0.05	−0.08	0.17	0.06	0.13		
Depression Symptoms	−0.18 **	−0.29	−0.06	0.06	−0.50 **		
Binge Eating Symptoms	0.09	−0.08	0.26	0.09	0.19		
Food Craving	0.01	−0.03	0.05	0.02	0.09		

Note. b = unstandardized beta, LL = Lower limit, UL = Upper limit, SE b = Standard error of unstandardized beta, B = standardized beta, adj.R^2 = adjusted R^2, R^2C = R^2 Change. ** $p < 0.01$; *** $p < 0.001$.

3.3.4. Environmental

The multiple regression model predicting environmental impairment was statistically significant, F(5,35) = 3.17, $p = 0.018$, adj. $R^2 = 0.21$. In this model, only symptoms of depression were significant. FA, binge eating, symptoms of anxiety, and food craving were not significant predictors of environmental impairments (Table 6). A post hoc power analysis indicated a power of 0.88 based on our results.

Table 6. Multiple regression results predicting environmental impairments measured using WHOQOL-bref.

Environmental Impairment	b	LL	UL	SE b	B	adj. R^2	R^2C
Model						0.21	0.31 *
Constant	14.51 ***	10.28	18.74				
Food Addiction	−0.01	−0.03	0.01	0.01	−0.16		
Anxiety Symptoms	−0.02	−0.10	0.06	0.04	−0.09		
Depression Symptoms	−0.11 **	−0.19	−0.03	0.04	−0.48 **		
Binge Eating Symptoms	−0.001	−0.12	0.12	0.06	−0.004		
Food Craving	0.01	−0.02	0.04	0.02	0.15		

Note. b = unstandardized beta, LL = Lower limit, UL = Upper limit, SE b = Standard error of unstandardized beta, B = standardized beta, adj.R^2 = adjusted R^2, R^2C = R^2 Change. * $p < 0.05$; ** $p < 0.01$; *** $p < 0.001$.

4. Discussion

The present study is, to our knowledge, the first to examine the clinical characteristics and psychosocial impairments of individuals for whom FA is the primary concern and reason for seeking treatment. Regarding demographic characteristics, the sample consisted mainly of women, consistent with previous studies reporting a higher prevalence of FA among women [4]. A potential explanation for this gender difference is that the weight gain associated with or expected to occur as a consequence of food addiction may be more distressing to women given they are under greater sociocultural pressure to conform to a thin body ideal [27]. As a result, women may be more likely to be distressed by and seek treatment for FA. Nonetheless, in the current study, roughly one in five participants seeking treatment were men, providing further evidence for the clinical significance of FA among individuals of both these genders. Future studies investigating gender differences in the clinical characteristics of those seeking treatment for FA would be highly informative. Indeed, to increase the generalizability of characterizations of FA across the gender spectrum, it is important to avoid under-representation of men and individuals who identify as transgender or gender non-binary in studies of FA.

Regarding the relationship between FA and binge eating, the mean score of the participants on the BES was in the severe range, and FA was moderately (r = 0.42) associated with binge eating, consistent with previous research [15]. These findings suggest binge eating disorder may be a common comorbidity; however, given that the correlation between FA and BES scores was far from perfect, there does not appear to be a complete overlap between these two constructs. Regarding other eating disorders, no participants met the diagnostic criteria for anorexia nervosa including the binge/purge subtype, and less than 1 in 5 participants met diagnostic criteria for bulimia nervosa. These results may be partly attributable to the low base rates of anorexia nervosa and bulimia nervosa and are consistent with prior evidence that FA can occur outside the context of eating disorders [28,29].

The majority of participants reported a current psychiatric condition, with patients meeting criteria for two diagnoses on average. However, it should be noted that 16.7% of the participants did not meet criteria for any current psychiatric conditions. This result suggests that there likely exists a group of individuals with FA who may not meet criteria for a recognized eating disorder or other psychiatric condition, yet still experience psychosocial impairment severe enough to warrant seeking treatment. Addictive disorders were not very common in the sample, which is surprising given the conceptualization of FA as an addiction and given that addictive disorders tend to co-occur [30,31]. Additionally, FA was not related to cravings, which is also a hallmark symptom of addictive disorders. A potential reason for this finding may be due to the relatively small sample size as the association between FA and craving was approaching significance with close to a moderate effect size (p = 0.087, r = 0.26). Thus, future research with large samples is needed to further investigate the association of FA with other addictive behaviors, to examine whether they are likely to co-occur, and whether FA is associated with hallmark characteristics of addictive disorders such as heightened levels of impulsivity.

The most frequent comorbid conditions were anxiety and mood disorders. Interestingly, however, FA was not significantly correlated with severity of depression in contrast to previous findings but in line with others [9]. Given the mixed findings in the literature regarding the association between FA and depression, further research is warranted. On the other hand, FA was significantly associated with severity of anxiety. Furthermore, anxiety disorders were the most frequent disorders in patients seeking treatment for FA. Longitudinal studies would be highly valuable in determining the temporal relationships between FA and anxiety.

FA was significantly associated with physical, psychological, and social impairment in our univariate analyses. FA remained a significant predictor of social impairment when controlling for binge eating, craving, depression, and anxiety. These results provide some support for the incremental clinical utility of FA, specifically in regard to social impairment, and suggest that individuals seeking treatment for FA may experience significant impairments in their social and interpersonal lives. These results are consistent with qualitative research [32], wherein people with FA described significant interpersonal difficulties as a result of FA. They reported that the shame, secrecy, and judgment by others regarding their difficulties with FA led them to withdraw from social situations, resulting in social and interpersonal harm.

Taken together, the results of the present research hold some implications for the clinical utility (i.e., prognosis, treatment plans, potential outcomes) of FA. Given the cross-sectional nature of our data, it would be premature to draw definitive conclusions regarding the prognosis or treatment of FA. Nonetheless, our findings identified factors worthy of further study using longitudinal and experimental designs, to examine whether they play a causal role in the generation or maintenance of FA symptoms or in recovery from FA. For example, given the significant association between FA and anxiety, it is plausible that excessive food consumption may represent a maladaptive coping mechanism to manage symptoms of anxiety, as was described by participants in an earlier qualitative study conducted by our team [32]. Using addictive behaviors to regulate one's emotions is a hallmark characteristic of addictions. Previous reports have distinguished two types of emotion regulation goals that may motivate addictive behavior: reducing aversive emotional states such as anxiety (a form of negative reinforcement) or increasing positive affect via the introduction of a pleasurable stimulus (a form of positive reinforcement). Some addictive behaviors such as alcohol abuse may be more motivated by the former goal, whereas others, such as gambling, may be motivated by the latter [33,34]. Our findings suggest that, in FA, eating may be used primarily as a means of reducing aversive emotional states, rather than for increasing positive affect. This finding is consistent with a prior qualitative study where participants emphasized eating as a means of temporarily reducing aversive emotional states [32].

From a potential treatment perspective, if addictive-like eating represents a maladaptive response to anxiety, then clinicians may wish to employ an integrated treatment model to address difficulties with anxiety and FA simultaneously, by the same team of clinicians. Indeed, an integrative approach has been associated with improved outcomes compared to a sequential or parallel treatment approach when addressing multiple concerns [35]. Regarding social impairments, should social functioning be identified as a causal or perpetuating factor in the development and maintenance of FA symptoms, incorporating aspects of social skill training into the treatment plan may lead to improved prognosis, and social impairment may represent an outcome to track in progress monitoring. That said, more research is needed regarding the associations between FA and anxiety as well as social impairments before recommending potential treatment strategies for FA. Lastly, the results suggest that it may be helpful to monitor treatment outcomes not only for FA but also for related conditions given the high rates of psychiatric conditions, in particular anxiety disorders, and the strong associations between FA, binge eating, and depression.

Limitations

Several limitations are worth noting. First, the cross-sectional design does not allow for causal inferences between FA and our variables of interest. Second, given the relatively small sample size, future research with larger samples is needed to replicate the findings of the present research. Having said that, the sample in the present study is one of the largest clinical samples of FA, and to our knowledge, the only study investigating clinical characteristics of people seeking treatment whose primary concern is FA. Third, the version of the MINI used in the present research captured DSM-IV diagnoses and as such did not capture binge eating disorder. Rather, in the present research, the well-known and used Binge Eating Scale was used to examine the relationship between FA and binge eating disorder. However, the BES was developed prior to the inclusion of binge eating disorder in the DSM-5 and thus was not designed to diagnose binge eating disorder [27]. Importantly, FA predicted social impairments when controlling for binge eating symptoms, providing some support for the clinical utility of FA. Lastly, although FA predicted social impairment when controlling for demographic factors and Body mass index, it is possible that other variables may have influenced the results. As such, future research controlling for other confounding variables would provide further support for our results.

5. Conclusions

In the past decade, there has been an increased empirical interest in FA. Although our knowledge of FA has grown exponentially, less is known regarding the clinical utility of FA, which impedes progress in developing efficacious treatments for this relatively common concern. The current study suggests that people seeking treatment for FA are likely to present with co-occurring psychiatric conditions and experience impairments in social functioning, over and beyond other psychopathology. Taken together, the results suggest FA holds some clinical utility. The results of the present research, as well as future research investigating the clinical utility of FA, may help in providing knowledge on the potential treatment possibilities for people with FA.

Author Contributions: Conceptualization, E.O., H.S.K., M.d.F.V., C.R.D., and E.L.; methodology, E.O. and H.T.; formal analysis, H.S.K.; investigation, C.R.D., D.P., J.R.C., and P.S.B.; resources, H.T.; data curation X.G. and E.V.R.; supervision, M.d.F.V. and H.T.; writing—original draft preparation, E.O., H.S.K., and E.L.; writing—review and editing, X.G., E.V.R., and H.T. All authors have read and agreed to the published version of the manuscript.

References

1. Ifland, J.R.; Preuss, H.G.; Marcus, M.T.; Rourke, K.M.; Taylor, W.C.; Burau, K.; Jacobs, W.S.; Kadish, W.; Manso, G. Refined food addiction: A classic substance use disorder. *Med. Hypotheses* **2009**, *72*, 518–526. [CrossRef]
2. Gearhardt, A.N.; Corbin, W.R.; Brownell, K. Food addiction: An examination ofthe diagnostic criteria for dependence. *J. Addict. Med.* **2009**, *3*, 1–7. [CrossRef] [PubMed]
3. Meule, A.; Gearhardt, A.N. Food addiction in the light of DSM-5. *Nutrients* **2014**, *6*, 3653–3671. [CrossRef]
4. Meule, A.; Gearhardt, A.N. Ten years of the Yale Food Addiction Scale: A review of Version 2.0. *Curr. Addict. Rep.* **2019**, *6*, 218–228. [CrossRef]
5. Nunes-Neto, P.R.; Köhler, C.A.; Schuch, F.B.; Solmi, M.; Quevedo, J.; Maes, M.; Murru, A.; Vieta, E.; McIntyre, R.S.; McElroy, S.L.; et al. Food addiction: Prevalence, psychopathological correlates and associations with quality of life in a large sample. *J. Psychiatr. Res.* **2018**, *96*, 145–152. [CrossRef] [PubMed]
6. Finlayson, G. Food addiction and obesity: Unnecessary medicalization of hedonic overeating. *Nat. Rev. Endocrinol.* **2017**, *13*, 493–498. [CrossRef] [PubMed]
7. Davis, C. Compulsive overeating as an addictive behavior: Overlap between food addiction and binge eating disorder. *Curr. Obes. Rep.* **2013**, *2*, 171–178. [CrossRef]
8. American Psychiatric Association. *Diagnostics and Statistical Manual of Mental Disorders*, 5th ed.; (DSM-5); American Psychiatric Publishing: Washington, DC, USA, 2013.
9. Long, C.G.; Blundell, J.E.; Finlayson, G. A systematic review of the application and correlates of YFAS-diagnosed "food addiction" in humans: Are eating-related "addictions" a cause for concern or empty concepts? *Obes. Facts* **2015**, *8*, 386–401. [CrossRef]
10. Schulte, E.M.; Gearhardt, A.N. Associations of food addiction in a sample recruited to be nationally representative of the United States. *Eur. Eat. Disord. Rev.* **2018**, *26*, 112–119. [CrossRef]
11. Wiedemann, A.A.; Lawson, J.L.; Cunningham, P.M.; Khalvati, K.M.; Lydecker, J.A.; Ivezaj, V.; Grilo, C.M. Food addiction among men and women in India. *Eur. Eat. Disord. Rev.* **2018**, *26*, 597–604. [CrossRef]
12. Raymond, K.L.; Lovell, G.P. Food addiction associations with psychological distress among people with type 2 diabetes. *J. Diabetes Complicat.* **2016**, *30*, 651–656. [CrossRef] [PubMed]
13. Koball, A.M.; Clark, M.M.; Collazo-Clavell, M.; Kellogg, T.; Ames, G.; Ebbert, J.; Grothe, K.B. The relationship among food addiction, negative mood, and eating-disordered behaviors in patients seeking to have bariatric surgery. *Surg. Obes. Relat. Dis.* **2016**, *12*, 165–170. [CrossRef] [PubMed]
14. Meadows, A.; Nolan, L.J.; Higgs, S. Self-perceived food addiction: Prevalence, predictors, and prognosis. *Appetite* **2017**, *114*, 282–298. [CrossRef]
15. Burrows, T.; Skinner, J.; McKenna, R.; Rollo, M. Food addiction, binge eating disorder, and obesity: Is there a relationship? *Behav. Sci.* **2017**, *7*, 54. [CrossRef]
16. Lacroix, E.; von Ranson, K. Prevalence of social, cognitive, and emotional impairment among individuals with food addiction. *Eat. Weight Disord.* **2020**. [CrossRef] [PubMed]
17. Cassin, S.E.; Sijercic, I.; Montemarano, V. Psychosocial interventions for food addiction: A systematic review. *Curr. Addict. Rep.* **2020**, *7*, 9–19. [CrossRef]
18. Vella, S.L.C.; Pai, N.B. A narrative review of potential treatment strategies for food addiction. *Eat. Weight Disord.* **2017**, *22*, 387–393. [CrossRef]
19. Gearhardt, A.N.; Corbin, W.R.; Brownell, K.D. Development of the Yale Food Addiction Scale Version 2.0. *Psychol. Addict. Behav.* **2016**, *30*, 113–121. [CrossRef]

20. Amorim, P. Mini International Neuropsychiatric Interview (MINI): Validação de entrevista breve para diagnóstico de transtornos mentais. *Rev. Braz. Psiquiatr.* **2000**, *22*, 106–115. [CrossRef]
21. Oliveira, E.; Lacroix, E.; Stravogiannis, A.; de Vasques, M.F.; Durante, C.R.; Duran, E.P.; Pereira, D.; Cabral, J.R.; Tavares, H. Treatment of food addiction: Preliminary results. *Arch. Clin. Psychiatry* **2020**, *47*, 163–164.
22. Freitas, S.R.; Lopes, C.S.; Appolinario, J.C.; Coutinho, W. The assessment of binge eating disorder in obese women: A comparison of the binge eating scale with the structured clinical interview for the DSM-IV. *Eat. Behav.* **2006**, *7*, 282–289. [CrossRef] [PubMed]
23. Queiroz de Medeiros, A.C.; Campos Pedrosa, L.F.; Hutz, C.S.; Yamamoto, M.E. Brazilian version of food cravings questionnaires: Psychometric properties and sex differences. *Appetite* **2016**, *105*, 328–333. [CrossRef]
24. Gomes-Oliveira, M.H.; Gorenstein, C.; Neto, F.L.; Andrade, L.H.; Wang, Y.P. Validação da versão Brasileira em Português do Inventário de Depressão de Beck-II numa amostra da comunidade. *Rev. Bras. Psiquiatr.* **2012**, *34*, 389–394. [CrossRef]
25. Quintão, S.; Delgado, A.R.; Prieto, G. Validity study of the beck anxiety inventory (Portuguese version) by the rasch rating scale model. *Psicol. Reflex. Crit.* **2013**, *26*, 305–310. [CrossRef]
26. Fleck, M.; Louzada, S.; Xavier, M.; Chachamovich, E.; Vieira, G.; Santos, L.; Pinzon, V. Application of the Portuguese version of the abbreviated instrument of quality life WHOQOL-bref. *Rev. Saude Publica* **2000**, *34*, 178–183. [CrossRef]
27. Polivy, J.; Herman, C.P. Sociocultural idealization of thin female body shapes: An introduction to the special issue on body image and eating disorders. *J. Soc. Clin. Psychol.* **2004**, *23*, 1–6. [CrossRef]
28. Gearhardt, A.N.; White, M.A.; Masheb, R.M.; Morgan, P.T.; Crosby, R.D.; Grilo, C.M. An examination of the food addiction construct in obese patients with binge eating disorder. *Int. J. Eat. Disord.* **2012**, *45*, 657–663. [CrossRef]
29. Avena, N.M.; Gearhardt, A.N.; Gold, M.S.; Wang, G.J.; Potenza, M.N. Tossing the baby out with the bathwater after a brief rinse? The potential downside of dismissing food addiction based on limited data. *Nat. Rev. Neurosci.* **2012**, *13*, 514. [CrossRef]
30. Konkolÿ Thege, B.; Hodgins, D.C.; Wild, T.C. Co-occurring substance-related and behavioral addiction problems: A person-centered, lay epidemiology approach. *J. Behav. Addict.* **2016**, *5*, 614–622. [CrossRef] [PubMed]
31. Kim, H.S.; Hodgins, D.C.; Kim, B.; Wild, T.C. Transdiagnostic or disorder specific? Indicators of substance and behavioral addictions nominated by people with lived experience. *J. Clin. Med.* **2020**, *9*, 334. [CrossRef]
32. Lacroix, E.; Oliveira, E.; Saldanha de Castro, J.; Cabral, J.R.; Tavares, H.; von Ranson, K.M. "There is no way to avoid the first bite": A qualitative investigation of addictive-like eating in treatment-seeking Brazilian women and men. *Appetite* **2019**, *137*, 35–46. [CrossRef]
33. De Castro, V.; Fong, T.; Rosenthal, R.J.; Tavares, H. A comparison of craving and emotional states between pathological gamblers and alcoholics. *Addict. Behav.* **2007**, *32*, 1555–1564. [CrossRef]
34. Tavares, H.; Zilberman, M.L.; Hodgins, D.C.; El-Guebaly, N. Comparison of craving between pathological gamblers and alcoholics. *Alcohol. Clin. Exp. Res.* **2005**, *29*, 1427–1431. [CrossRef] [PubMed]
35. Karapareddy, V. A review of integrated care for concurrent disorders: Cost effectiveness and clinical outcomes. *J. Dual Diagn.* **2019**, *15*, 56–66. [CrossRef]

8

Validation of the Japanese Version of the Yale Food Addiction Scale 2.0 (J-YFAS 2.0)

May Thet Khine [1], Atsuhiko Ota [1,*], Ashley N. Gearhardt [2], Akiko Fujisawa [1], Mamiko Morita [3], Atsuko Minagawa [3], Yuanying Li [1], Hisao Naito [1] and Hiroshi Yatsuya [1]

1 Department of Public Health, Fujita Health University School of Medicine, 1-98 Dengakugakubo, Kutsukake-cho, Toyoake, Aichi 470-1192, Japan; maythet7@gmail.com (M.T.K.); akifuji@fujita-hu.ac.jp (A.F.); liyy@fujita-hu.ac.jp (Y.L.); naitoh@fujita-hu.ac.jp (H.N.); yatsuya@fujita-hu.ac.jp (H.Y.)

2 Department of Psychology, University of Michigan, 2268 East Hall, 530 Church Street, Ann Arbor, MI 48109, USA; agearhar@umich.edu

3 Faculty of Nursing, Fujita Health University School of Health Sciences, 1-98 Dengakugakubo, Kutsukake-cho, Toyoake, Aichi 470-1192, Japan; mamorita@fujita-hu.ac.jp (M.M.); mina@fujita-hu.ac.jp (A.M.)

* Correspondence: ohtaa@fujita-hu.ac.jp

Abstract: The Yale Food Addiction Scale 2.0 (YFAS 2.0) is used for assessing food addiction (FA). Our study aimed at validating its Japanese version (J-YFAS 2.0). The subjects included 731 undergraduate students. Confirmatory factor analysis indicated the root-mean-square error of approximation, comparative fit index, Tucker–Lewis index, and standardized root-mean-square residual were 0.065, 0.904, 0.880, and 0.048, respectively, for a one-factor structure model. Kuder–Richardson α was 0.78. Prevalence of the J-YFAS 2.0-diagnosed mild, moderate, and severe FA was 1.1%, 1.2%, and 1.0%, respectively. High uncontrolled eating and emotional eating scores of the 18-item Three-Factor Eating Questionnaire (TFEQ R-18) ($p < 0.001$), a high Kessler Psychological Distress Scale score ($p < 0.001$), frequent desire to overeat ($p = 0.007$), and frequent snacking ($p = 0.003$) were associated with the J-YFAS 2.0-diagnosed FA presence. The scores demonstrated significant correlations with the J-YFAS 2.0-diagnosed FA symptom count ($p < 0.01$). The highest attained body mass index was associated with the J-YFAS 2.0-diagnosed FA symptom count ($p = 0.026$). The TFEQ R-18 cognitive restraint score was associated with the J-YFAS 2.0-diagnosed FA presence ($p < 0.05$) and symptom count ($p < 0.001$), but not with the J-YFAS 2.0-diagnosed FA severity. Like the YFAS 2.0 in other languages, the J-YFAS 2.0 has a one-factor structure and adequate convergent validity and reliability.

Keywords: food addiction; Japan; validation; Yale Food Addiction Scale 2.0

1. Introduction

The idea of food addiction (FA) is receiving increased interest [1]. Evidence is emerging that certain types of foods (e.g., highly processed foods with high levels of refined carbohydrates and/or added fat) may be capable of triggering addictive-like eating behaviors (e.g., loss of control, withdrawal, and cravings) in some individuals, which can lead to significant impairment or distress, [2,3]. Obesity and eating disorders such as bulimia nervosa (BN), binge eating disorders (BED), along with psychiatric disorders such as depression, posttraumatic stress disorder, attention-deficit hyperactivity disorder, have been reported as potential correlates with FA [4–6]. Relevant pharmacological findings have been reported. Highly processed sweetened and fatty foods trigger a rewarding effect through the release of dopamine [7]. Repeated eating of hyper-palatable food down-regulates the dopaminergic response, resulting in impulsive and compulsive responses to food cues [8]. Food craving—an intense desire to eat a specific food—activates the hippocampus, insula, and caudate nucleus, similar to drug craving [9]. On the other hand, there has been a lot of debate regarding the extent to which food can be addictive in the same way as drugs. Controversies exist, for instance, as to whether FA represents a specific construct as addiction that is distinct from other eating disorders, such as BED, and whether neurobiological changes underlying FA behaviors are sufficiently ascertained in humans [10,11].

The Yale Food Addiction Scale (YFAS) is the most commonly used measure to assess FA, although FA is not included in the Diagnostic and Statistical Manual of Mental Disorders, 5th edition (DSM-5) [12] and controversy exists regarding its definition [11]. The original YFAS applies the DSM 4th edition (DSM-IV) diagnostic criteria for substance dependence to the consumption of highly palatable foods (e.g., chocolate, ice cream, and pizza) [13,14]. Later, the scale was replaced with the Yale Food Addiction Scale 2.0 (YFAS 2.0) in response to the revision of the Substance-Related and Addictive Disorders criteria in the DSM-5 [15]. The YFAS 2.0 additionally introduced the following four diagnostic criteria: craving, use despite interpersonal or social consequences, failure in role obligations, and use in physically hazardous situations. It also introduced a severity classification. The YFAS 2.0 is available not only in English but also in German, French, Italian, Spanish, and Arabic [16–20]. The YFAS 2.0 exhibits good internal consistency, as well as convergent, discriminant, and incremental validity [15–20]. Associations of the YFAS-diagnosed FA with obesity, eating disorders, and psychiatric disorders have been accumulated. The YFAS 2.0-defined FA prevalence is supposed to draw a J-shape curve according to body mass index (BMI): 3.3–15.8% in healthy general populations [15–20], 17.2–47.4% in obese population [16,21], and 15.0% in underweight population [21]. Women and patients with eating disorders (BN and BED) and mental disorders (depression, sleep disturbance, and general psychiatric status) were more likely to have FA diagnosed with the YFAS 2.0 [15,17–19].

The current study aimed to validate the Japanese version of YFAS 2.0 (J-YFAS 2.0). Scant evidence regarding FA is available in Asia. The previous version of YFAS was translated into Chinese [22,23] and Malay [24]. Using these questionnaires, researchers reported that a FA diagnosis was assigned to 6.9–9.2% of Chinese teenage students [22,23] and 10.4% of Malay obese adults [24]. FA prevalence in Japan has not been reported so far, to the best of our knowledge. The YFAS 2.0 has not yet been translated into Asian languages. Development of the J-YFAS 2.0 enables examining the FA prevalence in Japan, comparing it with other countries and regions, and exploring the mechanism of FA. Referring to previous research [15–19], we hypothesized that (1) the J-YFAS has a one-factorial structure for the 11 J-YFAS 2.0 diagnostic criteria (structural validity); (2) underweight, overweight, obesity, uncontrolled and emotional eating, frequent desire to overeat, frequent snacking, and mood and anxiety disorders are associated with the J-YFAS 2.0-diagnosed FA (convergent validity); (3) cognitive restraint in eating is not associated with the J-YFAS 2.0-diagnosed FA (discriminant validity); and (4) the internal consistency is good for the 11 J-YFAS 2.0 diagnostic criteria (reliability).

2. Subjects and Methods

2.1. Study Design

We employed a cross-sectional design. All data were collected from a questionnaire survey. The present study was completed in accordance with the Declaration of Helsinki and the Ethical Guidelines for Medical and Health Research Involving Human Subjects established by the Ministry of Education, Culture, Sports, Science and Technology and the Ministry of Health, Labour and Welfare, Japan. We obtained the approval by the Ethics Review Committee of Fujita Health University, Japan (HM17-110 and HM18-155). All subjects provided their informed written consent for participation in the present study.

2.2. Subjects

This study was conducted with a convenience sample of undergraduate students from a private medical and health science university in Japan. The authors (A.O., M.M., and A.M.) explained the study purpose and methods to the students in the classes. Paper-based questionnaires were then distributed. Of the 759 students to whom the questionnaires were distributed, 752 (99%) were returned. Those who did not provide informed consent (n = 2) and who did not fully complete the J-YFAS 2.0 (n = 18) were excluded from the analysis. One student who replied to experience desire to overeat 50 times per week was excluded as this reply was a significant outlier. Consequently, we retained the remaining 731 students (96%) as the subjects.

2.3. *J-YFAS 2.0*

As with the YFAS 2.0 [15], the J-YFAS 2.0 is a 35-item self-administered questionnaire (Table S1). It assesses food consumption during the past 12 months. A Likert-scale ranging from 0 (never) through 7 (every day) is employed as a response option for each item. The items assess clinical impairment/distress and the following 11 diagnostic criteria: (1) eating larger amounts for a longer period than intended (consumed more than intended); (2) persistent desire or repeated unsuccessful attempts to quit eating (unable to cut down or stop); (3) spending considerable time or activity obtaining or eating food or recovering from eating (great deal of time spent); (4) giving up or reducing important social, occupational, or recreational activities due to eating (important activities given up); (5) continued eating despite knowledge of adverse consequences (use despite physical/emotional consequences); (6) development of tolerance (tolerance); (7) characteristic withdrawal symptoms (withdrawal); (8) continued eating despite interpersonal or social problems (use despite interpersonal/social problems); (9) failure to fulfil major role obligation at work, school, and home due to eating (failure in role obligation); (10) eating even in physically hazardous situations (use in physically hazardous situations); and (11) craving, strong desire, or urge for certain foods (craving). Each item is scored dichotomously based on the threshold determined by the YFAS 2.0 validation paper [15]. If any item that corresponds to the diagnostic criteria or clinical severity meets the clinical threshold, this criterion is endorsed. There are two scoring methods: the symptom count and the diagnostic threshold. For the symptom count scoring method, the diagnostic criteria for which the subjects meet are summed together. For the diagnostic threshold, the clinically significant impairment/distress criterion has to be met and two or more diagnostic criteria have to be met. The J-YFAS 2.0 FA diagnostic severity is classified as mild (2–3 criteria met plus impairment/distress), moderate (4–5 criteria met plus impairment/distress), and severe (6–11 criteria met plus impairment/distress).

For the development of the J-YFAS 2.0, the original English YFAS 2.0 [15] was translated into Japanese by the three Japanese authors (A.O., A.F., and H.Y.) and back-translated into English by an external professional translator who had no previous knowledge of the YFAS 2.0. Discrepancies between the back-translation and the original were resolved by consensus amongst the three Japanese authors and an American author (A.N.G.), who developed the original YFAS 2.0. We added two food examples, wagashi (Japanese traditional confectionery) and instant noodles (as salty snacks), in the introductory part, considering that food preference in Japan differs from western countries.

2.4. *Variables for Convergent and Discriminant Validity*

2.4.1. Body Mass Index (BMI)

Each subject self-reported their current and highest attained BMI. The questionnaire included a table indicating BMI from the weights and heights so that the subjects could choose their BMI from the following options: <16.0, 16.0–16.9, 17.0–18.4, 18.5–22.9, 23.0–24.9, 25.0–29.9, and ≥30.0 kg/m^2. No one chose <16.0 kg/m^2 for their current or highest attained BMI.

It was reported that Japanese tended to under-report their body weights and the tendency was more prominent among those with high BMI than those with low BMI [25]. We arranged the categorical response options for BMI to minimize the shame that subjects may feel for self-reporting their actual BMI.

2.4.2. Three-Factor Eating Questionnaire Revised 18-Item Version (TFEQ R-18)

The TFEQ R-18 is a self-assessment tool used to measure the following three types of eating behaviors: Cognitive restraint, uncontrolled eating, and emotional eating [26]. Cognitive restraint is a control over food intake in order to influence body weight and body shape [26]. Uncontrolled eating is a tendency to overeat food with the feeling of being out of control [27]. Emotional eating is a tendency to eat in response to negative emotions [27]. The higher the score is, the greater the levels of cognitive restraint, uncontrolled eating, and emotional eating are. We chose the corresponding items for the current study from the Japanese version of the original 51-item TFEQ [28].

2.4.3. Desire to Overeat

No validated questionnaire was available in Japanese to evaluate binge eating frequency. Thus, we asked the frequency of desiring to overeat with a single question, "How many times per week did you feel you wanted to eat more even after eating quite a lot of food during the last two hours?" The subjects filled in the number of the times.

2.4.4. Snacking Frequency

A frequency of snacking (eating and drinking outside of breakfast, lunch, or dinner) was self-reported. No validated questionnaire was available in Japanese to evaluate the frequency of snacking. Thus, we developed a single question, "How many days per week are you snacking?" for this evaluation. The subjects chose one of the following options: none, 2–3 days, 4–5 days, and almost every day. The snack included foods and drinks that contained any calories. Zero-calorie drinks, such as coffee and tea without milk and sugar, and vitamin and mineral supplements were excluded from the snack.

2.4.5. Kessler Psychological Distress Scale (K6)

The Japanese version of K6 was used as an indicator of mood and anxiety disorders [29]. A K6 score of 13 or greater was regarded as having such disorders.

2.5. Statistical Analyses

Confirmatory factor analysis (CFA) was conducted to assess the one-factor structure for the 11 J-YFAS 2.0 diagnostic criteria. Clinically significant impairment/distress was not included in this CFA analysis. The model fit was evaluated with the root-mean-square error of approximation (RMSEA), comparative fit index (CFI), Tucker–Lewis index (TLI), and standardized root-mean-square residual (SRMR). For assessing the reliability, internal consistency was calculated for the 11 J-YFAS 2.0 diagnostic criteria with Kuder–Richardson's α (KR-20). Convergent and discriminant validity was examined with chi-square test, *t*-test, analysis of variance (ANOVA), and Spearman's rank correlation. We examined whether the current and highest attained BMI, TFEQ R-18 cognitive restraint, uncontrolled eating, and emotional eating scores, frequency of desire to overeat, snacking frequency, and K6 score were associated with the J-YFAS 2.0-diagnosed FA. Not only the presence and severity (mild, moderate, and severe) but also the symptom count was used as the J-YFAS 2.0-diagnosed FA index, given the small numbers of subjects diagnosed as having FA. We could not apply the chi-square test to examine the associations of BMI, high K6 score, and the snacking frequency with the J-YFAS 2.0-diagnosed FA severity, since more than 20% of all cells had an expected frequency of less than five. Effect size indices were calculated [30–32]. Subjects with missing responses were excluded from the corresponding analyses. SPSS version 23.0 (IBM, Armonk, NY, USA) and Amos Version 23.0 (IBM, Chicago, IL, USA) were used for statistical calculations.

3. Results

3.1. Subjects' Characteristics

Most subjects were women (78.5%, n = 574) (Table 1). The mean (standard deviation) age was 20.8 (1.8) years. The years and majors included fourth-year medical technology students, first- to fourth-year nursing students, and third-year medical students. Around 80% of the subjects reported normal-weight BMI, 18.5–24.9 kg/m^2.

Table 1. Subject characteristics (n = 731).

Characteristics	Frequency (%) or Mean (SD)
Sex	
Men	156 (21.3%)
Women	574 (78.5%)
Age (year)	20.8 (1.8)
Years and Majors	
Fourth-year medical technology students	149 (20.4%)
First-year nursing students	142 (19.4%)
Second-year nursing students	132 (18.1%)
Third-year medical students	111 (15.2%)
Fourth-year nursing students	99 (13.5%)
Third-year nursing students	98 (13.4%)
Current body mass index (BMI) (kg/m^2)	
16.0–16.9	17 (2.3%)
17.0–18.4	108 (14.8%)
18.5–22.9	521 (71.3%)
23.0–24.9	57 (7.8%)
25.0–29.9	21 (2.9%)
30 and above	6 (0.8%)
Highest attained BMI (kg/m^2) *	
16.0–16.9	3 (0.4%)
17.0–18.4	60 (8.2%)
18.5–22.9	493 (67.4%)
23.0–24.9	117 (16.0%)
25.0–29.9	51 (7.0%)
30 and above	7 (1.0%)
Kessler Psychological Distress Scale (K6) score	4.6 (4.5)
13 or greater	45 (6.2%)
Three-factor Eating Questionnaire-R 18 (TFEQ R-18) score	
Cognitive restraint	37.0 (20.2)
Uncontrolled eating	35.5 (19.9)
Emotional eating	29.7 (27.5)
Desire to overeat	0.5 (1.0) (Range: 0–7)
Snacking frequency per week	
None	89 (12.2%)
2–3 days	276 (37.8%)
4–5 days	157 (21.5%)
Almost every day	208 (28.5%)
J-YFAS 2.0-diagnosed food addiction (FA)	
No FA	707 (96.7%)
Mild FA	8 (1.1%)
Moderate FA	9 (1.2%)
Severe FA	7 (1.0%)

SD: standard deviation. There were missing responses for sex (n = 1), age (n = 1), current BMI (n = 1), K6 (n = 4), the TFEQ R-18 cognitive restraint (n = 8), uncontrolled eating (n = 12), and emotional eating (n = 2), desire to overeat (n = 1), and snacking frequency (n = 1). * Highest attained BMI means the highest weight ever (when not pregnant) during the lifetime.

3.2. CFA and Internal Consistency

The RMSEA, CFI, TLI, and SRMR were 0.065, 0.904, 0.880, and 0.048, respectively. One diagnostic criterion (failure in role obligation) indicated a factor loading of 0.31 (Table 2). The other diagnostic criteria had factor loadings of 0.41 or higher. The KR-20 was 0.78 for the 11 diagnostic criteria.

Table 2. Diagnostic criteria of the Japanese version of the Yale Food Addiction Scale 2.0 ($n = 731$).

Diagnostic Criteria	Met Criteria	Did Not Meet Criteria	Factor Loading
Consumed more than intended	82 (11.2%)	649 (88.8%)	0.57 ***
Unable to cut down or stop	124 (17.0%)	607 (83.0%)	0.52 ***
Great deal of time spent	30 (4.1%)	701 (95.9%)	0.45 ***
Important activities given up	25 (3.4%)	706 (96.6%)	0.41 ***
Use despite physical/emotional consequences	45 (6.2%)	686 (93.8%)	0.55 ***
Tolerance	31 (4.2%)	700 (95.8%)	0.50 ***
Withdrawal	90 (12.3%)	641 (87.7%)	0.62 ***
Use despite interpersonal/social problems	98 (13.4%)	633 (86.6%)	0.54 ***
Failure in role obligation	29 (4.0%)	702 (96.0%)	0.31 ***
Use in physically hazardous situations	42 (5.7%)	689 (94.3%)	0.56 ***
Craving	21 (2.9%)	710 (97.1%)	0.50 ***
Impairment/distress	29 (4.0%)	702 (96.0%)	

*** $p < 0.001$, calculated with confirmatory factor analysis.

3.3. J-YFAS 2.0-Diagnosed FA Prevalence

The mean J-YFAS 2.0-diagnosed FA symptom count was 0.84 (SD = 1.61; range = 0–11). The proportions of the subjects who met the threshold for each diagnostic criterion ranged from 2.9–17.0% (Table 2). A total of 24 (3.3%) subjects were regarded as having FA: 8 (1.1%) received a mild, 9 (1.2%) a moderate, and 7 (1.0%) a severe FA diagnosis using the J-YFAS 2.0 (Table 1). All subjects who were diagnosed as FA with the J-YFAS 2.0 were women. Sex was significantly associated with the J-YFAS 2.0-diagnosed FA ($p = 0.004$, Fisher's Exact Test).

3.4. Convergent and Discriminant Validity

For convergent validity, neither the current nor the highest attained BMI was associated with the presence of J-YFAS 2.0-diagnosed FA (Table 3). The highest attained BMI was associated with the J-YFAS 2.0-diagnosed FA symptom count, while the current BMI was not (Table 4). The effect size was small for the association between the highest attained BMI and the J-YFAS 2.0-diagnosed FA symptom count—the η^2 was 0.02. A high K6 score and snacking frequency were significantly associated with the J-YFAS 2.0-diagnosed FA presence and the J-YFAS 2.0-diagnosed FA symptom count (Tables 3 and 4, respectively). TFEQ R-18 uncontrolled eating and emotional eating scores and desire to overeat were significantly associated with the J-YFAS 2.0-diagnosed FA presence, severity, and symptom count (Tables 5–7, respectively).

For discriminant validity, there was a significant association between the TFEQ R-18 cognitive restraint score and the J-YFAS 2.0-diagnosed FA presence (Table 5). Its effect size was small—the Cohen's d was 0.44. There was no significant association between the cognitive restraint score and the J-YFAS 2.0-diagnosed FA severity (Table 6). We found a significant correlation between the cognitive restraint score and the J-YFAS 2.0-diagnosed FA symptom count (Table 7). Its Spearman's rank correlation coefficient was 0.143.

Table 3. Associations of body mass index (BMI), the Kessler Psychological Distress Scale (K6) score, and snacking frequency with the J-YFAS 2.0-diagnosed food addiction (FA) absence/presence.

	FA Absent (n = 707)	FA Present (n = 24)	Chi-Square	p Value	Effect Size (V)
Current BMI (kg/m^2)					
16.0–16.9	16 (94.1%)	1 (5.9%)	1.421	0.922	0.04
17.0–18.4	105 (97.2%)	3 (2.8%)			
18.5–22.9	503 (96.5%)	18 (3.5%)			
23.0–24.9	55 (96.5%)	2 (3.5%)			
25.0–29.9	21 (100%)	0 (0%)			
30 and above	6 (100%)	0 (0%)			
Highest attained BMI (kg/m^2) *					
16.0–16.9	3 (100%)	0 (0%)	1.522	0.911	0.05
17.0–18.4	58 (96.7%)	2 (3.3%)			
18.5–22.9	478 (97.0%)	15 (3.0%)			
23.0–24.9	113 (96.6%)	4 (3.4%)			
25.0–29.9	48 (94.1%)	3 (5.9%)			
30 and above	7 (100%)	0 (0%)			
K6 score					
12 or less	665 (97.5%)	17 (2.5%)	22.565	<0.001	0.18
13 or greater	38 (84.4%)	7 (15.6%)			
Snacking Frequency Per Week					
None	89 (100%)	0 (0%)	13.855	0.003	0.14
2–3 days	272 (98.6%)	4 (1.4%)			
4–5 days	151 (96.2%)	6 (3.8%)			
Almost every day	194 (93.3%)	14 (6.7%)			

Chi-square test was used. The numbers of missing responses were as follows: current BMI (n = 1), K6 score (n = 4), and snacking frequency (n = 1). * Highest attained BMI means the highest weight ever (when not pregnant) during the lifetime.

Table 4. Associations of body mass index (BMI), the Kessler Psychological Distress Scale (K6) score, and snacking frequency with the J-YFAS 2.0-diagnosed food addiction (FA) symptom count (n = 731).

	FA Symptom Count	F/t Value	p Value	Pairwise Difference [a]	Effect Size (η^2)/(d)
Current BMI (kg/m^2)					
16.0–16.9	1.0 (2.7)	1.375	0.231		0.01
17.0–18.4	0.6 (1.2)				
18.5–22.9	0.8 (1.6)				
23.0–24.9	1.1 (1.8)				
25.0–29.9	1.4 (2.1)				
30 and above	1.3 (1.5)				
Highest attained BMI (kg/m^2) *					
16.0–16.9 (1)	0.7 (0.6)	2.555	0.026	(2), (3), (4) < (5)	0.02
17.0–18.4 (2)	0.6 (1.7)				
18.5–22.9 (3)	0.8 (1.6)				
23.0–24.9 (4)	0.7 (1.1)				
25.0–29.9 (5)	1.5 (2.3)				
30 and above (6)	1.1 (1.5)				
K6 score					
12 or less	0.8 (1.4)	−3.060	0.004		0.95
13 or greater	2.2 (3.2)				
Snacking frequency per week					
None (1)	0.4 (0.7)	15.986	<0.001	(1), (2) < (3), (4)	0.06
2–3 days (2)	0.5 (1.0)				
4–5 days (3)	1.0 (1.9)				
Almost every day (4)	1.4 (2.1)				

Analysis of variance (for BMI and snacking frequency) and t-test (for K6 score) were used. FA symptom counts are shown as mean (standard deviation). The numbers of missing responses were as follows: Current BMI (n = 1), K6 score (n = 4), and snacking frequency (n = 1). [a] Pairwise differences were of $p < 0.05$ (Bonferroni corrected). * Highest attained BMI means the highest weight ever (when not pregnant) during the lifetime.

Table 5. Associations of the 18-item Three-Factor Eating Questionnaire (TFEQ R-18) scores and frequency of desiring to overeat with the J-YFAS 2.0-diagnosed food addiction (FA) absence/presence.

	FA Absent (n = 707)	FA Present (n = 24)	t Value	p Value	Effect Size (d)
Cognitive restraint	36.7 (20.1)	45.7 (21.7)	−2.097	0.036	0.44
Uncontrolled eating	34.5 (19.1)	64.1 (23.1)	−7.246	<0.001	1.54
Emotional eating	28.6 (26.4)	63.9 (34.6)	−4.959	<0.001	1.32
Desire to overeat	0.41 (0.91)	1.7 (2.0)	−2.965	0.007	1.28

t-test was used. TFEQ R-18 scores and frequency of desiring to overeat are shown as mean (standard deviation). The numbers of missing responses were as follows: TFEQ R-18 cognitive restraint, n = 8 (7 from FA absent, 1 from FA present); uncontrolled eating, n = 12 (11 from FA absent, 1 from FA present); emotional eating, n = 2 (all from FA absent); and desire to overeat, n = 1 (from FA absent).

Table 6. Associations of the 18-item Three-Factor Eating Questionnaire (TFEQ R-18) scores and frequency of desiring to overeat with the J-YFAS 2.0-diagnosed food addiction (FA) severity.

	FA Absent (n = 707)	Mild FA (n = 8)	Moderate FA (n = 9)	Severe FA (n = 7)	F Value	p Value	Pairwise Difference [a]	Effect Size (η^2)
Cognitive restraint	36.7 (20.1)	43.1 (17.8)	48.6 (24.3)	45.2 (25.6)	1.56	0.197		0.01
Uncontrolled eating	34.5 (19.1)	56.0 (24.5)	62.5 (20.5)	75.1 (23.2)	18.80	<0.001	1 < 2,3,4	0.07
Emotional eating	28.6 (26.4)	43.1 (37.3)	74.1 (26.1)	74.6 (34.4)	16.06	<0.001	1 < 3,4	0.06
Desire to overeat	0.4 (0.9)	0.6 (1.2)	1.8 (1.5)	2.7 (2.9)	19.53	<0.001	1 < 3, 4; 2 < 4	0.07

Analysis of variance was used. TFEQ R-18 scores and frequency of desiring to overeat are shown as mean (standard deviation). The numbers of missing responses were as follows: TFEQ R-18 cognitive restraint, n = 8 (7 from FA absent, 1 from Moderate FA); uncontrolled eating, n = 12 (11 from FA absent, 1 from Moderate FA); emotional eating, n = 2 (all from FA absent); and desire to overeat, n = 1 (from FA absent). [a] Pairwise differences were of p < 0.05 (Bonferroni corrected). 1 = No FA, 2 = Mild FA, 3 = Moderate FA, 4 = Severe FA.

Table 7. Spearman's rank correlation coefficients among the J-YFAS 2.0-diagnosed food addiction (FA) symptom count, the 18-item Three-Factor Eating Questionnaire (TFEQ R-18) scores, and frequency of desiring to overeat (n = 731).

	FA Symptom Count	Cognitive Restraint	Uncontrolled Eating	Emotional Eating	Desire to Overeat
FA symptom count					
Cognitive restraint	0.143 ***				
Uncontrolled eating	0.403 ***	0.248 ***			
Emotional eating	0.296 ***	0.258 ***	0.619 ***		
Desire to overeat	0.277 ***	0.039	0.449 ***	0.361 ***	

*** p < 0.001. The numbers of missing responses were as follows: TFEQ R-18 cognitive restraint (n = 8), uncontrolled eating (n = 12), emotional eating (n = 2), and desire to overeat, (n = 1).

4. Discussion

We examined the J-YFAS 2.0's properties in a sample of healthy undergraduate students in Japan. The J-YFAS 2.0 had a one-factor structure and adequate convergent validity and reliability, like the YFAS 2.0 in other languages [15–20], whereas our results were not the same as hypothesized with regard to the associations of BMI and cognitive restraint in eating with the J-YFAS 2.0-diagnosed FA. The J-YFAS 2.0-diagnosed FA prevalence was 3.3% in our subjects. Similar findings were reported from Italian and Spanish young healthy samples [18,19].

A one-factor structure was confirmed for the J-YFAS 2.0, which is the same as for the English, German, French, Italian, and Spanish YFAS 2.0 [15–19]. Our findings did not strictly meet the Hu and Bentler criteria, i.e., RMSEA ≤ 0.06, CFI ≥ 0.95, TLI ≥ 0.95, and SRMR ≤ 0.08 [33]. However, one or more of the four indices do not often meet the criteria [34]. The French version of the YFAS 2.0 showed a CFI of 0.887 and RMSEA of 0.083 [17]. There is the criticism that the Hu and Bentler criteria may be too stringent [35]. Our fit indices did not deviate substantially from the Hu and Bentler criteria. We thus retained the one-factor structure of the J-YFAS 2.0. Regarding the reliability of the J-YFAS 2.0, KR-20 was 0.78. This suggests the acceptable internal consistency of the J-YFAS 2.0.

The J-YFAS 2.0-diagnosed FA prevalence was 3.3% in this study. A similar prevalence was observed in other developed countries: Italy (3.4%) and Spain (3.3%) [18,19]. The subjects' characteristics of these three studies bear some resemblance, which might account for the similar prevalence. They were mainly young (aged about 20) and normal-weight people. Like our study, the Italian study collected the subjects from a medical school. About 80% of the subjects were female in both the Spanish and our sample. On the other hand, a web-based survey found a much higher YFAS 2.0-diagnosed FA prevalence, 9.7%, among German-speaking university students with the similar age and BMI [16]. This could imply that not only biological characteristics but also cultural differences are associated with YFAS 2.0-diagnosed FA, although it is possible that the web-based survey received considerable attention from those with FA and obtained their participation. Similar to previous reports in the U.S. [15] and Italy [18], women exhibited a significantly greater YFAS 2.0-diagnosed FA prevalence than men in our study. This suggests a sex difference in YFAS 2.0-diagnosed FA, which should be further investigated in future studies.

The YFAS 2.0-diagnosed FA prevalence was high in overweight, obese, and underweight people in the U.S., Germany, France, Italy, Spain, and Egypt [15–21]. Contrary to these findings, both the current and highest attained BMI did not demonstrate an explicit association with the J-YFAS 2.0-diagnosed FA in the present study. We only found that the subjects with the highest attained BMI of 25.0–29.9 had a greater J-YFAS 2.0-diagnosed FA symptom count than those with the highest attained BMI of 17.0–24.9. However, its effect size was small—the η^2 was only 0.02. One possible reason for the finding might be the small numbers of our subjects with overweight, obesity, and extreme underweight. Current overweight and obesity were declared only by nearly 4% of the subjects. This reflected the fact that Japan has a much lower prevalence of overweight and obesity than other countries where the YFAS 2.0 has been validated [36]. Perhaps, some subjects in our study could have under-reported their BMI [37], although we arranged the categorical response options for BMI to minimize the shame that subjects may feel for self-reporting their actual BMI. Consequently, the low prevalence of overweight and obesity exerted a floor effect, diminishing the association between BMI, especially overweight and obesity, and the J-YFAS 2.0-diagnosed FA. Another possible reason is that the causes to affect BMI are multifactorial and different by region. We did not examine all causes that potentially affected BMI more strongly than FA. For instance, some researchers pointed out that social norms (pressure) might drive the young Japanese women's desire for slimming [38–40]. They could have more impact on BMI than FA among our subjects. Our subjects involved medical, nursing, and medical technology students. They must have a greater knowledge of health, nutrition, and exercise than the normal population, which may have skewed the association between BMI, especially the current BMI, and the J-YFAS 2.0-diagnosed FA. Development of the J-YFAS 2.0 improves the examination of FA in Japan where the prevalence of obesity is much lower than the western countries [36]. This may help elucidate our understanding of the impact of FA on body weight. Although FA was initially applied to understanding obesity, controversy remains over how much FA explains obesity [10,11].

Other variables hypothetically related to the convergent validity of the J-YFAS 2.0 showed significant associations with the J-YFAS 2.0-diagnosed FA as we expected. The TFEQ R-18 uncontrolled eating and emotional eating scores and desire to overeat were associated with the J-YFAS 2.0-diagnosed FA presence, severity, and symptom count in our study, as hypothesized based on the previous studies [15–19]. One study limitation is that we could not assess binge eating itself which was positively and moderately associated with the YFAS-diagnosed FA [41]. However, our findings regarding the desire to overeat and snacking would suggest the relationship between compulsive eating and FA. A desire to overeat forms a part of binge eating. Highly processed sweetened foods, which has been reported to be potentially related to FA [42–44], are often chosen for snacking in Japan [45]. We found that a high K6 score, which implied mood and anxiety disorders, is associated with the presence and higher symptom count of the J-YFAS 2.0-diagnosed FA. Some previous studies showed associations of psychopathological disorders [19] and depressive symptoms [18] with the YFAS 2.0-diagnosed FA.

A recent systematic review suggested a positive, moderate association of the YFAS-diagnosed FA with depression and anxiety [41]. Our finding was consistent with them.

Regarding the discriminant validity, we hypothesized that cognitive restraint in eating was a different entity from FA, referring to the idea that the YFAS 2.0 does not simply measure an intention and a failure to restrict food consumption [15,16]. Our findings exhibited an inconsistency in the association of cognitive restraint in eating with the FA presence, severity, and symptom count. In our sample, the association between cognitive restraint and the J-YFAS 2.0-diagnosed FA would not be so strong even if the association existed. Previous findings are also inconsistent regarding the association. It was reported in France and Italy that the YFAS 2.0-diagnosed FA was associated with a high level of cognitive restraint [17,18]. The Italian researchers mentioned the possibility that addictive-like eating and restricting food consumption could coexist in patients with anorexia nervosa [18]. We could not ascertain this possibility in our study since we did not examine whether the subjects suffered from anorexia. Further research would be necessary to examine the role of anorexia in the association between cognitive restraint and FA.

There are several limitations to the interpretation of our findings. First, the current study employed a convenience sample that was dominated by young, under- and normal-weight, female, healthy undergraduate students. For a generalization of the present findings, the J-YFAS 2.0 should be tested for different-age groups, obese individuals, and patients with eating disorders. Second, we were not able to include all kinds of validity and reliability. For instance, we did not address incremental validity and test-retest reliability. Third, we used our original questions to assess the desire to overeat and frequency of snacking. For instance, the Binge Eating Scale (BES) [46] and the Eating Behavior Patterns Questionnaire (EBPQ) [47] are the validated tools to evaluate binge eating and snacking, respectively. We did not use them since they were not translated into and validated in Japanese. This may limit the comparison of our results with the others. Finally, as FA has not yet been recognized in the DSM-5, we could not define the standard of psychiatrist-diagnosed FA.

As mentioned in the introduction, the conceptual construct of FA and the neurobiological changes underpinning it remain controversial [10,11]. Development of the J-YFAS 2.0 would facilitate research on FA in Japan where prevalence of overweight and obesity is much lower than the western countries [36]. This would contribute to specifying the conceptual construct of FA and the neurobiological changes related to FA.

5. Conclusions

The J-YFAS 2.0 had a one-factor structure and adequate convergent validity and reliability, like the YFAS 2.0 in other languages. Further studies are necessary to confirm the discriminant validity of the J-YFAS 2.0.

Author Contributions: M.T.K., A.O., A.N.G., and H.Y. designed the study plan. A.O., A.N.G., A.F., and H.Y. translated the English YFAS 2.0 into Japanese. M.T.K., A.O., A.F., M.M., A.M., Y.L., H.N., and H.Y. collected the data. M.T.K., A.O., and H.Y. analyzed the data and drafted the manuscript. A.N.G., A.F., M.M., A.M., Y.L., and H.N. critically reviewed and approved the manuscript. A.O. and H.Y. obtained the fund.

Acknowledgments: Data collection and processing were supported by Shunsuke Omura, Nozomi Furukawa, Yukino Onuma, Sho Nakahama, and Keigo Yamada.

References

1. Meule, A. Back by Popular Demand: A Narrative Review on the History of Food Addiction Research. *Yale J. Biol. Med.* **2015**, *88*, 295–302. [PubMed]
2. Schulte, E.M.; Smeal, J.K.; Gearhardt, A.N. Foods are differentially associated with subjective effect report questions of abuse liability. *PLoS ONE* **2017**, *12*, e0184220. [CrossRef] [PubMed]
3. Meule, A.; Hermann, T.; Kubler, A. Food addiction in overweight and obese adolescents seeking weight-loss treatment. *Eur. Eat. Disord. Rev. J. Eat. Disord. Assoc.* **2015**, *23*, 193–198. [CrossRef]
4. Meule, A.; Gearhardt, A.N. Five years of the Yale Food Addiction Scale: Taking stock and moving forward. *Curr. Addict. Rep.* **2014**, *1*, 193–205. [CrossRef]

5. Pursey, K.M.; Stanwell, P.; Gearhardt, A.N.; Collins, C.E.; Burrows, T.L. The prevalence of food addiction as assessed by the Yale Food Addiction Scale: A systematic review. *Nutrients* **2014**, *6*, 4552–4590. [CrossRef] [PubMed]
6. Brewerton, T.D. Food addiction as a proxy for eating disorder and obesity severity, trauma history, PTSD symptoms, and comorbidity. *Eat. Weight Disord.* **2017**, *22*, 241–247. [CrossRef]
7. Onaolapo, A.Y.; Onaolapo, O.J. Food additives, food and the concept of 'food addiction': Is stimulation of the brain reward circuit by food sufficient to trigger addiction? *Pathophysiology* **2018**, *25*, 263–276. [CrossRef]
8. Volkow, N.D.; Wise, R.A.; Baler, R. The dopamine motive system: Implications for drug and food addiction. *Nat. Rev. Neurosci.* **2017**, *18*, 741–752. [CrossRef]
9. Pelchat, M.L.; Johnson, A.; Chan, R.; Valdez, J.; Ragland, J.D. Images of desire: Food-craving activation during fMRI. *Neuroimage* **2004**, *23*, 1486–1493. [CrossRef]
10. Ziauddeen, H.; Farooqi, I.S.; Fletcher, P.C. Obesity and the brain: How convincing is the addiction model? *Nat. Rev. Neurosci.* **2012**, *13*, 279–286. [CrossRef]
11. Fletcher, P.C.; Kenny, P.J. Food addiction: A valid concept? *Neuropsychopharmacology* **2018**, *43*, 2506–2513. [CrossRef]
12. American Psychiatric Association (APA). Substance-related and addictive disorders. In *Diagnostic and Statistical Manual of Mental Disorders (DSM-5)*, 5th ed.; APA, Ed.; APA: Arlington, VA, USA, 2013; pp. 481–589.
13. Gearhardt, A.N.; Corbin, W.R.; Brownell, K.D. Preliminary validation of the Yale Food Addiction Scale. *Appetite* **2009**, *52*, 430–436. [CrossRef]
14. American Psychiatric Association (APA). Substance-related disorders. In *Diagnostic and Statistical Manual of Mental Disorders (DSM-IV)*, 4th ed.; APA, Ed.; APA: Arlington, VA, USA, 1994; pp. 175–272.
15. Gearhardt, A.N.; Corbin, W.R.; Brownell, K.D. Development of the Yale Food Addiction Scale Version 2.0. *Psychol. Addict. Behav.* **2016**, *30*, 113–121. [CrossRef] [PubMed]
16. Meule, A.; Müller, A.; Gearhardt, A.N.; Blechert, J. German version of the Yale Food Addiction Scale 2.0: Prevalence and correlates of 'food addiction' in students and obese individuals. *Appetite* **2017**, *115*, 54–61. [CrossRef] [PubMed]
17. Brunault, P.; Courtois, R.; Gearhardt, A.N.; Gaillard, P.; Journiac, K.; Cathelain, S.; Réveillère, C.; Ballon, N. Validation of the French Version of the DSM-5 Yale Food Addiction Scale in a Nonclinical Sample. *Can. J. Psychiatry* **2017**, *62*, 199–210. [CrossRef] [PubMed]
18. Aloi, M.; Rania, M.; Rodriguez Munoz, R.C.; Jimenez Murcia, S.; Fernandez-Aranda, F.; De Fazio, P.; Segura-Garcia, C. Validation of the Italian version of the Yale Food Addiction Scale 2.0 (I-YFAS 2.0) in a sample of undergraduate students. *Eat. Weight Disord.* **2017**, *22*, 527–533. [CrossRef] [PubMed]
19. Granero, R.; Jiménez-Murcia, S.; Gearhardt, A.N.; Agüera, Z.; Aymamí, N.; Gómez-Peña, M.; Lozano-Madrid, M.; Mallorquí-Bagué, N.; Mestre-Bach, G.; Neto-Antao, M.I.; et al. Validation of the Spanish Version of the Yale Food Addiction Scale 2.0 (YFAS 2.0) and Clinical Correlates in a Sample of Eating Disorder, Gambling Disorder, and Healthy Control Participants. *Front. Psychiatry* **2018**, *9*, 208. [CrossRef] [PubMed]
20. Fawzi, M.; Fawzi, M. Validation of an Arabic version of the Yale Food Addiction Scale 2.0. *East. Mediterr. Health J.* **2018**, *24*, 745–752. [CrossRef]
21. Hauck, C.; Weiß, A.; Schulte, E.M.; Meule, A.; Ellrott, T. Prevalence of 'Food Addiction' as Measured with the Yale Food Addiction Scale 2.0 in a Representative German Sample and Its Association with Sex, Age and Weight Categories. *Obes. Facts* **2017**, *10*, 12–24. [CrossRef] [PubMed]
22. Zhao, Z.; Ma, Y.; Han, Y.; Liu, Y.; Yang, K.; Zhen, S.; Wen, D. Psychosocial Correlates of Food Addiction and Its Association with Quality of Life in a Non-Clinical Adolescent Sample. *Nutrients* **2018**, *10*, 837. [CrossRef]
23. Chen, G.; Tang, Z.; Guo, G.; Liu, X.; Xiao, S. The Chinese version of the Yale Food Addiction Scale: An examination of its validation in a sample of female adolescents. *Eat. Behav.* **2015**, *18*, 97–102. [CrossRef] [PubMed]
24. Swarna Nantha, Y.; Abd Patah, N.A.; Ponnusamy Pillai, M. Preliminary validation of the Malay Yale Food Addiction Scale: Factor structure and item analysis in an obese population. *Clin. Nutr. ESPEN* **2016**, *16*, 42–47. [CrossRef]
25. Anai, A.; Ueda, K.; Harada, K.; Katoh, T.; Fukumoto, K.; Wei, C.-N. Determinant factors of the difference between self-reported weight and measured weight among Japanese. *Environ. Health Prev. Med.* **2015**, *20*, 447–454. [CrossRef] [PubMed]

26. Karlsson, J.; Persson, L.O.; Sjöström, L.; Sullivan, M. Psychometric properties and factor structure of the Three-Factor Eating Questionnaire (TFEQ) in obese men and women. Results from the Swedish Obese Subjects (SOS) study. *Int. J. Obes.* **2000**, *24*, 1715–1725. [CrossRef]
27. Anglé, S.; Engblom, J.; Eriksson, T.; Kautiainen, S.; Saha, M.-T.; Lindfors, P.; Lehtinen, M.; Rimpelä, A. Three factor eating questionnaire-R18 as a measure of cognitive restraint, uncontrolled eating and emotional eating in a sample of young Finnish females. *Int. J. Behav. Nutr. Phys. Act.* **2009**, *6*, 41. [CrossRef]
28. Adachi, Y.; Fujii, K.; Yamagami, T. Responses regarding restrained eating on the Three-Factor Eating Questionnaire and weight loss. *Jpn. J. Behav. Ther.* **1992**, *18*, 140–148.
29. Furukawa, T.A.; Kawakami, N.; Saitoh, M.; Ono, Y.; Nakane, Y.; Nakamura, Y.; Tachimori, H.; Iwata, N.; Uda, H.; Nakane, H.; et al. The performance of the Japanese version of the K6 and K10 in the World Mental Health Survey Japan. *Int. J. Methods Psychiatr. Res.* **2008**, *17*, 152–158. [CrossRef]
30. Cohen, J. A power primer. *Psychol. Bull.* **1992**, *112*, 155–159. [CrossRef]
31. Volker, M.A. Reporting Effect Size Estimates in School Psychology Research. *Psychol. Sch.* **2006**, *43*, 653–672. [CrossRef]
32. Lakens, D. Calculating and reporting effect sizes to facilitate cumulative science: A practical primer for t-tests and ANOVAs. *Front. Psychol.* **2013**, *4*, 863. [CrossRef]
33. Hu, L.-T.; Bentler, P.M. Cutoff criteria for fit indexes in covariance structure analysis: Conventional criteria versus new alternatives. *Struct. Equ. Model.* **1999**, *6*, 1–55. [CrossRef]
34. Bagozzi, R.P.; Yi, Y. Specification, evaluation, and interpretation of structural equation models. *J. Acad. Mark. Sci.* **2012**, *40*, 8–34. [CrossRef]
35. Barrett, P. Structural equation modelling: Adjudging model fit. *Pers. Individ. Dif.* **2007**, *42*, 815–824. [CrossRef]
36. Yatsuya, H.; Li, Y.; Hilawe, E.H.; Ota, A.; Wang, C.; Chiang, C.; Zhang, Y.; Uemura, M.; Osako, A.; Ozaki, Y.; et al. Global Trend in Overweight and Obesity and Its Association With Cardiovascular Disease Incidence. *Circ. J.* **2014**, *78*, 2807–2818. [CrossRef] [PubMed]
37. Elgar, F.J.; Roberts, C.; Tudor-Smith, C.; Moore, L. Validity of self-reported height and weight and predictors of bias in adolescents. *J. Adolesc. Health* **2005**, *37*, 371–375. [CrossRef] [PubMed]
38. Takimoto, H.; Yoshiike, N.; Kaneda, F.; Yoshita, K. Thinness Among Young Japanese Women. *Am. J. Public Health* **2004**, *94*, 1592–1595. [CrossRef] [PubMed]
39. Hayashi, F.; Takimoto, H.; Yoshita, K.; Yoshiike, N. Perceived body size and desire for thinness of young Japanese women: a population-based survey. *Br. J. Nutr.* **2007**, *96*, 1154–1162. [CrossRef]
40. Smith, A.R.; Joiner, T.E. Examining body image discrepancies and perceived weight status in adult Japanese women. *Eat. Behav.* **2008**, *9*, 513–515. [CrossRef] [PubMed]
41. Burrows, T.; Kay-Lambkin, F.; Pursey, K.; Skinner, J.; Dayas, C. Food addiction and associations with mental health symptoms: A systematic review with meta-analysis. *J. Hum. Nutr. Diet.* **2018**, *31*, 544–572. [CrossRef]
42. Schulte, E.M.; Avena, N.M.; Gearhardt, A.N. Which foods may be addictive? The roles of processing, fat content, and glycemic load. *PLoS ONE* **2015**, *10*, e0117959. [CrossRef]
43. Gearhardt, A.N.; Davis, C.; Kuschner, R.; Brownell, K.D. The Addiction Potential of Hyperpalatable Foods. *Curr. Drug Abuse Rev.* **2011**, *4*, 140–145. [CrossRef] [PubMed]
44. Lindgren, E.; Gray, K.; Miller, G.; Tyler, R.; Wiers, C.E.; Volkow, N.D.; Wang, G.J. Food addiction: A common neurobiological mechanism with drug abuse. *Front. Biosci. (Landmark Ed.)* **2018**, *23*, 811–836. [CrossRef] [PubMed]
45. Takeichi, H.; Taniguchi, H.; Fukinbara, M.; Tanaka, N.; Shikanai, S.; Sarukura, N.; Hsu, T.-F.; Wong, Y.; Yamamoto, S. Sugar intakes from snacks and beverages in Japanese children. *J. Nutr. Sci. Vitaminol. (Tokyo)* **2012**, *58*, 113–117. [CrossRef] [PubMed]
46. Gormally, J.; Black, S.; Daston, S.; Rardin, D. The assessment of binge eating severity among obese persons. *Addict. Behav.* **1982**, *7*, 47–55. [CrossRef]
47. Schlundt, D.G.; Hargreaves, M.K.; Buchowski, M.S. The Eating Behavior Patterns Questionnaire predicts dietary fat intake in African American women. *J. Am. Diet. Assoc.* **2003**, *103*, 338–345. [CrossRef] [PubMed]

9

Food Addiction is Associated with Binge Eating and Psychiatric Distress among Post-Operative Bariatric Surgery Patients and May Improve in Response to Cognitive Behavioural Therapy

Stephanie Cassin [1,2,3,*], Samantha Leung [3,4], Raed Hawa [2,3,4], Susan Wnuk [2,3,4], Timothy Jackson [4,5] and Sanjeev Sockalingam [2,3,4,6,*]

1. Department of Psychology, Ryerson University, Toronto, ON M5B 2K3, Canada
2. Department of Psychiatry, University of Toronto, Toronto, ON M5T 1R8, Canada; raed.hawa@uhn.ca (R.H.); susan.wnuk@uhn.ca (S.W.)
3. Centre for Mental Health, University Health Network, Toronto, ON M5T 2S8, Canada; samantha.leung@uhn.ca
4. Bariatric Surgery Program, Toronto Western Hospital, Toronto, ON M5T 2S8, Canada; timothy.jackson@uhn.ca
5. Division of General Surgery, University Health Network, University of Toronto, Toronto, ON M5T 2S8, Canada
6. Centre for Addiction and Mental Health, Toronto, ON M5S 2S1, Canada

* Correspondence: stephanie.cassin@psych.ryerson.ca (S.C.); sanjeev.sockalingam@camh.ca (S.S.)

Abstract: The current study examined clinical correlates of food addiction among post-operative bariatric surgery patients, compared the clinical characteristics of patients with versus without food addiction, and examined whether a brief telephone-based cognitive behavioural therapy (Tele-CBT) intervention improves food addiction symptomatology among those with food addiction. Participants ($N = 100$) completed measures of food addiction, binge eating, depression, and anxiety 1 year following bariatric surgery, were randomized to receive either Tele-CBT or standard bariatric post-operative care, and then, repeated the measure of food addiction at 1.25 and 1.5 years following surgery. Thirteen percent of patients exceeded the cut-off for food addiction at 1 year post-surgery, and this subgroup of patients reported greater binge eating characteristics and psychiatric distress compared to patients without food addiction. Among those with food addiction, Tele-CBT was found to improve food addiction symptomatology immediately following the intervention. These preliminary findings suggest that Tele-CBT may be helpful, at least in the short term, in improving food addiction symptomatology among some patients who do not experience remission of food addiction following bariatric surgery; however, these findings require replication in a larger sample.

Keywords: bariatric surgery; food addiction; Yale Food Addiction Scale; cognitive behavioural therapy; telephone therapy

1. Introduction

The increasing prevalence of obesity is a growing global concern [1]. Bariatric surgery remains the most durable intervention for severe obesity, with studies demonstrating significant weight loss and improvements in, or even resolution of, obesity-related comorbidities [2–4]. The period of most significant weight loss occurs within the first 12 months following surgery [5,6]; however, between 20% to 50% of patients experience weight regain during long-term follow-up [7–9]. Bariatric patients' weight change trajectories begin to diverge between 6 and 12 months following surgery [5,6] and different trajectories have an impact on the prevalence of comorbidities and corresponding health care costs [10]. Post-operative binge eating, loss of control eating, and grazing have been shown to predict poorer weight loss outcomes following surgery [11–13].

The concept of food addiction (FA) may help account for the divergent weight change trajectories observed following bariatric surgery. It has been proposed that certain foods (i.e., hyperpalatable foods with refined carbohydrates and/or added fats) share pharmacokinetic properties with drugs of abuse [14], and are capable of activating an addictive-like process in susceptible individuals that can cause weight-promoting eating behaviours such as compulsive overeating and binge eating [15]. Food addiction is not included as a diagnosis in the Diagnostic and Statistical Manual of Mental Disorders, 5th Edition (DSM-5) [16]; however, the term was first coined in the scientific literature in the 1950s [17] and is widely used by health care professionals, researchers, patients, and the general public. The Yale Food Addiction Scale (YFAS) [18] was developed to operationalize food addiction and identify individuals with addictive tendencies towards highly processed foods. Given the similarities between highly processed foods and drugs of abuse, the YFAS adapted the DSM-IV criteria for substance dependence to make them relevant to the consumption of certain foods such as sweets, salty snacks, fatty foods, and sugary drinks (e.g., consuming more of certain foods than intended or over a longer period of time, preoccupation with certain foods, craving or strong urge to consume certain foods, and continued consumption of certain foods despite knowledge of adverse effects).

Rates of food addiction in pre-operative bariatric surgery populations as determined by the YFAS [18] and its subsequent modifications range from 14% to 58% [19]. Food addiction has been found to be associated with increased psychosocial impairment, including higher rates of depression, anxiety, impulsivity, and eating psychopathology, particularly binge eating [20–25]. In fact, food addiction has been conceptualized as a more severe and compulsive subtype of binge eating disorder (BED) [26]. Although food addiction is positively associated with body mass index [25,27], pre-operative YFAS scores do not appear to be significantly associated with percentage total weight loss (% TWL) following surgery [24,28] and food addiction is not considered a contraindication for bariatric surgery [29].

To date, research on food addiction among post-operative bariatric surgery patients remains sparse. Rates of food addiction in post-operative bariatric surgery populations are much lower, ranging from 2% to 14%, with no de novo cases of food addiction identified following bariatric surgery [19]. These improvements in food addiction symptomatology as well as associated problematic eating behaviours have led some researchers to consider whether bariatric surgery could be used as a treatment for food addiction [29]. Despite the improvements in food addiction that generally occur following bariatric surgery, some patients do continue to experience significant food addiction symptomatology. Currently, very little is known about the clinical characteristics of this subgroup of patients; however, they likely represent a subgroup with a particularly severe form of food addiction that may require additional intervention.

A recent systematic review concluded that there are currently no evidence-based psychosocial interventions for food addiction [30]. To our knowledge, no studies conducted to date have examined therapeutic interventions for bariatric patients experiencing food addiction. However, previous studies have shown that a brief telephone-based cognitive behavioural therapy (Tele-CBT) intervention developed specifically for bariatric surgery patients is effective in improving binge eating, emotional eating, depression, and anxiety among both pre- and post-operative patients [31–33]. Given the close association between food addiction, other forms of disordered eating, and psychiatric distress that has been reported in the literature, it is possible that such an intervention may also be effective in improving food addiction symptomatology following surgery.

The current study had three aims: (1) to examine correlates of food addiction among post-operative bariatric surgery patients; (2) to compare the clinical characteristics of patients who meet "diagnosis" for food addiction at 1 year post-surgery to those who do not; and (3) to examine whether Tele-CBT improves food addiction symptomatology among the subset of individuals who meet "diagnosis" for food addiction at 1 year post-surgery. It was hypothesized that: (1) food addiction symptomatology would be strongly correlated with binge eating and moderately correlated with percentage total weight loss and measures of psychiatric distress at 1 year post-surgery; (2) patients meeting "diagnosis" for food addiction would have greater binge eating and psychiatric distress and lower percentage total weight loss compared to those who do not; and (3) patients meeting "diagnosis" for food addiction at 1 year post-surgery who received Tele-CBT would report greater improvements in food addiction symptomatology compared to those receiving standard care.

2. Materials and Methods

2.1. Study Setting

Patients were recruited between 2018 and 2020 from the University Health Network (Toronto Western Hospital) Bariatric Surgery Program (UHN-BSP) and from the Humber River Hospital Bariatric Surgery Program (HRH-BSP) as part of a larger multisite randomized controlled trial examining the efficacy of telephone-based cognitive behavioural therapy 1 year following bariatric surgery. This study was approved by the institutional Research Ethics Boards and all patients provided informed consent before commencing the study; ethical approval code: CTO #0942. Patients were eligible to participate in the study if they were 1 year post-bariatric surgery, fluent in English, and had access to a telephone and a computer with Internet connection to complete the questionnaires. Study exclusion criteria included active suicidal ideation and poorly controlled psychiatric illness that would preclude engaging in Tele-CBT (e.g., psychosis). Participants were between the ages of 18 and 65 years and had a pre-operative body mass index (BMI) of >40 or ≥35 kg/m^2 with at least one obesity-related comorbidity. Patients received a Roux-en-Y Gastric Bypass unless a sleeve gastrectomy was surgically indicated (e.g., if there was a history of previous abdominal surgeries resulting in extensive adhesions and/or distorted anatomy).

2.2. Study Procedures

A total of 100 patients completed all study procedures and were included in the analyses. Pre-surgery anthropomorphic data including height and weight were collected by a clinician during pre-surgery appointments. Subsequent post-surgery weights at 1 year post-surgery (henceforth, referred to as "baseline" for the purposes of the present study), post-intervention (1.25 years post-surgery), and follow-up (1.5 years post-surgery) were provided directly from participants via photo or self-report. Percent total weight loss (%TWL) was calculated by dividing the difference in weight at post-intervention by the pre-surgery weight and then multiplying by 100.

All participants completed questionnaires at baseline, post-intervention, and follow-up using Qualtrics (Provo, UT, USA). Upon completion of the baseline questionnaires, participants were randomized to either the Tele-CBT group or the standard care control group using a customized randomization application. Participants randomized to the Tele-CBT group received the intervention described below, whereas those randomized to the control group received standard post-operative care that consisted of routine clinic visits (including post-surgery psychosocial follow-up appointments) and the option of attending a monthly support group. Participants completed questionnaires again at post-intervention and follow-up. The total time interval between the baseline and post-intervention timepoints was 10 weeks.

The Tele-CBT intervention consisted of six 1-hour sessions conducted weekly followed by a 1-hour "booster" session 1 month after the sixth session. Four clinical psychology graduate students who had experience assessing and treating bariatric surgery patients conducted the sessions, and the first author provided clinical supervision. The Tele-CBT intervention introduced participants to a personalized cognitive behavioural model of obesity, and included a variety of clinical strategies such as setting goals, scheduling healthy meals and snacks throughout the day, identifying and planning for difficult eating scenarios, planning pleasurable activities and behavioural alternatives to overeating, engaging in self-care activities, and challenging maladaptive thoughts and solving problems in order to decrease vulnerability to overeating. Participants were asked to complete worksheets for homework between sessions (e.g., food records, thought records) and practice skills that were introduced during the sessions (e.g., engaging in self-care and pleasurable activities) (see full Tele-CBT protocol description) [34]. The final "booster" session served as a check-in for participants to review the skills learned, troubleshoot issues that arose in the month prior, and develop a relapse prevention plan to help maintain the improvements made following surgery.

2.3. Study Measures

The Modified Yale Food Addiction Scale Version 2.0 (mYFAS 2.0) [35] was used to assess food addiction symptoms. The mYFAS 2.0 is a 13-item self-report measure designed to assess indicators of addictive-like eating and is comprised of 11 questions assessing substance use disorders as outlined by the DSM-5 and two questions that evaluate clinically significant impairment and distress. Symptom scores on the mYFAS 2.0 range from 0 to 11, and "diagnosis" scores range from no food addiction (1 or fewer symptoms, or does not meet criteria for clinical significance) to mild (2 or 3 symptoms and clinical significance), moderate (4 or 5 symptoms and clinical significance), or severe food addiction (6 or more symptoms and clinical significance). The YFAS 2.0 has been validated in bariatric surgery patients [36], and the abbreviated version of the YFAS 2.0 (i.e., the mYFAS 2.0) has similar psychometric properties as the full version [35].

The Binge Eating Scale (BES) was used to assess binge eating symptoms [37,38]. The BES is a self-report measure that assesses the presence of binge eating characteristics suggestive of an eating disorder. It was designed for use with individuals with obesity. Total cores on the BES range from 0 to 46. Moderate and severe levels of binge eating correspond to cut-off scores of 18 and 27, respectively.

The Patient Health Questionnaire-9 (PHQ-9) [39] and the Generalized Anxiety Disorder-7 (GAD-7) [40] were used to assess psychological distress. The PHQ-9 is a self-report measure that assesses depressive symptoms on a scale ranging from 0 (not at all) to 3 (nearly every day). Total scores on the PHQ-9 range from 0 to 27. Mild, moderate, moderately severe, and severe levels of depressive symptoms correspond to cut-off scores of 5, 10, 15, and 20, respectively. The GAD-7 is a self-report measure that assesses anxiety symptoms on a scale ranging from 0 (not at all) to 3 (nearly every day). Total scores on the GAD-7 range from 0 to 21. Mild, moderate, and severe levels of anxiety symptoms correspond to cut-off scores of 5, 10, and 15, respectively. Previous studies have used the PHQ-9 and GAD-7 to assess changes in psychological distress among bariatric surgery patients [41–43].

2.4. Statistical Analysis

All statistical analyses were performed using SPSS Statistics for Windows (Version 23.0; SPSS, IBM Corp., Armonk, NY, USA). Descriptive statistics including means, standard deviations, and frequency counts were calculated to describe the participant sample. Bivariate correlational analyses were conducted to examine correlates of food addiction. A Pearson's r effect size of 0.1, 0.3, and 0.5 correspond to a small, medium, and large effect, respectively [44]. Change scores were calculated by comparing post-intervention and follow-up to baseline scores. The Shapiro–Wilk test was used to determine whether the data were normally distributed. Kruskal–Wallis H tests were conducted for clinical variables with non-normally distributed data to assesses differences between groups, and Wilcoxon Signed-Rank tests were conducted for clinical variables with non-normally distributed data to assess differences from baseline (pre-intervention) to post-intervention.

3. Results

3.1. Participant Flow and Characteristics

As mentioned, the current study examining the correlates of food addiction and changes in food addiction in response to cognitive behavioural therapy was part of a larger multisite randomized controlled trial. Of the 136 participants who consented to participate, 122 completed the baseline questionnaires and were randomized to either the Tele-CBT group ($n = 61$) or control group ($n = 61$).

Of the remaining participants, eight did not respond to phone calls or emails, two were excluded due to their screening results, and four dropped out due to time constraints. Twelve participants from the Tele-CBT group discontinued treatment due to time constraints and 10 participants from the control group were lost to follow-up due to non-response. Given that this was a pilot study, data analyses for the first and second study aims were conducted with only those who had complete data at baseline (n = 100). Participants had a mean age of 48.40 ± 8.51 years, and the majority were female (82%), Caucasian (84%), college or university graduates (68%), were employed full-time (74%), and either married or in a common-law relationship (62%) (see Table 1). Only the subgroup of patients who met "diagnosis" for food addiction at 1 year post-surgery was included in the data analyses for the third study aim (i.e., to examine whether Tele-CBT improves food addiction symptomatology).

Table 1. Participant Characteristics (n = 100).

Variable	M (SD) or n (%)
Age (years)	48.40 (8.51)
Gender (female)	82 (82%)
Race/Ethnicity	
Black	4 (4%)
East Asian	1 (1%)
Latin American	3 (3%)
South Asian	1 (1%)
White (Caucasian)	84 (84%)
Other	7 (7%)
Relationship Status	
Married/Common-Law	62 (62%)
Divorced/Separated	13 (13%)
Single	23 (23%)
Widowed	1 (1%)
Occupational status	
Full-Time	74 (74%)
Part-Time	6 (6%)
Retired	7 (7%)
Disability	7 (7%)
Unemployed	6 (6%)
Education	
Some High School	3 (3%)
High School Graduate	7 (7%)
Some College/University	22 (22%)
College or University Graduate	68 (67%)

3.2. Correlates of Food Addiction 1 Year Post-Surgery

The correlates of food addiction are presented in Table 2. As hypothesized, at 1 year post-surgery, mYFAS 2.0 symptom scores were significantly correlated with scores on the BES, PHQ-9, and GAD-7, as well as %TWL. Similarly, mYFAS 2.0 "diagnosis" scores were significantly correlated with scores on the BES, PHQ-9, and GAD-7, as well as %TWL.

Table 2. Correlates of Modified Yale Food Addiction Scale Version 2.0 (mYFAS 2.0) symptom and diagnosis scores at 1 year post-surgery.

Measure	mYFAS 2.0 Symptom Scores		mYFAS 2.0 Diagnosis Scores	
	r	*p*	r	*p*
BES	0.633	<0.001	0.365	<0.001
PHQ-9	0.459	<0.001	0.217	0.030
GAD-7	0.372	<0.001	0.239	0.016
%TWL	−0.293	0.003	−0.229	0.022

Note: BES—Binge Eating Scale; PHQ-9—Patient Health Questionnaire 9-Item Scale; GAD-7—Generalized Anxiety Disorder 7-Item Scale; %TWL—Percent Total Weight Loss; mYFAS 2.0 Symptomatology—Modified Yale Food Addiction Scale Version 2.0 Symptomatology Scores.

3.3. *Comparison of Participants with versus without Food Addiction 1 Year Post-Surgery*

Of the 100 participants in this study, 13 (13%) exceeded the cut-off for food addiction according to the mYFAS "diagnosis" score at 1 year post-surgery. Those who exceeded the cut-off for food addiction reported significantly higher scores on the BES ($p < 0.001$), PHQ-9 ($p = 0.006$), GAD-7 ($p = 0.027$), and mYFAS 2.0 symptoms ($p < 0.001$). Those with food addiction also reported greater %TWL; however, the difference between groups was non-significant ($p = 0.08$). Mean scores (and standard deviations) are presented in Table 3.

Table 3. Clinical characteristics of patients with food addiction (according to the mYFAS2.0), patients without food addiction, and the total sample assessed at 1 year post-surgery. Values represent mean ± standard deviation.

Measure	No Food Addiction ($n = 87$)	Food Addiction ($n = 13$)	Total Sample ($n = 100$)
BES	11.86 ± 7.85	20.46 ± 5.78	12.980 ± 8.12
PHQ-9	5.22 ± 4.60	8.54 ± 3.36	5.65 ± 4.59
GAD-7	4.40 ± 3.96	7.15 ± 4.20	4.76 ± 4.07
%TWL	29.91 ± 9.44	22.09 ± 14.91	28.89 ± 10.55
mYFAS 2.0 Symptomatology	0.72 ± 1.13	3.92 ± 1.44	1.14 ± 1.59

Note: BES—Binge Eating Scale; PHQ-9—Patient Health Questionnaire 9-Item Scale; GAD-7—Generalized Anxiety Disorder 7-Item Scale; %TWL—Percent Total Weight Loss; mYFAS 2.0 Symptomatology—Modified Yale Food Addiction Scale Version 2.0 Symptomatology Scores.

3.4. *Changes in Food Addiction Following Tele-CBT*

Changes in mYFAS 2.0 scores were examined among the subgroup of patients who met "diagnosis" for food addiction at 1 year post-surgery ($n = 13$). mYFAS 2.0 symptom scores were significantly lower in the Tele-CBT group (1.29 ± 1.38) than the control group (2.33 ± 3.33) at post-intervention ($p = 0.027$). Patients in the Tele-CBT group reported significant improvements in mYFAS 2.0 symptom scores from pre- to post-intervention ($p = 0.027$), whereas those in the control group did not report significant changes over the same period ($p = 0.246$). mYFAS 2.0 symptom scores were not significantly different between the Tele-CBT group (2.00 ± 1.826) and the control group (2.50 ± 2.429) at follow-up ($p = 0.772$). See Figure 1 for changes in mYFAS 2.0 symptom scores across time as a function of group.

Regarding mYFAS 2.0 "diagnosis" scores, only one patient in the Tele-CBT group met "diagnosis" for food addiction at post-intervention and follow-up. Only two patients in the control group met "diagnosis" for food addiction at post-intervention and they no longer met "diagnosis" at follow-up. However, one other patient reported a resurgence of food addiction despite having remitted at post-intervention.

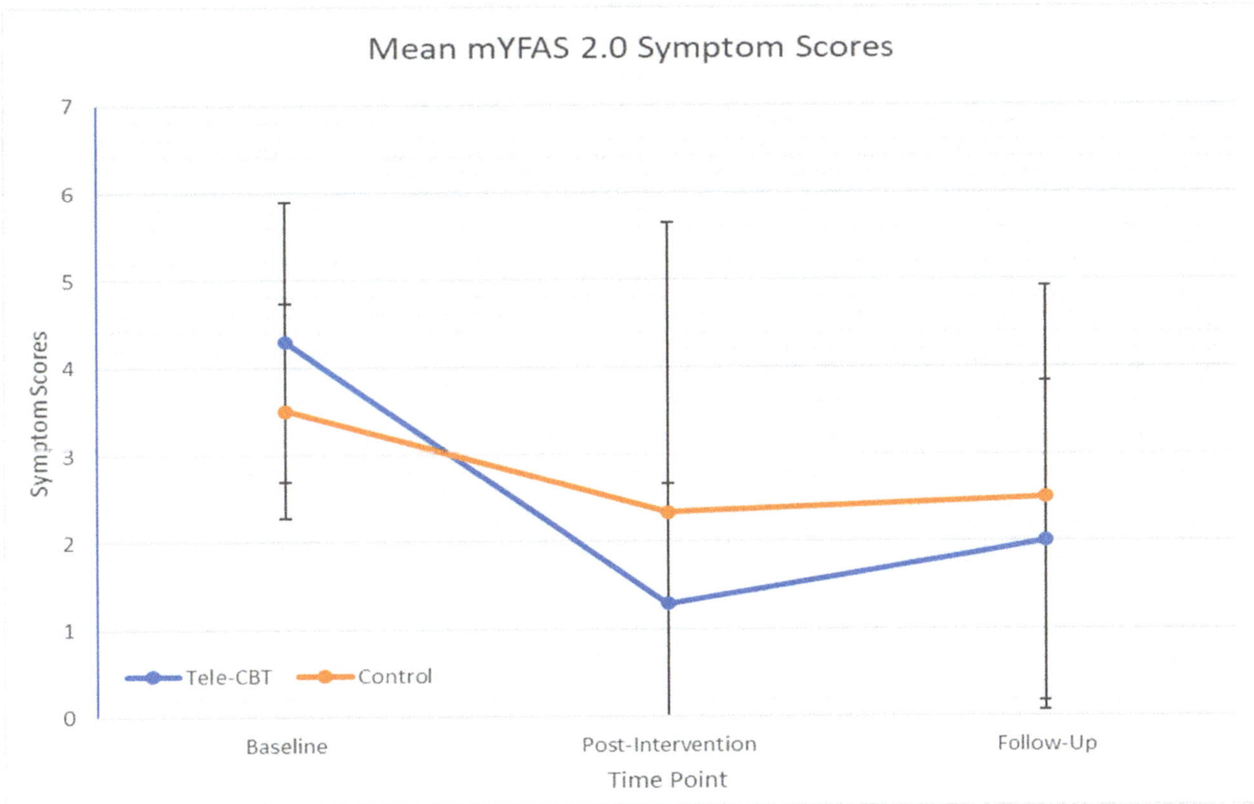

Figure 1. Changes in mYFAS 2.0 symptom scores over time as a function of treatment group among patients meeting "diagnosis" for food addiction at 1 year post-surgery ($n = 13$). Note: Baseline = 1 year post-surgery (prior to CBT); Post-intervention = 15 months post-surgery (immediately following CBT); Follow-up − 18 months post-surgery (3 months following CBT). mYFAS 2.0 Symptomatology—Modified Yale Food Addiction Scale Version 2.0 Symptomatology Scores. Tele-CBT—telephone-based cognitive behavioural therapy.

4. Discussion

The current study sought to examine clinical correlates of food addiction among post-operative bariatric surgery patients, to compare the clinical characteristics of patients with food addiction to those without food addiction, and to examine whether Tele-CBT improves food addiction symptomatology among those with food addiction. Our study hypotheses were largely supported. Consistent with the existing literature [20–25], food addiction symptomatology was strongly correlated with binge eating characteristics and psychiatric distress (i.e., depression and anxiety symptoms). It was also moderately correlated with %TWL. Thirteen percent of patients exceeded the mYFAS 2.0 cut-off for food addiction at 1 year post-surgery, and this subgroup of patients reported greater binge eating characteristics and psychiatric distress compared to patients without food addiction. They also reported almost 8% less total weight loss on average, though the difference was not statistically significantly likely due to the small sample size and variability in weight loss outcomes. Among those with food addiction, Tele-CBT was found to improve YFAS symptomatology immediately following the intervention.

The findings of this study add to the literature demonstrating that food addiction tends to improve following bariatric surgery [29]. The rate of mYFAS 2.0 "diagnosis" of 13% in the current study falls within the range of 2% to 14% that has previously been reported among post-operative patients [45,46], and below the range of 14% to 58% reported among pre-operative patients [19]. The mechanisms underlying this improvement are unclear; however, Koball and colleagues [29] identify a number of changes that occur following surgery, including cravings [47], rewarding properties of food [48], food preference and intolerance [49,50], and regulation of hunger and satiety [51,52], which may help account for improvements in food addiction symptomatology.

The impact of bariatric surgery on food addiction symptomatology is encouraging given the lack of empirical research on treatments for food addiction [30]. The subgroup of patients who meet "diagnosis" for food addiction following bariatric surgery appear to have more persistent and clinically significant binge eating characteristics (falling within the "moderate" range according to BES cut-offs in the current study), which may result in attenuated weight loss outcomes. The very limited research examining the association between post-operative YFAS scores and weight loss outcomes has generated mixed results, with one study reporting that post-operative YFAS score was not associated with the maximum %TWL achieved following surgery but was positively ($r = 0.22$, albeit not significantly, $p = 0.065$) associated with weight regain [53].

To our knowledge, this is the first study to examine the effect of a psychosocial intervention on food addiction symptomatology in a bariatric surgery population. Cognitive behavioural therapy has been suggested as a potential treatment for food addiction among bariatric surgery patients, given its efficacy in the treatment of binge eating disorder and substance use disorders [29,30,54]. Patients receiving Tele-CBT reported significant improvements in food addiction symptomatology immediately following the intervention. They improved to a greater extent than those receiving standard post-operative care alone; however, the group difference was no longer significant 3 months following the intervention. These preliminary findings suggest that Tele-CBT may be helpful, at least in the short term, in improving food addiction symptomatology among some patients who do not experience remission of food addiction following bariatric surgery. It is important to highlight that only one patient in each group met "diagnosis" for food addition at the follow-up assessment, which occurred 1.5 years following surgery. Thus, at least among this small group of study participants, it appears that the prevalence of food addiction may continue to decrease between 1 and 1.5 years post-surgery, even among those receiving standard post-operative bariatric care.

5. Limitations and Future Research Directions

The results of this study must be considered in light of a number of limitations. First and foremost, a relatively low percentage of patients met "diagnosis" for food addiction at 1 year post-surgery. This is a very encouraging finding; however, it meant that the sample size was very small ($n = 13$) to examine the efficacy of the Tele-CBT intervention among the subgroup of patients with food addiction. It will be important to replicate the findings of this pilot study in a much larger sample of patients with food addiction. If Tele-CBT is found to be effective in improving food addiction symptomatology in a larger replication study, it would be informative to examine the mechanisms of change and predictors of response, similar to studies in patients without food addiction [55]. Second, the Tele-CBT intervention did not have an explicit focus on food addiction. It focused predominantly on goal setting, normalized eating, self-care activities, alternative activities to replace overeating, planning for challenging eating situations, and challenging thoughts that may increase vulnerability for maladaptive behaviours, such as binge eating. It is noteworthy that the Tele-CBT intervention resulted in short-term improvements in food addiction symptomatology despite not explicitly addressing food addiction. However, whether incorporating food addiction into the treatment protocol, using models such as those proposed by Wiss and Brewerton [56] and Treasure and colleagues [57], results in larger and sustained improvements in food addiction symptomatology is an important question that could be empirically tested. Third, given that the intervention was delivered by telephone and thus, did not require patients to travel to the bariatric program, the post-operative weight data used to calculate %TWL were collected directly from patients via photo or self-report, which may impact the reliability of those calculations. Finally, the study sample was quite homogeneous with respect to participant ethnicity (Caucasian) and sex (female). Although this is typical of most bariatric surgery programs, the findings may not generalize to male patients and those of diverse racial and ethnic backgrounds. Regarding future research directions, it would also be informative to conduct a longitudinal study examining pre-operative and post-operative predictors of food addiction symptomatology, as well as the mechanisms that might account for improvements in food addiction symptomatology observed from pre- to post-surgery.

6. Conclusions

The findings of this study contribute to the body of literature suggesting that bariatric surgery improves food addiction symptomatology. Patients who continue to experience food addiction after undergoing surgery likely have a more severe form of food addiction that is characterized by greater binge eating characteristics and psychosocial distress. The results of this preliminary study suggest that Tele-CBT may result in short-term improvements in food addiction symptomatology among the subgroup of patients who continue to experience food addiction following surgery.

Author Contributions: Authors S.C., S.S., S.L. and S.W. contributed to the study conception and design, as well as the data analysis. All authors (S.C., S.S., S.L., S.W., R.H., and T.J.) contributed to the data interpretation and manuscript preparation. All authors have read and agreed to the published version of the manuscript.

Acknowledgments: The authors would like to thank the patients who participated in the study as well as the Toronto Western Hospital Bariatric Surgery Program team members for their support.

References

1. Arroyo-Johnson, C.; Mincey, K.D. Obesity epidemiology worldwide. *Gastroenterol. Clin. N. Am.* **2016**, *45*, 571–579. [CrossRef]
2. Karlsson, J.; Taft, C.; Ryden, A.; Sjostrom, L.; Sullivan, M. Ten-year trends in health-related quality of life after surgical and conventional treatment for severe obesity: The SOS intervention study. *Int. J. Obes.* **2007**, *31*, 1248–1261. [CrossRef]
3. Puzziferri, N.; Roshek, T.B., III; Mayo, H.G.; Gallagher, R.; Belle, S.H.; Livingston, E.H. Long-term follow-up after bariatric surgery: A systematic review. *JAMA* **2014**, *312*, 934–942. [CrossRef]
4. Sjöström, L.; Lindroos, A.K.; Peltonen, M.; Torgerson, J.; Bouchard, C.; Carlsson, B.; Dahlgren, S.; Larsson, B.; Narbro, K.; Sjöström, C.D.; et al. Lifestyle, diabetes, and cardiovascular risk factors 10 years after bariatric surgery. *N. Engl. J. Med.* **2004**, *351*, 2683–2693. [CrossRef]
5. Courcoulas, A.P.; Christian, N.J.; Belle, S.H.; Berk, P.D.; Flum, D.R.; Garcia, L.; Horlick, M.; Kalarchian, M.A.; King, W.C.; Mitchell, J.E.; et al. Weight change and health outcomes at 3 years after bariatric surgery among individuals with severe obesity. *JAMA* **2013**, *310*, 2416–2425. [CrossRef]
6. Courcoulas, A.P.; King, W.C.; Belle, S.H.; Berk, P.; Flum, D.R.; Garcia, L.; Gourash, W.; Horlick, M.; Mitchell, J.E.; Pomp, A.; et al. Seven-Year Weight Trajectories and Health Outcomes in the Longitudinal Assessment of Bariatric Surgery (LABS) Study. *JAMA Surg.* **2018**, *153*, 427–434. [CrossRef]
7. Dimeglio, C.; Becouarn, G.; Topart, P.; Bodin, R.; Buisson, J.C.; Ritz, P. Weight Loss Trajectories After Bariatric Surgery for Obesity: Mathematical Model and Proof-of-Concept Study. *JMIR Med. Inform.* **2020**, *8*, e13672. [CrossRef]
8. Monaco-Ferreira, D.V.; Leandro-Merhi, V.A. Weight Regain 10 Years After Roux-en-Y Gastric Bypass. *Obes. Surg.* **2017**, *27*, 1137–1144. [CrossRef]
9. Magro, D.O.; Geloneze, B.; Delfini, R.; Pereja, B.C.; Callejas, F.; Pereja, J.C. Longterm weight regain after gastric bypass: A 5-year prospective study. *Obes. Surg.* **2008**, *18*, 648–651. [CrossRef]
10. Davis, J.A.; Saunders, R. Impact of weight trajectory after bariatric surgery on co-morbidity evolution and burden. *BMC Health Serv. Res.* **2020**, *20*, 278. [CrossRef]
11. Devlin, M.J.; King, W.C.; Kalarchian, M.A.; Hinerman, A.; Marcus, M.D.; Yanovski, S.Z.; Mitchell, J.E. Eating pathology and associations with long-term changes in weight and quality of life in the longitudinal assessment of bariatric surgery study. *Int. J. Eat. Disord.* **2018**, *51*, 1322–1330. [CrossRef]
12. Meany, G.; Conceição, E.; Mitchell, J.E. Binge eating, binge eating disorder and loss of control eating: Effects on weight outcomes after bariatric surgery. *Eur. Eat. Disord. Rev.* **2014**, *22*, 87–91. [CrossRef]
13. Pizato, N.; Botelho, P.B.; Gonçalves, V.S.S.; Dutra, E.S.; de Carvalho, K.M.B. Effect of grazing behavior on weight regain post-bariatric surgery: A systematic review. *Nutrients* **2017**, *9*, 1322. [CrossRef]

14. Schulte, E.M.; Avena, N.M.; Gearhardt, A.N. Which foods may be addictive? The roles of processing, fat content, and glycemic load. *PLoS ONE* **2015**, *10*, e0117959. [CrossRef]
15. Gearhardt, A.N.; Davis, C.; Kuschner, R.; Brownell, K.D. The addiction potential of hyperpalatable foods. *Curr. Drug Abuse Rev.* **2011**, *4*, 140–145. [CrossRef]
16. American Psychiatric Association. *Diagnostic and Statistical Manual of Mental Disorders*, 5th ed.; American Psychiatric Association: Arlington, VA, USA, 2013.
17. Randolph, T.G. The descriptive features of food addiction; addictive eating and drinking. *Q. J. Stud. Alcohol.* **1956**, *17*, 198–224. [CrossRef]
18. Gearhardt, A.N.; Corbin, W.R.; Brownell, K.D. Preliminary validation of the Yale Food Addition Scale. *Appetite* **2009**, *52*, 430–436. [CrossRef]
19. Ivezaj, V.; Wiedemann, A.A.; Grilo, C.M. Food addiction and bariatric surgery: A systematic review of the literature. *Obes. Rev.* **2017**, *18*, 1386–1397. [CrossRef]
20. Davis, C.; Curtis, C.; Levitan, R.D.; Carter, J.C.; Kaplan, A.S.; Kennedy, J.L. Evidence that 'food addiction' is a valid phenotype of obesity. *Appetite* **2011**, *57*, 711–717. [CrossRef]
21. Ivezaj, V.; White, M.A.; Grilo, C.M. Examining binge-eating disorder and food addiction in adults with overweight and obesity. *Obesity* **2016**, *24*, 2064–2069. [CrossRef]
22. Benzerouk, F.; Gierski, F.; Ducluzeau, P.-H.; Bourbao-Tournois, C.; Gaubil-Kaladjian, I.; Bertin E' Kaladjian, A.; Ballon, N.; Brunault, P. Food addiction, in obese patients seeking bariatric surgery, is associated with higher prevalence of current mood and anxiety disorders and past mood disorders. *Pyschiatry Res.* **2018**, *267*, 473–479. [CrossRef] [PubMed]
23. Meule, A.; Heckel, D.; Jurowich, C.F.; Vogele, C.; Kubler, A. Correlates of food addiction in obese individuals seeking bariatric surgery. *Clin. Obes.* **2014**, *4*, 228–236. [CrossRef] [PubMed]
24. Koball, A.M.; Clark, M.M.; Collazo-Clavell, M.; Kellogg, T.; Ames, G.; Ebbert, J.; Grothe, K.B. The relationship among food addiction, negative mood, and eating-disordered behaviors in patients seeking to have bariatric surgery. *Surg. Obes. Relat. Dis.* **2016**, *12*, 165–170. [CrossRef] [PubMed]
25. Burrows, T.; Skinner, J.; McKenna, R.; Rollo, M. Food addition, binge eating disorder, and obesity: Is there a relationship? *Behav. Sci.* **2017**, *7*, 54. [CrossRef] [PubMed]
26. Davis, C. From passive overeating to "food addiction": A spectrum of compulsion and severity. *ISRN Obes.* **2013**, *2013*, 435027. [CrossRef]
27. Gearhardt, A.N.; Boswell, R.G.; White, M.A. The association of "food addiction" with disordered eating and body mass index. *Eat. Behav.* **2014**, *15*, 427–433. [CrossRef] [PubMed]
28. Clark, S.M.; Saules, K.K. Validation of the Yale Food Addiction Scale among a weight-loss surgery population. *Eat. Behav.* **2013**, *14*, 216–219. [CrossRef]
29. Koball, A.M.; Ames, G.; Goetze, R.E.; Grothe, K. Bariatric Surgery as a Treatment for Food Addiction? A Review of the Literature. *Curr. Addict. Rep.* **2000**, *7*, 1–8. [CrossRef]
30. Cassin, S.E.; Sijercic, I.; Montemarano, V. Psychosocial Interventions for Food Addiction: A Systematic Review. *Curr. Addict. Rep.* **2020**, *7*, 9–19. [CrossRef]
31. Cassin, S.E.; Sockalingam, S.; Du, C.; Wnuk, S.; Hawa, R.; Parikh, S.V. A pilot randomized controlled trial of telephone-based cognitive behavioural therapy for preoperative bariatric surgery patients. *Behav. Res. Ther.* **2016**, *80*, 17–22. [CrossRef]
32. Sockalingam, S.; Cassin, S.E.; Wnuk, S.; Du, C.; Jackson, T.; Hawa, R.; Parikh, S.V. A Pilot Study on Telephone Cognitive Behavioral Therapy for Patients Six-Months Post-Bariatric Surgery. *Obes. Surg.* **2017**, *27*, 670–675. [CrossRef] [PubMed]
33. Sockalingam, S.; Leung, S.E.; Hawa, R.; Wnuk, S.; Parikh, S.V.; Jackson, T.; Cassin, S.E. Telephone-based cognitive behavioural therapy for female patients 1-year post-bariatric surgery: A pitlo study. *Obes. Res. Clin. Pract.* **2019**, *13*, 499–504. [CrossRef] [PubMed]
34. Cassin, S.E.; Sockalingam, S.; Wnuk, S.; Strimas, R.; Royal, S.; Hawa, R.; Parikh, S.V. Cognitive behavioral therapy for bariatric surgery patients: Preliminary evidence for feasibility, acceptability, and effectiveness. *Cogn. Behav. Pract.* **2013**, *20*, 529–543. [CrossRef]
35. Schulte, E.; Gearhardt, A.N. Development of the Modified Yale Food Addiction Scale Version 2.0. *Eur. Eat. Disord. Rev.* **2017**, *25*, 302–308. [CrossRef] [PubMed]

36. Clark, S.M.; Martens, K.; Smith-Mason, C.E.; Hamann, A.; Miller-Matero, L.R. Validation of the Yale Food Addiction Scale 2.0 among a Bariatric Surgery Population. *Obes. Surg.* **2019**, *29*, 2923–2928. [CrossRef] [PubMed]
37. Gormally, J.; Black, S.; Daston, S.; Rardin, D. The assessment of binge eating severity among obese persons. *Addict. Behav.* **1982**, *7*, 47–55. [CrossRef]
38. Hood, M.M.; Grupski, A.E.; Hall, B.J.; Ivan, I.; Corsica, J. Factor structure and predictive utility of the Binge Eating Scale in bariatric surgery candidates. *Surg. Obes. Relat. Dis.* **2013**, *9*, 942–948. [CrossRef]
39. Kroenke, K.; Spitzer, R.L.; Williams, J.B. The PHQ-9: Validity of a brief depression severity measure. *J. Gen. Intern. Med.* **2001**, *16*, 606–613. [CrossRef]
40. Spitzer, R.L.; Kroenke, K.; Williams, J.B.; Lowe, B. A brief measure for assessing generalized anxiety disorder: The GAD-7. *Arch. Intern. Med.* **2006**, *166*, 1092–1097. [CrossRef]
41. Cassin, S.; Sockalingam, S.; Hawa, R.; Wnuk, S.; Royal, S.; Taube-Schiff, M.; Okrainec, A. Psychometric properties of the Patient Health Questionnaire (PHQ-9) as a depression screening tool for bariatric surgery candidates. *Psychosomatics* **2013**, *54*, 352–358. [CrossRef]
42. Sockalingam, S.; Wnuk, S.; Kantarovich, K.; Meaney, C.; Okrainec, A.; Hawa, R.; Cassin, S. Employment Outcomes One Year after Bariatric Surgery: The Role of Patient and Psychosocial Factors. *Obes. Surg.* **2015**, *25*, 514–522. [CrossRef] [PubMed]
43. Sockalingam, S.; Hawa, R.; Wnuk, S.; Santiago, V.; Kowgier, M.; Jackson, T.; Okrainec, A.; Cassin, S. Psychosocial predictors of quality of life and weight loss two years after bariatric surgery: Results from the Toronto Bari-PSYCH study. *Gen. Hosp. Psychiatry* **2017**, *47*, 7–13. [CrossRef] [PubMed]
44. Rice, M.E.; Harris, G.T. Comparing effect sizes in follow-up studies: ROC area, Cohen's *d*, and *r*. *Law Hum. Behav.* **2005**, *29*, 615–620. [CrossRef] [PubMed]
45. Pepino, M.Y.; Stein, R.I.; Eagon, J.C.; Klein, S. Bariatric surgery-induced weight loss causes remission of food addiction in extreme obesity. *Obesity* **2014**, *22*, 1792–1798. [CrossRef]
46. Sevincer, G.M.; Konuk, N.; Bozkurt, S.; Coskun, H. Food addiction and the outcome of bariatric surgery at 1-year: Prospective observational study. *Psychiatry Res.* **2016**, *244*, 159–164. [CrossRef]
47. Leahey, T.M.; Bond, D.S.; Raynor, H.; Roye, D.; Vithiananthan, S.; Ryder, B.A.; Sax, H.C.; Wing, R.R. Effects of bariatric surgery on food cravings: Do food cravings and the consumption of craved foods "normalize" after surgery? *Surg. Obes. Relat. Dis.* **2012**, *8*, 84–91. [CrossRef]
48. Berthoud, H.R.; Zheng, H.; Shin, A.C. Food reward in the obese and after weight loss induced by calorie restriction and bariatric surgery. *Ann. N. Y. Acad. Sci.* **2012**, *1264*, 36–48. [CrossRef]
49. Le Roux, C.W.; Bueter, M.; Theis, N.; Werling, M.; Ashrafian, H.; Löwenstein, C.; Athanasiou, T.; Bloom, S.R.; Spector, A.C.; Olbers, T.; et al. Gastric bypass reduces fat intake and preference. *Am. J. Physiol. Regul. Integr. Comp. Physiol.* **2011**, *301*, R1057–R1066. [CrossRef]
50. Thomas, J.R.; Marcus, E. High and low fat food selection with reported frequency intolerance following Roux-en-Y gastric bypass. *Obes. Surg.* **2008**, *18*, 282–287. [CrossRef]
51. Schultes, B.; Ernst, B.; Wilms, B.; Thurnheer, M.; Hallschmid, M. Hedonic hunger is increased in severely obese patients and is reduced after gastric bypass surgery. *Am. J. Clin. Nutr.* **2010**, *92*, 277–283. [CrossRef]
52. Thirlby, R.C.; Bahiraei, F.; Randall, J.; Drewnoski, A. Effect of Roux-en-Y gastric bypass on satiety and food likes: The role of genetics. *J. Gastrointest. Surg.* **2006**, *10*, 270–277. [CrossRef] [PubMed]
53. Yanos, B.R.; Saules, K.K.; Schuh, L.M.; Sogg, S. Predictors of lowest weight and long-term weight regain among Roux-en-Y gastric bypass patients. *Obes. Surg.* **2015**, *25*, 1364–1370. [CrossRef] [PubMed]
54. Schulte, E.M.; Joyner, M.A.; Potenza, M.N.; Grilo, C.M.; Gearhardt, A.N. Current conditions regarding food addiction. *Curr. Psychiatry Rep.* **2015**, *17*, 563. [CrossRef] [PubMed]
55. Costa-Dookhan, K.A.; Leung, S.E.; Cassin, S.E.; Sockalingam, S. Psychosocial predictors of response to telephone-based cognitive behavioural therapy in bariatric surgery patients. *Can. J. Diabetes* **2020**, *44*, 236–240. [CrossRef]
56. Wiss, D.A.; Brewerton, T.D. Incorporating food addiction into disordered eating: The disordered eating food addiction nutrition guide (DEFANG). *Eat. Weight Disord.* **2017**, *22*, 49–59. [CrossRef]
57. Treasure, J.; Leslie, M.; Chami, R.; Fernandez-Arand, F. Are trans diagnostic models of eating disorders fit for purpose? A consideration of the evidence for food addiction. *Eur. Eat. Disord. Rev.* **2018**, *26*, 83–91. [CrossRef]

Fat Addiction: Psychological and Physiological Trajectory

Siddharth Sarkar [1], Kanwal Preet Kochhar [2] and Naim Akhtar Khan [3,*]

1 Department of Psychiatry and National Drug Dependence Treatment Centre (NDDTC), All India Institute of Medical Sciences (AIIMS), New Delhi 110029, India; sidsarkar22@gmail.com
2 Department of Physiology, All India Institute of Medical Sciences (AIIMS), New Delhi 110029, India; kpkochhar6@gmail.com
3 Nutritional Physiology and Toxicology (NUTox), UMR INSERM U1231, University of Bourgogne and Franche-Comte (UBFC), 6 boulevard Gabriel, 21000 Dijon, France
* Correspondence: Naim.Khan@u-bourgogne.fr

Abstract: Obesity has become a major public health concern worldwide due to its high social and economic burden, caused by its related comorbidities, impacting physical and mental health. Dietary fat is an important source of energy along with its rewarding and reinforcing properties. The nutritional recommendations for dietary fat vary from one country to another; however, the dietary reference intake (DRI) recommends not consuming more than 35% of total calories as fat. Food rich in fat is hyperpalatable, and is liable to be consumed in excess amounts. Food addiction as a concept has gained traction in recent years, as some aspects of addiction have been demonstrated for certain varieties of food. Fat addiction can be a diagnosable condition, which has similarities with the construct of addictive disorders, and is distinct from eating disorders or normal eating behaviors. Psychological vulnerabilities like attentional biases have been identified in individuals described to be having such addiction. Animal models have provided an opportunity to explore this concept in an experimental setting. This discussion sheds light on fat addiction, and explores its physiological and psychological implications. The discussion attempts to collate the emerging literature on addiction to fat rich diets as a prominent subset of food addiction. It aims at addressing the clinical relevance at the community level, the psychological correlates of such fat addiction, and the current physiological research directions.

Keywords: diet; fat; food addiction; obesity

---

1. Introduction

Over the last half a century, many developing countries have seen rapid socio-economic development, resulting in a move from a traditional to a modern way of life, including changes in local dietary and culinary profiles [1–3]. Abundance and easy availability of food, especially the one that is rich in fat and carbohydrate, have resulted in changes of dietary patterns and preferences. Right from early childhood in developing brains, the exposure and imprinting to high sugar, high salt and high fat food (rich in saturated and trans-fat), which is cheap and easily available, are impacting the health of younger population. Trans fat may lead to its greater consumption than polyunsaturated fat, as the latter is more quicker than the former to trigger satiety [4]. The changes in dietary intake profile with cultural and societal transitions have gained traction [5]. The dietary profile and constitution have a role in the etiopathogenesis of lifestyle-related diseases like obesity, metabolic syndrome, coronary artery disease, gut motility disorders, psychosomatic, autoimmune as well as degenerative disorders. Major transition, noticed during the last couple of years, has been an increasing use of sugar, processed food, beverages, animal-fat based food rich in trans-fats that have impacted human health [6–10].

In the recent years, there is a growing interest in the concept of food addiction from both clinical and applied nutritional research perspectives [9,11–14]. The increase in obesity, and associated metabolic syndrome and diabetes mellitus have called into the questions about factors leading to genesis of obesity. The imbalance of energy intake has been proposed as one of the reasons of increasing prevalence of obesity, though there are other several factors, i.e., epigenetics, psychological trauma, use of medications and dieting, that may increase body weight gain. why do some individuals consume excess of certain types of food (including fat-rich food)? Hence, the phenomenon of addiction to food has been suggested to be one of the mechanisms. Food addiction can refer to a variety of substrates, but fat and sugars have been considered the typical prototype food items to which individuals develop addiction. The occurrence of distinct features of salience and inability to control intake of specific types of foods have been considered similar to addiction to other psychoactive substances. The adverse consequences of uncontrolled fat intake on the body metabolism have been documented [15,16]. This has implications in intervention modules for addressing this problem and promoting healthy lifestyles [17,18]. Yet, the understanding of fat addiction as a concept is still under evolution, and progress is being made to characterise and discern the psychology and physiology behind this condition.

Recent studies suggest that fat has its own metabolic, physiological and nutritional profiles, which are distinct from other macronutrients [19–21]. Fat accords palatability and organoleptic properties to food, and is consumed across all ages from infancy through adulthood to elderly. Evolutionarily, this confers survival benefit due to high energy density, more so in cultures with thrifty genotypes [22–24]. In recent years, the benefits of mono-unsaturated fatty acid and controlled amounts of saturated fat intake have been revisited, especially in the context of benefits in cognitive functioning, synaptic connectivity, and membrane stability for both brain and heart health [25,26].

In this context, taste for fat has been proposed as the sixth taste modality in recent years [27]. The interactions between fatty acids and specific receptors in taste bud cells elicit physiological changes that are implicated in dietary fat preference via the activation of tongue-brain-gut axis. This phenomenon has an implication in the genesis of obesity as oro-sensory detection of nutrients determines the 'liking' and 'wanting' of food products. It has been proposed that there are two components of eating behavior, represented in neuronal circuits, i.e., emotional (hedonic and affective) and metabolic (homeostatic). Obesity may arise due to the imbalance of these two eating motives.

Research on food addiction or eating addiction has not paid distinct attention to specific nutrients like dietary fat [9,10,12,13]. The concept of fat addiction would have important psychological determinants like motivation, depression, anxiety and reasoning that merit cautious evaluation. There is cognitive appraisal that makes an individual "like" and "want" a specific food product, and the reward obtained from the food is cognitively processed as well. Hence, the intertwined psychological and physiological aspects of addiction towards fat rich food must be considered and understood further. There is a lack of comprehensive synthesis of literature to provide an account of fatty food addiction. In this paper, we have aimed at providing an overview of the construct, the clinical relevance, the psychological correlates, and the current physiological research trajectory in the emerging area of fat addiction as a subset of food addiction. Wherever specific literature with regard to fat is not available, evidence related to food addiction will be alluded to. However, our main emphasis is to discuss about fat addiction as this phenomenon might lead to high dietary fat intake and, consequently, to obesity. The term "high fat" in this article would mean the diet where the calories brought by fat are more than 40% of total dietary calories as most of industrialized countries recommend to respect this limit. As we have mentioned in the title, our main emphasis is to shed light on fat addiction and we have excluded other addictive behaviors like sweet addiction.

2. The Construct of Fat Rich Food Addiction

Addressing the issue of obesity would require improved knowledge of pathophysiological and neurobehavioral mechanisms. This would help better target behaviors which predispose individuals to obesity [28]. Schmidt and Campbell argue that disordered eating cannot remain "brainless" [29], and the "psychological constructs", that define aberrant consumptive patterns of food, are relevant. In this regard, addiction to food explains hedonistic excess and uncontrolled consumption of food items which are associated with adverse consequences.

Addiction towards fat rich diet relates to the overall definition of addiction. Addiction has been conceptualized as a maladaptive pattern of substance intake or behavior that signifies neurobiological changes and is associated with adverse consequences. The nosological systems providing nomenclature to diagnosis has moved on from abuse and dependence to substance use disorders in DSM5. The criteria based evaluation of the cluster of symptomatology helps provide with coherent account of the disorder, and categorize individuals who meet a threshold for diagnosis and consequent potential treatment.

2.1. *Defining Fatty Food Addiction in the Context of Nutrient Intake*

Food addiction shares some of the commonalities with drug addiction like craving, bingeing and tolerance [30]. The DSM5 criteria for substance use disorders have been adapted and explored in the context of food addiction [31,32]. The 11 criteria for substance use disorders can be applicable to individuals with addiction to lipid dense foods (especially trans and saturated fat). The empirically supported criteria describe a substance (food) often taken in larger amounts or over a longer period of time than that was intended, persistent desire or unsuccessful efforts to cut down or control substance use (food), and continued use despite knowledge of having a persistent or recurrent physical or psychological problem. The plausible features include great deal of time being spent in activities necessary to obtain or use the substance (food) or recover from its effects, recurrent substance (food) use resulting in a failure to fulfil major role obligations, continued use despite having persistent or recurrent social or interpersonal problems, important social, occupational, or recreational activities are given up or reduced, and tolerance. What might be difficult to clearly clinically elicit are withdrawal (while differentiating from energy deficit), and recurrent use in physically hazardous situations. As with different substances, each of the criteria is endorsed to different extent by a sample of participants.

The diagnostic constructs related to food addiction include binge eating disorder and an eating disorder not otherwise specified. Binge eating disorder is characterised by repeated ingestion of eating in large amounts of food in a short amount of time, followed by intense guilt and attempts to either remove the food (by vomiting or using laxatives) or compensatory behaviors to increase the energy expenditure [33,34]. On the other hand, eating disorder not otherwise specified is a diagnostic rubric that resembles anorexia nervosa or binge eating disorder, but does not fulfil the diagnostic thresholds for these disorders. These disorders may have some overlap with food addiction from a phenomenological and behavioral perspective, but the constructs themselves are distinct. It has been seen that individuals with binge eating disorders have greater rates of food addiction, than expected by chance [35,36], though at the same time, not all individuals with binge eating disorders would have food addiction [36,37].The main point of divergence lies in the focus of the constructs: food addiction lays emphasis on the salience and loss of control of hedonic eating behaviors, while eating disorders are accompanied by intense immediate guilt after excessive food consumption and efforts are made to get rid of (effects of) the ingested food quickly.

2.2. *Clinical and Epidemiological Implications of Addiction towards Fat*

While limited literature has looked at addiction to fat rich foods per se, there is enough evidence that has ascertained the occurrence rate and determinants of food addiction in the community and clinical samples [38,39]. The questionnaires used to assess food addiction generally incorporate fat as a component of food that the respondents are asked to think about, when they answer the questions. The Yale Food Addiction Scale is perhaps the most commonly used instrument for the assessment of food addiction. The weighted mean prevalence of food addiction according to this instrument was 19.9% [38]. The prevalence of food addiction was high in women with obesity [38]. Also, food addiction was higher in clinical samples, as compared to community samples [37,38]. Food addiction was high in subjects that were either obese, or suffered from eating disorders. High scores of food addiction were associated with high depressive symptoms, food craving and impulsivity. Food addiction has not only been related to negative mood states, but also with poorer quality of life [40]. It has been seen that individuals with food addiction had higher dietary fat intake as compared to those without food addiction [41]. Similarly, Pursey et al reported that the subjects with high food addiction scores had high percentage of consumption of saturated fat [42]. Thus, food addiction provides a paradigm for identification of individuals with skewed dietary profiles with other psychological vulnerabilities, which might require concomitant attention.

Food addiction has also been studied in those individuals who have undergone bariatric surgery which is generally indicated for people with severe obesity [43]. The rates of food addiction in bariatric surgery population go down after the surgery. In one study, the proportion of individuals with food addiction reduced to 2% post-surgery from 32% pre-surgery [44]. Another long term follow-up suggested that the rates of food addiction reduced from 57.8% to 7.2% at 6 months and to 13.7% at 12 months after surgery [45]. In pre-operative cases of bariatric surgery, the dietary intervention is less effective in individuals with food addiction [46]. It has been seen that food addiction in bariatric surgery patients was associated with greater levels of depression, anxiety and binge eating episodes, though it did not predict the degree of weight loss. Thus, it seems that food addiction has some clinical prognostic influence with surgical intervention outcomes.

2.3. Measurement Approaches

Currently the standard of practice for determination of food addiction has been the diagnostic cut-off from the Yale Food Addiction Scale (YFAS) [47]. The YEAS is a 25 item self–reported questionnaire based scale that assesses various features of food addiction. There are two items that assess for clinically significant impairment or distress. The instrument looks at the past year pattern of food intake and includes fatty foods like steak, bacon, hamburgers, cheeseburgers, pizza, and French fries as one of the representative group of foods that are mentioned in the questionnaire. The instrument has become standard of use in the field of food addiction. The instrument has adequate internal reliability, good convergent validity and good discriminant validity. The instrument has been adapted for use in children [48]. The instrument has also been translated into several other languages like Chinese, French and Malay [49–51]. A newer version of the scale (YFAS 2.0) has been developed considering the changes in conjunction with the DSM5 [52]. The instrument has been used in studies of epidemiology, etiology, nosology and interventions of food addiction. While the YFAS addressed food as a whole, assessing fat addiction separately may have implications for interventions. This could be in terms of the type of food products that are focused upon in the intervention modules that are developed. This would have also a corollary for the investigation procedures that can include assessment of salience and behavioral neuroplasticity (eye tracking and neuroimaging) for different types of food products (fat rich versus carbohydrate rich, sweet versus savory fatty food) that are implicated in food addiction.

Other self-reported scales and questionnaires for assessment of aspects of food addiction are also available and have been validated, though they rely on features like craving and eating patterns. These include Eating Behaviors Questionnaire [53], Food Cravings Questionnaire [54], Eating Behaviors Patterns Questionnaire [55], and Power of Food Scale [56]. Many of these questionnaires are self-reported, i.e., the individual reads through the questions and responds through them. The responses are thereafter graded and interpreted based upon the cut-offs from the population scores.

3. Psychological Correlates of Addiction to Fat Rich Diets

3.1. Attentional Biases and Cognitive Functioning

Research has been carried out towards attentional biases and psychological processing in individuals with food addiction. Obese as compared to lean teens showed less activation of prefrontal regions (dorsolateral prefrontal cortex, ventral lateral prefrontal cortex) when trying to inhibit responses to high-calorie food images which suggest behavioral evidence of reduced inhibitory control [57]. Adults who had greater dorsolateral prefrontal cortex activation when instructed to "resist craving" after viewing food images had better weight loss success following gastric bypass surgery [58]. This suggests that visual cue induction paradigms have relevance to assessment of how food images are processed centrally.

Rodrigue et al. [59] compared those with higher and lower food addiction scores on cognitive processes of planning, inhibition, cognitive flexibility and error processing. The investigators found that high food addiction group differed from the low food addiction group only in terms of inhibition/cognitive flexibility scaled scores, but not in individual scores. The authors infer that though basic level processes are intact, individuals with higher food addiction scores experience greater difficulties in more challenging context where they had to simultaneously keep in mind to inhibit a behavior and switch their mind-set when the task required it. This might make it difficult for them to anticipate the long-term consequences of behavior. Also, individuals with symptoms of food addiction made more errors as the interference task became challenging, suggesting that those with food addiction might have greater difficulty in detecting and monitoring errors. Another study compared error monitoring among individuals with food addiction and healthy controls using the Eriksen flanker task [60]. The results suggested that food addiction group had higher number of errors on the flanker task, implying impaired performance monitoring and cognitive control, as seen with other addictions. In a study that included women with obesity, food addiction severity levels were negatively correlated with overall scores on the Iowa Gambling Task, which measures decision making capacity [61]. Also, those with food addiction had attentional deficits as reflected by more omissions and perseveration errors on the Continuous Performance Task. On the other hand, Blume et al. [62] compared response inhibition, attention, decision-making, and impulsivity among four groups of individuals, i.e., obesity and food addiction; obesity and binge eating disorder; obesity/food addiction and binge eating disorder; and obesity only. The authors did not find food addiction to be related to altered executive functioning.

Ruddock et al. [63] evaluated the attentional bias using eye tracking while showing pictures of chocolate among individuals with self-perceived food addiction in design that evaluated state factors like hunger or expectancy of reward or having food addiction. The authors found that the expectancy of receiving chocolate as reward was associated with attentional bias, while hunger state or having self-perceived food addiction was not associated with attentional bias toward food related cues. In another eye tracking paradigm, sad mood induction through showing of a video of child passing away with cancer was associated with attentional bias towards unhealthy food among those with food addiction, but such a change did not occur in those without food addiction [64]. This suggests that emotional cues may impel or prime those with food addiction towards specific food types. In another study, Gearhardt et al. [65] studied food-related visual attention and dwell time of food stuff among obese and overweight women. The authors reported that hunger was associated with attentional bias toward sweets, and trend level attentional bias towards fried (fatty) foods. On the other hand, hunger was associated with shorter dwell time on fried food. Taken together, literature suggests that hunger may be an important component that may influence attentional biases in individuals with food addiction. We acknowledge that though addiction has gained traction, fat addiction is an emerging concept, and nevertheless needs debate and discussion to inform lifestyle practices and research directions.

3.2. *Craving and Liking*

Craving and liking are related, but represent distinct terms that are linked to food addiction. While craving refers to desire or urge to eat a food item, liking refers to qualitative and affective evaluation of food [66–68]. Liking for fat has been evaluated in a large web-based study to examine the determinants of dietary patterns and nutritional status [69]. The investigators reported that individuals with a strong liking for fat had high total energy and fat intake, and high consumption of saturated fats, meat, butter, sweetened cream desserts and croissant-like pastries. Such individuals also consumed low quantities of fiber, fruits, vegetables and yogurt. It was highlighted that increased liking for fat, especially fat-and-salt liking, was associated with a lower intake of fruit and vegetables.

Gearhardt et al. [70] assessed craving for 180 food items among a sample of 105 obese or overweight women. The authors found that those with greater symptomatology of food addiction had higher craving ratings for fatty foods. However, as BMI increased, the craving decreased. In contrast to craving in this study, high fat content was not associated with high liking for food product, suggesting a dichotomy between craving and liking.

4. Understanding the Physiological and Neurobiological Processes of Fat Food Addiction

There have been considerable advances in understanding the mechanisms of addiction for food rich in lipids. Some of them were conducted on animals, particularly rodent models. Other directions of research, for example, genetics and neuroimaging have explored the origin of addiction towards fat and other palatable foods in human participants [71,72]. The reward pathway (schematically shown in Figure 1) is intricately linked to understanding the addiction to fatty food, though some differences have been reported in food addiction and substance use disorders [73].

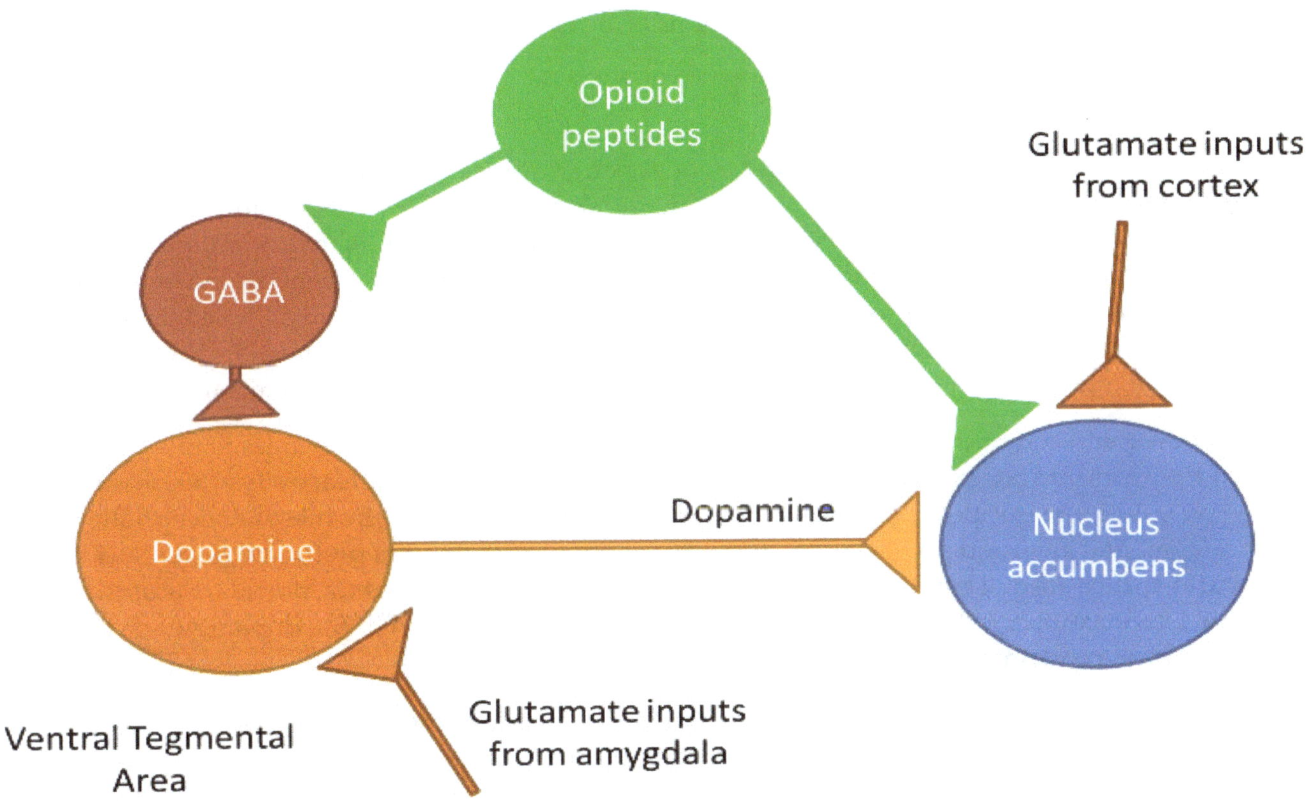

Figure 1. Schematic representation of the reward pathway. The figure shows the interplay between different neurons where the nucleus accumbens seems to be the central player, receiving the projection of dopaminergic, glutamatergic and opioidergic neurons. The model for food addiction might be quite different and is under examination [74].

4.1. Animal Models for Understanding the Addiction to Fat Rich Foods

The advantage of animal models is that they are able to develop addiction to fat as the diets given in animal models are homogenous [75–77]. This is not possible in human studies. The high-fat diet that generally comprises of 45% of energy from lipids is used to trigger obesity in rodents [78]. However, none of the experimental high-fat diets resembles closely to human diet fatty acid composition, though they are efficient to induce obesity.

Initially, Avena et al. [79] developed a model for sugar addiction which showed patterns of binge eating, withdrawal symptoms, and neurochemical changes similar to those observed with opiate addiction. The phenotype of animal was created by restricting the frequency, duration or access to sugar. Subsequently, fat models of bingeing have been developed in conjunction with carbohydrates, wherein corn oil is used as a reinforcing food item. However, the features of opiate-like withdrawal were not noted by Avena et al. [80] when animals were deprived of food after fat bingeing. This observation suggests that fat addiction may have different phenomenological aspects than the addiction to sugars. An alternate explanation could be that fat addiction might be more closely aligned to behavioral addiction like gambling disorder, while addiction to sugar rich food might be more closely aligned to substance use disorders. The development of animal models has the potential to advance the field substantially, by enabling to better understand the neurobiological alterations, and to assess the changes in bingeing behaviors with medications or other interventions [81]. Yet, one needs to be cognizant of the fact that translation of human behavior of food consumption is much more complex than animals, and is influenced by socio-economic and political environment, and the determinants like cost, availability and marketing. Furthermore, it is possible that modeling addiction in animals (especially rodents) might differ substantially from clinical situation [8]. It has been argued that simplistic experiments would need critical reflection about translational validity of patterns of eating behavior and food choice from animals to humans.

4.2. Neurotransmitters Including Dopamine

Animal studies have suggested implication of dopamine in the nucleus accumbens in the rat model of addictive behaviors towards fat [82]. Hence, microdialysis samples were taken in this model before, during and after sham feeding with corn oil. The study found an increase in dopamine in the sham licking group leading to the inference that corn oil increases dopamine concentrations in the nucleus accumbens in a manner similar to those induced by sucrose. In another study, low concentration of non-esterified fatty acid (linoleic acid) increased the dopamine levels in the nucleus accumbens and amygdala in a manner equivalent to those resulting from corn oil in the brain's reward system [83].

Dela Cruz and colleagues studied the expression of c-Fos in reward circuit areas in rats which were exposed to sugars and fats [84,85]. The authors reported c-Fos like immunoreactivity after consumption of corn oil solutions, isocaloric glucose and fructose, in the dopaminergic mesotelencephalic nuclei (ventral tegmental area) and projections (infralimbic and prelimbic medial prefrontal cortex, basolateral and central-cortico-medial amygdala, core of nucleus accumbens as well as the dorsal striatum), but not in the nucleus accumbens shell. This signified transcriptional activation of the dopaminergic pathway with exposure to certain nutrients including fat.

Dela Cruz et al aimed at investigating whether dopamine antagonists (D1 receptor antagonist SCH23390 and D2 receptor antagonist raclopride) attenuated the development of fat conditioned flavour preference among rats [86]. These investigators reported that, as compared to sucrose, the D1 and D2 receptor antagonists were not able to attenuate the fat conditioned flavor preference. They further suggested that fat addiction in rats could possibly have distinct mechanisms than sugars, which involved the post ingestive phase.

The role of opioid receptors and fatty food addiction has also been explored [76]. It has been seen that after injection of morphine, a mu-opioid receptor agonist, rats preferred fats over carbohydrates when both were available. Intra-accumbens administration of opioid agonists increased the consumption of fats, and the effect was blocked by the administration of naltrexone, an opioid antagonist [87]. The opioid receptors have been implicated in not only the 'liking' process, but also the 'wanting' process of excessive food consumption, and the effects are blocked by opioid antagonists.

Endocannabinoid system is another neurotransmitter system studied in relation with animal model of excessive fat consumptive behavior. Ward et al. [88] studied male, cannabinoid (CB1) knockout mice which were trained to respond to the sweet reinforcer (Ensure) or corn oil. The authors suggest that CB1 receptor antagonism selectively attenuated reinstatement of responding for Ensure. Interestingly, the genetic deletion of the CB1 receptor did not attenuate reinstatement of corn-oil seeking. The authors suggest that either CB1 receptor system does not play an equivalent role in modulating conditioned seeking or corn oil may serve as a robust reinforcer. Additionally, Brissard et al. [89] found that invalidation of CB1R gene was related to lower levels of fat preference among mice, and similar results were obtained after using rimonabant, a cannabinoid receptor antagonist. The authors reported that fat taste perception was mediated through calcium signaling and GLP-1 secretion in lingual taste bud cells. Peterschmitt et al. [90] looked at the link between the gustatory and the reward pathway with regard to fat intake. The authors observed that lipid taste perception was based upon the systematic activation of the major cerebral structures of the canonical gustatory pathway and was intricately linked to the reward pathway through the ventral tegmental area.

4.3. Neuroimaging Correlates

Though literature exists on the neuroimaging correlates of obesity [91,92], studies on the neuroimaging of food addiction have gradually started to come up. Gearhardt et al. [93] assessed the blood oxygen level-dependent functional magnetic resonance imaging (fMRI) activation in response to receipt and anticipated receipt of palatable food (chocolate milkshake) among adolescent female participants. The investigators demonstrated that food addiction scores correlated with greater activation in the anterior cingulate cortex, medial orbitofrontal cortex and amygdala, consequent to anticipated receipt of food. The participants with high food addiction scores had enhanced activation of dorsolateral prefrontal cortex and caudate, but less activation in lateral orbitofrontal cortex in response to anticipated receipt of food. These findings underscore the similarity of food addiction to other types of addictions, especially in relation to involvement of the reward pathway.

Hsu et al. [94] assessed response inhibition and error processing among subjects with obesity and sweet food addiction by fMRI. Women with obesity and food addiction had a higher score for impulsivity and lower brain activation (processing response inhibition over the right rolandic operculum and thalamus) than controls. The activation during error processing over the left insula, precuneus, and bilateral putamen were higher in the subjects with obesity and sweet food addiction than controls. These findings suggest that women with obesity and sweet food addiction have impaired rolandic operculum activation.

A further study looked at the relationship of food addiction and functional connectivity in the brain during fasting and fed state [95]. The authors found that high number of symptoms of food addiction were associated with ventral caudate-hippocampus hyperconnectivity in the fasted scan only. However, a significant reduction of this connectivity was observed in the fed scans, suggesting that heightened connectivity in the ventral striatum during a fasted state corroborated reward prediction signals, further lending credence to the involvement of the reward pathway.

A schematic representation of the neurobiological relationship of fatty food intake, mediated through gustatory signaling and reward pathway, is presented in Figure 2.

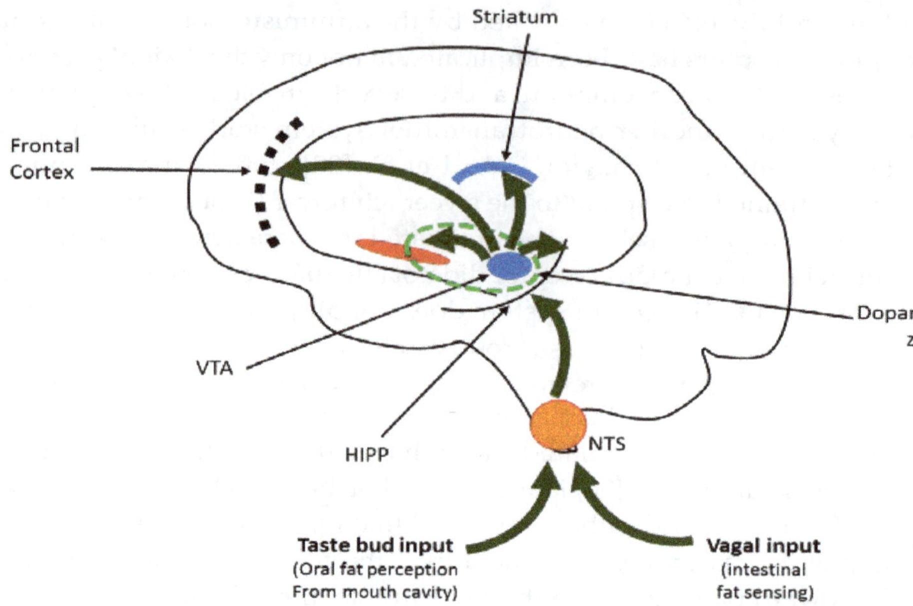

Figure 2. Relationship of food intake and reward pathway. The figure shows that the gustatory memory for fat and its implication would depend on the cues coming from taste bud cells, localized in the lingual papillae, and vagal nerve information from intestinal lipid sensing. Both kinds of information will ascend to different parts of the brain via NTS. Hippocampus will be involved in the learning of palatability of fat, and communicate to VTA which is sending its afferences to frontal cortex, straitum and other parts of the brain. Indeed, the dopaminergic zone covers VTA and NA. NTS: nucleus tractus solitaris; HIPP: hippocampus; VTA: ventral tegmental area.

4.4. Genetics Underpinnings

Several studies have also looked at the genetic associations of food addiction. A study evaluated whether a composite index of elevated dopamine signaling, a multilocus genetic profile score (MLGP) could segregate between those with food addiction and normal eating behavior [96]. The authors observed that MLGP score was high in subjects with food addiction, and it correlated positively with binge eating, food cravings, and emotional overeating. This finding supported the view that dopamine signaling genetic profile was different in subjects with food addiction.

Pedram et al. [97] studied food addiction in the Newfoundland population and observed the major allele A of rs2511521 located in DRD2 and the minor allele T of rs625413 located in TIR domain containing adaptor protein (TIRAP) to be significantly associated with food addiction. A study on the Asian American college students assessed the relationship of food addiction and a dopamine-resistant receptor (DRD2) polymorphism [98]. The authors reported that DRD2 A1 allele among Asian Americans (versus A2 allele) was associated with greater carbohydrate craving, but not fat craving. Cornelis et al. [99] presented genome wide analysis of food addiction in more than 9000 women with European ancestry. This study showed two loci significant at genome-wide level (17q21.31 and 11q13.4), but they did not have any obvious roles in eating behavior. The study did not find any candidate single nucleotide polymorphism or gene for drug addiction to be significantly associated with food addiction after correction for multiple testing.

There is accruing literature that suggests that reduced fat taste perception may contribute to increased fat consumption and, consequently, to obesity [100], and this might be influenced by the genetic polymorphisms. Studies from USA, Algeria and Tunisia seem to suggest that rs1761667-AA genotype of CD36 receptor is associated with obesity, and high thresholds for oro-sensory detection of dietary lipids [101–103]. Interestingly, Plesnik et al. [104] reported that another variant of CD36, i.e., rs1527483 SNP, was associated with greater body weight in young Czech participants. Thus, the taste threshold and preference for fat, mediated through specific genetic polymorphisms, may determine fat-eating behaviors that may lead to fat addiction.

5. Conclusions, Limitations and Future Directions

Addiction to food products, especially those rich in fat has received attention in recent decades. Figure 3 depicts the overall associations and implications of addiction to fat replete diets. The construct of food addiction has undergone sufficient scrutiny, and means and measures have been developed to reliably assess this condition. Fat as a component of food addiction itself has yet to find its niche, but has possible implications for the control and prevention of obesity. Research has elaborated on the attentional biases and cognitive functioning in individuals with food addiction, and has pitched varied findings. Animal models of food addiction, especially those which have used fat as a substrate, have expanded the scope of the field and have given an armamentarium of options for understanding the condition and interventional choices. Neuroimaging and genetic studies have also progressed, enriching the field.

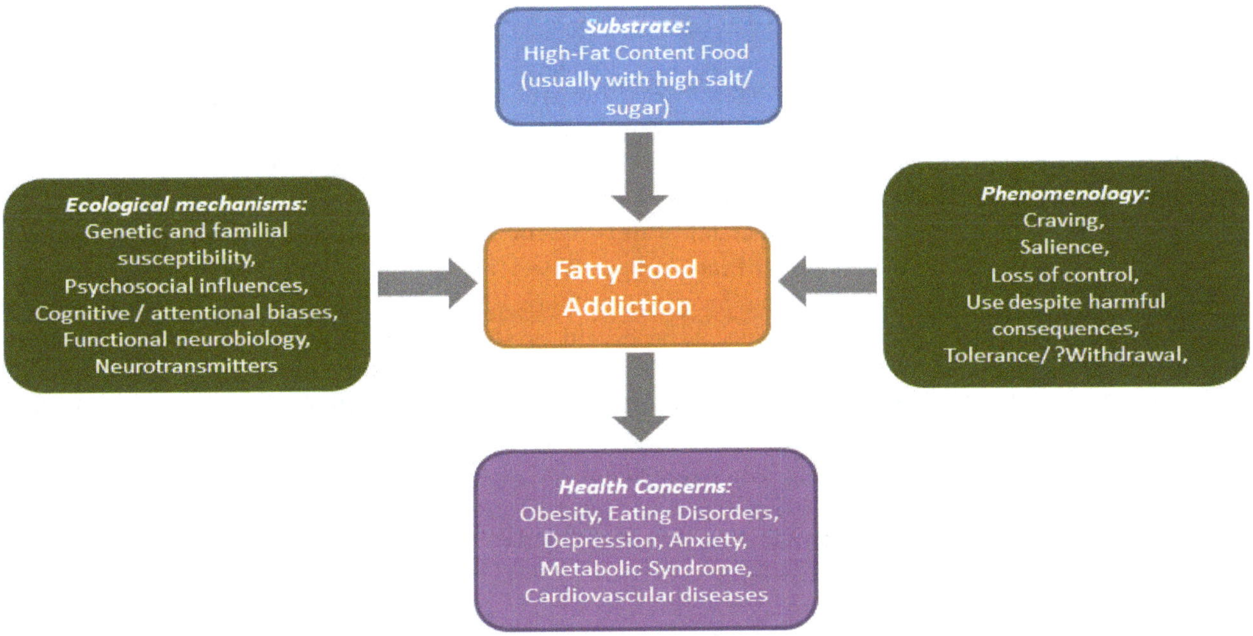

Figure 3. Schematic representation of addiction to fat.

Some of the limitations of the present paper should be born in mind while considering different observations. The present findings have not been synthesized as a systematic review, but are rather in the form of a narrative review. The advantage of narrative review is that broad range of findings can be presented to provide the reader with various dimension of the topic, but it may not be able to present all relevant literature in the field. The concept of food addiction, similar or different from other (substance/drug) addiction, as a continuum of behavioral addiction has been debated. Additionally, segregation of food addiction into a specific macronutrient based fat addiction may be difficult to operationalize clinically, as food products generally contain multiple elements together (fats, sugars and salt). Furthermore, food addiction as a concept has been criticized as pathologizing a normal behavior, and some researchers have questioned the validity and nomenclature of the construct [8].

Future research investigations are required to look at the stability of addiction to fat rich food over longitudinal course. The etiological understanding would be strengthened by foray into multi-modal assessment incorporating neuroimaging, genetic and psychological domains. Another aspect would be determining a threshold for fat composition in the food to qualify for fat addiction. Neurobiological studies would be strengthened if they incorporate the neuroimaging responses to palatable food taste, and cues (including visual cues). Neurobiological correlates of fat addiction and its persistence can be elicited by developing studies for individual nutrient components as well as combinations in sweet and savory food and linking it to markers of obesity. It would be pertinent to see how other neuropsychological functions like motivation, sensory processing in various domains and working memory interact with reward and homeostatic systems in controlling the various phenomenological aspects of fat addiction. Also, relationship of addictive behavior with intervention outcomes (for example, for obesity) needs to be looked into. The social impact of food addiction from a macro policy level, and the lived experience of the individual with 'food addiction' would help better understand the condition. Also, attempts to enhance the awareness of this condition and the harmful impact of trans-fat and saturated fat, coupled with greater funding to understand and address this issue would help both for primary and secondary prevention. Of course, the overarching aim would be to provide with relevant prevention for at-risk population, and suitable interventions for affected individuals.

Author Contributions: Conceptualization, S.S., K.P.K., and N.A.K.; review of literature, S.S., K.P.K., and N.A.K.; data curation, S.S.; writing—original draft preparation, S.S.; writing—review and editing, K.P.K. and N.A.K.; project administration, N.A.K.

References

1. Popkin, B.M.; Adair, L.S.; Ng, S.W. Global nutrition transition and the pandemic of obesity in developing countries. *Nutr. Rev.* **2012**, *70*, 3–21. [CrossRef] [PubMed]
2. Kochhar, K.P. Dietary spices in health and diseases: I. *Ind. J. Physiol. Pharmacol.* **2008**, *52*, 106–122.
3. Kochhar, K.P. Dietary spices in health and diseases (II). *Ind. J. Physiol. Pharmacol.* **2008**, *52*, 327–354.
4. Erlanson-Albertsson, C. Fat-rich food palatability and appetite regulation. In *Fat Detection: Taste, Texture, and Post Ingestive Effects*; CRC Press/Taylor & Francis: Boca Raton, FL, USA, 2010.
5. Drewnowski, A. Obesity, diets, and social inequalities. *Nutr. Rev.* **2009**, *67* (Suppl. 1), S36–S39. [CrossRef]
6. Popkin, B.M. Global nutrition dynamics: The world is shifting rapidly toward a diet linked with noncommunicable diseases. *Am. J. Clin. Nutr.* **2006**, *84*, 289–298. [CrossRef]
7. Popkin, B.M.; Gordon-Larsen, P. The nutrition transition: Worldwide obesity dynamics and their determinants. *Int. J. Obes.* **2004**, *28*, S2–S9. [CrossRef]
8. Hebebrand, J.; Albayrak, Ö.; Adan, R.; Antel, J.; Dieguez, C.; de Jong, J.; Leng, G.; Menzies, J.; Mercer, J.G.; Murphy, M.; et al. "Eating addiction", rather than "food addiction", better captures addictive-like eating behavior. *Neurosci. Biobehav. Rev.* **2014**, *47*, 295–306. [CrossRef]
9. Gordon, E.L.; Ariel-Donges, A.H.; Bauman, V.; Merlo, L.J. What Is the Evidence for "Food Addiction?" A Systematic Review. *Nutrients* **2018**, *10*, 477. [CrossRef]
10. Lerma-Cabrera, J.M.; Carvajal, F.; Lopez-Legarrea, P. Food addiction as a new piece of the obesity framework. *Nutr. J.* **2015**, *15*, 5. [CrossRef]
11. Bassareo, V.; Gambarana, C. Food and Its Effect on the Brain: From Physiological to Compulsive Consumption. *Front. Psychiatry* **2019**, *10*, 209. [CrossRef]
12. Fernandez-Aranda, F.; Karwautz, A.; Treasure, J. Food addiction: A transdiagnostic construct of increasing interest. *Eur. Eat. Disord. Rev. J. Eat. Disord. Assoc.* **2018**, *26*, 536–540. [CrossRef] [PubMed]
13. Pelchat, M.L. Food addiction in humans. *J. Nutr.* **2009**, *139*, 620–622. [CrossRef] [PubMed]
14. Shriner, R.; Gold, M. Food addiction: An evolving nonlinear science. *Nutrients* **2014**, *6*, 5370–5391. [CrossRef] [PubMed]
15. Golay, A.; Bobbioni, E. The role of dietary fat in obesity. *Int. J. Obes. Relat. Metab. Disord. J. Int. Assoc. Study Obes.* **1997**, *21* (Suppl. 3), S2–S11.
16. Smilowitz, J.T.; German, J.B.; Zivkovic, A.M. Food Intake and Obesity: The Case of Fat. In *Fat Detection: Taste, Texture, and Post Ingestive Effects*; Frontiers in Neuroscience; Montmayeur, J.-P., le Coutre, J., Eds.; CRC Press/Taylor & Francis: Boca Raton, FL, USA, 2010; ISBN 978-1-4200-6775-0.
17. Meule, A. A Critical Examination of the Practical Implications Derived from the Food Addiction Concept. *Curr. Obes. Rep.* **2019**, *8*, 11–17. [CrossRef]
18. Cassin, S.E.; Buchman, D.Z.; Leung, S.E.; Kantarovich, K.; Hawa, A.; Carter, A.; Sockalingam, S. Ethical, Stigma, and Policy Implications of Food Addiction: A Scoping Review. *Nutrients* **2019**, *11*, 710. [CrossRef]
19. Khan, N.A.; Besnard, P. Oro-sensory perception of dietary lipids: New insights into the fat taste transduction. *Biochim. Biophys. Acta* **2009**, *1791*, 149–155. [CrossRef]
20. Mattes, R.D. Fat taste and lipid metabolism in humans. *Physiol. Behav.* **2005**, *86*, 691–697. [CrossRef]

21. Drewnowski, A.; Mennella, J.A.; Johnson, S.L.; Bellisle, F. Sweetness and food preference. *J. Nutr.* **2012**, *142*, 1142S–1148S. [CrossRef]
22. Sellayah, D.; Cagampang, F.R.; Cox, R.D. On the evolutionary origins of obesity: A new hypothesis. *Endocrinology* **2014**, *155*, 1573–1588. [CrossRef]
23. Reddon, H.; Patel, Y.; Turcotte, M.; Pigeyre, M.; Meyre, D. Revisiting the evolutionary origins of obesity: Lazy versus peppy-thrifty genotype hypothesis. *Obes. Rev. Off. J. Int. Assoc. Study Obes.* **2018**, *19*, 1525–1543. [CrossRef] [PubMed]
24. Genné-Bacon, E.A. Thinking evolutionarily about obesity. *Yale J. Biol. Med.* **2014**, *87*, 99–112. [PubMed]
25. Clifton, P.M.; Keogh, J.B. A systematic review of the effect of dietary saturated and polyunsaturated fat on heart disease. *Nutr. Metab. Cardiovasc. Dis. NMCD* **2017**, *27*, 1060–1080. [CrossRef] [PubMed]
26. Power, R.; Prado-Cabrero, A.; Mulcahy, R.; Howard, A.; Nolan, J.M. The Role of Nutrition for the Aging Population: Implications for Cognition and Alzheimer's Disease. *Annu. Rev. Food Sci. Technol.* **2019**, *10*, 619–639. [CrossRef] [PubMed]
27. Besnard, P.; Passilly-Degrace, P.; Khan, N.A. Taste of Fat: A Sixth Taste Modality? *Physiol. Rev.* **2016**, *96*, 151–176. [CrossRef]
28. Val-Laillet, D.; Aarts, E.; Weber, B.; Ferrari, M.; Quaresima, V.; Stoeckel, L.E.; Alonso-Alonso, M.; Audette, M.; Malbert, C.H.; Stice, E. Neuroimaging and neuromodulation approaches to study eating behavior and prevent and treat eating disorders and obesity. *NeuroImage Clin.* **2015**, *8*, 1–31. [CrossRef]
29. Schmidt, U.; Campbell, I.C. Treatment of eating disorders can not remain "brainless": The case for brain-directed treatments. *Eur. Eat. Disord. Rev. J. Eat. Disord. Assoc.* **2013**, *21*, 425–427. [CrossRef]
30. Rogers, P.J. Food and drug addictions: Similarities and differences. *Pharmacol. Biochem. Behav.* **2017**, *153*, 182–190. [CrossRef]
31. Hone-Blanchet, A.; Fecteau, S. Overlap of food addiction and substance use disorders definitions: Analysis of animal and human studies. *Neuropharmacology* **2014**, *85*, 81–90. [CrossRef]
32. Meule, A.; Gearhardt, A.N. Food addiction in the light of DSM-5. *Nutrients* **2014**, *6*, 3653–3671. [CrossRef]
33. Schreiber, L.R.N.; Odlaug, B.L.; Grant, J.E. The overlap between binge eating disorder and substance use disorders: Diagnosis and neurobiology. *J. Behav. Addict.* **2013**, *2*, 191–198. [CrossRef] [PubMed]
34. Citrome, L. A primer on binge eating disorder diagnosis and management. *CNS Spectr.* **2015**, *20* (Suppl. 1), 44–50. [CrossRef] [PubMed]
35. Carter, J.C.; Van Wijk, M.; Rowsell, M. Symptoms of "food addiction" in binge eating disorder using the Yale Food Addiction Scale version 2.0. *Appetite* **2019**, *133*, 362–369. [CrossRef] [PubMed]
36. Linardon, J.; Messer, M. Assessment of food addiction using the Yale Food Addiction Scale 2.0 in individuals with binge-eating disorder symptomatology: Factor structure, psychometric properties, and clinical significance. *Psychiatry Res.* **2019**, *279*, 216–221. [CrossRef] [PubMed]
37. Burrows, T.; Skinner, J.; McKenna, R.; Rollo, M. Food Addiction, Binge Eating Disorder, and Obesity: Is There a Relationship? *Behav. Sci. Basel Switz.* **2017**, *7*, 54. [CrossRef] [PubMed]
38. Pursey, K.M.; Stanwell, P.; Gearhardt, A.N.; Collins, C.E.; Burrows, T.L. The prevalence of food addiction as assessed by the Yale Food Addiction Scale: A systematic review. *Nutrients* **2014**, *6*, 4552–4590. [CrossRef] [PubMed]
39. Penzenstadler, L.; Soares, C.; Karila, L.; Khazaal, Y. Systematic Review of Food Addiction as Measured With the Yale Food Addiction Scale: Implications for the Food Addiction Construct. *Curr. Neuropharmacol.* **2018**, *16*, 520. [CrossRef]
40. Zhao, Z.; Ma, Y.; Han, Y.; Liu, Y.; Yang, K.; Zhen, S.; Wen, D. Psychosocial Correlates of Food Addiction and Its Association with Quality of Life in a Non-Clinical Adolescent Sample. *Nutrients* **2018**, *10*, 837. [CrossRef]
41. Ayaz, A.; Nergiz-Unal, R.; Dedebayraktar, D.; Akyol, A.; Pekcan, A.G.; Besler, H.T.; Buyuktuncer, Z. How does food addiction influence dietary intake profile? *PLoS ONE* **2018**, *13*, e0195541. [CrossRef]
42. Pursey, K.M.; Collins, C.E.; Stanwell, P.; Burrows, T.L. Foods and dietary profiles associated with "food addiction" in young adults. *Addict. Behav. Rep.* **2015**, *2*, 41–48. [CrossRef]
43. Ivezaj, V.; Wiedemann, A.A.; Grilo, C.M. Food addiction and bariatric surgery: A systematic review of the literature. *Obes. Rev. Off. J. Int. Assoc. Study Obes.* **2017**, *18*, 1386–1397. [CrossRef] [PubMed]
44. Pepino, M.Y.; Stein, R.I.; Eagon, J.C.; Klein, S. Bariatric surgery-induced weight loss causes remission of food addiction in extreme obesity. *Obes. Silver Spring Md.* **2014**, *22*, 1792–1798. [CrossRef] [PubMed]

45. Sevinçer, G.M.; Konuk, N.; Bozkurt, S.; Coşkun, H. Food addiction and the outcome of bariatric surgery at 1-year: Prospective observational study. *Psychiatry Res.* **2016**, *244*, 159–164. [CrossRef]
46. Guerrero Pérez, F.; Sánchez-González, J.; Sánchez, I.; Jiménez-Murcia, S.; Granero, R.; Simó-Servat, A.; Ruiz, A.; Virgili, N.; López-Urdiales, R.; Montserrat-Gil de Bernabe, M.; et al. Food addiction and preoperative weight loss achievement in patients seeking bariatric surgery. *Eur. Eat. Disord. Rev. J. Eat. Disord. Assoc.* **2018**, *26*, 645–656. [CrossRef]
47. Gearhardt, A.N.; Corbin, W.R.; Brownell, K.D. Preliminary validation of the Yale food addiction scale. *Appetite* **2009**, *52*, 430–436. [CrossRef]
48. Gearhardt, A.N.; Roberto, C.A.; Seamans, M.J.; Corbin, W.R.; Brownell, K.D. Preliminary validation of the Yale Food Addiction Scale for children. *Eat. Behav.* **2013**, *14*, 508–512. [CrossRef] [PubMed]
49. Chen, G.; Tang, Z.; Guo, G.; Liu, X.; Xiao, S. The Chinese version of the Yale Food Addiction Scale: An examination of its validation in a sample of female adolescents. *Eat. Behav.* **2015**, *18*, 97–102. [CrossRef]
50. Nantha, Y.S.; Patah, N.A.A.; Pillai, M.P. Preliminary validation of the Malay Yale Food Addiction Scale: Factor structure and item analysis in an obese population. *Clin. Nutr. ESPEN* **2016**, *16*, 42–47. [CrossRef]
51. Brunault, P.; Ballon, N.; Gaillard, P.; Réveillère, C.; Courtois, R. Validation of the French version of the Yale Food Addiction Scale: An examination of its factor structure, reliability, and construct validity in a nonclinical sample. *Can. J. Psychiatry* **2014**, *59*, 276–284. [CrossRef]
52. Gearhardt, A.N.; Corbin, W.R.; Brownell, K.D. Development of the Yale Food Addiction Scale Version 2.0. *Psychol. Addict. Behav. J. Soc. Psychol. Addict. Behav.* **2016**, *30*, 113–121. [CrossRef]
53. Wardle, J.; Guthrie, C.A.; Sanderson, S.; Rapoport, L. Development of the children's eating behaviour questionnaire. *J. Child Psychol. Psychiatry* **2001**, *42*, 963–970. [CrossRef] [PubMed]
54. Cepeda-Benito, A.; Gleaves, D.H.; Williams, T.L.; Erath, S.A. The development and validation of the state and trait food-cravings questionnaires. *Behav. Ther.* **2000**, *31*, 151–173. [CrossRef]
55. Schlundt, D.G.; Hargreaves, M.K.; Buchowski, M.S. The eating behavior patterns questionnaire predicts dietary fat intake in African American women. *J. Am. Diet. Assoc.* **2003**, *103*, 338–345. [PubMed]
56. Cappelleri, J.C.; Bushmakin, A.G.; Gerber, R.A.; Leidy, N.K.; Sexton, C.C.; Karlsson, J.; Lowe, M.R. Evaluating the Power of Food Scale in obese subjects and a general sample of individuals: Development and measurement properties. *Int. J. Obes.* **2009**, *33*, 913–922. [CrossRef] [PubMed]
57. Batterink, L.; Yokum, S.; Stice, E. Body mass correlates inversely with inhibitory control in response to food among adolescent girls: An fMRI study. *NeuroImage* **2010**, *52*, 1696–1703. [CrossRef] [PubMed]
58. Goldman, R.L.; Canterberry, M.; Borckardt, J.J.; Madan, A.; Byrne, T.K.; George, M.S.; O'Neil, P.M.; Hanlon, C.A. Executive control circuitry differentiates degree of success in weight loss following gastric-bypass surgery. *Obes. Silver Spring Md.* **2013**, *21*, 2189–2196. [CrossRef]
59. Rodrigue, C.; Ouellette, A.-S.; Lemieux, S.; Tchernof, A.; Biertho, L.; Bégin, C. Executive functioning and psychological symptoms in food addiction: A study among individuals with severe obesity. *Eat. Weight Disord. EWD* **2018**, *23*, 469–478. [CrossRef]
60. Franken, I.H.A.; Nijs, I.M.T.; Toes, A.; van der Veen, F.M. Food addiction is associated with impaired performance monitoring. *Biol. Psychol.* **2018**, *131*, 49–53. [CrossRef]
61. Steward, T.; Mestre-Bach, G.; Vintró-Alcaraz, C.; Lozano-Madrid, M.; Agüera, Z.; Fernández-Formoso, J.A.; Granero, R.; Jiménez-Murcia, S.; Vilarrasa, N.; García-Ruiz-de-Gordejuela, A.; et al. Food addiction and impaired executive functions in women with obesity. *Eur. Eat. Disord. Rev. J. Eat. Disord. Assoc.* **2018**, *26*, 574–584. [CrossRef]
62. Blume, M.; Schmidt, R.; Hilbert, A. Executive Functioning in Obesity, Food Addiction, and Binge-Eating Disorder. *Nutrients* **2018**, *11*, 54. [CrossRef]
63. Ruddock, H.K.; Field, M.; Jones, A.; Hardman, C.A. State and trait influences on attentional bias to food-cues: The role of hunger, expectancy, and self-perceived food addiction. *Appetite* **2018**, *131*, 139–147. [CrossRef] [PubMed]
64. Frayn, M.; Sears, C.R.; von Ranson, K.M. A sad mood increases attention to unhealthy food images in women with food addiction. *Appetite* **2016**, *100*, 55–63. [CrossRef] [PubMed]
65. Gearhardt, A.N.; Treat, T.A.; Hollingworth, A.; Corbin, W.R. The relationship between eating-related individual differences and visual attention to foods high in added fat and sugar. *Eat. Behav.* **2012**, *13*, 371–374. [CrossRef] [PubMed]

66. Havermans, R.C. "You Say it's Liking, I Say it's Wanting ... ". On the difficulty of disentangling food reward in man. *Appetite* **2011**, *57*, 286–294. [CrossRef] [PubMed]
67. Mela, D.J. Why do we like what we like? *J. Sci. Food Agric.* **2001**, *81*, 10–16. [CrossRef]
68. Pelchat, M.L. Of human bondage: Food craving, obsession, compulsion, and addiction. *Physiol. Behav.* **2002**, *76*, 347–352. [CrossRef]
69. Méjean, C.; Deglaire, A.; Kesse-Guyot, E.; Hercberg, S.; Schlich, P.; Castetbon, K. Association between intake of nutrients and food groups and liking for fat (The Nutrinet-Santé Study). *Appetite* **2014**, *78*, 147–155. [CrossRef]
70. Gearhardt, A.N.; Rizk, M.T.; Treat, T.A. The association of food characteristics and individual differences with ratings of craving and liking. *Appetite* **2014**, *79*, 166–173. [CrossRef]
71. Volkow, N.; Wang, G.J.; Fowler, J.S.; Tomasi, D.; Baler, R. Food and drug reward: Overlapping circuits in human obesity and addiction. In *Brain Imaging in Behavioral Neuroscience*; Springer: Berlin, Germany, 2011; pp. 1–24.
72. Fortuna, J.L. Sweet preference, sugar addiction and the familial history of alcohol dependence: Shared neural pathways and genes. *J. Psychoact. Drugs* **2010**, *42*, 147–151. [CrossRef]
73. Ahmed, S.H.; Lenoir, M.; Guillem, K. Neurobiology of addiction versus drug use driven by lack of choice. *Curr. Opin. Neurobiol.* **2013**, *23*, 581–587. [CrossRef]
74. Ziauddeen, H.; Farooqi, I.S.; Fletcher, P.C. Obesity and the brain: How convincing is the addiction model? *Nat. Rev. Neurosci.* **2012**, *13*, 279–286. [CrossRef] [PubMed]
75. Morgan, D.; Sizemore, G.M. Animal models of addiction: Fat and sugar. *Curr. Pharm. Des.* **2011**, *17*, 1168–1172. [CrossRef] [PubMed]
76. Novelle, M.G.; Diéguez, C. Food Addiction and Binge Eating: Lessons Learned from Animal Models. *Nutrients* **2018**, *10*, 71. [CrossRef] [PubMed]
77. De Jong, J.W.; Vanderschuren, L.J.M.J.; Adan, R.A.H. Towards an animal model of food addiction. *Obes. Facts* **2012**, *5*, 180–195. [CrossRef]
78. Marques, C.; Meireles, M.; Norberto, S.; Leite, J.; Freitas, J.; Pestana, D.; Faria, A.; Calhau, C. High-fat diet-induced obesity Rat model: A comparison between Wistar and Sprague-Dawley Rat. *Adipocyte* **2016**, *5*, 11–21. [CrossRef]
79. Avena, N.M. Examining the addictive-like properties of binge eating using an animal model of sugar dependence. *Exp. Clin. Psychopharmacol.* **2007**, *15*, 481–491. [CrossRef]
80. Avena, N.M.; Rada, P.; Hoebel, B.G. Sugar and fat bingeing have notable differences in addictive-like behavior. *J. Nutr.* **2009**, *139*, 623–628. [CrossRef]
81. Wong, K.J.; Wojnicki, F.H.W.; Corwin, R.L.W. Baclofen, raclopride, and naltrexone differentially affect intake of fat/sucrose mixtures under limited access conditions. *Pharmacol. Biochem. Behav.* **2009**, *92*, 528–536. [CrossRef]
82. Liang, N.-C.; Hajnal, A.; Norgren, R. Sham feeding corn oil increases accumbens dopamine in the rat. *Am. J. Physiol. Regul. Integr. Comp. Physiol.* **2006**, *291*, R1236–R1239. [CrossRef]
83. Adachi, S.; Endo, Y.; Mizushige, T.; Tsuzuki, S.; Matsumura, S.; Inoue, K.; Fushiki, T. Increased levels of extracellular dopamine in the nucleus accumbens and amygdala of rats by ingesting a low concentration of a long-chain Fatty Acid. *Biosci. Biotechnol. Biochem.* **2013**, *77*, 2175–2180. [CrossRef]
84. Dela Cruz, J.A.D.; Coke, T.; Bodnar, R.J. Simultaneous Detection of c-Fos Activation from Mesolimbic and Mesocortical Dopamine Reward Sites Following Naive Sugar and Fat Ingestion in Rats. *J. Vis. Exp. JoVE* **2016**. [CrossRef]
85. Dela Cruz, J.A.D.; Coke, T.; Karagiorgis, T.; Sampson, C.; Icaza-Cukali, D.; Kest, K.; Ranaldi, R.; Bodnar, R.J. c-Fos induction in mesotelencephalic dopamine pathway projection targets and dorsal striatum following oral intake of sugars and fats in rats. *Brain Res. Bull.* **2015**, *111*, 9–19. [CrossRef]
86. Dela Cruz, J.A.D.; Icaza-Cukali, D.; Tayabali, H.; Sampson, C.; Galanopoulos, V.; Bamshad, D.; Touzani, K.; Sclafani, A.; Bodnar, R.J. Roles of dopamine D1 and D2 receptors in the acquisition and expression of fat-conditioned flavor preferences in rats. *Neurobiol. Learn. Mem.* **2012**, *97*, 332–337. [CrossRef] [PubMed]
87. Zhang, M.; Gosnell, B.A.; Kelley, A.E. Intake of high-fat food is selectively enhanced by mu opioid receptor stimulation within the nucleus accumbens. *J. Pharmacol. Exp. Ther.* **1998**, *285*, 908–914. [PubMed]

88. Ward, S.J.; Walker, E.A.; Dykstra, L.A. Effect of cannabinoid CB1 receptor antagonist SR141716A and CB1 receptor knockout on cue-induced reinstatement of Ensure and corn-oil seeking in mice. *Neuropsychopharmacol. Off. Publ. Am. Coll. Neuropsychopharmacol.* **2007**, *32*, 2592–2600. [CrossRef] [PubMed]
89. Brissard, L.; Leemput, J.; Hichami, A.; Passilly-Degrace, P.; Maquart, G.; Demizieux, L.; Degrace, P.; Khan, N.A. Orosensory Detection of Dietary Fatty Acids Is Altered in $CB_1R^{-/-}$ Mice. *Nutrients* **2018**, *10*, 1347. [CrossRef] [PubMed]
90. Peterschmitt, Y.; Abdoul-Azize, S.; Murtaza, B.; Barbier, M.; Khan, A.S.; Millot, J.-L.; Khan, N.A. Fatty Acid Lingual Application Activates Gustatory and Reward Brain Circuits in the Mouse. *Nutrients* **2018**, *10*, 1246. [CrossRef] [PubMed]
91. Patriarca, L.; Magerowski, G.; Alonso-Alonso, M. Functional neuroimaging in obesity. *Curr. Opin. Endocrinol. Diabetes Obes.* **2017**, *24*, 260–265. [CrossRef] [PubMed]
92. Brooks, S.J.; Cedernaes, J.; Schiöth, H.B. Increased prefrontal and parahippocampal activation with reduced dorsolateral prefrontal and insular cortex activation to food images in obesity: A meta-analysis of fMRI studies. *PLoS ONE* **2013**, *8*, e60393. [CrossRef]
93. Gearhardt, A.N.; Yokum, S.; Orr, P.T.; Stice, E.; Corbin, W.R.; Brownell, K.D. The Neural Correlates of "Food Addiction". *Arch. Gen. Psychiatry* **2011**, *68*, 808–816. [CrossRef]
94. Hsu, J.-S.; Wang, P.-W.; Ko, C.-H.; Hsieh, T.-J.; Chen, C.-Y.; Yen, J.-Y. Altered brain correlates of response inhibition and error processing in females with obesity and sweet food addiction: A functional magnetic imaging study. *Obes. Res. Clin. Pract.* **2017**, *11*, 677–686. [CrossRef] [PubMed]
95. Contreras-Rodriguez, O.; Burrows, T.; Pursey, K.M.; Stanwell, P.; Parkes, L.; Soriano-Mas, C.; Verdejo-Garcia, A. Food addiction linked to changes in ventral striatum functional connectivity between fasting and satiety. *Appetite* **2019**, *133*, 18–23. [CrossRef] [PubMed]
96. Davis, C.; Loxton, N.J.; Levitan, R.D.; Kaplan, A.S.; Carter, J.C.; Kennedy, J.L. "Food addiction" and its association with a dopaminergic multilocus genetic profile. *Physiol. Behav.* **2013**, *118*, 63–69. [CrossRef] [PubMed]
97. Pedram, P.; Zhai, G.; Gulliver, W.; Zhang, H.; Sun, G. Two novel candidate genes identified in adults from the Newfoundland population with addictive tendencies towards food. *Appetite* **2017**, *115*, 71–79. [CrossRef]
98. Yeh, J.; Trang, A.; Henning, S.M.; Wilhalme, H.; Carpenter, C.; Heber, D.; Li, Z. Food Cravings, Food Addiction, and a Dopamine-Resistant (DRD2 A1) Receptor Polymorphism in Asian American College Students. *Asia Pac. J. Clin. Nutr.* **2016**, *25*, 424–429.
99. Cornelis, M.C.; Flint, A.; Field, A.E.; Kraft, P.; Han, J.; Rimm, E.B.; van Dam, R.M. A genome-wide investigation of food addiction. *Obes. Silver Spring Md.* **2016**, *24*, 1336–1341. [CrossRef]
100. Khan, A.S.; Murtaza, B.; Hichami, A.; Khan, N.A. A cross-talk between fat and bitter taste modalities. *Biochimie* **2019**, *159*, 3–8. [CrossRef]
101. Love-Gregory, L.; Abumrad, N. CD36 genetics and the metabolic complications of obesity. *Curr. Opin. Clin. Nutr. Metab. Care* **2011**, *14*, 527–534. [CrossRef]
102. Mrizak, I.; Šerý, O.; Plesnik, J.; Arfa, A.; Fekih, M.; Bouslema, A.; Zaouali, M.; Tabka, Z.; Khan, N.A. The a allele of cluster of differentiation 36 (CD36) SNP 1761667 associates with decreased lipid taste perception in obese Tunisian women. *Br. J. Nutr.* **2015**, *113*, 1330–1337. [CrossRef]
103. Melis, M.; Carta, G.; Pintus, S.; Pintus, P.; Piras, C.A.; Murru, E.; Manca, C.; Di Marzo, V.; Banni, S.; Tomassini Barbarossa, I. Polymorphism rs1761667 in the CD36 Gene Is Associated to Changes in Fatty Acid Metabolism and Circulating Endocannabinoid Levels Distinctively in Normal Weight and Obese Subjects. *Front. Physiol.* **2017**, *8*, 8. [CrossRef]
104. Plesník, J.; Serý, O.; Khan, A.; Bielik, P.; Khan, N.A. The rs1527483, but not rs3212018, CD36 polymorphism associates with linoleic acid detection and obesity in Czech young adults. *Br. J. Nutr.* **2018**, *119*, 1–7. [CrossRef]

11

Food Addiction: Implications for the Diagnosis and Treatment of Overeating

Rachel C. Adams [1,*], Jemma Sedgmond [1], Leah Maizey [1], Christopher D. Chambers [1] and Natalia S. Lawrence [2]

1 CUBRIC, School of Psychology, Cardiff University, Maindy Road, Cardiff CF24 4HQ, UK
2 School of Psychology, College of Life and Environmental Sciences, University of Exeter, Exeter EX4 4QG, UK
* Correspondence: adamsrc1@cardiff.ac.uk

Abstract: With the obesity epidemic being largely attributed to overeating, much research has been aimed at understanding the psychological causes of overeating and using this knowledge to develop targeted interventions. Here, we review this literature under a model of food addiction and present evidence according to the fifth edition of the Diagnostic and Statistical Manual (DSM-5) criteria for substance use disorders. We review several innovative treatments related to a food addiction model ranging from cognitive intervention tasks to neuromodulation techniques. We conclude that there is evidence to suggest that, for some individuals, food can induce addictive-type behaviours similar to those seen with other addictive substances. However, with several DSM-5 criteria having limited application to overeating, the term 'food addiction' is likely to apply only in a minority of cases. Nevertheless, research investigating the underlying psychological causes of overeating within the context of food addiction has led to some novel and potentially effective interventions. Understanding the similarities and differences between the addictive characteristics of food and illicit substances should prove fruitful in further developing these interventions.

Keywords: food addiction; overeating; obesity; impulsivity; reward sensitivity; cognitive training; neuromodulation

---

1. Introduction

In 2003, obesity was declared a global epidemic by the World Health Organisation [1], and the prevalence of overweight and obesity in both developed and developing countries continues to increase [2,3]. In 2016, 39% of adults were estimated to be overweight and 13% to be obese [4]. Overweight and obesity present a substantial economic burden; in the UK, the total direct and indirect costs are expected to reach £37.2 billion by 2025 [5]. One of the common explanations for the increase in obesity over recent decades is the environment and, in particular, the availability of highly varied, palatable and fattening foods—which have been considered to be addictive [6–9]. While many individuals manage to resist these temptations and maintain a healthy weight, obese individuals have been shown to have a preference for such energy-dense foods compared to healthy-weight individuals [10–12]. The critical question is why some individuals are able to resist overeating while others cannot; what is the evidence for 'food addiction' and how can this be used to inform interventions for overeating.

The concept of 'food addiction' has been evident in the media and general public for some time and is gaining increasing interest in the scientific literature [13]. There are now numerous reviews discussing the diagnostic, neurobiological and practical aspects of food addiction, with arguments both for and against its utility and validity [14–20]. This surge of interest comes with the perspective that addiction can be conceptualised as a loss of control over intake for a particular substance or behaviour without the need to focus purely on psychoactive substances [21,22]. The fifth edition of the Diagnostic and Statistical Manual [23] acknowledged this shift in perspective, with the addition of gambling disorder as the first behavioural addiction. Acceptance of this disorder was based on evidence that gambling can produce behavioural symptoms that parallel those of substance addiction and can activate the same neural reward circuits as drugs of abuse [24,25]. There is now a large body of research documenting similar observations for overeating and obesity. Moreover, treatments developed for addictive disorders have also shown some efficacy for the treatment of obesity and overeating. These findings highlight how a model of food addiction may help us to understand elements of overweight/obesity beyond a simple lack of willpower and can also be used to inform effective interventions and policy [26–30].

Food addiction has not yet been recognised in the DSM; however, the similarities between some feeding and eating disorders and substance-use disorders (SUDs) have been acknowledged. These similarities include the experience of cravings, reduced control over intake, increased impulsivity and altered reward-sensitivity. Binge eating disorder (BED) and bulimia nervosa (BN) have been proposed as phenotypes that may reflect these similarities to the greatest extent [31–34]. Both BED and BN are characterised by recurrent episodes of binge eating in which large quantities of food are consumed in a short time accompanied by feelings of a lack of control, despite physical and emotional distress. Reports of food addiction have been shown to be particularly high amongst these individuals [32,35,36]. Food addiction has also been acknowledged with a standardised 'diagnostic' tool—the Yale Food Addiction Scale (YFAS) [37,38]. The YFAS is a questionnaire that parallels the diagnostic criteria for SUDs. The scale has so far been shown to exhibit good internal reliability as well as convergent, discriminant and incremental validity [37–40].

In this review, we first discuss the DSM-5 diagnostic criteria for SUDs to summarise evidence for food addiction. These criteria are defined as 'a cluster of cognitive, behavioural and physiological symptoms' [23]. More specifically, the following categories are considered: impaired control, social impairment, repeated use despite negative consequences and physiological criteria. However, it should be noted that the physiological criteria of tolerance and withdrawal—for which there is less evidence in relation to food—are not necessary for a diagnosis of SUD. The DSM-5 also states that although changes in neural functioning are a key characteristic of SUDs, the diagnosis is based on a pathological pattern of behaviours. Hence, we discuss the diagnostic criteria initially, followed by a review of neurobiological evidence. We then explore the question of how this information can be, and has been, applied to interventions for overeating.

1.1. Impaired Control

Taking larger amounts of the substance for longer periods than intended has been cited as one of the most commonly reported symptoms in overweight/obese and BED individuals [41,42]. Excessive and uncontrolled eating also forms the definition of binge eating in BED [23]. Although bingeing can be a planned behaviour, it has been shown that planned binges still result in a greater intake than initially intended [41]. Binge eating has also been documented in non-clinical samples [43,44]; however, in these individuals, occasions of impaired control are more likely to reflect unintentional snacking and excessive portion sizes [8,41,45].

Unsuccessful efforts to restrict food intake are also well documented, with many dieters failing to maintain their diet or even gaining weight in the long term [46–51]. In their paper reviewing evidence for refined food addiction (i.e., processed foods with high levels of sugars or sweeteners, refined carbohydrates, fat, salt and caffeine), Ifland et al. [52] report that 'Every refined food addict reports a series of attempts to cut back on eating. They have used a variety of techniques' (pg. 521). Curtis and Davis [41] also report similar anecdotes in women with BED who describe avoiding certain trigger foods to control their binges.

The third criterion of time spent obtaining, using and recovering from substance use also translates to BED and BN. These individuals may spend a lot of their time thinking about, engaging in and recovering from binge episodes. As mentioned earlier, bingeing is often a planned behaviour which may require a great deal of effort to purchase and store foods ready for a binge episode [41]. In addition, the criteria for BED emphasise the time spent bingeing, with the number of binge episodes per week determining the severity of the disorder [23]. Moreover, these individuals often experience physical and emotional distress following a binge eating episode. Recovery from food consumption has also been reported in self-identified food addicts with references to feeling sleepy or 'hung-over' [52,53].

Although evidence for food addiction directly related to the DSM-5 diagnostic criteria for impaired control is largely anecdotal, there is a considerable amount of empirical evidence for an association between overeating/obesity and impaired control generally. Two aspects of self-regulatory failure that are particularly pertinent in the case of substance use and overeating are impulsivity and reward sensitivity [54–56].

1.1.1. Impulsivity

Although impulsivity is a multi-faceted construct, it can be defined broadly as the tendency to think and act without sufficient forethought, which often results in behaviour that is discordant with one's long-term goals. The role of impulsivity in SUDs is well documented [55,57–60]. Many studies have reported higher impulsivity levels with increasing substance use across a wide range of questionnaires and behavioural tasks, and for a variety of different substances [61–66]. For example, Noël et al. [67] performed a series of behavioural tasks assessing the ability to suppress irrelevant responses (response inhibition) and irrelevant information (proactive interference) in a group of detoxified alcohol-dependent individuals and matched healthy controls. They found a statistically significant group difference for all three tests assessing response inhibition but no differences for proactive interference.

Impulsivity has also been implicated in overeating and obesity [54,68–71]. Overweight/obese individuals score higher on self-reported [72–74] and behavioural measures of impulsivity [75–77], whereas those high in self-control have been shown to be less likely to give in to temptation [78–80] and are more likely to maintain a healthy diet and engage in physical exercise [81–83] Impulsivity scores have also been shown to predict poor food choices [84] and correlate positively with food consumption [85–87]. For example, Guerrieri et al. [87] found that, in a sample of healthy-weight women, those with higher impulsivity scores ate more candy during a 'bogus' taste test than those with lower impulsivity scores. Churchill and Jessop [88] also showed a predictive relationship between impulsivity and snacking on high-fat foods over a two-week period. Scores on the YFAS have also been associated with various measures of impulsivity, such as motor and attentional impulsivity, mood-related impulsivity and delay discounting [89,90].

1.1.2. Reward Sensitivity

A heightened general sensitivity to reward has also been linked to both substance use and overeating [69,77,91–93]. In the food literature, self-report measures of reward sensitivity have revealed associations with BMI, food craving and preferences for foods high in fat and sugar [93–95]. Using two behavioural tasks, Guerrieri et al. [69] measured reward sensitivity and response inhibition in children aged 8–10. They subsequently measured food intake in a bogus taste test when the foods were either varied or monotonous. Their results revealed that reward-sensitive children consumed significantly more calories than non-reward sensitive children only when the food was varied. There was no effect of response inhibition on food intake, nor any interaction with variety; however, unlike reward sensitivity, deficient response inhibition was associated with being overweight. The authors suggested that reward sensitivity may play a causal role in overeating, whereas deficient inhibitory control may be more of a maintaining factor. This fits well with findings from a study demonstrating a role of reward sensitivity in the early onset of heroin use and a role of impulsivity in escalating use [92,96].

There is also evidence to suggest that reward sensitivity may decrease with more prolonged or established overeating, with studies showing anhedonia, or hypo-sensitivity to reward, in obese participants [97–100]. For example, Davis et al. [97] demonstrated that although overweight women were more sensitive to reward than healthy-weight women, those who were obese were significantly *less* reward sensitive than overweight women. Importantly, the earlier mentioned association between reward sensitivity and increased BMI was found in a sample of mainly healthy-weight women, with only 1% classified as obese [93]. Although there is a great deal of evidence to suggest that sensitivity to reward plays a role in substance abuse and overeating, the causal direction of this relationship remains unclear. On the one hand, increasing reward sensitivity may lead to overeating by increasing motivation towards pleasurable activities, such as consuming energy-dense foods that elicit dopamine and opioid activation. On the other hand, decreased reward sensitivity may cause individuals to seek out rewarding activities as a form of 'self-medication' in order to boost dopamine functioning (i.e., addictive behaviour is the result of a 'reward deficiency syndrome') [101,102]. These two arguments, and the relevant neuroimaging literature, are discussed further below (see the Neurobiological Similarities section below) and in more detail by Burger and Stice [103].

Burger and Stice [103] offer several theories for how these two causal directions combine to explain obesity. They propose that high sensitivity to reward may initially cause individuals to over-consume palatable foods, but this sensitivity is then modified over time as the brain's reward system adapts and shows divergent changes in food motivation ('wanting') versus hedonic pleasure ('liking'). According to Robinson and Berridge's [104–106] incentive-sensitisation theory, repeated intake results in an increased incentive value for these foods and their associated cues, which may be subjectively experienced as excessive wanting or craving. Moreover, this theory argues that with repeated presentations of palatable foods, the hedonic pleasure derived from consuming the food will decrease due to neural habituation, while the anticipation of reward increases. Hence, a vicious cycle emerges in which the individual will experience less pleasure from the food ('liking'), but will simultaneously experience an increased desire ('wanting') for the food, driving further food seeking and consumption [107–109] (see Figure 1). The experience of intense cravings is the third criterion of impaired control and is another symptom of substance addiction that can be readily applied to overeating and obesity.

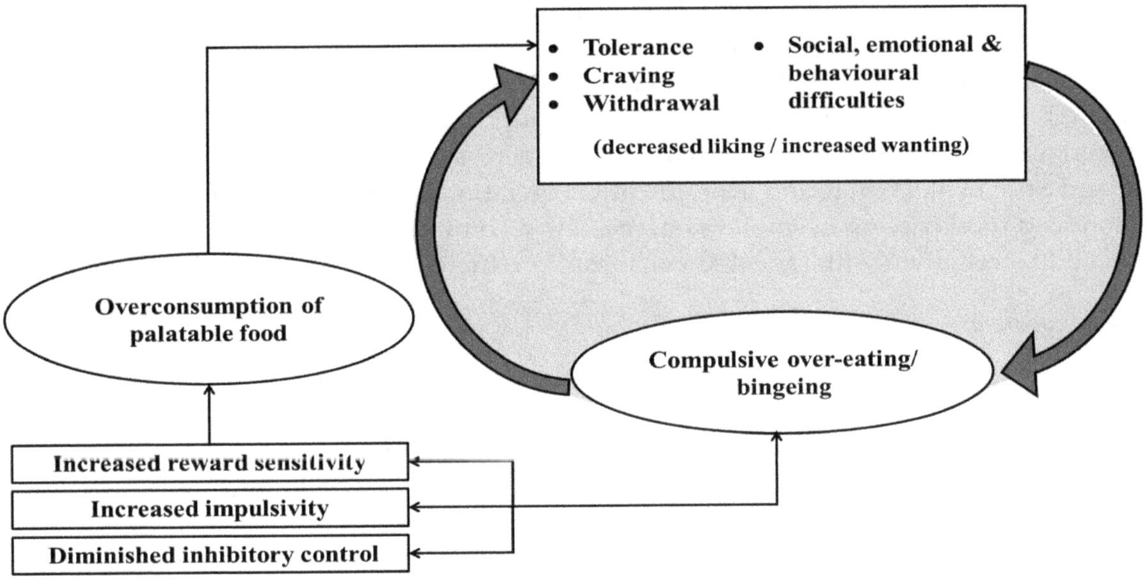

Figure 1. The proposed cycle of 'food addiction'. Initial vulnerability for the over-consumption of palatable food is marked by increased impulsivity and reward sensitivity, as well as a diminished capacity for inhibitory control. As a consequence of overconsumption, individuals experience tolerance, craving and withdrawal, along with a range of social, emotional and behavioural difficulties such as weight stigmatisation and feelings of guilt and shame. With repeated consumption of these foods, the individual is likely to habituate to the hedonic properties of the food, resulting in reduced enjoyment or liking. These changes are also accompanied by an increased desire or 'wanting' for the food [104–108]. In an attempt to relieve these symptoms, the individual 'self-medicates' by increasing food consumption, which can result in compulsive or binge eating behaviour, thus creating a cycle of addiction. It should be noted that the extent to which each of these mechanisms is experienced varies considerably across individuals. In particular, initial vulnerability to addiction may be related to individual differences in reward sensitivity, impulsivity and inhibitory control [110–113].

1.2. Craving

The term 'food craving' typically refers to an intense desire to consume a specific food [114,115]. Food cravings appear to be very common with reports of 100% of young women and 70% of young men experiencing a craving for at least one food in the past year [116,117]. The most commonly reported craved food is chocolate, although cravings for carbohydrates and salty snacks are also common [118–122]. The prevalence of food cravings has prompted the development of several standardised questionnaires that measure food cravings with a good degree of internal consistency and construct validity [123–127], including a specific questionnaire just for chocolate (Attitudes to Chocolate Questionnaire) [128]. Recurrent food cravings are of interest in relation to food addiction as they have been associated with binge eating, increased food intake and increased BMI [124,127,129–132]. Increased reports of food craving have also been demonstrated in individuals who score highly on measures of self-reported food addiction [133–135] and those with BED and BN [136–138]. Furthermore, just as drug craving is associated with an increased likelihood of relapse [139–141], food craving has been linked to poor dieting success [142–144].

Further support for the similarity between drug and food craving is evident in the findings of cue-reactivity research. The aphorism that cravings are most likely to occur in the presence of substance-related stimuli has been well documented, with cue-exposure paradigms showing significant effects of drug-related cues on self-reported and physiological measures of craving [145–148]. Similarly, exposure to food cues has also been shown to increase food cravings [149,150] and a recent systematic review of 45 studies (involving 3292 participants) concluded that 'food cue-reactivity' (physiological, neural and subjective reward-related responses to food cues) reliably and prospectively predicts both energy intake and weight gain, particularly over the longer-term, accounting for ~11% (7%–26%) of variance in these outcomes [129]. Food cue-induced craving is especially prevalent among binge eaters and those with BED [151,152] in whom it has been correlated with binge eating frequency and BMI [153]. It is possible, therefore, that certain individuals are more susceptible to cue-induced cravings, and also that this susceptibility may transfer across different substances. Both Mahler and de Wit [147] and Styn et al. [148] found a significant correlation between cue-induced cigarette craving and cue-induced food craving in smokers, suggesting a common mechanism. Cue-induced craving is also believed to strengthen with repeated consumption, fueling the vicious circle shown in Figure 1.

1.3. Social Impairment

Overeating and obesity have been associated with poor social functioning, especially among children and adolescents. When assessing quality of life with child and parent-proxy reports, social functioning is significantly lower for obese compared to healthy-weight children and is inversely correlated with BMI [154–156]. Poor social functioning in overweight children may be partly due to the overt victimisation and teasing experienced as a direct result of their weight status [157,158]. Hayden-Wade et al. [159] found that the degree of teasing experienced by overweight children was positively correlated with loneliness, an increased preference for isolative activities and a lower preference for social activities. This preference for being alone, along with the emotional difficulty of being victimised, fuels a vicious cycle as these circumstances are likely to promote further overeating and binge-eating—which, in turn, leads to increased weight gain and further teasing [42,160] (see Figure 1).

Weight stigmatisation may also affect interpersonal friendships and romantic relationships in adulthood with reports of discriminatory attitudes and behaviours in occupational [161,162] and romantic settings [158,162,163]. For example, Chen and Brown [164] reported that when making sexual choices about a partner, both male and female college students ranked an obese individual as the least liked. In a study focusing on the psychosocial correlates of food addiction, Chao et al. [165] found that, compared to control participants, those who met the YFAS criteria scored lower on physical, mental and social aspects of health-related quality of life. Social impairments were related to self-esteem, sexual life, public distress and work. Interpersonal problems have also been associated with binge eating—a relationship which is likely to be bidirectional [166,167].

1.4. Repeated Use Despite Negative Consequences

It has been noted that due to its increase in prevalence and associated comorbidities, obesity now appears to be a greater threat to the burden of disease than smoking [168]. The physical and psychological effects of overweight and obesity are well documented and include, but are not limited to, depression, an increased risk of diabetes, hypertension, cardiovascular disease and some cancers [169–177]. With pervasive warnings regarding the consequences of overeating, from the media, government, and the medical profession, it seems fair to assume that most overweight and obese individuals are aware of the negative outcomes associated with their dietary behaviour [41,52]. Critically, even those who have undergone weight loss treatment often fail to lose weight or gain weight following intervention [46,48,50,51]. Continued overeating also occurs in those who have received bariatric surgery with patients showing continued snacking and poor food choices [178,179]. There is, therefore, considerable evidence to support continued overeating despite negative consequences.

1.5. Physiological Criteria

Tolerance to a substance occurs when the same amount of the substance has an increasingly diminished effect with repeated use. This effect usually results in escalated use as the individual increases their dosage in order to recreate the original experience. There is some evidence of food tolerance in animal models of sugar addiction. Rats given intermittent and excessive access to sugar solution increase their intake significantly over time, and this is accompanied by neurochemical changes that are similar to those seen in drug abuse [180,181]. In humans, there is some indication that tolerance to sugar may occur in the first few years of life. The effectiveness of sucrose as an analgesic in young infants is reported to diminish after 18 months of age as sugar consumption increases [182–185]. The possibility of such early tolerance to palatable foods and the methodological difficulties of diet restriction in humans makes finding empirical evidence of tolerance in adults difficult and unlikely. However, statistics indicating increased consumption and portion sizes for these foods provide indirect evidence of tolerance to high-fat/high-sugar foods at a population level [52,186], and also at an individual level based on anecdotal reports. For example, Pretlow [42] found that 77% of overweight poll respondents reported eating more now than when they originally became overweight. Furthermore, in response to a follow-up question asking why they believed that they ate more, 15% indicated that they were less satisfied by food. Hetherington et al. [109] also found that when participants were provided with chocolate for three weeks, they increased their intake over time while simultaneously reporting a reduction in food liking.

Withdrawal is the second physiological criterion for substance abuse and is defined by the presence of physical or psychological symptoms in response to substance deprivation, or the use of the substance in order to relieve these symptoms. Evidence of withdrawal has also been found in the aforementioned animal models of sugar addiction. Under conditions of sugar deprivation, these animals show withdrawal symptoms similar to those seen with morphine and nicotine withdrawal, including physical symptoms of teeth chattering, forepaw tremor, head shaking and reduced body temperature [187,188] as well as increased aggression [189] and anxiety [190]. There are also anecdotal reports of withdrawal-like symptoms in humans, including persistent cravings and negative affects when attempting to reduce food intake [42,191], as well as the tendency to eat to avoid the emotional symptoms associated with withdrawal such as fatigue, anxiety and depression [52]. Using the YFAS, withdrawal symptoms (such as agitation, anxiety, or other physical symptoms) have been reported in up to 50% of individuals with obesity and BED [35].

2. Neurobiological Similarities between Palatable Foods and Drugs of Abuse

Just as altered brain functioning has been reported in SUDs, overeating and obesity have also been associated with changes in the neural processing of the motivational properties of food. This includes changes in systems coding the hedonic and rewarding aspects of the substance, as well as the systems involved in controlling these motivations [103,192–194]. Volkow and colleagues [195–199] have proposed a common model for addiction and obesity that involves two neural circuits that are both modulated by dopamine—increased reward sensitivity and diminished inhibitory control [70].

2.1. Neurobiology of Reward Sensitivity

Addictive drugs directly affect the mesolimbic dopamine system (MDS), which is thought to mediate the processing of motivational salience, pleasure and reward [200]. Animal studies have shown that, similar to drugs of abuse, palatable foods are capable of triggering dopamine release in the nucleus accumbens (NAc) and ventral tegmental area (VTA) [181,201–203]. Furthermore, activity in the MDS has been linked to the amount of food ingested and its rewarding properties [204,205]. However, distinct patterns of neuronal firing in the NAc to food and illicit substances have also been reported [206,207]. Increased activation of this reward system has also been shown in human participants during the presentation of food cues and meal consumption [96,208–211]. For example, Stoeckel et al. [212] demonstrated that when viewing images of high-calorie foods, obese women showed significantly greater activation in a number of regions associated with reward, compared to healthy-weight women. Obese participants have also demonstrated increased responsivity to food in gustatory and somatosensory regions [213,214], suggesting a heightened sensitivity to palatable food that may contribute to overeating and obesity.

Although an increased sensitivity to reward may initially drive individuals to consume calorific foods, it has been speculated that compulsive eating may develop as the pleasure derived from these foods diminishes with increased tolerance (see Figure 1). It has been argued that, just as with drugs of abuse, the chronic consumption of such rewarding foods may cause the downregulation of dopamine receptors in order to compensate for their overstimulation [215–217]. Decreased striatal dopamine receptor availability has frequently been observed in individuals with substance addictions [218–222], whereas increased receptor availability has been shown to have a protective role against alcoholism [223,224]. It has also been shown that striatal D2 receptor availability is significantly lower in severely obese individuals compared to controls and is significantly and negatively correlated with BMI [99,100].

It has been argued, therefore, that a reduction in dopamine receptor availability may subsequently cause or exacerbate overeating as a form of 'self-medication' in which the individual attempts to compensate for a diminished experience of reward [100,225–227] (see Figure 2). For example, Geiger et al. [228] found that rats fed on a cafeteria-style diet showed reduced baseline levels of mesolimbic dopamine activity. This activity was stimulated by cafeteria foods but not by their regular chow, thus suggesting that a preference for palatable food may develop as a consequence of its ability to increase dopamine release compared to other, less palatable, foods. Animal studies have also demonstrated causal effects of D2 receptor agonists and antagonists on overeating. The administration of D2 antagonists has been shown to increase meal size, meal duration and body weight, whereas treatment with D2 agonists can reduce hyperphagia and prevent weight gain [229–231]. The effects of such pharmaceutical interventions in humans, however, have been fairly mixed. The use of antipsychotic medication which blocks D2 receptors is typically associated with weight gain [232] and some D2 agonists have been found to reduce body weight [233]. A recent trial, however, found no effect of the dopamine agonist cabergoline on preventing weight regain [234,235] and there is some evidence that D2 agonists can promote weight gain in patients with anorexia nervosa [236]. More encouragingly, studies with gastric bypass patients have demonstrated increased D2 receptor availability following weight loss, indicating that the effects of overeating on dopamine receptor downregulation may be reversible [237–239].

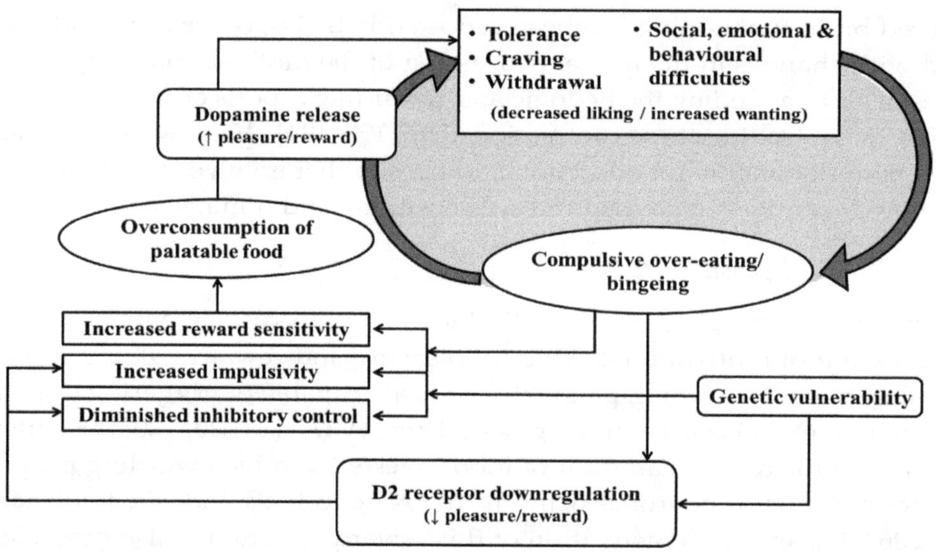

Figure 2. The proposed cycle of 'food addiction' including the role of dopamine. When palatable food is consumed, the brain releases the hormone dopamine (alongside other neurotransmitters such as opioids). Over time, this increase in dopamine leads to the downregulation of dopamine receptors, causing individuals to experience a reduction in pleasure during palatable food consumption. This decrease in pleasure, combined with symptoms of tolerance, craving, withdrawal and other social, emotional and behavioural difficulties, results in the individual engaging in compensatory behaviour by increasing food consumption. As a consequence, food consumption may become compulsive, thus creating a cycle of food addiction.

2.2. Neurobiology of Inhibitory Control

Dopamine receptor availability in obese individuals has also been shown to correlate positively with metabolism in prefrontal regions involved in inhibitory control (specifically the dorsolateral prefrontal cortex [DLPFC], medial orbitofrontal cortex [mOFC] and anterior cingulate gyrus, as well as the somatosensory cortices) [99]. Similar findings have been observed in healthy-weight participants, who demonstrated a positive correlation between dopamine receptor availability and inhibitory control performance on the stop-signal task [240]. Volkow et al. [99] hypothesised that altered dopamine functioning may play a role in overeating not only through altering the rewarding properties of food but also by reducing inhibitory control. A significant negative correlation between BMI and prefrontal activity has also been reported [75,241,242] along with reduced prefrontal activation following a meal in obese men and women [243–245]. Conversely, successful dieting has been positively associated with frontal activation [246–249].

In a study of healthy women, Lawrence et al. [96] reported an association between food cue reactivity in the NAc and later snack consumption [117]. They also found that this reactivity was associated with increased BMI for individuals who reported low self-control. The authors proposed a 'dual hit' of increased reward motivation and poor self-control in predicting increased food intake [250]. Similarly, reductions in frontal grey matter volume have also been linked to increased BMI, poor food choices and related deficits in executive functioning [251–258]. These findings are reflective of a growing literature on the cognitive dysfunction associated with drug abuse and obesity, although research indicates that the causal relationship is bidirectional [76,259–263].

Although it has been hypothesised that overeating is initially caused by a hyper-responsive reward circuitry and maintained by the subsequent degradation of this system [103], there is also evidence to suggest that some individuals may be genetically vulnerable to an impaired capacity for reward and inhibitory control. Genetics studies have revealed that both drug users and obese individuals have a significantly greater prevalence of the *Taq*I A1 allele polymorphism which can cause a 30%–40% reduction in striatal D2 receptors [213,264–269]. In addition, this polymorphism has been associated with behavioural measures of impulsivity and low reward sensitivity [270–272]. It has also been linked to low grey matter volume in the anterior cingulate cortex (ACC) [273], an area which is believed to be involved in executive control and reward expectancy [240,274,275], and has been shown to be active during resistance of cigarette craving [276]. Together these findings demonstrate that overeating and SUDs may share a common neurobiological mechanism involving altered dopamine functioning that subsequently disrupts mechanisms involved in reward sensitivity and inhibitory control.

Our review, considering each of the DSM-5 criteria for SUDs in isolation, suggests that there is considerable evidence for food addiction. Whether an individual meets clinical diagnostic criteria under an SUD model, and the severity of the disorder, however, is dependent on an individual presenting a number of symptoms (mild: two to three symptoms; moderate: four to five symptoms; severe: six or more symptoms). Studies utilising the YFAS (which uses diagnostic criteria for SUDs) have certainly suggested that a substantial proportion of the general population meet the diagnostic cut-off for food addiction (15%–20%), with approximately 11% of the population being classified as 'severe' [38,276]. The prevalence of food addiction in those with BED and BN has been reported as much higher, with estimates of 92% for BED and 96%–100% for BN [32,277,278]. Acknowledging the potential prevalence of food addiction, we next discuss a range of treatments for overeating that have been informed by the similarities between SUDs and overeating.

3. Treatment Implications

One of the greatest potential advantages of identifying the similarities between substance addictions and overeating is the development of effective interventions. The standard approach to weight loss, involving maintaining a healthy diet and physical exercise, is often associated with poor adherence rates and overall weight gain [46–51,279]. One possible reason for the ineffectiveness of dieting is that it is treating the outcome of overeating and not the underlying cause. Approaches that target increased impulsivity and reduced self-control may have more success. For example, Hall, Fong, Epp and Elias [280] showed that executive function on the go/no-go task (a measure of response inhibition) predicted unique variance for dietary behaviour and physical exercise, and also moderated the association between intentions and behaviour [117,281]. This suggests that individuals who are more capable of controlling their impulsive actions are more likely to successfully meet their goals. This also implies that techniques to improve such abilities may prove to be effective tools for aiding weight loss.

3.1. Cognitive Interventions

Increased motivation for illicit substances has been associated with several cognitive biases including attentional biases [282–287], approach biases [283,284,288–290] and affective biases [291–294]. One method for reducing this motivation, therefore, has been to use training tasks that are designed to reduce these cognitive biases, and recently, these training tasks have been explored as potential interventions for overeating.

Heightened attentional biases towards food have been demonstrated across various populations, including those with disordered eating patterns [295–300] and those who are overweight or obese [301–304]. Just as the addiction literature has explored whether attentional biases can be manipulated to reduce substance intake, this approach has also been explored with food consumption, although with mixed results [305–309]. Hardman et al. [305] trained undergraduate students on the visual probe task to either attend or avoid images of cake and stationery. They found a modest increase in attentional bias for the attend-cake group but no effects of bias training, for either group, on hunger or food consumption, suggesting that any attentional biases with food may be particularly difficult to modify. Using a female-only sample, Kemps et al. [306] demonstrated significant effects of a similar dot-probe training on attentional bias and food consumption. Effects on attention were found to generalise to novel pictures, however, effects on food intake were specific to the trained food and were undermined by participants consuming more of an equally unhealthy novel food. More recent results hold some promise for attentional bias modification, indicating that training can be used to decrease immediate calorie consumption in overweight and obese women [310] and can increase the consumption of healthy foods [311]. Multiple training sessions have also demonstrated that effects can persist beyond the period of training for up to a week [312].

There is also a small body of evidence demonstrating an approach tendency towards food for individuals with disordered eating [295,313,314], high trait food craving [315] and those who are overweight or obese [316–318]. For example, Veenstra and de Jong [313] showed that those who scored highly on a measure of dietary restraint (a measure for the chronic, cognitive limitation of food intake) were significantly faster to move a manikin towards than away from images of food. Using a different measure of approach bias, Kemps, Tiggemann, Martin and Elliott [319] also found that participants who liked chocolate were significantly faster at pairing images of chocolate with approach words compared to avoid words. Furthermore, they also demonstrated that participants who were trained to pair images of chocolate with either approach or avoid words increased and decreased their approach bias, respectively. The approach group also demonstrated a significant increase in chocolate cravings. Although the avoid group showed a decrease in reported craving, this finding was not statistically significant from baseline [320]. Similar training protocols have also been shown to be effective at reducing action tendencies towards high-calorie foods and reducing trait- and cue-induced craving in participants with subclinical eating disorders [321].

The use of addictive substances can also be motivated by the positive affect associated with them; therefore, reducing such an affective bias should discourage their use. Studies using evaluative (or affective) conditioning have shown initial promise. Here, the evaluation of a conditioned stimulus (CS) can be modified by consistently pairing it with a valenced unconditioned stimulus (US) [322,323]. In the food literature, negatively valenced stimuli are typically used to reduce the implicit liking of unhealthy foods [324–328]. Further, evaluative conditioning has been found to lead to more favourable food choices in some studies. For example, Walsh and Kiviniemi [329] found that participants were three times more likely to select fruit over a granola bar after receiving evaluative conditioning training where positive (relative to negative or neutral) words and images were paired with images of fruit. Similarly, Hollands et al. [325] showed that participants were more likely to select fruit over an unhealthy snack when snack images were repeatedly paired with negative body images compared to a blank screen. Interestingly, this effect was moderated by implicit attitudes towards the snack foods; participants with more favourable attitudes at baseline showed the greatest change in subsequent behaviour. Although these studies have involved healthy participants, this latter finding, in particular, suggests that evaluative conditioning may be an appropriate intervention for those with disordered eating who show strong preferences for unhealthy foods. However, the effects of evaluative conditioning training on reducing unhealthy food consumption are currently unclear. To date, only a limited number of studies have included post-intervention follow-up, and while some have found reduced consumption in the week following training [330], others have failed to show immediate effects [327,328,330]. It is likely that training effects are dependent on baseline strength of liking for specific foods [325,330], the specificity of the US used [331], and awareness of the CS-US contingencies [332–334]. To establish the therapeutic benefits of evaluative conditioning training, studies in overweight and disordered eating groups are required.

Another approach to cognitive training is to reduce such biases indirectly through tasks such as response inhibition training. Response inhibition refers to our ability to interrupt or override impulsive reactions in accordance with new information, and plays a key role in goal-directed behaviour [335–340]. Deficient response inhibition has been linked not only to the use of different addictive substances [70] but also to the severity of use [61,64,341], poor treatment outcomes [342] and likelihood of relapse [343]. Houben and Wiers [344] have also shown that positive implicit attitudes towards alcohol are only related to alcohol consumption when inhibitory control is low. These results suggest that an increased ability to inhibit responses may enable an individual to exert self-control over their behaviour, even when they possess strong implicit preferences [117].

Similar findings have also been replicated with overeating and obesity. Obese individuals have been shown to demonstrate less efficient response inhibition than their healthy-weight counterparts [69,251,345,346] and poor inhibitory control has been associated with increased unhealthy food consumption [86,347,348], high BMI [75,85,349,350], food cravings [351], unhealthy food choices [84,352] and binge-eating [353]. Moreover, as in the addiction literature, inhibitory control has also been shown to interact with implicit attitudes towards food, thus indicating that effective response inhibition may play a protective role against strong implicit preferences for unhealthy foods [80,117,250].

Simple tasks designed to train response inhibition to relevant cues or contexts have been shown to reduce gambling behaviour and alcohol consumption [354–359]—although available evidence suggests that the longevity of such effects may be limited [360]. These training tasks have also been adapted to train response inhibition to food stimuli and are showing encouraging effects across a range of eating-related behaviours including food consumption [361–365], food choices [365–371] and even weight loss [372–375]. For example, Lawrence et al. [376] trained participants to inhibit their responses towards either images of unhealthy snack foods (active group) or non-food items (control group). After four training sessions, they found that, compared to the control group, individuals in the active group showed reduced energy intake (220 kcal less per 24 h food diary) and reduced liking for unhealthy foods. Furthermore, participants in the active group showed significant weight loss; showing objectively measured weight loss of 0.7 kg after 2 weeks and self-reported weight loss of more than two kilograms after a six month follow up (2.66% decrease).

The cognitive training paradigms discussed above show promise but are currently in the early phases of testing. Before such training methods can be taken forward to clinical trials, researchers should further explore the effects of different experimental protocols with the aim of developing the most effective training techniques. One aspect of training that is likely to be important in determining successful behavior change is training performance. For example, the proportion of successful inhibitions on an inhibition training task and accuracy during attentional bias training have both been shown to moderate efficacy [308,375]. To establish whether effects can be long-lasting, we need to consider repeated testing sessions, personalised training stimuli and combining training techniques to simultaneously reduce cognitive biases and increase executive control [312,369,377,378]. Understanding the mechanisms that underlie such effects could also prove crucial. For example, the effects of inhibition training on food consumption may be due to the devaluation of inhibited stimuli. Several studies have shown that repeatedly pairing a stimulus with the inhibition of a response can reduce how much the image is liked or how attractive it was perceived to be [371,376]. Such devaluation could be the result of action conflict or inherent links between avoidance and aversion [371,379–382]. Designing interventions that promote automatic associations between stimuli and action tendencies may, therefore, prove fruitful, especially if training is performed accurately, personalised and delivered across multiple sessions. Combining cognitive training tasks with prefrontal brain stimulation is another avenue worthy of investigation. Brain stimulation methods have the potential to augment learning effects [383] and can also be used to reduce food consumption and craving in isolation; these methods are discussed below.

3.2. Neuromodulation Interventions

Non-surgical brain stimulation techniques have also been explored for their potential benefits in reducing craving and addictive behaviours by altering neural activity and increasing dopamine [384–388]. The most commonly applied stimulation methods are transcranial magnetic stimulation (TMS) and transcranial direct current stimulation (tDCS). These methods are used in awake participants and are generally considered to be safe when administered within recommended guidelines [389–394].

The use of TMS involves the delivery of electromagnetic pulses that penetrate the skull to induce electric current in the underlying cortex and cause short-term changes in cortical excitability. The modulation of cortical excitability can last beyond the period of stimulation by delivering trains of pulses, a technique known as repetitive TMS (rTMS) [395]. When applied to the DLPFC, rTMS has been shown to effectively reduce cravings for cigarettes, alcohol and drugs of abuse, especially when applied for multiple sessions [396–400]. The DLPFC is an area involved extensively in inhibitory control [401–404] and stimulation of this region may act to boost self-control, potentially by increasing dopamine release in the caudate nucleus [405,406].

Reductions in substance craving have also been demonstrated with stimulation of the DLPFC using tDCS [114,407–412]. The use of tDCS involves the application of a weak (typically 1–2mA) direct electrical current to the scalp via a pair of electrodes. The effect of tDCS on brain activity is dependent on the stimulation polarity; anodal stimulation is thought to increase cortical excitability by neuronal depolarisation whereas cathodal stimulation is believed to decrease excitability by hyperpolarising neurons [413–418]. Long-lasting effects on resting membrane potential have been shown with longer stimulation durations, for example, 13 min of anodal tDCS has been shown to increase motor cortical excitability for up to 90 min [419]. Compared to TMS, tDCS is a weaker form of stimulation with fewer incidental artefacts and is considered to be safer and more appropriate for reliable double-blinding [387,420,421]. It is also thought that tDCS can be used to potentiate learning [422], and may effectively enhance the effects of the aforementioned cognitive interventions [378,423].

These stimulation methods are currently being investigated for their potential to reduce food craving and consumption [424–429]. Using rTMS to the left DLPFC, Uher et al. [430] found an increase in cue-induced craving for palatable foods in the group who experienced sham stimulation but not the active group. However, no effect was found on ad-libitum food consumption, although this result may have been due to the limited time period (5 min) causing participants in both groups to consume a large amount of calories. Using a similar methodology, Van den Eynde et al. [431] demonstrated an increase in craving scores in the sham group, but a decrease in craving scores for the active group in a sample of participants with bulimic-type eating disorders. In addition, active rTMS was associated with a reduction in binge-eating episodes in the following 24 h period. However, blinding was only partially successful in this study with most participants correctly guessing whether they were receiving active or sham rTMS. In a later study, Barth et al. [432] used a within-subjects design with an improved sham condition in which they matched the perceived pain of active rTMS with scalp electrodes. They found an equal reduction in cravings for both conditions and attributed this effect to the experience of pain rather than prefrontal stimulation.

As mentioned, tDCS is believed to involve a more appropriately matched sham condition, especially when participants receive active stimulation for a short initial period [420,421]. When stimulating the DLPFC bilaterally using tDCS, Fregni et al. [433] found a significant increase in cue-induced craving, measured before and after stimulation, in the sham condition and a significant reduction when participants received anodal right/cathodal left stimulation. Compared to the sham condition, active stimulation was also associated with a reduction in food intake during an ad-libitum eating phase. Although the authors did not assess blinding in this study, they did report equal occurrences of mild adverse effects across conditions. Using the same montage, Goldman et al. [424] and Lapenta et al. [426] also found the same reduction in food craving, and an early meta-analysis revealed a medium effect-size favouring active over sham stimulation in the reduction of cravings [434]. However, as the number of studies utilizing tDCS in the exploration of its effects on food craving has increased, evidence of efficacy has weakened. A more recent meta-analysis, including eight experiments, found no effect of tDCS on food craving [386], and subsequent research, including a large pre-registered experiment, has also failed to replicate findings for both food craving and consumption [435,436].

Another neuromodulation intervention, which is worthy of a brief mention and gaining in popularity for the treatment of SUDs, is real-time fMRI (rt-fMRI) neurofeedback training. Neurofeedback training involves providing participants with feedback of their neural response to certain cues and instructing them to increase or decrease their response, so that they may gain volitional control over specific brain regions. In the treatment of SUDs, neurofeedback training typically involves increasing activity in control regions, such as the prefrontal cortex, or decreasing activity in regions associated with craving, such as the ACC. For example, it has been shown that decreasing activity in the ACC with rt-fMRI neurofeedback is significantly correlated with decreased nicotine craving in smokers [437–439]. Using a similar technique with electroencephalography (EEG) has also shown improvements in cravings, drug use and treatment outcomes for a range of different substances [440–443]. Although in its early days, the application of neurofeedback training to food consumption and obesity has already been proposed [444–446]; recent findings have also suggested that neurofeedback may be another method of decreasing activity in motivation- and reward-related regions [447] and increasing activity within critical prefrontal regions such as the DLPFC [448,449].

3.3. Therapeutic Interventions

Therapeutic interventions such as Overeaters Anonymous and cognitive behavioural therapy have taken a more holistic approach to the treatment of obesity. Overeaters Anonymous (OA) is based directly on the 12-step programme developed by Alcoholics Anonymous. The OA organisation promotes the central belief that obesity is a symptom of 'compulsive overeating', which is an addictive-like illness with physical, emotional and spiritual components [450]. Individuals are required to acknowledge that compulsive overeating is beyond their willpower to overcome and, therefore, they must attempt to control their intake by avoiding certain foods and surrendering to a 'higher power'. Just like Alcoholics Anonymous, OA involves group meetings for individuals to share their feelings and experiences. Although the way in which this programme influences outcomes is unclear [53], the group meetings may act to alleviate feelings of isolation and instead foster a sense of community. As discussed earlier, due to the feelings of shame and guilt and the weight teasing experienced, overweight and obesity are associated with a preference for isolative activities [159]. This social isolation can subsequently exacerbate overeating, creating a vicious cycle [42,160]. It is possible, therefore, that OA acts to break this cycle by providing a supportive and encouraging social environment. However, due to the anonymous nature of OA, there has been little research conducted on its efficacy and it is not understood exactly how OA affects overeating and the extent to which it may do so.

Cognitive behavioural therapy (CBT), on the other hand, is a therapeutic approach which is extensively informed by research. CBT requires patients to critically evaluate the thoughts, feelings and behaviours that result in maladaptive behaviour and then modify them through therapy. This therapy allows patients to recognise potential triggers and develop appropriate coping strategies. CBT interventions have been effective in the treatment of substance addictions [451] and have also demonstrated their potential in the treatment of obesity [452,453] and BED [453–456]. However, it has been argued that the success of treating overeating and BED with CBT refutes the food addiction model [30]. The food addiction model applied in OA requires complete avoidance of so-called trigger foods, thereby acting to increase dietary restraint, whereas a reduction in dietary restraint has been shown to moderate the increased effectiveness of CBT on binge eating in a sample of patients with BN [457]. The focus of CBT is to replace dysfunctional eating with more normalised eating behaviour, therefore, favouring moderation and flexibility rather than absolute restraint.

4. Conclusions

As the prevalence of obesity continues to increase and traditional weight loss methods appear to be largely unsuccessful, researchers and clinicians have begun to consider the addictive potential of food. There is a substantial body of evidence demonstrating the similarities between addictive drugs and food on reward and control pathways in the brain and subsequent behaviour such as craving and impulsivity. There is also limited evidence to indicate that in some circumstances, overeating meets the physiological criteria of substance dependence, although more research is necessary to determine the validity of these symptoms in human participants. More research is also required for other behavioural criteria such as social impairment and repeated use despite negative consequences, as the evidence to date is largely anecdotal. However, meeting the physiological criteria for addiction is not necessary for a DSM diagnosis, and as food is a legal substance, just like caffeine, tobacco and alcohol, not all criteria associated with SUDs [23] readily translate to food addiction. Nevertheless, the criterion of withdrawal in SUDs has been associated with clinical severity and the number of symptoms that an individual endorses is used to determine the disorder's overall severity [23].

With a number of these criteria having a limited application to food addiction, a clinical diagnosis appears unlikely in most cases of overeating; however, using the YFAS, it has been estimated that approximately 11% of the general population meet the criteria for a 'severe' food addiction [38]. It should also be made clear that the concept of food addiction does not equate with obesity. Obesity is a multifactorial condition determined by genetic, environmental, biological and behavioural components. For the majority of cases, obesity is caused by a steady increase in excess energy intake and it is not characterised by a compulsive drive for food consumption. Instead, it is thought that the concept of food addiction applies most appropriately to individuals with BED and BN [31,32,277,278].

Despite there being considerable parallels between substance use and compulsive overeating, there is still some concern regarding the use and validity of the term 'food addiction', which is unlikely to apply to the majority of cases [17]. There is also concern over the use of such terminology in the wider social context and whether the term may do more harm than good. While most people would believe that an addiction model reduces individual responsibility, it has also been argued that attributing the problem to a minority of individuals also reduces corporate responsibility [28,458]. As the majority of the population would not be considered 'food addicts', there would be less pressure for the food industry to reduce marketing or to promote healthier alternatives. Likewise, any environmental interventions to reduce access and availability may also seem less critical with a food addiction model.

There are also implications of such terminology for the diagnosed individual. Obesity is already associated with significant social stigmatisation [157–159,161–164] and an additional 'addict' label, which may invoke stereotypes of a person who is untrustworthy and inferior [459], may only serve to heighten the problem [460–462]. DePierre et al. [460] found that when an individual was labelled as an 'obese food addict' they were more stigmatised than when they received either label in isolation ('food addict' or 'obese'). However, a study investigating the effect of an addiction model on public perceptions found that it actually reduced stigma, blame and perceived psychopathology [463,464], suggesting that it may be beneficial in reducing weight-related prejudice. The 'addicted' individual described in the study was viewed as being less at fault for their weight. Although, it is unclear whether the fault then lies with the individual's biology (i.e., certain individuals are prone to becoming 'food addicts') or the industry that continues to promote potentially addictive foods. Although it is almost certain to be a combination of both entities, demonstrating that certain foods can be addictive should increase corporate responsibility and pressure on the food industry to regulate the availability, advertising and nutritional content of such palatable foods [9,458].

Despite these issues and concerns, it has also been acknowledged that for some individuals, 'food addiction' may be the most appropriate diagnosis for their symptoms and it may help to inform their treatment [34]. The available evidence suggests, therefore, that some individuals *are* capable of experiencing an addictive-type relationship with food, although the majority of individuals who compulsively overeat are unlikely to receive such a diagnosis. Considering the underlying causes of impulsive overeating has also led to the development of some exciting and potentially effective interventions. While there are differences between the addictive characteristics of food and illicit substances, there are many parallels that should not be ignored. These parallels have contributed greatly to our current knowledge of compulsive overeating and potential treatments. Both the similarities and differences should encourage more research, which is necessary to determine the extent and potential impact of such a disorder. Until then, the idea of 'food addiction' is expected to remain hotly debated [14,19,20].

Author Contributions: R.C.A. conceived, drafted and finalised the manuscript. J.S., L.M., C.D.C. and N.S.L. made substantial contributions to the manuscript drafts and final approval of the manuscript. All the authors agree to be accountable for all aspects of the work in ensuring that questions related to the accuracy or integrity of any part of the work are appropriately investigated and resolved.

References

1. WHO. *Obesity and Overweight*; World Health Organization: Geneva, Switzerland, 2003.
2. Global Burden of Disease Collaborative Network. *Global Burden of Disease Study. Obesity Prevalence 1990–2013*; Institute for Health Metrics and Evaluation (IHME): Seattle, WA, USA, 2014.
3. Ng, M.; Fleming, T.; Robinson, M.; Thomson, B.; Graetz, N.; Margono, C.; Mullany, E.C.; Biryukov, S.; Abbafati, C.; Abera, S.F.; et al. Global, regional, and national prevalence of overweight and obesity in children and adults during 1980–2013: A systematic analysis for the Global burden of disease study 2013. *Lancet* **2014**, *384*, 766–781. [CrossRef]
4. WHO. *Obesity and Overweight*; World Health Organization: Geneva, Switzerland, 2018.
5. Butland, B.; Jebb, S.; Kopelman, P.; McPherson, K.; Thomas, S.; Mardell, J.; Parry, V. *Tackling Obesities: Future Choices—Project Report*, 2nd ed.; Foresight Programme of the Government Office for Science: London, UK, 2007. Available online: www.bis.gov.uk/assets/bispartners/foresight/docs/obesity/17.pdf (accessed on 28 September 2018).
6. Cummins, S.; Macintyre, S. Food environments and obesity—Neighbourhood or nation? *Int. J. Epidemiol.* **2006**, *35*, 100–104. [CrossRef] [PubMed]
7. Jeffery, R.W.; Utter, J. The changing environment and population obesity in the United States. *Obes. Res.* **2003**, *11*, 12S–22S. [CrossRef] [PubMed]
8. Levitsky, D.A. The non-regulation of food intake in humans: Hope for reversing the epidemic of obesity. *Physiol. Behav.* **2005**, *86*, 623–632. [CrossRef] [PubMed]

9. Schulte, E.M.; Avena, N.M.; Gearhardt, A.N. Which foods may be addictive? The roles of processing, fat content, and glycemic load. *PLoS ONE* **2015**, *10*, e0117959. [CrossRef] [PubMed]
10. Blundell, J.E.; Burley, V.J.; Cotton, J.R.; Lawton, C.L. Dietary fat and the control of energy intake: Evaluating the effects of fat on meal size and postmeal satiety. *Am. J. Clin. Nutr.* **1993**, *57*, 772S–778S. [CrossRef] [PubMed]
11. Drewnowski, A.; Brunzell, J.; Sande, K.; Iverius, P.; Greenwood, M. Sweet tooth reconsidered: Taste responsiveness in human obesity. *Physiol. Behav.* **1985**, *35*, 617–622. [CrossRef]
12. Drewnowski, A.; Kurth, C.; Holden-Wiltse, J.; Saari, J. Food preferences in human obesity: Carbohydrates versus fats. *Appetite* **1992**, *18*, 207–221. [CrossRef]
13. Davis, C. An introduction to the Special Issue on 'food addiction'. *Appetite* **2017**, *115*, 1–2. [CrossRef] [PubMed]
14. Avena, N.M.; Gearhardt, A.N.; Gold, M.S.; Wang, G.-J.; Potenza, M.N. Tossing the baby out with the bathwater after a brief rinse? The potential downside of dismissing food addiction based on limited data. *Nat. Rev. Neurosci.* **2012**, *13*, 514. [CrossRef]
15. Corsica, J.A.; Pelchat, M.L. Food addiction: True or false? *Curr. Opin. Gastroenterol.* **2010**, *26*, 165–169. [CrossRef] [PubMed]
16. Meule, A.; Gearhardt, A. Food addiction in the light of DSM-5. *Nutrients* **2014**, *6*, 3653–3671. [CrossRef] [PubMed]
17. Rogers, P.J.; Smit, H.J. Food craving and food "addiction": A critical review of the evidence from a biopsychosocial perspective. *Pharmacol. Biochem. Behav.* **2000**, *66*, 3–14. [CrossRef]
18. Volkow, N.D.; Wise, R.A.; Baler, R. The dopamine motive system: Implications for drug and food addiction. *Nat. Rev. Neurosci.* **2017**, *18*, 741–752. [CrossRef] [PubMed]
19. Ziauddeen, H.; Farooqi, I.S.; Fletcher, P.C. Food addiction: is there a baby in the bathwater? *Nat. Rev. Neurosci.* **2012**, *13*, 514. [CrossRef]
20. Ziauddeen, H.; Farooqi, I.S.; Fletcher, P.C. Obesity and the brain: how convincing is the addiction model? *Nat. Rev. Neurosci.* **2012**, *13*, 279–286. [CrossRef] [PubMed]
21. Frascella, J.; Potenza, M.N.; Brown, L.L.; Childress, A.R. Carving addiction at a new joint? Shared brain vulnerabilities open the way for non-substance addictions. *Ann. N. Y. Acad. Sci.* **2010**, *1187*, 294–315. [CrossRef]
22. Orford, J. Addiction as excessive appetite. *Addiction* **2001**, *96*, 15–31. [CrossRef]
23. American Psychiatric Association. *Diagnostic and Statistical Manual of Mental Disorders*, 5th ed.; American Psychiatric Association: Washington, DC, USA, 2013.
24. Potenza, M.N. Biological contributions to addictions in adolescents and adults: Prevention, treatment and policy implications. *J. Adolesc. Health* **2013**, *52*, S22–S32. [CrossRef]
25. Worhunsky, P.D.; Malison, R.T.; Rogers, R.D.; Potenza, M.N. Altered neural correlates of reward and loss processing during simulated slot-machine fMRI in pathological gambling and cocaine dependence. *Drug Alcohol Depend.* **2014**, *145*, 77–86. [CrossRef]
26. Barry, D.; Clarke, M.; Petry, N.M. Obesity and its relationship to addictions: Is overeating a form of addictive behavior? *Am. J. Addict.* **2009**, *18*, 439–451. [CrossRef] [PubMed]
27. Cassin, S.E.; Buchman, D.Z.; Leung, S.E.; Kantarovich, K.; Hawa, A.; Carter, A.; Sockalingam, S. Ethical, Stigma, and policy implications of food addiction: A scoping review. *Nutrients* **2019**, *11*, 710. [CrossRef] [PubMed]
28. Gearhardt, A.N.; Grilo, C.M.; Dileone, R.J.; Brownell, K.D.; Potenza, M.N. Can food be addictive? Public health and policy implications. *Addiction* **2011**, *106*, 1208–1212. [CrossRef] [PubMed]
29. Volkow, N.D.; Wise, R.A. How can drug addiction help us understand obesity? *Nat. Neurosci.* **2005**, *8*, 555–560. [CrossRef] [PubMed]
30. Wilson, G.T. Eating disorders, obesity and addiction. *Eur. Eat. Disord. Rev.* **2010**, *18*, 341–351. [CrossRef] [PubMed]
31. Davis, C.; Carter, J.C. Compulsive overeating as an addiction disorder. A review of theory and evidence. *Appetite* **2009**, *53*, 1–8. [CrossRef] [PubMed]
32. Meule, A.; von Rezori, V.; Blechert, J. Food addiction and bulimia nervosa. *Eur. Eat. Dis. Rev.* **2014**, *22*, 331–337. [CrossRef] [PubMed]
33. Shell, A.G.; Firmin, M.W. Binge eating disorder and substance use disorder: A case for food addiction. *Psychol. Stud.* **2017**, *62*, 370–376. [CrossRef]
34. Smith, D.G.; Robbins, T.W. The neurobiological underpinnings of obesity and binge eating: A rationale for adopting the food addiction model. *Biol. Psychiatr.* **2013**, *73*, 804–810. [CrossRef]

35. Cassin, S.E.; Von Ranson, K.M. Is binge eating experienced as an addiction? *Appetite* **2007**, *49*, 687–690. [CrossRef]
36. Gearhardt, A.N.; White, M.A.; Masheb, R.M.; Morgan, P.T.; Crosby, R.D.; Grilo, C.M. An examination of the food addiction construct in obese patients with binge eating disorder. *Int. J. Eat. Dis.* **2012**, *45*, 657–663. [CrossRef] [PubMed]
37. Gearhardt, A.N.; Corbin, W.R.; Brownell, K.D. Preliminary validation of the Yale food addiction scale. *Appetite* **2009**, *52*, 430–436. [CrossRef] [PubMed]
38. Gearhardt, A.N.; Corbin, W.R.; Brownell, K.D. Development of the Yale food addiction scale version 2.0. *Psychol. Addict. Behav.* **2016**, *30*, 113–121. [CrossRef] [PubMed]
39. Gearhardt, A.N.; Roberto, C.A.; Seamans, M.J.; Corbin, W.R.; Brownell, K.D. Preliminary validation of the Yale food addiction scale for children. *Eat. Behav.* **2013**, *14*, 508–512. [CrossRef]
40. Murphy, C.M.; Stojek, M.K.; MacKillop, J. Interrelationships among impulsive personality traits, food addiction, and body mass index. *Appetite* **2014**, *73*, 45–50. [CrossRef]
41. Curtis, C.; Davis, C. A qualitative study of binge eating and obesity from an addiction perspective. *Eat. Dis.* **2014**, *22*, 19–32. [CrossRef]
42. Pretlow, R.A. Addiction to highly pleasurable food as a cause of the childhood obesity epidemic: A qualitative internet study. *Eat. Disord.* **2011**, *19*, 295–307. [CrossRef]
43. French, S.; Jeffery, R.; Sherwood, N.; Neumark-Sztainer, D. Prevalence and correlates of binge eating in a nonclinical sample of women enrolled in a weight gain prevention program. *Int. J. Obes.* **1999**, *23*, 576–585. [CrossRef]
44. Lu, H.K.; Mannan, H.; Hay, P. Exploring relationships between recurrent binge eating and illicit substance use in a non-clinical sample of women over two years. *Behav. Sci.* **2017**, *7*, 46. [CrossRef]
45. MacDiarmid, J.; Loe, J.; Kyle, J.; McNeill, G. "It was an education in portion size". Experience of eating a healthy diet and barriers to long term dietary change. *Appetite* **2013**, *71*, 411–419. [CrossRef]
46. Bacon, L.; Aphramor, L. Weight science: Evaluating the evidence for a paradigm shift. *Nutr. J.* **2011**, *10*, 9. [CrossRef] [PubMed]
47. Dansinger, M.L.; Gleason, J.A.; Griffith, J.L.; Selker, H.P.; Schaefer, E.J. Comparison of the Atkins, Ornish, Weight Watchers, and Zone Diets for Weight Loss and Heart Disease Risk Reduction. *JAMA* **2005**, *293*, 43. [CrossRef] [PubMed]
48. Jeffery, R.W.; Epstein, L.H.; Wilson, G.T.; Drewnowski, A.; Stunkard, A.J.; Wing, R.R. Long-term maintenance of weight loss: Current status. *Health Psychol.* **2000**, *19*, 5–16. [CrossRef] [PubMed]
49. Lowe, M.R.; Annunziato, R.A.; Markowitz, J.T.; Didie, E.; Bellace, D.L.; Riddell, L.; Maille, C.; McKinney, S.; Stice, E. Multiple types of dieting prospectively predict weight gain during the freshman year of college. *Appetite* **2006**, *47*, 83–90. [CrossRef] [PubMed]
50. Mann, T.; Tomiyama, A.J.; Westling, E.; Lew, A.-M.; Samuels, B.; Chatman, J. Medicare's search for effective obesity treatments: Diets are not the answer. *Am. Psychol.* **2007**, *62*, 220–233. [CrossRef] [PubMed]
51. Pietiläinen, K.H.; Saarni, S.E.; Kaprio, J.; Rissanen, A. Does dieting make you fat? A twin study. *Int. J. Obes.* **2012**, *36*, 456–464. [CrossRef] [PubMed]
52. Ifland, J.; Preuss, H.; Marcus, M.; Rourke, K.; Taylor, W.; Burau, K.; Jacobs, W.; Kadish, W.; Manso, G. Refined food addiction: A classic substance use disorder. *Med. Hypotheses* **2009**, *72*, 518–526. [CrossRef] [PubMed]
53. Russell-Mayhew, S.; Von Ranson, K.M.; Masson, P.C. How does overeaters anonymous help its members? A qualitative analysis. *Eur. Eat. Disord. Rev.* **2010**, *18*, 33–42. [CrossRef] [PubMed]
54. Dawe, S.; Loxton, N.J. The role of impulsivity in the development of substance use and eating disorders. *Neurosci. Biobehav. Rev.* **2004**, *28*, 343–351. [CrossRef]
55. Gullo, M.; Dawe, S. Impulsivity and adolescent substance use: Rashly dismissed as "all-bad"? *Neurosci. Biobehav. Rev.* **2008**, *32*, 1507–1518. [CrossRef] [PubMed]
56. Schulte, E.M.; Grilo, C.M.; Gearhardt, A.N. Shared and unique mechanisms underlying binge eating disorder and addictive disorders. *Clin. Psychol. Rev.* **2016**, *44*, 125–139. [CrossRef] [PubMed]
57. De Wit, H. Impulsivity as a determinant and consequence of drug use: A review of underlying processes. *Addict. Biol.* **2008**, *14*, 22–31. [CrossRef] [PubMed]
58. Hershberger, A.R.; Um, M.; Cyders, M.A. The relationship between the UPPS-P impulsive personality traits and substance use psychotherapy outcomes: A meta-analysis. *Drug Alcohol Depend.* **2017**, *178*, 408–416. [CrossRef] [PubMed]

59. Iacono, W.G.; Malone, S.M.; McGue, M. Behavioral disinhibition and the development of early-onset addiction: Common and specific influences. *Annu. Rev. Clin. Psychol.* **2008**, *4*, 325–348. [CrossRef]
60. Verdejo-García, A.; Lawrence, A.J.; Clark, L. Impulsivity as a vulnerability marker for substance-use disorders: Review of findings from high-risk research, problem gamblers and genetic association studies. *Neurosci. Biobehav. Rev.* **2008**, *32*, 777–810. [CrossRef]
61. Billieux, J.; Gay, P.; Rochat, L.; Khazaal, Y.; Zullino, D.; Van Der Linden, M. Lack of inhibitory control predicts cigarette smoking dependence: Evidence from a non-deprived sample of light to moderate smokers. *Drug Alcohol Depend.* **2010**, *112*, 164–167. [CrossRef] [PubMed]
62. Butler, G.; Montgomery, A. Impulsivity, risk taking and recreational 'ecstasy' (MDMA) use. *Drug Alcohol Depend.* **2004**, *76*, 55–62. [CrossRef]
63. García-Marchena, N.; De Guevara-Miranda, D.L.; Pedraz, M.; Araos, P.F.; Rubio, G.; Ruiz, J.J.; Pavón, F.J.; Serrano, A.; Castilla-Ortega, E.; Santín, L.J.; et al. Higher impulsivity as a distinctive trait of severe cocaine addiction among individuals treated for cocaine or alcohol use disorders. *Front. Psychol.* **2018**, *9*, 26. [CrossRef] [PubMed]
64. Lawrence, A.J.; Luty, J.; Bogdan, N.A.; Sahakian, B.J.; Clark, L. Impulsivity and response inhibition in alcohol dependence and problem gambling. *Psychopharmacology* **2009**, *207*, 163–172. [CrossRef]
65. Monterosso, J.R.; Aron, A.R.; Cordova, X.; Xu, J.; London, E.D. Deficits in response inhibition associated with chronic methamphetamine abuse. *Drug Alcohol Depend.* **2005**, *79*, 273–277. [CrossRef]
66. Verdejo-García, A.J.; Perales, J.C.; Pérez-García, M. Cognitive impulsivity in cocaine and heroin polysubstance abusers. *Addict. Behav.* **2007**, *32*, 950–966. [CrossRef] [PubMed]
67. Noël, X.; Van Der Linden, M.; Brevers, D.; Campanella, S.; Verbanck, P.; Hanak, C.; Kornreich, C.; Verbruggen, F. Separating intentional inhibition of prepotent responses and resistance to proactive interference in alcohol-dependent individuals. *Drug Alcohol Depend.* **2013**, *128*, 200–205. [CrossRef] [PubMed]
68. Emery, R.L.; Levine, M.D. Questionnaire and behavioral task measures of impulsivity are differentially associated with body mass index: A comprehensive meta-analysis. *Psychol. Bull.* **2017**, *143*, 868–902. [CrossRef] [PubMed]
69. Guerrieri, R.; Nederkoorn, C.; Jansen, A. The interaction between impulsivity and a varied food environment: Its influence on food intake and overweight. *Int. J. Obes.* **2008**, *32*, 708–714. [CrossRef] [PubMed]
70. Jentsch, J.D.; Pennington, Z.T. Reward, interrupted: Inhibitory control and its relevance to addictions. *Neuropharmacology* **2014**, *76*, 479–486. [CrossRef] [PubMed]
71. Meule, A. Impulsivity and overeating: A closer look at the subscales of the Barratt impulsiveness scale. *Front. Psychol.* **2013**, *4*, 177. [CrossRef]
72. Chalmers, D.K.; Bowyer, C.A.; Olenick, N.L. Problem drinking and obesity: A comparison in personality patterns and lifestyle. *Int. J. Addict.* **1990**, *25*, 803–817. [CrossRef]
73. Davis, C.; Levitan, R.D.; Carter, J.; Kaplan, A.S.; Reid, C.; Curtis, C.; Patte, K.; Kennedy, J.L. Personality and eating behaviors: A case-control study of binge eating disorder. *Int. J. Eat. Disord.* **2008**, *41*, 243–250. [CrossRef]
74. Rydén, A.; Sullivan, M.; Torgerson, J.S.; Karlsson, J.; Lindroos, A.-K.; Taft, C. Severe obesity and personality: A comparative controlled study of personality traits. *Int. J. Obes.* **2003**, *27*, 1534–1540. [CrossRef]
75. Batterink, L.; Yokum, S.; Stice, E. Body mass correlates inversely with inhibitory control in response to food among adolescent girls: An fMRI study. *NeuroImage* **2010**, *52*, 1696–1703. [CrossRef]
76. Davis, C.; Patte, K.; Curtis, C.; Reid, C. Immediate pleasures and future consequences. A neuropsychological study of binge eating and obesity. *Appetite* **2010**, *54*, 208–213. [CrossRef] [PubMed]
77. Nederkoorn, C.; Braet, C.; Van Eijs, Y.; Tanghe, A.; Jansen, A. Why obese children cannot resist food: The role of impulsivity. *Eat. Behav.* **2006**, *7*, 315–322. [CrossRef] [PubMed]
78. Friese, M.; Hofmann, W. Control me or I will control you: Impulses, trait self-control, and the guidance of behavior. *J. Res. Personal.* **2009**, *43*, 795–805. [CrossRef]
79. Friese, M.; Hofmann, W.; Wänke, M. When impulses take over: Moderated predictive validity of explicit and implicit attitude measures in predicting food choice and consumption behaviour. *Br. J. Soc. Psychol.* **2008**, *47*, 397–419. [CrossRef] [PubMed]
80. Hofmann, W.; Friese, M.; Roefs, A. Three ways to resist temptation: The independent contributions of executive attention, inhibitory control, and affect regulation to the impulse control of eating behavior. *J. Exp. Soc. Psychol.* **2009**, *45*, 431–435. [CrossRef]

81. Crescioni, A.W.; Ehrlinger, J.; Alquist, J.L.; Conlon, K.E.; Baumeister, R.F.; Schatschneider, C.; Dutton, G.R. High trait self-control predicts positive health behaviors and success in weight loss. *J. Health Psychol.* **2011**, *16*, 750–759. [CrossRef] [PubMed]
82. De Boer, B.J.; van Hooft, E.A.J.; Bakker, A.B. Stop and start control: A distinction within self-control. *Eur. J. Personal.* **2011**, *25*, 349–362. [CrossRef]
83. Gerrits, J.H.; O'Hara, R.E.; Piko, B.F.; Gibbons, F.X.; De Ridder, D.T.D.; Keresztes, N.; Kamble, S.V.; De Wit, J.B.F. Self-control, diet concerns and eater prototypes influence fatty foods consumption of adolescents in three countries. *Health Educ. Res.* **2010**, *25*, 1031–1041. [CrossRef]
84. Jasinska, A.J.; Yasuda, M.; Burant, C.F.; Gregor, N.; Khatri, S.; Sweet, M.; Falk, E.B. Impulsivity and inhibitory control deficits are associated with unhealthy eating in young adults. *Appetite* **2012**, *59*, 738–747. [CrossRef]
85. Allan, J.L.; Johnston, M.; Campbell, N. Unintentional eating. What determines goal-incongruent chocolate consumption? *Appetite* **2010**, *54*, 422–425. [CrossRef]
86. Allom, V.; Mullan, B. Individual differences in executive function predict distinct eating behaviours. *Appetite* **2014**, *80*, 123–130. [CrossRef] [PubMed]
87. Guerrieri, R.; Nederkoorn, C.; Jansen, A. How impulsiveness and variety influence food intake in a sample of healthy women. *Appetite* **2007**, *48*, 119–122. [CrossRef] [PubMed]
88. Churchill, S.; Jessop, D.C. Reflective and non-reflective antecedents of health-related behaviour: Exploring the relative contributions of impulsivity and implicit self-control to the prediction of dietary behaviour. *Br. J. Health Psychol.* **2011**, *16*, 257–272. [CrossRef] [PubMed]
89. Meule, A.; De Zwaan, M.; Müller, A. Attentional and motor impulsivity interactively predict 'food addiction' in obese individuals. *Compr. Psychiatr.* **2017**, *72*, 83–87. [CrossRef] [PubMed]
90. VanderBroek-Stice, L.; Stojek, M.K.; Beach, S.R.H.; Vandellen, M.R.; MacKillop, J. Multidimensional assessment of impulsivity in relation to obesity and food addiction. *Appetite* **2017**, *112*, 59–68. [CrossRef] [PubMed]
91. Appelhans, B.M.; Woolf, K.; Pagoto, S.L.; Schneider, K.L.; Whited, M.C.; Liebman, R. Inhibiting food reward: Delay discounting, food reward sensitivity, and palatable food intake in overweight and obese women. *Obesity* **2011**, *19*, 2175–2182. [CrossRef] [PubMed]
92. Dissabandara, L.O.; Loxton, N.J.; Dias, S.R.; Dodd, P.R.; Daglish, M.; Stadlin, A. Dependent heroin use and associated risky behaviour: The role of rash impulsiveness and reward sensitivity. *Addict. Behav.* **2014**, *39*, 71–76. [CrossRef]
93. Franken, I.H.; Muris, P. Individual differences in reward sensitivity are related to food craving and relative body weight in healthy women. *Appetite* **2005**, *45*, 198–201. [CrossRef]
94. Davis, C.; Patte, K.; Levitan, R.; Reid, C.; Tweed, S.; Curtis, C. From motivation to behaviour: A model of reward sensitivity, overeating, and food preferences in the risk profile for obesity. *Appetite* **2007**, *48*, 12–19. [CrossRef]
95. De Cock, N.; Van Lippevelde, W.; Goossens, L.; De Clercq, B.; Vangeel, J.; Lachat, C.; Beullens, K.; Huybregts, L.; Vervoort, L.; Eggermont, S.; et al. Sensitivity to reward and adolescents' unhealthy snacking and drinking behavior: The role of hedonic eating styles and availability. *Int. J. Behav. Nutr. Phys. Act.* **2016**, *13*, 17. [CrossRef]
96. Lawrence, N.S.; Hinton, E.C.; Parkinson, J.A.; Lawrence, A.D. Nucleus accumbens response to food cues predicts subsequent snack consumption in women and increased body mass index in those with reduced self-control. *NeuroImage* **2012**, *63*, 415–422. [CrossRef] [PubMed]
97. Davis, C.; Strachan, S.; Berkson, M. Sensitivity to reward: Implications for overeating and overweight. *Appetite* **2004**, *42*, 131–138. [CrossRef] [PubMed]
98. Volkow, N.D.; Fowler, J.S.; Wang, G.-J. The addicted human brain: Insights from imaging studies. *J. Clin. Investig.* **2003**, *111*, 1444–1451. [CrossRef] [PubMed]
99. Volkow, N.D.; Wang, G.-J.; Telang, F.; Fowler, J.S.; Thanos, P.K.; Logan, J.; Alexoff, D.; Ding, Y.-S.; Wong, C.; Ma, Y.; et al. Low dopamine striatal D2 receptors are associated with prefrontal metabolism in obese subjects: Possible contributing factors. *NeuroImage* **2008**, *42*, 1537–1543. [CrossRef] [PubMed]
100. Wang, G.J.; Volkow, N.D.; Logan, J.; Pappas, N.R.; Wong, C.T.; Zhu, W.; Netusil, N.; Fowler, J.S. Brain dopamine and obesity. *Lancet* **2001**, *357*, 354–357. [CrossRef]
101. Blum, K.; Braverman, E.R.; Holder, J.M.; Lubar, J.F.; Monastra, V.J.; Miller, D.; Lubar, J.O.; Chen, T.J.; Comings, D.E. The reward deficiency syndrome: A biogenetic model for the diagnosis and treatment of impulsive, addictive and compulsive behaviors. *J. Psychoact. Drugs* **2000**, *32*, 1–112. [CrossRef]

102. Bowirrat, A.; Oscar-Berman, M. Relationship between dopaminergic neurotransmission, alcoholism, and reward deficiency syndrome. *Am. J. Med. Genet. Part B Neuropsychiatr. Genet.* **2005**, *132*, 29–37. [CrossRef]
103. Burger, K.S.; Stice, E. Variability in reward responsivity and obesity: Evidence from brain imaging studies. *Curr. Drug Abus. Rev.* **2011**, *4*, 182–189. [CrossRef]
104. Robinson, T. The neural basis of drug craving: An incentive-sensitization theory of addiction. *Brain Res. Rev.* **1993**, *18*, 247–291. [CrossRef]
105. Robinson, T.E.; Berridge, K.C. Incentive-sensitization and addiction. *Addiction* **2001**, *96*, 103–114. [CrossRef]
106. Robinson, T.E.; Berridge, K.C. Addiction. *Annu. Rev. Psychol.* **2003**, *54*, 25–53. [CrossRef] [PubMed]
107. Berridge, K.C. 'Liking' and 'wanting' food rewards: Brain substrates and roles in eating disorders. *Physiol. Behav.* **2009**, *97*, 537–550. [CrossRef] [PubMed]
108. Berridge, K.C.; Ho, C.-Y.; Richard, J.M.; DiFeliceantonio, A.G. The tempted brain eats: Pleasure and desire circuits in obesity and eating disorders. *Brain Res.* **2010**, *1350*, 43–64. [CrossRef] [PubMed]
109. Hetherington, M.; Pirie, L.; Nabb, S.; Hetherington, M. Stimulus satiation: Effects of repeated exposure to foods on pleasantness and intake. *Appetite* **2002**, *38*, 19–28. [CrossRef] [PubMed]
110. Ersche, K.D.; Jones, P.S.; Williams, G.B.; Turton, A.J.; Robbins, T.W.; Bullmore, E.T. Abnormal brain structure implicated in stimulant drug addiction. *Science* **2012**, *335*, 601–604. [CrossRef] [PubMed]
111. Everitt, B.J.; Belin, D.; Economidou, D.; Pelloux, Y.; Dalley, J.W.; Robbins, T.W. Neural mechanisms underlying the vulnerability to develop compulsive drug-seeking habits and addiction. *Philos. Trans. R. Soc. B Biol. Sci.* **2008**, *363*, 3125–3135. [CrossRef] [PubMed]
112. Flagel, S.B.; Akil, H.; Robinson, T.E. Individual differences in the attribution of incentive salience to reward-related cues: Implications for addiction. *Neuropharmacology* **2009**, *56*, 139–148. [CrossRef]
113. Saunders, B.T.; Robinson, T.E. Individual variation in resisting temptation: Implications for addiction. *Neurosci. Biobehav. Rev.* **2013**, *37*, 1955–1975. [CrossRef] [PubMed]
114. Kekic, M.; McClelland, J.; Campbell, I.; Nestler, S.; Rubia, K.; David, A.S.; Schmidt, U. The effects of prefrontal cortex transcranial direct current stimulation (tDCS) on food craving and temporal discounting in women with frequent food cravings. *Appetite* **2014**, *78*, 55–62. [CrossRef]
115. Weingarten, H.P.; Elston, D. The phenomenology of food cravings. *Appetite* **1990**, *15*, 231–246. [CrossRef]
116. Pelchat, M.L. Food cravings in young and elderly adults. *Appetite* **1997**, *28*, 103–113. [CrossRef] [PubMed]
117. Lopez, R.B.; Hofmann, W.; Wagner, D.D.; Kelley, W.M.; Heatherton, T.F. Neural predictors of giving in to temptation in daily life. *Psychol. Sci.* **2014**, *25*, 1337–1344. [CrossRef] [PubMed]
118. Cocores, J.A.; Gold, M.S. The Salted Food Addiction Hypothesis may explain overeating and the obesity epidemic. *Med. Hypotheses* **2009**, *73*, 892–899. [CrossRef] [PubMed]
119. Corsica, J.A.; Spring, B.J. Carbohydrate craving: A double-blind, placebo controlled test of the self-medication hypothesis. *Eat. Behav.* **2008**, *9*, 447–454. [CrossRef] [PubMed]
120. Hill, A.J.; Heaton-Brown, L. The experience of food craving: A prospective investigation in healthy women. *J. Psychosom. Res.* **1994**, *38*, 801–814. [CrossRef]
121. Massey, A.; Hill, A.J. Dieting and food craving. A descriptive, quasi-prospective study. *Appetite* **2012**, *58*, 781–785. [CrossRef]
122. Rozin, P.; Levine, E.; Stoess, C. Chocolate craving and liking. *Appetite* **1991**, *17*, 199–212. [CrossRef]
123. Cepeda-Benito, A.; Gleaves, D.H.; Williams, T.L.; Erath, S.A. The development and validation of the state and trait food-cravings questionnaires. *Behav. Ther.* **2000**, *31*, 151–173. [CrossRef]
124. Hill, A.J.; Weaver, C.F.; Blundell, J.E. Food craving, dietary restraint and mood. *Appetite* **1991**, *17*, 187–197. [CrossRef]
125. Nicholls, W.; Hulbert-Williams, L. British english translation of the food craving inventory (FCI-UK). *Appetite* **2013**, *67*, 37–43. [CrossRef]
126. Nijs, I.M.; Franken, I.H.; Muris, P. The modified trait and state food-cravings questionnaires: Development and validation of a general index of food craving. *Appetite* **2007**, *49*, 38–46. [CrossRef] [PubMed]
127. White, M.A.; Whisenhunt, B.L.; Williamson, D.A.; Greenway, F.L.; Netemeyer, R.G. Development and validation of the food-craving inventory. *Obes. Res.* **2002**, *10*, 107–114. [CrossRef] [PubMed]
128. Benton, D.; Greenfield, K.; Morgan, M. The development of the attitudes to chocolate questionnaire. *Personal. Individ. Differ.* **1998**, *24*, 513–520. [CrossRef]
129. Boswell, R.G.; Kober, H. Food cue reactivity and craving predict eating and weight gain: A meta-analytic review. *Obes. Rev.* **2016**, *17*, 159–177. [CrossRef] [PubMed]

130. Burton, P.; Smit, H.J.; Lightowler, H.J. The influence of restrained and external eating patterns on overeating. *Appetite* **2007**, *49*, 191–197. [CrossRef] [PubMed]
131. Dalton, M.; Blundell, J.; Finlayson, G.S. Examination of food reward and energy intake under laboratory and free-living conditions in a trait binge eating subtype of obesity. *Front. Psychol.* **2013**, *4*, 757. [CrossRef] [PubMed]
132. Lafay, L.; Mennen, L.; Charles, M.A.; Eschwège, E.; Borys, J.-M. Gender differences in the relation between food cravings and mood in an adult community: Results from the Fleurbaix Laventie Ville Sant study. *Int. J. Eat. Disord.* **2001**, *29*, 195–204. [CrossRef]
133. Davis, C.; Curtis, C.; Levitan, R.D.; Carter, J.C.; Kaplan, A.S.; Kennedy, J.L. Evidence that 'food addiction' is a valid phenotype of obesity. *Appetite* **2011**, *57*, 711–717. [CrossRef]
134. Meule, A. Food cravings in food addiction: Exploring a potential cut-off value of the food cravings questionnaire-trait-reduced. *Eat. Weight Dis. Stud. Anorex. Bulim. Obes.* **2018**, *23*, 39–43. [CrossRef]
135. Meule, A.; Kübler, A. Food cravings in food addiction: The distinct role of positive reinforcement. *Eat. Behav.* **2012**, *13*, 252–255. [CrossRef]
136. Mussell, M.P.; Mitchell, J.E.; De Zwaan, M.; Crosby, R.D.; Seim, H.C.; Crow, S.J. Clinical characteristics associated with binge eating in obese females: A descriptive study. *Int. J. Obes. Relat. Metab. Disord. J. Int. Assoc. Stud. Obes.* **1996**, *20*, 324–331.
137. Ng, L.; Davis, C. Cravings and food consumption in binge eating disorder. *Eat. Behav.* **2013**, *14*, 472–475. [CrossRef]
138. Van den Eynde, F.; Koskina, A.; Syrad, H.; Guillaume, S.; Broadbent, H.; Campbell, I.C.; Schmidt, U. State and trait food craving in people with bulimic eating disorders. *Eat. Behav.* **2012**, *13*, 414–417. [CrossRef] [PubMed]
139. Bottlender, M.; Soyka, M. Impact of craving on alcohol relapse during, and 12 months following, outpatient treatment. *Alcohol Alcohol.* **2004**, *39*, 357–361. [CrossRef] [PubMed]
140. Litt, M.D.; Cooney, N.L.; Morse, P. Reactivity to alcohol-related stimuli in the laboratory and in the field: Predictors of craving in treated alcoholics. *Addiction* **2000**, *95*, 889–900. [CrossRef] [PubMed]
141. Paliwal, P.; Hyman, S.M.; Sinha, R. Craving predicts time to cocaine relapse: Further validation of the now and brief versions of the cocaine craving questionnaire. *Drug Alcohol Depend.* **2008**, *93*, 252–259. [CrossRef] [PubMed]
142. Gendall, K.A.; Sullivan, P.F.; Joyce, P.R.; Fear, J.L.; Bulik, C.M. Psychopathology and personality of young women who experience food cravings. *Addict. Behav.* **1997**, *22*, 545–555. [CrossRef]
143. Meule, A.; Lutz, A.; Vögele, C.; Kübler, A. Food cravings discriminate differentially between successful and unsuccessful dieters and non-dieters. Validation of the food cravings questionnaires in German. *Appetite* **2012**, *58*, 88–97. [CrossRef]
144. Meule, A.; Westenhöfer, J.; Kübler, A. Food cravings mediate the relationship between rigid, but not flexible control of eating behavior and dieting success. *Appetite* **2011**, *57*, 582–584. [CrossRef]
145. Carter, B.L.; Tiffany, S.T. Meta-analysis of cue-reactivity in addiction research. *Addiction* **1999**, *94*, 327–340. [CrossRef]
146. Davidson, D.; Tiffany, S.T.; Johnston, W.; Flury, L.; Li, T.-K. Using the cue-availability paradigm to assess cue reactivity. *Alcohol. Clin. Exp. Res.* **2003**, *27*, 1251–1256. [CrossRef]
147. Mahler, S.V.; De Wit, H. Cue-Reactors: Individual differences in cue-induced craving after food or smoking abstinence. *PLoS ONE* **2010**, *5*, e15475. [CrossRef] [PubMed]
148. Styn, M.A.; Bovbjerg, D.H.; Lipsky, S.; Erblich, J. Cue-induced cigarette and food craving: A common effect? *Addict. Behav.* **2013**, *38*, 1840–1843. [CrossRef] [PubMed]
149. Cornell, C.E.; Rodin, J.; Weingarten, H. Stimulus-induced eating when satiated. *Physiol. Behav.* **1989**, *45*, 695–704. [CrossRef]
150. Nederkoorn, C.; Smulders, F.; Jansen, A. Cephalic phase responses, craving and food intake in normal subjects. *Appetite* **2000**, *35*, 45–55. [CrossRef] [PubMed]
151. Meule, A.; Küppers, C.; Harms, L.; Friederich, H.-C.; Schmidt, U.; Blechert, J.; Brockmeyer, T. Food cue-induced craving in individuals with bulimia nervosa and binge-eating disorder. *PLoS ONE* **2018**, *13*, e0204151. [CrossRef] [PubMed]
152. Karhunen, L.J.; Lappalainen, R.I.; Tammela, L.; Turpeinen, A.K.; Uusitupa, M.I.J. Subjective and physiological cephalic phase responses to food in obese binge-eating women. *Int. J. Eat. Disord.* **1997**, *21*, 321–328. [CrossRef]

153. Sobik, L.; Hutchison, K.; Craighead, L. Cue-elicited craving for food: A fresh approach to the study of binge eating. *Appetite* **2005**, *44*, 253–261. [CrossRef]
154. Kjelgaard, H.H.; Holstein, B.E.; Due, P.; Brixval, C.S.; Rasmussen, M. Adolescent weight status: Associations with structural and functional dimensions of social relations. *J. Adolesc. Health* **2017**, *60*, 460–468. [CrossRef]
155. Schwimmer, J.B.; Burwinkle, T.M.; Varni, J.W. Health-Related quality of life of severely obese children and adolescents. *JAMA* **2003**, *289*, 1813. [CrossRef]
156. Williams, J.; Wake, M.; Hesketh, K.; Maher, E.; Waters, E. Health-Related quality of life of overweight and obese children. *JAMA* **2005**, *293*, 70–76. [CrossRef] [PubMed]
157. Griffiths, L.J.; Wolke, D.; Page, A.S.; Horwood, J.P. Obesity and bullying: Different effects for boys and girls. *Arch. Dis. Child.* **2006**, *91*, 121–125. [CrossRef] [PubMed]
158. Pearce, M.J.; Boergers, J.; Prinstein, M.J. Adolescent obesity, overt and relational peer victimization, and romantic relationships. *Obes. Res.* **2002**, *10*, 386–393. [CrossRef] [PubMed]
159. Hayden-Wade, H.A.; Stein, R.I.; Ghaderi, A.; Saelens, B.E.; Zabinski, M.F.; Wilfley, D.E. Prevalence, characteristics, and correlates of teasing experiences among overweight children vs. non-overweight peers. *Obes. Res.* **2005**, *13*, 1381–1392. [CrossRef] [PubMed]
160. Neumark-Sztainer, D.; Falkner, N.; Story, M.; Perry, C.; Hannan, P.J.; Mulert, S. Weight-teasing among adolescents: Correlations with weight status and disordered eating behaviors. *Int. J. Obes.* **2002**, *26*, 123–131. [CrossRef] [PubMed]
161. Puhl, R.; Brownell, K.D. Bias, Discrimination, and Obesity. *Obes. Res.* **2001**, *9*, 788–805. [CrossRef] [PubMed]
162. Puhl, R.M.; Heuer, C.A. The stigma of obesity: A review and update. *Obesity* **2009**, *17*, 941–964. [CrossRef] [PubMed]
163. Puhl, R.M.; Latner, J.D. Stigma, obesity, and the health of the nation's children. *Psychol. Bull.* **2007**, *133*, 557–580. [CrossRef]
164. Chen, E.Y.; Brown, M. Obesity stigma in sexual relationships. *Obes. Res.* **2005**, *13*, 1393–1397. [CrossRef]
165. Chao, A.M.; Shaw, J.A.; Pearl, R.L.; Alamuddin, N.; Hopkins, C.M.; Bakizada, Z.M.; Wadden, T.A. Prevalence and psychosocial correlates of food addiction in persons with obesity seeking weight reduction. *Compr. Psychiatr.* **2017**, *73*, 97–104. [CrossRef]
166. Blomquist, K.K.; Ansell, E.B.; White, M.A.; Masheb, R.M.; Grilo, C.M. Interpersonal problems and developmental trajectories of binge eating disorder. *Compr. Psychiatr.* **2012**, *53*, 1088–1095. [CrossRef] [PubMed]
167. Lo Coco, G.; Gullo, S.; Salerno, L.; Iacoponelli, R. The association among interpersonal problems, binge behaviors, and self-esteem, in the assessment of obese individuals. *Compr. Psychiatr.* **2011**, *52*, 164–170. [CrossRef] [PubMed]
168. Jia, H.; Lubetkin, E.I. Trends in quality-adjusted life-years lost contributed by smoking and obesity. *Am. J. Prev. Med.* **2010**, *38*, 138–144. [CrossRef] [PubMed]
169. Bray, G.A. Medical consequences of obesity. *J. Clin. Endocrinol. Metab.* **2004**, *89*, 2583–2589. [CrossRef] [PubMed]
170. Carpenter, K.M.; Hasin, D.S.; Allison, D.B.; Faith, M.S. Relationships between obesity and DSM-IV major depressive disorder, suicide ideation, and suicide attempts: Results from a general population study. *Am. J. Public Health* **2000**, *90*, 251–257. [PubMed]
171. Haslam, D.W.; James, W.P.T. Obesity. *Lancet* **2005**, *366*, 1197–1209. [CrossRef]
172. Kahn, S.E.; Hull, R.L.; Utzschneider, K.M. Mechanisms linking obesity to insulin resistance and type 2 diabetes. *Nature* **2006**, *444*, 840–846. [CrossRef] [PubMed]
173. Lopresti, A.L.; Drummond, P.D. Obesity and psychiatric disorders: Commonalities in dysregulated biological pathways and their implications for treatment. *Prog. Neuro Psychopharmacol. Biol. Psychiatr.* **2013**, *45*, 92–99. [CrossRef]
174. Luppino, F.S.; de Wit, L.M.; Bouvy, P.F.; Stijnen, T.; Cuijpers, P.; Penninx, B.W.J.H.; Zitman, F.G. Overweight, obesity, and depression: A systematic review and meta-analysis of longitudinal studies. *Arch. Gen. Psychiatr.* **2010**, *67*, 220–229. [CrossRef]
175. Mannan, M.; Mamun, A.; Doi, S.; Clavarino, A. Prospective associations between depression and obesity for adolescent males and females—A systematic review and meta-analysis of longitudinal studies. *PLoS ONE* **2016**, *11*, 0157240. [CrossRef]
176. Mokdad, A.H.; Ford, E.S.; Bowman, B.A.; Dietz, W.H.; Vinicor, F.; Bales, V.S.; Marks, J.S. Prevalence of obesity, diabetes, and obesity-related health risk factors, 2001. *JAMA* **2003**, *289*, 76–79. [CrossRef] [PubMed]

177. Van Gaal, L.F.; Mertens, I.L.; De Block, C.E. Mechanisms linking obesity with cardiovascular disease. *Nature* **2006**, *444*, 875–880. [CrossRef] [PubMed]
178. Elkins, G.; Whitfield, P.; Marcus, J.; Symmonds, R.; Rodriguez, J.; Cook, T. Noncompliance with behavioral recommendations following bariatric surgery. *Obes. Surg.* **2005**, *15*, 546–551. [CrossRef]
179. Toussi, R.; Fujioka, K.; Coleman, K.J. Pre- and postsurgery behavioral compliance, patient health, and postbariatric surgical weight loss. *Obesity* **2009**, *17*, 996–1002. [CrossRef] [PubMed]
180. Colantuoni, C.; Schwenker, J.; McCarthy, J.; Rada, P.; Ladenheim, B.; Cadet, J.-L.; Schwartz, G.J.; Moran, T.H.; Hoebel, B.G. Excessive sugar intake alters binding to dopamine and mu-opioid receptors in the brain. *NeuroReport* **2001**, *12*, 3549–3552. [CrossRef]
181. Rada, P.; Avena, N.; Hoebel, B. Daily bingeing on sugar repeatedly releases dopamine in the accumbens shell. *Neuroscience* **2005**, *134*, 737–744. [CrossRef] [PubMed]
182. Harrison, D.M. Oral sucrose for pain management in infants: Myths and misconceptions. *J. Neonatal Nurs.* **2008**, *14*, 39–46. [CrossRef]
183. King, J.M. Patterns of sugar consumption in early infancy. *Community Dent. Oral Epidemiol.* **1978**, *6*, 47–52. [CrossRef]
184. Rossow, I.; Kjaernes, U.; Holst, D. Patterns of sugar consumption in early childhood. *Community Dent. Oral Epidemiol.* **1990**, *18*, 12–16. [CrossRef]
185. Slater, R.; Cornelissen, L.; Fabrizi, L.; Patten, D.; Yoxen, J.; Worley, A.; Boyd, S.; Meek, J.; Fitzgerald, M. Oral sucrose as an analgesic drug for procedural pain in newborn infants: A randomised controlled trial. *Lancet* **2010**, *376*, 1225–1232. [CrossRef]
186. Nielsen, S.J.; Popkin, B.M. Patterns and trends in food portion sizes, 1977–1998. *JAMA* **2003**, *289*, 450–453. [CrossRef] [PubMed]
187. Wideman, C.H.; Nadzam, G.R.; Murphy, H.M. Implications of an animal model of sugar addiction, withdrawal and relapse for human health. *Nutr. Neurosci.* **2005**, *8*, 269–276. [CrossRef] [PubMed]
188. Avena, N.M.; Rada, P.; Hoebel, B.G. Evidence for sugar addiction: Behavioral and neurochemical effects of intermittent, excessive sugar intake. *Neurosci. Biobehav. Rev.* **2008**, *32*, 20–39. [CrossRef] [PubMed]
189. Galic, M.A.; Persinger, M.A. Voluminous sucrose consumption in female rats: Increased "nippiness" during periods of sucrose removal and possible oestrus periodicity. *Psychol. Rep.* **2002**, *90*, 58–60. [CrossRef] [PubMed]
190. Avena, N.M.; Bocarsly, M.E.; Rada, P.; Kim, A.; Hoebel, B.G. After daily bingeing on a sucrose solution, food deprivation induces anxiety and accumbens dopamine/acetylcholine imbalance. *Physiol. Behav.* **2008**, *94*, 309–315. [CrossRef] [PubMed]
191. Hetherington, M.M.; MacDiarmid, J.I. "Chocolate addiction": A preliminary study of its description and its relationship to problem eating. *Appetite* **1993**, *21*, 233–246. [CrossRef] [PubMed]
192. Carnell, S.; Gibson, C.; Benson, L.; Ochner, C.N.; Geliebter, A. Neuroimaging and obesity: Current knowledge and future directions. *Obes. Rev.* **2012**, *13*, 43–56. [CrossRef]
193. Parvaz, M.A.; Alia-Klein, N.; Woicik, P.A.; Volkow, N.D.; Goldstein, R.Z. Neuroimaging for drug addiction and related behaviors. *Rev. Neurosci.* **2011**, *22*, 609–624. [CrossRef] [PubMed]
194. Zhang, Y.; von Deneen, K.M.; Tian, J.; Gold, M.S.; Liu, Y. Food addiction and neuroimaging. *Curr. Pharm. Des.* **2011**, *17*, 1149–1157. [CrossRef] [PubMed]
195. Goldstein, R.Z.; Volkow, N.D. Drug addiction and its underlying neurobiological basis: Neuroimaging evidence for the involvement of the frontal cortex. *Am. J. Psychiatr.* **2002**, *159*, 1642–1652. [CrossRef]
196. Goldstein, R.Z.; Volkow, N.D. Dysfunction of the prefrontal cortex in addiction: Neuroimaging findings and clinical implications. *Nat. Rev. Neurosci.* **2011**, *12*, 652–669. [CrossRef] [PubMed]
197. Koob, G.F.; Volkow, N.D. Neurobiology of addiction: A neurocircuitry analysis. *Lancet Psychiatr.* **2016**, *3*, 760–773. [CrossRef]
198. Volkow, N.D.; Wang, G.-J.; Fowler, J.S.; Telang, F. Overlapping neuronal circuits in addiction and obesity: Evidence of systems pathology. *Philos. Trans. R. Soc. B Biol. Sci.* **2008**, *363*, 3191–3200. [CrossRef] [PubMed]
199. Volkow, N.D.; Wang, G.-J.; Tomasi, D.; Baler, R.D. The addictive dimensionality of obesity. *Biol. Psychiatr.* **2013**, *73*, 811–818. [CrossRef] [PubMed]
200. Pierce, R.C.; Kumaresan, V. The mesolimbic dopamine system: The final common pathway for the reinforcing effect of drugs of abuse? *Neurosci. Biobehav. Rev.* **2006**, *30*, 215–238. [CrossRef] [PubMed]

201. Hernández, L.; Hoebel, B.G. Food reward and cocaine increase extracellular dopamine in the nucleus accumbens as measured by microdialysis. *Life Sci.* **1988**, *42*, 1705–1712. [CrossRef]
202. Radhakishun, F.S.; Van Ree, J.M.; Westerink, B.H. Scheduled eating increases dopamine release in the nucleus accumbens of food-deprived rats as assessed with on-line brain dialysis. *Neurosci. Lett.* **1988**, *85*, 351–356. [CrossRef]
203. Yoshida, M.; Yokoo, H.; Mizoguchi, K.; Kawahara, H.; Tsuda, A.; Nishikawa, T.; Tanaka, M. Eating and drinking cause increased dopamine release in the nucleus accumbens and ventral tegmental area in the rat: Measurement by in vivo microdialysis. *Neurosci. Lett.* **1992**, *139*, 73–76. [CrossRef]
204. Martel, P.; Fantino, M. Influence of the amount of food ingested on mesolimbic dopaminergic system activity: A microdialysis study. *Pharmacol. Biochem. Behav.* **1996**, *55*, 297–302. [CrossRef]
205. Martel, P.; Fantino, M. Mesolimbic dopaminergic system activity as a function of food reward: A microdialysis study. *Pharmacol. Biochem. Behav.* **1996**, *53*, 221–226. [CrossRef]
206. Carelli, R.M.; Ijames, S.G.; Crumling, A.J. Evidence that separate neural circuits in the nucleus accumbens encode cocaine versus "natural" (water and food) reward. *J. Neurosci.* **2000**, *20*, 4255–4266. [CrossRef] [PubMed]
207. Caine, S.B.; Koob, G.F. Effects of mesolimbic dopamine depletion on responding maintained by cocaine and food. *J. Exp. Anal. Behav.* **1994**, *61*, 213–221. [CrossRef] [PubMed]
208. Rothemund, Y.; Preuschhof, C.; Bohner, G.; Bauknecht, H.-C.; Klingebiel, R.; Flor, H.; Klapp, B.F. Differential activation of the dorsal striatum by high-calorie visual food stimuli in obese individuals. *NeuroImage* **2007**, *37*, 410–421. [CrossRef]
209. Small, D.M.; Jones-Gotman, M.; Dagher, A. Feeding-induced dopamine release in dorsal striatum correlates with meal pleasantness ratings in healthy human volunteers. *NeuroImage* **2003**, *19*, 1709–1715. [CrossRef]
210. Volkow, N.D.; Wang, G.-J.; Fowler, J.S.; Logan, J.; Jayne, M.; Franceschi, D.; Wong, C.; Gatley, S.J.; Gifford, A.N.; Ding, Y.-S.; et al. Nonhedonic food motivation in humans involves dopamine in the dorsal striatum and methylphenidate amplifies this effect. *Synapse* **2002**, *44*, 175–180. [CrossRef] [PubMed]
211. Volkow, N.D.; Wang, G.-J.; Maynard, L.; Jayne, M.; Fowler, J.S.; Zhu, W.; Logan, J.; Gatley, S.J.; Ding, Y.-S.; Wong, C.; et al. Brain dopamine is associated with eating behaviors in humans. *Int. J. Eat. Disord.* **2003**, *33*, 136–142. [CrossRef] [PubMed]
212. Stoeckel, L.E.; Weller, R.E.; Cook, E.W.; Twieg, D.B.; Knowlton, R.C.; Cox, J.E.; Iii, E.W.C. Widespread reward-system activation in obese women in response to pictures of high-calorie foods. *NeuroImage* **2008**, *41*, 636–647. [CrossRef]
213. Stice, E.; Spoor, S.; Bohon, C.; Small, D.M. Relation between obesity and blunted striatal response to food is moderated by TaqIA A1 allele. *Science* **2008**, *322*, 449–452. [CrossRef]
214. Wang, G.-J.; Volkow, N.D.; Felder, C.; Fowler, J.S.; Levy, A.V.; Pappas, N.R.; Wong, C.T.; Zhu, W.; Netusil, N. Enhanced resting activity of the oral somatosensory cortex in obese subjects. *NeuroReport* **2002**, *13*, 1151–1155. [CrossRef] [PubMed]
215. Bello, N.T.; Lucas, L.R.; Hajnal, A. Repeated sucrose access influences dopamine D2 receptor density in the striatum. *NeuroReport* **2002**, *13*, 1575–1578. [CrossRef] [PubMed]
216. Johnson, P.M.; Kenny, P.J. Dopamine D2 receptors in addiction-like reward dysfunction and compulsive eating in obese rats. *Nat. Neurosci.* **2010**, *13*, 635–641. [CrossRef] [PubMed]
217. Volkow, N.D.; Wang, G.-J.; Fowler, J.S.; Tomasi, D.; Telang, F.; Baler, R. Addiction: Decreased reward sensitivity and increased expectation sensitivity conspire to overwhelm the brain's control circuit. *BioEssays* **2010**, *32*, 748–755. [CrossRef] [PubMed]
218. Fehr, C.; Yakushev, I.; Hohmann, N.; Buchholz, H.G.; Landvogt, C.; Deckers, H.; Eberhardt, A.; Smolka, M.N.; Scheurich, A.; Dielentheis, T.; et al. Association of low striatal dopamine D 2 receptor availability with nicotine dependence similar to that seen with other drugs of abuse. *Am. J. Psychiatr.* **2008**, *165*, 507–514. [CrossRef] [PubMed]
219. Heinz, A. Correlation Between Dopamine D2 Receptors in the Ventral Striatum and Central Processing of Alcohol Cues and Craving. *Am. J. Psychiatr.* **2004**, *161*, 1783–1789. [CrossRef] [PubMed]
220. Volkow, N.D.; Fowler, J.S.; Wang, G.-J.; Hitzemann, R.; Logan, J.; Schlyer, D.J.; Dewey, S.L.; Wolf, A.P. Decreased dopamine D2 receptor availability is associated with reduced frontal metabolism in cocaine abusers. *Synapse* **1993**, *14*, 169–177. [CrossRef]

221. Volkow, N.D.; Wang, G.-J.; Fowler, J.S.; Logan, J.; Hitzemann, R.; Ding, Y.-S.; Pappas, N.; Shea, C.; Piscani, K. Decreases in dopamine receptors but not in dopamine transporters in alcoholics. *Alcohol. Clin. Exp. Res.* **1996**, *20*, 1594–1598. [CrossRef] [PubMed]
222. Volkow, N.D.; Chang, L.; Wang, G.-J.; Fowler, J.S.; Ding, Y.-S.; Sedler, M.; Logan, J.; Franceschi, D.; Gatley, J.; Hitzemann, R.; et al. Low level of brain dopamine D2 receptors in methamphetamine abusers: Association with metabolism in the orbitofrontal cortex. *Am. J. Psychiatr.* **2001**, *158*, 2015–2021. [CrossRef]
223. Thanos, P.K.; Volkow, N.D.; Freimuth, P.; Umegaki, H.; Ikari, H.; Roth, G.; Ingram, D.K.; Hitzemann, R. Overexpression of dopamine D2 receptors reduces alcohol. *J. Neurochem.* **2001**, *78*, 1094–1103. [CrossRef]
224. Volkow, N.D.; Wang, G.-J.; Begleiter, H.; Porjesz, B.; Fowler, J.S.; Telang, F.; Wong, C.; Ma, Y.; Logan, J.; Goldstein, R.; et al. High levels of dopamine D2 receptors in unaffected members of alcoholic families. *Arch. Gen. Psychiatr.* **2006**, *63*, 999–1008. [CrossRef]
225. Reinholz, J.; Skopp, O.; Breitenstein, C.; Bohr, I.; Winterhoff, H.; Knecht, S. Compensatory weight gain due to dopaminergic hypofunction: New evidence and own incidental observations. *Nutr. Metab.* **2008**, *5*, 35. [CrossRef]
226. Wang, G.; Volkow, N.D.; Thanos, P.K.; Fowler, J.S. Similarity between obesity and drug addiction as assessed by neurofunctional imaging: A concept review. *J. Addict. Dis.* **2004**, *23*, 39–53. [CrossRef] [PubMed]
227. Hardman, C.A.; Herbert, V.M.; Brunstrom, J.M.; Munafò, M.R.; Rogers, P.J.; Brunstrom, J. Dopamine and food reward: Effects of acute tyrosine/phenylalanine depletion on appetite. *Physiol. Behav.* **2012**, *105*, 1202–1207. [CrossRef] [PubMed]
228. Geiger, B.M.; Haburcak, M.; Avena, N.M.; Moyer, M.C.; Hoebel, B.G.; Pothos, E.N. Deficits of mesolimbic dopamine neurotransmission in rat dietary obesity. *Neuroscience* **2009**, *159*, 1193–1199. [CrossRef] [PubMed]
229. Baptista, T.; Parada, M.; Hernández, L. Long term administration of some antipsychotic drugs increases body weight and feeding in rats. Are D2 dopamine receptors involved? *Pharmacol. Biochem. Behav.* **1987**, *27*, 399–405. [CrossRef]
230. Clifton, P.G.; Rusk, I.N.; Cooper, S.J. Effects of dopamine D1 and dopamine D2 antagonists on the free feeding and drinking patterns of rats. *Behav. Neurosci.* **1991**, *105*, 272–281. [CrossRef]
231. Scislowski, P.; Tozzo, E.; Zhang, Y.; Phaneuf, S.; Prevelige, R.; Cincotta, A. Biochemical mechanisms responsible for the attenuation of diabetic and obese conditions in ob/ob mice treated with dopaminergic agonists. *Int. J. Obes.* **1999**, *23*, 425–431. [CrossRef]
232. Goudie, A.J.; Cooper, G.D.; Halford, J.C.G. Antipsychotic-induced weight gain. *Diabetes Obes. Metab.* **2005**, *7*, 478–487. [CrossRef]
233. Cincotta, A.H.; Meier, A.H. Bromocriptine (Ergoset) reduces body weight and improves glucose tolerance in obese subjects. *Diabetes Care* **1996**, *19*, 667–670. [CrossRef]
234. Manning, P.J.; Grattan, D.; Merriman, T.; Manning, T.; Williams, S.; Sutherland, W. Pharmaceutical interventions for weight-loss maintenance: No effect from cabergoline. *Int. J. Obes.* **2018**, *42*, 1871–1879. [CrossRef]
235. Gibson, C.D.; Karmally, W.; McMahon, D.J.; Wardlaw, S.L.; Korner, J. Randomized pilot study of cabergoline, a dopamine receptor agonist: Effects on body weight and glucose tolerance in obese adults. *Diabetes Obes. Metab.* **2012**, *14*, 335–340. [CrossRef]
236. Frank, G.K.W.; Shott, M.E.; Hagman, J.O.; Schiel, M.A.; DeGuzman, M.C.; Rossi, B. The Partial Dopamine D2 Receptor Agonist Aripiprazole is Associated With Weight Gain in Adolescent Anorexia Nervosa. *Int. J. Eat. Disord.* **2017**, *50*, 447–450. [CrossRef] [PubMed]
237. Steele, K.E.; Prokopowicz, G.P.; Schweitzer, M.A.; Magunsuon, T.H.; Lidor, A.O.; Kuwabawa, H.; Kuma, A.; Brasic, J.; Wong, D.F. Alterations of central dopamine receptors before and after gastric bypass surgery. *Obes. Surg.* **2010**, *20*, 369–374. [CrossRef] [PubMed]
238. Van Der Zwaal, E.M.; De Weijer, B.A.; Van De Giessen, E.M.; Janssen, I.; Berends, F.J.; Van De Laar, A.; Ackermans, M.T.; Fliers, E.; La Fleur, S.E.; Booij, J.; et al. Striatal dopamine D2/3 receptor availability increases after long-term bariatric surgery-induced weight loss. *Eur. Neuropsychopharmacol.* **2016**, *26*, 1190–1200. [CrossRef] [PubMed]
239. Ochner, C.N.; Kwok, Y.; Conceição, E.; Pantazatos, S.P.; Puma, L.M.; Carnell, S.; Teixeira, J.; Hirsch, J.; Geliebter, A. Selective reduction in neural responses to high calorie foods following gastric bypass surgery. *Ann. Surg.* **2011**, *253*, 502–507. [CrossRef] [PubMed]

240. Ghahremani, D.G.; Lee, B.; Robertson, C.L.; Tabibnia, G.; Morgan, A.T.; De Shetler, N.; Brown, A.K.; Monterosso, J.R.; Aron, A.A.; Mandelkern, M.A.; et al. Striatal dopamine D_2/D_3 receptors mediate response inhibition and related activity in frontostriatal neural circuitry in humans. *J. Neurosci.* **2012**, *32*, 7316–7324. [CrossRef] [PubMed]
241. Lavagnino, L.; Arnone, D.; Cao, B.; Soares, J.C.; Selvaraj, S. Inhibitory control in obesity and binge eating disorder: A systematic review and meta-analysis of neurocognitive and neuroimaging studies. *Neurosci. Biobehav. Rev.* **2016**, *68*, 714–726. [CrossRef] [PubMed]
242. Volkow, N.D.; Wang, G.-J.; Telang, F.; Fowler, J.S.; Goldstein, R.Z.; Alia-Klein, N.; Logan, J.; Wong, C.; Thanos, P.K.; Ma, Y.; et al. Inverse association between BMI and prefrontal metabolic activity in healthy adults. *Obesity* **2009**, *17*, 60–65. [CrossRef] [PubMed]
243. Le, D.S.N.T.; Pannacciulli, N.; Chen, K.; Del Parigi, A.; Salbe, A.D.; Reiman, E.M.; Krakoff, J. Less activation of the left dorsolateral prefrontal cortex in response to a meal: A feature of obesity. *Am. J. Clin. Nutr.* **2006**, *84*, 725–731. [CrossRef]
244. Le, D.S.N.; Pannacciulli, N.; Chen, K.; Salbe, A.D.; Hill, O.J.; Wing, R.R.; Reiman, E.M.; Krakoff, J. Less activation in the left dorsolateral prefrontal cortex in the reanalysis of the response to a meal in obese than in lean women and its association with successful weight loss. *Am. J. Clin. Nutr.* **2007**, *86*, 573–579. [CrossRef]
245. Gautier, J.F.; Chen, K.; Salbe, A.D.; Bandy, D.; Pratley, R.E.; Heiman, M.; Ravussin, E.; Reiman, E.M.; Tataranni, P.A. Differential brain responses to satiation in obese and lean men. *Diabetes* **2000**, *49*, 838–846. [CrossRef]
246. Del Parigi, A.; Chen, K.; Salbe, A.D.; Hill, J.O.; Wing, R.R.; Reiman, E.M.; Tataranni, P.A. Successful dieters have increased neural activity in cortical areas involved in the control of behavior. *Int. J. Obes.* **2007**, *31*, 440–448. [CrossRef] [PubMed]
247. Hollmann, M.; Hellrung, L.; Pleger, B.; Schlögl, H.; Kabisch, S.; Stumvoll, M.; Villringer, A.; Horstmann, A. Neural correlates of the volitional regulation of the desire for food. *Int. J. Obes.* **2012**, *36*, 648–655. [CrossRef] [PubMed]
248. McCaffery, J.M.; Haley, A.P.; Sweet, L.H.; Phelan, S.; Raynor, H.A.; Del Parigi, A.; Cohen, R.; Wing, R.R. Differential functional magnetic resonance imaging response to food pictures in successful weight-loss maintainers relative to normal-weight and obese controls. *Am. J. Clin. Nutr.* **2009**, *90*, 928–934. [CrossRef] [PubMed]
249. Weygandt, M.; Mai, K.; Dommes, E.; Leupelt, V.; Hackmack, K.; Kahnt, T.; Rothemund, Y.; Spranger, J.; Haynes, J.-D. The role of neural impulse control mechanisms for dietary success in obesity. *NeuroImage* **2013**, *83*, 669–678. [CrossRef] [PubMed]
250. Nederkoorn, C.; Houben, K.; Hofmann, W.; Roefs, A.; Jansen, A. Control yourself or just eat what you like? Weight gain over a year is predicted by an interactive effect of response inhibition and implicit preference for snack foods. *Health Psychol.* **2010**, *29*, 389–393. [CrossRef] [PubMed]
251. Cohen, J.; Yates, K.F.; Duong, M.; Convit, A. Obesity, orbitofrontal structure and function are associated with food choice: A cross-sectional study. *BMJ Open* **2011**, *1*, e000175. [CrossRef] [PubMed]
252. Maayan, L.; Hoogendoorn, C.; Sweat, V.; Convit, A. Disinhibited eating in obese adolescents is associated with orbitofrontal volume reductions and executive dysfunction. *Obesity* **2011**, *19*, 1382–1387. [CrossRef] [PubMed]
253. Masouleh, S.K.; Arelin, K.; Horstmann, A.; Lampe, L.; Kipping, J.A.; Luck, T.; Riedel-Heller, S.G.; Schroeter, M.L.; Stumvoll, M.; Villringer, A.; et al. Higher body mass index in older adults is associated with lower gray matter volume: Implications for memory performance. *Neurobiol. Aging* **2016**, *40*, 1–10. [CrossRef]
254. Pannacciulli, N.; Del Parigi, A.; Chen, K.; Le, D.S.N.; Reiman, E.M.; Tataranni, P.A. Brain abnormalities in human obesity: A voxel-based morphometric study. *NeuroImage* **2006**, *31*, 1419–1425. [CrossRef]
255. Taki, Y.; Kinomura, S.; Sato, K.; Inoue, K.; Goto, R.; Okada, K.; Uchida, S.; Kawashima, R.; Fukuda, H. Relationship between body mass index and gray matter volume in 1428 healthy individuals. *Obesity* **2008**, *16*, 119–124. [CrossRef]
256. Walther, K.; Birdsill, A.C.; Glisky, E.L.; Ryan, L. Structural brain differences and cognitive functioning related to body mass index in older females. *Hum. Brain Mapp.* **2010**, *31*, 1052–1064. [CrossRef] [PubMed]
257. Yao, L.; Li, W.; Dai, Z.; Dong, C. Eating behavior associated with gray matter volume alternations: A voxel based morphometry study. *Appetite* **2016**, *96*, 572–579. [CrossRef] [PubMed]

258. Yokum, S.; Stice, E. Cognitive regulation of food craving: Effects of three cognitive reappraisal strategies on neural response to palatable foods. *Int. J. Obes.* **2013**, *37*, 1565–1570. [CrossRef] [PubMed]
259. Bechara, A. Decision making, impulse control and loss of willpower to resist drugs: A neurocognitive perspective. *Nat. Neurosci.* **2005**, *8*, 1458–1463. [CrossRef] [PubMed]
260. Davis, C.; Levitan, R.D.; Muglia, P.; Bewell, C.; Kennedy, J.L. Decision-making deficits and overeating: A risk model for obesity. *Obes. Res.* **2004**, *12*, 929–935. [CrossRef] [PubMed]
261. Elias, M.F.; Elias, P.K.; Sullivan, L.M.; Wolf, P.A.; D'Agostino, R.B. Obesity, diabetes and cognitive deficit: The Framingham heart study. *Neurobiol. Aging* **2005**, *26*, 11–16. [CrossRef] [PubMed]
262. Gunstad, J.; Paul, R.H.; Cohen, R.A.; Tate, D.F.; Spitznagel, M.B.; Gordon, E. Elevated body mass index is associated with executive dysfunction in otherwise healthy adults. *Compr. Psychiatr.* **2007**, *48*, 57–61. [CrossRef] [PubMed]
263. Lowe, C.J.; Reichelt, A.C.; Hall, P.A. The prefrontal cortex and obesity: A health neuroscience perspective. *Trends Cogn. Sci.* **2019**, *23*, 349–361. [CrossRef] [PubMed]
264. Blum, K.; Braverman, E.R.; Wood, R.C.; Gill, J.; Li, C.; Chen, T.J.; Taub, M.; Montgomery, A.R.; Sheridan, P.J.; Cull, J.G. Increased prevalence of the Taq I A1allele of the dopamine receptor gene (DRD2) in obesity with comorbid substance use disorder: A preliminary report. *Pharmacogenetics* **1996**, *6*, 297–305. [CrossRef] [PubMed]
265. Comings, D.E.; Muhleman, D.; Ahn, C.; Gysin, R.; Flanagan, S.D. The dopamine D2 receptor gene: A genetic risk factor in substance abuse. *Drug Alcohol Depend.* **1994**, *34*, 175–180. [CrossRef]
266. Han, D.H.; Yoon, S.J.; Sung, Y.H.; Lee, Y.S.; Kee, B.S.; Lyoo, I.K.; Renshaw, P.F.; Cho, S.C. A preliminary study: Novelty seeking, frontal executive function, and dopamine receptor (D2) TaqI A gene polymorphism in patients with methamphetamine dependence. *Compr. Psychiatr.* **2008**, *49*, 387–392. [CrossRef] [PubMed]
267. Jönsson, E.G.; Nöthen, M.M.; Grünhage, F.; Farde, L.; Nakashima, Y.; Propping, P.; Sedvall, G.C.; Nöthen, M.; Jönsson, E. Polymorphisms in the dopamine D2 receptor gene and their relationships to striatal dopamine receptor density of healthy volunteers. *Mol. Psychiatr.* **1999**, *4*, 290–296. [CrossRef]
268. Noble, E. Addiction and its reward process through polymorphisms of the D2 dopamine receptor gene: A review. *Eur. Psychiatr.* **2000**, *15*, 79–89. [CrossRef]
269. Spitz, M.R.; Detry, M.A.; Pillow, P.; Hu, Y.; Amos, C.I.; Hong, W.K.; Wu, X. Variant alleles of the D2 dopamine receptor gene and obesity. *Nutr. Res.* **2000**, *20*, 371–380. [CrossRef]
270. Eisenberg, D.T.; MacKillop, J.; Modi, M.; Beauchemin, J.; Dang, D.; Lisman, S.A.; Lum, J.K.; Wilson, D.S. Examining impulsivity as an endophenotype using a behavioral approach: A DRD2 TaqI A and DRD4 48-bp VNTR association study. *Behav. Brain Funct.* **2007**, *3*, 2. [CrossRef] [PubMed]
271. Kirsch, P.; Reuter, M.; Mier, D.; Lonsdorf, T.; Stark, R.; Gallhofer, B.; Vaitl, D.; Hennig, J. Imaging gene–substance interactions: The effect of the DRD2 TaqIA polymorphism and the dopamine agonist bromocriptine on the brain activation during the anticipation of reward. *Neurosci. Lett.* **2006**, *405*, 196–201. [CrossRef]
272. Klein, T.A.; Neumann, J.; Reuter, M.; Hennig, J.; Von Cramon, D.Y.; Ullsperger, M. Genetically determined differences in learning from errors. *Science* **2007**, *318*, 1642–1645. [CrossRef]
273. Montag, C.; Weber, B.; Jentgens, E.; Elger, C.; Reuter, M. An epistasis effect of functional variants on the BDNF and DRD2 genes modulates gray matter volume of the anterior cingulate cortex in healthy humans. *Neuropsychology* **2010**, *48*, 1016–1021. [CrossRef]
274. Gasquoine, P.G. Localization of function in anterior cingulate cortex: From psychosurgery to functional neuroimaging. *Neurosci. Biobehav. Rev.* **2013**, *37*, 340–348. [CrossRef]
275. Peoples, L.L. Will, anterior cingulate cortex, and addiction. *Science* **2002**, *296*, 1623–1624. [CrossRef]
276. Brody, A.L.; Mandelkern, M.A.; Olmstead, R.E.; Jou, J.; Tiongson, E.; Allen, V.; Scheibal, D.; London, E.D.; Monterosso, J.R.; Tiffany, S.T.; et al. Neural substrates of resisting craving during cigarette cue exposure. *Biol. Psychiatr.* **2007**, *62*, 642–651. [CrossRef] [PubMed]
277. Pursey, K.M.; Stanwell, P.; Gearhardt, A.N.; Collins, C.E.; Burrows, T.L. The prevalence of food addiction as assessed by the Yale food addiction scale: A systematic review. *Nutrients* **2014**, *6*, 4552–4590. [CrossRef] [PubMed]
278. Carter, J.C.; Van Wijk, M.; Rowsell, M. Symptoms of 'food addiction' in binge eating disorder using the Yale food addiction scale version 2.0. *Appetite* **2019**, *133*, 362–369. [CrossRef] [PubMed]

279. De Vries, S.-K.; Meule, A. Food addiction and bulimia nervosa: New data based on the Yale food addiction scale 2.0. *Eur. Eat. Disord. Rev.* **2016**, *24*, 518–522. [CrossRef] [PubMed]
280. Hall, P.A.; Fong, G.T.; Epp, L.J.; Elias, L.J. Executive function moderates the intention-behavior link for physical activity and dietary behavior. *Psychol. Health* **2008**, *23*, 309–326. [CrossRef] [PubMed]
281. Hall, P.A. Executive control resources and frequency of fatty food consumption: Findings from an age-stratified community sample. *Health Psychol.* **2012**, *31*, 235–241. [CrossRef] [PubMed]
282. Alcorn, J.L.; Marks, K.R.; Stoops, W.W.; Rush, C.R.; Lile, J.A. Attentional bias to cannabis cues in cannabis users but not cocaine users. *Addict. Behav.* **2019**, *88*, 129–136. [CrossRef] [PubMed]
283. Bradley, B.; Field, M.; Mogg, K.; De Houwer, J. Attentional and evaluative biases for smoking cues in nicotine dependence: Component processes of biases in visual orienting. *Behav. Pharmacol.* **2004**, *15*, 29–36. [CrossRef]
284. Field, M.; Eastwood, B.; Bradley, B.P.; Mogg, K. Selective processing of cannabis cues in regular cannabis users. *Drug Alcohol Depend.* **2006**, *85*, 75–82. [CrossRef]
285. Qureshi, A.; Monk, R.L.; Pennington, C.R.; Wilcockson, T.D.; Heim, D. Alcohol-related attentional bias in a gaze contingency task: Comparing appetitive and non-appetitive cues. *Addict. Behav.* **2019**, *90*, 312–317. [CrossRef]
286. Field, M.; Cox, W. Attentional bias in addictive behaviors: A review of its development, causes, and consequences. *Drug Alcohol Depend.* **2008**, *97*, 1–20. [CrossRef] [PubMed]
287. Franken, I.H. Drug craving and addiction: Integrating psychological and neuropsychopharmacological approaches. *Prog. Neuro Psychopharmacol. Biol. Psychiatr.* **2003**, *27*, 563–579. [CrossRef]
288. Detandt, S.; Verbanck, P.; Bazan, A.; Quertemont, E. Smoking addiction: The shift from head to hands: Approach bias towards smoking-related cues in low-dependent versus dependent smokers. *J. Psychopharmacol.* **2017**, *31*, 819–829. [CrossRef] [PubMed]
289. Weckler, H.; Kong, G.; Larsen, H.; Cousijn, J.; Wiers, R.W.; Krishnan-Sarin, S. Impulsivity and approach tendencies towards cigarette stimuli: Implications for cigarette smoking and cessation behaviors among youth. *Exp. Clin. Psychopharmacol.* **2017**, *25*, 363–372. [CrossRef] [PubMed]
290. Watson, P.; De Wit, S.; Hommel, B.; Wiers, R.W. Motivational mechanisms and outcome expectancies underlying the approach bias toward addictive substances. *Front. Psychol.* **2012**, *3*, 440. [CrossRef] [PubMed]
291. Beraha, E.M.; Cousijn, J.; Hermanides, E.; Goudriaan, A.E.; Wiers, R.W. Implicit Associations and Explicit Expectancies toward Cannabis in Heavy Cannabis Users and Controls. *Front. Psychol.* **2013**, *4*, 1–9. [CrossRef]
292. De Houwer, J.; Custers, R.; De Clercq, A. Do smokers have a negative implicit attitude toward smoking? *Cogn. Emot.* **2006**, *20*, 1274–1284. [CrossRef]
293. Houben, K.; Wiers, R.W. Are drinkers implicitly positive about drinking alcohol? Personalizing the alcohol-IAT to reduce negative extrapersonal contamination. *Alcohol Alcohol.* **2007**, *42*, 301–307. [CrossRef]
294. McCarthy, D.M.; Thompsen, D.M. Implicit and explicit measures of alcohol and smoking cognitions. *Psychol. Addict. Behav.* **2006**, *20*, 436–444. [CrossRef]
295. Brignell, C.; Griffiths, T.; Bradley, B.P.; Mogg, K. Attentional and approach biases for pictorial food cues. Influence of external eating. *Appetite* **2009**, *52*, 299–306. [CrossRef]
296. Deluchi, M.; Costa, F.S.; Friedman, R.; Gonçalves, R.; Bizarro, L. Attentional bias to unhealthy food in individuals with severe obesity and binge eating. *Appetite* **2017**, *108*, 471–476. [CrossRef] [PubMed]
297. Hardman, C.A.; Scott, J.; Field, M.; Jones, A. To eat or not to eat. The effects of expectancy on reactivity to food cues. *Appetite* **2014**, *76*, 153–160. [CrossRef] [PubMed]
298. Popien, A.; Frayn, M.; Von Ranson, K.M.; Sears, C.R. Eye gaze tracking reveals heightened attention to food in adults with binge eating when viewing images of real-world scenes. *Appetite* **2015**, *91*, 233–240. [CrossRef] [PubMed]
299. Field, M.; Werthmann, J.; Franken, I.; Hofmann, W.; Hogarth, L.; Roefs, A. The role of attentional bias in obesity and addiction. *Health Psychol.* **2016**, *35*, 767–780. [CrossRef] [PubMed]
300. Stojek, M.; Shank, L.M.; Vannucci, A.; Bongiorno, D.M.; Nelson, E.E.; Waters, A.J.; Engel, S.G.; Boutelle, K.N.; Pine, D.S.; Yanovski, J.A.; et al. A systematic review of attentional biases in disorders involving binge eating. *Appetite* **2018**, *123*, 367–389. [CrossRef]
301. Castellanos, E.H.; Charboneau, E.; Dietrich, M.S.; Park, S.; Bradley, B.P.; Mogg, K.; Cowan, R.L.; Bradley, B. Obese adults have visual attention bias for food cue images: Evidence for altered reward system function. *Int. J. Obes.* **2009**, *33*, 1063–1073. [CrossRef]

302. Iceta, S.; Benoit, J.; Cristini, P.; Lambert-Porcheron, S.; Segrestin, B.; Laville, M.; Poulet, E.; Disse, E. Attentional bias and response inhibition in severe obesity with food disinhibition: A study of P300 and N200 event-related potential. *Int. J. Obes.* **2019**, *1*. [CrossRef]
303. Nijs, I.M.; Muris, P.; Euser, A.S.; Franken, I.H. Differences in attention to food and food intake between overweight/obese and normal-weight females under conditions of hunger and satiety. *Appetite* **2010**, *54*, 243–254. [CrossRef]
304. Werthmann, J.; Roefs, A.; Nederkoorn, C.; Mogg, K.; Bradley, B.P.; Jansen, A. Can (not) take my eyes off it: Attention bias for food in overweight participants. *Health Psychol.* **2011**, *30*, 561–569. [CrossRef]
305. Hardman, C.A.; Rogers, P.J.; Etchells, K.A.; Houstoun, K.V.E.; Munafò, M.R. The effects of food-related attentional bias training on appetite and food intake. *Appetite* **2013**, *71*, 295–300. [CrossRef]
306. Kemps, E.; Tiggemann, M.; Orr, J.; Grear, J. Attentional retraining can reduce chocolate consumption. *J. Exp. Psychol. Appl.* **2013**, *20*, 94–102. [CrossRef] [PubMed]
307. Schmitz, F.; Svaldi, J. Effects of bias modification training in binge eating disorder. *Behav. Ther.* **2017**, *48*, 707–717. [CrossRef] [PubMed]
308. Werthmann, J.; Field, M.; Roefs, A.; Nederkoorn, C.; Jansen, A. Attention bias for chocolate increases chocolate consumption—An attention bias modification study. *J. Behav. Ther. Exp. Psychiatr.* **2014**, *45*, 136–143. [CrossRef] [PubMed]
309. Zhang, S.; Cui, L.; Sun, X.; Zhang, Q. The effect of attentional bias modification on eating behavior among women craving high-calorie food. *Appetite* **2018**, *129*, 135–142. [CrossRef] [PubMed]
310. Smith, E.; Treffiletti, A.; Bailey, E.P.; Moustafa, A. The effect of attentional bias modification training on food intake in overweight and obese women. *J. Health Psychol.* **2018**, 1–11. [CrossRef] [PubMed]
311. Kakoschke, N.L.; Kemps, E.; Tiggemann, M. Attentional bias modification encourages healthy eating. *Eat. Behav.* **2014**, *15*, 120–124. [CrossRef] [PubMed]
312. Kemps, E.; Tiggemann, M.; Elford, J. Sustained effects of attentional re-training on chocolate consumption. *J. Behav. Ther. Exp. Psychiatr.* **2015**, *49*, 94–100. [CrossRef] [PubMed]
313. Veenstra, E.M.; De Jong, P.J. Restrained eaters show enhanced automatic approach tendencies towards food. *Appetite* **2010**, *55*, 30–36. [CrossRef]
314. Becker, D.; Jostmann, N.B.; Wiers, R.W.; Holland, R.W. Approach avoidance training in the eating domain: Testing the effectiveness across three single session studies. *Appetite* **2015**, *85*, 58–65. [CrossRef]
315. Brockmeyer, T.; Hahn, C.; Reetz, C.; Schmidt, U.; Friederich, H.-C. Approach bias and cue reactivity towards food in people with high versus low levels of food craving. *Appetite* **2015**, *95*, 197–202. [CrossRef]
316. Havermans, R.C.; Giesen, J.C.; Houben, K.; Jansen, A. Weight, gender, and snack appeal. *Eat. Behav.* **2011**, *12*, 126–130. [CrossRef] [PubMed]
317. Mehl, N.; Mueller-Wieland, L.; Mathar, D.; Horstmann, A. Retraining automatic action tendencies in obesity. *Physiol. Behav.* **2018**, *192*, 50–58. [CrossRef] [PubMed]
318. Mogg, K.; Bradley, B.P.; O'Neill, B.; Bani, M.; Merlo-Pich, E.; Koch, A.; Bullmore, E.T.; Nathan, P.J. Effect of dopamine D_3 receptor antagonism on approach responses to food cues in overweight and obese individuals. *Behav. Pharmacol.* **2012**, *23*, 603–608. [CrossRef] [PubMed]
319. Kemps, E.; Tiggemann, M.; Martin, R.; Elliott, M. Implicit approach–avoidance associations for craved food cues. *J. Exp. Psychol. Appl.* **2013**, *19*, 30–38. [CrossRef] [PubMed]
320. Schumacher, S.E.; Kemps, E.; Tiggemann, M. Bias modification training can alter approach bias and chocolate consumption. *Appetite* **2016**, *96*, 219–224. [CrossRef] [PubMed]
321. Brockmeyer, T.; Hahn, C.; Reetz, C.; Schmidt, U.; Friederich, H.-C. Approach Bias Modification in Food Craving-A Proof-of-Concept Study. *Eur. Eat. Disord. Rev.* **2015**, *23*, 352–360. [CrossRef] [PubMed]
322. De Houwer, J. A conceptual and theoretical analysis of evaluative conditioning. *Span. J. Psychol.* **2007**, *10*, 230–241. [CrossRef] [PubMed]
323. De Houwer, J.; Thomas, S.; Baeyens, F. Association learning of likes and dislikes: A review of 25 years of research on human evaluative conditioning. *Psychol. Bull.* **2001**, *127*, 853–869. [CrossRef] [PubMed]
324. Dwyer, D.M.; Jarratt, F.; Dick, K. Evaluative conditioning with foods as CSs and body shapes as USs: No evidence for sex differences, extinction, or overshadowing. *Cogn. Emot.* **2007**, *21*, 281–299. [CrossRef]
325. Hollands, G.J.; Prestwich, A.; Marteau, T.M. Using aversive images to enhance healthy food choices and implicit attitudes: An experimental test of evaluative conditioning. *Health Psychol.* **2011**, *30*, 195–203. [CrossRef]

326. Lascelles, K.R.; Field, A.P.; Davey, G.C. Using foods as CSs and body shapes as UCSs: A putative role for associative learning in the development of eating disorders. *Behav. Ther.* **2003**, *34*, 213–235. [CrossRef]
327. Lebens, H.; Roefs, A.; Martijn, C.; Houben, K.; Nederkoorn, C.; Jansen, A. Making implicit measures of associations with snack foods more negative through evaluative conditioning. *Eat. Behav.* **2011**, *12*, 249–253. [CrossRef] [PubMed]
328. Wang, Y.; Wang, G.; Zhang, D.; Wang, L.; Cui, X.; Zhu, J.; Fang, Y. Learning to dislike chocolate: Conditioning negative attitudes toward chocolate and its effect on chocolate consumption. *Front. Psychol.* **2017**, *8*, 1–7. [CrossRef] [PubMed]
329. Walsh, E.M.; Kiviniemi, M.T. Changing how I feel about the food: Experimentally manipulated affective associations with fruits change fruit choice behaviors. *J. Behav. Med.* **2014**, *37*, 322–331. [CrossRef] [PubMed]
330. Shaw, J.A.; Forman, E.M.; Espel, H.M.; Butryn, M.L.; Herbert, J.D.; Lowe, M.R.; Nederkoorn, C. Can evaluative conditioning decrease soft drink consumption? *Appetite* **2016**, *105*, 60–70. [CrossRef]
331. Houben, K.; Havermans, R.C.; Wiers, R.W. Learning to dislike alcohol: Conditioning negative implicit attitudes toward alcohol and its effect on drinking behavior. *Psychopharmacology* **2010**, *211*, 79–86. [CrossRef] [PubMed]
332. Zerhouni, O.; Houben, K.; El Methni, J.; Rutte, N.; Werkman, E.; Wiers, R.W. I didn't feel like drinking, but I guess why: Evaluative conditioning changes on explicit attitudes toward alcohol and healthy foods depends on contingency awareness. *Learn. Motiv.* **2019**, *66*, 1–12. [CrossRef]
333. Hofmann, W.; De Houwer, J.; Perugini, M.; Baeyens, F.; Crombez, G. Evaluative conditioning in humans: A meta-analysis. *Psychol. Bull.* **2010**, *136*, 390–421. [CrossRef]
334. Benedict, T.; Richter, J.; Gast, A. The influence of misinformation manipulations on evaluative conditioning. *Acta Psychol.* **2019**, *194*, 28–36. [CrossRef]
335. Aron, A.R.; Robbins, T.W.; Poldrack, R.A. Inhibition and the right inferior frontal cortex. *Trends Cogn. Sci.* **2004**, *8*, 170–177. [CrossRef]
336. Aron, A.R.; Robbins, T.W.; Poldrack, R.A. Inhibition and the right inferior frontal cortex: One decade on. *Trends Cogn. Sci.* **2014**, *18*, 177–185. [CrossRef] [PubMed]
337. Logan, G.D. Executive control of thought and action. *Acta Psychol.* **1985**, *60*, 193–210. [CrossRef]
338. Logan, G.D.; Cowan, W.B. On the ability to inhibit thought and action: A theory of an act of control. *Psychol. Rev.* **1984**, *91*, 295–327. [CrossRef]
339. Logan, G.D.; Schachar, R.J.; Tannock, R. Impulsivity and inhibitory control. *Psychol. Sci.* **1997**, *8*, 60–64. [CrossRef]
340. Miyake, A.; Friedman, N.P.; Emerson, M.J.; Witzki, A.H.; Howerter, A.; Wager, T.D. The unity and diversity of executive functions and their contributions to complex "frontal lobe" tasks: A latent variable analysis. *Cogn. Psychol.* **2000**, *41*, 49–100. [CrossRef] [PubMed]
341. Nigg, J.T.; Wong, M.M.; Martel, M.M.; Jester, J.M.; Puttler, L.I.; Glass, J.M.; Adams, K.M.; Fitzgerald, H.E.; Zucker, R.A. Poor response inhibition as a predictor of problem drinking and illicit drug use in adolescents at risk for alcoholism and other substance use disorders. *J. Am. Acad. Child Adolesc. Psychiatr.* **2006**, *45*, 468–475. [CrossRef]
342. Krishnan-Sarin, S.; Reynolds, B.; Duhig, A.M.; Smith, A.; Liss, T.; McFetridge, A.; Cavallo, D.A.; Carroll, K.M.; Potenza, M.N. Behavioral impulsivity predicts treatment outcome in a smoking cessation program for adolescents. *Drug Alcohol Depend.* **2007**, *88*, 79–82. [CrossRef]
343. Czapla, M.; Simon, J.J.; Richter, B.; Kluge, M.; Friederich, H.C.; Herpertz, S.; Loeber, S. The impact of cognitive impairment and impulsivity on relapse of alcohol-dependent patients: Implications for psychotherapeutic treatment. *Addict. Biol.* **2016**, *21*, 873–884. [CrossRef]
344. Houben, K.; Wiers, R.W. Response inhibition moderates the relationship between implicit associations and drinking behavior. *Alcohol. Clin. Exp. Res.* **2009**, *33*, 626–633. [CrossRef]
345. Nederkoorn, C.; Smulders, F.T.; Havermans, R.C.; Roefs, A.; Jansen, A. Impulsivity in obese women. *Appetite* **2006**, *47*, 253–256. [CrossRef]
346. Price, M.; Lee, M.; Higgs, S. Food-specific response inhibition, dietary restraint and snack intake in lean and overweight/obese adults: A moderated-mediation model. *Int. J. Obes.* **2016**, *40*, 877. [CrossRef] [PubMed]
347. Houben, K. Overcoming the urge to splurge: Influencing eating behavior by manipulating inhibitory control. *J. Behav. Ther. Exp. Psychiatr.* **2011**, *42*, 384–388. [CrossRef] [PubMed]
348. Nederkoorn, C.; Dassen, F.C.; Franken, L.; Resch, C.; Houben, K. Impulsivity and overeating in children in the absence and presence of hunger. *Appetite* **2015**, *93*, 57–61. [CrossRef] [PubMed]

349. Houben, K.; Nederkoorn, C.; Jansen, A. Eating on impulse: The relation between overweight and food-specific inhibitory control. *Obesity* **2014**, *22*, e6–e8. [CrossRef] [PubMed]
350. Mühlberg, C.; Mathar, D.; Villringer, A.; Horstmann, A.; Neumann, J. Stopping at the sight of food—How gender and obesity impact on response inhibition. *Appetite* **2016**, *107*, 663–676. [CrossRef] [PubMed]
351. Meule, A.; Lutz, A.P.; Vögele, C.; Kübler, A. Impulsive reactions to food-cues predict subsequent food craving. *Eat. Behav.* **2014**, *15*, 99–105. [CrossRef] [PubMed]
352. Allan, J.L.; Johnston, M.; Campbell, N. Missed by an inch or a mile? Predicting the size of intention–behaviour gap from measures of executive control. *Psychol. Health* **2011**, *26*, 635–650. [CrossRef]
353. Rosval, L.; Steiger, H.; Bruce, K.; Israël, M.; Richardson, J.; Aubut, M. Impulsivity in women with eating disorders: Problem of response inhibition, planning, or attention? *Int. J. Eat. Disord.* **2006**, *39*, 590–593. [CrossRef]
354. Bowley, C.; Faricy, C.; Hegarty, B.; Johnstone, S.J.; Smith, J.L.; Kelly, P.J.; Rushby, J.A. The effects of inhibitory control training on alcohol consumption, implicit alcohol-related cognitions and brain electrical activity. *Int. J. Psychophysiol.* **2013**, *89*, 342–348. [CrossRef]
355. Di Lemma, L.C.G.; Field, M. Cue avoidance training and inhibitory control training for the reduction of alcohol consumption: A comparison of effectiveness and investigation of their mechanisms of action. *Psychopharmacology* **2017**, *234*, 2489–2498. [CrossRef]
356. Houben, K.; Havermans, R.C.; Nederkoorn, C.; Jansen, A. Beer à no-go: Learning to stop responding to alcohol cues reduces alcohol intake via reduced affective associations rather than increased response inhibition. *Addiction* **2012**, *107*, 1280–1287. [CrossRef] [PubMed]
357. Houben, K.; Nederkoorn, C.; Wiers, R.W.; Jansen, A. Resisting temptation: Decreasing alcohol-related affect and drinking behaviour by training response inhibition. *Drug Alcohol Depend.* **2011**, *116*, 132–136. [CrossRef] [PubMed]
358. Kilwein, T.M.; Bernhardt, K.A.; Stryker, M.L.; Looby, A. Decreased alcohol consumption after pairing alcohol-related cues with an inhibitory response. *J. Subst. Use* **2017**, *23*, 154–161. [CrossRef]
359. Verbruggen, F.; Adams, R.; Chambers, C.D. Proactive motor control reduces monetary risk taking in gambling. *Psychol. Sci.* **2012**, *23*, 805–815. [CrossRef] [PubMed]
360. Verbruggen, F.; Adams, R.C.; Van't Wout, F.; Stevens, T.; McLaren, I.P.L.; Chambers, C.D. Are the effects of response inhibition on gambling long-lasting? *PLoS ONE* **2013**, *7*, e70155. [CrossRef] [PubMed]
361. Adams, R.C.; Lawrence, N.S.; Verbruggen, F.; Chambers, C.D. Training response inhibition to reduce food consumption: Mechanisms, stimulus specificity and appropriate training protocols. *Appetite* **2017**, *109*, 11–23. [CrossRef] [PubMed]
362. Houben, K.; Jansen, A. Training inhibitory control. A recipe for resisting sweet temptations. *Appetite* **2011**, *56*, 345–349. [CrossRef]
363. Houben, K.; Jansen, A. Chocolate equals stop. Chocolate-specific inhibition training reduces chocolate intake and go associations with chocolate. *Appetite* **2015**, *87*, 318–323. [CrossRef]
364. Lawrence, N.S.; Verbruggen, F.; Morrison, S.; Adams, R.C.; Chambers, C.D. Stopping to food pictures reduces food intake: Effects of cue specificity, control conditions and individual differences. *Appetite* **2015**, *85*, 91–103. [CrossRef]
365. Oomen, D.; Grol, M.; Spronk, D.; Booth, C.; Fox, E. Beating uncontrolled eating: Training inhibitory control to reduce food intake and food cue sensitivity. *Appetite* **2018**, *131*, 73–83. [CrossRef]
366. Camp, B.; Lawrence, N.S. Giving pork the chop: Response inhibition training to reduce meat intake. *Appetite* **2019**, *141*, 104315. [CrossRef] [PubMed]
367. Chen, Z.; Holland, R.W.; Quandt, J.; Dijksterhuis, A.; Veling, H. When mere action versus inaction leads to robust preference change. *J. Personal. Soc. Psychol.* **2019**. [CrossRef] [PubMed]
368. Porter, L.; Bailey-Jones, C.; Priudokaite, G.; Allen, S.; Wood, K.; Stiles, K.; Lawrence, N.S. From cookies to carrots; the effect of inhibitory control training on children's snack selections. *Appetite* **2018**, *124*, 111–123. [CrossRef] [PubMed]
369. Van Koningsbruggen, G.M.; Veling, H.; Stroebe, W.; Aarts, H. Comparing two psychological interventions in reducing impulsive processes of eating behaviour: Effects on self-selected portion size. *Br. J. Health Psychol.* **2013**, *19*, 767–782. [CrossRef] [PubMed]
370. Veling, H.; Aarts, H.; Stroebe, W. Using stop signals to reduce impulsive choices for palatable unhealthy foods. *Br. J. Health Psychol.* **2013**, *18*, 354–368. [CrossRef] [PubMed]

371. Veling, H.; Aarts, H.; Stroebe, W. Stop signals decrease choices for palatable foods through decreased food evaluation. *Front. Psychol.* **2013**, *4*, 875. [CrossRef] [PubMed]
372. Gish, M.Y. Addiction to food: How go/no-go tasks affect appetite. *Biomed. Health Sci. Res.* **2015**, *6*, 221–231. [CrossRef]
373. Veling, H.; van Koningsbruggen, G.M.; Aarts, H.; Stroebe, W. Targeting impulsive processes of eating behavior via the internet. Effects on body weight. *Appetite* **2014**, *78*, 102–109. [CrossRef]
374. Allom, V.; Mullan, B.; Hagger, M. Does inhibitory control training improve health behaviour? A meta-analysis. *Health Psychol. Rev.* **2015**, *10*, 1–38. [CrossRef]
375. Jones, A.; Di Lemma, L.C.; Robinson, E.; Christiansen, P.; Nolan, S.; Tudur-Smith, C.; Field, M. Inhibitory control training for appetitive behaviour change: A meta-analytic investigation of mechanisms of action and moderators of effectiveness. *Appetite* **2016**, *97*, 16–28. [CrossRef]
376. Lawrence, N.S.; O'Sullivan, J.; Parslow, D.; Javaid, M.; Adams, R.C.; Chambers, C.D.; Kos, K.; Verbruggen, F. Training response inhibition to food is associated with weight loss and reduced energy intake. *Appetite* **2015**, *95*, 17–28. [CrossRef] [PubMed]
377. Kakoschke, N.L.; Kemps, E.; Tiggemann, M. The effect of combined avoidance and control training on implicit food evaluation and choice. *J. Behav. Ther. Exp. Psychiatr.* **2017**, *55*, 99–105. [CrossRef] [PubMed]
378. Schakel, L.; Veldhuijzen, D.S.; Van Middendorp, H.; Van Dessel, P.; De Houwer, J.; Bidarra, R.; Evers, A.W.M. The effects of a gamified approach avoidance training and verbal suggestions on food outcomes. *PLoS ONE* **2018**, *13*, e0201309. [CrossRef] [PubMed]
379. Chen, Z.; Veling, H.; Dijksterhuis, A.; Holland, R.W. Do impulsive individuals benefit more from food go/no-go training? Testing the role of inhibition capacity in the no-go devaluation effect. *Appetite* **2018**, *124*, 99–110. [CrossRef] [PubMed]
380. McLaren, I.P.L.; Verbruggen, F. Association and inhibition. In *The Wiley Blackwell Handbook on the Cognitive Neuroscience of Learning*; Murphy, R.A., Honey, R.C., Eds.; John Wiley and Sons: Chichester, UK, 2016.
381. Veling, H.; Holland, R.W.; Van Knippenberg, A. When approach motivation and behavioral inhibition collide: Behavior regulation through stimulus devaluation. *J. Exp. Soc. Psychol.* **2008**, *44*, 1013–1019. [CrossRef]
382. Verbruggen, F.; Best, M.; Bowditch, W.A.; Stevens, T.; McLaren, I.P. The inhibitory control reflex. *Neuropsychology* **2014**, *65*, 263–278. [CrossRef] [PubMed]
383. Alonso-Alonso, M. Translating tDCS into the field of obesity: Mechanism-driven approaches. *Front. Hum. Neurosci.* **2013**, *7*, 512.
384. Feil, J.; Zangen, A. Brain stimulation in the study and treatment of addiction. *Neurosci. Biobehav. Rev.* **2010**, *34*, 559–574. [CrossRef] [PubMed]
385. Hall, P.A.; Vincent, C.M.; Burhan, A.M. Non-invasive brain stimulation for food cravings, consumption, and disorders of eating: A review of methods, findings and controversies. *Appetite* **2018**, *124*, 78–88. [CrossRef]
386. Lowe, C.J.; Vincent, C.; Hall, P.A. Effects of noninvasive brain stimulation on food cravings and consumption: A meta-analytic review. *Psychosom. Med.* **2017**, *79*, 2–13. [CrossRef]
387. Nardone, R.; Bergmann, J.; Christova, M.; Lochner, P.; Tezzon, F.; Golaszewski, S.; Trinka, E.; Brigo, F. Non-invasive brain stimulation in the functional evaluation of alcohol effects and in the treatment of alcohol craving: A review. *Neurosci. Res.* **2012**, *74*, 169–176. [CrossRef] [PubMed]
388. Song, S.; Zilverstand, A.; Gui, W.; Li, H.J.; Zhou, X. Effects of single-session versus multi-session non-invasive brain stimulation on craving and consumption in individuals with drug addiction, eating disorders or obesity: A meta-analysis. *Brain Stimul.* **2018**, *12*, 606–618. [CrossRef] [PubMed]
389. Maizey, L.; Allen, C.P.; Dervinis, M.; Verbruggen, F.; Varnava, A.; Kozlov, M.; Adams, R.C.; Stokes, M.; Klemen, J.; Bungert, A.; et al. Comparative incidence rates of mild adverse effects to transcranial magnetic stimulation. *Clin. Neurophysiol.* **2013**, *124*, 536–544. [CrossRef] [PubMed]
390. Matsumoto, H.; Ugawa, Y. Adverse effects of tDCS and tACS: A review. *Clin. Neurophysiol. Pract.* **2017**, *2*, 19–25. [CrossRef] [PubMed]
391. Pascual-Leone, A.; Houser, C.; Reese, K.; Shotland, L.; Grafman, J.; Sato, S.; Valls-Sole, J.; Brasil-Neto, J.; Wassermann, E.; Cohen, L.; et al. Safety of rapid-rate transcranial magnetic stimulation in normal volunteers. *Electroencephalogr. Clin. Neurophysiol. Potentials Sect.* **1993**, *89*, 120–130. [CrossRef]
392. Poreisz, C.; Boros, K.; Antal, A.; Paulus, W. Safety aspects of transcranial direct current stimulation concerning healthy subjects and patients. *Brain Res. Bull.* **2007**, *72*, 208–214. [CrossRef] [PubMed]

393. Rossi, S.; Hallett, M.; Rossini, P.M.; Pascual-Leone, A. Safety, ethical considerations, and application guidelines for the use of transcranial magnetic stimulation in clinical practice and research. *Clin. Neurophysiol.* **2009**, *120*, 2008–2039. [CrossRef] [PubMed]
394. Taylor, R.; Gálvez, V.; Loo, C. Transcranial magnetic stimulation (TMS) safety: A practical guide for psychiatrists. *Australas. Psychiatr.* **2018**, *26*, 189–192. [CrossRef]
395. Fitzgerald, P.; Fountain, S.; Daskalakis, Z. A comprehensive review of the effects of rTMS on motor cortical excitability and inhibition. *Clin. Neurophysiol.* **2006**, *117*, 2584–2596. [CrossRef]
396. Amiaz, R.; Levy, D.; Vainiger, D.; Grunhaus, L.; Zangen, A. Repeated high-frequency transcranial magnetic stimulation over the dorsolateral prefrontal cortex reduces cigarette craving and consumption. *Addiction* **2009**, *104*, 653–660. [CrossRef]
397. Bolloni, C.; Panella, R.; Pedetti, M.; Frascella, A.G.; Gambelunghe, C.; Piccoli, T.; Maniaci, G.; Brancato, A.; Cannizzaro, C.; Diana, M. Bilateral transcranial magnetic stimulation of the prefrontal cortex reduces cocaine intake: A pilot study. *Front. Psychol.* **2016**, *7*, 101. [CrossRef]
398. Mishra, B.R.; Praharaj, S.K.; Katshu, M.Z.U.H.; Sarkar, S.; Nizamie, S.H. Comparison of anticraving efficacy of right and left repetitive transcranial magnetic stimulation in alcohol dependence: A randomized double-blind study. *J. Neuropsychiatry Clin. Neurosci.* **2015**, *27*, 54. [CrossRef] [PubMed]
399. Su, H.; Zhong, N.; Gan, H.; Wang, J.; Han, H.; Chen, T.; Li, X.; Ruan, X.; Zhu, Y.; Jiang, H.; et al. High frequency repetitive transcranial magnetic stimulation of the left dorsolateral prefrontal cortex for methamphetamine use disorders: A randomised clinical trial. *Drug Alcohol Depend.* **2017**, *175*, 84–91. [CrossRef] [PubMed]
400. Terraneo, A.; Leggio, L.; Saladini, M.; Ermani, M.; Bonci, A.; Gallimberti, L.; Information, P.E.K.F.C. Transcranial magnetic stimulation of dorsolateral prefrontal cortex reduces cocaine use: A pilot study. *Eur. Neuropsychopharmacol.* **2016**, *26*, 37–44. [CrossRef] [PubMed]
401. Beeli, G.; Casutt, G.; Baumgartner, T.; Jäncke, L. Modulating presence and impulsiveness by external stimulation of the brain. *Behav. Brain Funct.* **2008**, *4*, 33. [CrossRef] [PubMed]
402. Garavan, H.; Hester, R.; Murphy, K.; Fassbender, C.; Kelly, C. Individual differences in the functional neuroanatomy of inhibitory control. *Brain Res.* **2006**, *1105*, 130–142. [CrossRef] [PubMed]
403. Oldrati, V.; Patricelli, J.; Colombo, B.; Antonietti, A. The role of dorsolateral prefrontal cortex in inhibition mechanism: A study on cognitive reflection test and similar tasks through neuromodulation. *Neuropsychology* **2016**, *91*, 499–508. [CrossRef] [PubMed]
404. Zheng, D.; Oka, T.; Bokura, H.; Yamaguchi, S. The key locus of common response inhibition network for no-go and stop signals. *J. Cogn. Neurosci.* **2008**, *20*, 1434–1442. [CrossRef] [PubMed]
405. Diana, M. The dopamine hypothesis of drug addiction and its potential therapeutic value. *Front. Psychol.* **2011**, *2*, 64. [CrossRef] [PubMed]
406. Strafella, A.P.; Paus, T.; Barrett, J.; Dagher, A. Repetitive Transcranial Magnetic Stimulation of the Human Prefrontal Cortex Induces Dopamine Release in the Caudate Nucleus. *J. Neurosci.* **2001**, *21*, RC157. [CrossRef] [PubMed]
407. Batista, E.K.; Klauss, J.; Fregni, F.; Nitsche, M.A.; Nakamura-Palacios, E.M. A Randomized Placebo-Controlled Trial of Targeted Prefrontal Cortex Modulation with Bilateral tDCS in Patients with Crack-Cocaine Dependence. *Int. J. Neuropsychopharmacol.* **2015**, *18*, 066. [CrossRef] [PubMed]
408. Boggio, P.S.; Liguori, P.; Sultani, N.; Rezende, L.; Fecteau, S.; Fregni, F. Cumulative priming effects of cortical stimulation on smoking cue-induced craving. *Neurosci. Lett.* **2009**, *463*, 82–86. [CrossRef] [PubMed]
409. Boggio, P.S.; Sultani, N.; Fecteau, S.; Merabet, L.; Mecca, T.; Pascual-Leone, A.; Basaglia, A.; Fregni, F. Prefrontal cortex modulation using transcranial DC stimulation reduces alcohol craving: A double-blind, sham-controlled study. *Drug Alcohol Depend.* **2008**, *92*, 55–60. [CrossRef] [PubMed]
410. Boggio, P.S.; Zaghi, S.; Villani, A.B.; Fecteau, S.; Pascual-Leone, A.; Fregni, F. Modulation of risk-taking in marijuana users by transcranial direct current stimulation (tDCS) of the dorsolateral prefrontal cortex (DLPFC). *Drug Alcohol Depend.* **2010**, *112*, 220–225. [CrossRef] [PubMed]
411. Fecteau, S.; Agosta, S.; Hone-Blanchet, A.; Fregni, F.; Boggio, P.; Ciraulo, D.; Pascual-Leone, A. Modulation of smoking and decision-making behaviors with transcranial direct current stimulation in tobacco smokers: A preliminary study. *Drug Alcohol Depend.* **2014**, *140*, 78–84. [CrossRef] [PubMed]
412. Klauss, J.; Anders, Q.S.; Felippe, L.V.; Nitsche, M.A.; Nakamura-Palacios, E.M. Multiple sessions of transcranial direct current stimulation (tDCS) reduced craving and relapses for alcohol use: A randomized placebo-controlled trial in alcohol use disorder. *Front. Pharmacol.* **2018**, *9*, 716. [CrossRef] [PubMed]

413. Antal, A.; Terney, D.; Poreisz, C.; Paulus, W. Towards unravelling task-related modulations of neuroplastic changes induced in the human motor cortex. *Eur. J. Neurosci.* **2007**, *26*, 2687–2691. [CrossRef] [PubMed]
414. Liebetanz, D.; Nitsche, M.A.; Tergau, F.; Paulus, W. Pharmacological approach to the mechanisms of transcranial DC-stimulation-induced after-effects of human motor cortex excitability. *Brain* **2002**, *125*, 2238–2247. [CrossRef] [PubMed]
415. Nitsche, M.A.; Paulus, W. Excitability changes induced in the human motor cortex by weak transcranial direct current stimulation. *J. Physiol.* **2000**, *527*, 633–639. [CrossRef]
416. Nitsche, M.; Schauenburg, A.; Lang, N.; Liebetanz, D.; Exner, C.; Paulus, W.; Tergau, F. Facilitation of implicit motor learning by weak transcranial direct current stimulation of the primary motor cortex in the human. *J. Cogn. Neurosci.* **2003**, *15*, 619–626. [CrossRef]
417. Nitsche, M.A.; Seeber, A.; Frommann, K.; Klein, C.C.; Rochford, C.; Nitsche, M.S.; Fricke, K.; Liebetanz, D.; Lang, N.; Antal, A.; et al. Modulating parameters of excitability during and after transcranial direct current stimulation of the human motor cortex. *J. Physiol.* **2005**, *568*, 291–303. [CrossRef] [PubMed]
418. Priori, A. Brain polarization in humans: A reappraisal of an old tool for prolonged non-invasive modulation of brain excitability. *Clin. Neurophysiol.* **2003**, *114*, 589–595. [CrossRef]
419. Nitsche, M.A.; Paulus, W. Sustained excitability elevations induced by transcranial DC motor cortex stimulation in humans. *Neurology* **2001**, *57*, 1899–1901. [CrossRef]
420. Gandiga, P.C.; Hummel, F.C.; Cohen, L.G. Transcranial DC stimulation (tDCS): A tool for double-blind sham-controlled clinical studies in brain stimulation. *Clin. Neurophysiol.* **2006**, *117*, 845–850. [CrossRef] [PubMed]
421. Nitsche, M.A.; Cohen, L.G.; Wassermann, E.M.; Priori, A.; Lang, N.; Antal, A.; Paulus, W.; Hummel, F.; Boggio, P.S.; Fregni, F.; et al. Transcranial direct current stimulation: State of the art 2008. *Brain Stimul.* **2008**, *1*, 206–223. [CrossRef] [PubMed]
422. Stagg, C.J.; Nitsche, M.A. Physiological basis of transcranial direct current stimulation. *Neuroscience* **2011**, *17*, 37–53. [CrossRef]
423. Wiers, R.W.; Gladwin, T.E.; Hofmann, W.; Salemink, E.; Ridderinkhof, K.R. Cognitive bias modification and cognitive control training in addiction and related psychopathology: Mechanisms, clinical perspectives, and ways forward. *Clin. Psychol. Sci.* **2013**, *1*, 192–212. [CrossRef]
424. Goldman, R.L.; Borckardt, J.J.; Frohman, H.A.; O'Neil, P.M.; Madan, A.; Campbell, L.K.; Budak, A.; George, M.S. Prefrontal cortex transcranial direct current stimulation (tDCS) temporarily reduces food cravings and increases the self-reported ability to resist food in adults with frequent food craving. *Appetite* **2011**, *56*, 741–746. [CrossRef]
425. Kim, S.H.; Chung, J.H.; Kim, T.H.; Lim, S.H.; Kim, Y.; Lee, Y.A.; Song, S.W. The effects of repetitive transcranial magnetic stimulation on eating behaviors and body weight in obesity: A randomized controlled study. *Brain Stimul.* **2018**, *11*, 528–535. [CrossRef]
426. Lapenta, O.M.; Di Sierve, K.; De Macedo, E.C.; Fregni, F.; Boggio, P.S. Transcranial direct current stimulation modulates ERP-indexed inhibitory control and reduces food consumption. *Appetite* **2014**, *83*, 42–48. [CrossRef]
427. Ljubisavljevic, M.; Maxood, K.; Bjekic, J.; Oommen, J.; Nagelkerke, N. Long-Term effects of repeated prefrontal cortex transcranial direct current stimulation (tDCS) on food craving in normal and overweight young adults. *Brain Stimul.* **2016**, *9*, 826–833. [CrossRef] [PubMed]
428. Montenegro, R.A.; Okano, A.H.; Cunha, F.A.; Gurgel, J.L.; Fontes, E.B.; Farinatti, P.T. Prefrontal cortex transcranial direct current stimulation associated with aerobic exercise change aspects of appetite sensation in overweight adults. *Appetite* **2012**, *58*, 333–338. [CrossRef] [PubMed]
429. Ray, M.K.; Sylvester, M.D.; Osborn, L.; Helms, J.; Turan, B.; Burgess, E.E.; Boggiano, M.M. The critical role of cognitive-based trait differences in transcranial direct current stimulation (tDCS) suppression of food craving and eating in frank obesity. *Appetite* **2017**, *116*, 568–574. [CrossRef]
430. Uher, R.; Yoganathan, D.; Mogg, A.; Eranti, S.V.; Treasure, J.; Campbell, I.C.; McLoughlin, D.M.; Schmidt, U. Effect of left prefrontal repetitive transcranial magnetic stimulation on food craving. *Biol. Psychiatr.* **2005**, *58*, 840–842. [CrossRef]
431. Van den Eynde, F.; Claudino, A.M.; Mogg, A.; Horrell, L.; Stahl, D.; Ribeiro, W.; Uher, R.; Campbell, I.; Schmidt, U. Repetitive transcranial magnetic stimulation reduces cue-induced food craving in bulimic disorders. *Biol. Psychiatr.* **2010**, *67*, 793–795. [CrossRef]

432. Barth, K.S.; Rydin-Gray, S.; Kose, S.; Borckardt, J.J.; O'Neil, P.M.; Shaw, D.; Madan, A.; Budak, A.; George, M.S. Food Cravings and the Effects of Left Prefrontal Repetitive Transcranial Magnetic Stimulation Using an Improved Sham Condition. *Front. Psychol.* **2011**, *2*, 9. [CrossRef]
433. Fregni, F.; Orsati, F.; Pedrosa, W.; Fecteau, S.; Tome, F.A.; Nitsche, M.A.; Mecca, T.; Macedo, E.C.; Pascual-Leone, A.; Boggio, P.S. Transcranial direct current stimulation of the prefrontal cortex modulates the desire for specific foods. *Appetite* **2008**, *51*, 34–41. [CrossRef] [PubMed]
434. Jansen, J.M.; Daams, J.G.; Koeter, M.W.; Veltman, D.J.; Brink, W.V.D.; Goudriaan, A.E. Effects of non-invasive neurostimulation on craving: A meta-analysis. *Neurosci. Biobehav. Rev.* **2013**, *37*, 2472–2480. [CrossRef] [PubMed]
435. Ray, M.K.; Sylvester, M.D.; Helton, A.; Pittman, B.R.; Wagstaff, L.E.; McRae, T.R.; Turan, B.; Fontaine, K.R.; Amthor, F.R.; Boggiano, M.M.; et al. The effect of expectation on transcranial direct current stimulation (tDCS) to suppress food craving and eating in individuals with overweight and obesity. *Appetite* **2019**, *136*, 1–7. [CrossRef] [PubMed]
436. Sedgmond, J.; Lawrence, N.S.; Verbruggen, F.; Morrison, S.; Chambers, C.D.; Adams, R.C. Prefrontal brain stimulation during food-related inhibition training: Effects on food craving, food consumption and inhibitory control. *R. Soc. Open Sci.* **2019**, *6*, 181186. [CrossRef]
437. Hanlon, C.A.; Hartwell, K.J.; Canterberry, M.; Li, X.; Owens, M.; LeMatty, T.; Prisciandaro, J.J.; Borckardt, J.; Brady, K.T.; George, M.S. Reduction of cue-induced craving through realtime neurofeedback in nicotine users: The role of region of interest selection and multiple visits. *Psychiatr. Res.* **2013**, *213*, 79–81. [CrossRef] [PubMed]
438. Hartwell, K.J.; Prisciandaro, J.J.; Borckardt, J.; Li, X.; George, M.S.; Brady, K.T. Real-time fMRI in the treatment of nicotine dependence: A conceptual review and pilot studies. *Psychol. Addict. Behav.* **2013**, *27*, 501–509. [CrossRef] [PubMed]
439. Li, X.; Hartwell, K.J.; Borckardt, J.; Prisciandaro, J.J.; Saladin, M.E.; Morgan, P.S.; Johnson, K.A.; LeMatty, T.; Brady, K.T.; George, M.S. Volitional reduction of anterior cingulate cortex activity produces decreased cue craving in smoking cessation: A preliminary real-time fMRI study. *Addict. Biol.* **2012**, *18*, 739–748. [CrossRef] [PubMed]
440. Dehghani-Arani, F.; Rostami, R.; Nadali, H. Neurofeedback training for opiate addiction: Improvement of mental health and craving. *Appl. Psychophysiol. Biofeedback* **2013**, *38*, 133–141. [CrossRef] [PubMed]
441. Dehghani-Arani, F.; Rostami, R.; Nostratabadi, M. Effectiveness of neurofeedback training as a treatment for opioid-dependent patients. *Clin. EEG Neurosci.* **2010**, *41*, 170–177. [CrossRef] [PubMed]
442. Horrell, T.; El-Baz, A.; Baruth, J.; Tasman, A.; Sokhadze, G.; Stewart, C.; Sokhadze, E. Neurofeedback Effects on Evoked and Induced EEG Gamma Band Reactivity to Drug-related Cues in Cocaine Addiction. *J. Neurother.* **2010**, *14*, 195–216. [CrossRef] [PubMed]
443. Scott, W.C.; Kaiser, D.; Othmer, S.; Sideroff, S.I. Effects of an EEG biofeedback protocol on a mixed substance abusing population. *Am. J. Drug Alcohol Abus.* **2005**, *31*, 455–469. [CrossRef]
444. Dewiputri, W.I.; Auer, T. Functional Magnetic Resonance Imaging (fMRI) neurofeedback: Implementations and applications. *Malays. J. Med Sci.* **2013**, *20*, 5–15.
445. Frank, S.; Lee, S.; Preissl, H.; Schultes, B.; Birbaumer, N.; Veit, R. The obese brain athlete: Self-regulation of the anterior insula in adiposity. *PLoS ONE* **2012**, *7*, e42570. [CrossRef]
446. Frank, S.; Kullmann, S.; Veit, R. Food related processes in the insular cortex. *Front. Hum. Neurosci.* **2013**, *7*, 499. [CrossRef]
447. Ihssen, N.; Sokunbi, M.O.; Lawrence, A.D.; Lawrence, N.S.; Linden, D.E. Neurofeedback of visual food cue reactivity: A potential avenue to alter incentive sensitization and craving. *Brain Imaging Behav.* **2017**, *11*, 915–924. [CrossRef]
448. Kohl, S.H.; Veit, R.; Spetter, M.S.; Günther, A.; Rina, A.; Lührs, M.; Birbaumer, N.; Preissl, H.; Hallschmid, M. Real-time fMRI neurofeedback training to improve eating behavior by self-regulation of the dorsolateral prefrontal cortex: A randomized controlled trial in overweight and obese subjects. *NeuroImage* **2019**, *191*, 596–609. [CrossRef] [PubMed]
449. Spetter, M.S.; Malekshahi, R.; Birbaumer, N.; Lührs, M.; Van Der Veer, A.H.; Scheffler, K.; Spuckti, S.; Preissl, H.; Veit, R.; Hallschmid, M. Volitional regulation of brain responses to food stimuli in overweight and obese subjects: A real-time fMRI feedback study. *Appetite* **2017**, *112*, 188–195. [CrossRef] [PubMed]

450. Weiner, S. The addiction of overeating: Self-help groups as treatment models. *J. Clin. Psychol.* **1998**, *54*, 163–167. [CrossRef]
451. Magill, M.; Ray, L.A. Cognitive-behavioural treatment with alcohol and illicit drug users: A meta-analysis of randomized controlled trials. *J. Stud. Alcohol Drugs* **2009**, *70*, 516–527. [CrossRef] [PubMed]
452. Göhner, W.; Schlatterer, M.; Seelig, H.; Frey, I.; Berg, A.; Fuchs, R. Two-Year follow-up of an interdisciplinary cognitive-behavioral intervention program for obese adults. *J. Psychol.* **2012**, *146*, 371–391. [CrossRef] [PubMed]
453. Marchesini, G.; Natale, S.; Chierici, S.; Manini, R.; Besteghi, L.; Di Domizio, S.; Sartini, A.; Pasqui, F.; Baraldi, L.; Forlani, G.; et al. Effects of cognitive–behavioural therapy on health-related quality of life in obese subjects with and without binge eating disorder. *Int. J. Obes.* **2002**, *26*, 1261–1267. [CrossRef] [PubMed]
454. Linardon, J.; Wade, T.D.; Garcia, X.D.L.P.; Brennan, L. The efficacy of cognitive-behavioral therapy for eating disorders: A systematic review and meta-analysis. *J. Consult. Clin. Psychol.* **2017**, *85*, 1080–1094. [CrossRef] [PubMed]
455. Vanderlinden, J.; Adriaensen, A.; Vancampfort, D.; Pieters, G.; Probst, M.; Vansteelandt, K. A Cognitive-behavioral therapeutic program for patients with obesity and binge eating disorder: Short- and long- term follow-up data of a prospective study. *Behav. Modif.* **2012**, *36*, 670–686. [CrossRef] [PubMed]
456. Wilfley, D.E.; Welch, R.R.; Stein, R.I.; Spurrell, E.B.; Cohen, L.R.; Saelens, B.E.; Dounchis, J.Z.; Frank, M.A.; Wiseman, C.V.; Matt, G.E. A randomized comparison of group cognitive-behavioral therapy and group interpersonal psychotherapy fort the treatment of overweight individuals with binge-eating disorder. *Arch. Gen. Psychiatr.* **2002**, *59*, 713721. [CrossRef] [PubMed]
457. Wilson, G.T.; Fairburn, C.C.; Agras, W.S.; Walsh, B.T.; Kraemer, H. Cognitive-behavioral therapy for bulimia nervosa: Time course and mechanisms of change. *J. Consult. Clin. Psychol.* **2002**, *70*, 267–274. [CrossRef] [PubMed]
458. Gearhardt, A.N.; Corbin, W.R.; Brownell, K.D. Food addiction: An examination of the diagnostic criteria for dependence. *J. Addict. Med.* **2009**, *3*, 1–8. [CrossRef] [PubMed]
459. Earnshaw, V.; Smith, L.; Copenhaver, M. Drug addiction stigma in the context of methadone maintenance therapy: An investigation into understudied sources of stigma. *Int. J. Ment. Healthy Addict.* **2013**, *11*, 110–122. [CrossRef] [PubMed]
460. DePierre, J.A.; Puhl, R.M.; Luedicke, J. A new stigmatized identity? Comparisons of a "food addict" label with other stigmatized health conditions. *Basic Appl. Soc. Psychol.* **2013**, *35*, 10–21. [CrossRef]
461. Rasmussen, N. Stigma and the addiction paradigm for obesity: Lessons from 1950s America. *Addiction* **2015**, *110*, 217–225. [CrossRef] [PubMed]
462. Hardman, C.A.; Rogers, P.J.; Dallas, R.; Scott, J.; Ruddock, H.K.; Robinson, E. "Food addiction is real". The effects of exposure to this message on self-diagnosed food addiction and eating behaviour. *Appetite* **2015**, *91*, 179–184. [CrossRef] [PubMed]
463. Latner, J.D.; Puhl, R.M.; Murakami, J.M.; O'Brien, K.S. Food addiction as a causal model of obesity. Effects on stigma, blame, and perceived psychopathology. *Appetite* **2014**, *77*, 79–84. [CrossRef]
464. Reid, J.; O'Brien, K.S.; Puhl, R.; Hardman, C.A.; Carter, A. Food addiction and its potential links with weight stigma. *Curr. Addict. Rep.* **2018**, *5*, 192–201. [CrossRef]

12

Unexpected Association of Desacyl-Ghrelin with Physical Activity and Chronic Food Restriction: A Translational Study on Anorexia Nervosa

Philibert Duriez [1,2], Lauralee Robichon [1], Roland Dardennes [2], Guillaume Lavoisy [2], Dominique Grouselle [1], Jacques Epelbaum [1,3], Nicolas Ramoz [1], Philip Gorwood [1,2], Virginie Tolle [1,†] and Odile Viltart [1,4,*,†]

1 Institute of Psychiatry and Neuroscience of Paris (IPNP), Université de Paris, INSERM UMR-S 1266, F-75014 Paris, France; p.duriez@ghu-paris.fr (P.D.); lauralee.robichon@sfr.fr (L.R.); dominique.grouselle@inserm.fr (D.G.); jacques.epelbaum@inserm.fr (J.E.); nicolas.ramoz@inserm.fr (N.R.); p.gorwood@ghu-paris.fr (P.G.); virginie.tolle@inserm.fr (V.T.)
2 GHU Paris Psychiatrie et Neurosciences, Hôpital Sainte-Anne, F-75014 Paris, France; r.dardennes@ghu-paris.fr (R.D.); guillaumelavoisy@hotmail.com (G.L.)
3 UMR 7179 CNRS, MNHN, Adaptive mechanism and Evolution (MECADEV), 91800 Brunoy, France
4 Cité scientifique, SN4, Université de Lille, 59491 Villeneuve d'Ascq, France
* Correspondence: odile.viltart@univ-lille.fr
† Both authors contributed equally to this work.

Abstract: Anorexia nervosa (AN) is a severe metabopsychiatric disorder characterised by caloric intake restriction and often excessive physical exercise. Our aim is to assess in female AN patients and in a rodent model, the co-evolution of physical activity and potential dysregulation of acyl—(AG) and desacyl—(DAG) ghrelin plasma concentrations during denutrition and weight recovery. AN inpatients were evaluated at inclusion (T0, $n = 29$), half—(T1) and total (T2) weight recovery, and one month after discharge (T3, $n = 13$). C57/Bl6 mice with access to a running wheel, were fed ad libitum or submitted to short—(15 days) or long—(50 days) term quantitative food restriction, followed by refeeding (20 days). In AN patients, AG and DAG rapidly decreased during weight recovery (T0 to T2), AG increased significantly one-month post discharge (T3), but only DAG plasma concentrations at T3 correlated negatively with BMI and positively with physical activity. In mice, AG and DAG both increased during short- and long-term food restriction. After 20 days of ad libitum feeding, DAG was associated to persistence of exercise alteration. The positive association of DAG with physical activity during caloric restriction and after weight recovery questions its role in the adaptation mechanisms to energy deprivation that need to be considered in recovery process in AN.

Keywords: restrictive anorexia nervosa; weight recovery; animal models; acyl-ghrelin; desacyl-ghrelin; physical activity; chronic food restriction

1. Introduction

Anorexia nervosa (AN) is a psychiatric disorder where the severe weight loss due to a reduction on food intake is associated with high levels of physical activity. Indeed, 31% to 80% of AN patients display inappropriate quantity of exercise with respect to their energy resources [1,2]. Hyperactivity has been associated with an increase in the length of hospitalisation stay [3], a poor treatment outcome both interfering with refeeding therapies and increasing the risk of relapse [4]. One out of two patients relapses within a year following inpatient treatment and approximately 20% of patients experience recurrent patterns of remission and relapse or chronic disease [5,6]. The disorder affects predominantly women and girls, with female to male ratios of approximately 10/1 to 15/1 [7]. The etiology of AN is complex, but recent evidences emphasise metabolic and endocrine aspects as key pathophysiological determinants of the disorder [8–12].

Amongst many metabolic and endocrine factors, ghrelin a 28-amino-acid peptide orexigenic gut hormone produced by the X/A-like endocrine cells in the oxyntic glands of the gastric fundus [13–15], is involved in many physiological processes associated with feeding and exercise including the regulation of energy metabolism and appetite [16], the cardiovascular system as autonomic nervous system [17–20], and the modulation of reward and motivation [11,21,22]. Ghrelin has rapidly been considered as a biomarker of AN since its plasma concentrations are significantly increased in AN patients and return to control values after renutrition as also observed in animal models mimicking several symptoms of AN [23–25]. Acylation (on its third serine residue) by ghrelin O-acyl transferase allows acyl-ghrelin (AG) to bind to its receptor, the growth hormone secretagogue receptor (GHSR) type 1a that is widely distributed within the central nervous system [13,26]. Desacyl-ghrelin (DAG) is also present in the blood circulation [27]. Original studies using competition assays showed that DAG accounts for 80–90% of total circulating ghrelin [28]. More recently, using very selective sandwich immunoassays for AG and DAG, DAG accounted for 76% of the total circulating ghrelin (i.e., AG+DAG) [29]. Despite a number of studies reporting a physiological role for DAG, usually opposite to AG [27,30–32], its role remains elusive.

Beside appetite, many clinical and preclinical studies support an association of ghrelin with physical exercise. More particularly, in healthy subjects, acute or short-term exercise duration is associated with a decrease in ghrelin plasma concentrations while chronic physical activity is correlated with increased concentrations of ghrelin [33–35]. Increased ghrelin plasma concentrations are also described in rodents performing chronic treadmill exercise [36]. In pathological situations associated with excessive physical activity such as AN, total ghrelin is positively correlated with physical activity, measured by daily step counts [37]. In the activity-based anorexia (ABA) model, where time-restriction in food access is associated with running activity, mice display excessive daytime physical activity in the context of limited access to food [38,39]. Interestingly, in ABA mice, a single intracerebroventricular injection or chronic peripheral treatment with a GHS-R1a antagonist lead to a significant decrease of daytime activity [38]. Moreover, GHS-R KO mice show a more rapid exhaustion in an endurance exercise as compared to wild-type mice [40]. However, the differential effect or association of AG and DAG with chronic physical activity, in clinical or preclinical studies is controversial, because of the kind of exercise considered (acute, endurance, etc. ...) or the sex of the participants (usually males, in human or rodents). Furthermore, in healthy conditions, only plasma AG concentrations were modulated by exercise [41–43]. Finally, most of the studies that investigated the role of ghrelin in AN have focused on variations in plasma total ghrelin or AG, neglecting the potential involvement of DAG. To our knowledge, longitudinal data are not yet available on AG and DAG levels during a refeeding hospital program and after body weight recovery associated with physical activity. A standardised definition of remission, recovery and relapse is still lacking [44]. We thus hypothesised that in long-term food restriction and in nutritional recovery, AG and DAG plasma concentrations evolve differentially according to the level of physical activity. For this purpose, we first assessed the evolution of plasma concentrations of AG and DAG in ill- and recovered-AN patients, in relation with their physical activity. Then, we used a modified mouse ABA model of chronic quantitative food restriction associated with a voluntary running activity in a wheel, to determine whether AG and DAG plasma concentrations reflect the level of physical activity during the periods of chronic food restriction and nutritional recovery [45,46]. Here, "nutritional recovery" is used to identify patients or rodents that followed a program of refeeding and included weight restoration.

2. Materials and Methods

2.1. Experiment 1. Clinical Investigation

Participants. Twenty-nine female patients suffering from anorexia nervosa (AN) in undernourished state were included in the study (Table 1). Thirteen patients had full weight recovery during intensive in-patient program and were evaluated one-month post discharge. Participants, aged 18–37 years, fulfilled DSM-V criteria for AN (APA, 2013). All patients attended a structured in-patient program in the Eating Disorders Unit of *Clinique des Maladies Mentales et de l'Encéphale* (CMME, Sainte-Anne Hospital, Paris, France) and received behavioural nutritional rehabilitation program with progressive and controlled access to physical activity and were discharged after reaching their target weight and maintaining it for at least 2 weeks. We excluded patients with active malignancies, active inflammatory or infectious diseases, epilepsy, and other psychiatric disorders. Several clinical parameters were recorded at the different time-points. Patients were weighted at every inpatient and follow-up assessment, size was measured and corresponding body mass indexes (BMIs) were calculated. Physical activity was assessed with the self-reported International Physical Activity Questionnaire (IPAQ) [47]. The study protocol was approved by *Comité de Protection des Personnes Ile de France III* (EUDRACT N: 2008-A008 17–48; CPP N Am5355-2-2592). All patients gave written informed consent prior to participation. All data were recorded anonymously.

Table 1. Demographic, anthropometric and socio-economic characteristics of anorexia nervosa in the clinical samples. Data are presented as mean +/− SD. T0: at admission; T1: 50–70% of target BMI reached; T2-T3: weight recovered patients with evaluation one month post discharge; AN: anorexia nervosa; AN-R: anorexia nervosa restrictive type; AN-BP: anorexia nervosa binge-eating/purging type; BMI: body mass index; EDI2: Eating Disorder Inventory version 2.

	T0 (*n* = 29)		**T1 (*n* = 28)**		**T2-T3 (*n* = 13)**	
	Mean +/−SD	%	Mean +/−SD	%	%	%
Age (years)	25.8+/−6.8		26.2 +/−6.44		26+/−7	
AN-Duration (years)	7.4+/−5.4		7.4+/−5.5		8.8+/−6.5	
Age of onset	18.4+/−3.8		18.4 +/−3.9		17.2+/−1.9	
AN Subtype						
AN-R		59%		57%		60%
AN-BP		41%		43%		40%
BMI at inclusion (kg/m^2)	14.6+/−1.3		14.6+/−1.4		14.8+/−1.2	
Partner ship						
Single		79%		78%		69%
In a relationship		21%		22%		31%
Daily psychiatric drugs		62%		62%		62%
EDI-2 at inclusion						
Total	116+/−5		118+/−52		114+/−53.7	
Drive for thinness	11.9+/−7.4		12.2+/−7.3		11.5+/−8.6	
Bulimia	4.9+/−7		5.1+/−7.1		5+/−7.62	
Body dissatisfaction	17+/−6.9		17.1+/−7		17+/−6.7	
Ineffectiveness	16+/−8.9		16.5+/−8.7		15.5+/−9.3	
Perfectionism	7.5+/−4.4		7.3+/−4.4		7.7+/−4.6	
Interpersonal distrust	9.4+/−4.8		9.3+/−4.9		9.4+/−4.5	
Interoceptive awareness	14.7+/−7.3		14.8+/−7.4		14.2+/−5.9	
Maturity fears	8.3+/−6.5		8.6+/−6.4		8.2+/−7.5	
Asceticism	9+/−5.74		9.3+/−5.8		9+/−6.32	
Impulse Regulation	7+/−7.25		7+/−7.3		6+/−7.4	
Social Insecurity	11+/−5.52		10.8+/−5.4		11+/−6.3	

In order to assay hormonal longitudinal variations in different nutritional conditions, blood samplings were performed in undernourished conditions (T0) (5–8 days after the arrival at the Hospital) during the acute phase of the disorder, in the course of the refeeding process (T1: 50–70% target BMI of 20 kg/m^2), after complete weight recovery (T2: 90–100% target BMI) or during the stabilisation process (T3: 1 month following discharge).

Conditions of Blood Sampling, Processing and Storage of Blood. Blood sampling was performed after an overnight fast. Blood was collected on tubes containing 15% EDTA and Aprotinin 250 KIU (tube BD vacutainer EDTA K3 Aprotinin). Blood samples were immediately centrifuged at 4 °C (1000× *g* for 15 min). In addition, plasma samples were aliquoted and supplemented with HCl at a final concentration of 0.1 N immediately after collection in order to preserve acylation and frozen at −80 °C.

Acyl—and Desacyl-Ghrelin Immunoassays. Acyl- (AG) and desacyl-ghrelin (DAG) concentrations were assayed in duplicates with selective two-sites sandwich enzyme-immunoassays (EIA) using two different monoclonal antibodies for capture and revelation (human AG and DAG EIA Easy Sampling Elisa kits, Ref A05306 and Ref A05319, respectively, Bertin Bioreagent, Montigny-le-Bretonneaux, France). For AG, the limit of detection is 4 pg/mL. Intra- and inter-assay coefficients of variation are 9 and 16%, respectively. For DAG, the limit of detection is 10 pg/mL. Intra- and inter-assay coefficients of variation are 6 and 16%, respectively.

2.2. Experiment 2. Preclinical Investigation

Animals. Seven-week old C57BL/6J female mice (Charles River Laboratories, L'Arbresle, France) weighing 18.3 ± 0.1 g were housed by cages of two to avoid isolation stress and hypothermia [45]. They were kept in a pathogen-free barrier facility maintained at 22–24 °C with a 12:12-h dark-light cycle (lights on at 07:00 a.m.). During one week of habituation, mice were weighted every day to get acclimatised to handling. Mice within the same cage had a similar initial body weight. They had free access to water and to standard chow diet (3% fat, 16% protein, 60% carbohydrate, 4% fibres, 2.79 kcal/g; Safe A04). All experiments were carried out in accordance with the European Communities Council Directive (86/609/EEC) and approved by the Regional ethical committed of Paris Descartes University France.

Short-Term Food Restriction Protocol. In this first set of experiments, mice were randomised into two experimental groups according to their initial body weight. Mice of the group "ad libitum and wheel" (group ALW, n = 12) were placed in a cage equipped with a free running wheel (ActiviWheel Software; Intellibio, Seichamps, France) and had free access to food. In the group "food restriction and wheel" (group FRW, n = 12), mice were placed in a cage equipped with a free running wheel and exposed to a 30% quantitative food restriction for three days followed by 50% quantitative food restriction through the end of the protocol. This restriction was calculated every day from the total food consumed by each mouse in the ALW group the previous day, by weighing the whole pellets in the feeder. Food (on pellet per mouse) was distributed directly into the cage every day at 6:30 p.m. Body weight was monitored daily at the same time. In 8 out of the 12 cages, the locomotor activity was assessed daily with a running wheel (diameter: 230 mm; width: 50 mm; 1 revolution = 0.72 m) linked to a computer system that measured interval counts (10 min) per mean wheel revolution (ActiviWheel Software; Intellibio, Seichamps, France). In 4 out of the 6 cages of ALW mice, the physical activity was measured with a manual counter (Sigma Germany BC 9.16 ATS), which indicated total distance, mean speed, and maximum speed in 12-h periods. Manual counters were read twice per day: between 7:30 and 8:00 a.m. to evaluate ALW nocturnal activity and around 6:00 p.m., before the food distribution, for the diurnal activity. The wheel running activity was measured per cage, because ethologically speaking and for the welfare of the animals, we decided to avoid stress isolation and the hypothermia induced by our long-term caloric restriction protocol. The recording of physical activity thus reflected the activity of two mice that usually run two by two in the wheel (personal observation), resulting in 6 ALW and 6 FRW cages. Since we measured each animal body weight daily, we were able to detect changes in feeding or running activity and thus avoided the cage-effect of these analyses. As mentioned, weight loss in a same cage is usually similar (considering the standard deviation) leading us to consider the cage value of physical activity in wheel for each mouse. Data were extracted with an excel macro (Microsoft Office Standard, 2016) to obtain cumulative activity or day/night activity. To establish a link between plasma concentrations of AG and DAG with physical activity, blood samples were collected twice: in the morning (D11) at 9:00 a.m. and before food distribution (at D10) at 5:00 p.m., when the anticipatory food activity was developed in the FRW mice (see results).

Long-Term Food Restriction and Nutritional Recovery Protocols. In the second set of experiments, mice were randomised according to their initial body weight into two experimental groups FRW ($n = 6$) and ALW ($n = 6$) as described above. The experimental protocol was exactly similar to the short-term food restriction, except that we maintained the groups of mice in this protocol for 8 weeks. Body weight was monitored three times a week. The locomotor activity was assessed daily with a running wheel linked to a computer system that measured interval counts (10 min) per mean wheel revolution (ActiviWheel Software; Intellibio, Seichamps, France). After 8 weeks of this protocol, nutritional recovery was achieved by giving ad libitum access to standard diet to all FRW mice while free access to the running wheel was maintained. As mentioned above, the activity was evaluated per cage. Data were extracted with an Excel® macro (Microsoft Office Standard, 2016) to obtain cumulative activity or day/night activity. To evaluate the kinetic of plasma ghrelin concentrations during the refeeding period, two blood samples were withdrawn at 5:00 p.m.: on day 51, one day after the beginning of the refeeding, and on day 70, at sacrifice (after two weeks of nutritional recovery).

Blood Samples Collection. AG and DAG Plasma Assays. Blood samples were collected from the caudal vein with a 1-mL syringe in EDTA coated tubes (1 mg/mL final, Microvette® CB 300 μL, Sarstedt, Germany) containing p-hydroxy-mercuribenzoic acid (PHMB 0.4 mM final), which is a serine protease inhibitor, and kept at 4 °C until processing. At the end of the short- and long-term protocols, mice were deeply anesthetised with an overdose of ketamine (100 mg/kg) and xylazine (20 mg/kg) mix. Blood was collected through cardiac puncture with a 1-mL syringue and transferred into EDTA coated tubes. Samples were rapidly centrifuged (1000× g for 10 min, 4 °C), to collect plasma (around 80 μL), which was immediately acidified with HCl (0.1 N final) to preserve ghrelin acylation. Plasma aliquots were frozen in dry ice before being stored at −80 °C until they were assayed. Plasma AG and DAG concentrations were evaluated by specific EIA (A05118 for the acylated form and A05117 for the des-acylated form; Bertin Bioreagents, Montigny le Bretonneux, France). All samples were analysed in duplicates. Intra- and inter-assay coefficients of variations were 6.1% and 5.7% for AG and 5.5% and 4.8% for DAG, respectively.

Statistical Analysis. Analysis of normality and equality of variances were tested by Shapiro-Wilk test. Statistical analysis were performed using one-way ANOVA followed by a Fisher *post-hoc* test when the p value of the ANOVA was significant ($p < 0.05$) or a non-parametric ANOVA followed by Tukey or Bonferroni post hoc test was used when appropriate, using Statview® software (SAS institute Inc., Cary, NC, USA).

Clinical values are given as mean ±SD. Preclinical values are given as mean ±SEM. For both clinical and preclinical values correlations we used Pearson correlation test if normality is respected (Shapiro-Wilk $p > 0.05$) or Spearman's rank correlation coefficient if not (Shapiro-Wilk $p < 0.05$). We used Jamovi Softare (Version 1.1; R Core Team 2018). The level for significance was established at 5%. We considered a tendency at $0.1 > p > 0.05$. Graphs were generated using GraphPad Prism® 5.01 (Abacus Concepts, Berkeley, CA, USA).

3. Results

3.1. Experiment 1. Clinical Investigation

3.1.1. Longitudinal Evolution of BMI and Physical Activity during Inpatient Weight Recovery and One-Month Post Discharge

At inclusion (T0), 29 female patients were evaluated. Only one patient left the protocol before T1. Thirteen patients out of the 29 were re-evaluated both at T2 (90–100% target BMI) and one-month post-discharge (T3). Our analysis focused on recovery and early modifications of metabolic parameters after discharge (Time T3). We thus considered only patients who succeeded in obtaining "full" weight recovery during treatment in our clinical unit, namely the 13 patients presented in our study. The other patients ($n = 16$) did not fulfil the criteria and left hospital mainly after "partial" weight recovery (about 16 kg/m^2). Table 1 describes the clinical sample.

Between T0 and T2, patients increased their BMI according to the strict clinical protocol with weight therapeutic contract ($U = 51$, $p < 0.001$) and reduced their physical activity ($U = 53.5$, $p = 0.002$). The BMI significantly increased between T0 and T2 ($F_{(2\text{-}75)} = 186$, $p < 0.001$; Figure 1A). More specifically, post-hoc analysis revealed a significant increase between T0 and T1 ($p < 0.001$) and between T1 and T2 ($p < 0.001$). Physical activity was permitted after 50% of total expected weight gain, explaining no physical activity reported at T1 (Figure 1B).

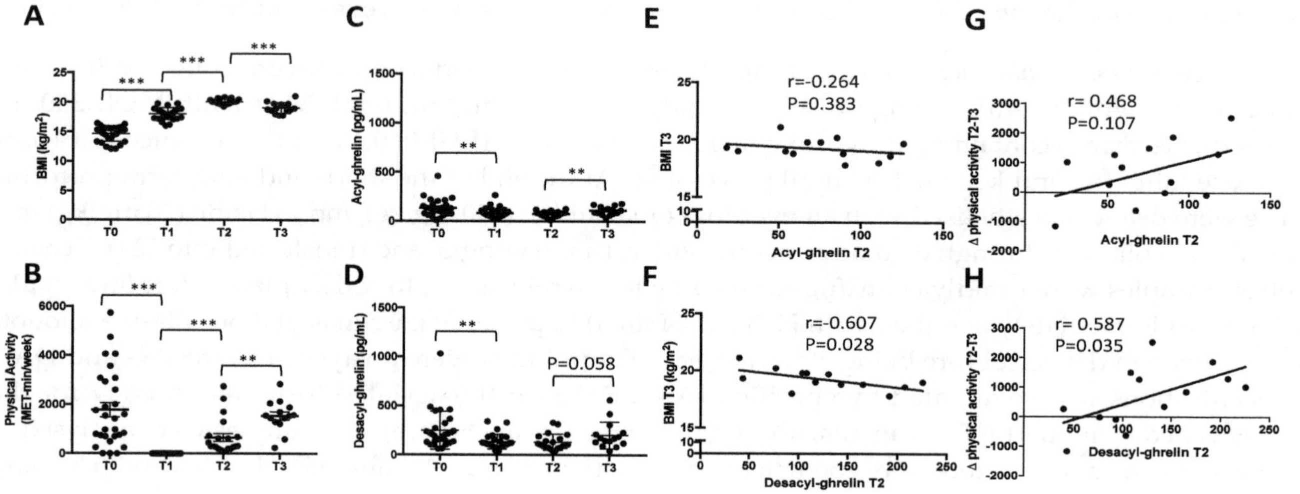

Figure 1. Longitudinal evolution of acyl-ghrelin (AG) and desacyl-ghrelin (DAG) during inpatient weight restoration and one-month post discharge. One-month post hospitalisation (T3), BMI (**A**) and physical activity (**B**) significantly decreased and plasma concentrations of AG (**C**) increased but not DAG (**D**). Plasma concentrations of DAG at the end of hospitalisation (T2) were negatively correlated to BMI one month later (T3,**F**), but not AG (**E**) and positively correlated to the increase of physical activity between the end of hospitalisation and one month later (**H**), but not AG (**G**). Only statistical differences between two consecutive time-points are reported. T0 = 1-week post-admission; T1 = 50–70% of target BMI reached; T2 = discharge BMI (close to target BMI); T3 = 1-month post-discharge visit. BMI: body mass index. MET: metabolic equivalent of task. ** $p < 0.01$; *** $p < 0.001$.

3.1.2. Rapid Decrease of Circulating AG and DAG during Refeeding Period

Both AG and DAG plasma concentrations significantly decreased during weight recovery (respectively $F_{(2\text{-}75)} = 7.68$, $p < 0.001$; $F_{(2\text{-}75)} = 6.86$, $p = 0.002$, Figure 1C,D). More specifically, post-hoc analysis revealed a significant decrease of these two forms of ghrelin between T0 and T1 (AG: $p = 0.006$; DAG: $p = 0.005$), T0 and T2 (AG: $p = 0.003$; DAG: $p = 0.009$) and T1 and T2 (AG: n.s.; DAG: n.s.). The AG/DAG ratio was calculated, and ANOVA analysis did not show any significant effect of time ($F_{(2\text{-}75)} = 0.04$, $p = 0.963$).

3.1.3. Early Increase of Circulating AG but Not DAG One Month after Discharge

One month after discharge (T3), patients BMI globally decreased (20.1 ± 0.09 vs. 19.1 ± 0.24; T2 vs. T3, $U = 51$, $p < 0.001$, Figure 1A). Physical activity was significantly increased (T2 vs. T3, $U = 53.5$, $p = 0.002$, Figure 1B). Plasma concentrations of AG were significantly increased (73.2 ± 30.9 vs. 111 ± 43.6; T2 vs. T3, $U = 79$, $p = 0.011$, Figure 1C), with mean circulating DAG at T3 was 153% of that at T2 ($U = 08$, $p = 0.058$, Figure 1D). The AG/DAG ratio was calculated and no significant difference was noted between T2 vs. T3 ($U = 146$, $p = 0.727$).

3.1.4. Correlations between Circulating DAG after Weight Recovery (T2) and BMI at T3

The correlations are presented in Table 2. At T2, AG and DAG plasma concentrations were not correlated to BMI (respectively: r = 0.107, $p = 0.73$; r = −0.378, $p = 0.202$). DAG plasma concentrations, but not AG, were positively correlated with physical activity (respectively: rho = −0.609, $p = 0.027$; rho = -0.322, $p = 0.283$). Furthermore, DAG value at T2 was negatively correlated with BMI at T3 (r = −0.607, $p = 0.028$, Figure 1F), while it was not the case for the AG value (r = −0.264, $p = 0.383$, Figure 1E). Finally, the increase of physical activity between T2 and T3 was significantly correlated to DAG value at T2 (r = 0.587, $p = 0.035$ Figure 1H), but not AG value at T2 (r = 0.468, $p = 0.107$, Figure 1G).

3.2. *Experiment 2. Preclinical Investigation*

3.2.1. Short Term Food Restriction Protocol: Link between AG, DAG and Physical Activity

At D0, the body weight was not significantly different between ALW and FRW mice (17.3 ± 0.25 vs. 17.0 ± 0.19 g). At D14, the body weight of FRW mice was significantly decreased (12.92 ± 0.21 g) compared to ALW mice (17.89 ± 0.27; t = 14.63, $p < 0.0001$; Figure 2A). Physical activity was evaluated per cage (2 mice per cage). Total 24 h activity was similar between ALW and FRW at D0 ($U = 71$, $p = 0.96$; ALW vs. FRW: 564,302 ± 196,102 vs. 348,602 ± 113,549) and at D14 ($U = 50$, $p = 0.22$; ALW vs. FRW: 1,032,292 ± 308,989 vs. 564,872 ± 183,051). From D8, only FRW mice developed a food anticipatory activity (FAA, $p < 0.01$ FRW vs. ALW; Figure 2B) 4 h 30 before the distribution of food (2:00 *p*.m. to 6:30 p.m.). From D10 to D14, ANOVA analysis for repeated measures revealed an interaction between group and day/night activity ($F_{(1\text{-}160)} = 8.86$, $p = 0.049$). When considering the cumulative activity between D10 and D14, post-hoc analysis indicated that ALW showed the highest activity during the night (day vs. night: 52,178 ± 18,874 cm vs. 4,850,005 ± 1,358,516 cm, $p = 0.008$), and FRW mice did not show any significant differences between day and night activity (day vs. night: 877,885 ± 189,871 cm vs. 1,026,869 ± 189,585 cm, $p = 0.61$) reflecting the FAA.

Plasma ghrelin concentrations were measured when the FAA was clearly developed: before distribution of food for FRW (at 5:00 p.m.) and when mice were fed (at 9:00 a.m.). At 9:00 a.m. AG plasma concentrations in fed mice were not different between ALW and FRW ($p = 0.15$), but were significantly increased only for FRW mice at 5:00 p.m. as compared to ALW mice ($U = 79.5$, $p < 0.0001$, Figure 2C). DAG plasma concentrations were significantly higher in FRW mice both at 9:00 a.m. ($U = 151$, $p = 0.0041$) and at 5:00 *p*.m. ($U = 32$, $p < 0.0001$) than in ALW mice (Figure 2D). Finally, AG and DAG were significantly increased between morning and afternoon ($p < 0.0001$, Figure 2C,D). The AG/DAG ratio was significantly different between ALW and FRW at 9:00 a.m. (0.22 ± 0.02 vs. 0.13 ± 0.01, $U = 140$, $p = 0.0018$), but not at 5:00 p.m. (0.25 ± 0.04 vs. 0.24 ± 0.03, $U = 250.5$, $p = 0.44$).

The high quantity of physical activity performed by FRW mice during FAA (day 12) was correlated with high plasma concentrations of AG (Figure 2E, rho = 0.661, $p = 0.001$) and DAG (Figure 2F; rho = 0.614, $p = 0.002$).

Table 2. Correlations between BMI, physical activity, AG and DAG plasma concentrations in the clinical samples after weight restoration and one-month post discharge.

	BMI T2	PA T2 [1]	AG T2	DAG T2	BMI T3	PA T3	AG T3	DAG T3 [1]	Δ BMI	Δ PA	Δ AG	Δ DAG
BMI T2	—											
PA T2 [1]	0.007	—										
AG T2	0.107	−0.322	—									
DAG T2	−0.378	**−0.609** *	0.205	—								
BMI T3	0.533	0.111	−0.264	**−0.607** *	—							
PA T3	−0.188	0.165	0.159	0.192	−0.038	—						
AG T3	−0.107	0.146	0.369	0.186	−0.510	0.527	—					
DAG T3 [1]	−0.302	0.069	0.346	0.319	−0.494	0.301	0.445	—				
Δ BMI	0.087	0.141	−0.369	−0.511	**0.890** ***	0.050	−0.543	−0.278	—			
Δ PA	−0.121	**−0.664** *	0.468	**0.587** *	−0.204	**0.613** *	0.412	0.159	−0.175	—		
Δ AG	−0.190	0.085	−0.492	0.002	−0.257	0.344	**0.628** *	0.143	−0.200	−0.006	—	
Δ DAG	−0.222	0.198	0.355	−0.063	−0.101	−0.015	−0.072	**0.791** **	0.001	−0.113	−0.364	—

T2: after weight restoration (90–100% BMI target); T3: one-month post discharge. BMI: body mass index; PA: physical activity measured by IPAQ; AG: acyl-ghrelin; DAG: desacyl-ghrelin.
[1] Shapiro-Wilk $p < 0.05$: Spearman's rank correlation coefficient is indicated; Δ: delta between T2 and T3. * $p<0.05$; ** $p<0.01$; *** $p<0.001$.

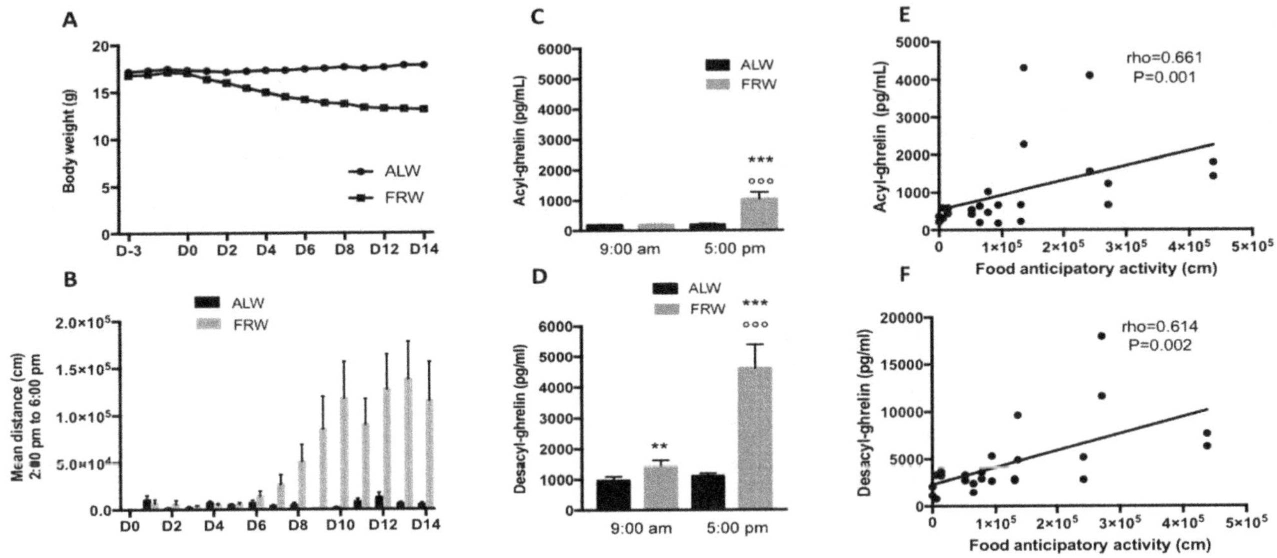

Figure 2. Short-term food restriction protocol. (**A**) Body weight evolution with a significant decrease from D2 to D14 for FRW vs. ALW mice. (**B**) Implementation of the food anticipatory activity (FAA, day activity) in the FRW mice from D6 to D14. (**C**) Mean plasma concentrations of acyl- (AG) and (**D**) desacyl-ghrelin (DAG) sampled at D10 (5:00 p.m.) and D11 (9:00 a.m.). Significant increases of AG and DAG were observed between morning and late afternoon samples only for FRW mice. (**E**,**F**) Plasma concentrations of AG (**E**) and DAG (**F**) were positively correlated with food anticipatory activity. Data are expressed as mean ± SEM; n = 24/group. °°° $p < 0.001$ 9 h vs. 17 h; ** $p < 0.01$, *** $p < 0.001$ ALW vs. FRW. ALW: ad libitum and wheel; FRW: food restriction and wheel.

3.2.2. Long Term Food Restriction Protocol and Refeeding

Fifty days after the beginning of quantitative food restriction for the FRW group, ad libitum food regimen was fully restored. The body weight of the FRW mice was rapidly restored after one day of refeeding (Figure 3A). In 4 days, FRW mice exhibited higher food intake as compared to the ALW group (D1: 213% of ALW food intake, D2: 167%, D3: 147%, Figure 3B).

It was not possible to properly measure physical activity during early refeeding from D51, because of the high binge-eating-like behaviour that interfered with FRW mice daily exercise. However, at D70, when FRW mice body weight was completely restored, activity in running wheels was significantly lower as compared to ALW mice during night-time only ($U = 0$, $p = 0.007$, Figure 3C).

On the first day of the refeeding period (D51), AG and DAG plasma concentrations were significantly decreased in FRW mice compared to ALW mice (respectively $U = 3$, $p = 0.015$; $U = 3$, $p = 0.015$, Figure 3D,E), whereas at D70, no difference was noted between the two groups for AG ($U = 13$, $p = 0.792$, Figure 3F) and DAG ($U = 10$, $p = 0.429$, Figure 3G).

At D70, night and total activities in ALW mice were positively correlated to AG (respectively, rho = 0.887, $p = 0.018$; rho = 0.888, $p = 0.018$), but not DAG. In contrast, total activity in FRW mice was positively correlated to DAG (rho = 0.96, $p = 0.01$) with a tendency only for day activity (rho = 0.820, $p = 0.089$) but not AG (Table 3).

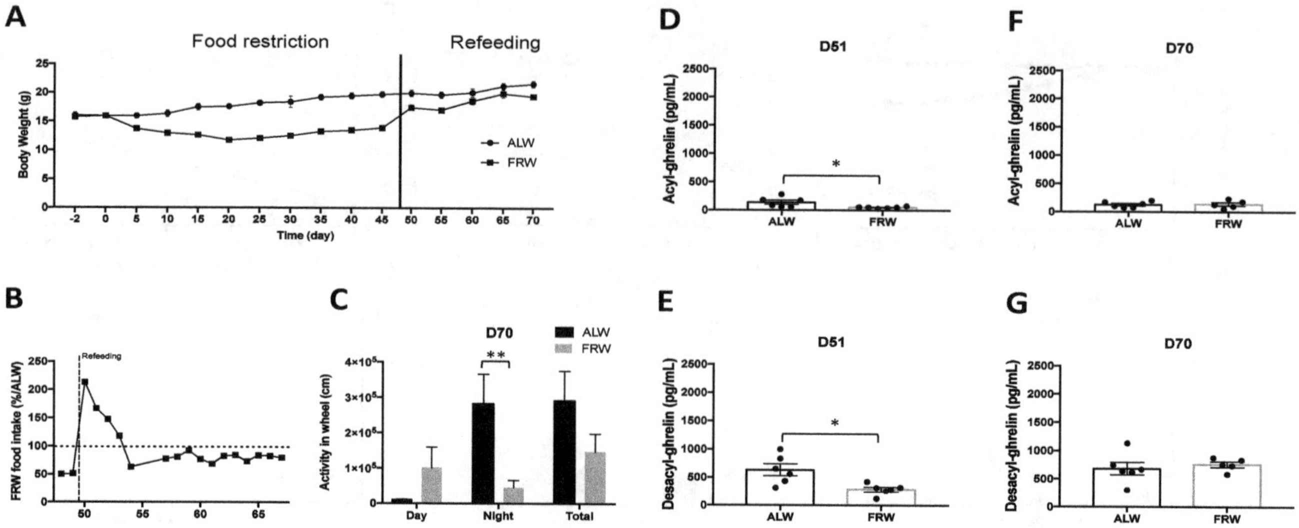

Figure 3. Long-term food restriction protocol and nutritional recovery (refeeding). (**A**) Longitudinal evolution of body weight during long term protocol. (**B**) Evolution of food intake during the refeeding period. (**C**) Total, day and night voluntary exercise in wheel at the end of the refeeding period; FRW mice showed an alteration in the daily distribution of their physical activity. (**D**,**E**) Acyl- (**D**) and desacyl-ghrelin (**E**) after one day of refeeding (D51). (**F**,**G**) Acyl- (**F**) and desacyl-ghrelin (**G**) after 20 days of refeeding (D70). Data are expressed as mean ± SEM; $n = 6$/group. Dotted lines in **B** represent the percentage value corresponding to the food eaten by ALW mice. * $p < 0.05$; ** $p < 0.01$. ALW: ad libitum and wheel; FRW: food restriction and wheel.

Table 3. Correlation between physical activity in wheel (total, day and night) and acyl- and desacyl-ghrelin plasma concentrations, in FRW and ALW mice at D70 (20 days of refeeding). Spearman's rank correlation coefficient is indicated by rho.

		ALW		FRW	
		AG	DAG	AG	DAG
Activity in Wheel	*Total*	**0.887** *	0.609	0.699	**0.960** *
	Day	−0.297	−0.407	0.569	0.820
	Night	**0.888** *	0.614	0.117	0.049

* $p < 0.05$. Significant values are indicated in bold. AG: acyl-ghrelin; DAG: desacyl-ghrelin; ALW: ad libitum and wheel; FRW: food restriction and wheel.

4. Discussion

In the present study, we aimed to improve our understanding of the link between plasma concentrations of the two isoforms of ghrelin and the level of physical activity in condition of chronic food restriction and during nutritional recovery. In AN patients, under an inpatient therapeutic program, we observed that one month after discharge only plasma DAG concentrations were negatively correlated to BMI and positively to the level of physical activity. In keeping with this observation in AN patients, we also showed in mice that after two weeks of nutritional recovery, plasma DAG concentrations were positively correlated with diurnal physical activity.

In AN, refeeding is accompanied by a significant reduction in plasma ghrelin concentrations [23,48]. To our knowledge, only one study reported a differential evolution of plasma AG and DAG concentrations during nutritional recovery in five women with restrictive-type AN [49]. Plasma DAG concentrations decreased more rapidly than AG in the early stage of hospitalisation and after 8 weeks they remained significantly lower than in ten control subjects [49].

Relapse after hospitalisation is a major clinical challenge, especially within the first year following treatment [44,50]. Thus, the identification of factors influencing recovery is a research priority for AN [51]. During hospitalisation, the therapeutic program followed by our AN patients involves reduction of exercise and physical activity limitations and both quantitative and qualitative food intake modifications. During this period, we observed that plasma concentrations of total ghrelin, AG and DAG decreased rapidly, as previously demonstrated in longitudinal studies [23,49]. The therapeutic program includes a progressive exposure to home after weight recovery and before discharge, with regular home visits. However, the period following weight recovery remains a challenge both for patients and caregivers, most patients losing weight one month after discharge and resuming their physical hyperactivity routine. In the present study plasma AG concentrations increase faster than DAG after return in an ecological environment. More specifically, BMI and DAG are negatively correlated. Recent data showed that physical activity correlated positively with total plasma ghrelin levels in acute state of AN [37]. Here, only DAG plasma concentrations at discharge were associated with increased physical activity one month later. Although the follow-up was too short to conclude about a possible relapse, our data further support that early variations of body weight and physical activity may be influenced by metabolic factors at discharge. Length of hospitalisation and balance between inpatient and intensive outpatient treatment might benefit from objective metabolic biomarkers, such as AG and DAG.

To better decipher the potential interaction between daily physical activity and metabolic alterations, we used a preclinical mouse model of chronic food restriction associated with voluntary physical activity, in which metabolic parameters have been characterised previously following either a short- (2 weeks) or long-term (8 weeks) protocol [45,46]. In the present study, AG and DAG plasma concentrations were assessed at different key stages of the protocol, using selective and sensitive immunoassays [29]. We first assessed such variations in mice submitted to a two-week food restriction that had the ability to run in a wheel. The association between ghrelin and exercise had previously been demonstrated in the "activity-based anorexia" (ABA) model. Indeed during 5 days of ABA protocol, GHRS-R1a antagonism inhibited food anticipatory activity (FAA) in mice [38] and the motivational drive to eat in rats [52]. Moreover, ghrelin knockout mice exhibited a lower FAA in wheel during a time-restricted feeding protocol and acute administration of GHRP-6, a GHSR-1a agonist, was sufficient to enhance the amount of voluntary exercise in ghrelin KO mice [53]. This increase of FAA induced by GHRP-6 is mediated by an increase of dopaminergic activity in the nucleus accumbens [53]. These data are of importance since they emphasise how ghrelin, usually studied for its involvement in the modulation of food intake [54], is essential to initiate voluntary exercise in parallel to feeding behaviour. Here, in our quantitative food-restricted model, we consolidated the data obtained by Mifune et al. in their time-food restricted model [53]. Indeed, only the food-restricted mice that developed the highest FAA displayed the highest plasma concentrations of both AG and DAG. The mechanisms by which animals anticipate feeding remain yet unresolved (see. Mistlberger (1994) for review) [55]. Food anticipatory activity might be induced by both food-inducible oscillators—the precise location into the brain of which remains to be determined [56,57]—and circadian-clocks located in the suprachiasmatic nucleus [58]. LeSauter et al. (2009) suggested that stomach-producing ghrelin cells contain food-entrainable oscillators [59]. They showed that intraperitoneal ghrelin administration in non-deprived mice, but in the absence of food, induced an increase in the locomotor activity while mice lacking ghrelin receptors displayed a significant reduction of FAA. Acylated ghrelin appears to stimulate both the appetitive (anticipatory locomotor behaviour) and the consummatory component (food intake) of feeding behaviour. However, AG does not appear to be necessary for FAA although anticipatory activity rhythms may exhibit a reduced peak level or duration in *ghsr* −/− mice; supporting a modulatory influence of ghrelin rather than a full food-inducible oscillator role [56,60–63]. Although the potential role of DAG as a hormone remains a matter of debate, DAG is suggested to be a signalling molecule that has specific targets, including the brain, with mostly opposite and independent effects to AG on food intake and glucose homeostasis [27,30,64,65]. To our knowledge, a relation between DAG and physical activity anticipatory to feeding had not been previously demonstrated in food-restricted rodents. An elegant study on bird migratory behaviours demonstrated that injections of DAG decrease food intake and increase migratory restlessness [66]. Indeed, ethologic condition of migration associates voluntary exercise to voluntary immediate food renunciation permitting long-term gain for the species [67]. As mentioned by Guisinger et al. (2003) "AN's distinctive symptoms of restricting food, denial of starvation, and hyperactivity are likely to be evolved adaptive mechanisms that facilitated ancestral nomadic foragers leaving depleted environments; genetically susceptible individuals who lose too much weight may trigger these archaic adaptations." [67]. Although highly speculative and lacking enough empirical substantiation, these findings prompted us to determine whether the evolution of AG and DAG in relation with physical activity during and after feeding evolved similarly to establish them as reliable post-remission predictors.

The food restriction protocol was thus extended to 50 days followed by a long-term nutritional recovery protocol. Such a protocol better mimicked the physiological changes that occur during weight recovery in AN patients. In this perspective, our preclinical model may fulfil face validity (phenomenological similarities for the physiological alterations) and predictive validity, criteria that are essential to model pathology [68]. After long-term food restriction, plasma AG and DAG concentrations remained elevated. Then, the prolongation of the protocol impacted the day-night exercise setting out even after 20 days of nutritional recovery, despite the technical necessity of maintaining two mice per cage to limit social stress. Nevertheless, this suggested that after 20 days of nutritional recovery, the voluntary physical activity remained differentially correlated with AG or DAG, in control or food restricted mice respectively. Indeed, DAG positively correlated with exercise performed during the day, only in the FRW group.

The effects of exercise on plasma total or AG plasma ghrelin levels have been investigated in multiple human and rodent studies although the results have been inconsistent, demonstrating either a decrease, increase, or no change [40,69]. Only total and AG concentrations have been measured. To our knowledge, no study described the impact of physical activity on DAG. Here, we benefited from the development of selective and sensitive assays, validated both in humans (personal data) and rodents [29]. Our results converge in both rodents and humans and highlight the importance of the balance between AG and DAG. Indeed on one side, AG is rapidly converted into a DAG because of the rapid action of blood esterases [70]. On the other side, the ghrelin *O*-acyl transferase (GOAT) that permits the octanoylation of ghrelin (AG) is now considered to be a key regulator in energy metabolism and hedonic feeding [71–73]. DAG has long been considered to be an inactive product of degradation of AG but subsequent data suggest that it is a metabolically active peptide acting through a yet unknown receptor [27]. Mostly, DAG antagonises but sometimes acts synergistically with AG, since it can bind and activate the AG receptor but with a lower affinity in vitro and in vivo [74]. However, DAG does not reach the necessary concentrations in tissues to do so, at least under physiological conditions [27]. Overall, studies in rodents and humans support a role of DAG to decrease body weight, food intake and body fat [75,76]. Indeed, DAG overexpressing mice exhibit a decrease in body weight, food intake, fat pad mass weight accompanied by a modest decrease in linear growth [76]. These physiological changes are attributable to (1) the decrease in gastric emptying and (2) an anorexigenic effect of DAG mediated by a specific activation of hypothalamic neurons [76,77]. In the present FRW model, intraperitoneal injection of DAG increased physical activity [78]. Therefore, we hypothesise an indirect action of DAG on physical activity. Indeed, GOAT activity has been detected in the hypothalamus and pituitary and its hypothalamic expression is nutritionally regulated [73,79]. Thus, increased DAG plasma concentrations during chronic food restriction might indirectly activate GHS-R via a local hypothalamic conversion into AG, leading to an adaptive increase of physical activity [80].

The present clinical data enlightened the potential role of DAG in recovery processes in AN and suggested a potential negative impact of DAG on weight recovery. Such interpretation might be paralleled with data obtained from the mouse model where increased plasma DAG correlated with an unusual physical activity during daytime, since rodents are used to exercise during night-time. This may reflect a sustainable alteration of physiological regulation of feeding-relative behaviours away from a long- period of caloric restriction that can interfere with a proper recovery. DAG has also been implicated in myogenesis and thus may protect the muscle integrity along weight loss [54,81]. Finally, we cannot exclude the role of elevated DAG plasma concentrations in the development of osteopenia and osteoporosis even if DAG effects on bone physiology are currently very limited and contradictory. On one side, DAG stimulates human osteoblasts proliferation in the absence of GHS-R1a [82]. On the other side, mice overexpressing DAG show a moderate decrease in their linear growth suggesting an impairment of the skeletal integrity [76]. Further mechanistic studies will help to decipher how AG and DAG modulate both muscle and bone integrity and functioning.

Translational data might be a prerequisite to stress the mechanisms that support a successful recovery in AN. On one hand, ghrelin agonists induced motivation to exercise through activation of the central reward circuit [53]. Furthermore, central administration of ghrelin enhances exercise through dopamine release in the nucleus accumbens [83]. In AN, an alteration of the reward circuit is now well accepted [11]. Further studies are needed to determine the action of DAG on this brain circuit. On the other hand, several data have linked the body temperature with the level of activity both in mice, in rats and in AN patients [84,85]. Thus, increasing physical activity through a direct or indirect action of AG or DAG could maintain appropriate body temperature in AN.

Limitations and perspectives. There are several limitations to this study. First, the small size of the clinical sample prevents generalisation and calls for replication. Second, we need to be cautious with the interpretation of data related to physical activity measurement in clinical and preclinical experiments. In the clinical sample, we used an internationally valid self-report assessment (IPAQ). Actimetry, heart rate monitoring, and recent progress on portable devices would allow investigating physical activity based on objective measures, which would be more accurate. Indeed, physical activity in AN patients is underestimated by subjective assessment (IPAQ) when compared with objective (Actiheart) measurement [86]. We also confirmed that objective assessment of physical activity could be more informative than subjective ratings, to reflect for example cognitive specificities of anorexia nervosa [87]. As surprising as it may seem, physical activity assessment in AN is so far not well defined, and there is currently no real consensus on how to measure it. In future research, it seems necessary to assess the different aspects of physical exercise conjointly (obligatory exercise, addiction exercise, commitment for exercise, reasons for exercise, isometry. . .) [88]. Recent studies support the need to investigate more in depth this unsuitable behaviour in a condition of reduced energy supplies [2,89]. Third, the choice to maintain as long as possible two restricted mice in a cage equipped with a wheel to avoid social stress and hypothermia, could limit the measurement of physical activity. However, separate experiments done in metabolic cages (where the ALW and FRW mice were singly housed for 5 to 6 days), validated that singly housed FRW mice exhibited similar FAA after 15 days of protocol (Duriez et al., unpublished data, [45]). For the welfare of the animals and to avoid stress isolation and hypothermia induced by a long-term caloric restriction, mice were maintained as two per cage. The recording of physical activity reflected the activity of two mice that usually run two by two in the wheel (ALW or FRW, personal observation). We also observed that the nutritional recovery was extremely rapid in our animal experiment, with a rapid body weight gain, that is consistent with a faster metabolism observed in rodents than in human. It might be interesting to validate another protocol of slow nutritional refeeding monitored by the investigator. Altogether, this reflects the limitations of animal modelling of psychiatric disorders. The rapid decrease of AG and DAG plasma concentrations, rapid weight gain and binge-eating like behaviour in the first three days of nutritional recovery suggest the persistence of food directed motivation after a long caloric restriction period. However, our conclusion asks the question to compare progressive to rapid weight recovery in mice. Indeed, clinical practice reported in some cases a rapid weight recovery in AN, especially in the case of clinical switch from AN to bulimia nervosa [90,91]. Ghrelin gene variants may also predict crossover rate from restricting-type AN to binge-purging subtype or bulimia nervosa [92]. We need to know whether the changes in AG and DAG during a rapid or a progressive weight recovery associated or not with binge-eating crisis forecast sustainable altered eating behaviour. Finally, weight gain cannot be considered as the unique remission factor. Preclinical models appear then to be crucial tools to decipher long-term metabolic alterations after full weight recovery and despite their limitations, they could permit to test pharmacological options. Shall DAG-signalling be a pharmacological target in AN?

Author Contributions: O.V. was responsible for the study concept and design of animal experiments and R.D., G.L. and J.E. for the study concept and design of the clinical protocol. V.T. was responsible for the design and analyses of biomarkers assays in both experimental and clinical protocols. O.V., P.D. and V.T. wrote the paper. P.D., L.R., V.T. and O.V. performed animal experimentations. D.G. performed immunoassays. P.D., P.G., N.R., L.R., V.T. and O.V. contributed to data analysis and interpretation of findings. R.D., G.L. were in charge of the recruitment of patients and data analysis. All authors have read and agreed to the published version of the manuscript.

Acknowledgments: We first warmly acknowledge Cécile Bergot and Emilie Grasset (CMME, Ste Anne Hospital) for the care of the patients and their contribution to the clinical study. We are grateful to the staff in the animal experimentation platform at the Institute of Psychiatry and Neurosciences of Paris (IPNP) for the care of the animals and to the PhenoBrain phenotyping for providing a platform for animal experimentation. We are grateful to Bertin Biotechnologies (Montigny-le-Bretonneaux, France) for providing the acyl-ghrelin and desacyl-ghrelin assays.

References

1. Hebebrand, J.; Exner, C.; Hebebrand, K.; Holtkamp, C.; Casper, R.C.; Remschmidt, H.; Herpertz-Dahlmann, B.; Klingenspor, M. Hyperactivity in patients with anorexia nervosa and in semistarved rats: Evidence for a pivotal role of hypoleptinemia. *Physiol. Behav.* **2003**, *79*, 25–37. [CrossRef]
2. Rizk, M.; Mattar, L.; Kern, L.; Berthoz, S.; Duclos, J.; Viltart, O.; Godart, N. Physical Activity in Eating Disorders: A Systematic Review. *Nutrients* **2020**, *12*, 183. [CrossRef]
3. Solenberger, S.E. Exercise and eating disorders: A 3-year inpatient hospital record analysis. *Eat. Behav.* **2001**, *2*, 151–168. [CrossRef]
4. Taranis, L.; Meyer, C. Associations between specific components of compulsive exercise and eating-disordered cognitions and behaviors among young women. *Int. J. Eat. Disord.* **2011**, *44*, 452–458. [CrossRef]
5. Steinhausen, H.-C. The outcome of anorexia nervosa in the 20th century. *Am. J. Psychiatry* **2002**, *159*, 1284–1293. [CrossRef]
6. Strober, M.; Freeman, R.; Morrell, W. The long-term course of severe anorexia nervosa in adolescents: Survival analysis of recovery, relapse, and outcome predictors over 10–15 years in a prospective study. *Int. J. Eat. Disord.* **1997**, *22*, 339–360. [CrossRef]
7. Treasure, J.; Zipfel, S.; Micali, N.; Wade, T.; Stice, E.; Claudino, A.; Schmidt, U.; Frank, G.K.; Bulik, C.M.; Wentz, E. Anorexia nervosa. *Nat. Rev. Dis. Primers* **2015**, *1*, 15074. [CrossRef]
8. Duncan, L.; Yilmaz, Z.; Gaspar, H.; Walters, R.; Goldstein, J.; Anttila, V.; Bulik-Sullivan, B.; Ripke, S.; Eating Disorders Working Group of the Psychiatric Genomics Consortium; Thornton, L.; et al. Significant Locus and Metabolic Genetic Correlations Revealed in Genome-Wide Association Study of Anorexia Nervosa. *Am. J. Psychiatry* **2017**, *174*, 850–858. [CrossRef]
9. Schorr, M.; Miller, K.K. The endocrine manifestations of anorexia nervosa: Mechanisms and management. *Nat. Rev. Endocrinol.* **2017**, *13*, 174–186. [CrossRef]
10. Watson, H.J.; Yilmaz, Z.; Thornton, L.M.; Hübel, C.; Coleman, J.R.I.; Gaspar, H.A.; Bryois, J.; Hinney, A.; Leppä, V.M.; Mattheisen, M.; et al. Genome-wide association study identifies eight risk loci and implicates metabo-psychiatric origins for anorexia nervosa. *Nat. Genet.* **2019**, *51*, 1207–1214. [CrossRef]
11. Duriez, P.; Ramoz, N.; Gorwood, P.; Viltart, O.; Tolle, V. A Metabolic Perspective on Reward Abnormalities in Anorexia Nervosa. *Trends Endocrinol. Metab.* **2019**, *30*, 915–928. [CrossRef] [PubMed]
12. Viltart, O.; Duriez, P.; Tolle, V. Metabolic and neuroendocrine adaptations to undernutrition in anorexia nervosa: From a clinical to a basic research point of view. *Horm. Mol. Biol. Clin. Investig.* **2018**, *36*. [CrossRef] [PubMed]
13. Kojima, M.; Hosoda, H.; Date, Y.; Nakazato, M.; Matsuo, H.; Kangawa, K. Ghrelin is a growth-hormone-releasing acylated peptide from stomach. *Nature* **1999**, *402*, 656–660. [CrossRef] [PubMed]
14. Date, Y.; Kojima, M.; Hosoda, H.; Sawaguchi, A.; Mondal, M.S.; Suganuma, T.; Matsukura, S.; Kangawa, K.; Nakazato, M. Ghrelin, a novel growth hormone-releasing acylated peptide, is synthesized in a distinct endocrine cell type in the gastrointestinal tracts of rats and humans. *Endocrinology* **2000**, *141*, 4255–4261. [CrossRef] [PubMed]

15. Müller, T.D.; Nogueiras, R.; Andermann, M.L.; Andrews, Z.B.; Anker, S.D.; Argente, J.; Batterham, R.L.; Benoit, S.C.; Bowers, C.Y.; Broglio, F.; et al. Ghrelin. *Mol. Metab.* **2015**, *4*, 437–460. [CrossRef]
16. De Vriese, C.; Perret, J.; Delporte, C. Focus on the short- and long-term effects of ghrelin on energy homeostasis. *Nutrition* **2010**, *26*, 579–584. [CrossRef]
17. Pradhan, G.; Samson, S.L.; Sun, Y. Ghrelin: Much more than a hunger hormone. *Curr. Opin. Clin. Nutr. Metab. Care* **2013**, *16*, 619–624. [CrossRef]
18. Tajiri, Y. Ghrelin and exercise: A possible virtuous circle. *Diabetol. Int.* **2017**, *8*, 347–349. [CrossRef]
19. Tokudome, T.; Otani, K.; Miyazato, M.; Kangawa, K. Ghrelin and the heart. *Peptides* **2019**, *111*, 42–46. [CrossRef]
20. Camargo-Silva, G.; Turones, L.C.; da Cruz, K.R.; Gomes, K.P.; Mendonça, M.M.; Nunes, A.; de Jesus, I.G.; Colugnati, D.B.; Pansani, A.P.; Pobbe, R.L.H.; et al. Ghrelin potentiates cardiac reactivity to stress by modulating sympathetic control and beta-adrenergic response. *Life Sci.* **2018**, *196*, 84–92. [CrossRef]
21. Perello, M.; Dickson, S.L. Ghrelin signalling on food reward: A salient link between the gut and the mesolimbic system. *J. Neuroendocrinol.* **2015**, *27*, 424–434. [CrossRef] [PubMed]
22. Bake, T.; Edvardsson, C.E.; Cummings, C.J.; Dickson, S.L. Ghrelin's effects on food motivation in rats are not limited to palatable foods. *J. Neuroendocrinol.* **2018**, e12665. [CrossRef]
23. Tolle, V.; Kadem, M.; Bluet-Pajot, M.-T.; Frere, D.; Foulon, C.; Bossu, C.; Dardennes, R.; Mounier, C.; Zizzari, P.; Lang, F.; et al. Balance in ghrelin and leptin plasma levels in anorexia nervosa patients and constitutionally thin women. *J. Clin. Endocrinol. Metab.* **2003**, *88*, 109–116. [CrossRef] [PubMed]
24. Pardo, M.; Roca-Rivada, A.; Al-Massadi, O.; Seoane, L.M.; Camiña, J.P.; Casanueva, F.F. Peripheral leptin and ghrelin receptors are regulated in a tissue-specific manner in activity-based anorexia. *Peptides* **2010**, *31*, 1912–1919. [CrossRef]
25. Méquinion, M.; Chauveau, C.; Viltart, O. The use of animal models to decipher physiological and neurobiological alterations of anorexia nervosa patients. *Front. Endocrinol. (Lausanne)* **2015**, *6*, 68. [CrossRef] [PubMed]
26. Zigman, J.M.; Jones, J.E.; Lee, C.E.; Saper, C.B.; Elmquist, J.K. Expression of ghrelin receptor mRNA in the rat and the mouse brain. *J. Comp. Neurol.* **2006**, *494*, 528–548. [CrossRef]
27. Delhanty, P.J.; Neggers, S.J.; van der Lely, A.J. Des-acyl ghrelin: A metabolically active peptide. *Endocr. Dev.* **2013**, *25*, 112–121. [CrossRef]
28. Hosoda, H.; Kojima, M.; Matsuo, H.; Kangawa, K. Ghrelin and des-acyl ghrelin: Two major forms of rat ghrelin peptide in gastrointestinal tissue. *Biochem. Biophys. Res. Commun.* **2000**, *279*, 909–913. [CrossRef]
29. Hassouna, R.; Grouselle, D.; Chiappetta, G.; Lipecka, J.; Fiquet, O.; Tomasetto, C.; Vinh, J.; Epelbaum, J.; Tolle, V. Combination of Selective Immunoassays and Mass Spectrometry to Characterize Preproghrelin-Derived Peptides in Mouse Tissues. *Front. Neurosci.* **2017**, *11*, 211. [CrossRef]
30. Stevanovic, D.M.; Grefhorst, A.; Themmen, A.P.N.; Popovic, V.; Holstege, J.; Haasdijk, E.; Trajkovic, V.; van der Lely, A.-J.; Delhanty, P.J.D. Unacylated ghrelin suppresses ghrelin induced neuronal activity in the hypothalamus and brainstem of male rats [corrected]. *PLoS ONE* **2014**, *9*, e98180. [CrossRef]
31. Allas, S.; Caixàs, A.; Poitou, C.; Coupaye, M.; Thuilleaux, D.; Lorenzini, F.; Diene, G.; Crinò, A.; Illouz, F.; Grugni, G.; et al. AZP-531, an unacylated ghrelin analog, improves food-related behavior in patients with Prader-Willi syndrome: A randomized placebo-controlled trial. *PLoS ONE* **2018**, *13*, e0190849. [CrossRef] [PubMed]
32. Beauloye, V.; Diene, G.; Kuppens, R.; Zech, F.; Winandy, C.; Molinas, C.; Faye, S.; Kieffer, I.; Beckers, D.; Nergårdh, R.; et al. High unacylated ghrelin levels support the concept of anorexia in infants with prader-willi syndrome. *Orphanet J. Rare Dis.* **2016**, *11*, 56. [CrossRef] [PubMed]
33. King, J.A.; Deighton, K.; Broom, D.R.; Wasse, L.K.; Douglas, J.A.; Burns, S.F.; Cordery, P.A.; Petherick, E.S.; Batterham, R.L.; Goltz, F.R.; et al. Individual Variation in Hunger, Energy Intake, and Ghrelin Responses to Acute Exercise. *Med. Sci. Sports Exerc.* **2017**, *49*, 1219–1228. [CrossRef]
34. Dundar, A.; Kocahan, S.; Sahin, L. Associations of apelin, leptin, irisin, ghrelin, insulin, glucose levels, and lipid parameters with physical activity during eight weeks of regular exercise training. *Arch. Physiol. Biochem.* **2019**, 1–5. [CrossRef] [PubMed]

35. Sartorio, A.; Morpurgo, P.; Cappiello, V.; Agosti, F.; Marazzi, N.; Giordani, C.; Rigamonti, A.E.; Muller, E.E.; Spada, A. Exercise-induced effects on growth hormone levels are associated with ghrelin changes only in presence of prolonged exercise bouts in male athletes. *J. Sports Med. Phys. Fit.* **2008**, *48*, 97–101.
36. Fathi, R.; Ghanbari-Niaki, A.; Kraemer, R.R.; Talebi-Garakani, E.; Saghebjoo, M. The effect of exercise intensity on plasma and tissue acyl ghrelin concentrations in fasted rats. *Regul. Pept.* **2010**, *165*, 133–137. [CrossRef]
37. Hofmann, T.; Elbelt, U.; Haas, V.; Ahnis, A.; Klapp, B.F.; Rose, M.; Stengel, A. Plasma kisspeptin and ghrelin levels are independently correlated with physical activity in patients with anorexia nervosa. *Appetite* **2017**, *108*, 141–150. [CrossRef]
38. Verhagen, L.A.W.; Egecioglu, E.; Luijendijk, M.C.M.; Hillebrand, J.J.G.; Adan, R.A.H.; Dickson, S.L. Acute and chronic suppression of the central ghrelin signaling system reveals a role in food anticipatory activity. *Eur. Neuropsychopharmacol.* **2011**, *21*, 384–392. [CrossRef]
39. Wu, H.; van Kuyck, K.; Tambuyzer, T.; Luyten, L.; Aerts, J.-M.; Nuttin, B. Rethinking food anticipatory activity in the activity-based anorexia rat model. *Sci. Rep.* **2014**, *4*, 3929. [CrossRef]
40. Mani, B.K.; Castorena, C.M.; Osborne-Lawrence, S.; Vijayaraghavan, P.; Metzger, N.P.; Elmquist, J.K.; Zigman, J.M. Ghrelin mediates exercise endurance and the feeding response post-exercise. *Mol. Metab.* **2018**, *9*, 114–130. [CrossRef]
41. Mackelvie, K.J.; Meneilly, G.S.; Elahi, D.; Wong, A.C.K.; Barr, S.I.; Chanoine, J.-P. Regulation of appetite in lean and obese adolescents after exercise: Role of acylated and desacyl ghrelin. *J. Clin. Endocrinol. Metab.* **2007**, *92*, 648–654. [CrossRef] [PubMed]
42. Shiiya, T.; Ueno, H.; Toshinai, K.; Kawagoe, T.; Naito, S.; Tobina, T.; Nishida, Y.; Shindo, M.; Kangawa, K.; Tanaka, H.; et al. Significant lowering of plasma ghrelin but not des-acyl ghrelin in response to acute exercise in men. *Endocr. J.* **2011**, *58*, 335–342. [CrossRef] [PubMed]
43. Tiryaki-Sonmez, G.; Ozen, S.; Bugdayci, G.; Karli, U.; Ozen, G.; Cogalgil, S.; Schoenfeld, B.; Sozbir, K.; Aydin, K. Effect of exercise on appetite-regulating hormones in overweight women. *Biol. Sport* **2013**, *30*, 75–80. [CrossRef]
44. Khalsa, S.S.; Portnoff, L.C.; McCurdy-McKinnon, D.; Feusner, J.D. What happens after treatment? A systematic review of relapse, remission, and recovery in anorexia nervosa. *J. Eat. Disord.* **2017**, *5*, 20. [CrossRef] [PubMed]
45. Méquinion, M.; Caron, E.; Zgheib, S.; Stievenard, A.; Zizzari, P.; Tolle, V.; Cortet, B.; Lucas, S.; Prévot, V.; Chauveau, C.; et al. Physical activity: Benefit or weakness in metabolic adaptations in a mouse model of chronic food restriction? *Am. J. Physiol. Endocrinol. Metab.* **2015**, *308*, E241–E255. [CrossRef]
46. Duriez, P.; Eddarkaoui, S.; Blum, D.; Dickson, S.L.; Gorwood, P.; Tolle, V.; Viltart, O. Does physical activity associated with chronic food restriction alleviate anxiety like behaviour, in female mice? *Horm. Behav.* **2020**, *124*, 104807. [CrossRef]
47. Craig, C.L.; Marshall, A.L.; Sjöström, M.; Bauman, A.E.; Booth, M.L.; Ainsworth, B.E.; Pratt, M.; Ekelund, U.; Yngve, A.; Sallis, J.F.; et al. International physical activity questionnaire: 12-country reliability and validity. *Med. Sci. Sports Exerc.* **2003**, *35*, 1381–1395. [CrossRef]
48. Otto, B.; Cuntz, U.; Fruehauf, E.; Wawarta, R.; Folwaczny, C.; Riepl, R.L.; Heiman, M.L.; Lehnert, P.; Fichter, M.; Tschöp, M. Weight gain decreases elevated plasma ghrelin concentrations of patients with anorexia nervosa. *Eur. J. Endocrinol.* **2001**, *145*, 669–673. [CrossRef]
49. Koyama, K.-I.; Yasuhara, D.; Nakahara, T.; Harada, T.; Uehara, M.; Ushikai, M.; Asakawa, A.; Inui, A. Changes in acyl ghrelin, des-acyl ghrelin, and ratio of acyl ghrelin to total ghrelin with short-term refeeding in female inpatients with restricting-type anorexia nervosa. *Horm. Metab. Res.* **2010**, *42*, 595–598. [CrossRef]
50. Keel, P.K.; Dorer, D.J.; Franko, D.L.; Jackson, S.C.; Herzog, D.B. Postremission predictors of relapse in women with eating disorders. *Am. J. Psychiatry* **2005**, *162*, 2263–2268. [CrossRef]
51. Van Furth, E.F.; van der Meer, A.; Cowan, K. Top 10 research priorities for eating disorders. *Lancet Psychiatry* **2016**, *3*, 706–707. [CrossRef]
52. Merkestein, M.; Brans, M.A.D.; Luijendijk, M.C.M.; de Jong, J.W.; Egecioglu, E.; Dickson, S.L.; Adan, R.A.H. Ghrelin mediates anticipation to a palatable meal in rats. *Obesity (Silver Spring)* **2012**, *20*, 963–971. [CrossRef] [PubMed]

53. Mifune, H.; Tajiri, Y.; Sakai, Y.; Kawahara, Y.; Hara, K.; Sato, T.; Nishi, Y.; Nishi, A.; Mitsuzono, R.; Kakuma, T.; et al. Voluntary exercise is motivated by ghrelin, possibly related to the central reward circuit. *J. Endocrinol.* **2020**, *244*, 123–132. [CrossRef] [PubMed]
54. Yanagi, S.; Sato, T.; Kangawa, K.; Nakazato, M. The Homeostatic Force of Ghrelin. *Cell Metab.* **2018**, *27*, 786–804. [CrossRef]
55. Mistlberger, R.E. Circadian food-anticipatory activity: Formal models and physiological mechanisms. *Neurosci. Biobehav. Rev.* **1994**, *18*, 171–195. [CrossRef]
56. Mistlberger, R.E. Neurobiology of food anticipatory circadian rhythms. *Physiol. Behav.* **2011**, *104*, 535–545. [CrossRef]
57. Chen, Y.; Lin, Y.-C.; Zimmerman, C.A.; Essner, R.A.; Knight, Z.A. Hunger neurons drive feeding through a sustained, positive reinforcement signal. *Elife* **2016**, *5*. [CrossRef]
58. Challet, E. Circadian clocks, food intake, and metabolism. *Prog. Mol. Biol. Transl. Sci.* **2013**, *119*, 105–135. [CrossRef]
59. LeSauter, J.; Hoque, N.; Weintraub, M.; Pfaff, D.W.; Silver, R. Stomach ghrelin-secreting cells as food-entrainable circadian clocks. *Proc. Natl. Acad. Sci. USA* **2009**, *106*, 13582–13587. [CrossRef]
60. Blum, I.D.; Patterson, Z.; Khazall, R.; Lamont, E.W.; Sleeman, M.W.; Horvath, T.L.; Abizaid, A. Reduced anticipatory locomotor responses to scheduled meals in ghrelin receptor deficient mice. *Neuroscience* **2009**, *164*, 351–359. [CrossRef]
61. Gunapala, K.M.; Gallardo, C.M.; Hsu, C.T.; Steele, A.D. Single gene deletions of orexin, leptin, neuropeptide Y, and ghrelin do not appreciably alter food anticipatory activity in mice. *PLoS ONE* **2011**, *6*, e18377. [CrossRef] [PubMed]
62. Patton, D.F.; Katsuyama, A.M.; Pavlovski, I.; Michalik, M.; Patterson, Z.; Parfyonov, M.; Smit, A.N.; Marchant, E.G.; Chung, S.H.; Chung, J.; et al. Circadian mechanisms of food anticipatory rhythms in rats fed once or twice daily: Clock gene and endocrine correlates. *PLoS ONE* **2014**, *9*, e112451. [CrossRef] [PubMed]
63. Dailey, M.J.; Stingl, K.C.; Moran, T.H. Disassociation between preprandial gut peptide release and food-anticipatory activity. *Endocrinology* **2012**, *153*, 132–142. [CrossRef] [PubMed]
64. Toshinai, K.; Yamaguchi, H.; Sun, Y.; Smith, R.G.; Yamanaka, A.; Sakurai, T.; Date, Y.; Mondal, M.S.; Shimbara, T.; Kawagoe, T.; et al. Des-acyl ghrelin induces food intake by a mechanism independent of the growth hormone secretagogue receptor. *Endocrinology* **2006**, *147*, 2306–2314. [CrossRef] [PubMed]
65. Delhanty, P.J.D.; Neggers, S.J.; van der Lely, A.J. Should we consider des-acyl ghrelin as a separate hormone and if so, what does it do? *Front. Horm. Res.* **2014**, *42*, 163–174. [CrossRef]
66. Goymann, W.; Lupi, S.; Kaiya, H.; Cardinale, M.; Fusani, L. Ghrelin affects stopover decisions and food intake in a long-distance migrant. *Proc. Natl. Acad. Sci. USA* **2017**. [CrossRef]
67. Guisinger, S. Adapted to flee famine: Adding an evolutionary perspective on anorexia nervosa. *Psychol. Rev.* **2003**, *110*, 745–761. [CrossRef]
68. Willner, P. Validation criteria for animal models of human mental disorders: Learned helplessness as a paradigm case. *Prog. Neuropsychopharmacol. Biol. Psychiatry* **1986**, *10*, 677–690. [CrossRef]
69. Holliday, A.; Blannin, A. Appetite, food intake and gut hormone responses to intense aerobic exercise of different duration. *J. Endocrinol.* **2017**, *235*, 193–205. [CrossRef]
70. Hosoda, H.; Doi, K.; Nagaya, N.; Okumura, H.; Nakagawa, E.; Enomoto, M.; Ono, F.; Kangawa, K. Optimum collection and storage conditions for ghrelin measurements: Octanoyl modification of ghrelin is rapidly hydrolyzed to desacyl ghrelin in blood samples. *Clin. Chem.* **2004**, *50*, 1077–1080. [CrossRef]
71. Yang, J.; Brown, M.S.; Liang, G.; Grishin, N.V.; Goldstein, J.L. Identification of the acyltransferase that octanoylates ghrelin, an appetite-stimulating peptide hormone. *Cell* **2008**, *132*, 387–396. [CrossRef] [PubMed]
72. Davis, J.F.; Perello, M.; Choi, D.L.; Magrisso, I.J.; Kirchner, H.; Pfluger, P.T.; Tschoep, M.; Zigman, J.M.; Benoit, S.C. GOAT induced ghrelin acylation regulates hedonic feeding. *Horm. Behav.* **2012**, *62*, 598–604. [CrossRef] [PubMed]
73. Kirchner, H.; Gutierrez, J.A.; Solenberg, P.J.; Pfluger, P.T.; Czyzyk, T.A.; Willency, J.A.; Schurmann, A.; Joost, H.G.; Jandacek, R.; Hale, J.E.; et al. GOAT links dietary lipids with the endocrine control of energy balance. *Nat. Med.* **2009**, *15*, 741–745. [CrossRef]

74. Heppner, K.M.; Piechowski, C.L.; Müller, A.; Ottaway, N.; Sisley, S.; Smiley, D.L.; Habegger, K.M.; Pfluger, P.T.; Dimarchi, R.; Biebermann, H.; et al. Both acyl and des-acyl ghrelin regulate adiposity and glucose metabolism via central nervous system ghrelin receptors. *Diabetes* **2014**, *63*, 122–131. [CrossRef] [PubMed]
75. Delhanty, P.J.D.; Neggers, S.J.; van der Lely, A.J. Mechanisms in endocrinology: Ghrelin: The differences between acyl- and des-acyl ghrelin. *Eur. J. Endocrinol.* **2012**, *167*, 601–608. [CrossRef] [PubMed]
76. Asakawa, A.; Inui, A.; Fujimiya, M.; Sakamaki, R.; Shinfuku, N.; Ueta, Y.; Meguid, M.M.; Kasuga, M. Stomach regulates energy balance via acylated ghrelin and desacyl ghrelin. *Gut* **2005**, *54*, 18–24. [CrossRef]
77. Asakawa, A.; Ataka, K.; Fujino, K.; Chen, C.-Y.; Kato, I.; Fujimiya, M.; Inui, A. Ghrelin family of peptides and gut motility. *J. Gastroenterol. Hepatol.* **2011**, *26* (Suppl. 3), 73–74. [CrossRef]
78. Robichon, L.; Adda, S.; Tolle, V.; Viltart, O. Deacyl-ghrelin: A potential role on the food anticipatory activity in a mouse model of chronic food restriction? *Eur. Neuropsychopharmacol.* **2019**, *29*, S189–S190. [CrossRef]
79. Gahete, M.D.; Córdoba-Chacón, J.; Salvatori, R.; Castaño, J.P.; Kineman, R.D.; Luque, R.M. Metabolic regulation of ghrelin O-acyl transferase (GOAT) expression in the mouse hypothalamus, pituitary, and stomach. *Mol. Cell. Endocrinol.* **2010**, *317*, 154–160. [CrossRef]
80. Hopkins, A.L.; Nelson, T.A.S.; Guschina, I.A.; Parsons, L.C.; Lewis, C.L.; Brown, R.C.; Christian, H.C.; Davies, J.S.; Wells, T. Unacylated ghrelin promotes adipogenesis in rodent bone marrow via ghrelin O-acyl transferase and GHS-R1a activity: Evidence for target cell-induced acylation. *Sci. Rep.* **2017**, *7*, 45541. [CrossRef]
81. Gortan Cappellari, G.; Zanetti, M.; Semolic, A.; Vinci, P.; Ruozi, G.; Falcione, A.; Filigheddu, N.; Guarnieri, G.; Graziani, A.; Giacca, M.; et al. Unacylated Ghrelin Reduces Skeletal Muscle Reactive Oxygen Species Generation and Inflammation and Prevents High-Fat Diet-Induced Hyperglycemia and Whole-Body Insulin Resistance in Rodents. *Diabetes* **2016**, *65*, 874–886. [CrossRef]
82. Delhanty, P.J.D.; van der Eerden, B.C.J.; van der Velde, M.; Gauna, C.; Pols, H.A.P.; Jahr, H.; Chiba, H.; van der Lely, A.J.; van Leeuwen, J.P.T.M. Ghrelin and unacylated ghrelin stimulate human osteoblast growth via mitogen-activated protein kinase (MAPK)/phosphoinositide 3-kinase (PI3K) pathways in the absence of GHS-R1a. *J. Endocrinol.* **2006**, *188*, 37–47. [CrossRef] [PubMed]
83. Jerlhag, E.; Egecioglu, E.; Dickson, S.L.; Douhan, A.; Svensson, L.; Engel, J.A. Ghrelin administration into tegmental areas stimulates locomotor activity and increases extracellular concentration of dopamine in the nucleus accumbens. *Addict. Biol.* **2007**, *12*, 6–16. [CrossRef]
84. Carrera, O.; Adan, R.A.H.; Gutierrez, E.; Danner, U.N.; Hoek, H.W.; van Elburg, A.A.; Kas, M.J.H. Hyperactivity in anorexia nervosa: Warming up not just burning-off calories. *PLoS ONE* **2012**, *7*, e41851. [CrossRef] [PubMed]
85. Inoue, Y.; Nakahara, K.; Maruyama, K.; Suzuki, Y.; Hayashi, Y.; Kangawa, K.; Murakami, N. Central and peripheral des-acyl ghrelin regulates body temperature in rats. *Biochem. Biophys. Res. Commun.* **2013**, *430*, 278–283. [CrossRef] [PubMed]
86. Alberti, M.; Galvani, C.; El Ghoch, M.; Capelli, C.; Lanza, M.; Calugi, S.; Dalle Grave, R. Assessment of physical activity in anorexia nervosa and treatment outcome. *Med. Sci. Sports Exerc.* **2013**, *45*, 1643–1648. [CrossRef]
87. Di Lodovico, L.; Gorwood, P. The relationship between moderate to vigorous physical activity and cognitive rigidity in anorexia nervosa. *Psychiatry Res.* **2020**, *284*, 112703. [CrossRef]
88. Rizk, M.; Lalanne, C.; Berthoz, S.; Kern, L.; EVHAN Group; Godart, N. Problematic Exercise in Anorexia Nervosa: Testing Potential Risk Factors against Different Definitions. *PLoS ONE* **2015**, *10*, e0143352. [CrossRef] [PubMed]
89. Meyer, C.; Taranis, L.; Touyz, S. Excessive exercise in the eating disorders: A need for less activity from patients and more from researchers. *Eur. Eat. Disord. Rev.* **2008**, *16*, 81–83. [CrossRef]
90. Eddy, K.T.; Dorer, D.J.; Franko, D.L.; Tahilani, K.; Thompson-Brenner, H.; Herzog, D.B. Diagnostic crossover in anorexia nervosa and bulimia nervosa: Implications for DSM-V. *Am. J. Psychiatry* **2008**, *165*, 245–250. [CrossRef]

91. Schaumberg, K.; Jangmo, A.; Thornton, L.M.; Birgegård, A.; Almqvist, C.; Norring, C.; Larsson, H.; Bulik, C.M. Patterns of diagnostic transition in eating disorders: A longitudinal population study in Sweden. *Psychol. Med.* **2019**, *49*, 819–827. [CrossRef] [PubMed]
92. Ando, T.; Komaki, G.; Nishimura, H.; Naruo, T.; Okabe, K.; Kawai, K.; Takii, M.; Oka, T.; Kodama, N.; Nakamoto, C.; et al. A ghrelin gene variant may predict crossover rate from restricting-type anorexia nervosa to other phenotypes of eating disorders: A retrospective survival analysis. *Psychiatr. Genet.* **2010**, *20*, 153–159. [CrossRef] [PubMed]

13

Food Addiction Symptoms and Amygdala Response in Fasted and Fed States

Kirrilly M. Pursey [1,2], Oren Contreras-Rodriguez [3], Clare E. Collins [1,2], Peter Stanwell [1] and Tracy L. Burrows [1,*]

1 Faculty of Health and Medicine, The University of Newcastle, University Drive, Callaghan, NSW 2308, Australia; kirrilly.pursey@newcastle.edu.au (K.M.P.); Clare.Collins@newcastle.edu.au (C.E.O.); peter.stanwell@newcastle.edu.au (P.S.)

2 Priority Research Centre for Physical Activity and Nutrition, The University of Newcastle, University Drive, Callaghan, NSW 2308, Australia

3 Department of Psychiatry, Bellvitge Biomedical Research Institute (IDIBELL), and CIBERSAM, 08907 Barcelona, Spain; orencoro@gmail.com

* Correspondence: Tracy.Burrows@newcastle.edu.au

Abstract: Few studies have investigated the underlying neural substrates of food addiction (FA) in humans using a recognised assessment tool. In addition, no studies have investigated subregions of the amygdala (basolateral (BLA) and central amygdala), which have been linked to reward-seeking behaviours, susceptibility to weight gain, and promoting appetitive behaviours, in the context of FA. This pilot study aimed to explore the association between FA symptoms and activation in the BLA and central amygdala via functional magnetic resonance imaging (fMRI), in response to visual food cues in fasted and fed states. Females (n = 12) aged 18–35 years completed two fMRI scans (fasted and fed) while viewing high-calorie food images and low-calorie food images. Food addiction symptoms were assessed using the Yale Food Addiction Scale. Associations between FA symptoms and activation of the BLA and central amygdala were tested using bilateral masks and small-volume correction procedures in multiple regression models, controlling for BMI. Participants were 24.1 ± 2.6 years, with mean BMI of 27.4 ± 5.0 kg/m^2 and FA symptom score of 4.1 ± 2.2. A significant positive association was identified between FA symptoms and higher activation of the left BLA to high-calorie versus low-calorie foods in the fasted session, but not the fed session. There were no significant associations with the central amygdala in either session. This exploratory study provides pilot data to inform future studies investigating the neural mechanisms underlying FA.

Keywords: Food addiction; Yale Food Addiction Scale; functional magnetic resonance imaging; basolateral amygdala

1. Introduction

There is increasing scientific interest in the possible role of "food addiction" (FA) underlying particular patterns of overeating, dietary relapse and weight gain in vulnerable individuals. Neuroimaging techniques, such as functional magnetic resonance imaging (fMRI), have provided insight into this phenomenon in humans. Visual food cues and consumption of palatable, energy-dense foods have been shown to activate reward-related brain circuits in humans in a similar way to substances of abuse [1]. Despite accumulating evidence supporting FA as a phenomenon in preclinical [2] and behavioural research [3], few studies have investigated the potential underlying neural substrates in humans. Many studies have used obesity as a proxy for addictive-like eating in lieu of a recognised assessment tool for FA, such as the Yale Food Addiction Scale (YFAS) [4]. Using obesity as a proxy for

FA could result in inconsistent neuroimaging findings as it is unclear as to the proportion of participants truly affected by addictive-like eating in these samples.

In one neuroimaging study using a recognised FA assessment tool, YFAS symptoms were associated with greater activation in response to a visual milkshake cue in brain areas encoding the reward value of foods and craving (amygdala, anterior cingulate cortex (ACC), medial orbitofrontal cortex (OFC), and the dorsolateral prefrontal cortex (DLPFC)) in young females [5]. In another study, while main effects were found activation in the amygdala, OFC, nucleus accumbens and inferior frontal cortex in response to the taste of sugar-sweetened beverages, no relationships were observed between YFAS symptoms and neural response in male and female adolescents [6]. The divergence in previous studies may be related to the limited range of food cues used, which have often been restricted to sweetened beverages [5,6]. These previous studies have also not studied participants in different motivational states (i.e., fasted and fed), which is important given the differences in responsivity in reward-related networks in these states [7,8].

The amygdala has been implicated in previous FA neuroimaging research [5] and plays a role in regulating the hedonic impact of salient stimuli and coordinating appetitive behaviours, with studies reporting selective sensitivity of the amygdala to food cues in the fasted state [9,10]. The amygdala has also been shown to integrate interoceptive states and sensory cues along the ventral visual stream [9] and has been implicated in drug cue reactivity and drug craving [11,12]. While the amygdala may play an important role in the context of FA, no studies have explored the potential role of distinct subregions of the amygdala. The basolateral amygdala (BLA) is of particular interest as it has been shown to drive external cues to the hypothalamic feeding centres in both humans and rats [13,14], consistent with the role in processing high-level sensory input and stimulus-value associations in humans [15]. In animal studies, the BLA has been implicated in reward-seeking behaviours in response to food-related stimuli [16] and relapse to food seeking [17]. In the satiated state, the BLA has also been associated with eating in the absence of homeostatic needs in rats [18] as well as predicting weight gain susceptibility in males and females [13]. In addition, the central amygdala has been reported to have a role in increasing reward saliency, modulating food consumption and promoting appetitive behaviours in mice [19]. While these previous studies of the BLA and central amygdala were not conducted in FA populations specifically, these findings suggest that there is a need to study the subregions of the amygdala in relation to FA in different motivational states.

This pilot study aimed to explore the association between YFAS assessed FA symptoms and activation in the central and BLA, assessed via functional MRI, in response to visual food cues in fasted and fed states. It was hypothesised that FA symptoms would be associated with greater activation in the BLA in response to high-calorie vs low-calorie foods in both the fasted and fed states, based on the findings of previous neuroimaging research [7,9,10].

2. Materials and Methods

2.1. Participants

Australian females aged 18–35 years were recruited to the current study from an existing pool of participants who had completed an online FA survey, which aimed to determine FA prevalence and associations with dietary intake in Australian adults [20]. At the end of the survey, participants could exit the survey with no further contact or could volunteer to be recontacted for future research. Full details regarding the FA survey are published elsewhere [20]. This study was approved by the University of Newcastle Human Research Ethics Committee (Approval number H-2012-0419) and was conducted in accordance with the ethical standards of the 1964 Helsinki Declaration.

Participants were eligible for the current study if they were female, aged 18–35 years, lived within a one-hour proximity to the imaging facility (Newcastle, NSW, Australia) and elected to be contacted for future research at the end of the online survey. Eligibility for this pilot study was restricted to females only in order to reduce potential inter-person variation in appetite and neural activation to visual food cues associated with sex-related differences [21]. Seventy-seven participants from the original survey volunteered for future research and were recontacted via email to participate in the fMRI component of the study. Of those recontacted, 35 responded that they were interested in participating in the fMRI study and were screened via telephone. Exclusion criteria for the current study included pregnancy, body mass >150 kg due to weight limitations for the MRI scanner, contraindications to MRI, left handedness, pre-existing medical or Axis 1 disorders, disordered eating behaviour, medications affecting appetite, history of substance abuse or head injury with loss of consciousness, allergy to any beverage ingredients, risk of adverse medical events as a result of fasting (e.g., diabetes), or inability to refrain from cigarette smoking. Seventeen participants did not meet the inclusion criteria for the current study, and five participants were not able to be contacted for screening, resulting in a final sample of thirteen participants. Written informed consent was obtained from all participants in the current study.

2.2. Procedures

The study procedure is outlined in Figure 1. Participants attended a single session where they underwent two fMRI scans of the brain, the first in the fasted state and the second in the fed state. Four hours prior to the first scan, participants consumed a standardised pre-fast meal (237 mL Ensure Plus; 1485 kJ/355 kcal). Participants then fasted for four hours, excluding water, to capture the hunger-state experienced when approaching the next meal. Participants were instructed to avoid caffeinated and alcoholic beverages, and smoking for twelve hours prior to the scan. Compliance with the pre-scan protocol was checked via verbal self-report upon arrival at the imaging facility prior to scanning. The session included anthropometric measurements, a demographic survey, hunger and image ratings, and the first of two fMRI scans. Following the first scan, participants drank a second Ensure Plus drink with compliance monitored by the research team. Participants again completed the hunger and image ratings before undertaking a second fMRI scan approximately 45 min following the completion of the second meal replacement beverage. Participants were not able to be scanned at the same time of day due to scheduling at the imaging facility.

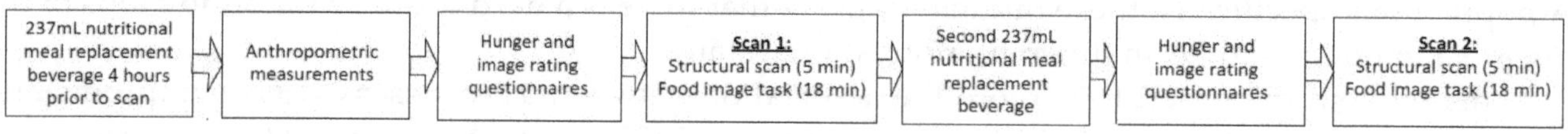

Figure 1. Flow diagram of the study procedure.

2.3. Measures

Demographics: Demographic data including sex, age, indigenous status, marital status and highest qualification were collected. Current and previous dieting history [22] was also assessed.

Yale Food Addiction Scale: The YFAS is a 25-item questionnaire which assesses addictive-like eating according to the diagnostic criteria for substance dependence. The YFAS has been shown to have adequate psychometric properties [4]. The tool includes two scoring options, a symptom score from 0–7 based on the DSM criteria for substance dependence, as well as a diagnosis of FA if ≥3 symptoms are reported as well as clinical impairment or distress. Cronbach α for the current sample was 0.93.

Anthropometrics: Height was taken using a BSM370 stadiometer, while weight and body composition (% body fat, fat free mass) was assessed using the InBody720 bioelectrical impedance analyser (Biospace, Seoul, Korea) using a standardised protocol. Body mass index (BMI) was subsequently calculated.

Hunger and Image Ratings: Participants completed a set of ratings related to hunger and appetite, as well as rating a subset of images shown to them in the MRI scanner (n = 20; n = 10 high-calorie, n = 10 low-calorie), using a 10 cm visual analogue scale. Participants completed the set of ratings in the fasted state at baseline (prior to Scan 1) and in the fed state (prior to Scan 2). Hunger and appetite ratings included self-reported (i) hunger, (ii) satiety, (iii) fullness and (iv) prospective food consumption [23]. For the image ratings, participants were asked to rate the (i) appeal of the food, (ii) desire to eat the food, (iii) whether the food increased their appetite and (iv) perceptions of prospective food consumption amount related to each of the food images.

2.4. Imaging Paradigm

Food images were chosen from a standardised database [24] and foods representative of the Australian food environment. Images were matched for brightness, complexity, resolution and size. Two groups of images were created according to nutrient composition, (i) appetising high-calorie foods (e.g., chocolate, chips, pizza, ice cream) and (ii) low-calorie foods (fruits and vegetables). The selected images were informed by the foods commonly reported in the original FA online survey. Food images were piloted on a sample of six university students independent of the study sample (mean age 27 years) regarding recognisability, familiarity and appeal. Those foods with low pilot ratings for recognisability and familiarity were excluded ($n = 27$). A final sample of 150 single food images were selected for the study including $n = 75$ high-calorie and $n = 75$ low-calorie foods. Nutritional composition of the food images can be found in Table S1.

Visual stimuli were presented in a block design format using Presentation software (Neurobehavioral Systems, Inc, Berkley, USA) and NordicNeuroLab sync box (NordicNeuroLab AS, Bergen, Norway), and consisted of two 18 min 20 s runs. Each run consisted of 15 epochs each of (i) low-calorie foods, (ii) high-calorie foods and (iii) fixation cross. Within each 20 s epoch of food images, five images were presented for four seconds each. A 20 s central fixation cross was presented as a control, and each epoch was separated by a four second blank screen. Each run consisted of 440 volumes over the scanning period. Images were presented onto an MRI compatible screen via a projector, and viewed via a mirror attached to the head coil. Standardised instructions to remain still focus on the visual stimuli were provided by the radiographer during the scan.

2.5. Imaging Data Collection

Structural and task-related functional scans were acquired using a Siemens 3-tesla MRI (Siemens AG, Germany). Structural images were acquired with a three-dimension (3D) magnetisation-prepared rapid gradient-echo (MP-RAGE) sequence with the following parameters: TE = 3.5 ms, TR = 2 s, 7° excitation flip angle, 160 slices with 1mm isotropic resolution. Task-related functional MR images were acquired using a T2*-weighted gradient-echo echo planar imaging (EPI) pulse sequence. The parameters were TE = 24 ms, TR = 2.5 s, 90° excitation flip angle, 47 axial slices 3 mm thick with a 0 mm interslice gap, in-plane resolution of 3 × 3 mm, covering from vertex to cerebellum. Axial slices were angled to the anterior cranial floor for to limit distortions that may impact on imaging of the orbito-frontal region.

2.6. Statistical Analysis

Participant characteristics, hunger and image ratings were analysed descriptively using Stata13. Differences in hunger and image ratings between the first and second scan were assessed using paired t-tests. Task-related functional MR images were processed and analysed using MATLAB version R2017a (The MathWorks Inc, Natick, Mass, USA) and Statistical Parametric Software (SPM12; The Welcome Department of Imaging Neuroscience, London, UK). Preprocessing steps involved motion correction, spatial normalization and smoothing using a Gaussian filter (FWHM 8 mm). The realigned functional sequences were coregistered to each participant's anatomical scan, which had been previously coregistered and normalized to the SPM-T1 template. Normalization parameters were then applied to the coregistered functional images, which were then resliced to a 2 mm isotropic resolution in Montreal Neurological Institute (MNI) space.

First-level (single-subject) SPM contrasts images were estimated for each of the fasted and fed scans for the following task main effects of interest: high-calorie > low-calorie foods, and low-calorie > high-calorie foods. Changes in brain activation between sessions were computed by the creation of the following contrasts: (Fasted scan (high-calorie > low-calorie foods) – Fed scan (high-calorie > low-calorie foods)) and (Fed scan (high-calorie > low-calorie foods) – Fasted scan (high-calorie > low-calorie foods)). The same contrasts were created to explore the between session effects on the activation of low-calorie > high calorie foods. Three regressors were used in these analyses to model conditions separately corresponding to high-calorie and low-calorie foods, and the fixation cross. Furthermore, to correct for subtle in-scanner movements from volume-to-volume scans, we identified the outlier scans present in the realigned task-related functional scans as determined using the CONN toolbox (Whitfield-Gabrieli and Nieto-Castanon, 2012). For each participant, the actual removal of outlier scans was completed by entering the subject-specific variables identifying the outlier scans (i.e., one regressor per outlier) in the first-level models as covariates of no interest, so these outlier scans were removed from these and subsequent analyses. We excluded one subject that had 19.8% of outlier scans. A hemodynamic delay of 4 s and a high-pass filter (1/120 Hz) were considered. The resulting first-level contrasts images were then carried forward to subsequent second-level random-effects (group) analyses. One-sample t-tests were used to assess the main task effects in the fasted and fed sessions. Multiple regression models were used to assess associations between FA symptoms and whole-brain activation under the main task effects in the fasted and fed sessions, and the change between sessions. These analyses were controlled for the subject-specific number of outlier scans, BMI, hunger and dieting when the association with FA symptoms was explored. Results were considered significant when surviving a $p > 0.001$ and a determined cluster-extent using Monte Carlo simulations implemented in the AlphaSim thresholding approach [25] (94 voxels and 135 voxels for the fasted and fed sessions, respectively incorporating a 2×2×2mm grey matter mask of 128,190 voxels). However, we specifically tested for associations between FA symptoms and the activation of the basolateral and central amygdala using bilateral masks and small-volume correction procedures in the multiple regression models. To that end, we defined bilateral basolateral and centromedial amygdala masks comprising 3.5 mm radial spheres cantered at left basolateral (x = −26, y = −5, z = −23) and right BLA (x = 29, y = −3, z = −23), and the left centromedial amygdala (x = −19, y = −5, z = −15) and right centromedial amygdala (x = 23, y = −5, z = −13) following previous research [26,27].

3. Results

Participant characteristics can be found in Table 1. The mean YFAS symptom score for the group was 4.1 ± 2.2 (range 1–7), with six participants classified as having a YFAS FA diagnosis. Hunger and image ratings are presented in Table 2. Hunger ratings were not significantly different between the fasted and fed scans ($p = 0.13$); however, ratings of fullness and satisfaction increased, and prospective food consumption decreased (all $p < 0.05$). Image ratings were significantly reduced from the fasted to fed scans ($p < 0.05$). FA symptoms were not associated with hunger or image ratings ($p > 0.05$)

Table 1. Participant characteristics at baseline ($n = 12$).

Characteristic	**Total Sample**
Age (years)	24.1 ± 2.6 (range 21–29)
Aboriginal or Torres Strait Islander background *n* (%)	0 (0)
Highest level of education *n* (%)	
Higher school certificate	2 (17)
Diploma	2 (17%)
University degree	8 (67%)
Body mass index (BMI) (kg/m^2)	27.4 ± 5.0 (range 21.7–39.0)
Body fat (%)	32.5 ± 9.8 (range 18.7–50.1)
Symptom score	4.1 ± 2.2 (range 1–7)
Current dieting *n* (%)	6 (50)
Previous dieting *n* (%)	12 (100)

Data is presented as mean ± SD unless otherwise specified.

Table 2. Hunger, appetite and image ratings in the fasted and fed states.

	Rating		p
	Fasted Scan	**Fed Scan**	
Hunger and appetite ratings			
Self-reported hunger	5.8 ± 1.9	4.2 ± 3.0	0.13
Self-reported satisfaction	3.1 ± 2.4	5.4 ± 2.6	0.03
Self-perceived fullness	2.1 ± 2.3	5.8 ± 3.1	0.003
Prospective food consumption amount	7.2 ± 1.8	4.8 ± 2.7	0.02
Image ratings			
Appeal of food	6.0 ± 1.6	4.5 ± 1.3	0.02
Desire to eat food	5.2 ± 1.7	3.8 ± 1.2	0.03
Effect of food in increasing appetite	4.5 ± 1.6	3.1 ± 1.1	0.02
Prospective consumption amount of food depicted in image	5.2 ± 1.3	3.2 ± 1.0	<0.001

Ratings completed using a 10 cm visual analogue scale. Results are presented as mean ± SD.

Brain Activation and Association with FA Symptoms

Visual cues of high-calorie vs low-calorie foods activated a cluster in the right amygdala, the left hippocampus, the fusiform gyrus, and in bilateral occipital cortex in the fasted session, and the left amygdala in the fed session (Table 3, Figure 2). No significant activations were recorded in the contrast low-calorie vs high-calorie foods in the fasted and fed sessions.

Table 3. Brain regions showing significant activation in response to the sight of high-calorie vs low-calorie foods in the fasted and fed sessions.

Brain Activation	Coordinates (x, y, z)	t-Value	CS
Fasted session			
Amygdala	14, −6, −18	6.1	111
Hippocampus	−36, −18, −16	6.7	243
Fusiform gyrus	32, −46, −16	5.2	127
Occipital cortex	42, −88, 6	8.3	434
	−34, −94, 2	7.9	165
Fed session			
Amygdala	−24, 14, −20	7.5	314

Coordinates are given in Montreal Neurological (MNI) Atlas space. The results for the fasted session surpassed a $p < 0.001$ and a cluster size (CS) of 94 voxels and 135 voxels, for the fasted and fed session, respectively. The t-values refer to the comparison of the activation of each of the listed brain regions to the high-calorie vs low-calorie food images.

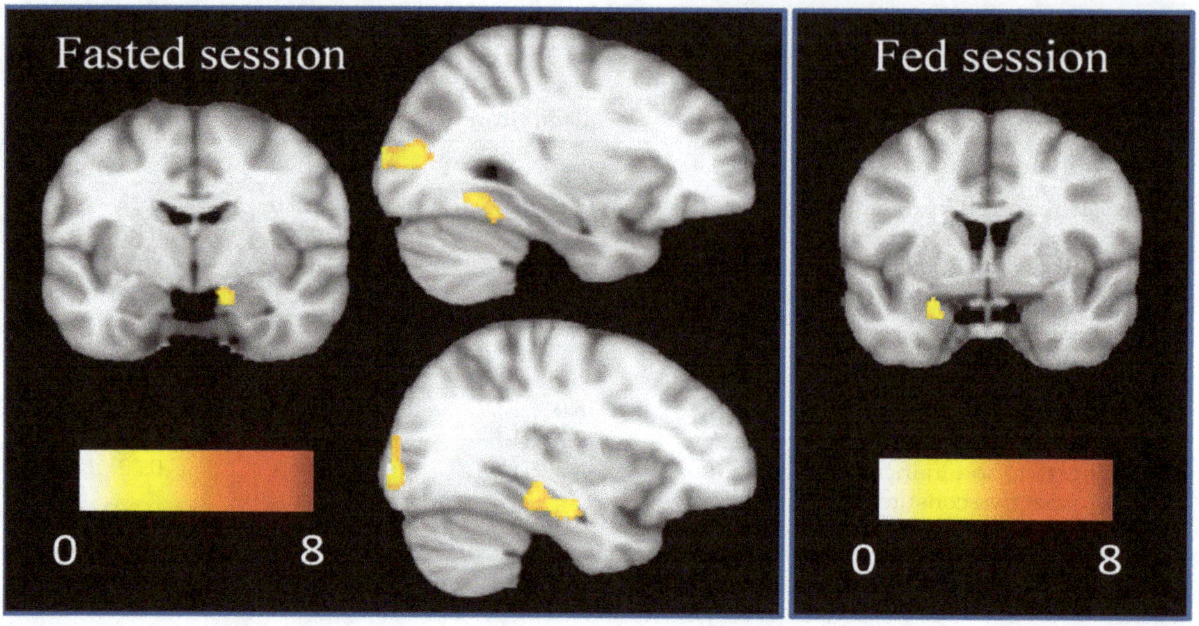

Figure 2. Increased brain activation to "high-calorie vs low-calorie" foods during the fasted and the fed sessions. Right side of the figure corresponds to the right hemisphere in the coronal views. In sagittal views, the upper figure corresponds to the right hemisphere, whereas the lower figure corresponds to the left hemisphere. Colour bar displays t-values for the comparison of activation in response to high-calorie vs low-calorie food cues.

No significant associations with FA symptoms were found using whole-brain corrections, but a significant association between the FA symptoms and higher activation of the left BLA to high-calorie vs low-calorie foods in the fasted session (x = −26, y = −4, z = −26, t = 3.45, 11 voxels, $p_{SVC\text{-}FWE<0.05} = 0.042$) were identified using small-volume correction procedures. Importantly, this association was found regardless of the body mass index of the participants, and it also remained statistically significant after controlling for hunger reported by the participants during the fasted session and current dieting status. No significant associations were identified between FA symptoms and the activation of the central amygdala in the fasted session, and the activation of the basolateral and central amygdala in the fed session (all $p_{SVC\text{-}FWE} > 0.05$). The change in the magnitude of activation from the fasted to the fed sessions of the left BLA showed a significant association with FA symptoms, controlling for BMI (x = −26, y = −4, z = −26, t = 3.77, 8 voxels, $p_{SVC\text{-}FWE<0.05} = 0.027$) (Figure 3).

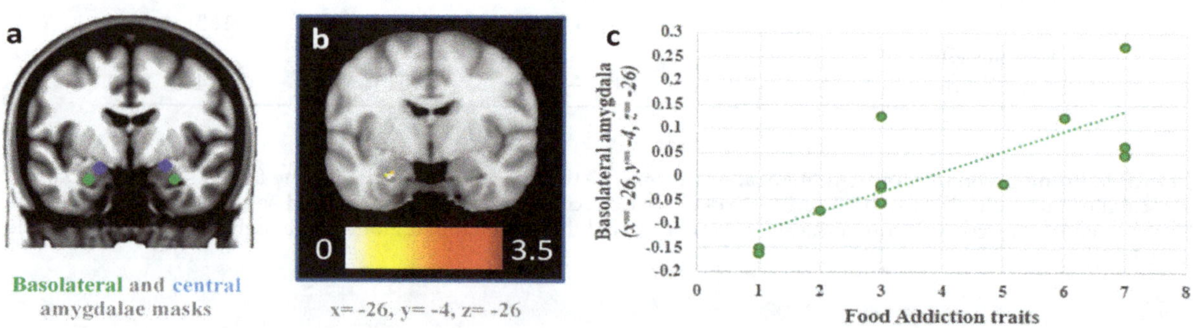

Figure 3. Association between the activation of the left basolateral amygdala and food addiction traits, (**a**) location of the basolateral (green) and central (blue) amygdala seeds, used as a mask for small-volume corrections; (**b**) left basolateral amygdala significantly associated with food addiction traits during the fasted session ($p_{SVC\text{-}FWE<0.05} = 0.042$); (**c**) scatter plot represents the correlation between the change in the activation of the left basolateral amygdala from the fasted to the fed sessions (y-axis) and food addiction traits (x-axis) (x = −26, y = −4, z = −26, t = 3.77, $p_{SVC\text{-}FWE<0.05} = 0.027$).

4. Discussion

This is the first study to use fMRI to investigate activation in distinct subregions of the amygdala in response to visual food cues in relation to FA symptoms in both fasting and fed states. In line with the hypothesis, activation in the BLA in response to high-calorie foods versus low-calorie foods was found to be associated with higher FA symptoms in the fasted state, which is consistent with previous research [7,9,10]. Furthermore, participants with greater FA symptoms showed higher activation in the BLA in the fasted than in the fed scans to the sight of high-calorie vs low-calorie foods. One possible mechanism consistent with this is that the amygdala boosts activation in the ventral stream [9,28], increasing food salience in the hunger state. Individual differences in BLA response in the hunger state to appetizing, high-calorie foods may therefore be associated with susceptibility to overeating.

The findings of the current study suggest that those with higher FA symptoms may be vulnerable to environmental food cues of energy-dense, nutrient-poor, high-calorie food when hungry compared to those with lower FA symptoms. This may lead those vulnerable individuals to greater desire to eat, hence leading to food seeking and consumption, which is consistent with previous research [16,17]. It is possible that FA may play a mediating role in non-homeostatic eating, dietary relapse and other longer-term issues such as weight gain. This may be an important consideration in future interventions targeting FA, suggesting a regular meal pattern that uses strategies to avoid long periods of fasting may be warranted. This may also suggest that further consideration to reducing environmental food cues (e.g., food advertisements) in treatment approaches may be warranted for those vulnerable to addictive-like eating.

The second hypothesis was not supported, with no significant associations found between FA symptoms and BLA activation in the fed state. This is divergent previous work investigating the role of the amygdala in eating in the absence of hunger and weight gain susceptibility [13]. However, the study by Sun and colleagues [13] did not recruit a sample to investigated FA, in contrast to the current study. These differences may also be due to the study samples (i.e., inclusion of males in the previous study) and use of different food cues (i.e., taste vs sight). Alternatively, this may be related to the standardised meal not significantly reducing self-reported hunger from baseline in the current study, although fullness was increased, and prospective food consumption was decreased. Of note, the standardised meal would have contributed a relatively small proportion of total daily energy intake (TEE) for participants (<30%). Future studies should therefore consider the use of a standardised meal with greater contribution to %TEE.

The strengths of the current study include the use of a recognised assessment tool for FA and investigation of participants in fasted and fed states. Food images were informed by previous research and selected from a standardised database [24], which was found to be a limitation of previous studies [21]. This current exploratory study is limited by the small sample size and inclusion of females only. Additionally, participants could not be scanned at the same time of day, however, a standardised meal replacement was provided to reduce inter-individual variation. Self-reported hunger was not significantly different between the fasted and fed states, however, other measures of appetite were significantly reduced. Future studies should consider standardised meals with greater calorie content, to ensure hunger is significantly different between the two conditions. As the scans were not conducted in a counterbalanced order, it is possible that the lack of associations may be attributed to a habituation effect. A further limitation is the lack of control condition in the cue reactivity task, and the addition of a control condition should be considered in future studies. Although participants were asked about disordered eating behaviours during the screening process, a clinical interview to identify eating disorder was not included in the baseline assessment. Future studies should use a clinical eating disorder assessment to better control for underlying disordered eating. This study used the original YFAS tool as the updated YFAS 2.0 tool had not been released at the time of the study. Future imaging studies should consider the use of the YFAS 2.0, which aligns with the DSM-5 criteria [29]. The current study also investigated associations between neural activation and FA symptoms, however, future studies may consider analysing according to the dichotomous YFAS diagnosis and in those with higher FA symptoms to better understand addictive-like eating.

5. Conclusions

This study demonstrates that activation of the BLA, which has been linked to reward-seeking behaviours and susceptibility to weight gain, was associated with FA symptoms in the fasted state. This study provides pilot data to inform future studies with larger sample sizes investigating the neural mechanisms associated with FA.

Author Contributions: Conceptualization, K.M.P., T.L.B., P.S. and C.E.C.; Analysis, O.C.-R., K.M.P.; Writing—Original Draft Preparation, K.M.P.; Writing—Review and Editing, T.L.B., O.C.-R., C.E.C., P.S.; Funding Acquisition, T.L.B. All authors have contributed to the development of the manuscript and have approved the final version.

Acknowledgments: K.M.P. is supported by a Hunter Medical Research Institute Greaves Family Early Career Support Grant. O.C.-R. is funded by the postdoctoral contract "PERIS" (SLT006/17/00236) from the Catalan Government. T.L.B. is supported by University of Newcastle Brawn Research Fellowship.

References

1. Kenny, P.J. Reward mechanisms in obesity: New insights and future directions. *Neuron* **2011**, *69*, 664–679. [CrossRef] [PubMed]
2. Avena, N.M.; Rada, P.; Hoebel, B.G. Evidence for sugar addiction: Behavioral and neurochemical effects of intermittent, excessive sugar intake. *Neurosci. Biobehav. Rev.* **2008**, *32*, 20–39. [CrossRef] [PubMed]
3. Pursey, K.M.; Stanwell, P.; Gearhardt, A.N.; Collins, C.E.; Burrows, T.L. The prevalence of food addiction as assessed by the Yale Food Addiction Scale: A systematic review. *Nutrients* **2014**, *6*, 4552–4590. [CrossRef] [PubMed]
4. Gearhardt, A.N.; Corbin, W.R.; Brownell, K.D. Preliminary validation of the Yale Food Addiction Scale. *Appetite* **2009**, *52*, 430–436. [CrossRef] [PubMed]
5. Gearhardt, A.N.; Yokum, S.; Orr, P.T.; Stice, E.; Corbin, W.R.; Brownell, K.D. Neural correlates of food addiction. *Arch. Gen. Psychiatry* **2011**, *68*, 808–816. [CrossRef]
6. Feldstein Ewing, S.W.; Claus, E.D.; Hudson, K.A.; Filbey, F.M.; Yakes Jimenez, E.; Lisdahl, K.M.; Kong, A.S. Overweight adolescents' brain response to sweetened beverages mirrors addiction pathways. *Brain Imaging Behav.* **2017**, *11*, 925–935. [CrossRef] [PubMed]
7. Siep, N.; Roefs, A.; Roebroeck, A.; Havermans, R.; Bonte, M.L.; Jansen, A. Hunger is the best spice: An fMRI study of the effects of attention, hunger and calorie content on food reward processing in the amygdala and orbitofrontal cortex. *Behav. Brain. Res.* **2009**, *198*, 149–158. [CrossRef]
8. Tomasi, D.; Volkow, N.D. Striatocortical pathway dysfunction in addiction and obesity: Differences and similarities. *Crit. Rev. Biochem. Mol. Biol.* **2013**, *48*, 1–19. [CrossRef]
9. LaBar, K.S.; Gitelman, D.R.; Parrish, T.B.; Kim, Y.-H.; Nobre, A.C.; Mesulam, M.M. Hunger selectively modulates corticolimbic activation to food stimuli in humans. *Behav. Neurosci.* **2001**, *115*, 493–500. [CrossRef]
10. Mohanty, A.; Gitelman, D.R.; Small, D.M.; Mesulam, M.M. The spatial attention network interacts with limbic and monoaminergic systems to modulate motivation-induced attention shifts. *Cereb. Cortex* **2008**, *18*, 2604–2613. [CrossRef]
11. Childress, A.R.; Mozley, P.D.; McElgin, W.; Fitzgerald, J.; Reivich, M.; O'Brien, C.P. Limbic activation during cue-induced cocaine craving. *Am. J. Psychiatry* **1999**, *156*, 11–18. [CrossRef] [PubMed]
12. Wilson, S.J.; Sayette, M.A.; Fiez, J.A. Prefrontal responses to drug cues: A neurocognitive analysis. *Nat. Neurosci.* **2004**, *7*, 211–214. [CrossRef] [PubMed]
13. Sun, X.; Kroemer, N.B.; Veldhuizen, M.G.; Babbs, A.E.; de Araujo, I.E.; Gitelman, D.R.; Sherwin, R.S.; Sinha, R.; Small, D.M. Basolateral amygdala response to food cues in the absence of hunger is associated with weight gain susceptibility. *J. Neurosci.* **2015**, *35*, 7964–7976. [CrossRef] [PubMed]

14. Petrovich, G.D.; Setlow, B.; Holland, P.C.; Gallagher, M. Amygdalo-hypothalamic circuit allows learned cues to override satiety and promote eating. *J. Neurosci.* **2002**, *22*, 8748–8753. [CrossRef] [PubMed]
15. Bzdok, D.; Laird, A.R.; Zilles, K.; Fox, P.T.; Eickhoff, S.B. An investigation of the structural, connectional, and functional subspecialization in the human amygdala. *Hum. Brain Mapp.* **2013**, *34*, 3247–3266. [CrossRef]
16. McLaughlin, R.J.; Floresco, S.B. The role of different subregions of the basolateral amygdala in cue-induced reinstatement and extinction of food-seeking behavior. *Neuroscience* **2007**, *146*, 1484–1494. [CrossRef] [PubMed]
17. Campbell, E.J.; Barker, D.J.; Nasser, H.M.; Kaganovsky, K.; Dayas, C.V.; Marchant, N.J. Cue-induced food seeking after punishment is associated with increased Fos expression in the lateral hypothalamus and basolateral and medial amygdala. *Behav. Neurosci.* **2017**, *131*, 155–167. [CrossRef]
18. Weingarten, H.P. Conditioned cues elicit feeding in sated rats: A role for learning in meal initiation. *Science* **1983**, *220*, 431–433. [CrossRef]
19. Douglass, A.M.; Kucukdereli, H.; Ponserre, M.; Markovic, M.; Gründemann, J.; Strobel, C.; Alcala Morales, P.L.; Conzelmann, K.-K.; Lüthi, A.; Klein, R. Central amygdala circuits modulate food consumption through a positive-valence mechanism. *Nat. Neurosci.* **2017**, *20*, 1384. [CrossRef]
20. Pursey, K.M.; Collins, C.E.; Stanwell, P.; Burrows, T.L. Foods and dietary profiles associated with 'food addiction' in young adults. *Addict. Behav. Rep.* **2015**, *2*, 41–48. [CrossRef]
21. Pursey, K.; Stanwell, P.; Callister, R.J.; Brain, K.; Collins, C.E.; Burrows, T.L. Neural responses to visual food cues according to weight status: A systematic review of functional magnetic resonance imaging studies. *Front. Nutr.* **2014**, *1*, 7. [CrossRef] [PubMed]
22. Meule, A.; Lutz, A.; Vogele, C.; Kubler, A. Self-reported dieting success is associated with cardiac autonomic regulation in current dieters. *Appetite* **2012**, *59*, 494–498. [CrossRef] [PubMed]
23. Flint, A.; Raben, A.; Blundell, J.E.; Astrup, A. Reproducibility, power and validity of visual analogue scales in assessment of appetite sensations in single test meal studies. *Int. J. Obes. Relat. Metab. Disord.* **2000**, *24*, 38–48. [CrossRef] [PubMed]
24. Blechert, J.; Meule, A.; Busch, N.A.; Ohla, K. Food-pics: An image database for experimental research on eating and appetite. *Front. Psychol.* **2014**, *5*, 617. [CrossRef] [PubMed]
25. Song, X.-W.; Dong, Z.-Y.; Long, X.-Y.; Li, S.-F.; Zuo, X.-N.; Zhu, C.-Z.; He, Y.; Yan, C.-G.; Zang, Y.-F. REST: A toolkit for resting-state functional magnetic resonance imaging data processing. *PLoS One* **2011**, *6*, e25031. [CrossRef] [PubMed]
26. Baur, V.; Hanggi, J.; Langer, N.; Jancke, L. Resting-state functional and structural connectivity within an insula-amygdala route specifically index state and trait anxiety. *Biol. Psychiatry* **2013**, *73*, 85–92. [CrossRef]
27. Pico-Perez, M.; Alonso, P.; Contreras-Rodriguez, O.; Martinez-Zalacain, I.; Lopez-Sola, C.; Jimenez-Murcia, S.; Verdejo-Garcia, A.; Menchon, J.M.; Soriano-Mas, C. Dispositional use of emotion regulation strategies and resting-state cortico-limbic functional connectivity. *Brain Imaging Behav.* **2018**, *12*, 1022–1031. [CrossRef]
28. Kravitz, D.J.; Saleem, K.S.; Baker, C.I.; Ungerleider, L.G.; Mishkin, M. The ventral visual pathway: An expanded neural framework for the processing of object quality. *Trends Cogn. Sci.* **2013**, *17*, 26–49. [CrossRef]
29. Gearhardt, A.N.; Corbin, W.R.; Brownell, K.D. Development of the Yale Food Addiction Scale Version 2.0. *Psychol. Addict. Behav.* **2016**, *30*, 113–121. [CrossRef]

14

Assessment of Physical Activity Patterns in Adolescent Patients with Anorexia Nervosa and their Effect on Weight Gain

Miriam Kemmer [1], Christoph U. Correll [1,2,3], Tobias Hofmann [4], Andreas Stengel [4,5], Julia Grosser [1] and Verena Haas [1,*]

1 Department of Child and Adolescent Psychiatry, Charité-Universitätsmedizin Berlin, Corporate Member of Freie Universität Berlin, Humboldt-Universität zu Berlin, and Berlin Institute of Health, 13353 Berlin, Germany; miriam.kemmer@charite.de (M.K.); CCorrell@northwell.edu (C.U.C.); julia.grosser@charite.de (J.G.)

2 Donald and Barbara Zucker School of Medicine at Hofstra/Northwell, Hempstead, NY 11549, USA

3 Department of Psychiatry, The Zucker Hillside Hospital, Glen Oaks, NY 11004, USA

4 Center for Internal Medicine and Dermatology, Department for Psychosomatic Medicine, Charité-Universitätsmedizin Berlin, Corporate Member of Freie Universität Berlin, Humboldt-Universität zu Berlin, and Berlin Institute of Health Berlin, 12200 Berlin, Germany; tobias.hofmann@charite.de (T.H.); Andreas.Stengel@med.uni-tuebingen.de (A.S.)

5 Department of Psychosomatic Medicine and Psychotherapy, Medical University Hospital Tübingen, 72076 Tübingen, Germany

* Correspondence: verena.haas@charite.de

Abstract: (1) Background: Altered physical activity (PA) affects weight recovery in anorexia nervosa (AN) patients. The study aimed to objectively characterize PA patterns and their effect on weight trajectory in adolescent AN patients. (2) Methods: PA was assessed in 47 patients on admission to inpatient treatment, in $n = 25$ of these patients again 4 weeks after discharge (follow-up, FU), as well as in 20 adolescent healthy controls using the Sense Wear™ armband. The following PA categories were defined by metabolic equivalent (MET) ranges: sedentary behavior (SB), light (LPA), moderate (MPA), vigorous (VPA), and high-level PA (HLPA= MPA + VPA). (3) Results: LPA on admission was significantly higher in AN patients than in controls (103 vs. 55 min/d, $p < 0.001$), and LPA in AN decreased over time to 90 min/d ($p = 0.006$). Patients with higher admission LPA ($n = 12$) still had elevated LPA at FU ($p = 0.003$). High admission LPA was associated with a higher inpatient BMI percentage gain (ΔBMI%; 18.2% ± 10.0% vs. 12.0% ± 9.7%, $p = 0.037$) but with a loss of ΔBMI% at FU (−2.3% ± 3.6% vs. 0.8% ± 3.6%, $p = 0.045$). HLPA at baseline was associated with a lower inpatient ΔBMI% ($p = 0.045$). (4) Conclusion: Elevated LPA in AN patients decreased after inpatient treatment, and PA patterns had an impact on weight trajectory.

Keywords: anorexia nervosa; physical activity; accelerometry; weight gain

---

1. Introduction

Anorexia nervosa (AN) is characterized by the restriction of energy intake, low body weight, fear of weight gain, and distorted body image [1]. Increased physical activity (PA) has been observed in 31–80% of patients suffering from AN [2], yet varying definitions and terminology, such as hyperactivity [3], excessive activity, and problematic exercise [4], are used in the literature to describe this phenomenon. These definitions include different types of PA, ranging from light PA, such as standing and walking, to high-level PA, such as running or biking. Due to the lack of a common definition, the AN-specific PA patterns as well as the effect of these PA patterns on the illness course are difficult to discern [4].

Additionally, when assessing PA in AN patients, there is a discrepancy between self-reported and objectively measured PA; patients tend to both either over- or underestimate their PA [5–7]. Despite the high clinical relevance of objectively measured PA in AN patients, considering its impact on weight recovery [8,9], few studies have objectively assessed PA in AN patients.

In the present study, the terms high-level PA and light PA will be used to distinguish between high and low intensity PA. In previous studies, average total PA did not vary between AN patients and healthy controls [5,10], but high-level PA was both higher [11] and lower [12] than in healthy controls. Several studies demonstrated increased light PA in AN patients, such as more time on feet during daytime [8], more time spent in PA intensities of between 1.8 and 3 metabolic equivalents (METs) [12], and more time 'fidgeting' compared to healthy controls [8,13]. However, varying definitions for fidgeting have been used, such as changes in body position while seated per time unit, and average acceleration from both feet in meters/second^2/minute. There is high interpersonal variation in PA patterns among AN patients [11,12]. Longitudinal PA assessment indicated a link between pre-hospital exercise behavior and objectively measured total PA at the time of admission [14]. The findings on long-term patterns of the PA behavior of AN patients during and after treatment are controversial, as some studies state that total PA increased during weight restoration [8,15], while in others total PA decreased [16]. After discharge from inpatient treatment, both light PA and high-level PA remained constant [16], and, overall, PA did not vary between recovered AN patients and healthy controls [17]. Little data exist on how objectively measured PA affects weight trajectory. One study found no association between light PA (<3 METs) and BMI trajectory in adult AN patients [18], while others found that BMI trajectories were associated with time on feet when weight restored [8], the number of steps per day, the time spent in light PA (1.8–3.0 METs) [12], and the time spent in high-level PA (3–6 METs) [12,19]. In an outpatient setting, higher levels of total PA were associated with higher BMI values [20]. While this finding is somewhat counterintuitive, i.e., more PA that may have been driven by the desire to lose weight did not reduce BMI, it also highlights the bidirectional interdependence of BMI and PA, as it is also possible that a higher BMI reflects a healthier state that can result in higher and healthy activity.

Prior studies in an inpatient setting have shown that even under PA restricted inpatient conditions, there is a high variance in regards to PA amongst AN patients [11,12,16]. In one study, steps ranged from 2479 to 31,876 per day [12]. This variance is observable even when PA is specifically restricted as part of the treatment program [16]. Our study aims to better characterize these PA patterns and to assess their impact on weight trajectory in order to identify subgroups of patients at risk for a poorer treatment outcome. Identifying these patients at the beginning of treatment may allow for future studies to explore new approaches to treatment tailored to the needs of patients with specific types of hyperactivity.

We propose that PA levels impact weight trajectory, while not all physical activity levels will have the same impact on the weight recovery of patients. Based on our prior research [12], we hypothesize that high light physical activity will correlate with a poorer weight trajectory while increased high level physical activity will not have this same impact. We also propose that physical activity patterns are closely linked to the phenotype of AN; therefore, PA patterns will vary between adolescent AN patients and healthy controls. To pursue these aims, the following hypotheses were tested:

- Similar to adults, inpatient adolescent AN patients spend more time in light PA than age-matched healthy controls, while moderate PA and vigorous PA will be lower in AN patients.
- Within AN patients, different subgroups exist with respect to PA patterns (i.e., increased light PA or high-level PA defined as moderate PA + vigorous PA), and this PA pattern is an individual trait that remains constant over time, irrespective of therapy.
- More time spent in light PA, but not in high-level PA, on admission is a significant risk factor for lower inpatient weight gain and greater weight loss between discharge and outpatient follow-up.

2. Experimental Section

2.1. Study Populations

Adolescent female patients (age 12–18 years) hospitalized between 2014–2018 in the Department of Child and Adolescent Psychiatry, Psychosomatic Medicine and Psychotherapy at Charité-Universitätsmedizin Berlin were enrolled in this study. The inclusion criteria were: AN diagnosis (restricting, purging, and atypical subtype) according to International Statistical Classification of Diseases and Related Health Problems, 10th Revision (ICD-10). Patients diagnosed with a condition in addition to AN, which might significantly affect PA behavior (e.g., half-sided paralysis) were excluded. During the inpatient stay aimed at medical stabilization and weight recovery, all patients received psychotherapy, nutrition counselling, and body-oriented therapy. According to current German guidelines, target weight for discharge was set at the 25th BMI percentile, with an expected rate of weekly weight gain between 500 and 1000 g/week. PA was limited as part of the treatment program. Patients under the 3rd BMI percentile were given strict resting hours, one hour of sitting still after each mealtime and half an hour after each in-between meal. Resting times may have been prolonged based on individual treatment decisions. PA was limited to a 15-min walk a day and a one-hour yoga class per week focusing on relaxation techniques. Patients over the 3rd percentile were allowed to attend hospital school on an hourly basis. There was no mandatory bed rest, no one-on-one surveillance of patients, and patients were able to move freely in the ward. Patients over the 15th percentile were not given specific resting times and were able to attend a physical therapy group once a week. Additionally, patients who were clinically stable had the possibility to be granted a two-day leave. Patients were given dietary plans at the beginning of the program that they were instructed to adhere to, and mealtimes were supervised by clinical staff. On average, patients were given a plan of 1860 kilocalories (kcal) per day (range: 800–2600 kcal). The daily intake was increased by 200 kcal/ week in order to enable the targeted weight gain of 500g/week. Once patients achieved this weight gain, the meal plan was adjusted accordingly. In the patients participating in the study, no feeding tubes were used during the treatment. By the end of treatment program patients were free to make their own decisions about meals and did not have a specific dietary plan. Instead, patients were encouraged to stabilize their weight by making healthy choices about their food intake based on the nutritional training they had received during the treatment program. Information about illness duration, medication, admission weight and height, comorbidities, and length of stay was obtained from medical records.

We also recruited sex- and age-matched healthy controls between 2017–2018. The Sick, Control, One stone (14 lbs./6.5 kg.), Fat, Food (SCOFF) questionnaire was used in the screening process to identify and exclude all possible participants that exhibited early signs of altered eating behavior and/or negative body perception linked to body weight. Further exclusion criteria for healthy controls were any other physical or psychiatric diseases with a significant impact on PA behavior.

In total, 106 patients were approached about participating in the study, and 56 agreed to participate. Four patients were excluded retrospectively from analysis, because they were male, 5 datasets were excluded due to being incomplete. Forty-seven patient data sets were included in this analysis.

Forty-five possible participants for the control group responded to our informational online pamphlet. All of them received the screening questionnaire and 35 returned screening questionnaires to the study office. Of the healthy participants who completed the screening, 11 were excluded as part of the screening process. Twenty-five girls participated in the study assessment and in total 20 data sets were complete and included in the data analysis.

All participants and their legal guardians (if patients were <18 years old) provided written informed consent before participating in this study. The study was approved by the institutional ethics committee of the Charité-Universitätsmedizin Berlin (Identification code: EA2/034/14; date of approval 06/24/2014) and is in accordance with the Declaration of Helsinki on 'Ethical Principles for Medical Research Involving Human Subjects'.

2.2. Anthropometry

Height and weight were measured in undergarments and empty-stomached during morning weigh-ins (7–8 a.m.) for patients at admission/discharge, and during the afternoon at follow-up, and similarly for healthy controls using a digital scale (KERN, MCB, Berlin, Germany) and a stadiometer (Sicca 2016, Hamburg, Germany).

2.3. Physical Activity Assessment

The SenseWear™ Pro3 Armband was used to assess PA. The SenseWear™ Pro3 is a two-axis accelerometer that also measures skin temperature, galvanic skin response and heat flux in order to calculate PA. It has been previously used in several studies to assess PA objectively both in controlled and free-range settings [21–23]. PA was assessed for three consecutive days, with recordings always taking place on Friday to Sunday, at the first study assessment and at outpatient follow-up. The same patients were given the SenseWear™ Pro3 within an average of 21 days of admission (first study assessment) and at the post- discharge outpatient follow-up visit, as described before [24], in order to assess longitudinal changes in activity; at both time points, patients were asked to wear the SenseWear™ Pro3 device on their dominant arm continuously for three consecutive days (data admissible if worn >20, 5 h on at least two out of the three days), except when showering, bathing, or swimming. As part of the inpatient treatment program, PA was limited; meanwhile, during post-discharge follow-up, PA was unrestricted. Healthy controls were given the SenseWear™ Pro3 Armband on one occasion on the day of their assessment and were instructed to wear the device for three consecutive days (Friday to Sunday) continuously except when showering, bathing, or swimming. PA was unrestricted in the control group.

In accordance with previous work [12,19], we defined PA intensity levels as follows:

- Sedentary behavior: ≥ 1.1 to ≤ 1.8 METs
- Light-intensity PA: > 1.8 and < 3 METs
- Moderate intensity PA: ≥ 3 to < 6 METs
- Vigorous-intensity PA: ≥ 6 METs

For the purpose of this paper, the category very light PA used previously was renamed as sedentary behavior, as new research suggests that 1.1–1.8 METs are more in line with this terminology [25]. The following activities are associated with each category. Sedentary behavior (SB) includes behavior such as lying down, watching television, eating, sitting, reading, and standing. LPA includes light physical work, walking slowly (less than 2.0 miles per hour), household errands and activities of daily life such as getting ready for bed. MPA involves activities such as descending stairs, walking for pleasure, dance practice, low impact aerobics, and bicycling (less than 10 miles per hour). Vigorous PA (VPA) includes running (<15 min/mile), competitive football or dance and high intensity cycling [26].

2.4. Statistical Analysis

A p-value of 0.05 was set as the significance threshold. All variables were tested two-sided. Analyses were conducted using R version 3.5.3 (2019-03-11). Comparing high vs. low physical activity was limited to AN patients and was calculated via median split. Descriptive statistics were selected according to scale level as absolute and relative frequencies for categories, median, the 25th/75th percentile, and extreme values for ordinal data, and the mean, standard deviation, and extreme values for normally distributed continuous measures. Group comparisons were performed using Fisher's exact test, the Wilcoxon rank sum test, and a t-test, accordingly. Correlations between measures were computed using the Spearman rank correlation. Range-based variability was calculated using the Siegel-Tukey test for equality in variability with adjustments for the median.

3. Results

3.1. Characterization of the Study Population

Within the study population of 47 patients, 25 patients (53%) were diagnosed with restrictive, 11 (23%) with purging, and 11 (23%) with atypical AN. Twenty-eight patients (60%) had their first inpatient admission, and, for the remaining patients, the number of prior inpatient therapies varied from 1 to 4. The mean illness duration was 11 months, ranging from 6.2–16.8 months. Thirty patients (64%) had comorbidities, including major depression ($n = 9$; 19%), borderline personality disorder ($n = 3$; 6%), anxiety disorders ($n = 5$; 11%), and obsessive-compulsive disorder ($n = 5$; 11%). Only eight patients (17%) received psychopharmacological medications, i.e., stimulating antidepressants ($n = 4$; 9%) and antipsychotics ($n = 2$; 4%). Three patients received oral contraceptives (6%). None of the healthy controls took any psychopharmacological medication, and 4 participants (20%) took oral contraceptives. The time between admission and first study assessment was on average 21 (2–50) days, and during this time, the patients' weight had increased by 0.9 ± 1.1 (−2.6–3.5) kilogram (kg). Table 1 shows the clinical characteristics and PA parameters of the AN patients on admission compared to healthy controls. The number of steps was significantly lower in AN patients ($p = 0.048$), but there was no between-group difference in the range of steps. AN patients spent significantly more time in light PA ($p < 0.001$) and less in moderate PA ($p = 0.009$) than healthy controls.

Table 1. General characteristics and physical activity parameters of patients with AN at first study assessment compared to healthy controls.

Participant Characteristics and PA	AN Total ($n = 47$)	Healthy Controls ($n = 20$)	p-Value
Age, years	15.70 (14.68/16.64) (12.44–17.85)	15.02 (13.59/15.84) (12.07–17.86)	0.139
Height, centimeters	164.3 ± 6.4 (150.2–183.0)	165.1 ± 7.1 (153.0–178.0)	0.672
Weight, kilograms	42.2 ± 6.0 (31.3–58.2)	57.3 ± 9.4 (38.8–70.8)	<0.001
BMI, kilogram/meter^2	15.60 ± 1.78 (12.80–20.40)	20.96 ± 2.88 (16.00–27.60)	<0.001
BMI, percentile	4.6 ± 9.9 (0.0–43.0)	51.8 ± 25.5 (7.0–93.0)	<0.001
Steps	8430 (6522/10398) (2026–26439)	11390 (8261/13680) (4427–23139)	0.048
Sedentary behavior (min) (≥1.1 to ≤1.8 METs)	705 (624/765) (189–868)	647 (557/732) (386–853)	0.118
Light PA (min) (>1.8 and <3 METs)	105 (73/204) (41–530)	55 (42/88) (14–303)	<0.001
Moderate PA (min) (≥3 to <6 METs)	77.0 (44.3/114.2) (3.0–268.0)	121.5 (82.3/188.2) (25.0–302.0)	0.009
Vigorous PA (min) (≥6 METs)	2.0 (0.0/10.2) (0.0–212.0)	2.0 (0.4/15.8) (0.0–55.0)	0.697

Values are means ± SDs (range) (first quartile/ third quartile). AN, anorexia nervosa; BMI, body mass index; MET, metabolic equivalent of task; PA, physical activity.

3.2. General Parameters and Physical Activity of AN Patients and Healthy Controls

The median length of stay for all patients was 17.0 weeks (range: 9.0 to 28.4 weeks), with a weight change from admission to discharge from 42.2 ± 6.0 to 48.1 ± 4.8 kg (total weight gain: 5.96 ± 3.62 kg; rate of weight gain: 391 ± 245 g/week). Of the 47 patients, 25 (53%) returned for outpatient follow-up, 36 days (range: 27–119 days) after discharge. This subgroup had a body weight increase from 41.9 ± 4.4 kg to 48.9 ± 3.1 kg during hospitalization that lasted 17.0 (9.0 to 28.4) weeks, which translates into an increase of 6.98 ± 3.45 kg and a rate of weight gain of 445 ± 241 g/week. Compared to the patients who returned, the patients not returning for a follow-up visit had similar admission BMI and PA parameters, but were significantly younger ($p = 0.006$). On average, weight between discharge and follow-up remained constant at 48.3 ± 3.8 kg ($p = 0.102$; range: −3.8 to +3.4). However, at follow-up, body weight and BMI of the AN patients remained significantly lower than in healthy controls ($p < 0.001$).

Clinical characteristics and PA of the patient subgroup returning for their follow-up in comparison with healthy controls are shown in Table 2. At the first study assessment, AN patients had significantly lower body weight ($p < 0.001$), BMI ($p < 0.001$), and BMI percentile ($p < 0.001$), and spent significantly more time in light PA than healthy controls ($p < 0.001$). At outpatient follow-up, AN patients were significantly older ($p < 0.001$), had a significantly lower body weight ($p < 0.001$), BMI ($p < 0.001$), BMI percentile ($p < 0.001$), and spent more time in light PA ($p = 0.039$) and vigorous PA ($p = 0.006$) than healthy controls. From admission to follow-up, AN patients gained significant weight ($p < 0.001$), BMI ($p < 0.001$) and BMI percentile ($p < 0.001$), had higher number of daily steps ($p = 0.037$), and spent significantly less time in light PA ($p = 0.008$) and more time in vigorous PA ($p < 0.001$).

Table 2. General characteristics and PA parameters for AN patients at first study assessment, AN patients at outpatient follow-up and healthy controls °.

Participant Characteristics and PA	AN (First Study Assessment) ($n = 25$)	AN (Follow-Up) ($n = 25$)	Healthy Controls ($n = 20$)
Age, years	16.49 (15.08/17.38) (12.44–17.85)	16.90 (15.49/17.82) [b] (12.88–18.20)	15.02 (13.59/15.84) [2] (12.07–17.86)
Height, centimeters	165.4 ± 5.5 (156.3–183.0)	164.9 ± 5.1 [a] (156.6–181.3)	165.1 ± 7.1 (153.0–178.0)
Weight, kilograms	41.9 ± 4.4 (35.3– 53.0)	48.3 ± 3.8 [b] (41.1–56.6)	57.3 ± 9.4 [II 2] (38.8–70.8)
BMI, kilogram/meter^2	15.34 ±1.72 (12.80–20.40)	17.87 ± 1.56 [b] (14.50–21.80)	20.96 ± 2.88 [II 2] (16.00–27.60)
BMI, percentile	2.8 ± 8.9 (0.0–43.0)	13.2 ± 13.7 [b] (0.0–61.0)	51.8 ± 25.5 [II 2] (7.0–93.0)
Steps	7821 (5948/9296) (2753–23923)	10475 (8612/14975) [a] (646–23273)	11390 (8261/13680) (4427–23139)
Sedentary behavior (min) (≥1.1 to ≤ 1.8 METs)	712 (634/760) (483–868)	681 (636/747) (499–848)	647 (557/732) (386–853)
Light PA (min) (>1.8 and < 3 METs)	103.0 (89.7/155.7) (41.0–293.0)	90.0 (64.0/117.7) [a] (49.0–162.0)	55.0 (41.8/88.1) [II 2] (14.0–303.0)
Moderate PA (min) (≥3 to < 6 METs)	73.0 (35.7/108.7) (22.0–268.0)	96.0 (73.0/132.3) (3.0–275.0)	121.5 (82.3/188.2) (25.0–302.0)
Vigorous PA (min) (≥6 METs)	1.0 (0.0/3.3) (0.0–23.0)	13.0 (5.0/33.3) [b] (0.0–116.0)	2.0 (0.4/15.8) [1] (0.0–55.0)

° The values are means ± SDs (range) (first quartile/ third quartile). AN, anorexia nervosa; BMI, body mass index; MET, metabolic equivalent of task; PA, physical activity; AN (first study assessment) vs. AN (follow-up): [a], $p < 0.05$; [b], $p < 0.01$; AN (first study assessment) vs. healthy controls: [II], $p < 0.01$; AN (follow-up) vs. healthy controls: [1], $p < 0.05$; [2], $p < 0.01$.

3.3. Light PA in AN Patients Over Time

As shown in Figure 1, total time spent in light PA in AN patients decreased significantly between the first study assessment and follow-up ($p = 0.008$). Nevertheless, at follow-up a significant difference between low light PA and high light PA patients remained, as high light PA patients continued to show higher levels of light PA at follow-up ($p = 0.003$). When analyzing the subgroups separately, the decrease in light PA over time was only significant in the group with high baseline light PA ($n = 12$, $p < 0.001$), and not in the low light PA group ($n = 13$, $p = 0.147$).

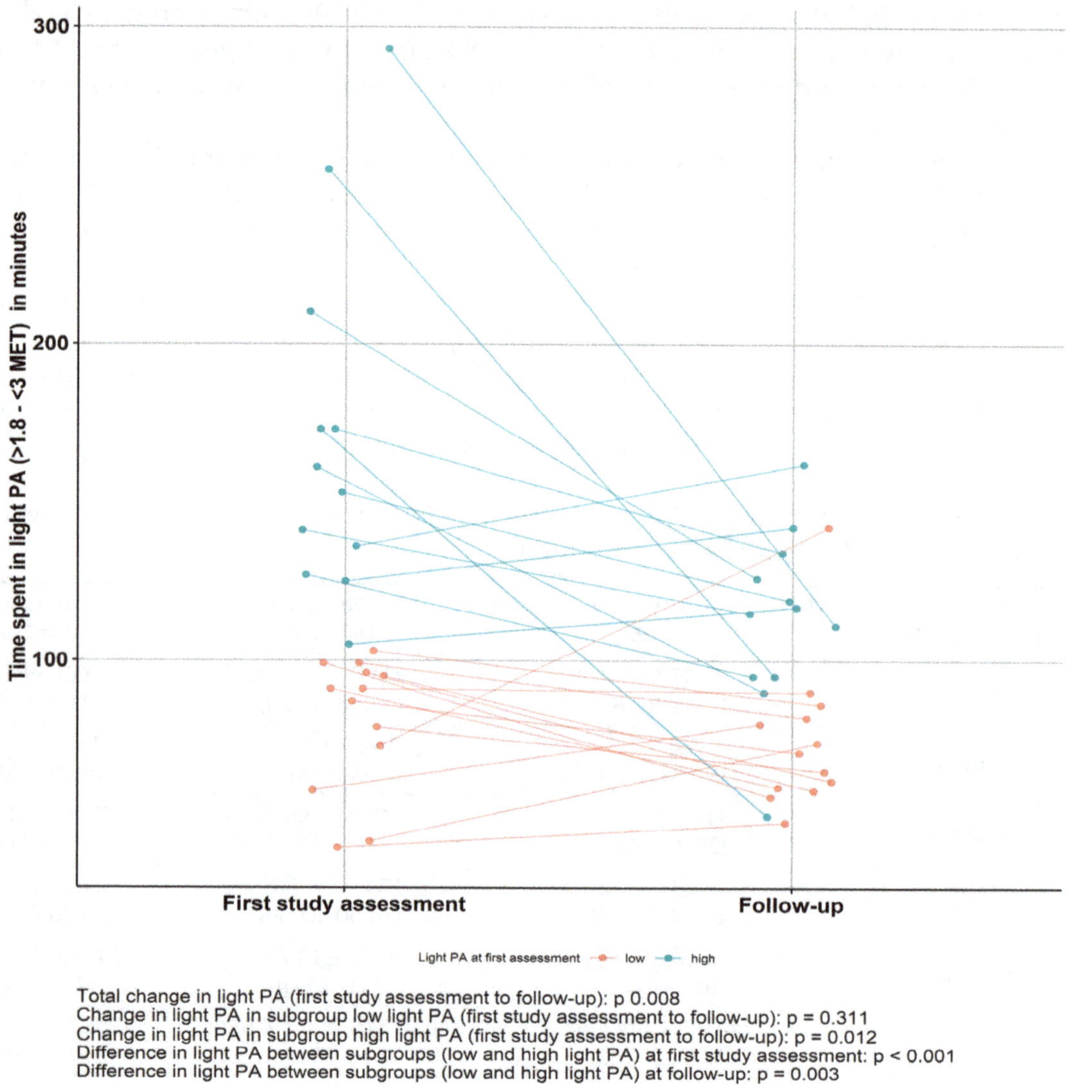

Figure 1. Light physical activity (PA) patterns in anorexia nervosa (AN) patients over time grouped by median split based on light PA at first study assessment (low light PA, $n = 13$; high light PA, $n = 12$).

3.4. Impact of light PA/ High-Level PA at Admission on Weight Trajectory

Compared to patients with low baseline light PA ($n = 13$), those with high baseline light PA ($n = 12$) showed a significantly higher inpatient BMI percentage increase, but less significant outpatient BMI percentage improvement (Table 3). Although the average time spent in high-level PA was short, increased high-level PA had a negative impact on inpatient BMI percentage change, as patients with higher baseline levels of high-level PA ($n = 11$) had significantly lower inpatient BMI percentage change than those with lower baseline levels of high-level PA ($n = 14$). Nevertheless, there were no differences in BMI percentage change in the outpatient setting (Table 3).

Table 3. Impact of light PA and high-level PA in anorexia nervosa patients at admission on BMI trajectory (BMI percentage change) from admission to discharge and from discharge to outpatient follow-up.

Weight Trajectory in PA Subgroups	Low Light PA (n = 13)	High Light PA (n = 12)	p-value	Low HLPA (n = 14)	High HLPA (n = 11)	p-value
Inpatient BMI percentage change (admission to discharge)	12.0 ± 9.7 (−3.6–33.6)	18.2 ± 10.0 (−0.5–38.6)	0.037	21.3 ± 9.7 (7.7–38.6)	13.43 ± 8.50 (−0.52–25.83)	0.045
Outpatient BMI percentage change (discharge to follow-up)	0.80 ± 3.61 (−3.70–9.42)	−2.28 ± 3.63 (−7.59–4.49)	0.045	−0.91 ± 3.90 (−6.25–9.42)	−0.38 ± 4.02 (−7.59–5.96)	0.740

Values are means ± SDs (range) (first quartile/ third quartile); unit = %; BMI, body mass index; HLPA, high level physical activity; PA, physical activity.

3.5. Characteristics of Patients Grouped by Low/High Levels of Light PA and Longitudinal Impact of Time Spent in Light PA

Comparing the two subgroups of patients (low light PA, n = 23; high light PA, n = 24) at admission, there were no differences with regards to AN subtype, comorbidities, medication, the presence of amenorrhea, hormonal contraception, age, and duration of illness (Ref. Table A1). The two subgroups presented a similar duration of inpatient stay and height. However, patients with high levels of light PA did have a significantly lower weight ($p = 0.015$), BMI ($p < 0.001$), and BMI percentile ($p = 0.026$) than low light PA patients. This difference was still present at discharge, where high light PA AN patients continued to present a significantly lower weight ($p < 0.001$), BMI ($p < 0.001$), and BMI percentile ($p = 0.018$). There was no significant difference in the BMI change between the first study assessment and discharge, or in daily steps. High light PA AN patients spent less time in sedentary behavior than low light PA AN patients ($p < 0.001$), but had similar levels of moderate PA and vigorous PA.

At outpatient follow-up, there was no significant difference with regards to age and height between the two subgroups. High light PA AN had significantly lower weight ($p = 0.003$) and BMI percentile ($p = 0.042$); but there was no significant difference in the BMI. High light PA AN patients had a lower BMI percentage change between discharge and outpatient follow-up ($p = 0.045$). There was no significant difference in daily steps and sedentary behavior. High light PA AN patients continued to present significantly higher light PA values ($p = 0.003$). Moderate PA was comparable and high light PA AN patients presented lower amounts of vigorous PA ($p = 0.034$).

The time spent in light PA at first study assessment showed a significant association with BMI at admission ($p = 0.041$), while time spent in light PA at admission and the BMI at outpatient follow-up were only associated trend-level significance ($p = 0.059$) (Figure 2).

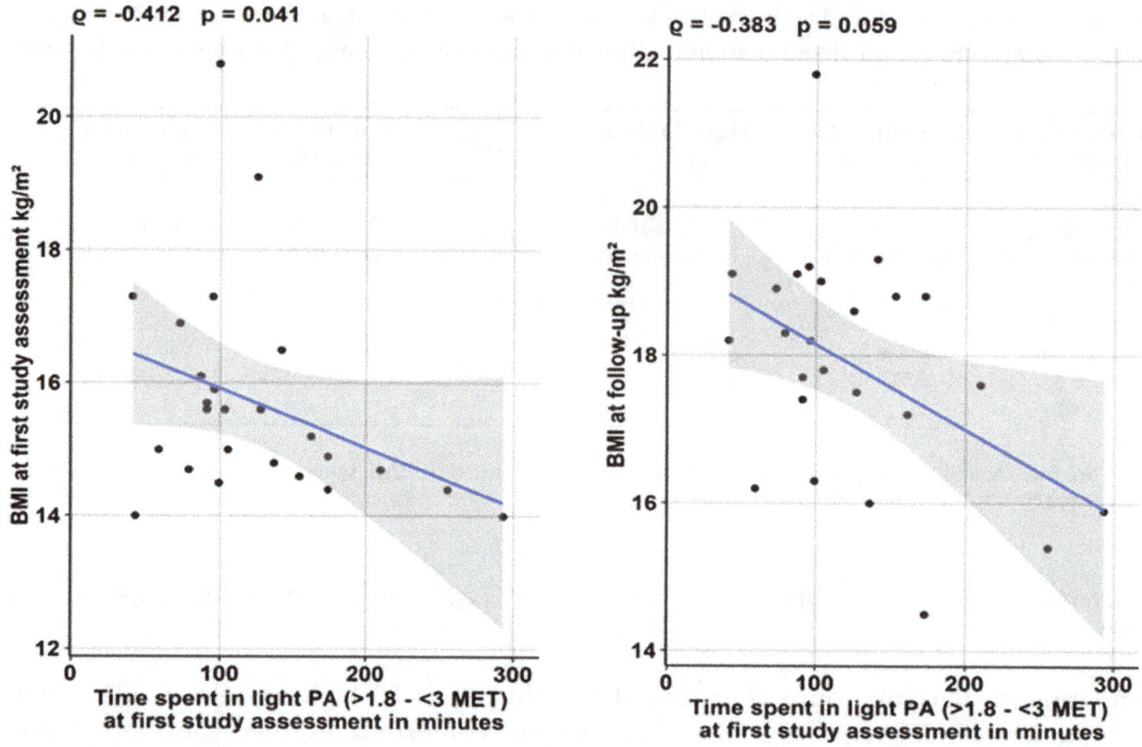

(a) (b)

Figure 2. Impact of time spent in light physical activity (PA) at first study assessment (**a**) on admission BMI and (**b**) BMI at outpatient follow-up.

4. Discussion

Objectively assessing PA patterns in adolescent AN patients compared to healthy controls and their impact on the weight trajectories of AN patients yielded following results: (1) There was no difference in sedentary behavior, AN inpatients exhibited more light PA, less moderate PA, and similar vigorous PA compared to healthy controls; (2) The time spent in light PA by AN patients decreased between admission and outpatient follow-up, but patients who had spent relatively more time in light PA on admission continued to do so at outpatient follow-up; (3) The decrease in light PA over time was only significant in the subgroup with high baseline light PA; (4) Contrary to our hypothesis, high baseline light PA was associated with a higher inpatient BMI percentage change, but as expected, with a poorer outpatient BMI percentage change; (5) High-level PA had a negative impact on inpatient but not on outpatient BMI percentage change.

4.1. Comparison of Activity Patterns Between AN Patients and Healthy Controls

Consistent with our previous study in adult AN inpatients [19], adolescent AN patients in the present study spent significantly more time in light PA than healthy, age-matched controls. High light PA was not mirrored by a high daily step count, pointing out the importance of a detailed PA assessment using intensity categories. In the literature, "fidgeting" assessed using a shoe-based monitor was higher in AN inpatients [13] than in controls and was similar when assessed using the Intelligent Device for Energy Expenditure and Activity (IDEEA™) accelerometer [8]. A comparison of data is difficult due to inconsistent definitions of light PA and different PA dimensions being assessed with varying devices. 'Fidgeting' in the second study may be more similar to sedentary behavior in the present study, which was similar between the two groups. For high-level PA, controversial results have been reported. In the present study, AN patients spent less time in moderate PA, and similar time in vigorous PA. A previous study using the Actiwatch™ (AW7) in a day hospital setting found similar amounts of high-level PA in AN and control subjects (no distinction was made between moderate PA and vigorous PA) [27], while a study using the SenseWear™ Armband in inpatient adolescent and adult AN patients reported higher high-level PA than in controls (3–6 METs, which corresponds to the category of moderate PA in the present study) [11]. The different amounts of high-level PA may be a result of different treatment programs and varying approaches to PA restriction. No information about the handling of PA during treatment was given in the cited studies. Furthermore, a variation in PA behavior patterns within the different control groups and different recruitment locations may have impacted the results.

4.2. Longitudinal Development of Light PA in AN Patients

The current study assessed light PA longitudinally at the beginning of inpatient treatment and at outpatient follow-up. While on average, light PA decreased over time, there were two characteristic subgroups: patients grouped in either high or low light PA at the first study assessment continued to exhibit these same PA patterns at follow-up. These findings lead to the question as to whether time spent in high or low light PA is an individual trait, which persists over time, regardless of therapy and setting, or whether the time needed to normalize varies and takes up more than a median of 36.0 days. Casper et al. proposed a dysregulation of PA called 'restless activation' as a phenotype of AN and hypothesized that it may be linked to improved self-esteem and wellbeing [28]. In rodent models, PA has been linked to dopamine and endocannabinoid signaling networks that suggest an addictive property [29]. Similar findings using MRI imagining in AN patients have linked altered neurological responses in the reward system to excessive exercise [30]. We are only aware of one comparable study, which reported a trend for increased time spent on feet between low-weight and weight restored AN patients, while 'fidgeting' did not vary when using the IDEEA™ [8]. The varying age of the study populations (adolescent and adult patients vs. only adolescents in the present study), the different admission BMIs (16.1 ± 1.0 vs. 15.6 ± 1.8 in the current study), and the different measurement instruments may have impacted PA behaviors and readings.

4.3. Impact of PA Patterns on Weight Trajectory

Contrary to our hypothesis, increased time spent in light PA was linked to a higher inpatient BMI percentage change. Previous studies on the impact of light PA on inpatient weight trajectory have yielded mixed findings. In an exploratory, non-linear model based on 50 adult AN patients, time spent in light PA was a potential predictor for poor BMI increase during inpatient treatment [19]. In adolescent and adult AN patients, time spent in light PA was inversely linked to BMI at discharge, while there was no significant relationship to BMI percentage change [19]. No association between 'fidgeting', assessed with a shoe based accelerometer, and weight gain was found in a group of 11 adolescent and adult AN patients [13]. Age differences may have led to different results, as in healthy participants, PA behaviors vary between adolescents and adults. Healthy adolescents are more active and spent more time in high-level PA than adults [31,32]. Additionally, some of these previous studies were small. In the present study, the group of patients with high light PA had a significantly lower BMI at admission; a higher BMI increase in this group may have been caused the program's discharge weight target at the 25th BMI percentile requiring more weight gain in this group in order to be discharged. There also might be a link between increased LPA and muscle gain as it has been shown that LPA can improve muscle strength [33], which may contribute to the increased BMI percentage change within the high LPA group. The present study found a statistical trend ($p = 0.059$) for an inverse association between high light PA at admission and inpatient BMI gain, as well as a significant inverse association with BMI percentile at follow-up. Therefore, the assessment of PA patterns at admission might hold the potential to identify patients at risk of poor weight gain. The time spent on feet in 61 AN patients at the assessment point weight, but not at low weight, was linked to a poorer weight trajectory at the 12 month follow-up [8]. Heterogeneous results may thus be caused either by different time points of PA assessment during treatment or by different follow-up durations. Consistent with our previous study [19], high-level PA was inversely associated with inpatient BMI change. Conversely, in a group of 88 AN patients in a day hospital setting, high-level PA assessed using an Actiwatch™ (AW7) was directly associated with achieving BMI > 18.5 and with decreased AN-specific cognitions and reduced binge/purge behavior [27]. Different settings (inpatient vs. day hospital treatment) may have impacted the patients' ability to exercise at higher intensities and the impact high-level PA had on the weight trajectory.

When assessing the impact of PA patterns on weigh status in healthy adolescents, two trends can be observed: high levels of high-level PA (HLPA) are associated with a lower BMI and a lower body fat mass. Additionally, more time in sedentary behavior is linked to a higher BMI and higher body fat [34–36]. These trends are also replicable when analyzing only healthy female participants [37,38]. Further sedentary behavior in both gender-mixed groups and female-only groups was also linked to a higher BMI increase in the long run [39,40]. However, in a sample of female secondary school students, there was no correlation between being underweight and PA patterns (both SB and HLPA) [41].

4.4. Limitations

The limitations of this study first include the prolonged and variable times between the admission and the first study assessment, and between discharge and the follow-up assessment. Second, a high drop-out (n = 22) may have reduced the generalizability of the findings, yet comparable studies had both similar (n = 26) [8] and lower (n = 3) [16] drop-outs. Third, there was a significant age difference between the patients at follow-up and the healthy controls. Fourth, the validity of the SenseWear™ Pro 3 Armand has not been assessed for PA parameters in underweight AN patients; thus, the validity of the obtained data is unknown. Fifth different cutoff points for PA are used in the literature. We used a definition for sedentary behavior (very low PA) with a cutoff point at 1.8 METs [42] to establish compatibility with our previous work [12,19], but a new definition proposed a cutoff point at 1.5 METs [25]. Therefore, the actual activities associated with sedentary behavior in this study may not fully represent all aspects of sedentary behavior. Sixth, it is unknown if wearing a SenseWear™ Armand affects PA behavior. Seventh, no data about the caloric intake of patients after discharge were obtained. Finally, potential differences in PA based on socioeconomic status were not assessed. However, despite these limitations, this is one of the first studies to assess the longitudinal development of light PA and its impact on weight trajectories in adolescent AN patients.

5. Conclusions

In summary, PA patterns vary between AN patients and healthy controls and impact weight trajectories in AN patients. Our study aims to raise awareness of the different types of hyperactivity and their impact on the weight development of AN patients. Our research may provide a foundation for future research into the benefit of objectively measured PA patterns in AN patients and may allow for a better understanding of PA as a disease maintaining factor as well as the identification of high risk patients at the beginning of treatment. This could enable research into new treatment interventions that are tailored to the different PA subgroups of patients, such as high light PA patients. An early intervention that focuses on reducing light PA hyperactivity from the beginning of the treatment program on may positively impact short- and long-term weight development. Our study shows that the detailed assessment of PA patterns, rather than general PA parameters, such as steps or activity counts, provides valuable insight into PA behavior of AN patients.

Author Contributions: Conceptualization, V.H., T.H., A.S.; Methodology, V.H., T.H., A.S.; Formal analysis and investigation, M.K.; Resources, Swiss Anorexia Nervosa Foundation (Project Number 23-13); Data curation, J.G., M.K.; writing-original draft preparation, M.K.; writing-review and editing, V.H., C.U.C., T.H. and A.S.; visualization, M.K.; supervision, V.H., C.U.C.; project administration, V.H.; funding acquisition, V.H. All authors have read and agreed to the published version of the manuscript.

Acknowledgments: We thank Andreas Busjahn for assistance with biostatistical analysis and Nathalie Engelhaus for support with data assessment of healthy controls.

Appendix A

Table A1. General characteristics and PA parameters of AN patients at admission, first study assessment and discharge grouped by a low/high level of light PA (median split).

Participant Characteristics and PA	Low Light PA (n = 23)	High Light PA (n = 24)	p-value
Duration of illness, months	12.0 (7.3/15.8) (3.0–64.0)	9.0 (4.0/17.6) (1.0–56.0)	0.176
Admission age, y	15.82 (14.87/16.64) (13.78–17.85)	15.11 (13.89/16.70) (12.44–17.82)	0.250
Admission height, cm	166.7 ± 6.4 (159.0–183.0)	164.1 ± 4.3 (156.3–170.0)	0.253
Admission weight, kg	43.9 ± 4.1 (39.6–53.0)	39.8 ± 3.8 (35.3–46.5)	0.015
Admission BMI, kg/m^2	15.84 ± 1.73 (13.90–20.40)	14.80 ± 1.61 (12.80–19.10)	0.135
Admission BMI percentile (%)	4.1 ± 11.7 (0.0–43.0)	1.33 ± 4.31 (0.00–15.00)	0.443
Steps	8586 (7136/9735) (2753–24536)	7870 (6159/12179) (2026–26439)	0.882
Sedentary behavior (min) (≥1.1 to ≤1.8 METs)	730 (698/789) (581–856)	646 (497/715) (189–868)	<0.001
Light PA (min) (>1.8 and <3 METs)	73.0 (54.3/93.5) (41.0–103.0)	192 (146/273) (105–530)	<0.001
Moderate PA (min) (≥3 to <6 METs)	73.0 (46.5/103.5) (22.0–268.0)	89.5 (39.3/120.8) (3.0–241.0)	0.663
Vigorous PA (min) (≥6 METs)	2.0 (1.0/10.0) (0.0–54.0)	1.5 (0.0/8.9) (0.0–212.0)	0.729
Time between admission and discharge, days	95.0 (74.8/118.8) (47.0–225.0)	121.0 (88.8/135.6) (41.0–171.0)	0.097
Discharge weight, kg	51.4 ± 3.3 (45.3–61.1)	45.0 ± 3.9 (36.6–52.5)	<0.001
Discharge BMI, kg/m^2	18.38 ± 0.96 (16.50–20.50)	17.31 ± 1.15 (15.50–19.40)	<0.001
Discharge BMI percentile (%)	18.4 ± 11.1 (0.0–45.0)	11.4 ± 8.4 (0.0–36.0)	0.018
BMI change from first study assessment to discharge kg/m^2	1.85 ± 1.41 (−0.70–4.70)	2.60 ± 1.36 (−0.10–5.40)	0.072
BMI percentile change from first study assessment to discharge (%)	12.0 ± 9.7 (−3.6–33.6)	18.2 ± 10.0 (−0.5–38.6)	0.037

Values are means ± SDs (range) (first quartile/ third quartile). AN, anorexia nervosa; BMI, body mass index; METs, metabolic equivalents; PA, physical activity.

References

1. Association, American Psychiatric. *Diagnostic and Statistical Manual of Mental Disorders: Dsm-5;* Amer Psychiatric Pub Incorporated: Washington, DC, USA, 2013.
2. Solenberger, S.E. Exercise and eating disorders: A 3-year inpatient hospital record analysis. *Eat. Behav.* **2001**, *2*, 151–168. [CrossRef]
3. Achamrah, N.; Coeffier, M.; Dechelotte, P. Physical activity in patients with anorexia nervosa. *Nutr. Rev.* **2016**, *74*, 301–311. [CrossRef] [PubMed]

4. Rizk, M.; Lalanne, C.; Berthoz, S.; Kern, L.; Godart, N. Problematic Exercise in Anorexia Nervosa: Testing Potential Risk Factors against Different Definitions. *PLoS ONE* **2015**, *10*, e0143352. [CrossRef] [PubMed]
5. Keyes, A.; Woerwag-Mehta, S.; Bartholdy, S.; Koskina, A.; Middleton, B.; Connan, F.; Webster, P.; Schmidt, U.; Campbell, I.C. Physical activity and the drive to exercise in anorexia nervosa. *Int. J. Eat. Disord.* **2015**, *48*, 46–54. [CrossRef] [PubMed]
6. Alberti, M.; Galvani, C.; Capelli, C.; Lanza, M.; El Ghoch, M.; Calugi, S.; Dalle Grave, R. Physical fitness before and after weight restoration in anorexia nervosa. *J. Sports Med. Phys. Fit.* **2013**, *53*, 396–402.
7. Bratland-Sanda, S.; Sundgot-Borgen, J.; Ro, O.; Rosenvinge, J.H.; Hoffart, A.; Martinsen, E.W. "I'm not physically active - I only go for walks": Physical activity in patients with longstanding eating disorders. *Int. J. Eat. Disord.* **2010**, *43*, 88–92. [CrossRef]
8. Gianini, L.M.; Klein, D.A.; Call, C.; Walsh, B.T.; Wang, Y.; Wu, P.; Attia, E. Physical activity and post-treatment weight trajectory in anorexia nervosa. *Int. J. Eat. Disord.* **2016**, *49*, 482–489. [CrossRef]
9. Gummer, R.; Giel, K.E.; Schag, K.; Resmark, G.; Junne, F.P.; Becker, S.; Zipfel, S.; Teufel, M. High Levels of Physical Activity in Anorexia Nervosa: A Systematic Review. *Eur. Eat. Disord. Rev.* **2015**, *23*, 333–344. [CrossRef]
10. Hechler, T.; Rieger, E.; Touyz, S.; Beumont, P.; Plasqui, G.; Westerterp, K. Physical activity and body composition in outpatients recovering from anorexia nervosa and healthy controls. *Adapt. Phys. Act. Q.* **2008**, *25*, 159–173. [CrossRef]
11. El Ghoch, M.; Calugi, S.; Pellegrini, M.; Milanese, C.; Busacchi, M.; Battistini, N.C.; Bernabe, J.; Dalle Grave, R. Measured physical activity in anorexia nervosa: Features and treatment outcome. *Int. J. Eat. Disord.* **2013**, *46*, 709–712. [CrossRef]
12. Lehmann, C.S.; Hofmann, T.; Elbelt, U.; Rose, M.; Correll, C.U.; Stengel, A.; Haas, V. The Role of Objectively Measured, Altered Physical Activity Patterns for Body Mass Index Change during Inpatient Treatment in Female Patients with Anorexia Nervosa. *J. Clin. Med.* **2018**, *7*, 289. [CrossRef] [PubMed]
13. Belak, L.; Gianini, L.; Klein, D.A.; Sazonov, E.; Keegan, K.; Neustadt, E.; Walsh, B.T.; Attia, E. Measurement of fidgeting in patients with anorexia nervosa using a novel shoe-based monitor. *Eat. Behav.* **2017**, *24*, 45–48. [CrossRef] [PubMed]
14. Klein, D.A.; Mayer, L.E.; Schebendach, J.E.; Walsh, B.T. Physical activity and cortisol in anorexia nervosa. *Psychoneuroendocrinology* **2007**, *32*, 539–547. [CrossRef] [PubMed]
15. Bratland-Sanda, S.; Sundgot-Borgen, J.; Ro, O.; Rosenvinge, J.H.; Hoffart, A.; Martinsen, E.W. Physical activity and exercise dependence during inpatient treatment of longstanding eating disorders: An exploratory study of excessive and non-excessive exercisers. *Int. J. Eat. Disord.* **2010**, *43*, 266–273. [CrossRef]
16. Kostrzewa, E.; van Elburg, A.A.; Sanders, N.; Sternheim, L.; Adan, R.A.; Kas, M.J. Longitudinal changes in the physical activity of adolescents with anorexia nervosa and their influence on body composition and leptin serum levels after recovery. *PLoS ONE* **2013**, *8*, e78251. [CrossRef]
17. Dellava, J.E.; Hamer, R.M.; Kanodia, A.; Reyes-Rodriguez, M.L.; Bulik, C.M. Diet and physical activity in women recovered from anorexia nervosa: A pilot study. *Int. J. Eat. Disord.* **2011**, *44*, 376–382. [CrossRef]
18. El Ghoch, M.; Calugi, S.; Pellegrini, M.; Chignola, E.; Dalle Grave, R. Physical activity, body weight, and resumption of menses in anorexia nervosa. *Psychiatry Res.* **2016**, *246*, 507–511. [CrossRef]
19. Großer, J.; Hofmann, T.; Stengel, A.; Zeeck, A.; Winter, S.; Correll, C.H. *Psychological and Nutritional Correlates of Objectively Assessed Physical Activity in Patients with Anorexia Nervosa, Submitted*; German Association for Psychiatry, Psychotherapy and Psychosomatics Congress: Berlin, Germany, 12 January 2018.
20. Bouten, C.V.; van Marken Lichtenbelt, W.D.; Westerterp, K.R. Body mass index and daily physical activity in anorexia nervosa. *Med. Sci. Sports Exerc.* **1996**, *28*, 967–973. [CrossRef]
21. Calabro, M.A.; Lee, J.M.; Saint-Maurice, P.F.; Yoo, H.; Welk, G.J. Validity of physical activity monitors for assessing lower intensity activity in adults. *Int. J. Behav. Nutr. Phys. Act.* **2014**, *11*, 119. [CrossRef]
22. van Hoye, K.; Mortelmans, P.; Lefevre, J. Validation of the SenseWear Pro3 Armband using an incremental exercise test. *J Strength Cond. Res.* **2014**, *28*, 2806–2814. [CrossRef]
23. Johannsen, D.L.; Calabro, M.A.; Stewart, J.; Franke, W.; Rood, J.C.; Welk, G.J. Accuracy of armband monitors for measuring daily energy expenditure in healthy adults. *Med. Sci. Sports Exerc.* **2010**, *42*, 2134–2140. [CrossRef] [PubMed]

24. Stengel, A.; Haas, V.; Elbelt, U.; Correll, C.U.; Rose, M.; Hofmann, T. Leptin and Physical Activity in Adult Patients with Anorexia Nervosa: Failure to Demonstrate a Simple Linear Association. *Nutrients* **2017**, *9*, 1210. [CrossRef] [PubMed]
25. Tremblay, M.S.; Aubert, S.; Barnes, J.D.; Saunders, T.J.; Carson, V.; Latimer-Cheung, A.E.; Chastin, S.F.M.; Altenburg, T.M.; Chinapaw, M.J.M. Sedentary Behavior Research Network (SBRN)—Terminology Consensus Project process and outcome. *Int. J. Behav. Nutr. Phys. Act.* **2017**, *14*, 75. [CrossRef] [PubMed]
26. Ainsworth, B.E.; Haskell, W.L.; Herrmann, S.D.; Meckes, N.; Bassett, D.R.J.; Tudor-Locke, C.; Greer, J.L.; Vezina, J.; Whitt-Glover, M.C.; Leon, A.S. 2011 Compendium of Physical Activities: A second update of codes and MET values. *Med. Sci. Sports Exerc.* **2011**, *43*, 1575–1581. [CrossRef]
27. Sauchelli, S.; Arcelus, J.; Sanchez, I.; Riesco, N.; Jimenez-Murcia, S.; Granero, R.; Gunnard, K.; Banos, R.; Botella, C.; de la Torre, R.; et al. Physical activity in anorexia nervosa: How relevant is it to therapy response? *Eur. Psychiatry J. Assoc. Eur. Psychiatr.* **2015**, *30*, 924–931. [CrossRef]
28. Casper, R.C. Not the Function of Eating, but Spontaneous Activity and Energy Expenditure, Reflected in "Restlessness" and a "Drive for Activity" Appear to Be Dysregulated in Anorexia Nervosa: Treatment Implications. *Front. Psychol.* **2018**, *9*, 2303. [CrossRef]
29. Garland, T.J.; Schutz, H.; Chappell, M.A.; Keeney, B.K.; Meek, T.H.; Copes, L.E.; Acosta, W.; Drenowatz, C.; Maciel, R.C.; van Dijk, G.; et al. The biological control of voluntary exercise, spontaneous physical activity and daily energy expenditure in relation to obesity: Human and rodent perspectives. *J. Exp. Biol.* **2011**, *214*, 206–229. [CrossRef]
30. Kullmann, S.; Giel, K.E.; Hu, X.; Bischoff, S.C.; Teufel, M.; Thiel, A.; Zipfel, S.; Preissl, H. Impaired inhibitory control in anorexia nervosa elicited by physical activity stimuli. *Soc. Cogn. Affect Neurosci.* **2014**, *9*, 917–923. [CrossRef]
31. Gordon-Larsen, P.; Nelson, M.C.; Popkin, B.M. Longitudinal physical activity and sedentary behavior trends: Adolescence to adulthood. *Am. J. Prev. Med.* **2004**, *27*, 277–283. [CrossRef]
32. Nelson, M.C.; Gordon-Larsen, P.; Adair, L.S.; Popkin, B.M. Adolescent physical activity and sedentary behavior: Patterning and long-term maintenance. *Am. J. Prev. Med.* **2005**, *28*, 259–266. [CrossRef]
33. Chantler, I.; Szabo, C.P.; Green, K. Muscular strength changes in hospitalized anorexic patients after an eight week resistance training program. *Int. J. Sports Med.* **2006**, *27*, 660–665. [CrossRef] [PubMed]
34. Werneck, A.O.; Silva, E.C.A.; Bueno, M.R.O.; Vignadelli, L.Z.; Oyeyemi, A.L.; Romanzini, C.L.P.; Ronque, E.R.V.; Romanzini, M. Association(s) Between Objectively Measured Sedentary Behavior Patterns and Obesity Among Brazilian Adolescents. *Pediatric Exerc. Sci.* **2019**, *31*, 37–41. [CrossRef] [PubMed]
35. Augustin, N.H.; Mattocks, C.; Cooper, A.R.; Ness, A.R.; Faraway, J.J. Modelling fat mass as a function of weekly physical activity profiles measured by actigraph accelerometers. *Physiol. Meas.* **2012**, *33*, 1831–1839. [CrossRef] [PubMed]
36. Machado-Rodrigues, A.M.; Coelho-e-Silva, M.J.; Mota, J.; Padez, C.; Ronque, E.; Cumming, S.P.; Malina, R.M. Cardiorespiratory fitness, weight status and objectively measured sedentary behaviour and physical activity in rural and urban Portuguese adolescents. *J. Child Health Care Prof. Work. Child. Hosp. Community* **2012**, *16*, 166–177. [CrossRef] [PubMed]
37. Allender, S.; Kremer, P.; de Silva-Sanigorski, A.; Lacy, K.; Millar, L.; Mathews, L.; Malakellis, M.; Swinburn, B. Associations between activity-related behaviours and standardized BMI among Australian adolescents. *J. Sci. Med. Sport* **2011**, *14*, 512–521. [CrossRef] [PubMed]
38. Jones, M.A.; Skidmore, P.M.; Stoner, L.; Harrex, H.; Saeedi, P.; Black, K.; Barone Gibbs, B. Associations of accelerometer-measured sedentary time, sedentary bouts, and physical activity with adiposity and fitness in children. *J. Sports Sci.* **2020**, *38*, 114–120. [CrossRef]
39. Altenburg, T.M.; Singh, A.S.; van Mechelen, W.; Brug, J.; Chinapaw, M.J. Direction of the association between body fatness and self-reported screen time in Dutch adolescents. *Int. J. Behav. Nutr. Phys. Act.* **2012**, *9*, 4. [CrossRef]
40. Hands, B.P.; Chivers, P.T.; Parker, H.E.; Beilin, L.; Kendall, G.; Larkin, D. The associations between physical activity, screen time and weight from 6 to 14 yrs: The Raine Study. *J. Sci. Med. Sport* **2011**, *14*, 397–403. [CrossRef]

41. Kantanista, A.; Osinski, W. Underweight in 14 to 16 year-old girls and boys: Prevalence and associations with physical activity and sedentary activities. *Ann. Agric. Environ. Med. Aaem* **2014**, *21*, 114–119.
42. Ainsworth, B.E.; Haskell, W.L.; Whitt, M.C.; Irwin, M.L.; Swartz, A.M.; Strath, S.J.; O'Brien, W.L.; Bassett, D.R.J.; Schmitz, K.H.; Emplaincourt, P.O.; et al. Compendium of physical activities: An update of activity codes and MET intensities. *Med. Sci. Sports Exerc.* **2000**, *32*, S498–S504. [CrossRef]

Permissions

All chapters in this book were first published by MDPI; hereby published with permission under the Creative Commons Attribution License or equivalent. Every chapter published in this book has been scrutinized by our experts. Their significance has been extensively debated. The topics covered herein carry significant findings which will fuel the growth of the discipline. They may even be implemented as practical applications or may be referred to as a beginning point for another development.

The contributors of this book come from diverse backgrounds, making this book a truly international effort. This book will bring forth new frontiers with its revolutionizing research information and detailed analysis of the nascent developments around the world.

We would like to thank all the contributing authors for lending their expertise to make the book truly unique. They have played a crucial role in the development of this book. Without their invaluable contributions this book wouldn't have been possible. They have made vital efforts to compile up to date information on the varied aspects of this subject to make this book a valuable addition to the collection of many professionals and students.

This book was conceptualized with the vision of imparting up-to-date information and advanced data in this field. To ensure the same, a matchless editorial board was set up. Every individual on the board went through rigorous rounds of assessment to prove their worth. After which they invested a large part of their time researching and compiling the most relevant data for our readers.

The editorial board has been involved in producing this book since its inception. They have spent rigorous hours researching and exploring the diverse topics which have resulted in the successful publishing of this book. They have passed on their knowledge of decades through this book. To expedite this challenging task, the publisher supported the team at every step. A small team of assistant editors was also appointed to further simplify the editing procedure and attain best results for the readers.

Apart from the editorial board, the designing team has also invested a significant amount of their time in understanding the subject and creating the most relevant covers. They scrutinized every image to scout for the most suitable representation of the subject and create an appropriate cover for the book.

The publishing team has been an ardent support to the editorial, designing and production team. Their endless efforts to recruit the best for this project, has resulted in the accomplishment of this book. They are a veteran in the field of academics and their pool of knowledge is as vast as their experience in printing. Their expertise and guidance has proved useful at every step. Their uncompromising quality standards have made this book an exceptional effort. Their encouragement from time to time has been an inspiration for everyone.

The publisher and the editorial board hope that this book will prove to be a valuable piece of knowledge for researchers, students, practitioners and scholars across the globe.

List of Contributors

Howard Steiger
Eating Disorders Continuum, Douglas University Institute, Montreal, Quebec H4H 1R3, Canada
Douglas Institute Research Centre, McGill University, Montreal, Quebec H4H 1R3, Canada
Department of Psychiatry, McGill University, Montreal, Quebec H3A 1A1, Canada

Linda Booij
Department of Psychiatry, McGill University, Montreal, Quebec H3A 1A1, Canada
Department of Psychology, Concordia University, Montreal, Quebec H4B 1R6, Canada
Sainte-Justine Hospital Research Centre, University of Montreal, Montreal, Quebec H3T 1C5, Canada

Shanon L. Casperson
USDA, Agricultural Research Service, Grand Forks Human Nutrition Research Center, 2420 2nd Ave. North, Grand Forks, ND 58203-9034, USA

Lisa Lanza, Eram Albajri and Jennifer A. Nasser
College of Nursing and Health Professions, Drexel University, 1601 Cherry St MS31030 RM 389, Philadelphia, PA 19102-1320, USA

Verónica Parent Mathias
Department of Human Physiology, Histology, Pathological Anatomy and Physical Education and Sport, University of Málaga-Andalucía Tech, 29071 Málaga, Spain

Jerónimo C. García-Romero
Department of Human Physiology, Histology, Pathological Anatomy and Physical Education and Sport, University of Málaga-Andalucía Tech, 29071 Málaga, Spain
The Biomedical Research Institute of Málaga (IBIMA), 29010 Málaga, Spain

José Ramón Alvero-Cruz
Department of Human Physiology, Histology, Pathological Anatomy and Physical Education and Sport, University of Málaga-Andalucía Tech, 29071 Málaga, Spain
The Biomedical Research Institute of Málaga (IBIMA), 29010 Málaga, Spain
Edificio López de Peñalver, Campus de Teatinos, Universidad de Málaga, 29071 Málaga, Spain

Tracy Burrows and Megan Whatnall
Priority Research Centre for Physical Activity and Nutrition, University of Newcastle, Callaghan, NSW 2308, Australia
School of Health Sciences, Faculty of Health and Medicine, University of Newcastle, Callaghan, NSW 2308, Australia

Antonio Verdejo-Garcia and Adrian Carter
Turner Institute for Brain and Mental Health, Monash University, Clayton, VIC 3800, Australia

Robyn M. Brown
Florey Institute of Neuroscience and Mental Health, University of Melbourne, Parkville, VIC 3052, Australia

Zane B. Andrews
Florey Institute of Neuroscience and Mental Health, University of Melbourne, Parkville, VIC 3052, Australia
Monash Biomedicine Discovery Institute and Department of Physiology, Monash University, Clayton, VIC 3800, Australia

Chris V. Dayas
School of Biomedical Sciences & Pharmacy, Faculty of Health and Medicine, University of Newcastle, Callaghan, NSW 2308, Australia
Hunter Medical Research Institute (HMRI), New Lambton Heights, NSW 2305, Australia

Charlotte A. Hardman
Department of Psychology, Institute of Population Health, University of Liverpool, Liverpool L69 7ZA, UK

Natalie Loxton
School of Applied Psychology, Griffith University, Brisbane, QLD 4122, Australia
Centre for Youth Substance Abuse Research, University of Queensland, Brisbane, QLD 4072, Australia

Priya Sumithran
Department of Medicine (Austin), University of Melbourne, Heidelberg, VIC 3084, Australia
Department of Endocrinology, Austin Health, Heidelberg Heights, VIC 3081, Australia

David Wiss
Department of Community Health Sciences, Fielding School of Public Health, University of California Los Angeles, Los Angeles, CA 90025, USA

Timothy Brewerton
Department of Psychiatry and Behavioral Sciences, Medical University of South Carolina, Charleston, SC 29425, USA

Mohamed Abdulkadir
Department of Psychiatry, Faculty of Medicine, University of Geneva, CH–1205 Geneva, Switzerland

Bianca L. De Stavola
Great Ormond Street Institute of Child Health, University College London, London WC1N 1EH, UK

Moritz Herle
Great Ormond Street Institute of Child Health, University College London, London WC1N 1EH, UK
Department of Biostatistics & Health Informatics, Institute of Psychiatry, Psychology & Neuroscience, King's College London, London SE5 8AB, UK

Christopher Hübel
Social, Genetic & Developmental Psychiatry Centre, Institute of Psychiatry, Psychology & Neuroscience, King's College London, London SE5 8AF, UK
UK National Institute for Health Research (NIHR) Biomedical Research Centre, South London and Maudsley Hospital, London SE5 8AF, UK
Department of Medical Epidemiology and Biostatistics, Karolinska Institutet, SE-171 77 Stockholm, Sweden

Diana L. Santos Ferreira
Medical Research Council Integrative Epidemiology, University of Bristol, Bristol BS8 2BN, UK
Population Health Sciences, Bristol Medical School, University of Bristol, Bristol BS8 2PS, UK

Ruth J. F. Loos
The Charles Bronfman Institute for Personalized Medicine, The Mindich Child Health and Development Institute, Icahn School of Medicine at Mount Sinai, New York, NY 10029, USA

Rachel Bryant-Waugh
Maudsley Centre for Child and Adolescent Eating Disorders, Michael Rutter Centre for Children and Young People, Maudsley Hospital, London SE5 8AZ, UK

Cynthia M. Bulik
Department of Medical Epidemiology and Biostatistics, Karolinska Institutet, SE-171 77 Stockholm, Sweden
Department of Psychiatry, University of North Carolina at Chapel Hill, Chapel Hill, NC 27599, USA
Department of Nutrition, University of North Carolina at Chapel Hill, Chapel Hill, NC 27599, USA

Nadia Micali
Department of Psychiatry, Faculty of Medicine, University of Geneva, CH–1205 Geneva, Switzerland
Great Ormond Street Institute of Child Health, University College London, London WC1N 1EH, UK
Department of Pediatrics, Gynecology and Obstetrics, University of Geneva, CH–1205 Geneva, Switzerland

Edgar Oliveira, Mária de Fátima Vasques, Cristiane Ruiz Durante, Daniela Pereira, Janice Rico Cabral, Paula Sanches Bernstein and Hermano Tavares
Department of Psychiatry, University of São Paulo, Rua Artur de Azevedo, 145, Cerqueira Cesar, São Paulo CEP 05404-010, SP, Brasil

Hyoun S. Kim
Department of Psychology, Ryerson University, 350 Victoria Street, Toronto, ON M5B 2K3, Canada

Emilie Lacroix and Ximena Garcia
Department of Psychology, University of Calgary, 2500 University Drive, NW, Calgary, AB T2N 1N4, Canada

Emma V. Ritchie
Department of Psychology, York University, 4700 Keele St, Toronto, ON M3J 1P3, Canada

May Thet Khine, Atsuhiko Ota, Akiko Fujisawa, Yuanying Li, Hisao Naito and Hiroshi Yatsuya
Department of Public Health, Fujita Health University School of Medicine, 1-98 Dengakugakubo, Kutsukake-cho, Toyoake, Aichi 470-1192, Japan

Ashley N. Gearhardt
Department of Psychology, University of Michigan, 2268 East Hall, 530 Church Street, Ann Arbor, MI 48109, USA

Mamiko Morita and Atsuko Minagawa
Faculty of Nursing, Fujita Health University School of Health Sciences, 1-98 Dengakugakubo, Kutsukake-cho, Toyoake, Aichi 470-1192, Japan

Stephanie Cassin
Department of Psychology, Ryerson University, Toronto, ON M5B 2K3, Canada
Department of Psychiatry, University of Toronto, Toronto, ON M5T 1R8, Canada
Centre for Mental Health, University Health Network, Toronto, ON M5T 2S8, Canada

Samantha Leung
Centre for Mental Health, University Health Network, Toronto, ON M5T 2S8, Canada
Bariatric Surgery Program, Toronto Western Hospital, Toronto, ON M5T 2S8, Canada

Raed Hawa and Susan Wnuk
Department of Psychiatry, University of Toronto, Toronto, ON M5T 1R8, Canada
Centre for Mental Health, University Health Network, Toronto, ON M5T 2S8, Canada
Bariatric Surgery Program, Toronto Western Hospital, Toronto, ON M5T 2S8, Canada

Timothy Jackson
Bariatric Surgery Program, Toronto Western Hospital, Toronto, ON M5T 2S8, Canada
Division of General Surgery, University Health Network, University of Toronto, Toronto, ON M5T 2S8, Canada

Sanjeev Sockalingam
Department of Psychiatry, University of Toronto, Toronto, ON M5T 1R8, Canada
Centre for Mental Health, University Health Network, Toronto, ON M5T 2S8, Canada
Bariatric Surgery Program, Toronto Western Hospital, Toronto, ON M5T 2S8, Canada
Centre for Addiction and Mental Health, Toronto, ON M5S 2S1, Canada

Roland Dardennes and Guillaume Lavoisy
GHU Paris Psychiatrie et Neurosciences, Hôpital Sainte-Anne, F-75014 Paris, France

Kanwal Preet Kochhar
Department of Physiology, All India Institute of Medical Sciences (AIIMS), New Delhi 110029, India

Naim Akhtar Khan
Nutritional Physiology and Toxicology (NUTox), UMR INSERM U1231, University of Bourgogne and Franche-Comte (UBFC), 6 boulevard Gabriel, 21000 Dijon, France

Rachel C. Adams, Jemma Sedgmond, Leah Maizey and Christopher D. Chambers
CUBRIC, School of Psychology, Cardiff University, Maindy Road, Cardiff CF24 4HQ, UK

Natalia S. Lawrence
School of Psychology, College of Life and Environmental Sciences, University of Exeter, Exeter EX4 4QG, UK

Philibert Duriez and Philip Gorwood
Institute of Psychiatry and Neuroscience of Paris (IPNP), Université de Paris, INSERM UMR-S 1266, F-75014 Paris, France
GHU Paris Psychiatrie et Neurosciences, Hôpital Sainte-Anne, F-75014 Paris, France

Lauralee Robichon, Dominique Grouselle, Nicolas Ramoz and Virginie Tolle
Institute of Psychiatry and Neuroscience of Paris (IPNP), Université de Paris, INSERM UMR-S 1266, F-75014 Paris, France

Siddharth Sarkar
Department of Psychiatry and National Drug Dependence Treatment Centre (NDDTC), All India Institute of Medical Sciences (AIIMS), New Delhi 110029, India

Jacques Epelbaum
Institute of Psychiatry and Neuroscience of Paris (IPNP), Université de Paris, INSERM UMR-S 1266, F-75014 Paris, France
UMR 7179 CNRS, MNHN, Adaptive mechanism and Evolution (MECADEV), 91800 Brunoy, France

Odile Viltart
Institute of Psychiatry and Neuroscience of Paris (IPNP), Université de Paris, INSERM UMR-S 1266, F-75014 Paris, France
Cité scientifique, SN4, Université de Lille, 59491 Villeneuve d'Ascq, France

Peter Stanwell and Tracy L. Burrows
Faculty of Health and Medicine, The University of Newcastle, University Drive, Callaghan, NSW 2308, Australia

Kirrilly M. Pursey and Clare E. Collins
Faculty of Health and Medicine, The University of Newcastle, University Drive, Callaghan, NSW 2308, Australia
Priority Research Centre for Physical Activity and Nutrition, The University of Newcastle, University Drive, Callaghan, NSW 2308, Australia

Oren Contreras-Rodriguez
Department of Psychiatry, Bellvitge Biomedical Research Institute (IDIBELL), and CIBERSAM, 08907 Barcelona, Spain

Miriam Kemmer, Julia Grosser and Verena Haas
Department of Child and Adolescent Psychiatry, Charité-Universitätsmedizin Berlin, Corporate Member of Freie Universität Berlin, Humboldt-Universität zu Berlin, and Berlin Institute of Health, 13353 Berlin, Germany

Christoph U. Correll
Department of Child and Adolescent Psychiatry, Charité-Universitätsmedizin Berlin, Corporate Member of Freie Universität Berlin, Humboldt-Universität zu Berlin, and Berlin Institute of Health, 13353 Berlin, Germany
Donald and Barbara Zucker School of Medicine at Hofstra/Northwell, Hempstead, NY 11549, USA
Department of Psychiatry, The Zucker Hillside Hospital, Glen Oaks, NY 11004, USA

Tobias Hofmann
Center for Internal Medicine and Dermatology, Department for Psychosomatic Medicine, Charité-Universitätsmedizin Berlin, Corporate Member of Freie Universität Berlin, Humboldt-Universität zu Berlin, and Berlin Institute of Health Berlin, 12200 Berlin, Germany

Andreas Stengel
Center for Internal Medicine and Dermatology, Department for Psychosomatic Medicine, Charité-Universitätsmedizin Berlin, Corporate Member of Freie Universität Berlin, Humboldt-Universität zu Berlin, and Berlin Institute of Health Berlin, 12200 Berlin, Germany
Department of Psychosomatic Medicine and Psychotherapy, Medical University Hospital Tübingen, 72076 Tübingen, Germany

Index

A

Addictive Eating Behaviours, 37-39, 48

Adverse Childhood Experience, 52, 66

Alcohol Abuse, 24, 100, 104

Altered Physical Activity, 210, 222

Anorexia Nervosa, 1-2, 8-10, 12-13, 15, 26-27, 33, 35, 52, 54-55, 70, 82, 95-96, 100, 103, 116, 132, 152, 169, 181, 183, 193-199, 210, 215-216, 220, 222-223

Anti-inflammatory Properties, 59

Anxiety Symptoms, 59, 97, 100-102, 122, 125

Attention Deficit Hyperactivity Disorder, 60, 66, 77

B

Bariatric Surgery, 56, 59, 69, 73, 77, 105, 119-122, 125-129, 133, 141-142, 150, 167, 169

Barratt Impulsiveness Scale, 66, 79, 162

Beck Depression Inventory, 66, 79, 99, 101

Binge Eating Disorder, 2, 9, 22, 25, 38, 44, 50, 52, 54-55, 70-73, 75, 80, 103-106, 120, 126-128, 132, 134, 141, 146, 160-162, 165-166, 170-171, 173, 180

Biomedical Research, 26, 34, 81, 200

Bipolar Disorder, 6, 12

Bulimia Nervosa, 1-2, 9, 15, 22, 26, 38, 52, 54, 62, 70-71, 73-75, 82, 97, 100, 103, 107, 146, 160, 165, 172, 180, 193, 198

C

Caloric Restraint, 1-3, 7-8

Cardiovascular Disease, 118, 150, 167

Childhood Trauma Questionnaire, 57, 66, 74

Cognitive Behavioural Therapy, 119-122, 125-126, 128-129, 157-158

Cognitive Flexibility, 134

Comorbidities, 49, 99-100, 119, 130, 150, 212

Coronary Artery Disease, 130

D

Depression, 4, 10-11, 15, 26, 33, 38, 49, 58-59, 64-67, 76-77, 79, 97-104, 107-108, 116, 119-120, 125, 129, 131, 133, 150-151, 166

Diabetes Mellitus, 4, 131

Dietary Intake Profile, 130, 141

Dietary Restraint, 8, 52-55, 59, 61-69, 72, 154, 158, 164, 174

Disordered Eating, 9, 26-29, 31, 33, 35-36, 39-41, 44, 48-50, 53-54, 60, 66, 68, 71, 75, 77-79, 81-82, 88-89, 91, 94-96, 120, 128-129, 132, 154-155, 166, 202, 207

Dna Methylation, 1, 3-6, 10-12

Dopamine-mediated Retinal Signal, 22

Dopaminergic Response, 22, 55, 107

E

Eating Disorder Pathology, 71, 75

Epidemiological, 66, 75, 92-93, 132

F

Feeding And Eating Disorders, 2, 35, 146

Food Craving Questionnaire, 101

G

Gambling Disorder, 117, 136, 146

Gene-environment Interactions, 1, 4, 7, 10

Generalized Anxiety, 77, 79, 100, 122, 124, 129

Glutamate, 6

H

Heredity And Environmental Activation, 1, 34

Hyperpalatable, 118, 120, 128, 130

I

Insulin Resistance, 3, 166, 198

L

Linoleic Acid, 136, 144

M

Maladaptive, 1, 7, 55, 67, 79, 104, 121, 126, 132, 158

Medical Specialists, 43, 46

Mental Disorders, 2, 9, 26, 34, 38, 52, 98, 105, 108, 117, 120, 128, 160, 197

Metabolic Equivalent, 186, 210, 215

Metabolic Factors, 3, 191

Mini International Neuropsychiatric Interview, 98, 100, 106

Morphine-benzedrine Group, 14-16, 18

N

Neuroimaging, 22, 55, 57, 71-73, 75, 77, 133, 135, 137, 139, 141, 144, 148, 167, 170-171, 200-201

Neuropsychological, 74, 140, 162

Neuropsychopharmacological, 172

Neurotransmitter, 5, 15-16, 20, 137

O

Obsessive Compulsive Disorder, 100

Orthorexia, 68, 80

P

Patient Health Questionnaire, 66, 122, 124, 129

Personality Disorder, 5, 11, 61, 71, 98

Phenotype, 3, 56-64, 73-74, 91, 128, 136, 165, 211, 219
Polygenic Score, 81-82, 88-89, 91
Polyunsaturated Fat, 130, 141
Posttraumatic Stress Disorder, 52-53, 69, 74-75, 79, 107
Prefrontal Cortex, 133-134, 136-137, 153, 157, 164, 167, 170-171, 177-179, 201
Proinflammatory Phenotype, 57, 74
Psychiatric Comorbidity, 52, 55
Psychological Impairment, 101
Psychopathology, 9, 11, 35, 53, 55, 70, 94, 97-98, 105, 120, 159, 165, 178, 180
Psychophysical Effects Questionnaire, 16-18
Psychosocial Interventions, 38, 50, 79, 105, 120, 128
Psychostimulant Effects, 14, 21

R

Restrictive Food Intake Disorder, 2, 26
Risk Factors, 9, 35-36, 53-54, 69, 72, 76, 82, 93, 96, 127, 166, 198, 222

S

Sedentary Behavior, 210, 213, 215, 218, 220, 223
Self-induced Vomiting, 2, 83
Social Anxiety, 59, 77, 100
Somatotype Components, 26-27, 29-33
Substance Use Disorder, 52, 65-66, 70, 72-73, 77, 97, 99, 105, 160-161, 171
Suicidality, 5-6, 11, 100
Symptomatology, 36, 54, 60, 72, 78, 119-121, 123-127, 132, 135, 141

T

Telephone-based Cognitive Behavioural
Therapy, 119-121, 125, 128-129
Theobromine, 21, 24

www.ingramcontent.com/pod-product-compliance
Lightning Source LLC
LaVergne TN
LVHW082208200926
848484LV00008B/2233